'The new Women's Liberation Movement that has been developing in the last few years badly needs feminist theory. This book is very welcome. With all her usual clarity and readability, Denise has set out to create a thorough analysis of the workings of male domination fit for our times. This is an excellent compendium of insights that can be returned to again and again to shed light on how the system works, and therefore provide some hope of how to begin dismantling it'.
Sheila Jeffreys, author of *Gender Hurts: a Feminist Analysis of the Politics of Transgenderism* (2014) and *The Lesbian Revolution: Lesbian Feminism in the UK 1970-1990* (2018).

'Denise Thompson's new book *Masculinity and the Ruling of the World* is an important book. Many scholars and activists have exposed, analysed, denounced and sought to correct systems of oppression, but what most of them do is either
- ignore or misidentify what it is that oppresses in the first place;
- consider manifestations of oppression as aberrations from an already-accepted norm, either individual (through words or acts) or group (through ideological tenets and systems);
- treat ideology, structure, culture and society as somehow discrete entities; or
- think in terms of concurrent and/or intersecting systems (race, 'gender', class, capitalism and so on).

What Thompson's book does is provide an in-depth and historically, experientially and theoretically grounded analysis of masculinity as systemic and totalising, as the ruling principle that underpins all logics and practices of domination. An essential read for anyone who wishes to better understand both male domination and feminism'.
Bronwyn Winter, Professor of Transnational Studies, Faculty of Humanities and Social Sciences, University of Sydney.

'This impressive tome gallantly explores the threat posed to humanity by masculine entitlement in various manifestations. Thompson has the honesty and courage to expose the trans juggernaut for the fraud that it is. Thompson is a sane voice of resistance at a time when the very definition of woman is imperiled and our sex-based rights are being rapidly eroded'.
Anna Kerr, Principal Solicitor, Feminist Legal Centre, Sydney

by the same author

Reading Between the Lines: A Lesbian Feminist Critique of Feminist Accounts of Sexuality
(1991, Spinifex Press, Melbourne)

Against the Dismantling of Feminism: A Study in the Politics of Meaning
(1996, PhD thesis, University of New South Wales)

Radical Feminism Today
(2001, Sage)

http://users.spin.net.au/~deniset/index.htm

Masculinity
and
the Ruling
of the World

DENISE THOMPSON

Sydney, Australia
2020

Cover design: Ally Taylor (allymosher.com)

Book design: Robbie Daley and the author

Publisher: The author

ISBN: 978-0-6488036-0-7

Subjects: radical feminism, male domination, masculinity, culture, right wing, entitlement, dissociation, sex differences, capitalism, socialist feminism, feminist economics, wealth, accumulation by dispossession, inequality, tax havens, poverty, finance capital, Modern Money Theory, fascism, surrogacy, transsexualism, US welfare reform, PRWORA, TANF

Acknowledgements

Many thanks to Robbie Daley, not only for his help in getting this book out, but also for many insightful conversations over the years.

My gratitude also to those feminist authors whose writings defined the 'second wave' of feminism, among them: Kathleen Barry, Susan Brownmiller, Mia Campioni, Phyllis Chesler, Mary Daly, Andrea Dworkin, Marilyn French, Marilyn Frye, Germaine Greer, Susan Griffin, Sarah Hoagland, Sheila Jeffreys, Gerda Lerner, Catharine MacKinnon, Maria Mies, Kate Millett, Robyn Morgan, Mary O'Brien, Carol Pateman, Julia Penelope, Janice Raymond, Adrienne Rich, Joanna Russ, Diana Russell and Bronwyn Winter.

The Ruling of the World is borrowed from the title of Dorothy Dinnerstein's book, *The Rocking of the Cradle and the Ruling of the World*.

And special thanks to Margaret Roberts, my friend for life, who listened until she understood and then continued the dialogue.

Table of Contents

Abbreviations

ABS	Australian Bureau of Statistics
ACLU	American Civil Liberties Union
ACOSS	Australian Council of Social Service
ACT	Australian Capital Territory
ADC	Aid to Dependent Children (US)
AFSCME	The American Federation of State, County and Municipal Employees
AFDC	Aid to Families with Dependent Children (US)
AHRC	Australian Human Rights Commission
AIFS	Australian Institute for Family Studies
AIHW	Australian Institute of Health and Welfare
ART	assisted reproductive treatment
BEGIN	Begin Employment, Gain Independence Now ('welfare' program, New York)
CBO	Congressional Budget Office (US)
CC	clomiphene citrate
CDC	Center for Disease Control (US)
CDO	collateralised debt obligation
CDS	credit default swap
CEO	Chief Executive Officer
CLASP	Center for Law and Social Policy (US)
CSE	Child Support Enforcement (Office of, US)
DES	Diethylstilbestrol
DHHS	Department of Health and Human Services (US)
DRA	Deficit Reduction Act (US)
DSM	Diagnostic and Statistical Manual of Mental Disorders
ESP	Employment Services and Placement (New York City)
Fannie Mae (FNMA)	Federal National Mortgage Association
FAO	Food and Agricultural Organization
FAP	Family Assistance Plan (US)
FICA	Federal Insurance Contributions Act (US)
FINRRAGE	Feminist International Network of Resistance to Reproductive and Genetic Engineering
Freddie Mac (FHMC)	Federal Home Mortgage Corporation
FSA	Family Support Act (US)

FTC	Failed to Comply (US 'welfare' sanctions)
GAIN	Greater Avenues for Independence (US)
GAO	Government Accountability Office (US)
GD	gender dysphoria
GFC	global financial crisis
GID	Gender Identity Disorder
GNI	gross national income
GRA	Gender Recognition Act (UK, 2004)
HHS	Health and Human Services (US Department of)
HRA	Human Resources Administration (New York City)
IMF	International Monetary Fund
IVF	in-vitro fertilisation
IWF	Institute for Wisconsin's Future
JOBS	Job Opportunities and Basic Skills (US)
LAB	Legislative Audit Bureau (Wisconsin)
MDRC	Manpower Demonstration Research Corporation (US)
MMT	Modern Money Theory
MOE	Maintenance of Effort
NAIRU	non-accelerating rate of unemployment
NAS	National Academy of Science (US)
NBCC	National Bioethics Consultative Committee (Australia)
NINJA	no income, no job or assets (loan)
NSW ADB	New South Wales Anti-Discrimination Board
NTER	Northern Territory Emergency Response (Australia)
OBRA	Omnibus Budget Reconciliation Act (US)
OECD	Organisation for Economic Co-operation and Development
OED	Oxford English Dictionary
OESSS	Office of Emergency Shelter and Support Services (Washington DC)
OFA	Office of Family Assistance (US)
OHSS	ovarian hyperstimulation syndrome
OIC-GM	Opportunities Industrialization Center of Greater Milwaukee
PIC	Private Industry Council (Milwaukee County)

PRWORA	Personal Responsibility and Work Opportunities Reconciliation Act (US)
PwC	PricewaterhouseCoopers
RMB	renminbi (Chinese currency)
RSC	Republican Study Committee (US)
SART	Society for Assisted Reproductive Technology
SBS	Special Broadcasting Service (Australia's multicultural broadcaster)
SIPP	Survey of Income and Program Participation (US Census Bureau)
SMH	Sydney Morning Herald
SNAP	Supplemental Nutrition Assistance Program (US)
SSI	Supplemental Security Income (US)
TANF	Temporary Assistance to Needy Families
TJN	Tax Justice Network
UK	United Kingdom
UMOS	United Migrant Opportunity Services (Milwaukee)
UN	United Nations
UNDP	United Nations Development Programme
UNSW	University of New South Wales
UP	Unemployed Parent (AFDC)
US	United States
USDA	US Department of Agriculture
W-2	Wisconsin Works
WAGES	Work And Gain Economic Self-Sufficiency ('welfare' program, Florida)
WEP	Work Experience Program (New York)
WHEDCO	Women's Housing and Economic Development Corporation (New York City)
WHO	World Health Organization
WIC	Women, Infant and Children (Food Program, US)
WIN	Work Incentive Program (US)
YWCA	Young Women's Christian Association

Prologue

Masculinity & the Ruling of the World argues that male domination not only subordinates women, it distorts the whole of the social world. It is the root cause of the current parlous state of the world. Male domination creates a culture of masculinity that breeds arrogant dissociated men who are the prime culprits in the depredations that have brought humanity to its present grievous condition (aided by those few women allowed into positions of power because they embrace the same system despite the misogyny at its core). At the same time, I argue, male supremacy is not the whole of the social world. There is also something I've called 'genuine humanity', which provides a life-affirming force that resists the impositions and seductions of male supremacy.

In order to illustrate some of the ways in which male domination permeates the social world, I have chosen to discuss five institutions that are rarely, if ever, considered in terms of masculinity. The first and most relevant of these institutions is capitalism, the economic system that is the form currently taken by male power. Among other things in this context, I discuss the male ownership of wealth, capitalism's origins in destruction, despoliation and slavery, 'inequality', poverty, the finance industry, and a theory of money (Modern Money Theory) that has the potential to democratise that crucial element of male wealth and power. I then discuss fascism, arguing not only that the fascist ethos centres around a particularly virulent form of dissociated masculinity, but also that it is compatible with capitalism. Just as fascism creates categories of people defined as 'non-human' and hence undeserving of any right to life, so capitalism creates categories of people who are 'superfluous' to its requirements, and hence undeserving of those resources necessary for human existence.

The other three institutions I discuss are surrogacy, transsexualism and US 'welfare reform'. Like capitalism and fascism, surrogacy, transsexualism and

US 'welfare reform' display the arrogant entitlement and crazed dissociation from reality characteristic of the male supremacist culture of masculinity.

Surrogacy gives men permission to take advantage of women's poverty and desperation to exploit their bodies as production-line incubators, obliterating women's knowledge of what bearing a child means to themselves and to the babies they give birth to. Although there are women who have availed themselves of surrogacy arrangements—as women have availed themselves of other male supremacist institutions of one form or another—there are indications that the surrogacy institution is by, for and about men. Certainly, it manifests those typical male supremacist values of overblown entitlement (for men) and dissociation from not only the reality of women, but also of their own humanity. To use women as objects for male satisfaction without any consideration of what women might need—and let's not forget the children who will never know their birth mothers, or their genetic mothers in most cases—is classic male supremacy.

Transsexualism (or transgender or just 'trans') gives men permission to say they are women. It is true that such individuals constitute a miniscule proportion of the population (although their numbers are growing fast, as are the numbers of young girls insisting they are boys) (Littman, 2018). The problem arises from the enormity of the influence of the transsexual agenda on the social world of all of us: the legal system (e.g. the UK Gender Recognition Act; the falsification of birth certificates); the justice system (e.g. crimes committed by 'transwomen' recorded as crimes committed by women; men being put into women's jails); the education system (e.g. pro-transgender resources being introduced into schools; universities and other organisations censoring critics of transsexualism); the health system (the acceptability of medical, surgical and chemical mutilations of healthy bodies); the anti-discrimination system (e.g. men claiming, and being given, access to positions reserved for women); the mass media, including social media, giving a positive spin to the transsexual agenda and its 'transitioning'; and the very meaning of what it is to be human.

And US 'welfare reform' (that is neither welfare nor reform) must be one of the cruelest (and most spiteful) pieces of legislation ever passed by the legislature of a so-called 'developed' country. The US 'welfare' system has always been woefully inadequate. But even that inadequacy was made infinitely worse by the Personal Responsibility and Work Opportunities Reconciliation Act passed in 1996 by the Bill Clinton administration. Powerful wealthy men deliberately set out to step up the financial abuse of the poorest people in the land, those already victimised by the system that made those men so rich at the expense of most of the citizens of their own country.

It might seem at first sight that these five institutions have nothing in common, either with each other or with masculinity. But I argue that all of them are characterised by male entitlement and dissociation from reality. There is no particular reason why I chose these institutions rather than any other forms of institutionalised masculinity to illustrate its prevalence throughout culture and society, apart from the fact that they are all of particular relevance at the moment. I could have chosen any number of other examples that are more obviously characteristic of male supremacy, such as the widespread occurrence of outright male violence against women, for example, or militarism, or US gun culture, or the rise and rise of neo-liberal governance and the right wing worldwide, or rape, or child sexual abuse, or pornography and prostitution and paedophilia and their acceptance into the mainstream. But the five institutions I do discuss are just as male supremacist as these more obvious examples, and they have received little attention as forms of male supremacy.

These five institutions are not the whole of male supremacy. But they do illustrate the callous brutality of the world men have made by obliterating the humanity of women. In a world of common human decency, none of them would exist (and neither would other bastions of male supremacy: war; rape; prostitution; pornography; sex trafficking; sexual abuse of children; etc.). Male supremacy does not have it all its own way, and common humanity can be found under even the worst of conditions. But male supremacy is still powerful enough to destroy the earth, and lethal enough to try. The first step in resisting it is to expose it for what it is—make it take off its disguises and show its ugly face.

What I have to say here follows on from what I have already written about male domination, while insisting that male domination is not the whole of social reality. If it had been, the human race would already have ceased to exist because male domination is lethal. These days the ruling of the earth is in the hands of arrogant, dissociated men for whom power over others is the supreme motivating force, including the power of brutal violence and destruction. It looks as though humanity has finally reached the point where either male supremacy ends, or civilisation does.

Chapter One: Introduction

We cannot gain a realistic understanding of who rules the world while ignoring the "masters of mankind," as Adam Smith called them: in his day, the merchants and manufacturers of England; in ours, multinational conglomerates, huge financial institutions, retail empires, and the like. Still following Smith, it is also wise to attend to the "vile maxim" to which the "masters of mankind" are dedicated: "All for ourselves and nothing for other people"—a doctrine known otherwise as bitter and incessant class war, often one-sided, much to the detriment of the people of the home country and the world (Chomsky, 2016).

There is something wrong with men—something obviously, undeniably, tragically wrong ... the dictates of masculinity in their most concentrated form: Demand what you want. Use violence to take it. Destroy what you can't have. This is the ideology of manhood ... The liberal notion of "healthy" masculinity is either a distraction, or a lie. It can be ahistorical and meaningless, by turning masculinity into an empty term indistinguishable from "decent human," or it can be a benign patriarchy that confirms the sex stratification at the heart of male power. But what it cannot be is an effective antidote to the militarized psychology of domination that drives male atrocities from mass shootings to genocide' (Mix, 2016).

That the world is in a parlous state is well known (except by those in denial). Global warming is destroying the biosphere and inequality has reached unprecedented proportions. Men's wars never cease; somewhere in the world there are always men killing each other en masse, along with any women and children within reach. Pornography has become mainstream, prostitution has come to be seen as just a job of work, and women and children are still being trafficked and enslaved to gratify men's sexual desires and nobody seems to be able to stop it. Capitalist greed has wrecked national economies, deprived the home countries of the much-vaunted 'jobs' by taking them offshore, destroyed people's livelihoods, impoverished billions while amassing obscene accumulations of wealth in the hands of the few, and now poses grave threats to the environment of all of us. The legacies of colonialism and the continued rapacious depredations of multinational corporations have devastated the Third World,[1] destroying the environment and entrenching poverty, and given rise to some of the vilest dictators the world has ever seen.

There are those who argue that things are improving. One commentator (Matthews, 2015), for example, gives us 26 reasons why 'the world is getting much, much better'. There are falls in rates of maternal and infant mortality, increases in literacy, education and life expectancy, and reductions in rates of violent crime worldwide (including in the US). However, some of his claims of improvement are debatable. For example, he says that the incidence of violent crime against women has fallen, but it is not clear how he or anyone else knows that. One of his references for the decline in violence is Steven Pinker's 2010 book, *The Better Angels of Our Nature: Why Violence Has Declined*. In that book, Pinker says that 'the women's-rights movement has helped to shrink the incidence of rape and the beating and killing of wives and girlfriends' (Pinker, 2011). But until very recently, rape and the beating and killing of women by men in the privacy of their own homes was acceptable and nobody noticed, much less counted, not even when he killed her; and there was no notion of marital rape. Before the advent of the women's movement, women's injuries and deaths at the hands of men were not seen as a demographic fact and hence would not have appeared in official statistics. Thus there is no 'before' data with which to compare current figures.

To give another example, he says that 'more and more countries are democracies', but the actual policies and practices of so-called 'democratic' governments are anything but democratic. They routinely support powerful vested interests against the common good, gerrymander elections, ignore

---

1   The term 'Third World' is at best meaningless, especially as the implied terms 'Second World' and 'First World' are rarely if ever used. At worst, it is imperialist. 'The South' is an alternative name, but two of the most important countries of 'the South'—China and India—are not in the southern hemisphere at all. The term, 'the South', dates from at least 1987, with the formation of the South Commission (South Commission, 1990), perhaps as a reference to Gramsci's The Southern Question, although this was an argument confined to Italy and its division into two regions, north and south. Alternative names are 'developing' or 'industrialising countries' (in contrast with the industrialised West). But 'developing' deletes the Western imperialism that expropriates these nations' resources in its own interests; and 'industrialising' deletes the shift in industrial capacity from the formerly industrialised nations to the Third World in order to exploit its cheaper labour power. I will continue to use the term, 'Third World', because I'm used to it, because none of the other terms is any great improvement and constantly changing the names does not address the underlying reality, and because 'Third World' at least has the virtue of being instantly recognisable.

people's protests, and rarely if ever consult with their constituencies. And then there is the oft-repeated claim that 'extreme poverty has fallen'. As I argue later (in chapter 8), this claim is suspect because the criterion used to measure extreme poverty—'the share of the world population living on less than is $1.25-a-day'—is meaningless. Moreover, he barely mentions global warming before hurrying on to say that it is getting cheaper to produce solar panels, and doesn't mention pollution or environmental destruction at all.

But whether or not things are improving (and global warming, depletion of the earth's resources and wild places, the resurgence of the rabid right wing, and the increasing belligerence and technological sophistication of the US war machine suggest otherwise), there are worldwide movements of resistance with a global awareness of the problems and a willingness to do whatever is necessary to solve them. Inspired by what I have termed 'genuine humanity' which works for the common good, that awareness has had little impact on the ruling elites—whether governments or corporations—who have the power to mend matters. But it does exist and we are not all going meekly to the slaughter.

There are many critiques of this state of affairs, the most relevant of which is the critique of neo-liberalism and the capitalist economy it serves to justify. I agree with these critiques (as far as they go), but I would add that behind the governmentality of neo-liberalism lies masculinity. The reality Chomsky refers to (above)—'bitter and incessant class war' waged by the 'masters of mankind' against everyone else—is what passes for normal. As normality, the fact that it is a war, and one waged by the powerful against the powerless must be denied. It must be called something else: 'the market' perhaps, or 'freedom', or, because the effects of that war are too obvious to be denied completely, 'inequality'; and it must be purveyed as though it were in the interests of all: 'jobs and growth' perhaps.[2] What Chomsky did not acknowledge, although it is implicit in his terminology ('*masters* of mankind'), is that the war against humanity is being waged by men made arrogant by the kind of masculinity needed to maintain the culture of domination that has brought us all to this point. That masculinity is characterised by an overweening sense of entitlement and an insane dissociation from humanity, their own as well as anyone else's. As a cultural imperative, that masculinity

---

2   'Jobs and growth' was a slogan much favoured by the Australian government in 2016-17 (according to the Commonwealth Government's 'Budget' website: https://budget.gov. au/2016-17/content/glossies/jobs-growth/html/ – viewed 8.8.2018). [I give the URLs of the references in the text to indicate where they originated, even though it is unlikely that readers of the hard copy of this book will type the URL into a search engine.]

can be resisted. But resistance needs to start by challenging the denial that disguises the true nature of the problem.

It is that denial I want to challenge in this present work, by excavating commonly-held beliefs about the way the world is, in order to expose them as justifications for male tyranny. The primary denial is the silence about the existence of male domination.[3] For it is men who are destroying the earth. No, not all men, and perhaps not even most men, and some men are valiantly trying to halt the destruction. Men, after all, do have a choice. But, as Jonah Mix points out (see above), there is something about a certain sort of masculinity that, at the very least, is heedless of the wilfully-caused destruction, at worst, glories in it. That 'something', I suggest, is a dissociated and arrogant sense of entitlement working for the perceived benefit of (some) men (aided by the women who also embrace the system of male supremacy) at the expense of the rest of us.

I agree that the current desperate state of the world is a consequence of the standard operating procedures of the capitalist economic system. For that reason, I discuss capitalism at some length (in chapters 5 to 11), arguing that capitalism is the modern form of male domination and clearly displays its arrogance and dissociation. As well, I discuss another four institutions to illustrate dissociated masculine entitlement in action—fascism, surrogacy, transsexualism and US 'welfare reform'. This is a disparate grouping, and at first sight it might seem that they have nothing in common. I argue, however, that what they have in common is a culture of masculinity that operates to privilege men at the expense, not only of women, but of humanity as a whole. In other words, male supremacy is bad for men too because it is dehumanising. But apart from capitalism as the current form of male power, there is no particular reason why I chose these other four institutions rather than any others to illustrate the prevalence of masculinity throughout culture and society. Institutionalised masculinity is everywhere. I could have chosen any number of other examples that are more obviously characteristic of male supremacy, such as the widespread occurrence of outright male violence against women, for example, or militarism, or US gun culture, or the rise and rise of neo-liberal governance and the right wing worldwide, or rape,

---

3. 'Patriarchy' is a common alternative term for the phenomenon. However, I prefer to call it 'male domination' (or 'male supremacy'). 'Patriarchy' means rule of the father, and men rule not because they are fathers, but because they are men (Thompson, 2001: 59-63).

or child sexual abuse, or pornography and prostitution and paedophilia and their acceptance into the malestream.[4]

I do have something to say about these issues, but I do not discuss them at any length because they have already been extensively criticised. The feminist critiques do not attribute the genesis of these phenomena to masculinity's dissociation and arrogant entitlement, but they do identify men as the perpetrators. In contrast, the five institutions I discuss have rarely, if ever, been linked to male entitlement and dehumanised dissociation. There is a mainstream critique of fascism as an extreme form of masculinity (see chapter 12); there is also a feminist critique of surrogacy and transsexualism as male entitlement (see chapters 13 and 14); and US 'welfare reform' has been extensively criticised for its effects on poor women and children (see chapters 15-19) (although not in terms of the masculinity of its framers). But capitalism has not to my knowledge been addressed as a culture of masculinity. However, all five, I hope to show, more or less avidly embrace the meanings and values of masculinity, namely, dissociation from a common humanity by way of an overweening entitlement on the part of powerful men and concomitant *dis*entitlement for those defined as less than human and either exploited or excluded from human rights altogether. Moreover, all are particularly pertinent at this point in time. Capitalism has created a level of inequality that threatens the very existence of society. Surrogacy and transsexualism are recent phenomena, products of two of male supremacy's more triumphant confidence tricks: a neo-liberalism that reduces people to nothing but commodities, and a post-structuralism that sneers at notions of humanity, reality and truth. Fascism is always with us and it is rearing its ugly head again in many countries, especially the US. And so-called 'welfare reform' in the US is one of the most spiteful pieces of victim-blaming to be found in the Western world, devised by powerful men and imposed on economically powerless women. Its viciousness is surpassed only by the US military industrial complex, which kills women and children directly, rather than through the indirect method of starvation and exclusion from health care. In the case of 'welfare', there is nothing left for the Trump administration to do. The US has a 'welfare' system in name only; the reality has already gone.

---

4. The term 'malestream' is Mary O'Brien's. She uses it to refer to the ideology 'which buttresses and justifies ... male dominant culture' (O'Brien, 1981: 5). It is derived from the term 'mainstream' and has the same connotation of widely-held beliefs, but with the added dimension that these are beliefs that uphold and justify male domination. I use it when the meanings and values espoused are clearly male supremacist, although I also continue to use the term 'mainstream' in its ordinary sense.

What I have to say here follows on from what I have already written about male domination, but it also postulates another reality existing alongside the male supremacist world, a genuinely human one that is a source of resistance to male domination. The notion of the 'genuinely human' is intended as a contrast to the dehumanisation of male supremacy, and as an acknowledgement that male domination can be challenged and resisted (see chapter 3).

Both personal and political

This present project is an attempt to theorise a feminist personal-political account of male domination, using a feminist focus to identify the sex-specific nature of social arrangements largely presented as gender-neutral.

The personal aspect involves a character structure by, for and about men, that both advantages men and creates the kind of men who believe they are entitled to all that the system promises them. One striking example of this personal aspect is Donald Trump (and the henchmen he surrounds himself with, including the women), brought to the world's attention during the 2016 US presidential campaign and his subsequent election to the US presidency. Other examples (discussed in subsequent chapters) are the men who generate and profit from capitalism's wealth accumulation, fascist men, those who exploit women's bodies in the surrogacy industry, those who embrace the transsexual agenda to obliterate the category of 'women', and the right-wing men in the US Congress responsible for 'welfare reform'.

The personal aspect also involves resistance. Domination is hegemonic as well as violent, i.e. it operates most efficiently to the extent that people 'consent' to its social arrangements (Chomsky, 1988). That 'consent' is elicited and managed through the meanings and values through which we come to understand the world. But if we can consent, we can also refuse and resist, even though that resistance might amount to no more than a reluctance to engage with what we are forced to be complicit with. For male supremacy is not the whole of social life. The more men are influenced by the genuine humanity of the common good, the less these personality characteristics hold sway. Humanised, such characteristics transmute into ordinary detachment and justified entitlement. Detachment is not pathologically oppressive— sometimes it's simply the most appropriate response for both sexes. And there are certain entitlements we all share simply because we're human. Nonetheless, the misogyny, dissociation and arrogant entitlement characteristic of male supremacist men is a cultural norm, far more widespread than the individuals who are its most brutal exemplars.

My primary concern here, then, is the political aspect, or more precisely the institutional aspect, of the system of male domination. Although it is men who are threatening life on the planet, it is not men as such but those men who embrace the meanings and values of male supremacy as their own (aided by the few token women who are allowed into the boys' games as long as they play by the boys' rules). I am not talking about what masculinity *is* (full stop), but about what masculinity is when it serves the purposes of male domination. I am using it in the sense alluded to by Mary Daly in *Gyn/Ecology*, when she said: 'I use both of these terms [feminine and masculine] to refer to roles/stereotypes/sets of characteristics which are essentially distorted and destructive' (Daly, 1978: 26). Or as Gena Corea (1985: 4) put it: 'When I write the word "men" in this book, I am writing about some individuals, but also about the institution of masculinist politics, about men as a social category and dominant class'.

So the masculinity I am talking about is both the character structure required of men under conditions of male supremacy, and a cultural imperative of meanings and values comprising an institutional framework for organising the social world of all of us in the interests of the powerful. My emphasis on the cultural (see chapter 3) is intended to avoid individualising[5] masculinity in any sense that implies that it originates in something inherent in male individuals. This tendency to see anything said about people in individualistic terms elides the social aspects of what it is to be human. Seeing masculinity as simply a characteristic of individuals identified as 'men' tends to understate the extent of the problem, even when those characteristics are acknowledged to originate with male supremacy. One cannot, for example, avoid this masculinity by avoiding interpersonal interactions with men, or, in the case of men, avoiding its worst manifestations, although that is a necessary part of any resistance. As meaning and value, that is, as culture, masculinity permeates the social world throughout, structuring institutions, creating the world-taken-for-granted, and presenting itself as a harmless 'difference' while disguising its true nature as the prerogative of men made powerful by a system whose reason for existence is to do exactly that.

I am talking about 'masculinity' in two senses—as a personality characteristic demanded of men by male domination, and as a cultural imperative structuring the everyday lives of all of us. I am saying that the male supremacist culture I call 'masculinity' is embedded within individuals (within men, but also within women although differently, to the extent

---

5.   For an extended critique of individualism, see: Thompson, 1997, 1998a, 1999, 2005b.

that either sex subscribes to its meanings and values), an embedding that takes the form of such 'subjective' phenomena as ideas, feelings, emotions, understandings, etc. In saying that, I am saying that we are creatures of our social environment in a quite literal sense, in that the way we understand the world is created within us by the society into which we are born (just as the language we speak is). But my use of the term 'masculinity' is not confined to male individuals. I am more concerned with its institutionalisation, its imperative of dissociation and unwarranted entitlement that structures the moral and political environment and gives meaning to the social world. With the concept of 'genuine humanity', however, I am also saying that we are not only male supremacy's creatures, that we do have choices.

In making these distinctions, I am not suggesting that my usage is correct and other usages are wrong. I am merely clarifying the way I use the word in this present work. 'Masculinity' meaning simply 'ways of being a man' without further qualification is the most widely accepted usage, and it will continue to be so, but that is not the meaning I am using. My usage is admittedly idiosyncratic. It is intended to go beyond the everyday usage by identifying male domination as the meaning both of personality characteristics and of institutions; at the same time it remains connected to that everyday usage by using the same term, because male domination is not something other than the everyday, but permeates the mundane existence of all of us.

The 'masculinities' literature

It might be assumed that the place to look for an account of masculinity is the literature on 'masculinities', but I have found this literature unhelpful for my purposes. Much of it does acknowledge male domination, but the focus still remains on male individuals. This is of course the corollary of feminism's focus on women, and it is only to be expected given that men are the bearers of masculinity however characterised. This work has produced some important insights.[6] But important as it is to account for male implication in the social relations of male supremacy, it needs to be complemented by a perspective based on the premise that masculinity manifests institutionally as well as through individual behaviour. In that sense, it becomes an issue not only for men (although it is that), but also an issue about the way society is structured and about the meanings and values which inform and shape the institutional realities we all live under. While it is true that masculinity is a characteristic

---

6. e.g. Schrock and Schwalbe, 2009; Schwalbe, 2014; Stoltenberg, 1989; Theweleit, 1987, 1989; the work of Jeff Hearne, Michael Kimmel and Michael Flood.

of individuals, a political analysis needs to investigate it as an institutional phenomenon as well. The 'masculinities' literature tends to focus simply on ways of being a man, on how male individuals are shaped by society or (in a more feminist vein) by male domination (or 'gender inequality'). There is too little emphasis on the meanings and values that animate both personalities and institutions, that permeate the whole of society (notwithstanding investigations of the media and educational practices). Keeping the analysis at the level of the personality characteristics or behaviour of individuals, even when they are acknowledged to be the result of male domination, is too narrow a focus.

However, another reason why the 'masculinities' literature is unhelpful is its use of the terms 'gender' and 'masculinities'.

'Gender'

The ubiquitous use of the word 'gender' is something the 'masculinities' literature has in common with both feminism and the malestream. The ease with which 'gender' has been adopted as a designator of the feminist enterprise should be a source of unease within feminism (as indeed it is, within radical feminism). It does nothing to expose the continued widespread existence of all the male supremacist evils exposed by feminism, much less curb them. The term's popularity neither guarantees its usefulness in clarifying what is at stake, nor its accuracy in identifying the problem. For a number of reasons, I would argue that it is meaningless: it falls into the same essentialist trap it was supposedly designed to avoid; it has so many meanings it is often unclear what is being appealed to; and, most importantly, it euphemises the real subject of feminism—male domination.

The distinction between sex and gender was supposedly designed to make the point that the differences between the sexes were socially constructed, not the result of biology. But by separating 'sex' out from 'gender' and assigning the social aspect of the relationship between the sexes to 'gender', the sex/gender distinction implies that sex isn't social—only 'gender' is. At the time the sex/gender distinction was being established, there was still a tendency to appeal to biology as the truth of sex differences, and they could be argued away if it could be shown that they didn't have a biological basis (Thompson, 1989, 1991a, 2001). More recently, with the arrival of the transsexualism phenomenon, it might seem as though biology has finally been vanquished. 'Gender' reigns, emotional feelings override any other kind of reality, and the biologically sexed body is argued away by changing the terminology—'he'

9

becomes 'she', the penis becomes female, etc.—and by bullying the reluctant into compliance.

This process has been enabled by liberal use of the word 'gender'. Unhooked from any reference to biological sex, it can mean anything. Because it has so many meanings it's often difficult to decide which one is being referred to: whether it's a synonym for 'sex' ('the gender of the fœtus'), or a substitute for 'women' (or more rarely, 'men') or for 'sex differences' or 'relations between the sexes', or whether it's a direct euphemism for male domination, or whether it denotes either some variety of misogynist ideology or alternatively, a feminist discourse. So malleable is the term 'gender' that its connotations are seemingly endless.

Whatever its referent, the main reason 'gender' is meaningless is because it obliterates the real political problem—male domination. The social problem uncovered by feminism is male supremacy, not 'gender' (or even 'women'). 'Gender' waters down the feminist message to incoherence. It may be that using 'gender' has enabled some of the more anodyne aspects of the feminist message to enter the mainstream. But without the concept of domination, at the very least it leads to confusion. Just being a man (or a woman) is not in itself a problem, and neither are relationships between the sexes. At worst, 'gender' allows anti-feminism to masquerade as feminism because it deletes the reason for the feminist enterprise. 'Gender' may not frighten, but neither does it enlighten.

'Masculinities'

Another reason why I find the 'masculinities' literature unhelpful is the use of the term 'masculinities' itself. The postmodern tendency to cast important words into the plural ('feminisms', 'sexualities', 'knowledges', 'logics', 'positionings', 'learnings', 'violences') trivialises and diminishes their significance. As Susan Hawthorne noted, 'What is presented as postmodern "feminisms" is a massive distortion of feminism and of the history of feminism'. This, too, has a euphemising function. It is, as Hawthorne pointed out, as though 'we are begging to be accepted'.[7] (See also: Hawthorne, 2016). It serves to soften references to a harsh reality by dissolving the phenomenon under discussion into fragments that disallow any overarching framework through which that reality might be named and challenged. As Schrock and Schwalbe said, it 'make[s] it hard to see what it is that masculinities have in common' (Schrock and Schwalbe, 2009: 280). These authors also point out

---

7. http://susanspoliticalblog.blogspot.com/2014/10/fragmented-feminisms.html – viewed 8.8.2018.

that it 'has fostered a kind of categorical essentialism in studies of men', by sorting men into 'conventional categories of race, ethnicity, sexuality, religion, or class'.

More importantly for my purposes, the use of the term 'masculinities' does not allow any distinction to be made between the masculinity required of men by male supremacy, and masculinity as simply a characteristic of men because they're men. R. W. Connell said that using the term 'masculinities' meant it was possible to 'recognize more than one kind of masculinity' (Connell, 1995: 76), but it is not clear on the face of it why that might be a political enterprise. The political task is not to identify ways of being a man since, in and of itself, being a man (or a woman) is not a social problem. The fact that men are different from each other is trivially true, i.e. it has no political implications. The political problematic is male domination, and the political task of analysing masculinity as a personality characteristic of male individuals is to identify only those ways of being a man which are complicit with domination. The concept of genuine humanity which I have introduced accepts the existence of male ways of being human which are not complicit with masculinity in the male supremacist sense. But these ways of being male and human do not need to be theorised because they have no relevance for an analysis of domination. The 'masculinities' literature tends on the whole to confuse the two—male supremacist masculinity and ways of being a male human being—and hence misrepresents the political project of identifying and resisting domination. Because the focus in this context is on the logic of domination which remains coherent no matter how multifarious its manifestations, the singular term, 'masculinity', is more appropriate.

Feminism and male domination

I regard this present project as an exercise in feminist theory because it follows on from a vast body of feminist work. However, this project differs from most of that prior feminist work because my focus is not primarily on women.[8] I do not ignore the harm done to the female half of the human race by the male supremacist system and the men who embrace it. The feminist focus on the harm done to women by men in, for example, rape, femicide (the murder of women by men because they can, and the leniency with which it is treated by the law), prostitution, pornography, the euphemistically termed 'domestic violence', exposes the system and its denial by the malestream. It

---

8. For a discussion of the limitations of defining feminism only in terms of 'women', see: Thompson, 2001: 64-72.

is an important and necessary focus, and it does bring public attention to bear on the most violent and degrading effects of the system. My primary focus, however, is on the system that wreaks the harm, a system that, while it oppresses women, is primarily concerned with stoking male power, often without any reference to women (e.g. that chief modern form of male power, capitalism). The feminist focus on women is perfectly valid, indeed vitally important, given that women are male supremacy's primary target of attack and exploitation. The very word 'feminism' means 'woman' after all (from the Latin word 'femina'). But the focus on concern for women can displace attention away from male domination as a system.

Moreover, as we've discovered, the malestream can acknowledge women and even the harms, as well as the need to do something about it, while ignoring the real problem. Take the example of 'domestic violence' (sometimes referred to as 'family violence', or worse, 'intimate partner violence'). Every government in the world, developed or developing, along with the United Nations, has taken it on board with policies, programs, projects, initiatives, political commitments, joint efforts, state responsibilities, etc., supposedly for dealing with it. But there is little or no discussion of the culture that condones and even encourages the violence. Of the systematic ways in which men are given permission to treat women with contempt—with pornography, prostitution, pop culture and advertising filling public spaces everywhere you look—little or nothing is said in the context of 'violence against women', much less anything done to change those cultural imperatives.

Even the fact that the perpetrators of 'domestic violence' are men is often absent from the policy discourses. For example, The NSW government's domestic violence 'blueprint for reform' (NSW Ministry of Health, 2016) lists 'women, men and children' as the victims whose lives are supposedly to be made 'safer' by this government initiative. But the text reveals the reality. 'Male victims' appears only once (on p.2), and there is no mention of whom they are victimised by (women? other men? the children? the furniture?). But there is a fairly large section devoted to 'men's behaviour change interventions' (p.3), in accordance with the reality that the main 'domestic violence' problem is the violence of men. In accordance with that same reality, women are not mentioned in this context of 'behaviour change', except for Aboriginal women (p.3). So the only female perpetrators of 'domestic violence', according to the NSW government's Ministry of Health, are Aboriginal women. Presumably the authors of this document were oblivious to this instance of racism. Men are finally acknowledged as perpetrators on p.7, in the section on 'Holding perpetrators accountable', which does not mention women at all. An earlier NSW government web page had not only explicitly denied that the systematic problem was the violence perpetrated by men, it even denied that women were the main victims. 'Domestic violence can happen to anyone', it said in a bold typeface headline,[9] thus expunging the system of male culpability and female victimisation altogether.

The United Nations is somewhat better. The description of the UN study of violence against women, *Ending Violence Against Women: from Words to Action*. Study of the Secretary-General,[10] launched on 9 October 2006, does include the phrase 'male violence against women' (once). But most of the time it is simply called 'violence against women' with the male agency deleted. Given this bowdlerisation and euphemisation, while the feminist focus on the harms to women was (and remains) important, there is a need to move beyond it as well, to expose every aspect of the system of domination that continues to harm not only women, but the whole human race, indeed, all life on the planet.

The recognition of male domination as the system that oppresses women is not absent from feminist accounts, of course. That is where I found it after all. As Mary O'Brien said: 'It is an axiom of feminist understanding that the dogmas of male supremacy invade all human institutions and pervade all modes of discourse' (O'Brien, 1986: 16). It is usually clear in feminist accounts (although surprisingly, not always) that the cause of women's oppression is male domination and the men who treat women with the violence and contempt mandated by the system. But I don't find feminism, even so-called 'radical feminism',[11] entirely adequate as an account of male domination, despite the fact that it was feminism that discovered the phenomenon.

Male violence against women is not the whole of male supremacy. Male domination is not always violent (although it is always corrupt and corrupting). It also seduces and presents itself as normality while disguising the harm it

---

9. http://www.domesticviolence.nsw.gov.au/ – viewed 26.8.2013. The website has since been changed.

10. http://www.un.org/womenwatch/daw/vaw/v-sg-ov.htm. I have been unable to find the full study on the UN website.

11. I am using the inverted commas because I do not agree that there are different forms of feminism. What is usually referred to as 'radical feminism' is simply feminism that needs no further modification (Thompson, 2001; MacKinnon, 1987). Prefacing feminism with a modifier, although well-intentioned in many cases (e.g. socialist feminism), modifies the feminist message, even to the extent that malestream discourses have been allowed to override the feminist message in the name of 'feminism'. The title of my 2001 book, *Radical Feminism Today*, was demanded by the publisher, despite the fact that it undermined the main argument of the book.

does by defining it as necessary, or even beneficial. The feminist critiques of the five institutional manifestations of male supremacy I discuss critically in what follows tend to focus on the harms done to women, and necessarily so, given how severely men exploit and harm women in these institutional arrangements, and how little women's interests are taken into account. My emphasis, however, (and it is an emphasis, not a disagreement or a criticism) is on the institutions themselves, sometimes on the ways they harm women (and humanity overall), but also on the fact that these institutions owe everything to the culture of masculinity that embraces the values of arrogant dissociation that create the kinds of men that wreak the harm.

Chapter Two: A Question of Culture

In talking about a culture of male supremacist masculinity, I am using the term 'culture' in the anthropological sense of a symbolic universe of meaning, not in the ordinary language sense of something other than, and superior to, everyday life. When I say 'a universe' of meaning, I don't mean something absolute. I use the term 'universe' to indicate something all-encompassing, certainly, something like Habermas' 'life worlds', Wittgenstein's 'forms of life' or Bourdieu's 'fields'. But its comprehensiveness does not mean that there are no alternatives, but rather that it is systematic, coherent and influential, and manifests itself in similar if not identical ways in individuals who have no tangible connection with each other. Culture is the common understanding of our shared reality, how we interpret what is happening and what we do.

The literature on 'culture', in anthropology, sociology and (more recently) cultural studies, is vast, and the debates about the concept's meaning, usage, scope and nature are by no means resolved to this day. I do not intend to review this literature.[12] In referring to masculinity as a kind of culture, I am not concerned with, for example, the foundational role of Marxism in the debates, with questions about the 'relative autonomy' of culture ('the superstructure') from the economic 'base' (in the Marxist version) or from 'society' (in the liberal democratic version) (e.g. Alexander, 1990; Sahlins, 1976). Neither am I concerned with the 'woman=nature'/'man=culture' debate, although I do think there is some truth in the latter homology. As far as I know, every culture that has ever existed has been male supremacist in the sense that its central organising principles revolve around what men want, or rather, what they should want in order to maintain masculinity as the 'human' norm. This is not inevitable. There are feminist accounts presenting evidence of early, pre-patriarchal societies where the culture was not male supremacist (e.g. Dexter, 1990; Gimbutas, 1989, 1991; the work of Max

---

12. For a classic account, see: Kroeber and Kluckhohn, 1963.

Dashu).[13] But we are all cultural beings anyway. We all make sense of the world through the meanings and values we are familiar with, and the genuine humanity I mentioned above is also a cultural phenomenon. So I am using the word 'culture' in a neutral sense, signifying simply meanings, values and understandings, i.e. the domain of the symbolic. In that sense, both feminism and the malestream are cultural.

Calling masculinity 'cultural' is intended to emphasise the fact that, like women, men are made not born. Or rather, masculinity is like femininity in that both are social phenomena not biological drives. Masculinity has nothing to do with hormones, for example (the usual culprit when one or another instance of egregious male behaviour is under discussion), and everything to do with how maleness is understood, valued, required and sanctioned. Calling it 'cultural' is more precise than calling it 'social' because of the importance of meaning and value in structuring worldviews, including that of masculinity. My purpose in using the term 'culture' rather than 'social' as a description of what masculinity 'is', is simply to underline the fairly limited point that what is at issue is a system of meanings and values—the symbolic. The term 'social' is not inappropriate for this purpose, but the term 'culture' is better.

This means that both the masculinity I am talking about and the genuine humanity are understandable only as social phenomena. Men are not violent and destructive because of something inherent in them. Violence and destruction are a consequence of a social environment of domination which gives men an inflated sense of their own importance (because they aren't women, the proof of which is their penis-possession), and denies them any grounding in genuine humanity. Men exercise violence for a variety of reasons: because they can; because the connection between violence and masculinity is encouraged even though it is also deplored; out of aggrieved resentment that they are not being given what they feel they're entitled to— sex or money or power or prestige; because violence is the default option in response to insult, real or perceived. Men's violence is a question of meaning and value, of choice and responsibility. There is always an alternative based in genuine humanity, if only they could see it.

Culture and social order

It is generally agreed that culture involves the establishment and maintenance of social order. To quote just one of the many commentators on this issue,

---

13. http://suppressedhistories.net/

Ernest Gellner: 'Social order requires a shared culture … any culture is a systematic prejudgement. Society needs entrenched paradigms … No society without culture, no culture without enforced prejudgement. Prejudgement alone makes social life and order possible' (Gellner, 1994: 32).[14] But a social order that needs to be enforced is a precarious one. Gellner did not discuss the implications of his use of the term 'enforced'. On the contrary, in true liberal fashion he remained focused on what he believed to be the bright side, the good society he called 'Civil Society' (caps in the original), i.e. the modern capitalist social democratic nation state. He argued that this was the kind of society where the prejudgement required for social order was less brutal than in any previous social arrangements. It 'was made milder and flexible, and yet order was maintained'. He referred to this as 'a miracle' (Gellner, 1994: 32).

However, Gellner's assumption that social order needs to be enforced is based on the belief that men (and it is men) need to be controlled. This belief is expressed in Hobbes's idea that man's natural state is a 'war of all against all' in which men would be constantly killing each other in struggles for ascendancy. This primal state of affairs is curbed by 'Leviathan', the strong central state which has the power to deter wrong-doers by imposing legitimate sanctions. The sociological question asked from this Hobbesian starting point is: 'How is social order possible?' (Gellner says it is enforced; other liberal theorists have said it comes about through a 'contract', a general agreement entered into when men realise that living together peaceably is preferable to constant strife). For example, Dennis Wrong couches the sociological question thus: 'How are men capable of uniting to form enduring societies in the first place? … How is man's animal nature domesticated by society?' (Wrong, 1961: 184). Wrong's assumption is that, if men need to unite then their original condition must be separation; and if they need to be domesticated, then they must originally be wild. The first question assumes that divisiveness not unity is the primal human condition; the other assumes that there's an animal aspect to being human that is prior to society and that needs to be 'domesticated' and therefore must be savage and dangerous.

This kind of questioning about the nature of society focuses on social order as the problem to be addressed ('How are men capable of uniting to form enduring societies in the first place?'), while finding the *breakdown* of social order theoretically unproblematic—that's just what men are like, or

---

14. Gellner, who died in 1995, was a philosopher, social anthropologist and all-round *enfant terrible* and scourge of the British intellectual elite (or at least, so his supporters believed) (http://gellnerpage.tripod.com/PStirlingObit.html – viewed 8.8.2018)

what they would be like if it were not for that puzzling ability they have to live together peaceably. It is theorising that is shaped and motivated by the symbolic violence of the culture of masculinity. It assumes that men are each others' natural enemies, and that Hobbes' 'war of all against all' is perfectly understandable (if reprehensible) and there is therefore no need to question it any further. This kind of theorising finds peace and goodwill curious and inexplicable, and violence, hatred, contempt and vicious conflict for control of 'scarce resources' only what is to be expected of men. It participates in masculinity's dissociated detachment by ignoring everyday existence where infants normally grow into social beings without the imposition of any strict methods of social control, and where people, men and women, get along together fairly well most of the time. And it participates in the inflated sense of entitlement by insisting that aggressive competitiveness is natural to 'human beings' (read: men), and hence that it is understandable that they might behave violently to get what they want, even though that violence must be restrained for the collective good. It regards the character structure of masculinity, with its 'unlimited resort to fraud and violence in pursuit of their ends' (Wrong, 1961: 185), not as the *product* of socialisation, but as a result of its failure.[15]

In contrast to the Hobbesian assumption of an innate lethal competitiveness, it is possible to assume instead a basic sociability that is disrupted by varying degrees of violence and aggression. The question then changes from 'How is social order possible?' to 'Why does social order break down?' Assuming an original cooperativeness is as plausible as assuming an original aggressiveness, if not more so, as anyone who has ever had any extended connection with infants would know. Alison Jaggar (among others) refers to this as 'human interdependence', pointing out that human infants need a long period of dependence on others within cooperative communities if they are to survive. If this were to be taken as the starting point for theorising society (she is speaking particularly of liberal theories of society), it would

---

15. To be fair, this does not apply to Wrong's main argument (although it *does* apply to his introduction to his argument). His main argument is a critique of those theories of human nature which give a simplistic answer to Hobbes' question about how social order is possible, by interpreting human beings as wholly socially determined, 'totally shaped by common norms or "institutionalized patterns"' (p.186). If that is so, he asks (quite rightly), 'How is it that violence, conflict, revolution, and the individual's sense of coercion by society manage to exist at all?' (p.186). He suggests that there are 'forces in man [sic] that are resistant to socialization' (p.191), and argues correctly that there is no socialisation without the possibility of resistance. However, he does start from the Hobbesian standpoint and thus accepts its basic premise that it is human sociability that is puzzling, not violence.

be 'egoism, competitiveness and conflict' which would become 'puzzling and problematic', not cooperation and community (Jaggar, 1983: 41. See also: Flax, 1983; Hartsock, 1985: 42; Hoagland, 1988: 250).

In contrast to the male supremacist assumption of inherent aggression, it is possible to take the assumption of an original cooperativeness as a starting point. Instead of assuming that human beings need to be tamed and domesticated, we can assume that we have an inherent propensity for sociability (men too), just as we have an innate propensity for language (and perhaps they are different aspects of the same thing). I do not intend to argue for this—it is just as plausible as the opposite assumption of inherent aggression. Neither is empirically testable because they are both assumptions about the whole of humanity and there is no control group.

But anyway (as Wrong points out), it is not a question of either/or— *either* human beings (or men) are innately aggressive, *or* they are innately sociable. Hobbes' question is the wrong question. That it should continue to be so influential is a consequence of the continuing influence of male supremacist beliefs about what men are like. The question is neither: what makes social order possible? nor: what makes social order break down? at least in part because social order and the culture which sustains it is not always a good thing. The term 'culture', as I am using it, does not necessarily refer to a pacifying and peaceable influence. It refers simply to a coherent structure of meanings and values. Sometimes the coherent culture can serve bad purposes. Capitalism, for example, is a source of exploitation and degradation, and yet it is coherent and influential. Dehumanisation can be embraced as a virtue, rather than being condemned as evil; and prevalent, widely accepted meanings (that is, ways in which the world is understood) can justify exploitation, oppression and degradation.

To take another example, slavery in the US was justified by appeals to custom, usage or tradition, that is, to culture (Binder, 1996; Wolff 2002). More precisely, the Reconstruction Amendments to the US Constitution had to defy custom and traditional usage in order to ban slavery and give all adult males equal rights including the right to vote.[16] As Guyora Binder has pointed out:

---

16. The Reconstruction Amendments are: the Thirteenth Amendment (1865) which abolished slavery; the Fourteenth Amendment (1868) which granted citizenship and equal protection to former slaves; and the Fifteenth Amendment (1870) which granted voting rights to all adult males. Women in the US did not get the vote until the Nineteenth Amendment was ratified in 1920 (another defiance of customary usage).

the institution of slavery was deeply and persistently entrenched in American society and culture … [and hence] the condemnation of slavery challenged the legitimacy of the very traditions and customs on which constitutional interpreters had always relied for guidance. It was the Reconstruction Amendments' command to abolish one of American culture's defining customs that rendered them peculiarly uninterpretable … [because] [t]o constitutionally abolish slavery was to disestablish and repudiate existing and enduring custom (Binder, 1996: 2066).

Male supremacy's masculinity is also 'existing and enduring custom'. The worst manifestations of anti-social activity, what Freud called the 'death instinct', are a consequence of the culture of male domination. Masculinity's 'fraud and violence' is a product of male supremacist socialisation, and not a failure of attempts to civilise him.

Feminism has long pointed out the ways in which culture is enforced through the subordination of women. I would also argue that the culture of masculinity as I describe it here is the source of the savagery that malestream thought has always located elsewhere than the social order. That 'elsewhere' is still 'nature', testosterone being the designation of choice these days although 'human nature' is still popular. But it is my contention that it is the culture of masculinity itself that is the source of the violence. It is a culture of *dis*order (always potential and sometimes actual) because it is a culture of domination. That disorder is not always catastrophic, although the frequency with which man-made catastrophes happen is the main reason for assuming the existence of an innate aggression. Sometimes, however, social breakdown is so subliminal that it is hardly noticed, felt simply through a persistent niggling sense of disquiet, alienation, depression or anxiety. But in its most extreme form masculinity is lethal because it is life-denying, savage and dangerous and not peaceable at all. On the contrary, a culture of male supremacist masculinity is responsible for all kinds of mayhem—war, bullying, torture, atrocities, mass murder, extermination, genocide, mass starvation, destitution alongside immense wealth. (See, for example: Barry, 2010, 2013; Hawthorne and Winter, eds, 2002; Morgan, 1990).

That the culture of male supremacy is deadly is common knowledge. Feminism has been saying it for years and is still saying it. Simone de Beauvoir, for example, attributed male domination (the 'understandable' belief that 'man would wish to dominate woman') (Beauvoir, 1972: 93) to the fact that men in prehistoric times put their lives at risk in hunting wild animals and fighting enemies. Men were 'the sex … which kills':

it is not in giving life but in risking life that man is raised above the animal; that is why superiority has been accorded in humanity not to the sex that brings forth but to that which kills (Beauvoir, 1972: 95-6).

While Beauvoir's appeal to 'prehistory' is wrong—men are trained to kill, it's not a genetic characteristic (Barry, 2010)—she clearly saw a connection between men and killing and was struggling to understand it.

For Andrea Dworkin the connection between men and killing was both age-old and ever-present:

> Men love death. In everything they make, they hollow out a central place for death … Men especially love murder. In art they celebrate it, and in life they commit it … as if murder were solace, stilling their sobs as they mourn the emptiness and alienation of their lives. Male history, romance, and adventure are stories of murder, literal or mythic … In male culture, slow murder is the heart of eros, fast murder is the heart of action, and systematized murder is the heart of history (Dworkin, 1977: 214-15).

The belief in culture as the source of social order takes this murderous imperative as 'natural', as an original human predisposition to aggressive competition. It is the business of 'society'/'culture' to curb this predisposition and create social order by making men (and the discussion is always about men) more or less forcibly into social beings.

The good news is that the terrible things that human beings do fall within the domain of human action and need not be so. What I am talking about in this present work is the preventable evil (i.e. evil that is the result of human action) that is male supremacy. I do not know if male supremacy can be held responsible for all forms of inhumanity. I do not know if humanly-devised evil would vanish from the human race if male supremacy were to be abolished. But it does seem clear to me that the dehumanisation, the dissociation, the overweening entitlement and the violence characteristic of male supremacist masculinity, is at the very least a major contributory factor to the age-old problem of 'man's inhumanity to man'.

Symbolic violence

Bourdieu's 'symbolic violence'[17] is a useful name for culture as a source of domination. It says that the cultural meanings and values that make the world comprehensible to us can harm people. It's a better name than 'ideology' to

---

17. e.g. Bourdieu, 1977: 171-97; 1990: chapter 7 'Symbolic capital' & chapter 8 'Modes of domination'; 1991: chapter 7, 'On symbolic power'; 2001.

describe the justifying of powerful vested interests,[18] both because it makes the harm explicit and because the meaning of 'ideology' has been euphemised to mean simply any set of ideas. It also acknowledges that socialising men and embedding them within culture does not stop the violence; it merely takes another form—through structured hierarchies of entitlement and deprivation communicated through the meanings and values of a world-taken-for-granted, rather than through the literal violence of person-to-person physical brutality.

'Symbolic power',[19] said Bourdieu, 'is that invisible power which can be exercised only with the complicity of those who do not want to know that they are subject to it or even that they themselves exercise it' (Bourdieu, 1991: 161). Again, '*symbolic violence* is that form of domination which ... is ... exerted *through* the communication in which it is disguised ... [It is] *censored*, *euphemized*, i.e. unrecognizable, socially recognized violence' (Bourdieu, 1977: 191—emphases in the original). Bourdieu called this form of domination 'gentle', because there is no physical coercion involved. It operates through 'acts of communication', through kinship networks, patronage and mentoring, and through 'gifts' which set up relationships of obligation and dependence. It is not usually regarded as domination at all (much less as violence), but as the world-taken-for-granted and, under normal conditions, it doesn't occur to anyone to question it. People's understanding of those normal conditions, however, needs to be manipulated in order for symbolic violence to function. That manipulation is rarely if ever deliberate, but current social arrangements must be 'disguised', 'censored' and 'euphemised', their real nature hidden if they are to be presented as the interests of all.

But the way in which Bourdieu used the concept of symbolic violence is unsatisfactory as an account of the kind of domination I am talking about, despite suggestive hints. The domination I am talking about does not happen only through complicity, but also through powerlessness. That powerlessness is rarely absolute: it may pertain only in one domain and not in others, for example. But domination would not be domination if it didn't make people powerless, that is part of what the word means. Refusing to be complicit is important if domination is to be resisted, and it may be the only form of resistance available for most people most of the time. But domination is

---

18. Thompson 2001: 22-9. Indeed, Bourdieu himself discusses symbolic power in the context of the concept of ideology (Bourdieu, 1991: 167).

19. Bourdieu uses 'symbolic power' and 'symbolic violence' interchangeably, e.g. '"symbolic systems" fulfil their political function ... as instruments which help to ensure that one class dominates another (symbolic violence)' (Bourdieu, 1991: 167).

not overcome simply by refusing compliance. For example, the globalised industry which is the origin of the clothing and textiles sold in the rich nations of the West is horrendously exploitative, but we are all complicit with that exploitation to the extent that we have no other source of clothing. We have to buy it if we don't want to walk around naked; and in buying the clothes (and other commodities), we at least enable the people who make them to stay in work, exploitative, underpaid and sometimes dangerous though it might be. People have demonstrated all over the world that they don't want garments made under dangerous sweat-shop conditions; but the industry carries on regardless, with or without token gestures towards regulation. Within the capitalist ethos firms have no choice if they want to stay ahead in the competition to keep costs down, a competition that involves scrimping and saving on the health and safety of non-unionised workers. Symbolic violence makes us complicit, but sometimes we have little or no choice. Again, that is what domination does—it deprives people of the resources and capabilities for making informed choices.

Another reason for the inadequacy of Bourdieu's concept is that his symbolic violence does no harm, or none that he tells us about. His is a rather pallid account of domination involving simply differences of aesthetic taste between 'classes' or 'groups' of people. As he put it in the Preface to *Distinction*, the book is 'seeking in the structure of the social classes the basis of the systems of classification which structure perception of the social world and *designate the objects of aesthetic enjoyment*' (Bourdieu, 1984: xv—emphasis added). He was, as one commentator put it, 'centrally preoccupied with the sociology of taste' (Bennett, 2013: xvii). Because they involve hierarchy and privilege, those distinctions might be invidious, but Bourdieu gives us no account of how they are harmful or even if they are.

But whatever the limitations of the way in which Bourdieu uses it, the term 'symbolic violence' neatly sums up the normal mode of operation of the modern form of domination, which does not assert its power through overt physical violence. The prevalence of war and mass murder, and the continuing male violence against women, are not always how domination is maintained. They are manifestations of domination and evidence of the ever-present threat of its essential violence. Men who bash and kill women, rape, pillage, commit mass slaughter and otherwise run amok, are given permission by a culture of male entitlement and dissociation from genuine humanity. But for the most part most of the time, overt violence is not necessary to keep society under conditions of domination; that maintenance is effected symbolically, through meanings and values, through the ways in which we understand the world and act within it, and through the reasons we find for doing what we do.

A culture of masculinity

The culture of masculinity, then, is symbolic violence. It is violent because of the harm it does; and it is 'symbolic' because that harm is not confined to physical violence but happens through other means whose violent nature is euphemised and denied. Capitalism, for example, does not by and large operate through physical violence (although it is not averse to doing so when it can get away with it, sometimes using the state's institutions of legitimate violence, the police and the military). Its domination operates through control over the production and distribution of wealth, of the material conditions of the lives of everyone, and of influential means of mass communication.

As culture, masculinity is a shared commonality which all its native inhabitants can understand and recognise (although not necessarily put into words), women as well as men, and children as well as adults. This culture establishes and maintains a character structure which defines what men are, how they ought to make sense of their lives, and what they ought to be if they are to qualify as masculine. This culture is meant for men and men embrace it, even if not all men do so all the time, even though men can be ambivalent, resistant or opposed to it, and even though its most extreme forms are infrequent,[20] at least in the privileged nations most of the time. At the same time, not only men embrace the culture of masculinity. Women too

---

20. However, male violence against women is not infrequent. In Australia around one woman a week, on average, is killed by her (male) 'intimate partner' (https://www.whiteribbon. org.au/understand-domestic-violence/facts-violence-women/domestic-violence-statistics/ – viewed 8.8.2018). This figure was widely reported in the Australian media when anti-domestic violence campaigner, Rosie Batty was named Australian of the Year on Australia Day 2015. Her husband had killed their eleven-year-old son in front of dozens of witnesses. The source is a report on homicide from the Australian Institute of Criminology (Chan and Payne, 2013), which said that, during the two years 2008-09 and 2009-10, 116 women were killed 'by an offender with whom they shared a principal domestic relationship' (p.18) (i.e. 58 women a year on average). Like all official reports, this publication is frustratingly limited in the information it provides. For example, it said that there were also 75 men who were killed by an 'intimate partner' in the same period (p.18), but the sex of the killers wasn't mentioned in the case of either sex. So 39% of those killed by an 'intimate partner' were men (75 of 191 people). Neither the report nor the media commented on this latter statistic. On the face of it, it looks as though nearly two-fifths of the 'intimate partner' killers were women. But given that the vast majority of killers are men (88% during these two years in Australia), this figure needs explaining. Perhaps these are men who were killed by female partners who fought back after years of abuse, but it is not possible to find out from this report. It does have a section on 'Motive' (p.15), but the motives are not broken down by sex; and anyway, there is no category for women who kill abusive male partners.

can be complicit, not in the sense that they can successfully 'be' masculine (although they can ape men), but in the sense that they can shore up the male sense of self-importance and entitlement ('reflect men at twice their natural size'), in the sense that they can supply without reciprocity the human reality men are detached from, in the sense that they can embrace femininity, masculinity's handmaiden, and in the sense that women, too, are participants in the institutions designed to purvey male domination as the interests of all. The system makes us all complicit, although not to the same degree or with the same awareness. It is possible to be more or less complicit, and to be more or less aware of what we cannot change (yet) but would if we could.

Character structure

One of the more insightful accounts of the kind of character structure required of men by male supremacy was given by Sandra Harding (1981). There are problems with her account, not least of which is the attributing of male supremacy to the fact that mothering is done by women.[21] This is her account of 'the natures of the humans who design and control patriarchy and capital':

> The frantic maintenance of dualisms between mind and body, between culture and nature, between highly-valued self and devalued others, take their first forms in the process of becoming a male person who must individuate himself from a devalued woman. Thus infant boys' psychological birth in families with our division of labor by gender produces men who will be excessively rationalistic [i.e. dissociated], who will need to dominate not only others but also their feelings, their physical bodies, and other bodies—nature—in general. They will be excessively competitive and concerned primarily with their own projects. They will maintain an excessive separation or distance from the concerns of those around them, especially those unlike themselves. It produces misogyny and male-bonding as prototypes of appropriate social relations with others perceived to be respectively unlike and like themselves. And, as Jane Flax argues, our division of labor by gender itself produces the repression of infantile experience in both boys and girls and consequently a great deal of covert adult acting out of unresolved infantile projects (Harding, 1981: 152-3).

As I have already noted, there are problems with this account. As well as the problem of blaming male supremacy on mothering by women, there is the use of the word 'gender' and 'our division of labor by gender' instead of

---

21. This was a common argument in the academic feminism of the time—see: Benjamin, 1988; Chodorow, 1978; Dinnerstein, 1976; Flax, 1990.

the naming of male domination. There's also too much importance given to 'dualisms' (another preoccupation of the time)—it comes first in the list of personality characteristics. Nonetheless, this is a good succinct summary of the character structure of male supremacy—the hyper-valuation of self and the devaluation of others, the hyper-rationalism to the point of dissociation, the need to dominate, the competitiveness and self-absorption, the distancing and separation from self and others, the misogyny and male-bonding, the location of the origin of the problem in infancy (although it should be the helplessness of infancy, not the fact that women mother), and the adult acting out of infantile projects.

So although 'masculinity' as I am using the term does not refer to men as such, it does refer to a certain kind of character structure required of all men, although not always in the same way because male domination establishes dehumanising hierarchies of worth and worthlessness among men, as well as between men and women. As I am using the term 'masculinity', it refers to the persona of the dominator under conditions of male supremacy, whether the system automatically grants him what he feels he is entitled to, or whether he has to use violence to get what he wants or to express his rage at being deprived.

That character structure is not confined to obviously privileged men (the male desire to prostitute women, for example, can be found at all levels of the hierarchy of masculinist privilege), and it manifests differently depending on where a man is located on that hierarchy. All men have access to a kind of subjectivity—desires, motivations, beliefs, actions, sense of self—which both requires and is required by a world social order structured around the meanings and values of male domination. All men have access to a 'human' status bought at women's expense, to a sense of self which depends on contempt for women, whose comfort, peace and security require the subordination of women, and whose rage at their perceived grievances is disproportionately directed towards women.

Kalish and Kimmel (2010) introduced the concept of 'aggrieved entitlement' in the context of mass shootings in the US, to describe what the authors felt was motivating the young men who were committing the murders. All were at the bottom of the hierarchy of masculine entitlement at their respective schools—outcasts who were viciously bullied daily while the relevant authorities turned a blind eye—and all used the typically masculine way of getting revenge—violence. Although these boys were dominated not dominating, their response was typically male supremacist. (The authors called it 'heteronormative') (p.455). The bullying they were subjected to is also male supremacist. It is male supremacy's way of socialising men into accepting violence as the only solution. In the case of boys and men who become mass murderers, it is wildly successful (as it is in the case of the men who own, control, wield and deploy the weapons of mass destruction routinely used to 'solve' perceived threats, whether domestically or internationally) (See also: Ford, 2016; Hamby, 2012; Katz, 2012).

The character structure of domination is something that men who embrace its meanings and values strive to be, but it is also something which, to the extent that they attain it, dehumanises them. To the extent that men are human beings, they are not like this. The version of reality that I call male supremacist is lethal for men too, as well as being lethal for women. At the same time, however, men do participate in that structure, embrace it as their own and defend it to the death. It does have its effects on the male psyche, because it presents itself as male, because it promises certain powerful benefits, and because it is the status quo. Men flock to its upper echelons—as amassers of wealth, CEOs of gigantic corporations, famous and revered historical personages, and leaders of all kinds, military, political, religious, cultural—and those who can't make it to the top honour, worship and envy those who do, or react with aggrieved resentment and murderous violence at their exclusion from what they are convinced they are entitled to. Men are expected, and expect themselves, to behave in accordance with this character structure that scrambles for power at any cost. Men can also resist it and refuse to be implicated, especially in its most obviously dehumanised forms.

'A huge thing'

So at the centre of the symbolic violence that is male supremacist masculinity stands the penis (Thompson, 1991a, 1996). A fascinating description of this centrality can be found in a passage from Jung's autobiography, *Memories, Dreams, Reflections*. Jung is reporting a dream he had when he was 'between three and four years old'. In the dream he was in a large room underground, at one end of which was a low platform on which stood 'a wonderfully rich golden throne'. There was something standing on the throne, which the little dreamer at first thought was a tree trunk. It was 'twelve to fifteen feet high and about one to two feet thick … a huge thing, reaching almost to the ceiling'. But it was also not like a tree trunk because 'it was made of skin and naked flesh, and on top there was something like a rounded head with no face and no hair', while on 'the very top of the head was a single eye, gazing motionlessly upwards'. The child was paralysed with fear because he thought the thing might get off the throne and come towards him. Then he heard his mother's voice saying: "'Yes, just look at him. That is the man-eater'". The child's terror intensified and he was afraid to go to sleep for many nights afterwards. Jung said that it wasn't until years later that he recognised the thing on the throne as a phallus (quoted in Jung, 1989: ix).

Jung himself did not interpret this dream in terms of the foundational myth of penis-possession under male supremacy—gigantic, many times its natural size, horrendously powerful and terrifying in its cannibalistic destruction of human life. He cogitated about the fact that it was upright and about the possibility that the room under the ground was a grave, and said that he didn't 'know where the anatomically correct phallus can have come from'. He eventually came to the odd conclusion that the phallus was an 'underground counterpart' for 'the Lord Jesus', 'a subterranean God "not to be named"', because the image had occurred to him throughout his childhood whenever 'anyone spoke too loudly about the Lord Jesus'. But he made no comment about what his 'mother' had said.

The German word his 'mother' used would have been 'Menschenfresser', which literally means 'human being-eater'. So does the English word 'man-eater', neither word being sex-specific. Both words also refer to the 'man-eater' as something non-human, an animal like a shark or a tiger, because both languages have another word for people who eat people, namely 'cannibal'/'Kannibale'. So what Jung's infant psyche was saying in the person of his 'mother' was: 'Here is what feeds off and destroys human life—male power become monstrous, subterranean and inhuman'.

Of course, the dream could have another, more mundane interpretation. Jung's father was a pastor, and although he was losing his faith during Carl Gustav's childhood, it is likely that the loud voice speaking about the Lord Jesus would have been his father's. In fact, it's possible that his father's voice was the loudest when he was least sure about the reality of the Lord Jesus, as he desperately tried to convince himself and everyone else that he did believe after all. Perhaps Carl Gustav picked up the anguish his father was feeling because of the doubt and the dishonesty of the attempt to hide it. However, that doesn't explain the fact that the phallus was enthroned.

His relationship with his mother when he was a child was not good. She was clearly depressed and spent much of the time in her own room, and she probably blamed men in general, and marriage to his father in particular, for the dreary emptiness of her life. And she would have been right about that. Carl Gustav was the only one of four children born to her that survived, and she was trapped in the marriage as women were in the nineteenth century.

Perhaps the child had picked up his mother's frustration and the reasons she gave herself for it. But is this another interpretation or the same one from a slightly different perspective?

The reason middle-class women's lives were tightly restricted in the nineteenth century was their subordination to men. (John Stuart Mill and Harriet Taylor had a great deal to say about this). Whether or not Jung's mother would have put it in terms of a monstrous phallus, Carl Gustav certainly did. And whether the monstrosity was an intimation of social reality in general, or simply a small boy's subliminal perception of his mother's despair, we'll never know. In fact, I'm not concerned about the epistemological status of Jung's dream. It serves merely as a word picture portraying the most extreme form of the character structure of male supremacist masculinity—an overweening entitlement that is monstrously arrogant, terrifying, lethal and inhuman. Jung's dream was unique to him, and yet it expressed more clearly than his waking mind was ever to let him know, the phallic monstrosity that looms over all of us.

The right wing

«la droite est une forme idéologique propre aux relations de domination» ('the Right is an ideological form belonging to relations of domination') (Guillaumin, 1986, 1995).

'[the British Conservative Party] has begun to see itself as the defender of individual freedom against the encroachments of the state … [whereas in Scruton's view] the conservative attitude seeks above all for government, and regards no citizen as possessed of a natural right that transcends his obligation to be ruled (Roger Scruton, quoted in Edgar, 1984: 45).

It is not immediately apparent why a spatial metaphor ('left' and 'right') is used to denote differing political positions. However, according to Seymour Martin Lipset, it originated in the seating arrangements of the delegates to the National Convention of the First French Republic (1792-1804):

The political and sociological analysis of modern society in terms of left, center, and right goes back to the days of the first French Republic when the delegates were seated, according to their political coloration, in a continuous semi-circle from the most radical and egalitarian on the left to the most moderate and aristocratic on the right. The identification of the left with advocacy of social reform and egalitarianism; the right, with aristocracy and conservatism, deepened as politics became defined as the clash between classes. Nineteenth-century conservatives and

> Marxists alike joined in the assumption that the socioeconomic cleavage
> is the most basic in modern society (Lipset 1981: 127-8).

There are some problems with this account of Lipset's. There is his assumption that such a thing as a political 'centre' exists, whereas it is more likely that left and right are so antithetical as to have no common meeting ground:

> The center does not exist in politics … Every Center is divided against itself and remains separated into two halves, Left-Center and Right-Center … The dream of the Center is to achieve a synthesis of contradictory aspirations; but synthesis is a power only of the mind. Action involves choice and politics involve action … There are no true Centers, only superimposed dualisms.[22]

There cannot be a political 'centre' when the interests involved are irreconcilable.

Again, Lipset's placing of moderation in the right-wing camp, even historically, is strange and he does not explain it. While the French revolutionary government were certainly far from moderate—their Orwellian 'Committee of Public Safety' instigated the earliest reign of terror of the modern world—there was nothing moderate about the earlier absolutist monarchy either.

His account, however, does contain the conventional connotations of the distinction between left and right: that it crucially revolves around class (i.e. economic) interests, with egalitarianism, social reform and concern with the interests of the economically disadvantaged on the left, and support for the powerful and privileged on the right. The distinction is most commonly characterised in terms of 'equality' and 'inequality', with the left in favour of equality and the right defending inequality. As Anthony Giddens put it: 'On the whole, the right is more happy to tolerate the existence of inequalities than the left, and more prone to support the powerful than the powerless' (Giddens, 1994: 251).

However, 'inequality' is a euphemism for domination, a world economy which ensures that some become unimaginably wealthy while others starve (as I argue in chapters 7 and 8). The right wing's defence of 'inequality' is actually a defence of power and privilege at the expense of those whom the system deprives of basic human necessities. Right-wing meanings and values justifying 'inequality' serve to justify domination.

---

22. M. Duverger *Political Parties: Their Organization and Activity in the Modern State* 1964: 215, quoted in Daalder, 1984: 92.

As well as the euphemising function of the term 'inequality', the use of the terms 'left' and 'right' themselves is a euphemism. The terms have never been an adequate designation of the political reality of liberal democracy. As a horizontal spatial metaphor, 'left' and 'right' imply an equivalence that is spurious. They flatten out what is actually a hierarchical relation of power. Because the right wing is the party of power and the left is the resistance to that power, they are not just two evenly matched discourses. There is no equality between left and right. This is the reason why the political left is in such disarray. As an apologia for domination, the right wing benefits from the power of the powerful; the left wing on the other hand, because it challenges that power, is constantly embattled, trivialised and derided, and constantly compromised by having to make accommodations with the manipulated consent that dominates the mass media. Governments which have traditionally been seen to lean towards the left of a purported spectrum of politics (e.g. New Labour in the UK, the Australian Labor Party) have embraced policies differing in no substantive way from those of the right-wing. The ease with which this has happened suggests that the social democratic attempt to compromise with capitalism has failed.

Marxism has argued for generations that the state must serve capital, all governments, liberal democratic or not, self-styled 'left-wing' or not: 'The executive of the modern state is but a committee for managing the common affairs of the whole bourgeoisie' (*The Communist Manifesto*). The consequence of not complying is exclusion from parliamentary politics altogether. In the last several decades of the neo-liberal hegemony, parliamentary politics has shamelessly moved even further to the right, blatantly working in the interests of the rich and powerful to an extent not seen since before World War II. As a consequence, the right is flourishing.

But domination is first and foremost male domination (whatever else it may be as well). So the right wing is the culture that most clearly expresses the symbolic violence of masculine entitlement and dissociation. The right wing is also defending the prerogatives of masculine entitlement when it defends 'inequality' and power and privilege at others' expense.

Two right wings

There are currently two strands of the right wing,[23] which can conflict with each other although in the functions they serve for domination they are as one. One strand is what is called 'neo-liberalism', the other strand is an old-

---

23. Barry, 1987; Bosanquet, 1983; Green, 1987; Hall and Jacques, 1983; Levitas, 1986a, b; Loxley and Thomas, 2001; Sawer, ed., 1982

style conservatism, which has a longer history but which is still useful as a form of social control. Both strands find a common cause in the functions they serve in presenting domination ('inequality') as the interests of all.

Neo-liberalism is the most recent name for the right-wing beliefs and practice.[24] Earlier names are: the New Right; Thatcherism; Reaganism; Rogernomics (in New Zealand); and the Washington consensus. It is the ideology of a resurgent, unfettered capitalism. It rose to prominence in the 1980s both as a backlash to the counter-cultural agitation of the 1960s and 1970s, and as an apologia for the unleashing of capital, which had been somewhat reined in since the end of the Second World War by regulation and the welfare state. Lulled into a false sense of security by the twentieth-century post-war interregnum of (relative) social peace, capitalism has thrown caution and Keynesianism to the winds, growing more and more avid and excessive ever since the 1970s. Neo-liberalism is the justification used by ideologues, including 'democratic' governments, to pander capitalism's ever more shameless depredations to electorates; or as Loïc Wacquant put it: 'neoliberalism [is] *an articulation of state, market and citizenship* that harnesses the first to impose the stamp of the second onto the third' (Wacquant, 2012: 66—original emphasis). Its purpose has been to make the rich richer, or in other words, to extend the logic of masculine entitlement and dissociation without limit. In that, it has been phenomenally successful. The male power that is wealth is now more monstrous than ever before in history—and humanity is paying the price.

Neo-liberalism, at least in the form it has taken in the last three or four decades, might seem like a new development. However, it is in fact not new (as Ruth Levitas has pointed out), even though the free-market ideas of neo-liberalism are 'newly ascendant' and 'accompanied by a qualitative shift against government intervention'. These ideas date back at least to the end of the nineteenth century: 'private capital has always defended itself against socialism and organized labour in this way', she said (Levitas, 1986a: 3). Moreover, however passé some tenets of old-style conservatism might appear—the distrust of libertarianism, the belief in moral decay, the defence of religion and the patriarchal family—it, too, presents ideological justifications for the maintenance of domination, especially for male control over women and their reproductive capacities.

---

24. The term 'alt-right' (short for 'alternative right'), a name the far-right in the US have given themselves, doesn't cover the whole spectrum on the political right, only the most extreme version.

Rebecca Klatch's research with women of the New Right in the US (1987, 1994) showed the distinction between two types of right-wing particularly clearly. The women, Klatch said, divided into two distinct groups on the basis of their beliefs about human nature, the family, society, women and the state. On the surface the two sets of views were not only different, they were in opposition, even though all of the women identified as 'conservative' and all had supported the 1980 election of Ronald Reagan. Klatch called these two groups of women the 'social conservatives' and the 'laissez-faire conservatives' (i.e. what has subsequently become known as neo-liberalism).

The social conservative set of beliefs sees the world, and US society in particular, in religious terms and regards the family as the building-block of society. Both family and religion are vitally important because human beings (aka men, but covertly) are believed to have no natural limits on their appetites and instincts, and only the family and religion can tame human passions and transform self-interest into the larger good. The chief concern is what is seen as the moral decay of America, caused by the disintegration of the basic unit of society, the family. The relationship between the sexes is one of rigid distinction ordained by Scripture. Men are the leaders, especially in the spiritual domain. They are also the decision-makers within the family, and it is women's duty to defer to men and support them through altruism and self-sacrifice.

In the laissez-faire conservative worldview, the highest value is the liberty of the individual, seen primarily as the economic liberty of the free market and the political liberty of a minimal state. It is the individual, not the family, that is the basic unit of society; and it is the erosion of liberty, not moral decay, which is the main concern. The top priorities for the nation are the economy and military 'defence' (because liberty requires the nation to be 'strong'). There is no concern about men's and women's roles nor about any need for male authority and female submission. In fact, such beliefs are antithetical to the laissez-faire worldview, which regards women as well as men as self-interested agents with free will, fully capable of and responsible for their own actions. Both sexes are threatened when freedom is eroded, not just women.

Given these differences between two varieties of New Right thought, it is difficult to see what they might have in common. Klatch said that they agreed on who the enemy is—'Communism and Big Government'—but even here they disagreed about what these might mean (Klatch, 1987: 5-6). However, Ruth Levitas (1986a, b), who characterised the two strands of New Right thought within the context of Thatcherism in the UK as neo-liberal economics and social authoritarianism (or neo-conservatism), argued that, although they were often incompatible, their common interests overrode their differences. Even though their basic principles—'freedom' for the former, 'authority' for the latter—were in conflict, they were rarely in disagreement about policy, and what seemed like contradictions on the surface masked deeper continuities. Both were in favour of a strong state, for example, in the areas of national 'defence' and law enforcement.

The neo-liberal putative detestation of 'big government' does not conflict with the neo-conservative veneration of authority when 'big government' is re-named 'strong government'. 'Big government' is applauded by the right-wing when it consists of actual or potential violence exercised against an enemy without (by the 'defence forces') or against those within the nation state who can be portrayed as undeserving—hooligans, rioters, criminals, the unemployed, terrorists, indigenous peoples, and others seen as feckless and improvident such as single mothers. Those who 'choose' not to exercise their economic freedom (and both strands agree that it is a matter of choice) cannot expect to evade the dictates of authority—the neo-liberal policy of 'welfare reform' is crystal clear on this. Neo-liberal liberty is not for those who have failed to take advantage of the economic opportunities regarded as equally available to all. In their case, they must submit to the authority of the state if they want to be supplied with the resources they should have acquired by their own unaided efforts. In this use of authority—against the powerless and against a real or imagined 'enemy' without—neo-liberalism and neo-conservatism are at one.

Nonetheless, although the liberty venerated by neo-liberalism is not the 'licence' feared by the conservative right, there is an aspect of neo-conservatism which is still uncomfortable with the liberty and individualism of neo-liberalism. Since liberty is something that belongs only to individuals, neo-liberalism is essentially individualistic and this brings it into conflict with neo-conservatism because conservatism's reverence for tradition commits it to an anti-individualism which subordinates the individual to the collective. In the conservative tradition, the liberty of the individual is a chimera.

Edmund Burke, for example, argued in his philippic against the French Revolution and its rallying cry of 'liberty' and the 'Rights of Man', that men who acted as if they were their own masters 'would become little better than the flies of a summer', because they took no account of what they had received from their ancestors or what they owed to posterity (Waldron, ed., 1987: 116). Worse, without the continuity provided by law, custom and tradition they become 'a nation of gross, stupid, ferocious, and at the same time, poor and sordid barbarians, destitute of religion, honour, or manly pride' (Waldron, ed., 1987: 113). Or to quote a more recent epigone (with a less colourful line in political invective): 'in a society where individuality seeks to realize itself independently of the institutions and traditions that have nurtured it … the civil order is threatened' (Scruton, 1984: 34).

Moreover, the conservative branch of the right-wing rejects neo-liberalism's embrace of economic freedom at any cost. One conservative UK commentator in the 1970s said he knew that any reassertion of state authority could mean curtailing the liberty of businessmen to 'pursue profit regardless of … the possible social repercussions', but he believed that that was the price that had to be paid for social stability and giving people what they really wanted:

> The spectre haunting most people is neither that of a totalitarian state nor of Big Brother but of other ordinary people being allowed to run wild. What they are worried about is crime, violence, disorder in the schools, promiscuity, idleness, pornography, football hooliganism, vandalism, and urban terrorism … for Mrs Thatcher to tell a party indignant at the collapse of all forms of authority, and longing for the smack of firm government, that the country is suffering from a lack of liberty makes her seem out of touch with reality … The urgent need today is for the state to regain control over "the people", to reassert its authority, and it is useless to imagine that this will be helped by some libertarian mishmash (Peregrine Worsthorne, quoted in Edgar, 1984: 44-5).

In the US, too, neo-conservatives were unhappy with unbridled capitalism. Irving Kristol, for example (labelled 'the godfather of neo-conservatism' and its 'leading architect' in his obituary in the *Washington Post*) (Bernstein, 2009), was known to be highly critical of the free-market panegyrics of Hayek and the Friedmans. Although the chief target of his opprobrium was the new left radicalism of the 1960s, which he regarded as the source of the "'self-destructive nihilism'" that was threatening American society, he was not very enthusiastic about capitalism either—one of his books is called *Two Cheers for Capitalism*. He believed that it was now "'a system for the impersonal liberation and satisfaction of appetites'", and that it had therefore "'inexorably eroded … self government, the basic principle of the republic … in favour of self-seeking, self-indulgence and just plain selfishness'" (quoted in Edgar, 1984: 47). So while neo-liberalism is quite comfortable with neo-conservatism's central defining characteristic, 'authority' (as long as it is visited only on the helpless within and the enemy without), neo-conservatism is less happy with neo-liberalism's central defining characteristic, 'freedom'.

But despite the essential individualism of liberty, the 'liberty' which is so crucial to the ethos of neo-liberalism is not at all what it is made out to be. First and foremost it is the freedom of 'the market' and not of individuals at all. As a British government document from the 1980s put it, 'economic freedom is the essence of personal freedom' (quoted in Levitas, 1986b: 91). With its 'invisible hand' and its 'laws' that cannot be flouted, or not with impunity, it is the very antithesis of individual liberty. The contradiction is managed by being ignored, and the emphasis on the individual remains untroubled by awkward questions about the nature of human agency in the face of a phenomenon ('the market') that remains impervious to any human action except obedience to its rulings. It will not allow people to plan their material existence collectively (e.g. by way of a socialist state); nor will it allow people to make reparation for the damage caused by uncontrolled market forces (e.g. through mandatory restrictions on carbon emissions, or through a welfare state). And yet, neo-liberalism purveys 'the market' as the very fount and origin of liberty. The market's capacity to create enormous wealth and concentrate it in the hands of the few is portrayed as the skill, intelligence and daring of individuals who are entitled to claim it as 'private property' because they have 'earned' it, while its equally great capacity to create poverty is seen as the fault of those who find themselves poor. Neo-liberalism's 'individualism', then, inalienable aspect of its ideology though it might be, is spurious and flawed.

It is unlikely that arguments to the effect that neo-liberalism's 'liberty' is not liberty at all would mitigate social authoritarianism's distaste for the libertarianism claimed in the name of neo-liberalism. But reconciliation on this point is not really necessary, given their agreement about the need for 'authority'. Both are staunch advocates of law and order, social conservatism explicitly so—vide Worsthorne's assertion above about 'crime, violence' (etc.). Neo-liberalism's support for liberty vanishes, and its true authoritarian colours show in its detestation of the welfare state (people who are poor must be punished for their poverty), its 'counter-terrorism' policies and practices, and its warmongering towards anything that stands in the way of capitalist expansion.

And it does have a predilection for jailing people. Over the decades of neo-liberal rule, the numbers of people in prison populations have grown, especially in the US, where the number of prison inmates grew by 274% between 1980 and 2009 (Pew Center, 2009). In Australia the number of prisoners increased by 36% between 1999 and 2009 (ABS, 2009), and continues to rise. Between 2014 and 2015, the numbers in custody increased by 7%, while the numbers of those in custody waiting to be sentenced increased by 21% (ABS, 2015). In the UK the prison population of England and Wales also increased between 1993 and 2012, both because of 'tougher sentencing and enforcement outcomes', and because the offences coming before the courts were more serious (although drug offences were included among the 'more serious' offences) (UK Government, 2013: 2).[25]

This growth is not the result of rising crime rates, at least in the US, which were already falling before the introduction of harsher penalties. It is the result of deliberate government increases in penalties, such as mandatory sentencing, 'truth in sentencing', 'three-strike laws', etc. The latter are statutes that mandate long prison sentences, frequently life imprisonment, for offenders who are convicted of a third offence. (The terminology comes from baseball—'three strikes and you're out'—although the US prison system is hardly a game). Not all of those convicted under 'three-strike' laws are innocent. Some of these men have committed horrendous crimes. However, while the 'three-strike' law is supposedly intended only for serious crimes, violent felonies rather than misdemeanours, in some states the statutes are so broadly defined that someone can be sent to prison for life for minor offences: 'In 1997 [in California], over 60 percent of all Third Strike offenders were sentenced for nonviolent and nonserious offenses' (Males and Macallair, 1999: 65).

This is the strong state so cherished by both old-style conservatism and neo-liberalism. It is a state that makes examples of 'those unwilling to accept the brisk logic of unfettered capitalism' (Edgar, 1984: 54) (or those unable to). It is a state that reassures those made fearful by the consequences of that same logic—poverty, desperation, degradation and violence—by providing scapegoats and demonstrating that they have been summarily dealt with. It is a state informed by the logic of an unfettered capitalism that requires others to be fettered. It is a state that increasingly regulates the rest of us the more it deregulates capitalism. It is a state that punishes those who can least help themselves, and rewards those who have the power to impose their demands

_____

25. In contrast, there are some countries where prison populations have diminished so much that other uses have been found for the prisons. In the Netherlands, for example, prisons are being used to house refugees. They are not, however, incarcerated (unlike the policy in Australia), but are free to come and go as they please while they wait for the results of their applications for asylum (https://news.nationalgeographic.com/2016/05/160517-refugees-netherlands-prisons/ – viewed 8.8.2018).

on society. It is a state with a selective emphasis on liberty, as devoted to law and order as any explicitly authoritarian discourse.

As well as jailing people, neo-liberalism's authoritarianism shows itself through such policies as 'welfare reform', 'mutual obligation', 'workfare', 'active labour market', 'social inclusion' (originally 'social exclusion'). These neo-liberal policies (and others) locate the responsibility for any failure to succeed squarely on the shoulders of those who have failed. These are the people who must be strictly controlled, their conduct monitored, their activities tracked, their defalcations noted and sanctioned, their dependency deplored, until they enter the labour force (which has its own forms of law and order—and of dependence), or they become dependent on emergency services instead (hospitals, crisis accommodation, refuges, police cells and prisons, charity), or they drop out of the system altogether,[26] or they die. These are the people—the unemployed, single mothers, the disabled, the mentally-ill, the young and the old (the latter constituting the 'dependency ratio' when their numbers are compared with those of workforce age)—who feel the weight of an authority dictated by the requirements of a market economy to which they cannot contribute.

As well as agreement on the need for a strong state, the two strands of the New Right find common cause in the moralism that social conservatism espouses explicitly. The social conservative praise for 'family values', for example, suits neo-liberal purposes well. Neo-liberalism needs 'the family' (i.e. the caring work of women) to perform the services made scarcer, or altogether unavailable, by its 'welfare reform'. The family can also be called upon as a haven in a heartless world, not only when the economy declines or goes into crisis, but also when it is working at its optimum best, e.g. a housing market which benefits property owners, speculators and landlords, and sends prices (including rents) out of the reach of a large proportion of the population. The two strands of right-wing thought are also mutually supportive in their explanations for the failure of the economy to provide basic necessities for all, by redirecting concern away from the economy and towards scapegoats—'the ageing population', 'boat people', 'terrorists', 'the unemployed', 'welfare dependency', and increasingly, 'Muslims'.

---

26. 'A small minority of former welfare recipients [in the US] is "disconnected" from the labor market and the welfare system, and the size of this group [has grown] over time. [It is] strictly defined … as individuals who, in the year being examined, had no employment income, no working spouse, and no TANF [Temporary Assistance to Needy Families] or public disability benefits. The size of this group increased from 9.8 percent of those leaving welfare in 1999 to 13.8 percent in 2002' (Golden, 2005: 9. See also: Zedlewski and Nelson, 2003).

But as one commentator put it: 'All of that said, it is right to question how much it matters' (Edgar, 1984: 53). Holding two contradictory positions at one and the same time is a characteristic of ideological thinking (because it operates through expression and denial at the same time). It is quite possible for neo-liberalism to argue for free trade and deregulation of the finance sector, while at the same time arguing for the hyper-regulation of the everyday life of those with no power to argue back. This hyper-regulation is explicit policy in the neo-liberal state. As the Brookings Institution, publisher of Lawrence M. Mead's anthology, *The New Paternalism* (Mead, ed., 1997), put it: 'The drift in antipoverty policy is toward paternalism—the close supervision of the dependent'.[27] As long as the right wing have the power to dictate the conditions of social life, logic and truth are irrelevant. The contradiction vanishes anyway, once it is realised that domination lies at the centre of the right-wing project. As the justification for power-over-others, the right wing will use any means at its disposal to maintain it.

The right-wing and the subordination of women

The subordination of women is a crucial aspect of right-wing meanings and values. Both strands of right-wing thought attempt to justify women's subordination to men, although in different ways. The social conservative variety is explicit in its validation of outright male domination: women exist to serve men and nurture men's children, and men have a right to expect that service. The neo-liberal version expects women to be like men, to conform to a pattern of consciousness and behaviour that used to be typical of men during the hegemony of the male breadwinner model of family life. Neo-liberalism still requires women's exploitation, both in the service of capital (having dispensed with the housewife role by commodifying the services that used to be produced domestically, e.g. the fast food industry), and as women in the service of men (e.g. prostitution, pornography, surrogacy), but now disguised behind a mantra of 'choice'.

The fact that explicitly male supremacist beliefs can be strongly held by women themselves makes those beliefs no less male supremacist. Although from a feminist standpoint it is not in women's interests to be subservient to men, women do embrace right-wing meanings and values. Their motivation to defend their own oppression, feminists have argued, is fear and a desire for protection. As Beatrix Campbell found in her research with right-wing women in Britain, although the right-wing women she interviewed tended

27. https://www.brookings.edu/book/the-new-paternalism/ – viewed 8.8.2018.

to distrust all political parties, the Conservative Party won their allegiance because they saw its emphasis on law and order and moral authoritarianism as at least an attempt to control forces that frightened them: 'It was *women's fear* which provided the emotional ignition for the law and order debates' (Campbell, 1987: 4—original emphasis). What they feared, those forces that victimised them, were men, and only men were strong enough to protect them from other men. These men could be distinguished from the men they looked to for protection by the fact that the protectors were familiar: 'Tory women have located their feminine grievances in the image of woman as a victim, not only of men but of the pathologies of nature: only men rape, but only mad men rape' (Campbell, 1987: 295).

These are not weak women. Campbell referred to them as 'iron ladies', and they are acknowledged to be the backbone of the Tory Party, although they have little power within the Party. (Margaret Thatcher was a single exception who rhetorically reinforced the right-wing belief in all women as housewives while ignoring her own exceptional status). But their strength is placed in the service of what they most fear: the social order of domination that is the prime cause of the violence and degradation they want to be protected from. As Andrea Dworkin put it:

> So the woman hangs on, not with the delicacy of a clinging vine, but with a tenacity incredible in its intensity, to the very persons, institutions, and values that demean her, degrade her, glorify her powerlessness, insist on constraining and paralyzing the most honest expressions of her will and being. She becomes a lackey, serving those who ruthlessly and effectively aggress against her and her kind (Dworkin, 1983:17).

The treatment of women in the other variety of right-wing thought—neo-liberalism—would seem at first sight to be the diametric opposite of the social conservative version. There is no overt expectation that women will be subservient to men. The emphasis on 'liberty' forbids any explicit validation of women's subordination. Neither are women expected to be housewives or full-time mothers. On the contrary, all women, like all men (apart from rich rent-seekers), are expected to be in paid employment, preferably full-time as the best way to avoid poverty, and uninterrupted throughout the working-age years so as to provide for retirement oneself rather than being 'dependent on the state'. But neo-liberalism remains male supremacist because it expects women to be like men—free of domestic and unpaid caring responsibilities towards the young, the old, the ill and the disabled, free (i.e. constantly available) for participation in the world of work, and free of any restraints on self-interest and wealth accumulation. At the same time, women's subordination, and subordination and exploitation more generally, are relabelled 'freedom' with the proliferation of the notion of 'choice'—people don't just simply do things any more, they 'choose to' do them—and the rebadging of such exploitative institutions as pornography and prostitution as 'free speech' and 'sex work'.

The right wing and masculinity

The right wing is the most blatant expression of the dissociation and arrogant entitlement of the character structure of male supremacist masculinity. The right-wing defence of masculinity is most frequently expressed through justifications for the subordination of women to men. But a direct connection has also been drawn between right-wing ideology and masculinity, especially in relation to fascism. In fact, fascism is the usual context within which connections are drawn explicitly between the right-wing and masculinity (see chapter 12), although there are those who argue that there is a left-wing form of fascism too. Alice Kaplan (1986), for example, argued that the left and the right could co-exist in fascism because it 'appeal[ed] to all people, to all classes … to both revolutionary and conservative', and was able to 'reconcile the nationalism of the right and the syndicalist revolt of the left' (Kaplan, 1986: 7, 14, 32). Lipset (1981) too believed that both left and right could be fascist because both were violent in their more extreme forms. But although it is true that extremist movements or regimes identifying themselves as left-wing can be violent, it could also be argued that, because violence is a form of domination, it is always right-wing whatever the stated reasons for the violence.

R. W. Connell finds a link between masculinity and the right wing in neo-liberalism, the most recent variety of right-wing thought justifying domination. Connell has pointed out that, not only has neo-liberalism been disproportionately detrimental for women both in Eastern Europe with the restoration of capitalism and in rich Western countries (e.g. 'welfare reform'), its hegemony has also meant that state power has remained 'overwhelmingly the province of men—indeed, men of a particular character: power oriented and ruthless'. Connell also noted that 'there has been a sharp remasculinization of political rhetoric and a turn to the use of force as a primary instrument in policy' (Connell, 2005: 1815).

The right-wing character structure is, first and foremost, bullying and punitive, whether as a personality trait or as political policy. The most immediate and only response by right-wing men and their political institutions, to any perceived slight or wrong-doing, is to punish the perpetrator, real or imagined; and there must always be a perpetrator, so any innocent scapegoat will do, because the desire to punish and bully overrides everything else. If the first level of punishment doesn't work, its severity is increased again, and then again and again and again, endlessly. The right-wing mindset ignores any evidence of the obvious failure of violent retaliation to achieve its aims; it also ignores the obvious fact that violence only begets violence, solves nothing, and brings worse problems in its wake.

The US policy in relation to criminal offending discussed above is a good example of this. Its reaction to crime is to increase penalties, rather than attempting to improve the social conditions, especially the poverty, that have been found over and over again to correlate with levels of crime. Another example is the US government's invasion of Iraq in retaliation for the destruction of the World Trade Center towers, even though there was no evidence that Iraq or Saddam Hussein had anything to do with it (Roy, 2003). As David Harvey (among others) has pointed out:

> Iraq was central [to the plans of the US neo-conservatives and the military-industrial complex], in part because of its geopolitical position and dictatorial regime, which was immune to financial disciplining because of its oil wealth, but also because it threatened to lead a secular pan-Arab movement that might dominate the whole of the Middle Eastern region and be able to hold the global economy hostage to its powers over the flow of oil … After 9/11, the neo-conservatives had had their "Pearl Harbor" [i.e. their excuse] … [even though] Iraq plainly had no connection with al Qaeda and the fight against terrorism had to take preference (Harvey, 2003: 195).

The US invasion bears a great deal of responsibility for subsequent events, most recently the rise of the brutal, dehumanised Islamic State movement.[28] But right-wing masculinity doesn't care; punishment is the only solution he can see to any and every problem, and his only response to the constant threat of war he has engineered is to increase the lethal technological sophistication of his weaponry. His desire is for violence for its own sake, because that is the most direct and immediate proof of his power.

Tom Engelhardt[29] described this as a refusal to learn from the terrible consequences of constantly increasing the level of violence:

---

28. Cockburn, 2014; Floyd, 2015; Robinson, 2014; Street, 2015.

29. Tom Engelhardt is the originator of an epublication, 'Tomdispatch', launched in November 2001 and intended as 'a regular antidote to the mainstream media' (http://www.tomdispatch.com/post/175971/tomgram%3A_rebecca_gordon%2C_it_didn%27t_work_in_afghanistan%2C_so_let%27s_do_it_in_mexico/#more – viewed 8.8.2018

One of the mysteries of our era is why there seems to be no learning curve in Washington. Over the last 13 years, American wars and conflicts have repeatedly helped create disaster zones, encouraging the fragmentation of whole countries and societies in the Greater Middle East and Northern Africa. In the process, such American wars, drone assassination campaigns, raids, and conflicts have acted as recruitment posters for and aided and abetted the growth of terror outfits. And here's where the genuine strangeness begins to enter the picture: after all of this is absorbed and assessed in Washington, the response is regularly more of what hasn't worked and a clamoring for yet more of it.

He did not, of course, identify the masculinity behind this refusal to learn; he was talking about the US government. But the US government's war-mongering is a prime example of the rampant masculinity created by male supremacy's dissociated entitlement. There are women who embrace the US government's war-mongering as well—Madeleine Albright, Condoleezza Rice, Hillary Clinton, etc.—but the meanings and values originated in and remain those of a masculinity obsessed with power.

The character structure espoused by the right-wing with its one overarching value—wealth and violence and the superordinate power both bring—is presented as gender-neutral. But women cannot don this masculine persona because they do not have the social power and the vitally necessary although covert support networks (with a few isolated exceptions permitted to occupy power positions created for men). But even if women could become more like neo-liberal men, that would not mean an end to male supremacy. Nor would it be 'freedom' in any genuinely human sense. Men cannot don the neo-liberal persona either if they are to remain in touch with their own humanity.

Not many men achieve the highest levels of wealth accumulation, although many more honour and glorify it and aspire to it vicariously, even though they will never personally achieve it. But even those who do not worship wealth must struggle with the character structure required for wealth accumulation and ruthless power (including outright physical violence). While it is lethal in its most extreme forms, two of its most common forms are bullying and media depictions of male triumph and entitlement at someone's expense. It is required of all males but inculcated in numerous ways which will be different for each person. However, it can also be entwined with a genuine humanity which leavens and mitigates its worst effects. This is discussed more fully in the next chapter.

Chapter Three: Domination and its Other

The arguments here follow on from my work theorising male domination.[30] I see male domination as the primary form of domination and the source from which all other forms of domination flow. I sometimes drop the qualifier 'male' because using it implies that there are other forms of domination than male domination and I am not concerned with other forms of domination, always supposing such exist. Those other two great loci of oppression—race and class—or rather, their concomitant forms of domination, I investigate under the rubric of male domination since, however else they may be characterised, both are forms of it.[31] What structures those social arrangements which ensure that some will prosper at others' expense is essentially masculine: the personnel at the top are largely men; the social order accords an overweening entitlement to powerful and privileged men while creating categories of disadvantage where entitlement even to basic necessities is minimal or non-existent; the violence is largely male; and the social arrangements are dissociated from everyday life and human need. This includes the chief form domination takes in the liberal democracies, capitalism.

I know of no social theory that deals adequately with the notion of male domination.[32] So absolute is this lack in malestream sociological theory that I have been known to wonder whether I'm hallucinating its existence. But

---

30. Thompson, 1991b, 2001 and 2005a, many of the other papers included on UNSWorks, and especially Thompson, 2005c.

31. For race, see: Thompson, 2001: chapter 9. For 'class', i.e. capitalism, see: Thompson, 2005c. The relevance of 'class' to male domination is also addressed in the following chapters on capitalism.

32. Or even domination, which tends to be discussed as an interaction between individuals (e.g. Simmel, 1908; Weber, 1976), rather than as a cultural imperative largely beyond the awareness of those caught up in it. Maintaining this ignorance is the function of ideology/symbolic violence. For a discussion of the limitations of sociology for any

not only have I found that other people can see it too, malestream theory itself exposes this lack through its dissociated detachment from anything that looks like real life. While a lack does not in and of itself indicate what it is that is lacking, hypothesising a need to justify and disguise domination does make intelligible much that is confusing.

Harm

For however much the perpetrators and upholders of the character structure of male supremacist masculinity might deny or downplay it, that masculinity is harmful. Masculine arrogance rides roughshod over the rights and needs of others, and the dissociation deprives him of any empathy or fellow feeling that might restrain him. Domination follows a logic that obliterates the principle of doing no harm. That principle would probably meet with general agreement, including from those who do the most damage (although that agreement comes in the form of a denial that what they are doing is harmful). But the primary importance of doing no harm is not often stated explicitly and it needs to be. Under conditions of domination, so much of what is presented as harmless, even beneficial, is harmful.

Fascism is the most extreme example of the cruelty and destructiveness of dissociated masculinity, but there is a connection between fascism and capitalism (see chapter 12). Both of them exclude categories of people from humanity, capitalism with its 'superfluous people' (Arendt, 1951) and 'wasted lives' (Bauman, 2004), fascism with its racism and its need for a target for its brutality. Moreover, although capitalism is usually presented (although not under that name) as the provider of jobs and commodities that everyone wants, it would destroy the biosphere if it could, with its coal mining and the burning of fossil fuels, fracking for coal seam gas, deforestation for timber and palm oil plantations, etc. It is also cruel, with its workforce exploitation and resource extraction in the Third World, and unemployment, starvation wages, 'welfare reform' in the rich nations of the West, and the 'austerity' measures imposed on populations beggared by the greed engendered by the global financial system.

Pornography and prostitution are both harmful for women;[33] their symbolic violence recommends the objectification of women as things for

---

account of male domination, despite the suggestive insights it can provide, see: Thompson, 1996: 15-20.

33. They are harmful for men too, but men are addicted to them and defend them vociferously against any perceived threat.

men's use, and in doing so, contributes to the actual male violence against women. Surrogacy also harms women and that has influenced some governments to pass legislation banning it as a commercial transaction, although the male sense of entitlement keeps the industry in existence (see chapter 13). US 'welfare reform' is also harmful for women and there is a substantial literature exposing that harm, although that exposure has had no influence on those with the power to modify its worst aspects (see chapters 15-19). As for transsexualism, while it doesn't physically harm anyone except the person himself, it is still symbolically violent in its arrogant demand that men be recognised as 'women' and its consequent obliteration of what it is to be female (see chapter 14).

Domination is cruel and destructive. Destruction makes men feel powerful, whether it is wreaked on other human beings, on animals or on the environment, war being the most obvious example. Cruelty and destructiveness are central to the character structure of male domination, reined in only by that genuine humanity that persists even through the worst that men riddled with male supremacist beliefs and values can do. But there are so many instances of cruelty that are not recognised as such, masquerading as policy or common sense, or justified with lies: the Australian government's treatment of refugees, or the Trump administration's treatment of 'Muslims'. Domination must be resisted because it is harmful, but resistance can only happen when domination is recognised for what it is.

Another reality—the genuinely human

But domination is not the whole of social reality. Alongside the masculinist culture of the male supremacist world ruled by men there is another reality, which I have called the 'genuinely human' (and sometimes 'a common humanity' or the common good). It is intended as a contrast to the dehumanisation of male supremacy, and as an acknowledgement that male domination is not inevitable. It is characterised by the absence of domination and subordination and doesn't involve the dehumanisation of anybody. It says that there is an alternative, or rather, that there are many alternative ways of being which are not male supremacist. These ways of being are defined negatively—they do not dehumanise anyone, they are not dissociated from the common human condition, and they do not exercise the unwarranted entitlement of some at others' expense.

The concept is not meant to imply unfailing goodness on the part of what is genuinely-human-because-it-is-not-male-supremacist—it can include badness as well as goodness, meanness as well as generosity, betrayal as well as loyalty, stupidity as well as intelligence, etc. It is 'the right and the good' of moral philosophy, but it is also simply any aspect of human existence that doesn't involve domination, including negative traits (e.g. unkindness, stupidity or meanness). I don't want to make too much of this phenomenon I have called the 'genuinely human'. I don't intend it as an absolute contrast to male domination in some Manichean contrast between good and evil. The function of the term 'genuinely human' is simply to emphasise the fact that male domination is not the whole of the social world, by giving a name to that other-than-male-domination reality. It is possible that not all bad behaviour is a consequence of male domination. In other words, I do not know if getting rid of male supremacy would mean an end to all wrong-doing. I am not saying that male domination is the source of all evil, simply that it is a source of evil. However, I am saying that it is the source of the worst humanly-contrived evils the world has ever seen, that behind those evils lies the masculinity demanded of men by male domination with its dissociation from humanity and its overweening sense of entitlement.

This 'other' reality is not a world of women since women participate in the male supremacist world too (and men need not). Still less is this other world 'feminine'. As I use the term, 'femininity' refers to the character structure demanded of women by male supremacy, just as 'masculinity' is the character structure demanded of men. Femininity requires women to be subservient as masculinity requires men to be dominant. It is what is required of women if men are to be masculine (in the male supremacist sense I am using here). In that sense, femininity is not a contrast to masculinity but a subset of it.[34]

This 'other' reality is other than the grotesqueries of both masculinity and femininity. It is not femininity that I contrast with masculinity, but this other, the common humanity we recognise in each other. Both masculinity and femininity are dehumanised in comparison with the genuinely human, not only because they circumscribe both sexes and limit their human potential, but because what they require of people is life-denying. With violence, an arrogant sense of entitlement, and a wasteland devoid of human decency on the one side, and fear, subservience and superficiality on the other, no one can live in comfort and dignity.

---

34. That femininity is a subset of masculinity and another type of character structure required by male supremacy is shown, not only by the functions it serves in the subduing of women, but also by the phenomena of transvestism ('drag', 'cross-dressing') and transsexualism. In these cases, femininity is avidly embraced by men themselves, rather than being required of women.

In calling the alternative reality to male supremacy 'genuinely human' or a common humanity, I do not mean to imply that the dehumanisation inherent in male supremacy is not a human phenomenon. It is established and maintained by people, it is not the consequence of something other than human, like natural laws for example. It is, therefore, as genuinely human as its opposite. But the world of domination is a world driven by destruction and death. There must be some countervailing force that has kept the human race in existence throughout the murderous millennia of male rule. That countervailing force is what I'm calling 'genuine humanity'. It has enabled the continuation of an alternative reality, where men do not rule, where people are not controlled by powerful vested interests, and where no one prospers at anyone else's expense, however much we may squabble among ourselves and however badly we may behave towards each other. In order to be identified, it needs to be named, and 'genuinely human' or a common humanity is the name I have given it.

The two 'realities'—common humanity and male supremacy—are not separate and distinct. They exist together in the same hearts and minds and the same society and it is not always possible to say which is which (or so I have found), largely because notions of domination are so seldom acknowledged and hence so little known. The two realities are, however, ethically mutually exclusive and logically incompatible—it is not possible to hold at one and the same time that only (some) men count as 'human' *and* that everyone is, or that some people are more worthwhile than others *and* that everyone has a right to human dignity and recognition. That incompatibility contains the possibility and actuality of resistance and refusal. It must also be managed by the male supremacist system if that system is to continue its masquerade as the interests of all.

For a number of reasons, I do not discuss this postulated alternative 'other' reality at any length. The alternative, 'genuinely human' reality I am postulating does not need theorising because ordinary daily life is simply lived, not theorised; and although bad behaviour and unhappiness do need to be explained, if they are not a consequence of male domination the explanations will be idiosyncratic and confined to each particular occasion. Only what is systematic can be theorised. So the first reason why I am not going to provide any account of what might be involved in a common humanity—that 'other' reality to male supremacy—is that ordinary life can't be theorised to the extent that its problems are not systematic.

Moreover, with the theorists of the Frankfurt School I see social theory as essentially critical theory. It aims to expose relations of ruling as domination in order to end them; it is not a theory of 'society' per se. As Max Horkheimer has said, 'There is … no theory of society … that does not contain political motivations' (Horkheimer, 1972: 222). The political motivation of critical theory is a concern with human dignity for all. This is a concern of liberalism too, but unlike liberalism, critical theory combines the concern with human dignity with a stance of overt opposition to current social arrangements which maintain wretchedness, injustice, exploitation and oppression. Critical theory is intended as 'transformative activity' (p.232). It investigates 'society as it is' from a standpoint of moral and political opposition to those aspects of the status quo which serve to maintain relations of ruling. In sum: 'Critical theory maintains: it need not be so; man [sic] can change reality, and the necessary conditions for such change already exist' (p.227n20). It is those already existing 'necessary conditions' that constitute what I am calling the genuinely human, the 'other' reality to male supremacy.

This present project differs from the standpoint of the Frankfurt School which remained focused on a critique of capitalism, in that, behind the dehumanising processes of capitalism, it finds the social relations of male supremacy, an aspect of social domination to which the Frankfurt School were largely oblivious (as is every other variety of malestream thought). But if it is the case that male domination is the primary form of social domination, then a critique of male supremacy is also a critique of capitalism anyway. So I am not theorising 'society' in any general sense. Rather, my project is an attempt to expose the systematic ways in which human actions, meanings and values serve those inhuman purposes generated by the social relations of male supremacy.

The 'genuinely human' I am talking about is not only a reference to the good life (in the ethical not the hedonistic sense). It can also include human weakness, stupidity, nastiness and sheer bloody-mindedness as long as these are not male supremacist. (The political/theoretical/ethical task is deciding which is which). I would argue, though, that the genuinely human is the source of all goodness because no good can come from male supremacy. However, I am not going to theorise the nature of that goodness even though theorising 'the right and the good' has always been the usual method of procedure in discussing social issues, from before the time of Plato to the present day. But such depictions are invariably blind to the systemic nature of domination, and hence, to important reasons why the good life might be out of reach, not only for the disadvantaged but also for those whose privilege depends on others having none.

Furthermore, devising ever more detailed accounts of what might be required for harmony and social order, is more often than not a way of avoiding acknowledging domination. It conveys the impression that problems can be rectified with more information or good will or through a process of rational argument. At its worst it implies that all is right with the world as it is and that whatever suffering exists is the fault of those who are suffering. This is my chief objection to liberalism—the endless reiteration of what is entailed by notions of the good society, with no account of the systematic reasons why that good society is constantly being undermined. So another reason why I am not concerned to depict the genuinely human is that it tends to take the focus away from the more immediate task, which is to expose the ways in which domination operates.

But there is yet another reason, and that is the fact that the social theorist has neither the responsibility nor the power to tell people how to live their lives. Despite prevalent misinterpretations of feminism as a series of authoritarian demands, how each personal life is lived is the responsibility of the one whose life it is and each of us lives that reality in our own unique way. Mitchell Dean expressed this reluctance to tell people what to do in the following terms:

> It may be that intellectuals can no longer stand at the barricades leading the masses. It may be that they can no longer in good faith tell others how to act and live, or what to change or leave alone (Dean, 1999: 7).

I would argue that it has never been the task of the theorist to 'lead the masses' or to tell others how to live. The theorist's task is to expose, to the best of one's ability, what 'need not be so'. It is the patterns of harm that need to be theorised, together with the ways in which the existence of that harm is constantly being denied. That is usually interpreted as 'telling people what to do', but the social theorist has no power to compel. Agreement cannot be coerced and attempts to do so are either futile or catastrophic, depending on how powerful are the forces that are trying to do the convincing. What others do with the knowledge once it has been produced is up to them, including ignoring it. As Marilyn Frye put it:

> illumination cannot be delivered complete & clear by one individual onto another's history & situation, not even if the two are very similar. If one person's theorizing is sound & correct enough to be useful to another, the other still has to make use of her own knowledge to transpose & interpret it, to adapt it to the details of her own life & circumstances, to make it her own (Frye, 1983: xiii).

But having said that the genuinely human doesn't need theorising, I do need to say that, to the extent that it is morally 'the right and the good', it centrally involves personal integrity and respect for others. Or to put this another way, 'the concept of responsibility [is] the foundation of human existence' (Frankl, 2004: 39).

Feminism and humanism

Feminism does not have an explicit account of dehumanisation because it does not on the whole have an account of a common humanity. Having said that, however, I must also say that resistance to the dehumanisation of women is a constant thread running through feminism, whether explicit or not. Sometimes it is made explicit. For example, in her critique of economic orthodoxy, Julie Nelson (1996b) calls for 'an economics would be neither masculine nor feminine but would be a human science in the pursuit of human ends' (Nelson, 1996b: 199). Again, Kathleen Barry (2010) talks about 'the value of human life', a 'shared human consciousness' and 'empathy', as a contrast to the kind of masculinity demanded of men in the making of war.

However, for the most part feminism has explicitly rejected any such notion in its rejection of 'humanism' as just one more disguise for masculine interests masquerading as 'humanity' in general. Celia Kitzinger (1987) used the term 'liberal humanism' pejoratively, although she used it interchangeably with 'individualism', and hence it was not the notion of a common humanity she was criticising, but rather the liberal notion of the atomised self.[35] Still, she saw no difference between humanism and individualism, nor any need to retrieve the notion of humanism for feminist purposes. As Mary O'Brien said: 'the word "human" is now regarded in feminist circles with some suspicion, on the grounds that it is just as spurious in its claim to generic inclusiveness as the ubiquitous "man"' (O'Brien, 1986: 14).

Another aspect of feminism that excludes any notion of a common humanity is the concept of 'false universalism'. This is meant as a rejection of the kind of feminism perceived 'to reflect the viewpoints of white, middle-class women of North America and Western Europe' (Nicholson, 1990: 1. For an extended critique of this argument, see: Thompson, 1994b, c, d; Thompson, 2001: 116-23). If there can be no common humanity even among women, there is no chance of any commonalty among the human race as a whole. Moreover, feminism's concern for women, although a necessary

---

35. For the use of 'humanism' in just this sense, see the discussion of the UK Ethical Society in chapter 14.

concern given the harms done to women by men under conditions of male domination, has tended to keep feminism focused on a particular category of human being ('women') and their particular needs, rather than adopting its own stance of the universal human with which to counter the male supremacist claims. Consequently, this feminist focus has tended to deflect attention from the fact that, not only do we share a common humanity, but also that feminism speaks from a position of the universal human. In other words, feminism has universal human relevance, not just for women.

This notion has been criticised on the grounds that feminism, either in whole or in part, speaks only from the position of privileged women. That may be true in some instances. It is unlikely that Betty Friedan's 'feminine mystique' would strike a chord with women in those countries still colonised, exploited and impoverished by the West (although the idea of women being subordinated to the needs and wants of men and children might be familiar, however differently that might be manifested elsewhere than in white, middle-class America). But feminism's central tenet of insisting on the humanity of women has relevance for everyone, for women because of the myriad ways in which male supremacy dehumanises women, and for men because men can't be fully human unless women are too.

Personal integrity

By personal integrity I mean being honest with oneself. This is difficult because 'democratic' domination requires 'consent'. It needs its citizens (i.e. all of us) to deceive ourselves, and being honest with oneself is a task that will remain unfinished as long as we live under conditions of domination. Its psychic mechanisms of denial, repression, dissociation, hysteria, etc., enable me to survive in a world of pain. But they also prevent me from realising my human potential and they damage and distort me. 'Democracy's' communication media are dominated by advertising, whose functions are deception, spin-doctoring and managing appearances, either with scant regard for what is really happening, or with the deliberate intention of denying it and convincing people to accept the unacceptable. While I can ignore the advertising up to a point, the barrage is relentless, with yet another sales pitch everywhere I look. Dissociation is a common and understandable reaction to such incessant battering. But reaching out to the genuinely human possibilities beyond the barrage means being honest with oneself, both about the wounding effects and about the possibilities for healing.

Domination destroys personal integrity. When people are powerless we can't take responsibility for ourselves or exercise our responsibilities towards others. So an important aspect of the concept of the responsibility that lies at the heart of human existence is the ability to recognise when we are *not* responsible. Women who are raped, for example, or bashed by their 'intimate (male) partners', need to be able to recognise that they are not responsible for the violence, that nothing they said or did caused it, that it is the result of *his* deficiency, his dehumanisation. This recognition is very difficult. It would seem that there is nothing human beings hate more than helplessness. We would rather find ourselves responsible for the harm than acknowledge that we were powerless to prevent it. In fact however, my responsibility only switches in when I react to the harm, although even then I can hardly be blamed if I don't survive. Under conditions of domination, there are limits to personal responsibility.[36] People must not be made responsible for what they have no control over.

Respect for others

> Respect … is a kind of "friendship" without intimacy and without closeness; it is a regard for the person from the distance which the space of the world puts between us, and this regard is independent of qualities which we may admire or of achievements which we may highly esteem. Thus, the modern loss of respect, or rather the conviction that respect is due only where we admire or esteem, constitutes a clear symptom of the increasing depersonalization of public and social life (Arendt, 1958: 243).

As in the case of personal integrity, respect for others is also diminished by domination. For example, the US system of 'welfare reform' treats with the utmost contempt those for whom 'welfare' is the only mainstream source of income. By denying people the means of subsistence it denies their humanity in the sense of their right to live lives of comfort and security. Not only does it pay benefits below the official poverty line (itself far below what is required for even a minimally decent standard of living), it subjects people, largely poor women, to an endless stream of impossible bureaucratic demands which disqualify the majority of applicants from receiving even this measly pittance. A nation state which not only will not compensate its citizens for the damage wreaked by its economic system, but which also blames the victims of the system for the poverty they cannot avoid, has no respect for persons. The US is not alone in this but it is the most extreme example, which has come

---

36. This is something Victor Frankl did not address, despite (or more likely because of) the three years he spent in Auschwitz and Dachau concentration camps. Having experienced the absolute worst form of man's inhumanity to man, his focus was on moving as far away from that as possible by clarifying the best that humanity is capable of.

to be surpassed with the election of Donald Trump to the US presidency and the ascendance of the extremist right wing within the US governmental apparatus. This is an unsurprising outcome in a nation that wages war against other peoples who have no hope of defending themselves, much less retaliating, namely the civilian populations massacred by US weapons of mass destruction 'defending' US corporate interests (Blum, 2003a, b, 2014; Ferguson, 2012). The US does not respect the humanity of people in other countries, but neither does it respect its own citizens. 'Welfare reform' is a telling example of the contempt with which the US ruling class treats its most vulnerable citizens.

Conduct of conduct

It is with some hesitation that I use the term 'respect for others', because it seems to have become yet another piece in the 'conduct of conduct' armoury of policies the neo-liberal democratic state is attempting to use as a substitute for the post-war welfare state.[37] 'Conduct of conduct' involves government attempts to manage people, not just for a specific purpose (e.g. in the workplace) but in any aspect of their lives at all, including the most intimate and personal. As Dean put it:

> From the perspective of those who seek to govern, human conduct is conceived as something that can be regulated, controlled, shaped and turned to specific ends … [It] entails an attempt to affect and shape … who and what we are and should be … This is a perspective … that seeks to connect questions of government, politics and administration to the space of bodies, lives, selves and persons (Dean, 1999: 11-12).

A politics that seeks to administer 'the space of bodies, lives, selves and persons' is literally totalitarian. It involves controlling people in their private lives. It is most evident in the treatment of 'the unemployed' and 'welfare' recipients—those who apply for government income support when they are unable to get income from a job (see, for example, the later discussion of US 'welfare reform', chapters 15 to 19). This kind of neo-liberal governmental focus on the lives and behaviour of those who fail to thrive in regimes of liberal democracy has intensified in recent years along with the erosion of people's

---

37. The term 'conduct of conduct' refers to Foucault's concept of 'governmentality'. He did not use the actual term itself, although he did use 'conduct' in the double sense of directing others and comporting the self. My use of the term differs from Foucault's for the usual reason: his equivocation on, and sometimes outright denial of, the existence of domination (Foucault, 1978, 1983, 1991. For more on 'governmentality', see: Bevir, 1999; Burchell, 1993; Burchell et al, eds, 1991; Dean, 1994, 1995, 1999; Hindess, 1997; Lemke, 2001; Miller and Rose, 1995; Rose, 1993, 1996; Stenson, 1993; Walters, 1994).

entitlement to the benefits of the welfare state. But the hyper-regulation of everyday life has increased for everyone, even as the prerogatives of the rich and powerful have been progressively deregulated.

Whatever my disagreements with the originator of the notion of 'conduct of conduct' (if not the exact terminology), it nicely expresses what is involved in the social policies of so-called 'democracies' under the neo-liberal hegemony. Those 'technologies of the self' employed by neo-liberal governments, while presented as attempts to deal with social problems, are actually ways of evading the real issues. Either they are punitive forms of social control imposed on those most harmed by the system (as in US 'welfare reform' and its facsimiles throughout the world, e.g. Australia's 'mutual obligation' regime), or they miss the target altogether. The Victorian government's 'Respect Agenda', for example, barely acknowledges the fact that the reprehensible behaviours it hopes to eradicate are largely perpetrated by men, e.g. 'alcohol-related violence in public places', 'violence against women' (Victorian Government, 2010). Women can of course disrespect others, just as they can be complicit with male supremacy more broadly. But one of the characteristics of the masculine sense of overweening entitlement is its psychopathic lack of consideration for others. Disrespect comes naturally to those who feel entitled to take what they want no matter who gets hurt in the process, or to lash out violently at anyone in the vicinity.

Still, despite its function as a feel-good term covering up governmental evasion of responsibility for citizens' welfare, 'respect' is exactly what I mean in characterising part of what is involved in what I am calling 'genuine humanity'. The fact that the word is used for purposes I cannot condone is no reason to abandon it and leave it for the exclusive use of the ignorant.

Chapter Four: Entitlement and Dissociation

Elsewhere (Thompson, 1991b, 1994a, 1998b, 2000a, 2001, 2005c) I have argued that the central cultural imperative of male supremacy is the principle that only men count as 'human'. Here, I am developing that insight by arguing that the belief that only men count as 'human' forms a masculinist character structure consisting of two primary value orientations: dissociation from the human condition, and an unwarranted sense of entitlement. By 'dissociation', I mean a crazed detachment from and a consequent blindness to reality,[38] and from an ethical commitment to the common good, what I am calling the 'genuinely human' (Thompson, 2005c); and by 'unwarranted entitlement' I mean the belief that anything he wants is his for the taking without any consideration of the needs of others and no matter who gets hurt in the process. As such, it is combined with the disentitlement of those who are harmed by masculinity's rapacious demands. This is a dehumanised character (because no one can be fully human as long as categories of people, women in the first place, are excluded from full human status).[39] But although he is dominant his power is not absolute. He exists side-by-side with genuine humanity's embrace of the common good, which constantly challenges him and ensures the continuation of the human race despite the power bestowed by ruthlessness and callous disregard of the rights of others.

---

38. By 'reality' I mean 'a quality appertaining to phenomena that we recognize as having a being independent of our own volition (we cannot "wish them away")' (Berger and Luckmann, 1967: 13). I am aware that such a concept is frowned upon in these days of the postmodernist hegemony. However, as with most of the targets of postmodernism's scorn, notions of reality are a necessary counterweight to the influence of dissociated discourses which serve the interests of domination by denying what is actually going on. The notion of 'truth' is another useful concept serving the same purpose, as a counterweight to the lies that are becoming normal part of public discourse.

39. For an account of masculinity and dehumanisation in the context of racism, see: Thompson, 2001: chapter 9.

I will begin by discussing entitlement and dissociation separately, although this is a matter of emphasis rather than any real separation. The entitlement I am talking about is only possible to the extent that the entitled one is dissociated from any sense of a common humanity, of himself as one among many. Entitlement and dissociation are inextricably intertwined, each feeding the other in a grotesque denial of all that is good in humanity.

Entitlement

Rights

The notion of entitlement implies the notion of rights. Someone who is entitled to something is someone who has a right to something. But the arrogant entitlement I am referring to does not involve rights as they are commonly understood. Because of the existence of this arrogant male entitlement, the notion of 'rights' has to be carefully used.

I have argued elsewhere (Thompson, 2000b) that rights claims only make sense when the existence of social domination is acknowledged. They are a humanitarian response to social evils and a well-intentioned attempt to rectify social wrongs. But without the recognition that violations of human rights are the consequence of inequalities of power, rights claims are useless for redressing social wrongs, or worse, they are complicit with domination because they focus solely on the victims and fail to identify the real source of the violations. There is no point in insisting on people's human rights if nothing is done to identify the source of the wrongs, much less redress it.

The United Nation's Universal Declaration of Human Rights,[40] for example, is a fine feel-good document detailing what people ought to be entitled to, but it has nothing to say about the reasons why everybody doesn't already enjoy these rights. Take Article 23, which enshrines a 'right to work', including 'free choice of employment', 'just and favourable conditions of work' and 'protection against unemployment'. The Declaration includes no acknowledgement of the reasons why that right cannot become a reality as long as the economy which provides the jobs remains capitalist. In fact there is no right to work under capitalist conditions of production and distribution, much less a right to a living wage. The function of employment under capitalist conditions is not to provide people with either a free choice of employment or just and favourable conditions of work; nor is it to provide 'just and favourable remuneration ensuring for himself and his family an

---

40. http://www.un.org/en/universal-declaration-human-rights/index.html – viewed 9.8.2018.

existence worthy of human dignity' (as Article 23 continues). The function of employment is to generate profit, and in the interest of generating the highest possible profit, employers pay the least they can get away with. This is especially the case in the low-wage economy in the US and in the use of 'off-shore' workers in the Third World on the part of multi-national corporations everywhere (see chapter 7). Moreover, as I argue in chapter 8, capitalism demands a certain level of unemployment in order to keep labour costs down. Given the lack of acknowledgement of standard operating procedures like these, and in the absence of any concerted efforts to challenge them, it is not clear what purpose is being served by declarations of any 'right to work'.

The concept of power is crucial to any discourse on rights because only the powerless need rights; those who have the resources to provide for themselves have no need of rights claims, and to the extent that they make them—to be permitted to make money unhindered by any environmental or humanitarian considerations, or to be free from taxation—they are claiming a right to harm others with impunity. The powerless need rights because they do not have the power-as-capability to acquire for themselves basic necessities like a living wage or protection from violence or unjust imprisonment. Powerlessness is not an attribute of individuals, it is situational, an effect of social arrangements, not something people carry around with them. Those who are powerless in one sphere may be reasonably capable, even pre-eminent in another. For example, wealthy and well-connected Jews had no need of rights in Weimar Germany, but once the Nazis came to power, they were subjected to power consisting of naked terror and outright, lethal violence. It was at that point that the question of the human rights of the comfortable, cultured, middle- to upper-class Jews became shockingly relevant.

The kind of entitlement I am talking about here has nothing to do with rights. Or rather, it is the kind of entitlement that violates the rights of others. It is a sense of entitlement heedless of the consequences to others and oblivious to the harm it causes. Prostitution and pornography provide the occasion for using others (mainly women) as objects for sexual gratification; capitalism uses people to generate profit for the few; US 'welfare reform' disentitles millions of women and children while the ruling class amasses wealth beyond belief; and fascism provides an object lesson in what happens when male supremacist dehumanisation is given free rein.

Disentitlement

Masculinist entitlement brings along with it *dis*entitlement—of those people, predominantly but not only women, who are used, exploited, abused and discarded by the male supremacist system. Masculinist entitlement must not be hindered by any needs any other person might have, including the right to be treated with respect and kindness, to be free from pain, to be paid a living wage, or even to survive. Trafficked and enslaved women and children are deprived of their right to bodily security in order to service the limitless male entitlement to sex; low-wage workers are deprived of a living wage in order to swell the profits of the already very rich; 'off-shore' workers in the Third World are paid even less, much, much less, than workers in the rich developed nations. Disentitlement is a form of harm imposed by powerful men (and those few women who have gained access to the upper echelons of the system).

Male entitlement

> Most social destructiveness is done by people who feel they have some kind of permission for what they do, even to the point of feeling righteous, and who commonly regard their victims as less than human or otherwise beyond the pale (Sanford et al, 1971: ix).

> I would annex the planets if I could (Cecil Rhodes, quoted by Hannah Arendt as the epigraph to 'Imperialism', section 2 of *The Origins of Totalitarianism*, taken from S. Gertrude Millin *Rhodes* London, 1933, p.138).

> The power of men is first a metaphysical assertion of self, an I am that exists a priori, bedrock, absolute, no embellishment or apology required, indifferent to denial or challenge … This self is not merely subjectively felt. It is protected by laws and customs, proclaimed in art and literature, documented in history, upheld in the distribution of wealth … When the subjective sense of self falters, institutions devoted to its maintenance buoy it up … It is entitled to take what it wants to sustain or improve itself, to have anything, to requite any need at any cost … The self is the conviction, beyond reason or scrutiny, that there is an equation between what one wants and what one is (Dworkin, 1981: 13-14).

The statement above by Cecil Rhodes—that he would annex the planets if he could, rather than being satisfied with annexing the continent of Africa—is typical of the kind of arrogant entitlement I am talking about. It is boundless, literally 'out of this world'. Although Rhodes did not of course mean it literally, it does express the limitless nature of that masculine sense of entitlement. Arendt saw this comment by Rhodes as evidence of his 'wisdom' because he had 'discovered the moving principle of the new, the imperialist era' (i.e. that '"expansion is everything"'), and also 'its inherent insanity and its contradiction to the human condition' (Arendt, 1951: 124) (in other words, its dissociation). However, there is no hint in the text quoted that Rhodes was aware of the inhumanity of his yearning to acquire the universe for England. His biographer said he 'fell into despair, for every night he saw overhead "these stars ... these vast worlds which we can never reach. I would annex the planets if I could"'. What he is expressing here is intense regret ('despair') that male power has limits beyond which it cannot go. That these limits are seen in purely physical terms—the limits of earth-bound nations and their ruling classes—rather than in genuinely human terms—what ought and ought not to be permitted in relations with other human beings—is certainly evidence of its inhumanity; it is not, however, evidence of Rhodes' awareness of this fact. The imperialism within which Rhodes was a leading figure knew no limits to its belief in its own entitlement. It was not held back by any consideration for the autonomy, the traditions or even the lives of the conquered peoples. Rhodes could express this so clearly because he believed it so utterly. This is not wisdom, however, but an arrogance dehumanised by a sense of entitlement that will allow nothing to stand in its way.

The quote from Andrea Dworkin refers to men who desire and consume pornography and use women in prostitution. While the wealth capitalism produces belongs only to ruling class men, sexuality is the area where men from all walks of life can exercise their sense of entitlement, a sense generated by the importance allotted to penis-possession under conditions of male supremacy. Those who desire to use human beings in this way are motivated by an overweening sense of entitlement, whether they actually act on it (prostitution) or whether they simply interpret other human beings as things to be used (pornography), and most of the men who feel so entitled do both. Their dissociation come from their callous disregard of the rights of others, and their obliviousness to the fact that what they are doing is wrong. What they believe and what they feel is 'beyond reason or scrutiny', and they never learn. While prostitution and pornography are the recognisable institutions buoying up the male sense of entitlement to sexual gratification at others' expense, both are legitimised by a more pervasive culture of male entitlement to sex.

One example of this is what might be called the 'de-moralising' of these two institutions. I am using the term in a different sense from the usual meaning of 'demoralise', hence the hyphen. The usual meaning is 'to lower or destroy someone's morale' (i.e. their self-confidence and ability to cope) (Shorter Oxford). I intend the term to mean refusing to repudiate moral scandals such as prostitution and pornography. I mean exactly what Janice

Raymond means with the term 'de-ethicize' in relation to transsexualism: 'De-ethicization occurs when problems that have moral implications are defined as if they had none' (Raymond, 1980: 125). I prefer the term 'de-moralisation' to 'de-ethicisation' just because of the connotations of the usual meaning of the word. De-moralising prostitution and pornography has a demoralising effect on society—if there is nothing wrong with prostitution and pornography, how is it possible to make any ethical judgements at all? If the harm done by prostitution and pornography is ignored, how is it possible to recognise anything as harmful?

This de-moralisation is a recent development, historically speaking, and it appears to be one of the main consequences of the sexual liberation movements (Dines, 2010; Jeffreys, 2008a; Tankard Reist and Bray, eds, 2011). Whereas prostitution and pornography used to be regarded with moral disapproval, it is now common practice to regard them in morally neutral terms. Prostitution is now called 'sex work', supposedly no different in its ethical implications from any other type of work. There may indeed be a sense in which prostitution is not very different from a great deal of the work available in an economy based on profit not need, and that is the sense in which both involve affronts to human dignity. But that is not what is meant by the equation between prostitution and paid labour. Instead, 'work' is assumed to be morally neutral, even praiseworthy, and likening prostitution to 'work' is intended to 'de-moralise' prostitution, not to question the morality of 'work'.

But this attempt to take the moral disapproval out of prostitution has not succeeded in re-valuing the women prostituted in 'sex work'. If they are still 'whores', it is not just a job of work they are doing. A genuinely human re-moralising of the sex industry would see the opprobrium directed towards the men who use women, not the women who are used. But what the recent de-moralising process has done is to bolster men's sense of entitlement to sexual access to women. It has enabled men to feel even less guilty about sexually using women. If the prostituted woman (Jeffreys, 2008a) is only doing a job of work, he is entitled to use her 'services' as long as he pays, even if she is semi-comatose under the effects of drugs, or trafficked or enslaved, or a child, and even though it is not the sex she wants but his money.

But male sexual entitlement is not confined to the bodies of women. Even child pornography (paedophilia) has become mainstream, although so far it is confined to the 'softer' end of the spectrum, i.e. the public face of the advertising industry does not depict the children in explicit sexual acts. The usual term for this, 'the sexualisation of children', does not do justice to what is actually happening. The problem is not the sexuality of children, but the sexuality of (some) adult men. The children, who are mainly girls, are presented in the mass media (in advertising, magazines for pre-teenage girls as young as the age of five, and in children's television) as sexual objects for the benefit of men. It is not women or other children who want to be given permission for sex with children by seeing it portrayed as normal and unremarkable, it is men. Of course, paedophilia is still disapproved of and illegal. But presenting children as desirable and desiring sexual objects contradicts the disapproval (not to mention the law).

The Australia Institute report criticising 'the sexualisation of children in Australia' (Rush and La Nauze, 2006. See also: Hamilton, 2008) acknowledged the connection with the sexual desires of adult men. 'The representation of children as miniature adults playing adult sexual roles', the authors said, 'sends a message to paedophiles that, contrary to laws and ethical norms, children are sexually available' (Rush and La Nauze, 2006: ix). While noting that 'strong evidence is difficult to obtain about the risks of the sexualisation of children promoting paedophilia and child sexual abuse', they argued that, nonetheless, 'society has an obligation to adopt a precautionary approach given the particular vulnerability of children' (p.41). In the final analysis they tended to attribute the phenomenon of sexualising children to 'the relentless drive of business for new markets' (p.48).

This is of course correct. That relentless drive is yet another aspect of the masculine sense of entitlement that powers the capitalist system, and the normalisation of children as erotically available was preceded by the normalisation of adult pornography and the prostitution of adult women (and other formerly disreputable activities such as gambling and depictions of violence in the media). This was just such a drive for new markets, and it was necessitated by what Harry Shutt called 'the relative stagnation of effective consumer demand' (Shutt, 1998: 184). Shutt (1998: 37, 184) has argued that it is the market saturation of the more conventional industries in the wealthy nations of the West after the surge of growth in the 1950s, that has led to such previously disreputable occupations as prostitution and pornography (and gambling) becoming respectable 'industries'. There is a limit to how many white goods, motor cars, television sets, furniture, soda pop, exotic fruit, etc., people want, or can be made to want, despite planned obsolescence, technical innovation and a proliferation of advertising at double the average rate of economic growth in the OECD countries. But although ordinary comfortably-off citizens are not insatiable, capital is. It must keep the sources of profit coming. Capital requires ever new outlets in which to invest the oceans of profit that the system produces.

The demand that is pandered to by prostitution and pornography was there. Throughout the recorded history of the West (and probably elsewhere as well), men have demanded and been supplied with women (and children) for use as sexual objects. These activities have usually been disapproved of, but all that was required to create these new areas of consumption and profit generation was to relax community standards and government restraints. So legal restrictions on the production and consumption of pornography were abolished, gambling was legalised, and prostitution was 'decriminalised' (i.e. the women were no longer automatically arrested—the men never had been, until the introduction of the Nordic model whereby it is made a criminal offence to buy sex but not to sell it).

This deregulation of enterprises formerly anathematised by the social conservative right wing is justified by the neo-liberal right wing in the name of 'freedom', although women's subordination continues under the neo-liberal hegemony. Male supremacy's most vicious forms—prostitution, pornography, sex trafficking, sex tourism, rape, child sexual abuse, other forms of male violence against women, children and each other, and one of the newest forms of male entitlement, surrogacy—have not abated. They may even have worsened in the last few decades with the power of capital behind them and the consequent blossoming of male entitlement. The fact that paedophilia harms children is ignored by the advertising industry, which has developed highly sophisticated methods for arguing away anything that stands in the way of profit, and whose ethical standards at the best of times are abysmal.

Dissociation

There is nothing as dangerous as an unembodied principle: no matter what blood flows, the principle comes first (Dworkin, 1988b: 212)

Implicit in all these criticisms [on the part of the women's movement] was a criticism of abstraction as a strategy in male hegemony. This was a movement that always wanted to know where the women were, substantively. Where was *women's* "choice"? Where was *women's* "consent"? Where was equality as *women* define it? What did freedom for *women* mean? As we criticized male reality in this movement that was, we always looked for the prick in the piece. We found that abstractions were a coverup for the gendered reality that was really going on. On this basis, this movement produced a systematic, relentless, deeply materially based and empirically rigorous critique of the male-dominated reality of women's lives and the glossy abstractions that made it seem not male-dominated (MacKinnon, 1990: 4—original emphases).

If I had to name one quality as the genius of patriarchy, it would be compartmentalization, the capacity for institutionalizing disconnection … survival requires a coarsening of the sensibility … We justify our lies, in business, in friendship, in love. We're accustomed to atrocity on our nightly television news, sandwiched between heartwarming "human interest" stories and headache-remedy commercials. We think little—or nothing—of it. We fear that to dwell on it, to truly notice and connect, is to invite madness. Hannah Arendt was not the first to perceive this state of being, but the name she gave to it is so precise as to be a candidate for describing the entire twentieth century—and, to me, a phrase synonymous with patriarchy: *the banality of evil* (Morgan, 1990: 51-2—emphases in the original).

What does it mean that a man's most routine, most repeated, most reliable, perhaps even most intensely "personal" erotic experiences are those that happen in relation to things, to bodies perceived and regarded as things, to images depicting bodies as things, to memories of images of bodies as things? … Acculturated phallic eroticism is genital-centric; all sense of life is centered in the phallus; the rest of the body is armoured and kept relatively dead. The phallus thus seems to have an independent life and will of its own, autonomous and unpredictable, and the man is at pains to control it, to make it do what he wants … As father right serves dead fathers, so also does father right serve men whose bodies are dead while their penises are alive (Stoltenberg, 1990: 44, 67).

The first quotation above comes from a short article by Andrea Dworkin criticising the American Civil Liberties Union for its embracing of the principle of 'free speech' at the expense of those harmed by what that 'speech' recommends. She was referring to the ACLU's defence of pornography, Nazism and the race hatred espoused by the Ku Klux Klan. Dissociation in this case takes the form of rigid adherence to a principle which takes no account of the harmfulness of what is said. The ACLU's absolutist defence of 'free speech' is dissociated from a stance of genuine humanity which would recognise that these discourses are hateful and damaging, and should be denounced, not defended.

The notion of 'free speech' is ideological. Rarely is it applied to the speech of or on behalf of the powerless: 'When I give food to the poor, they call me a saint. When I ask why they are poor, they call me a communist'.[41] As Dworkin herself was well aware, the ACLU's defence of 'free speech' is intimately connected with the masculinist interest in allowing pornography

---

41. Attributed to Hélder Pessoa Câmara, Brazilian Catholic Archbishop of Olinda and Recife between 1964 to 1985, during the military regime.

free rein. Pornography is male supremacy's dominant ideology justifying the use of the penis as the primary instrument for the subjugation of women by men dehumanised by being reduced to nothing but their penises. The dissociation involved in the ACLU's defence of 'free speech' no matter what is said, exposes the male supremacist interests it actually espouses, interests that involve hyper-valuation of penis-possession as the symbol of 'human' status, and which obliterate consideration for others and any fellow feeling of a shared humanity. It is nicely expressed by John Stoltenberg in the third quotation, with his reference to 'men whose bodies are dead while their penises are alive' (Stoltenberg, 1990: 44, 67)

The second quotation, from a critique by Catharine MacKinnon of liberalism as an attack on feminism, referred to another variant of dissociation—'abstraction as a strategy in male hegemony'. She gave a number of examples of the kinds of standpoints that amounted to abstractions in this sense, together with the genuinely human standpoint that would see these phenomena for what they really are: the dissociated view that rape is only sex (rather than sexual terrorism and violence against women); the dissociated view that prostitution stems from the nature of women (rather than from the interests of the johns and pimps who demand it, use it and profit from it); the dissociated view that incest and the helplessness of children are sexy (instead of focusing on the perpetrators); the dissociated view that battery expresses the intensity of love (again instead of focusing on the perpetrators); the dissociated belief in choice (which ignores a reality which makes any genuine choice impossible); the dissociated belief in consent (which ignores the reality of coercion); the dissociated belief in equality (which fails to see that the only two alternatives offered—sameness to or difference from men—both reproduce male standards). Dissociation involves being unable to acknowledge both realities: the reality where women exist only to serve and service men and men harm women because they can, and the reality where women are human beings in their own right. Being able to recognise both realities is the first step towards resisting the first and embracing the second.

Other common, everyday examples of dissociation in the cultural sense I am using here are: aerial bombing of civilians (or of anyone else); drones that kill people at a distance from the actual perpetrators; suicide bombing; war in general;[42] pouring pollutants into the atmosphere, the waterways and

---

42. MacKinnon (1990: 3) said that feminism 'criticized war as male ejaculation'. Or to put it another way, the meaning given to ejaculation by male supremacy is symbolic violence, while war is its actual violence. They are different expressions of the inherent violence of

the oceans; amassing gigantic stockpiles of lethal weapons; building nuclear power plants; extracting fossil fuels from the earth and burning them in the atmosphere and spilling them in the sea; a global economy that enables vast accumulations of wealth alongside desperate poverty for hundreds of millions of people; a world food-distribution network based on profit not need; a 'welfare reform' that makes things worse for the people most directly affected; advertising; surrogacy; transsexualism; and of course, pornography and prostitution.

These are all phenomena where humanity—people's right to comfort, safety, security, even their very lives—is sacrificed in the interests of power-as-domination. What is but ought not to be, is 'compartmentalisation', 'institutionalising disconnection' and 'a coarsening of the sensibility'. What ought to be but is not, is acknowledgement of the harm. What ought to be is the recognition that, not only is the harm caused by human actions and hence not inevitable, the 'humans' who cause the harm are those caught up in the masculine character structure of male supremacy. Women can aid men in such enterprises, but the motivating force of such humanitarian disasters is dissociated masculinity.

Psychiatric concept

By 'dissociation' I mean not just disaffection, but an actual divorce from the realities of human existence. I could have used the traditional sociological terms 'alienation' or 'anomie' to denote this aspect of the character structure of male supremacist masculinity. But I prefer the term 'dissociation' because of its connotations of insanity, even though my usage differs from the 'dissociative disorders' described in the fourth edition of the American Psychiatric Association's *Diagnostic and Statistical Manual of Mental Disorders*. In the DSM-IV, dissociation is a psychiatric and hence individualistic concept, whereas I am arguing that the dissociation characteristic of masculinity is a cultural phenomenon. It has its effects on individual men (and women) but it can only be adequately accounted for by exposing its meaning and purpose for the wider system of male supremacy, that is, for all of us.

When I say that the DSM-IV classification is individualistic, I don't mean that it suggests that dissociative disorders are inherent in individuals (like the outmoded 'degeneracy' theory of mental disorders). DSM-IV[43] acknowledges

---

male supremacy. For an account from a genuinely human standpoint of the possibility of 'unmaking war' by 'remaking men', see: Barry, 2010.

43. And the 'mental health' profession more generally: 'psychiatrists, other physicians, psychologists, social workers, nurses, occupational and rehabilitation therapists,

that dissociative disorders are the result of something 'stressful' and 'traumatic' in the environment. But because the classification is concerned with identifying the damage to individuals, the source is deemed irrelevant to the description of the disorder.

All four types of dissociative disorder—amnesia, fugue, identity disorder and depersonalisation—specify characteristics of individuals. Dissociated people forget (amnesia), they flee from their familiar environments (fugue), they fragment into two or more personalities (identity disorder), and they feel detached from their mental processes or their bodies (depersonalisation). The classification focuses on the sufferer's reactions ('the symptoms'), and on their 'distress or impairment' for the purposes of curing particular individuals. In contrast, I am interested in a cultural phenomenon which certainly affects individuals and to which they react, but which also structures institutions, and hence cannot be explained, much less rectified, by remaining focused on individuals. I am not concerned to explicate the level of the individual at all, neither people nor particular isolated events they might have been subjected to, except insofar as individuals are bearer of social relations, and either victors or victimised under dehumanising conditions. I am concerned to identify structures of meanings and values which exist whether or not any particular individual reacts to them or is affected by them, and which maintain an underlying consistency despite the diverse ways people deal with them.

Another way in which my account of dissociation differs from the dissociative disorders defined in the DSM-IV is that the latter are distinguished from normality. Dissociative amnesia, for example, is contrasted with 'ordinary forgetfulness', while the various mental functions are 'usually' integrated (whereas in dissociative disorders they are not). A classification of *dis*order implies the existence of an *order* whereby most people are healthy most of the time, and those diagnosed with disorders can be returned to that state. My usage, in contrast, finds dissociation to be normal—widespread, predominant, unquestioned and institutionalised—although it is still pathological and undesirable from any genuinely human point of view. I even regard dissociation, not as a disorder, but as an ordering principle in itself, as part of the character structure demanded of men by the culture of masculinity. While acknowledging the reality of individual experiences of dissociation so extreme that they require intervention from the mental

---

counselors, and other health and mental health professionals' (DSM-IV, Introduction).

health professions, I do not find such reactions surprising in a culture where dissociation is the norm.

So my usage of 'dissociation' diverges from that of the DSM-IV definitions—from the individualistic focus and from the assumption that dissociation is in itself abnormal (although I do agree that it is pathological). But I still find useful the notion of 'a disruption' in what should be integrated but is not, although I place a different emphasis from the DSM-IV on what it is that needs to be integrated. The DSM-IV specifies this as 'the usually integrated functions of consciousness, memory, identity, or perception'. I agree that dissociation involves the disruption of these functions (although I am not so sure that they are 'usually' integrated—vide the concept of the unconscious). However, I am interested in a different kind of integration, which has something to do with the ethical concept of integrity, which in turn is connected with such notions as truth, honesty, honourableness, trust, reliability, dependability, as well as being connected with something like a true perception of what is really going on. Dissociation in this context is a disruption of the integration between what something is (including a person) from the standpoint of the genuinely human, and what it is said to be and how it is felt within the dominant malestream discourse.

Feminist theories

There are a number of feminist accounts of the dissociated character structure of male supremacist masculinity. There is Carol Gilligan's argument that there are differences between the sexes in the way they form their identities and develop a moral sense:

> Since masculinity is defined through separation while femininity is defined through attachment, male gender identity is threatened by intimacy while female gender identity is threatened by separation. Thus males tend to have difficulty with relationships, while females tend to have problems with individuation (Gilligan, 1982: 8, citing the work of Nancy Chodorow).

These differences are benign to the extent that they are not complicit with the norms and mores of domination. Detachment is not in itself pathological (and neither is connection). It is the dehumanisation characteristic of the culture of male supremacy that demands dissociation and makes it a cultural imperative for everyone—for men as part of their identity, for both sexes as a way of managing a world of disrespect, misrecognition and violence. The crucial difference between women and men under conditions of male supremacy revolves around power. Neither sex has sufficient access to power-as-capability—to the capacity to live a life of comfort, peace, dignity and security, to make a difference in one's own world, and to be recognised and appreciated for oneself and one's achievements. But dissociation is a norm for men, even to the extent that the most ruthless have the power to make what they believe to be their interests prevail, with a callous disregard of the needs and rights of others; and men in general tend to be oblivious to the extent to which they receive recognition as human beings in their own right in ways that women do not.

The separative self

Another account is Catherine Keller's notion of the 'separative self' to refer to a self that was characteristically masculine.[44] This self she characterised as:

> [a being who is] armoured against the outer world and the inner depths … the Other, and even its own body … self-reifying and other-exclusive … [which] makes itself the absolute in that it absolves itself from relation … [and] brooks no other subjects and so it turns them into the nonsubjective other, the object, whenever it can … [It has a] need to posit the submissive other, be it male opponent or female property … [and a] lust for power over the other, the enemy, the woman, and the world … [Men who embrace the persona of the separative self] are quite literally less in touch with reality insofar as they are less prone to feel it … [and] in *danger of* (and dangerous with) too much blockage of feeling … Domination is its best defense, and retreat its familiar back-up plan (Keller, 1986: xix, 9, 200, 26, 31, 137, 189, 200—original emphasis).

She was not suggesting that these characteristics were inherent in men. She used the term 'separative' (rather than simply 'separate') in order to indicate that the self she was describing was 'an activity or an intention rather than any fundamental state of being' (p.9).

Up to this point her account of the separative self accords with the dissociated masculinity I have been discussing. But she has an unsatisfactory account of the origins of the power wielded by this 'self'. She seems to believe that the separative self asserts power over others because he is incapable of interacting with them. He has a 'need to posit the submissive other' as a way of 'mak[ing] up for the lack, the despair implicit in his triumphant defiance—the fundamental anxiety that he may be no one'. It is this 'lack' which 'motivate[s] [his] violence of conquest and domination'. 'Power *over* the other', she says, 'makes up for the lost sense of relation *with* the other' (Keller, 1986: 137-8—original emphases).

---

44. She called the self that was characteristically feminine, 'soluble'.

But it makes more sense to see the power-over as the *cause* of the loss, not as its consequence. The separative self lacks the ability to relate to others because of his violence—it is not the case that he is violent because he can't relate to others. The violence precedes the lack and leads to the loss of the capacity for relationship. The violence is the consequence of the male supremacist culture into which we are born. It is that which destroys the possibility of relationships, not the impossibility of relationships which gives rise to violence. Nonetheless, the notion of a 'separative self' armoured against self and other with a lust for power and a propensity for violence, is precisely what I mean by the dissociation characteristic of male supremacist masculinity.

Feminist object relations

As I have argued elsewhere (Thompson, 1991a: 17-22), feminist object relations theory shows the most promise as a starting point for theorising the ways in which males are inculcated into dissociated modes of being (or as I put it there, for theorising 'the making of men'). It is only a hint— the theory was not primarily concerned with masculinity. But it is worth developing further the little it had to say about how men are inculcated with the culture of masculinity and made into the dissociated, over-entitled beings required by male supremacy (although it has little or nothing to say about the development of genuine humanity).

The insight centres around the idea of separateness. Feminist object relations theory sees males as more able to remain separate and detached from others than females can. The theory does not regard detachment in relation to others as a problem, as indeed it is not in any absolute sense. But it is a problem in inappropriate circumstances, i.e. in circumstances where some form of connection is called for, where what is required are caring, empathy, fellow-feeling or identification, not distance or indifference. It is in such circumstances that detachment becomes dissociation.

Feminist object relations theory accounts for the greater detachment on the part of men in terms of women's mothering. Both sexes are mothered by women, but because males are a different sex from the one with whom they first experience a human relationship, they cannot identify with her. Because they are not like her, they must not be like her. They must repudiate her. On this point, however, the point where the imperative of masculinity switches in, feminist object relations theory is less than satisfactory. It underestimates the centrality of the meaning of penis-possession in the constitution of masculinity, and as a consequence it lays too much responsibility on the women who mother.

Nancy Chodorow explicitly rejects any explanation in terms of penis-possession. She says:

> Freud "explains" the development of boys' contempt for mothers as coming from their perception of genital differences, particularly their mother's "castration". He takes this perception to be unmediated by social experience, and not in need of explanation … it did not occur to Freud that such differential evaluation and ensuing contempt were not in the natural order of things (Chodorow, 1978: 182).

She goes on to cite Freud's 'Little Hans' case study as evidence that such attitudes on the part of boys were not natural at all, but the result of 'social experience': 'in fact Hans's father perpetuated and created such beliefs in his son'.

This is, of course, true enough. Freud's naturalising tendencies are a problem, and he did find the hyper-valuation of penis-possession to be not in need of explanation. But what is at issue here is not his appeal to 'nature'. That can be rejected without diminishing the significance of what he discovered. The 'differential evaluation and ensuing contempt' Freud uncovered among men were indeed 'not in the natural order of things', as Chodorow said. But that doesn't mean that the valorisation of penis-possession entailed by the 'masculine oedipus complex' is not real. Its 'curtailment' of 'relational capacities' (Chodorow, 1978: 93) doesn't come from male biology, but as a cultural imperative it has a profound influence on social life.

The Freudian Oedipus complex is not just a story about 'parent'-child relationships. It is also a story about the structuring of human relationships so they will take on the lineaments and serve the purposes of male supremacy. The meaning of penis-possession is central to that process: the male child must learn that the only truly 'human' thing about him is his penis. The Oedipus complex is an account of how (masculine) sex acquires meaning. It is the male infant which is targeted as *the* sex by way of his *sex*, that is, his penis. He must learn that the penis comes first, that all love, desire, connection, recognition and identification must be channelled through it.

This sets up a conflict in the masculine psyche. Freud interpreted this conflict as one between the male infant and his father for sexual possession of the mother. The father threatens castration if the son does not relinquish his desire for the mother, and the conflict is resolved by the son's internalisation of and identification with the powerful, punitive father. But prior to the onset of any Oedipus complex there already exists a human relationship between mother and child, a relationship of burgeoning mutual recognition, of a balancing of holding and letting go.[45] The theory of the Oedipus complex says that male phallic desire must be introduced into this relationship if the (male) child is to grow up to be a fully functioning adult. But the memory lingers on, even if only in the unconscious, and provides an alternative to phallic reality. The conflict in the male psyche is between the humanity of the child's mother and her dehumanisation within male supremacy.

I am not suggesting that the original bond between mother and child is some kind of exemplar of the genuinely human. This is not a distinction between genuine humanity on the one hand, and male supremacy on the other. Not only does this bond take place under conditions which ensure that male supremacy itself will be reproduced, it is also the kind of relationship that must be left behind, and by no means a model of what an adult human being might be. It is a relationship of 'symbiosis', as Margaret Mahler called it, of what might also be called 'merger or boundarylessness or undifferentiatedness' (Pine, 2004: 513). While there are more or less genuinely human ways for both mother and child, in which infancy can be lived out, in itself infancy does not provide a model of the genuinely human.

Nonetheless, the conflict which is introduced into the masculine psyche through the inculcation of male supremacy is one between a 'human' status based on penis-possession and a genuine humanity to which the penis-possession is irrelevant. Male supremacy engineers the hyper-valuation of penis-possession by defining genuine humanity as 'castration'. If the male child persists in identifying with his mother as his first fully human other, he will 'lose' his penis by being denied access to what it signifies, the world of men. He must take on the meanings and values of penis-possession and turn them against his first love object. He must repudiate her and come to hold her in contempt because she lacks what is so highly valued in a culture of male supremacy.

Dissociated masculinity lacks a moral compass, that sense of right and wrong arising out of connection with others. It is the domination by dissociated masculinity that has led to so many of the world's ills. It is dissociated masculinity that is responsible, for example, for Donald Trump's election to the US presidency (however else it might be characterised). It was the strict adherence to the rules ('the Electoral College') that elected him, rather than the actual number of votes and despite the fact that he had demonstrated over and over again his unfitness for the position. It is true that

---

45. For accounts of this, see: Benjamin, 1988—'The First Bond', and the work of Margaret Mahler: Mahler, 1967, 1974; Mahler et al, 2000; Pine, 2004.

a Hillary Clinton administration would not have been any more progressive (or genuinely human) than preceding administrations. But she did gain more votes than Trump, a criterion that has often been touted as the basis of democratic elections. Perhaps the US ruling class believes they can control Trump. For example, a right-wing correspondent for the *Los Angeles Times* said, 'Many movement conservatives, including Vice President-elect Mike Pence, operate under the assumption that Trump is essentially content-free and can be brought around to support the conventional conservative agenda' (Boot, 2016). But the German ruling class thought they could control Hitler and they were wrong. But whatever the consequences of a US presidency with Donald Trump at the head, and Republican control of all three branches of the federal government and a majority of State governments, it didn't come out of nowhere. It is a triumph for the arrogant, dissociated masculinity that has been driving the neo-liberal agenda for decades in the interests of amassing gigantic accumulations of wealth in the hands of a few ruthless men ('inequality').

Conclusion

As cultural phenomena, these masculinist characteristics of dissociation and overweening entitlement shape both psyches and institutions, including dominant justificatory ideological discourses. This present project is an exercise in critical theory intended to expose the male supremacist nature of some dominant institutions in our society, which present themselves as beneficial, necessary for the greater good, or harmless, while actually operating in the service of the privileged few. I recognise the possibility and actual existence of alternatives, not by specifying what those alternatives are, but as a way of acknowledging that resistance to domination is possible on the part of anyone, both as a lone objector and in concert with like-minded others. Everyone, by virtue of being human, is able to sort out truth from lies and think things through (Arendt, 1971). Resisting the conditions of domination requires a dialogue with the self and hence a kind of a doubled consciousness. There is the reality of male supremacy and there is the reality of what I have called the genuinely human—the reality structured by the requirements of domination on the one hand, and on the other, an alternative reality of genuine humanity which reaches beyond domination at the same time as it exists alongside it. This is not a distinction between the 'is' of domination and the 'ought' of its overcoming, because both domination and its absence are real and both involve an ethical standpoint. The ethics of domination is 'might makes right', while the ethics of its absence is human dignity for all. Dissociation is the disjunction between the two, between what is but ought not to be, and what ought to be but too often is not.

The overall message is that the reign of men must end in favour of human beings living together, not in any unrealistic 'equality' but in ways which exploit no one. Keeping the current system in check can no longer be dependent on sporadic appearances of genuine humanity.

Chapter Five: Capitalism

Adam Smith wrote the definitive one-sentence treatment: "Wealth, as Mr. Hobbes says, is power." (Galbraith, 2014b).[46]

From the late nineteenth century onwards, the US gradually learned to mask the explicitness of territorial gains and occupations under the mask of a spaceless universalization of its own values, buried within a rhetoric that was ultimately to culminate ... in what came to be known as "globalization" (Harvey, 2003: 47).

Capitalism is the form male domination takes under conditions of modernity. I have argued elsewhere (Thompson, 2005c) that current world economic arrangements can be seen as male supremacist because men are paid most of the world's income and own most of the world's wealth while doing a fraction of the work women do.[47] Here, I am extending that insight by pointing out that, behind the ownership and control of the world's wealth, lies dissociated masculine arrogance. Feminist accounts of capitalism focus on the ways in which capitalism exploits women (and other categories of the oppressed in some accounts). But capitalism is vastly more than that, indeed vastly more than the exploitation of workers in its industries. There is the accumulation of wealth in the hands of a few men (and their female relatives); there is the finance industry and its propensity to crash the world economy; and there is the way banks and corporations dictate to nation states at the expense of the interests citizens have in living in peace, comfort and security. My purpose is to do what Maria Mies said she was *not* doing in *Patriarchy & Accumulation*, namely, 'to produce a grand theory on the functioning of capitalist patriarchy' (Mies, 1998: vii). While I am not sure how 'grand' the theory is, and I prefer

---

46. This is James Kenneth Galbraith, the son of John Kenneth Galbraith.

47. This information was included in a 1980 UN publication, *Report of the World Conference of the United Nations Decade for Women: Equality, Development and Peace*, Copenhagen, 14 to 30 July 1980. I haven't been able to find any updating of this information by the UN.

the term 'male domination' to 'patriarchy', this is the task I am engaged upon here

Capitalism has been defined as 'the satisfaction of human needs and wants by industrial production undertaken by bureaucratic enterprises in which net profit is rationally calculated' (as Geoffrey Ingham put it, ascribing this view to Max Weber) (Ingham, 2008: 25). Described thus, capitalism appears admirable, even benign. Satisfying human needs and wants can only be a good thing, and even more so when that satisfaction happens rationally.

But despite the neutrality of this definition, and of most of Weber's account of capitalism, he was aware that there was more to it than 'the satisfaction of human needs and wants' and rational calculation. Take, for example, his famous 'iron cage' metaphor[48] from *The Protestant Ethic*:

> when asceticism was carried out of monastic cells into everyday life, and began to dominate worldly morality, it did its part in building the tremendous cosmos of the modern economic order. This order is now bound to the technical and economic conditions of machine production which to-day determine the lives of all the individuals who are born into this mechanism, not only those directly concerned with economic acquisition, with irresistible force. Perhaps it will so determine them until the last ton of fossilized coal is burnt ... the care for external goods should only lie on the shoulders of the "saint like a light cloak, which can be thrown aside at any moment". But fate decreed that the cloak should become an iron cage (Weber, 1976: 181).

Most commentaries attribute this rigid structure of capitalism to its bureaucratic rationalisation, but the 'iron cage' metaphor is first introduced in the context of 'the care for external goods', i.e. wealth. The view of wealth of Weber's Puritan informants was that:

> [w]ealth as such is a great danger; its temptations never end, and its pursuit is not only senseless as compared with the dominating importance of the Kingdom of God, but it is morally suspect (Weber, 1976: 156-7).

This is not, of course, the view of wealth that has prevailed in capitalist society. The Puritan distrust of wealth was circumvented by the Protestant ethic that bolstered capitalist acquisition through the notion of 'the calling' and hard work. The main Puritan objection to wealth was that it led to idleness. If a man amassed great wealth while engaging in his God-given calling, as long as he '"do the works of him who sent him"' (p.157) his accumulation of wealth

---

48. The original German, *stahlhartes Gehäuse*, translates literally as 'housing hard as steel'— 'iron cage' was Talcott Parsons' translation.

was at the very least irrelevant to his 'state of grace'. At most, it was a sign of God's love and proof that he was among the elect destined to be saved.

So despite the neutrality of much of his discussion of capitalism, Weber was not an unquestioning supporter. 'No one knows who will live in this cage in the future', he said,

> For of the last stage of this cultural development, it might truly be said: "Specialists without spirit, sensualists without heart; this nullity imagines that it has attained a level of civilization never before achieved" (Weber, 1976: 182).[49]

For Weber, in this context the 'iron cage' was wealth. It was the accumulating of wealth that imprisoned the whole society ('all the individuals who are born … not only those directly concerned with economic acquisition') in a rigid structure of soulless, heartless emptiness.

Weber did not, however, discuss capitalism as a system of domination (much less of male domination). His definition of 'domination' (*Herrschaft*) as 'the probability that a command with a given specific content will be obeyed by a given group of persons' (Weber, 1978: 53), was too narrow to encompass the notion of a system that results in massive levels of inequality—great wealth for the few and destitution for the many—without anyone giving any direct commands at all. Indeed, the word 'wealth' often appears in inverted commas throughout *Economy and Society*, as though it were not a thing in itself, but something that needed to be interpreted before it could be seen clearly. Moreover, sociologist though he was, his individualistic ethos prevented him from seeing forms of social control that need not be deliberately imposed by anyone, that are 'tolerable only on condition that it mask a substantial part of itself' (Foucault, 1984: 86). Not only did he define domination in terms of explicit commands given by identifiable individuals, he also defined the economy as activity by individuals: 'All economic activity in a market economy is undertaken and carried through by individuals acting to provide for their own ideal or material interests' (Weber, 1978: 202). Seeing the economy in terms of activities where everyone does their own thing precludes any account of domination. Thus did Weber forget the insights into capitalist accumulation he learned from his Puritan informants.

It is true that that was long ago and far away. Nowadays the pursuit of wealth is 'stripped of its religious and ethical meaning', especially 'in the field of its highest development, in the United States' (Weber, 1976: 182). Puritan strictures against wealth accumulation are now laughable, reduced to

---

49. This is a quotation from Goethe (Giddens, 1976: 9).

quaint anachronisms no longer relevant to a global economy where wealth accumulation is the highest good and ethical resistance to it is absent. But there is still a need for ethical resistance to capitalism because capitalism is not just an economy, still less is it adequately described as 'activity'. Whatever else it might be, it is also a system of domination which enables a small number of men to amass wealth and hence power at the expense of the common good. It supplies them and their apologists with the meanings and values of disproportionate entitlement at the expense of large segments of populations everywhere, and ultimately to the detriment of all of us. Capitalist domination has commodified the basic necessities of human existence while depriving segments of populations of the resources to buy them. It destroys subsistence livelihoods—generations ago in the industrialised nations, currently in the Third World—replacing them with unreliable wages frequently below subsistence. It is structured around 'the market' which is 'free' only in the sense that it is ungoverned, and not in the sense that it is available to all. It produces commodities and offers services only for profit, and any concern it displays for people is ill-considered, opportunistic and hypocritical (Chomsky, 1999).

For present-day capitalism, what kinds of commodities are produced is a matter of indifference, as long as they make a profit. It produces damaging garbage—weapons, fossil fuels, junk food, soda pop, advertising, plastic bags, Barbie dolls, nuclear reactors—to mention just a few of the commodities which produce wealth while actually undermining well-being; and such production is justified to the voting public on the grounds that it creates 'jobs'. That such jobs are expendable when maintaining or increasing the rate of profit requires it, is not mentioned. Humanising such a system would not be easy. As Susan George put it, 'you can't have a global economy which enriches a few beyond any historical parallel, which pushes wealth inexorably upwards and creates losers by the tens of millions—all that and a pristine environment and a clean conscience besides' (George 1999a: 180). All this is well known among those with the willingness to see.[50] What is less well known is that the drive for wealth and power is masculine, a system by, for and about men dehumanised by their own grandiose sense of entitlement.

The word 'capitalism' isn't used much any more. As Raymond Williams said: '[In the mid-twentieth century,] in reaction against socialist argument,

---

50. For some randomly chosen, recent critiques of capitalism and of neo-liberalism as its justificatory ideology, see: Ahmed, 2014; Brown, 2015; Cahill, 2004; Connell and Dados, 2014; Deeming, 2014; Dobbin, 2015a, b, c; Ferguson, 2012; George, 1976, 1984, 1990, 1999a, b, 2008; Harvey, 2003, 2005, 2006, 2007, 2011, 2014; Haseler, 2000; Hedges, 2016a,

the words **capitalism** and **capitalist** have often been deliberately replaced by such phrases as "private enterprise" and "free enterprise"' (Williams, 1986: 51). Earlier, Berthold Brecht put it more succinctly: 'capitalism is a gentleman who doesn't like to be called by that name', he is reported to have said (cited in Boron, 2006: 32). The most commonly used alternative name is 'markets' (the preferred term in the UN's 2010 *Human Development Report*, discussed below), but references to 'the free market' or 'firms' or 'investors' or 'business' or 'the business community' or 'the big end of town', or 'industry', or 'growth', or simply 'the economy', are also references to capitalism.

The following is a typical example of how to avoid naming capitalism:

> Growth produces progress and wealth, but in unforeseeable ways and in discrete lumps that create many small winners (for example, the people who can now buy their shirts at Wal-Mart for $8.99 as opposed to $12.99 at its less-efficient competitors), a few huge winners (for example, the Walton family of Bentonville, Ark.), and notable substantial losers (the Main Street merchants [i.e. small businesses] of the Mississippi Valley, the Great Plains, and the Sun Belt) (Delong, 2007).

This could be rewritten as follows: 'Capitalism produces material progress and wealth but not for everyone. While it appears to provide benefits for all, e.g. cheap clothing, it actually benefits only the few like the Walmart family, while destroying the livelihoods of many more, e.g. small business owners'. The author might also have listed among the losers, subsistence farmers, and the employees who produced the growth but received none of the wealth—the low-wage workforce at home, and the offshore workers in dangerous, substandard factories in Bangladesh, China and elsewhere in the Third World. Also among the losers not listed are the populations—eventually all of us—affected by environmental pollution, global warming and the exhaustion of natural resources brought about by that growth which rewarded those 'few huge winners' at the expense of the rest of us. This sort of wilful ignorance is the denial that functions to hide, not only the detrimental effects of unfettered capitalism, but also the male entitlement and dissociation that motivate the ceaseless drive for profit.

---

b; Higgs, 2014; Ingham, 2008; Isquith, 2015; Klein, 1999, 2008, 2014, 2017; Knight, 2008, 2009a, b, c, d, e, 2013; Leys, 2006; Lohmann, 2015; Lyngar, 2015; Madeley, 1999; Martinez and García, 2000; Motesharrei et al, 2014; Patience, 2015; Peck, 2001, 2010; Peck et al, 2012; Roy, 2002; Stuckler and Basu, 2013; Wacquant, 2009, 2010, 2012, 2013; Wallerstein et al, 2013. For a glimmer of optimism, see: the Global Justice Movement, and Monbiot, 2015.

There is also a new term—'Anthropocene'—now being used in discussions of the environmental destruction capitalism has wrought. The term means 'human geologic epoch' and it refers to 'overwhelming global evidence that atmospheric, geologic, hydrologic, biospheric and other earth system processes are now altered by humans' (Ellis, 2011, 2013). This new 'geologic era' is widely believed to date from the beginning of the 'Industrial Revolution' (Ellis, 2013), and the 'Industrial Revolution' is capitalism. The usual euphemisms apply in the use of this new term: the destructive processes are not named as 'capitalist' (nor, unsurprisingly, are they recognised as a consequence of male supremacy); there is much use of neutral terminology ('change', 'altered', 'influence', 'the effects of humans'); and the whole human race ('mankind') is held responsible (Crutzen, 2002), rather than that particular segment of the human race driven by arrogant entitlement and obliviousness to genuine humanity. It is true that some of the industrial destruction happened under so-called communist regimes, but they used the same methods as capitalism and displayed the same heedlessness towards the consequences. Moreover, I argue that the destructiveness is not in the first place a consequence of any particular economic regime, but rather, of an economy that establishes and maintains male domination.

The reluctance to name capitalism is partly in response to the criticism it has received, notably in the Marxist tradition (although not only there); capitalism's defenders can avoid answering those criticisms by the simple expedient of not using the same name. The Acton Institute (which is affiliated with the Tea Party Republicans) states this reason explicitly: 'If we want to give up the term capitalism to appease its critics, so be it' (Sirico, 2007). This dissociated statement is typical of the right-wing apologia for domination. Giving up the name 'capitalism' is hardly likely 'to appease its critics'; they are not objecting to the name, but rather to the reality, whatever it is called.

Another reason why the word 'capitalism' isn't used any more is that it is the only economic system we have. That capitalism is the only form an economy can take under present historical conditions is the foundational premise of the discipline of economics. As Robert Heilbroner said:

> Economics is the name we give to our attempts to understand the capitalist world ... economics, despite its sometimes self-proclaimed universal character, is by its very nature inextricably entwined with the institutions and values of the social order we call capitalism (Heilbroner, 1996: viii).

There is no point in naming it as a particular kind of economy when there isn't any other kind. For the most part this is not seen as a reason for dismay; on the contrary, not only is capitalism in fact the only economy in existence, it is regarded as the only economy that *ought* to be in existence. As the UN's 2010 *Human Development Report* put it, the way 'markets' organise production, involving 'extensive private ownership', is 'an indispensable component of any economic system capable of supporting the sustained dynamism necessary for transformative changes in most dimensions of human development' (UNDP, 2010: 61). For the UN, there is its 'sustained dynamism', which is guaranteed by its system of private ownership; but there are other reasons given for the undoubted success of capitalism in coming to monopolise humanity's economic arrangements.

According to Ross Gittins, economics editor at *The Sydney Morning Herald*, the reason why capitalism is the only economy we have is its efficiency in providing things we want:

> Economics is about efficient materialism; making sure the natural, man-made and human resources available to us are used in ways that yield maximum satisfaction of our material wants. It argues that economies based on private ownership and freely operating markets – "capitalist" economies – are the most efficient (Gittins, 2014).

It is true Gittins has always been critical (in an understated, euphemised kind of way) of some of the ways in which capitalism actually operates; on one occasion in the context of a critique of mainstream economics, for example, he referred approvingly to Adam Smith's 'powerful condemnation of business people's propensity to engage in rent-seeking' (Gittins, 2015a). He has also been critical of the economics profession for its sycophantic support of big business. On another occasion he said: 'we mustn't forget that, these days, the economy is run for the benefit of business, not the rest of us' (Gittins, 2015b). But these are also examples of some of the ways in which his criticism is euphemised. Referring to 'business people's propensity' makes it sound like a personality defect, rather than a system that allows people to acquire money they haven't earned ('rent-seeking'). Again, the use of the phrase 'these days' implies that there was a time when 'big business' was run for the benefit of the rest of us, and if it was once then it could be again, whereas it has never been the case that capitalism operated in the interests of all. However, it is also true that he has argued (in a euphemised kind of way) that the discipline of economics is the ideological justification for capitalism. He did not of course use that terminology; instead, he said that economists were 'apologists for business' (and that they ought not to be), but it amounts to the same thing. But no matter how critical he might be of capitalism or of economics, for him and for all other experts capitalism remains the only possible economic system.

Another reason given for capitalism's pre-eminence as the only possible form of economy is that it creates the wealth. Amanda Vanstone, a long-term member of the right wing in Australian politics,[51] told us: 'The plain truth is that if business is not going well there are less profits, fewer jobs and less tax paid ... To do something effective for those at the lower end of the economic luck spectrum you need to keep the economy vibrant ... make no mistake, we need Australians to get rich, and the sooner the better' (Vanstone, 2014). There are numerous problems with Vanstone's account: her use of the right-wing construct, the 'politics of envy', to individualise the issue ('All this stupid rich-versus-poor debate does is stir up the politics of envy'); her attributing poverty to (bad) 'luck' ('the economic luck spectrum'); her acceptance of economic inequality as necessary for the optimum working of the economy.[52] But she is not alone in her belief in the rightness of the system (although she does not of course see it as a system, but as a series of individuals who do things and own things and who just happen to be rich or poor, lucky or unlucky).

But perhaps the most frequently heard mantra is that capitalism provides jobs. This was one of the main reasons given by a number of corporations and audit firms as they argued their case to the Australian Senate inquiry into corporate tax avoidance.[53] 'Google's submission,' said one commentator, was 'particularly nauseating on this front' (West, 2015a. See also: Khadem, 2015). Google Australia's submission to the Inquiry made this their first point. 'Our employees' appears in the second sentence, while 'job(s)' appears six times

---

51. She was a Senator in the Australian federal parliament from 1984 to 2007, and a Minister from 1996 to 2007 in the Coalition government when John Howard was Prime Minister, holding various portfolios: Employment, Education, Training and Youth Affairs; Justice; Family and Community Services; and Immigration and Multicultural Affairs. She was still an influential voice in political affairs in 2014. At the time she wrote the opinion piece in the SMH, she was a member of the right-wing Coalition government's commission of audit appointed to 'rein in government spending' (Hurst, 2014).

52. This sets her at odds with the UN and the OECD (the Organisation for Economic Cooperation and Development), hardly hot-beds of left-wing radicalism: 'increasing income inequality has slowed the pace of poverty reduction' (UNDP, 2013: 78); 'Sustained inequality inhibits growth and social cohesion. It is a real "live" economic issue ... the economic crisis has added urgency to the need to address inequality ... The benefits of economic growth DO NOT trickle down automatically ... Greater inequality DOES NOT foster social mobility' (Gurría, 2011—original emphases. See also: Hardoon, 2015).

53 .https://www.aph.gov.au/About_Parliament/Parliamentary_Departments/ Parliamentary_Library/FlagPost/2014/December/Senate_inquiry_into_corporate_tax_ avoidance – viewed 9.8.2018.

in the first four pages, along with 'workforce', 'training', 'internship' and 'entrepreneurs'. (Google argued that they were good for small business, too) (Google Australia, 2015).

Google's submission omitted the word 'avoidance'. They called it an inquiry into 'corporate tax' rather than its correct title, 'Senate inquiry into corporate tax avoidance'. They also lied about the amount of tax they paid in Australia: 'Globally, Google pays billions of dollars of corporate tax every year, in fact our overall corporate tax rate in 2014 was about 19%, a few percent lower than the OECD average of 25%', they said. In the first place, the inquiry was not about how much tax Google paid globally, but how much it paid on income earned within Australia. In fact, most of that 19% (actually 18.18%) was paid in the US (Khadem, 2014). Secondly, 19% is not 'a few percent lower' than 25%, it's 24% lower; and finally, it paid no tax in Australia on the advertising revenue it earned in Australia, estimated to be around $2 billion (West, 2015b).

But capitalism's apologists don't always need to resort to outright lies to justify its existence. Half-truths will do. All the above is true—capitalism *is* an efficient creator of wealth, the most efficient ever known, and it does provide jobs. But it is not a system devised for the common good. The wealth is grossly inequitably distributed; many of the jobs are unfit for human employment and they can be taken away without warning, without acknowledgement and without recompense, and the system can't provide jobs for all anyway; and there are many people who can't (or won't) get jobs and the only source of income capitalism offers, but they also have a right to life even though they have no access to the means to supply themselves with basic necessities. Moreover, capitalism has always proceeded, at least in part and wherever it is convenient, by way of brutal expropriations, while its standard operating procedures are threatening to destroy the environment of all of us (Oxfam, 2015).

To put the matter bluntly, capitalism is the material basis of the modern ruling class. Capitalism is the way male power manifests itself now that the traditional forms (royalty, aristocracy, chieftainship) have vanished or become impotent. As Joseph Schumpeter put it: 'what may be attained by industrial or commercial success is still the nearest approach to medieval lordship possible to modern man' (from *The Theory of Economic Development* (1983), quoted in Watson, 2015, p.220 of 268). Schumpeter's use of the term 'man' was not meant literally, of course; he did not mean that 'industrial or commercial success' was peculiarly masculine. He would probably agree that those who 'attained industrial or commercial success' were almost all men, but he was oblivious to the question. His point was simply that the source of the power of the ruling class had changed, not that that ruling class continues to be male.

John Maynard Keynes also saw capitalism as a form of domination although, ironically, by making a distinction between wealth and outright tyranny. 'It is better than a man should tyrannize over his bank balance that over his fellow citizens', he said.

> [D]angerous human proclivities can be canalized into comparatively harmless channels by the existence of opportunities for money-making and private wealth, which, if they cannot be satisfied in this way, may find their outlet in cruelty, the reckless pursuit of personal power and authority, and other forms of self-aggrandisement (from *The General Theory of Employment Money and Interest*, quoted in Watson, 2015, p.220 of 268).

Keynes clearly believed that wealth-production was different from, and preferable to, overt and direct forms of domination and outright violence. But he also believed that it sprang from the same motivations—tyranny, cruelty, power and aggrandisement.

Could it be, though, that capitalism might be humanised? Could the good aspects be retained—the efficiency, the dynamism, the wealth and employment creation, the innovation—while the bad aspects are abolished or at least minimised? This is a question that was answered in the affirmative, at least in the developed nations, with the creation of the welfare state after the two world wars and the Great Depression. But the welfare state has been under sustained attack since the 1970s; and the ease with which governments and electorates have caved in to the neo-liberal agenda and its apologia for the resurgence of unfettered capitalism since that time, does not give cause for optimism.

I discuss the question of whether capitalism should be abolished or retained in more detail in chapter 11. The next section of this chapter discusses what feminism has had to say (or not) about masculinity and capitalism.

Feminism and capitalism

There is a great deal of important feminist work that might appear at first sight to have something of relevance to say about a critique of capitalism as an institutionalised expression of masculinity. There are many feminist critiques of the depredations of a capitalism recently unleashed by neo-liberalism, commonly referred to as 'globalisation',[54] as well as an extensive socialist feminist literature[55] and an established discipline of feminist economics.[56]

Globalisation

However, insightful though they are, and vitally important as exposés of the depredations of globalisation, these criticisms do not link capitalism with masculinity, or even (in some cases) with male domination. The work of Maria Mies and others (see footnote 9), for example, has exposed the multitude of ways in which the globalised economy not only exploits women, but depends on that exploitation for its very existence. Because the exploitation of women is so crucial to the continued existence of the globalised economy, the system is obviously male supremacist. But their concern with the masculinity of the system is confined to the consequences for women, or alternatively, to a detailed exposure of the system's inhumanity and destructiveness. Beyond its effect on women (and humanity and the earth more generally), they do not identify the system as inherently masculine in its arrogant dissociation.

Again, Susan Hawthorne (2002) refers to the system of global domination, not as male domination but as 'western global culture'; and those she sees exploited and harmed by the system are not only women, but also a series of other categories of the oppressed—'indigenous peoples, the poor, the marginalised, including lesbians, the disabled and refugees' (p.140)—which she refers to as the 'diversity matrix'. While it is certainly true that the global system of domination harms not only women, there are good reasons for feminism's focus on women. It helps expose aspects of domination that would otherwise not be apparent. It is a focus, not a total explanation attempting to account for every aspect of reality, but to dispense with it in favour of a plethora of oppressions weakens that distinctive feminist focus

---

54. e.g. Bennholdt-Thomsen et al, 1988, 2001; Mies, 1982, 1998; Mies and Shiva, 1993; Roy, 2002; Salleh, ed., 2009; Shiva, 1992, 1997, 2000, 2001, 2002, 2005, 2008, 2012; Werlhof, 2015.

55. e.g. Barrett, 1980; Beechey and Perkins, 1987; Benston, 1970; Burton, 1985; Coote and Campbell, 1982; Dalla Costa and James, 1975; Edmond and Fleming, eds, 1975; Eisenstein, ed., 1979; Guettel, 1974; Jaggar, 1983; Kuhn and Wolpe, eds, 1978; Mitchell, 1966, 1971, 1984; Mitchell and Oakley, eds, 1976, 1986; Oakley, 1974, 1981; Phelps, 1975; Phillips, 1987; Red Collective, 1973; Rowbotham, 1972, 1973, 1974, 1977; Rubin, 1975; Sachs, 1975; Sargent, ed., 1981; Segal, 1987; Segal, ed., 1983; Weinbaum, 1978.

56. e.g. Bergmann, 1990; Ferber and Nelson, eds, 1993, 2003; Folbre, 1994; Hewitson, 1999; Meagher, 1996; Meagher and Nelson, 2004; Nelson, 1993, 1996a, b; Peterson and Lewis, eds, 2000; Waring, 1985, 1988; the journal *Feminist Economics*; the International Association for Feminist Economics. The tags for this blog site contain no mention of male domination, or even of capitalism.

and fragments the core of feminism's critique. While I too have dispensed with the focus on women as the core of my critique, I have replaced it with the focus on male domination, on the system that gives rise to the need to focus on women. In doing so, I do not claim that I can thereby account for every form of oppression, exclusion or discrimination. It is simply a way of bringing a feminist focus to bear on capitalism (and the other four institutions discussed herein).

In the case of the global domestic-labour market (Ehrenreich and Hochschild, eds, 2003), where women are shipped from their homes in Mexico, Sri Lanka, the Philippines and Eastern Europe to western nations (and the Middle East) to work as cleaners, maids, carers and nannies, it might seem that it is women, not men, who are the dominators. Domestic labour is women's work, after all, and it is (comparatively) wealthy women whose time is freed up by the employment of these women. But there are a number of reasons why this global domestic labour market is as male supremacist as any other aspect of the globalised economy. Making domestic labour 'women's work' is in the interests of men, who don't do it but who benefit from its being done, whether by their wives or by immigrant workers; and a labour market that leaves employees with no resources to care for others is typical of the dissociation of male supremacist arrangements of the social world. Moreover, the global domestic labour industry is dominated by multinational corporations that exploit and degrade their employees just like any other globalised business (Ehrenreich, 2003).

My comments are not intended as criticism. These accounts are valuable records of what is being done to the earth and humankind by capitalist domination. My emphasis is simply different, namely, to expose capitalism as a system of male supremacy that both mimics and creates the masculine character structure necessary to establish and maintain itself.

Socialist feminism

Socialist feminism was not concerned with a critique of capitalism, much less with the ways in which capitalism institutionalised the arrogant entitlement and dissociation of male supremacist masculinity. It did draw attention to a number of important issues in relation to the economic situation of women under capitalism, especially the fact that women's domestic labour was a valuable part of the capitalist economy even though it was unpaid.[57] It was also an exposure of the male domination of left-wing politics and

---

57. For a more recent account of the domestic labour debate, see: Federici, 2010.

its contemptuous treatment of women as unpaid domestic labourers and sex objects. There was also an attempt to adapt Marxist theory for feminist purposes, but the overall conclusion of this aspect of the socialist feminist endeavour was that it was unable to account for the situation of women. It was 'sex blind', as Heidi Hartmann (1981) put it.[58] It was not possible to incorporate into a single theoretical schema both capitalism and patriarchy (the latter being theorised as the situation of women in relation to such non-Marxist categories as biological reproduction, the family, sexuality, male violence, sexism, misogyny, etc.). Attempts to do so either tended to subordinate feminist concerns to Marxist theory and leave large areas of the situation of women unaccounted for, or capitalism and patriarchy remained separate systems with different logics of domination (with racism a third such system).

Feminist economics

As in the case of socialist feminism, feminist economics is not a critique of the masculinity of capitalism either. Instead, it focuses on the discipline of economics. As the editor of the journal *Feminist Economics* said in the first issue of the journal: 'In founding *Feminist Economics* our intent is to enable new and important economic conversations to flourish' (Strassmann, 1995: 1). It is true that the discipline of economics is intimately connected to capitalism because capitalism is the only economy in existence. But feminist economics does not make that connection.

However, feminist economics does come close to a criticism of the masculinity of capitalism in its critique of 'rational economic man'. Analysing this concept exposes the assumptions about human nature made by the discipline of economics, and hence about the kind of human nature necessary for success in the capitalist economy. This is not a persona that ever appears in economics textbooks, but rather a model that theorists have uncovered by reading between the lines of economic theory. He is, as Martin Hollis and Edward J. Nell put it, 'introduced furtively and piece by piece … He lurks in the assumptions leading an enlightened existence between input and output, stimulus and response' (Hollis and Nell, 1975: 53-4).

Not surprisingly given the role economics plays as the justificatory ideology of capitalism, that model of rational economic man expresses the dissociation and arrogant entitlement I have argued is central to the masculinity of capitalism. He is a separative self who is beholden to no one

---

58. For critiques of attempts to theorise feminism through a Marxist lens, see: Campioni and Gross, 1983; Jónasdóttir, 1994; MacKinnon, 1991.

and relates to no one except as a buyer or a seller, a producer or consumer. The dissociation is also shown in the kind of human nature espoused within economics, which bears no relationship to what human beings actually do, want and need. The arrogance is shown in the notion of the self-interested 'utility maximiser'—he whose wants are endless while their satisfaction, although not guaranteed (there are 'constraints' after all), is the dynamism that keeps the system in existence. As Hollis and Nell (1975) said: 'We do not know what [rational economic man] wants. But we do know that, whatever it is, he will maximise ruthlessly to get it' (Hollis and Nell, 1975: 54). Or as Chris Hedges said: 'The rich never have enough. The more they get, the more they want' (Hedges, 2016b). As such, he must be allowed to do whatever he wants to do, and if he causes harm in the process, that can always be either ignored, denied, excused as an inescapable necessity, or deplored with promises to do better that never eventuate.

England

Paula England (1993) found the rational economic man construct in the '[t] hree most basic assumptions underlying economic theory'. These are: 'that interpersonal utility comparisons are impossible, that tastes are exogenous to economic models and unchanging, and that actors are selfish (have independent utilities) in markets (England, 1993: 37). These assumptions, she said, reveal 'the androcentric biases in the deep theoretical structure of neoclassical economics'.

The wording of these three basic assumptions of economics is so obscure that they are probably deliberately designed to obfuscate (not by England, but by the discipline of economics). The notion of selfishness is clear enough, and equally clearly it denotes a separative self in the sense of someone who is only interested in themselves and what they want, and who shows no consideration for others. The rest of the language is esoteric jargon— 'independent utilities', 'interpersonal utility comparisons', 'exogenous tastes', 'markets'—and that fact alone dissociates it from any everyday needs and interests people might have, even without knowing what it means.

Once you know what it means, however, the dissociated nature of economic theory becomes even clearer. 'Utility', for example, means someone getting what they want. England says: 'Since the 1930s, utility has been conceived [within the discipline of economics] as the satisfaction of an individual's subjective desires' (p.41). The impossibility of interpersonal utility comparisons means that you can't compare what one person wants with what someone else wants. Because everyone is assumed to be free and equal, it is impossible to know which particular 'wants' (or 'tastes' or 'preferences') should be served by economic arrangements, so all 'wants' (etc.) are treated alike.

'Utility' also means that the fact that someone gets something (or more precisely, buys something) proves that they want it. And by the same token, if they don't buy it they don't want it. This is what is meant by the notion that 'tastes' are 'exogenous'—they are 'outside' the theory until they appear in the area the theory is designed to account for, i.e. in the economy, 'the market'. The only way of deciding whether or not something is indeed a 'taste' is economic exchange, i.e. 'price', the measurable trace of someone buying something; and 'price', i.e. money, the universal medium of exchange, irons out all differences. Economics treats all 'wants' as equal and excludes the possibility of evaluating them, of deciding whether some 'wants' might be more worthwhile, or some more damaging, than others. The terminology of 'utility' ('wants' or 'tastes' or 'preferences' or 'desires') implies something non-essential, something 'the individual' could do without if reluctantly, or something for which a substitute could be found. It also implies the capability for making choices between equally desirable alternatives.

Rational economic man is the individual par excellence. He doesn't have any relationships apart from those necessary to get his desires satisfied. Those desires ('utilities', 'wants', 'tastes', 'preferences') are his alone, self-engendered, unknowable by anyone else (until they appear in 'the market'). This theory is useful for a system of domination because, in treating all 'utilities' (etc.) alike, such a theory makes it impossible to acknowledge the existence of inequality or to advocate policies of redistribution (as England quite rightly points out). The utility to a rich man of an updated executive jet, for example, is no different from the utility to a single mother of food and housing for herself and her children. The rich man's jet is a known to be a 'utility' (because he bought it), whereas the single mother is not known to have any utility for food and accommodation because she hasn't bought any. The theory assumes that commodities go to people who want them, and people who don't buy them don't want them.

The theory cannot allow that there are some things that no one can do without and that are matters of necessity, not choice. Because 'tastes' are 'exogenous' and it is not possible to make 'interpersonal utility comparisons', neo-classical economics excludes any discussion of need, of what Julie Nelson described as 'the provisioning of human life, that is … the commodities and processes necessary to human survival' (Nelson, 1993: 31). In the discourse of economics, need becomes just another 'taste'. Economics can give no account of what people's needs are, or of how they might be satisfied, or of whether or not they are being met, and if not, why not. Neither can it give any account of the powerlessness of not being able to get access to basic material necessities. There are some material things that people *need* if they are to be healthy and live in comfort, security and dignity, or even simply to remain alive—food and clean water, for example, and clothing and housing, and education, work, income and health care. And because people need them, there is no question of choice. If someone cannot get access to food or clothing or housing, it is not because they have 'chosen' not to; and neither is it because they have 'chosen' something else instead. The reality is that they do not have the money to buy them because the economy is organised in such a way that they are systematically deprived of the means for acquiring that money.

Referring to the need for these things as 'tastes' or 'desires' or 'utilities' turns them into something random and arbitrary. If I am said to want something rather than to need it, it becomes something I can do without. This, of course, is the logic of 'the market', of the capitalist system of production and distribution which turns basic necessities into commodities no different from any other commodity. Their only value is a monetary one, and any function they might have in fulfilling human need is irrelevant. Access to them requires money. They are available to anyone who can pay for them, but not to everyone who needs them if they cannot pay. Referring to the need for these things as 'tastes' is the logic of domination. In obliterating any distinction between need and 'desire' or 'preference', no matter how trivial the latter or how desperate the former, it says that everyone's circumstances are equal. The single mother's need for a home for herself and her children free from the violence that forced her to leave her previous home, is no different from the rich man's desire for another dwelling place when he already has a dozen or so investment properties. Both are simply 'preferences' and the fact that the single mother hasn't bought herself a house is proof that she doesn't want one. This spurious equality masks the real purpose of the system—wealth creation and accumulation and the power and inequality that go with it. By-passing the concept of need is the logic of the separative self dissociated from what is really going on, i.e. a system for the production and distribution of basic necessities that ignores human need in favour of profit.

England says that the rational economic man construct serves the interests and experiences of men. She argues that the three basic assumptions of economic theory are '"androcentric" or male-centered' because they reinforce the ways in which relations between the sexes are currently arranged ('had the existing system of gender relations not been seen as the only possible or desirable arrangement, these particular assumptions would not have been chosen') (England, 1993: 37). In doing so, they ignore men's power, the disadvantages women suffer, and women's contributions (p.38). She doesn't use the word 'domination', but she does acknowledge it when she says that 'the existing system of gender relations' involves male power and women's disadvantage. She also acknowledges domination when she says that the three assumptions 'explain why positive neoclassical theories harmonize so well with conservative normative positions on distributional issues' (p.43), or in other words, why economics is compatible with right-wing views on wealth and poverty. So 'neoclassical' and 'conservative' are equivalent to 'androcentric', 'male-centered' and 'the existing system of gender relations'; or in other (less ponderous) words, the discipline of economics, at least in its neo-classical form, supports both male domination and class society.

But there is a sense in which it is not strictly correct to say that the basic meanings and values of economics operate in the interests of men. Domination is no more in the interests of men (as human beings) than it is in the interests of women; and the persona portrayed in these accounts is not really like anyone at all, not even powerful men, because it is dehumanised. The construct is not a true depiction of human existence; rather, it exemplifies the dissociation I have argued is characteristic of male supremacist masculinity.

Moreover, while feminist economists have exposed the male supremacist meanings at the heart of the discipline of economics, they do not link that insight to the standard operating procedures of capitalism and government policies subservient to the needs of capital. The fact that rational economic man is not constructed from observations of actual human behaviour, even economic behaviour, does not mean that he has no relevance for human existence. On the contrary, despite the fact that he exists nowhere in reality, he is what men must aspire to. He is the model that expresses the values that drive that economy, that justifies and gives permission for its profit-maximisation, its accumulation of wealth in the hands of the few, its massive inequalities.

Hartsock

In contrast to both socialist feminism and feminist economics, Nancy Hartsock (1985) does have an account of capitalist society as a culture of masculinity (although she didn't use that terminology nor define her task in those terms). A society based on market exchange, such as that portrayed by neo-classical economic theory, she said, is the community of rational economic man of neo-classical economics—'arbitrary and fragile, structured fundamentally by competition and domination' (Hartsock, 1985: 38), where victory for some means defeat for others. It is an 'agonal model of community',[59] a community based on conflict and struggle. It is also a community which condones, even encourages, the kind of sexuality required of men under male supremacy:

> the culturally produced dynamics of hostility that structure sexual excitement correspond to a masculine sexuality that depends on defiling or debasing a fetishized sexual object (Hartsock, 1985: 164).

Hartsock argues quite rightly that this kind of sexuality is the heterosexual male norm and finds its clearest expression in pornography. A community that allows it to happen,

> emerges only through conquest, struggle, and even the potential death of its members. These dynamics of conquest and domination mean that the gain of one participant can come only at the expense of the other's submission, humiliation, or even death (Hartsock, 1985:177).

But in the final analysis she does not manage to bring together the masculine eros of hostility and degradation on the one hand, and the competitive ethic of market exchange on the other. Indeed, her discussion of market exchange is devoted to showing that the neo-liberal discourses which justify it give a *false* picture of social reality: 'The model of rational economic man in the market … gives us little insight into the working of actual human relations' (p.38). But that statement is only half true. Neo-classical economics does not portray the type of human relations we experience within an ethic of genuine humanity; but the human relations it portrays do exist. Characterised by entitlement for the ruthless few and dissociation from human need, those relations are imposed on us all. Hartsock is of course aware of this. '[T] he market account', she says, 'legitimizes (by obfuscating and concealing) relations of domination, presents coercion as choice, and ultimately justifies domination' (p.49). But it can only do that if the social relations it endorses take effect in the real world, and are not just confined to the discourse of neo-classical economics. We may not like those social relations and we may try to resist them to the best of our ability. But market relations are actual human relations, too, no matter how dehumanised.

---

59. 'Agonal' comes from the Greek word meaning 'contest' or 'struggle': 'the public realm itself, the *polis*, was permeated by a fiercely agonal spirit, where everybody had constantly to distinguish himself from all others, to show through unique deeds or achievements that he was the best of all' (Arendt, 1958: 41).

Hartsock understandably wants to identify an alternative reality to that of male supremacy. This she does by postulating a feminist standpoint based in 'women's life activity'.[60] A lot of her time and attention is devoted to that task, rather than to the task of elucidating the nature of domination. It is this focus which leads her to assert (not unreasonably) that neo-liberal ideology gives little insight into actual social relations. Nonetheless, despite these limitations of Hartsock's account, she did at least attempt to interpret capitalism as a central aspect of the construction and maintenance of male domination.

However, such an interpretation requires that the focus be taken away from women (although never completely). It is an interpretation which starts from the premise that capitalism's primary reason for existence is not because it enables men's access to and control over women (that is the function of pornography, prostitution, sex trafficking, 'the family', rape, sexual harassment, discrimination, etc.), but because it is the way in which men's arrogant, dissociated entitlement is institutionalised. It is the source of male power, privilege and prestige in the present day when sources such as aristocracy, royalty and martial honour have died out or become irrelevant. Male domination is not the same as women's oppression, even though the latter is a consequence of the former. Male domination is not just the domination of women by men (or sometimes, even at all). It is a system for the grotesque glorification of men, far beyond what is humanly feasible. The denigration of women is central to the glorification of men, and it manifests itself in the capitalist system in various ways: through lesser pay and grossly lesser access to wealth; through discriminatory exclusion from the upper echelons of the workforce or from the workforce altogether; and through contempt for the caring which produces the workforce and sustains the lives of those for whom capitalism cannot provide, largely done by women. But these manifestations, although helpful for capitalism's primary process, the generation of profit, are not essential to that process. Women are even sometimes permitted to participate in the upper reaches of the capitalist system as highly paid CEOs and owners and managers of enormous fortunes. But their numbers are small and they must play by the same rules devised by men for men. And in the finance sector, the 'headquarters of capitalism' as Schumpeter called it (Ingham, 2008: 36-8), women are few and far between. Capitalism, like war, is a struggle for ascendency among men, but this was

---

60. For a discussion of the limitations of women's life activity as the basis for a feminist standpoint, because women's life activity, too, can be permeated with domination, see: Thompson, 2001: 17-21.

not addressed, either by socialist feminism or by feminist economics or by the feminist globalisation literature.

The sex of wealth

Although the capitalist system of wealth production is not a question of types of persons but of culture—of meanings and values, institutions and a world-taken-for-granted—the chief beneficiaries of the economic system of capitalism are men. Or rather, capitalism is a social and economic system which enables (some) men to become unimaginably wealthy, while (some) other men envy and worship that same wealth and power. In that sense, capitalism is the form of masculinity demanded by conditions of male domination, and capitalism's primary function is to service that masculinity. Servicing masculinity is also the primary function of the sex industry (as radical feminism has been arguing for years). But that is obvious, or it should be, to anyone not blinded by the libertarian ideology that sees the sex industry as simply a matter of 'freedom' (for men) and 'choice' (for women). What is not so obvious is that the capitalist economy is by, for and about men.

That it is men who own the wealth created by the capitalist system of entitlement should come as no surprise, although it is rarely mentioned, much less commented upon. The information has to be garnered by reading between the lines. For example, in his critique of offshore 'tax havens', James Henry (2012) called its 'key clients' 'people', and described them as

> the world's wealthiest individuals and companies, as well as its worst villains. Numbering just a few million of the world's 6.5 billion people, they are an incredibly diverse group, from 30-year old Chinese real estate speculators and Silicon-Valley software tycoons to Dubai oil sheiks, Russian Presidents, mineral-rich African dictators and Mexican drug lords (Henry, 2012: 9).

While some of these people might be women—the real-estate speculators or the software tycoons, perhaps (although the word 'tycoon' doesn't sit easily with the word 'woman', so it would be modified with 'female' if any of them were indeed women). But the others clearly are not. And it is difficult to imagine that the world's 'worst villains' are women, not because women can't be villainous, but because women do not have the social power to be seen as the world's worst (or best) anything.

Nicholas Shaxson seems initially to be more upfront about the sex of those who accumulate the world's wealth in their own hands. The subtitle of his book on 'tax havens' (2012) is 'the men who stole the world', and they are mostly men he is talking about. He does mention a few women. Some of them are staunch supporters of the offshore wealth-producing system: a member of a right-wing think tank; a couple of private bankers, one of them in the Cayman Islands, the other in Jersey, the latter quoted saying that she "'didn't give a shit about Africa'" (p.228); Ayn Rand; and a woman at a gathering for 'politicians and decision makers' in Jersey, who 'primly dismiss[ed]' the methods employed by a TV journalist critical of the island's tax regime (p.233). Other women mentioned are critical of the system: a former private banker who 'had left private banking and joined the non-government sector … [and] hated what she had seen [when she worked in private banking]' (p.215); 'a tough and fearless union activist … and single mother … [who] described what it is like to live without money in Jersey' (p.238); a deputy in the States Assembly, Jersey's parliament, who described the island's domestic tax regime—zero tax for corporations and a consumption tax for the poor— as 'the "tax-the-poor-to-save-the-rich" approach' (p.239); and a *Financial Times* journalist who was '[o]ne of the few people to have sounded a clear early warning about the impending financial crisis' (p.244). But although there were women on both sides—for the system and against it—the vast majority of people mentioned were men, thus reflecting the reality of the offshore, 'tax haven' business of wealth accumulation.

However, Shaxson appears not to be aware of that fact. At one point he does say: 'Offshore sometimes feels like a *Boys' Own* fantasy of the world, in which white men sort things out over Scotch whisky and see the rest of the world as a consumable resource' (p.229). But that is the only explicit mention within the text of the male domination of the offshore finance industry, and he doesn't comment on it or bring out any of the implications. He even makes gratuitous use of the feminine personal pronoun (although only once), as though he were aware of an imbalance between the sexes and trying to rectify it: 'Take … a practice known as reinvoicing … The exporter invoices the London importer for $120 million, asking that $20 million of that is quietly deposited in *her* London account' (p.191—emphasis added). The point being made about reinvoicing is a general one, it doesn't refer to any particular person. Presumably the use of the feminine pronoun is a response to the feminist protest against the ubiquity of the masculine pronoun. But it's a lazy response asserting a false kind of 'equality' that ignores the ongoing reality. It is a facile reaction to the feminist protest, which was not simply about language but about the reality the language was expressing, that is, male domination; and by changing only the language, it misrepresents the continuing reality of male domination. A more cogent response would be to acknowledge the male domination of the finance industry and expose it for what it is. But that is too much to ask of any social theorist or commentator, no matter how insightful, after so many years of anti-feminist backlash. Shaxson's work, along with that of the Tax Justice Network with which he is affiliated, is timely and a necessary counterweight to the neo-liberal glorification of wealth accumulation at any price. But it is as oblivious to male domination as any other non-feminist discourse on the state of the world.

The word 'gender' plays its usual obfuscatory role here. One commentator noted that '[t]here is a growing, male-dominated Superclass of the very rich', but he did not draw any conclusions from this except to say that global inequality is not just about class, that it has 'gendered, racialized and ethnicized features' as well (Johnson, 2007: 107). Again, David Harvey says that he doesn't include 'gender' (or race, nationalism, ethnicity or religion) in his study of the contradictions of capital, because they are not specific to capitalism (Harvey, 2014: 9-10). He is technically correct, male domination (*not* 'gender') is not confined to capitalist society. But capitalism is still a variant of male domination, a system of unjustified male entitlement divorced from any genuine human reality. Using 'gender' masks the male entitlement of the system. He says that '[c]ontemporary capitalism plainly feeds off gender discriminations and violence' (p.10). But this is at best meaningless; at worst, it's pernicious because it enables men to argue that they are discriminated against too because they also have a 'gender' (as happens, for example, in the transsexual agenda), and that they, too, are subjected to violence (as indeed they are, usually from other men, although that is rarely mentioned).

This approach also seduces Harvey into the solecism of referring to 'the capitalist' as 'she' (Harvey, 2014: 43-4), in yet another example of that lazy response to the feminist protest. Yes, there are some women who are capitalists, just as there are some women who have been allowed entry into other hitherto male-dominated spheres. But 'the capitalist' is typically male, and the system's primary reason for existence is to enable (some) men to amass the wealth that gives them power to dictate other people's conditions of life, even to the point of destruction.

Women are largely absent from the ranks of the owners of the gargantuan accumulations of wealth created by capitalism. That doesn't mean that there are no wealthy women. Nor does it mean that the problem would be solved if more women were included in these ranks. The system remains male supremacist in its arrogance and dissociation even when women are participating in it. But most of the obscenely wealthy people named in 'rich lists' are men anyway. Oxfam (Hardoon, 2015), for example, said that 90% of the 1,645 billionaires listed by Forbes in 2014 were men.

Moreover, most of the women who do appear in 'rich lists' did not originally create the source of the wealth; they are the relatives or heirs of the men who did. For example, six of the 29 of 'the world's youngest billionaires' listed on Forbes website in the middle of 2013 were women, four of whom were described as 'daughter of …', while the other two were members of wealthy families. While many of the men also belonged to wealthy families, many others had made it on their own, e.g. 'the hottest young money manager on the planet', 'an emerging face of irresponsible capitalism in Africa', and the founders of Facebook and Google.[61]

Again, among a 'select group of 50 billionaires' listed on the Forbes website at the end of 2012 there were only three women, all of whom were related to the rich men who founded the fortunes: Alice Walton (Source of Wealth: Walmart); Christy Walton 'and family' (Source of Wealth: Walmart); and Laurene Powell Jobs (Source of Wealth: Apple, Disney). As Forbes put it in a discussion of '78 billionaire moms in the world' in the middle of 2011: 'Most inherited their fortunes from their fathers or husbands'. There is also Abigail Johnson, whom Oxfam (Hardoon, 2015) included in a list of 10 of the richest billionaires in the world in 2014 who had made at least part of their fortunes in the financial sector. She is CEO of the US investment firm, Fidelity Investments, but again she is not the originator of the wealth. Her grandfather founded the company and her father is still chairman. No doubt she is an able money manager, but it is unlikely that she would have become so wealthy without the men in her family, especially as, according to Forbes, just who owns what in the family is 'a mystery'.

It is true that women can support the system that makes them so rich just as enthusiastically as men do. One example is Gina Rinehart, often cited as the richest person in Australia.[62] As a journalist reporting her success said: 'Rinehart's wealth is based on inherited royalties from Hamersley Iron but she has built on it big time' (Murphy, 2010). Nonetheless, she did not make the original fortune herself (however astute she has been in increasing

61. information on Forbes' website changes daily, so the original URL for the information cited in this paragraph is no longer available. However, similar information is constantly provided on the internet, both on the Forbes website and elsewhere.

62. For many decades the honour (if that's the right word) of being 'Australia's richest man' belonged to Frank Packer and then to his son, Kerry, although Kerry's son, James, has lost that title, despite the fact that his fortune comes from such guaranteed money-spinners as gambling and advertising revenue.

it). She is the daughter of the original founder, Lang Hancock. Himself born into a wealthy family, he was the beneficiary of a system of property entitlement which allows men to own land that should belong to everybody or nobody, and to exploit it for financial gain by destroying it mining for iron ore. Rinehart's wealth was inherited from her father, and her 'building on it big time' is the result of the 'minerals boom' in Australia. She could have sat back and done nothing but watch the grass grow and the fortune would still have increased. And she is still trivialised and demeaned in the press for being a woman. To quote that same journalist: 'She's still daddy's little girl'.

Neither capitalism nor any other social institution of domination is the result of something inherent in men. But because the system centres around the principle that only men count as 'human', it is only to be expected that men would predominate in its upper reaches. Women do not reach the upper echelons of the capitalist system unaided because, I would suggest, women lack that overweening sense of entitlement that comes along with penis-possession (see: Thompson, 1991a: 14-23). For that reason, women are unlikely to succeed in the system in numbers equal to men, or in the same ways men do. But anyway, admitting women to those upper echelons would not render such a grossly inequitable system any less dissociated and arrogant, or more humanly acceptable.

Private ownership

Without private ownership, it would not be possible for men to accumulate wealth. As Gittins (2014) rightly pointed out, private ownership is central to capitalism (along with those 'freely operating markets'). Reference to private ownership, of 'property', of 'the means of production', and of the wealth produced by the economy, is the most common definition of capitalism. And it is quite right to give primary importance to private ownership—without it there could be no accumulation of wealth in the hands of the few.

But whether or not this aspect of capitalism is efficient in providing 'our material wants' is debatable. The entitlement that capitalist private ownership bestows means that others are disentitled. This is not necessarily a problem, it is simply what 'ownership' means. I am not entitled to someone else's personal possessions and they are not entitled to mine. But it is a problem when the ownership deprives others of basic necessities, and when ownership of those resources which generate profit ('the means of production') stands in the way of, or actively destroys, the public good.

The usual contrast to private ownership is state ownership, but there is another contrast to 'private' and that is 'the public' or 'the commons', goods and services that no one owns and everyone shares. Democratic governments are supposed to protect these public goods because they are supposed to act in the interests of all.[63] The right-wing hatred of government 'interference', and especially of taxation and 'government spending', is a hatred of this public interest aspect of democratic government. The 'government spending' which is so detested by right-wing apologists for wealth and power is spending for this common good. The dominators (and their apologists) do not see themselves as members of any community of interests, and they demand of the state that it not provide aid and sustenance to those who fall by the capitalist wayside. As Margaret Thatcher put it, 'The error to which I was objecting [with her comment 'There is no such thing as society'] was the confusion of society with the state as the helper of first resort'" (*The Downing Street Years* New York: Harper Collins, p.626, quoted in Watson, 2015). 'The state as the helper of first resort' that makes the rich richer, or preserves their prerogatives at others' expense, or destroys the common good including people's lives ('defence'), receives no condemnation from the right-wing.

Private ownership is deeply entrenched in capitalist society, as it must be if the modern form of wealth and power is to prevail. The neo-liberal 'privatisation' drive proceeds apace, justified by the insistence that private ownership of public services ('the market') is more efficient and cheaper for the 'consumer' and the 'taxpayer' than public ownership. This has frequently been shown to be false even in their own terms (i.e. profit and efficient production of goods and services), much less in terms of the public service they are supposedly so much better at providing than government.[64] For example, an article in the *Sydney Morning Herald* (Robins, 2015) quoted a report from the St Vincent de Paul Society saying that '"[t]he retail component of [gas and electricity] bills is too high in the deregulated, competitive electricity market'". The researchers estimated that the 'retail component' could amount to 45% in Victoria and 30% in NSW. But as Ian Milliss pointed out, 'The "retail component" should in fact be absolutely zero, it is a tax extorted by the rent seeking parasites that privatisation inserted into the system. There

---

63. For example, the US Constitution instructs the US government to 'establish Justice, insure domestic Tranquility, provide for the common defence, promote the general Welfare, and secure the Blessings of Liberty to ourselves and our Posterity', for 'we the people of the United States'.

64. The failure of many of the privatisations in the UK is documented on the website of the non-profit organisation, 'We Own It', devoted to resisting privatisation (We Own It, no date).

is no reason whatsoever for retailers to exist'.[65] Energy was cheaper when energy suppliers were public utilities owned and operated by government. There was no need for profit because there was no private owner to profiteer.

But the evidence is either routinely ignored by governments in the grip of powerful vested interests, or reinterpreted as a temporary setback. To make matters worse for the public good, some forms of privatisation (if not all of them) demand government guarantees that any financial risks will be borne by the public. Contracts typically specify that firms will be compensated for any adverse events, that there will be no competition, and that the firm can object to and receive compensation for any legislative, administrative and judicial decisions that might reduce their profits (Dannin, 2011, discussing the privatisation of the building of infrastructure in the US). Government still has responsibility for these 'privatised' goods and services, because market failures of such enterprises mean they are no longer available for the public to use. For example, railways in the UK were privatised in 1993 and by 2012 (if not earlier) it had become clear that the system was in disarray. It was 'failing society, the economy and the environment, whilst draining taxpayers' money into the pockets of private shareholders' (Taylor and Sloman, 2012: 4). This report not only documents the failures of the rail privatisation: the doubling or tripling of the cost to the UK government partly made up of subsidies that go to shareholders; the highest passenger fares in Europe; increased complexity in ticket purchases; increased staffing costs with the multiplication of managerial staff positions; the abolition of any overarching oversight with 16 different franchises throughout the country; and the destruction of a once-successful rail manufacturing industry. It also suggests solutions. But typically, no lessons are learned by governments enamoured of the privatisation agenda. In 2009, the British government had to re-nationalise one of the fragments of the disordered system (the East Coast main line rail service between London and Edinburgh),[66] only to re-privatise it once the problems had been remedied under public management (We Own It, no date).

So the financial risk is still public, while only the profits are privatised. This is so detrimental to the common good, that the fact that it can be taken seriously, much less implemented over and over again with no foreseeable end in sight, is scandalous. But the governments of the neo-liberal 'democracies'

---

65. Comment on Facebook, 12.10.2015.

66. http://news.bbc.co.uk/2/hi/business/8127851.stm – viewed 9.8.2018.

are impervious to any ethical considerations to the extent that they embrace the interests of big corporations.

As Bill Mitchell has pointed out, it is now abundantly clear (as it should have been right at the very beginning) that privatisation has failed to fulfil its promises about lower prices and costs and improved services:

> The reality now some 35 years or so into the privatisation experiment is that none of these claims have been realised. In many cases, costs are higher and the privatised firms rely on higher public subsidies than was the case when the operations were completely in public hands ... There is a litany of evidence after 30-40 years of practice to show that the promises held out for privatisation of large state enterprises have not been delivered (Mitchell, 2016. See also: Meek, 2012; Mitchell, 2009).

Strictly speaking, the proponents of privatisation were not making promises, they were telling lies. The way the privatisation agenda has played out is exactly what was intended all along—with the rich richer than ever, 'democratic' governments conned into withdrawing from provision for the common good (or embracing that withdrawal with enthusiasm), public services in disarray, and the public purse providing a gaping cornucopia for powerful men.

To the extent that capitalism's private ownership destroys the public good, it is far from efficient as a method for creating human well-being, however efficient it might be in increasing productivity and profitability. Indeed, its much-touted efficiency at wealth creation happens at the expense of the rest of us, even those of us who have materially benefited in the short term, and ultimately at the expense of all of us. Unregulated private profit breeds greed; and in the long term, unchecked greed can only lead to disaster. Even in the short term, the greed for money and its power fuelled by masculine entitlement is has disastrous consequences, although not, it would seem, for those whose greed and crazed dissociation caused the crisis.[67]

The numerical preponderance of men among the owners of wealth is not the only sign of the masculinity of capitalism. The system is also marked by the same values required of the masculine character structure of male supremacy. Overweening entitlement and dissociation from any genuine humanity are the hallmarks of capitalism, as they are of the male character structure created by and serving to maintain domination. Capitalism did not originate in freedom, and there is no sign of any respect for the human rights supposedly created by bourgeois society. It is the kind of economic system

---

67. For an account of the implication of the banking, finance and arms industries in the Greek economic crisis, see: Anderson, 2011; Leopold, 2012. The Greek people neither bought the arms nor took out the loans, but they are the ones suffering the consequences.

we might expect from the dissociated male arrogance that rules the world and both structures it in its own image and is structured by it. The fact, then, that it is the only economy in existence is no cause for congratulation; on the contrary, it is terrifying.

In what follows, I discuss some of the standard operating procedures of capitalism—'primitive accumulation', inequality, poverty, and the finance industry—that mark it as a system of unwarranted entitlement for the privileged few and which divorce it from the possibilities contained in genuine humanity. I could have discussed any number of other aspects— wage labour, individualism, competition, 'risk', 'innovation' and 'creative destruction', or its claims to 'freedom'.[68] But what I do discuss are some of its standard operating procedures, without which capitalism would cease to exist (or would not have started in the first place).

I conclude my discussion of capitalism with a chapter on money (chapter 10), with the help of what has come to be known as Modern Money (or Monetary) Theory (MMT). This framework doesn't directly challenge capitalism. In fact, Modern Money Theorists themselves see their framework as neither left wing nor right wing. As Wray said, 'On one level, MMT, by itself, is neither left nor right. It is a description: how "modern money" works' (Wray, 2011-12: #Blog 37). In other words, it is as applicable to an economy of domination as it is to an economy of emancipation and equality. However, as he himself went on to say, if it were generally acknowledged that governments were not constrained in their spending by any need to balance budgets or avoid inflation, then spending for such left-wing public purposes as health, education and welfare would become acceptable: 'MMT helps us to find a way to achieve [the] public purpose by quickly disposing of the notion that government cannot "afford" such policies' (Wray, 2011-12: #Blog 37).

As long as capitalism provisions male power, as it has been doing to an unprecedented extent under the regime of neo-liberalism, government spending for the common good is not likely to happen. Nonetheless, whatever its proponents might believe about its compatibility with capitalism, Modern Money Theory makes more sense than orthodox economics. It focuses on the crucial role sovereign currency-issuing governments play in the creation of money, and reminds us that governments are the original source of

---

68. 'let us replace [the term capitalism] with something even more poignant and descriptive of the reality of which we speak: freedom' (Sirico, 2007). See also: Chamberlain, 1965[1959], who prefers capitalism to any form of socialism because of his 'mature preference for the uncoerced man ... [Our society] is affluent because it has been free' (pp.viii, ix).

money, not private enterprise. It says that governments are not constrained in their spending by 'budgets', and hence they do not need to work towards 'surpluses', avoid 'deficits', or make 'savings'. It also says that taxation is not revenue and hence that taxes don't fund anything, although taxation is crucial for maintaining the demand for money, as well as serving a number of other economic functions. These arguments are largely unknown to the general public and the mainstream media; and orthodox economists reject them out of hand, or ignore them:

> There was an Op Ed last week from an Australian academic who attacked Modern Monetary Theory (MMT) along the lines that its proponents are "a bunch of cranks" and practice "charlatanism". He also considers us to be sellers of "snake oil" and other nasty things … MMT is now clearly at the stage of development where the mainstream think they have to attack us and put us down. That is the next stage in our development (following years of being totally ignored). Progress is being made (Mitchell, 2017).

But it is a framework that contradicts the neo-liberal agenda that has dominated the world economy for so many decades, and it provides governments with an economic model that is genuinely democratic. Ignoring it or sneering at it is a political decision, not an economic one.

Chapter Six: Capitalism's Origins

Capitalism generates wealth by re-investing profits in enterprises that produce more wealth. But capitalism cannot do this unless there is a stock of wealth with which to establish those profit-making enterprises in the first place. As Maria Mies has pointed out:

> Before the capitalist mode of production could establish and maintain itself as a process of extended reproduction of capital – driven by the motor of surplus value production – enough capital had to be accumulated to start this process (Mies, 1998: 88-9).

Wealth has always been a feature of large-scale human societies, and some of those forms (e.g. wealth accumulated from merchant trading or money-lending) became capital once the necessary social relations were in place. But early capitalism acquired its wealth in other ways, too, not just through inheritance from feudal, pre-capitalist or mercantile progenitors (whose own methods of accumulation leave much to be desired from a genuinely human standpoint). Those other ways were as ruthless as anything a feudal landowner might have employed, and as oblivious to the freedom and human rights supposedly introduced to the world by the bourgeois revolution.

For Mies (1998), the early accumulation of capital was largely accomplished through the western European colonisation of the rest of the world during the sixteenth and seventeenth centuries, 'by way of brigandage, piracy, forced and slave labour' (p.89). However, she also argued that the confiscation of the property of the 'witches' hunted and murdered during the seventeenth century contributed to early capitalism's wealth accumulation, if to a lesser extent: 'This blood money fed the original process of capital accumulation, perhaps not to the same extent as the plunder and robbery of the colonies, but certainly to a much greater extent than is known today' (p.87). But whatever method capitalism used (and continues to use) to accumulate the necessary resources, its origins do not bode well for the humanity of the system.

The process whereby the prerequisites of a capitalist economy—both the historical amassing of capital and the necessary social arrangements—come into being in the first place is referred to (largely in Marxist circles) as 'primitive accumulation'. The concept was originally Marx's, although he was picking up on a remark of Adam Smith's referring to 'previous accumulation' in the Introduction to Bk II of *The Wealth of Nations*: "The accumulation of stock must, in the nature of things, be previous to the division of labour" (Marx, 1976: 873; Smith, 2007: 221 of 754). Ignoring Smith's priority (Smith put the 'accumulation of stock' before the 'division of labour'), Marx's main focus of attention was the 'division of labour', the kinds of social arrangements that ensured the availability of people to work producing commodities to be sold for profit. Marx called these social arrangements 'free workers'. Industrial capital could not have developed unless there were large numbers of people who were 'free', both in the positive sense that they were not beholden to the rigid social statuses of feudalism, and in the negative sense that they had 'nothing left to lose' (as the song says), that is, they had no access to the resources necessary for sustaining their lives and hence no alternative but to work for capital.

Nonetheless, Marx did have something to say about the 'accumulation of stock', and he condemned outright the methods employed to acquire it:

> The spoliation of the Church's property, the fraudulent alienation of the state domains, the theft of the common lands, the usurpation of feudal and clan property and its transformation into modern private property under circumstances of ruthless terrorism, all these things were just so many idyllic methods of primitive accumulation. They conquered the field for capitalist agriculture, incorporated the soil into capital, and created for urban industries the necessary supplies of free and rightless proletarians (Marx, 1976: 895).

Enclosures

The best known form of primitive accumulation involved the enclosure movement, whereby wealthy nobles and other landowners usurped the common land and forcibly evicted the peasantry who traditionally had had as much right to the land as the nobles (Marx, 1976: 878-80). One of the main motivations for these enclosures was the money to be made from wool. The land could be more profitably used for raising sheep than for producing any other kind of agricultural product or for peasant subsistence farming. This created terrible social dislocation. People were torn from their livelihoods as arable land was turned into pasture, their dwellings demolished or allowed to fall into ruin. Marx quoted Francis Bacon on the enclosures at the end of the fifteenth century in England: "'This bred a decay of people, and, by consequence, a decay of towns, churches, tithes, and the like'" (Marx, 1976: 879).

Marx dated the enclosures from the last third of the fifteenth century to the first few decades of the sixteenth, long before the advent of capitalism per se. This process involved (as Marx put it) 'great masses of men ... suddenly and forcibly torn from their means of subsistence' (Marx, 1976: 876). But it was a necessary precursor to capitalism because it produced a sufficiently large proportion of the population who had nowhere else to turn to earn their daily bread and hence were available to work for industry.

Polanyi

When people are 'torn from their means of subsistence' they starve. So what industrial capital needed (and still needs) is a population whose only alternative to working in the factories is starvation.

Karl Polanyi saw the problem as a consequence of treating labour as a commodity. He argued that labour was a 'fictitious commodity',[69] along with land and money,[70] because all three lacked the basic prerequisite of a commodity. They were not the kinds of things that were produced in order to be bought and sold: 'the postulate that anything that is bought and sold must have been produced for sale is emphatically untrue in regard to them' (Polanyi, 1957: 72). To turn land and labour into commodities was to divest them of their meaning and use for human life (although 'fictitious' doesn't seem to be the right word, given the very real effects of this way of operating, and its dominance). Capitalism (his preferred term was 'the self-regulating market') sees only commodities and their monetary value; nothing else is of any use to it. To the extent that land and labour are incorporated into its system, they are detached from any other purpose; and to the extent that their commodity functions dictate to society, to that extent does human life become subordinated to the requirements of the market:

> labor and land are no other than the human beings themselves of which every society consists and the natural surroundings in which it exists.

---

69. Perhaps with reference to the concept of 'fictitious capital' used in the nineteenth century by Marx among others (see below), although Polanyi doesn't say so.

70. Polanyi's account of money and its commodification, as I understand it, focuses on the problems of using a commodity as money (i.e. 'the gold standard'), rather than on the use of money, or rather debt, as a commodity, such as happens in the finance industry. I discuss the finance industry and the buying and selling of debt in more detail below.

To include them in the market mechanism means to subordinate the substance of society itself to the laws of the market (Polanyi, 1957: 71).

Using labour as a commodity means buying human beings, or at least their time and energy—their 'labour power'; but people have to be willing, or compelled, to sell their labour power if it is to be available to be bought. For the early apologists for capitalism, hunger was the most efficient way human beings could be made to sell their labour power in the labour market. In order to make people hungry enough to sell their labour power ('job seek' in the current parlance), the land had to be made unavailable to them, and the communities which provided the traditional modes of sustenance and support (i.e. society) had to be destroyed. As Polanyi put it: 'In order to release … "nature's penalty," hunger … it was necessary to liquidate organic society, which refused to permit the individual to starve' (Polanyi, 1957: 165). This has been referred to as 'the whip of hunger',[71] a description that shamelessly exposes the dehumanised values driving the capitalist mode of production.

'Liquidating organic society' in order to deprive people of any alternative means of feeding themselves, involved turning land into a commodity. Commodifying land abolished subsistence farming and people's access to common land, as well as the basis on which human existence depended prior to the maturation of the self-regulating market. It is true that, once capitalism had matured, it provided wages for buying the necessities of life. But wages have never been a guaranteed means of subsistence. In the first place, they have never been available to everyone. Until the second half of the twentieth century wages were rarely available for women (and when they were, they were a fraction of what men were paid), and the fact that capital requires unemployment, underemployment and unemployability means that there are always people who cannot get access to them (Marx's 'reserve army of labour').

Moreover, wages are often inadequate, even for buying necessities. Currently, wages are so low in the US, for example, that many workers are eligible for welfare benefits. A study by researchers at the University of California, Berkeley, found that 56% of the money spent on welfare went to people who were in employment. This included the Earned Income Tax Credit, which is not available to anyone who is not working, but it also

---

71. 'Rational capitalistic calculation is possible only on the basis of free labor; only where in consequence of the existence of workers who in the formal sense voluntarily, but actually under the compulsion of the whip of hunger, offer themselves, the costs of products may be unambiguously determined by agreement in advance' (Weber, 1927).

included food stamps. In other words, these people were not being paid enough to feed themselves or their families (Morath, 2015). And yet wages are even lower in the Third World, capitalism's world of 'offshore', where industrial capital has moved most of its production processes.

It is true that access to land did not always guarantee a livelihood either, and the work was back-breaking and leisure was rare. Pre-capitalist life on the land tended to be nasty, brutish and short. But the fact that it could seriously be argued that starvation was a necessary prerequisite for a capitalist labour force, indicates a fatal moral flaw at the heart of the capitalist enterprise. Writing in the early 1940s before the end of the Second World War, Polanyi, like Arendt, argued that there was a connection between fascism and capitalism (see chapter 12). The values that underpin capitalism, to the extent that they show contempt for human life, are not dissimilar to fascism. Admittedly, Polanyi argued that fascism was a consequence of capitalism's *failure*. But capitalism's failures are a consequence of its normal operating procedures—its boom and bust crises.

Polanyi was convinced that the events of the early twentieth century—two world wars and a Great Depression—signalled the end of capitalism, of the self-regulating market economy. 'The end of this venture', he said, 'has come in our time; it closes a distinct stage in the history of industrial civilization' (Polanyi, 1957: 5). However, he was wrong. 'Subordinating the substance of society itself to the laws of the market' is exactly what has happened under the neo-liberal governmental consensus since the late twentieth century.

Slavery

> [N]othing in history ever seems to fully go away (Martin et al, 2008: 129).

In what follows I put the word 'free' in inverted commas in order to indicate that I am not using it literally. While modern work conditions are technically 'free' in contrast to slavery or serfdom, there is nothing free about work that is the only alternative to starvation or penury. Nor can work that is tedious, dehumanising or morally repugnant be called 'free'. Such work is more accurately described as coerced.

Throughout this section I use the masculine personal pronoun because it is mainly men who are discussed in this context. Although sometimes women and children worked alongside men under slavery, and hence were subjected to the same kinds of conditions, slave-owners preferred men and tended to regard women and children as uneconomic burdens (Weber, 1964:

276).[72] Moreover, the enslavement of women as women takes a different form from that of men. While in prostitution there is the same forced/'free' dichotomy as in productive labour—trafficked women (and children) versus 'sex workers'—the profits of prostitution are not enhanced by 'free' labour. On the contrary, given the market for coerced sex among men who will pay to rape, the supplier and customer would probably prefer slaves over 'consenting' 'sex workers'. But wherever it is a question of exploiting labour for gain, using the masculine pronoun is appropriate because it is largely men we are talking about, or women only if they fit a male paradigm.

Slavery was an especially egregious method for accumulating the wealth that fed into industrial capitalism. As Marx pointed out: 'Liverpool [in England] grew fat on the basis of the slave trade. This was its method of primitive accumulation' (Marx, 1976: 924).[73] He also reminded us that 'the cotton industry introduced child-slavery into England', while in the US that same industry could rely on 'more or less patriarchal slavery' for its workforce. 'If money', Marx said, '"comes into the world with a congenital blood-stain on one cheek,"[74] capital comes dripping from head to toe, from every pore, with blood and dirt' (p.926).

Industrial capitalism these days relies on formally 'free' labour, but slavery was one of the original sources of capitalist wealth. Although not typical of fully-developed capitalism, slavery in the eighteenth and early nineteenth centuries produced much of the accumulated wealth that fueled the capitalist expansion of the nineteenth century. It is true that slavery was characteristic of the mercantile period in European history, an era that preceded the growth of capitalism proper with its reliance on formally 'free' labour. But the profits of the slave trade and of the sugar islands in the Caribbean and the tobacco and cotton plantations on the American mainland provided much of the capital that financed the Industrial Revolution in England. As one seventeenth-century British government document put it, 'The Negro

---

72. This was the case on the Caribbean sugar plantations (Williams, 1944: 38; Weber, 1964: 276). However, in the southern states on the American mainland, the slave labour force was 'internally generated', rather than having to rely on 'fresh African cargoes' (Fox-Genovese and Genovese, 1983: 44). In that case, women would have been necessary to produce the children of the next generation of slaves, as well as for their usefulness as domestic servants in the slaveholders' mansions and as sexual resources for the slave master.

73. For a fictionalised account of the slave trade carried on from Liverpool, England, in the 18th century, see: Unsworth, 1992.

74. Quoting Marie Augier (1842) *Du crédit public et de son histoire depuis les temps anciens jusqu'à nos jours* ('On public credit and its history from ancient times to today').

slaves were "the strength and sinews of this western world"' (Williams, 1944: 29); and a certain Sir Dalby Thomas, Bristol sugar merchant and shareholder in the Royal African Company and its agent general from 1703-11, wrote in his 1690 history of the English West Indian colonies that '[t]he pleasure, glory and grandeur of England has been advanced more by sugar than by any other commodity, wool not excepted' (Williams, 1944: 55; Ellis, 1905: 82). In the latter half of the eighteenth century, Adam Smith was less sanguine about the economic efficiency of slavery, but he did concede that '[t]he profits of a sugar plantation in any of our West Indian colonies are generally much greater than those of any other cultivation that is known either in Europe or America' (Smith, 2007: 303).

If chattel slavery, the absolute ownership of human beings that existed on the great plantations cultivating sugar, tobacco and cotton, was so profitable, why was it replaced with the waged labour of 'free' men? The usual answer is that 'free' labour is actually more profitable. Slave labour is only profitable under certain conditions: when there is no 'free' labour available; when only unskilled labour such as agricultural work is required; and only then as long as there is a supply of new land once the soil of the old has been exhausted by the inefficiency of slave labour (Williams, 1944).

According to Adam Smith, 'free' labour was cheaper both because it cost the master less to pay wages than to buy slaves and supply them with basic necessities, and because slaves worked less efficiently. Wages were likely to be managed much more economically by a poor person himself, and hence cost the master less, than the costs disbursed by 'a negligent master or careless overseer' responsible for provisioning the slaves: 'The disorders which generally prevail in the economy of the rich, naturally introduce themselves into the management of the [slave]: The strict frugality and parsimonious attention of the poor as naturally establish themselves in that of the [free man]' (Smith, 2007: 67). This is a strange argument, since 'masters' and 'overseers' are hardly likely to be more profligate in supplying slaves with basic necessities than in paying wages. Still, this was not Smith's only argument. He also said that slave labour was less efficient than wage labour because the slave had no incentive to work hard. He was not going to improve his position no matter how hard he worked, and hence he had no motivation to do so, apart from the inefficient and expensive methods of compulsion and violence. As well, slaves 'are very seldom inventive' and hence they use more labour and take more time to produce the same amount as 'free' men do (p.531).

Marx agreed with Adam Smith that 'free' labour was more productive than slave labour (Marx, 1976: 1031-3). In the first place, it gave the worker a sense of self-determination (not wholly illusory, at least in comparison with slavery or serfdom) and hence a sense of ownership of the work process. It also meant that he himself was responsible for the quality of his work because he could be fired if he failed to satisfy the capitalist, and because he was in competition with other sellers of labour-power who could be hired in his stead. Moreover, while the slave knows that the quality of his work will make no difference to what he receives in return for it (but only to his purchase price), the 'free' worker can improve his position relative to other workers (even if ever so slightly) by greater 'diligence, skill or strength' (p.1032). Marx also agreed with Smith that it was to the benefit of the capitalist to make the worker responsible for his own subsistence and that of his family by providing him with a wage that he could spend as he pleased (although not for the reason Smith gave, i.e. that poor people are more likely to be frugal than rich people). There was also the possibility (unlikely though it might be) that a worker could become a capitalist, whereas a slave could never become a slave owner. And finally, the 'free' worker is more versatile than the slave because he can exercise some degree of choice about who he works for. He can move (or more likely, be moved) from one branch of industry to another and change with changing skill requirements, whereas slave labour is typically 'monotonous and traditional … [and] does not vary with changes in production' (p.1034). 'The effect of all these differences', said Marx, 'is to make the free worker's work more intensive, more continuous, more flexible and skilled than that of the slave' (pp.1032-3).

Max Weber (1964: 276-7) gave a number of reasons why slavery was 'less favourable to rationality and efficiency than the employment of free labour'. He agreed with Smith and Marx that it cost more to buy and maintain slaves than to pay wages, in part because the master was responsible for the maintenance of unproductive 'wives' and children 'when slaves have been permitted to enjoy family relationships'. He also agreed that slaves did not work as well as 'free' men, especially in operating machinery because it 'required responsibility and self-interest on the part of the operator'; and that slavery allowed for no flexibility in hiring and firing. (He regarded this as the most important difference from wage labour). He also saw slavery as politically riskier than 'free' labour, presumably because the moral disgracefulness of slavery gave rise to rebellions and political movements to end it. Moreover, slave labour-forces were harder to 'recruit' than 'free' labour, and when they were not 'permitted to enjoy family relationships', harsher disciplinary methods had to be imposed, thus 'greatly accentuat[ing] the difficulties of the problem of recruitment'. As Hannah Arendt summed it up: 'all the known disadvantages of slave labor … [are] lack of initiative, laziness, neglect of tools, and general inefficiency' (Arendt, 1951: 193).

The common theme running through all these arguments is that the profitability of 'free' labour lies in making the worker himself responsible both for the production process and for the reproduction of labour power (i.e. looking after his own subsistence and providing for the next generation). In other words, 'free' labour makes the exploited embrace his own exploitation of his own free will. He 'chooses' work over non-work, he 'chooses' one job and one employer over another, he can 'choose' to leave at any time, and he 'chooses' the basic necessities required for his survival and that of his family. 'Free' labour makes the labour process more efficient than coerced labour because the worker can be fired when the firm no longer needs him or if he doesn't give satisfaction, but also because people work more efficiently if they are not overtly coerced.

But isn't that ancient history? Capitalism nowadays uses 'free' labour, not slaves, indeed wage labour is one of capitalism's central defining characteristics. Well, not quite. Slavery has survived into the modern capitalist world,[75] although most of it involves women and children trafficked for sex (UN, 2000). While this says a great deal about the inherent brutality of male supremacist sexuality, capitalist industrial and service enterprises tend on the whole not to avail themselves of chattel slavery. What is called 'slavery' in the media (e.g. Kanj, 2013), hyper-exploitative though it is because of the abysmally low wages, still has all the characteristics of wage labour because the workers are paid and are technically 'free' to leave, or more to the point, to be dispensed with. When they are not free to leave—when they are undocumented migrants, or foreign workers whose employers confiscate their identification papers or threaten to report them to the authorities—such practices come close to slavery. But the fact that they are paid wages and that they are discarded when their labour is no longer needed, indicates that these are hyper-exploitative procedures of capitalism, and not strictly speaking slavery. But the difference is academic. The kind of wage labour that capitalism will get away with if it can—the payment of a pittance that comes nowhere near providing the worker with a living wage—differs from slavery hardly at all. And wage-diminishing procedures such as the moving 'off-shore' of industrial capital, and the illegal though rampant under-paying

---

75. http://borgenproject.org/seven-facts-modern-day-slavery/ – viewed 9.8.2018.

of foreign and immigrant workers, are standard operations of a capitalism grown monstrously out of control under the current neo-liberal hegemony.

The heyday of slavery was the colonial era in European history, largely dating from the eighteenth century to the beginning of the nineteenth century. Slavery was abolished in England in 1833 (the trade itself had been abolished in 1807) (Williams, 1944: 136), although the slave owners were compensated for the loss of their 'property' to the tune of £20 million. This was the equivalent of £16 billion 2015 pounds, and was the largest government bailout in British history until the bailouts of the finance industry following the 2008 global financial crisis. The slaves themselves not only received no compensation, they were even required to work for their masters for a further four years after their supposed emancipation (Olusoga, 2015). But although chattel slavery was no longer a source of wealth for the ruling class, capitalism didn't abandon it for genuinely human reasons. It didn't reject it because it was an evil that ought to be eradicated from the face of the earth, but because it was less efficient when there was a freely available alternative. Capitalism has no genuinely human morality. It is not devoted to human well-being, simply to profit. And chattel slavery was eventually found to be not very profitable.

Accumulation by dispossession

But even without slavery, the original entitlement to the ownership of wealth that marks the capitalist system, its primitive accumulation, was the kind of 'entitlement' characteristic of domination, where the spoils go to the most powerful, the most ruthless, the most heedless of human need. It was a 'might makes right' kind of entitlement, where other forms of entitlement, even to life itself, are obliterated in the relentless amassing of wealth. As one commentator put it: 'Marx defined "primitive accumulation" as the seizure of land and other communally held assets by raiders and the subsequent extraction of tribute or rent' (Hudson, 2010).

But primitive accumulation—the appropriation of what are originally non-wealth-producing resources in order to produce capital—is not confined to capitalism's beginnings. Because of capital's need for constant growth and expansion, it is still part of the capitalist mode of production today. The best known of the methods of primitive accumulation, the enclosures of the Commons by rich landlords, find their counterpart in present-day 'land grabs'. 'Primitive accumulation' can also refer to those methods of accumulation whereby big business takes resources hitherto beyond its reach without adequate (or any) compensation. As one commentator put it:

When Western capital sucks Third World labour power, whose costs of reproduction it did not pay for, into the world division of labour, whether in Indonesia or in Los Angeles, that's primitive accumulation. When capital loots the natural environment and does not pay the replacement costs for that damage, that's primitive accumulation. When capital runs capital plant and infrastructure into the ground (the story of much of the US and the UK economies since the 1960's) that's primitive accumulation. When capital pays workers non-reproductive wages, (wages too low to produce a new generation of workers) that's primitive accumulation too (Goldner, 2007).

Because such methods are still current as capitalism's standard operating procedures, David Harvey has called this 'accumulation by dispossession'.

accumulation based upon predation, fraud, and violence [is not confined] to an "original stage" that is considered no longer relevant or ... as being somehow "outside" of capitalism as a closed system. A general re-evaluation of the continuous role and persistence of the predatory practices of "primitive" or "original" accumulation within the long historical geography of capital accumulation is, therefore, very much in order ... Since it seems peculiar to call an ongoing process "primitive" or "original" I shall, in what follows, substitute these terms by the concept of "accumulation by dispossession" (Harvey, 2003: 144).

The reason for this new round of primitive accumulation, Harvey argues, was the need to do something productive with yet another over-accumulation of capital, which began to reach crisis point by the early 1970s when neo-liberalism began to establish its pre-eminence as government policy across the globe.

Land grabs are rife in the Third World because people's entitlements there tend to be traditional or customary, a form of entitlement that capital has always treated with contempt. These forms of expropriation involve the taking-over of indigenous people's land by powerful multi-national companies. These are modern forms of primitive accumulation in the Third World, where the multi-national company's 'entitlement' to the using the land is simply taken, with little or no recognition of any prior rights of the people who lived on the land before the exploiter took over, often with little or no compensation, scant regard for the natural environment ruined by the exploitation, and the corrupt complicity of the government of the host country.

Phnom Penh Sugar in Cambodia, for example, partly financed by Australia's ANZ Bank, is owned by one of Cambodia's richest men, a senator belonging to the country's ruling party, and a close associate of the Prime

Minister. The Cambodian government gave the company a concession to establish two sugar plantations on 20,000 hectares of farmland in one of the country's most impoverished regions. In 2010 more than 1,000 families were forcibly moved off the land by a former Khmer Rouge battalion[76] to make way for the plantation. The people said that they were given compensation of only $100 a family, even though they were losing land that had provided them with food and livelihood. They were now short of food because the resettlement sites were located on infertile land and their community forests and crops had been destroyed. Moreover, school-aged children were working in the cane fields in order to contribute to their families' income. (It was this aspect, the 'child labour', which most disturbed the Australian press). Not surprisingly, the company has denied all charges.[77]

Another example of corrupt acquisition concerns a Malaysian group of logging companies, the WTK Group, involved in illegal logging in rainforest areas in Borneo, the Sundaland area and Papua New Guinea. WTK is involved in a number of projects permitted under the Special Agricultural and Business Lease scheme in Papua New Guinea, whereby 'customary land' is 'acquired by the State and leased back to the customary landowners or their nominees … [in order to] facilitate agriculture and business activities' (Numapo, 2013: 3-4). But the company had made little attempt to plant anything while at the same time continuing to cut down the rainforest for the timber. Their operations have caused rivers to dry up, and they have been known to use armed police to threaten villagers, and to exploit local women as domestic servants and prostitute them to its expatriate workers (Narayanasamy, 2014: 14).

Multinational capitalism does not refrain from using methods of outright violence. Phnom Penh Sugar had access to the former Khmer Rouge in its new role of 'legitimate' defence force, and there are alarming levels of violence linked to sugar-related land conflict in Brazil. This is the country with the highest number of murders connected with land grabs by multinational companies (although that might be because killings in Brazil are more likely to be reported publicly because of the work of the Catholic Land Commission) (Global Witness, 2012: 4). An Amnesty International report said that 'landowners and ranchers' in the Brazilian state of Mato Grosso do Sul 'frequently use hired gunmen and private security companies

---

76. 'in the late 1990s … the Khmer Rouge collapsed and rebel fighters were incorporated into the government defence forces' (UN FAO, 2013: 63).

77. Baker and McKenzie, 2014a, b; Eyres, 2014; Quinlan et al, 2014.

to intimidate indigenous communities fighting for their constitutional rights to their ancestral lands' (Amnesty International, 2011). To cite just one instance: in the early morning of 18 November 2011, some 40 gunmen arrived at an indigenous encampment outside a sugar plantation owned by Bunge, one of the top three sugar producers in the world, on land which officially belonged to the indigenous people. The gunmen shot the leader of the indigenous protesters and dragged his body away, together with three indigenous children who have not been seen since (Global witness, 2012: 10; Amnesty International, 2011).

Between 2002 and 2011, 711 protesters worldwide—locals, community activists, NGO workers and journalists—were killed, either in deliberately targeted attacks or in violent clashes as a result of protests, investigating or taking grievances against mining operations, logging operations, intensive agriculture including ranching, tree plantations, hydropower dams, urban development and poaching (Global Witness, 2012: 2). It is true that murder is not one of capitalism's standard operating procedures, but the sense of entitlement that comes along with the drive to accumulate wealth does not stop at murder, especially in the Third World. Slavery and imperialism did not baulk at mass murder either.

Oxfam has released a series of reports on these land grabs.[78] They say that, since 2000, between 35.6 and 45 million hectares of large-scale farmland acquisitions have shifted the ownership of land away from small farmers and local communities, as well as from uses such as carbon sinks or retaining biodiversity, largely into the hands of foreign companies producing food for their own domestic populations and to commercial enterprises producing cash crops like sugar, palm oil, soy beans for animal feed, biofuel and timber (Narayanasamy, 2014: 9). Citing the Tirana Declaration issued by the International Land Coalition,[79] Oxfam lists a number of characteristics of 'land grabs'. These are acquisitions of land

- that violate human rights, especially those of women;
- that do not seek free, prior, and informed consent;
- that do not assess the social, economic, and environmental impacts of the uses to which the land is to be put;
- that do not involve transparent contracts with clear and binding commitments on employment and benefit sharing; and

---

78. Geary, 2012; Oxfam, 2013; Zagema, 2011.

79. http://www.landcoalition.org/en/resources/tirana-declaration – viewed 9.8.2018.

- that evade democratic planning, independent oversight and meaningful participation (Narayanasamy, 2014: 9. See also: Ahlers, 2010).

So the world knows what is happening and deplores it, but exposure does not shame the perpetrators nor empower those who would prevent it if they could.

Multinational agribusiness and mining companies could not do this without the active cooperation of the respective governments. This includes governments of rich developed countries like Australia, where state and federal governments have embraced the interests of coal mining and coal-seam gas extraction companies. Not only have Australian state governments granted mining licences to operate in state forests, water catchment areas and farming country,[80] with no consideration for the rights of the farmers who own the land, or for the environmental destruction to the pristine wilderness, the underground water tables, and the nation's food-producing resources; at the time of writing, those governments are passing laws mandating harsh penalties for activists protesting against the destruction wreaked by coal mining and coal-seam gas extraction in NSW and Western Australia (Mitchell, 2016) and the forestry industry in Tasmania (Gogarty, 2015).

The privatisation that has been so much a part of the neo-liberal agenda worldwide is another aspect of capitalism's rapacious siphoning up of the world's resources. Harvey called it 'the cutting edge of accumulation by dispossession' (Harvey, 2003: 157). The effect of putting these policies into practice, he said,

> was to make a new round of "enclosure of the commons" into an objective of state policies. Assets held by the state or in common were released into the market where overaccumulating capital could invest in them, upgrade them, and speculate in them (Harvey, 2003: 158).

Wherever capital sees an opportunity to aggrandise itself, it grabs it, with complete disregard for any prior forms of entitlement that might exist.

Capitalism has its roots in slavery, imperialism and primitive accumulation, and from such compromised origins no good thing can grow. There are numerous signs that the standard operating procedures of capitalism are so dissociated from human well-being, that it threatens to destroy the very civilisation it is supposedly responsible for creating: the growing reality of global warming created by a fossil fuel industry fighting savagely to retain its pre-eminence in the world economy; industrial capital and 'service' industries that beggar people because they cannot provide jobs at a living wage; a finance

---

80. http://www.lockthegate.org.au/fact_sheets – viewed 9.8.2018.

industry that produces nothing but more money and whose fictitious capital periodically throws the global economy into crisis; a US military-industrial complex grown more and more bloated and killing and maiming people daily. These and other signs indicate that, whatever capitalism once promised (and it never promised it to everyone anyway), that promise is rapidly being eroded.

Chapter Seven: Capitalism and Inequality

Nonetheless, the term used for the consequences of the blatant neo-liberal political partiality for economic power is 'inequality'. The consequences of government initiatives that work shamelessly in the interests of big business and are viciously punitive towards those protesting the destruction, are not referred to as 'domination', but as 'inequality'. This is an inadequate term to describe what has been happening throughout the world in the last few decades. Referring to the enormous discrepancies between one end of the wealth and income spectrum and the other as 'inequality' is a euphemism. There is nothing wrong with inequality per se. There are many forms of inequality which are inevitable, even beneficial, for example, prowess in sports or excellence in any other field of endeavour not available to everyone. Even the fact that some are very rich is not necessarily a pernicious form of inequality, as long as no one is harmed and everyone has access to sufficient resources to live in comfort and dignity (and the accumulation of wealth is not destroying the earth). If the recent enormous increase in income and wealth inequality caused no harm, then there would be no reason to criticise it. However, that is not the case, and 'domination' is a more accurate term than 'inequality' to the extent that the world's wealth is produced, distributed and consumed at the expense of a large proportion of the population for the benefit of the few. I will continue to use the term 'inequality' in what follows, since that is the term used in the literature. But what is really being discussed is a system of domination created by and creating powerful men (sometimes aided by a few women).

Inequality, it has been said, is 'the defining challenge of our time' (Dabla-Norris et al, 2015: 4, 5). Important multinational organisations like the United Nations, the World Bank, the International Monetary Fund and the World Economic Forum, and even the Pope, have all expressed their concern. The UN has referred to a 'growing global consensus on the need to bridge the divide between the haves and the have-nots', and calls on governments to implement 'a set of cohesive, coherent and complementary policies … to combat inequality in all its dimensions' (UN, 2013: 7, 23). Inequality has also been included among the 17 goals of the new UN Sustainable Development Goals (see below). The World Bank dates a renewed interest in 'inequality and equity issues' from 2011, when the debate 'left the academic seminar rooms to permeate the streets, the popular media, and the blogosphere'.[81] The IMF sees links between rising inequality on the one hand, and economic crises and threats to sustainable growth on the other, and notes that 'equality seems to drive higher and more sustainable growth' (Ostry et al, 2014: 5). The World Economic Forum puts inequality at the top of its list of the ten major trends facing the world in 2015 (Mohammed, 2015). Pope Francis did not mince words. 'Inequality is the root of social evil' he tweeted on 28 April 2014; and he devoted a significant proportion of his 'apostolic exhortation', *Evangelii Gaudium*, to condemning 'an economy of exclusion', 'the new idolatry of money', 'a financial system which rules rather than serves', and 'the inequality which spawns violence' (Pope Francis, 2013: 45-51). And then there is the reception of Thomas Piketty's 2013 book on inequality, *Capital in the Twenty-First Century*. It was frequently referred in the media to as 'a sensation', and was so popular soon after it was published that Amazon temporarily ran out of copies (Kilian, 2014).

Certainly, there is something seriously wrong when, by the end of 2015, the richest 1% of the world's population owned more than the other 99% of the people in the world (Hardoon, 2015), and by the beginning of 2017, just eight men owned as much as the poorest 3.6 billion people (Oxfam, 2017) (and Oxfam did say 'men', not 'people').

Not everyone agrees that such extreme inequality is a bad thing. The right wing, not surprisingly, defends it as the source of innovation and the good life. Not only is it not harmful, they argue, it is a result of the progress that creates material well-being for everyone. William Watson (2015) has provided a recent version of this kind of argument. A self-acknowledged 'conservative', he concedes that some kinds of inequality are harmful—the kind that 'emerges from transactions or arrangements that are not truly voluntary but rather are anti-competitive, corrupt, coercive, or criminal'.[82] (His main example concerned the 'transactions or arrangements' engaged in

---

81 .http://siteresources.worldbank.org/EXTPOVERTY/Resources/Inequality_in_Focus_April2012.pdf – viewed 9.8.2018.

82. My copy is an ebook with no pagination, but this statement appeared on p.33 of 268 pages.

by Bernie Madoff, creator of what is considered to be the largest financial fraud in history (to date), and one of the few architects of the 2008 global financial crisis to actually go to gaol) (Reuters, 2011). But, Watson argues, there are good kinds of inequality, namely the kind that 'emerges from market transactions almost everyone will approve of: unusual effort, ingenuity, imagination, innovation, or perseverance'. Such forms of inequality, he says, 'result … in goods or services that make the millions of people who buy them at least slightly better off … [and] no one in society … worse off' (Watson, 2015: 33). Moreover, in attacking inequality per se, rather than only the harmful kinds, critics run the risk of undermining capitalism, and hence destroying the engine of the prosperity that has marked economic progress since the middle of the eighteenth century. Capitalism, he said, is

> the social system whose advent coincided (almost certainly not coincidentally) with … our species' dramatic leave-taking from the more or less perpetually low incomes and high death rates, especially among young children, that until 1750 or so had been our fate for the 5,000 years of our written history and … for all our millennia before that (Watson, 2015: p.11 of 268).

He acknowledges that '[c]apitalism does generate inequality – that is how it works' (p.12), but he also insists that it provides the only way to abolish poverty: 'by unrelentingly expanding what is possible in terms of living standards, it … enables people to pull themselves up from poverty' (p.12); and it is poverty that is 'our true enemy', not inequality and certainly not capitalism. Moreover, capitalism enables the reduction of poverty in the best possible way, in his view: by expanding the size of the pool of resources, rather than by redistributing wealth by taxing the rich to give to the poor, a strategy that Watson refers to as 'taxing all successful entrepreneurs or investors as if they were thieves' (p.17).

But as with so many right-wing defences of domination, Watson's ignores those crucial aspects of reality that give the lie to his argument. To take just one example, in his discussion of the wealth of Steve Jobs (one of four examples of what he regards as good inequality because the wealth was 'honestly earned')[83] (p.58), he ignores a number of factors which suggest otherwise. There are the environmental consequences of IT devices, both in their production and in their eventual disposal; and there is the hyper-

---

83. The other three are: a highly paid athlete whose wealth comes from his athletic prowess (or rather, the media frenzy that accompanies it); a lottery winner; and Jamie Dimon, 'America's most prominent banker … [and] CEO of Morgan Chase' (Watson, 2015: 58) (although he acknowledges that 'some people will consider Jamie Dimon's case debatable') (p.112).

exploitation of the workers whose labour produces the devices, and whom he cavalierly dismisses in a single sentence.

All the stages of the production of the materials used in making IT devices (called 'rare earth elements')—mining them, refining them and disposing of them—are environmentally disastrous because they release poisonous contaminants into the air, ground and water around them.[84] Moreover, Apple (along with every other capitalist firm that produces material goods) takes no responsibility for the eventual disposal of the products that so enrich the firms' owners, their managers and major shareholders, when they become obsolete. This is despite the fact that such obliviousness works to their own detriment in the case of e-waste, because many of the materials used in making them are rare, running out and irreplaceable,[85] and recycling them would at least delay their depletion. Even when e-waste is re-cycled, it is done in such a way that it harms the workers, including many children, who do the processing (Borromeo, 2013; Upadhayaya, 2013).

In typical right-wing fashion, Watson studiously ignores the working conditions of the people who actually produce the devices. He says that they're better off working for Apple (or more precisely, for the firms Apple contracts to employ them) than they would otherwise be: 'Even the Chinese supposedly exploited in Foxconn plants that supply Apple likely are doing better than they would in alternative employment or, more likely, unemployment' (Watson, 2015: 69).[86] (Note that '*supposedly* exploited'). 'Better' is a relative term (to state the obvious), and it depends on your standard of comparison. It is not clear what Watson's standard is (apart from 'alternative employment' and 'unemployment'), but by any genuinely human standard, the treatment of the Chinese workers in Foxconn plants is appalling, even if the treatment of workers elsewhere is worse.

For example, the following account appeared in the *New York Times* (Duhigg and Bradsher, 2012). At a dinner with Silicon Valley's top executives in California in February 2011, President Obama was reported to have asked

---

84. http://web.mit.edu/12.000/www/m2016/finalwebsite/problems/environment.html – viewed 9.8.2018

85. https://www.gizmodo.com.au/2013/12/the-metals-in-your-phone-arent-just-rare-theyre-irreplacable/ – viewed 9.8.2018.

86. Foxconn is the world's largest contract electronics manufacturer and China's largest exporter with 1.2 million workers. It makes the products sold by Apple, HP, Dell, IBM, Samsung, Nokia, Hitachi and other electronic giants, including assembling the iPod, iPad and iPhone (Chan and Pun, 2010) which have made so much money for Steve Jobs (and others).

Steve Jobs 'what would it take to make iPhones in the United States ... Why can't that work come home?' Jobs' reported answer was simply "'Those jobs aren't coming back'". However, the article quoted a story told by 'a former [Apple] executive', which illustrated the reasons why Apple had no option but to take its manufacturing operations overseas instead of setting up in the US. The story involved the sudden redesign of the iPhone screen which, under the production conditions in the US, would have meant a long delay in getting the product onto the market. The order for the redesigned screens arrived at the factory in China at midnight, but that did not mean that the production process was delayed, even until the next day. Rather,

> [a] foreman immediately roused 8,000 workers inside the company's dormitories ... Each employee was given a biscuit and a cup of tea, guided to a workstation and within half an hour started a 12-hour shift fitting glass screens into beveled frames. Within 96 hours, the plant was producing over 10,000 iPhones a day (Duhigg and Bradsher, 2012).

The former executive was reported to have said, "'The speed and flexibility is breathtaking ... There's no American plant that can match that'". Another former executive was reported to have said, "'They could hire 3,000 people overnight ... What U.S. plant can find 3,000 people overnight and convince them to live in dorms?'"

The fact that Apple's former executive could express admiration for these conditions rather than condemnation, is typical of right-wing obliviousness to the humanity of the workers (and typical of masculinist dissociation from any genuine humanity). It is also an example of what Marx called 'the fetishism of commodities'. Nothing matters but the commodity and its profit-making capacities. Anything is justified in the name of 'efficiency': keeping costs down, prices competitive, and constant innovation (i.e. planned obsolescence) in order to keep the product in the eyes of the consumer. The people who make the product are simply means of production, to be used like any other means in the interests of the most 'efficient' production of the commodity. If that means that the US-based multinational drives down as low as possible the profit margins of the local contractor (who is the direct face-to-face employer), and hence the wages paid to the workers, that is simply the logic of capitalist efficiency.

Despite the exploitation involved in America's own low wage economy, the fact that this kind of thing cannot happen in the US ought to be a reason for congratulation, not criticism. As one author commented:

> The implication ... is that such manufacturing jobs have gone overseas because Americans don't want to work that hard. Take a moment

and think about the deeper implications of the situation. Imagine an employer that can wake you at midnight after a full day of work and pull you in for a 12 hour shift. Note that the situation—a last minute product change—virtually guarantees that it won't be your only 12 hour shift that week; it's on top of the 72+ hours you regularly work. Apple officially requires Chinese suppliers to restrict workers to 60 hours a week, [but] paystub checks by investigative journalists reveal this is generally ignored (Hruska, 2012).

Apple has denied the incident occurred. They are reported to have said that such an incident was impossible, "'because we have strict regulations regarding the working hours of our employees based on their designated shifts, and every employee has computerized timecards that would bar them from working at any facility at a time outside of their approved shift'". However, Foxconn employees have confirmed the story (Duhigg and Bradsher, 2012); and China Labor Watch found that the intensity of the work process had certainly increased between 2006 and 2011. In 2006, 150 workers assembled just over 2000 computers in a day; by 2011, this had increased to 3,500 computers. Part of the increase was due to improved technology, but the intensity of the work itself also increased significantly (China Labor Watch, 2012: 4).

Although Apple has a written Code of Conduct, manufacturers routinely breach it without sanction. The code is supposed to ensure that "'working conditions in Apple's supply chain are safe, that workers are treated with respect and dignity, and that manufacturing processes are environmentally responsible'". It also states that workers are not to work more than 60 hours a week, except in emergencies or under unusual circumstances (Musil, 2012). But Apple's own audits have consistently uncovered breaches every year since the audits started in 2007 (probably in response to the Western media exposure of working conditions and a number of widely reported suicides in Apple's supply chain) (China Labor Watch, 2012: 4).

Every year, half or more of the audits found that large numbers of employees worked more than six days a week and put in extended overtime. The audits also found that some workers had been paid less than the minimum wage or had had pay withheld as punishment. There were also 70 core violations by employers over that period, including involuntary (i.e. forced) labour, under-age workers, record falsifications, and improper disposal of hazardous waste. Over a hundred workers had been injured by exposure to toxic chemicals.[87] Audits in 2011 found slight improvements in some categories and the rate of core violations had declined. But that year, four employees were killed and 77 injured in workplace explosions (Musil, 2012). And why is a 60-hour work-week regarded as fair by Apple's code of conduct? Not only is it half as long again as the standard work-week in Western nations, according to Chinese law normal working hours are eight hours a day and 40 hours a week, and overtime should be no more than three hours a day (Chan and Pun, 2010: 27).

It is true that such working conditions are not unique to Apple, and that the pay at Foxconn[88] is better than in some other work places at a base rate of 2000 yuan ($US320) a month in 2015, a higher wage than any available in many other regions of the country, although it is still not a living wage in China.[89] To compare wage rates with those in the US, figures released by the Social Security Administration showed that 51% of the employed population earned less than $30,000 in 2014 (i.e. around $2,500 a month before tax). While this is not an adequate wage in the US either (Snyder, 2015), it clearly costs capitalism much less to hire workers in China than in the US.

But the bad inequality in Apple's supply chain is not confined to the pitiful pay levels. Because the factories are often built in remote rural areas with little infrastructure, the company has to supply living quarters for its workers. The accommodation consists of dormitories, initially rooms of up to 300 beds, then after the workers' living conditions were exposed in the Western media, rooms of six to 12 bunk beds. But the workers are still treated like things to be managed as cheaply and efficiently as possible. They have none of the rights to their living space that are common in Western nations. There is no privacy; there are no married quarters and couples have to share a single bed; people working different shifts are placed in the same room and disturb each others' sleep; accommodation is frequently reassigned so that people cannot form friendship networks; cooking is not allowed and neither is clothes-washing or the use of electrical appliances like hair-dryers; friends and family cannot stay overnight; the water and the electricity often fail; and

---

87. http://www.zonaeuropa.com/20060623_1.htm (viewed 9.8.2018); Chan and Pun, 2010; Frost and Burnett, 2007; Kahney, 2006; Millard, 2006; Pun, 2012; Pun and Chan, 2012; SACOM, 2010, 2011a, b, 2013; Schofield, 2006; Webster, 2006.

88. https://www.marketwatch.com/story/it-would-take-25-years-of-foxconn-wages-to-afford-10000-apple-watch-2015-03-10 – viewed 9.8.2018.

89. The activist group, 'Labour Behind the Label', estimated a living wage in China in 2012 at 2333 yuan a month. (This figure was subsequently updated to 3847 RMB in 2015) (http://labourbehindthelabel.org/campaigns/living-wage/ – viewed 9.8.2018).

the dormitory buildings are like jails, with bars on the windows, netting slung between the buildings (to prevent people committing suicide by jumping from the building), and 24-hour security guards (SACOM, 2011a, b; Pun, 2012; China Labor Watch, 2012).

Conditions for Foxconn workers are not the worst to be found in China. As a reporter for *China Labour Bulletin* put it:

> "I'm not going to condemn Foxconn for appalling conditions because there are certainly worse places to work in China. The pay is basic, they do pay overtime according to the proper rates, and they pay social insurance. The work environment is clean and the food is not too bad ... But there is a peculiar dynamic. The company is obsessed with security, and I must say that, from the outside, the place looks like a prison" (Demick and Sarno, 2010).

China Labor Watch (2012: 121) also said that Foxconn was not the worst of Apple's suppliers, largely because of the public scrutiny it had been under for years, although there were still serious problems at Apple's other suppliers. Even so, while Foxconn may have improved in comparison with Apple's other suppliers, those improvements do not go very far. They cannot, because none of them address the push to keep costs down.

The fact that the working class in the West has managed to win concessions from employers is exactly why Apple (and most of the industrial capacity of Western nations) has moved to China (and Bangladesh, and India, and Cambodia, etc., etc.). People in the Third World can be exploited to a much greater extent than workers in the rich nations of the West because Third World situations are even more desperate (largely, because of colonialism and imperialism and their corrupting influence on the native ruling classes). When labour costs become too high, the firm can simply move elsewhere. Those who have the power to make and enforce decisions in capitalist workplaces are endlessly inventive at finding ways to circumvent any restrictions on profit-making. While Foxconn may have acquiesced in demands to improve conditions, that acquiescence appears to make it too expensive for Apple's profit margin. It would seem that labour costs were too high even in China, where Foxconn 'battle[d] rising wage costs and labor disputes'.[90] So Apple shifted its iPhone orders to an even cheaper supplier, Pegatron (Chew, 2013), and Foxconn moved some of its facilities to India where they could pay people even less and not be bothered by the gains the Chinese workers had

---

90. https://www.cnbc.com/2015/07/14/apple-manufacturer-foxconn-to-build-12-factories-employ-1m-in-india.html – viewed 9.8.2018.

made. Thus does the logic of capitalist accumulation override any gestures towards a common humanity.

In his insistence that the 'inequality' exemplified by the wealth of Steve Jobs is good, Watson shows that he is wilfully ignorant of the actual state of affairs. He makes a fetish of the commodity form and focuses only on the pleasure it brings to consumers, while ignoring the conditions under which it is produced and how the people whose labour creates the wealth are treated. There is nothing good about the labour practices of multinational capitalist enterprises. They treat people as a means towards enriching those who already have plenty, exhausting people's time, energy and labour while paying them as little as they can get away with. And in those parts of the world where labour laws are non-existent, inadequate or not enforced, that is very, very little indeed.

But while concern about rising levels of inequality might be widespread, among those with the power to make their voices heard there is by no means agreement that the cause is capitalism. For example, the 2013 UN *Human Development Report* (UNDP, 2013) discussing improvements in living standards in 'the South', asserts that 'inequality holds back human development'. But it employs the usual tactic of avoiding referring to current economic arrangements as 'capitalism' (although 'capital' is an acceptable usage—'short-term capital flows', for example). The preference is for terms such as 'globalisation' or 'markets' or 'corporations' or 'firms' or 'business', terms which prohibit the identification of any overarching system, as well as disconnecting the economy of the present day from historical critiques of capitalism. Some of the worst consequences of an unbridled capitalism are presented as though they had nothing to do with the way the economy is organised. For example, 'environmental crises' (p.3) or '[g]lobal challenges such as climate change and stressed ecosystems' (p.2) appear in the text as though they were something other than the result of capitalism's business-as-usual. Hence, the texts cannot say that income and wealth inequality are the consequence of the standard operating procedures of capitalism (because there is no such word in the authors' vocabulary). Read carefully, however, the text says exactly that, as long as the missing term is supplied (because the only 'economy' around is a capitalist one). And the report does identify continued increases in income inequality as part of the standard operating procedures of the global economy:

> Under worst case scenarios, [capitalism's] business as usual approach to development combined with environmental crises [caused by capitalism's

business as usual approach] could reverse human development gains in the South or make this progress unsustainable (UNDP, 2013: 3).

Tax havens

One of the reasons given for the gross inequality worldwide is the existence of tax havens (Henry, 2012). Economically powerful individuals and corporations can legally avoid paying tax, and illegally evade it, by moving revenues from the country in which they were earned to other jurisdictions with lower (or no) tax liabilities. The conventional view is that refusing to pay tax is a refusal to give the government the money needed to fund public services: the money parked offshore is not available to fund the infrastructure and services such as schools, hospitals, health care and social security.

For example, a report by the Tax Justice Network argued that, even while the rich in a sub-group of 139 countries were hiding their wealth in 'tax havens', 'their public sectors were borrowing themselves into bankruptcy, enduring agonizing "structural adjustment" and low growth, and holding fire sales of public assets' (Henry, 2012: 6). The author pointed out that, if the offshore wealth were included as part of the assets of indebted Third World countries, they would not be debtors at all, but lenders to the rest of the world 'to the tune of $10.1 to $13.1 trillion'. He commented:

> The problem here is that the assets of these countries are held by a small number of wealthy individuals while the debts are shouldered by the ordinary people of these countries through their governments ... *developing countries as a whole didn't really face a "debt" problem, but a huge "offshore tax evasion" problem* (Henry, 2012: 6, 20—original emphasis).

Another example is Christian Aid's (2008) argument that tax evasion by multinational corporations was responsible for continuing poverty in the Third World. More starkly, they said that, by 2015 when progress towards UNDP's Millennium Development Goals is to be assessed, 5.6 million children would have died since 2000, denied basic medical care because the tax revenues were not there to pay for it. 'Half are already dead', they say. Christian Aid point out that this paucity of tax revenues is not only a consequence of corrupt dictators siphoning off the country's wealth; more importantly, it results from the practices, both legal and illegal, of multinational corporations concerned to extract as much wealth as they can from a country's natural resources at the least cost. One of the legal ways of doing this is through Special Economic Zones (or free trade zones or export processing zones). These are geographical areas handed over to foreign companies whom the government exempts from paying taxes, as well as from 'restrictive' laws regulating hiring practices and working conditions. Not only does the government allow the company these concessions, the land is taken away from the people who used to work on it. These people receive no compensation because they were not owners of the land, but landless labourers who earned a subsistence living to feed themselves and their families. Without the land on which to grow food, they become even poorer and move to the cities in search of work. As one Indian academic commented: 'what they used to be able to get from the land is not available to them now. Urban poverty is much harsher' (Christian Aid, 2008: 34).

The tax-avoiders also subscribe to this conventional view. They 'know' that their use of tax havens is depriving government of the necessary resources to fund public goods (or they think they do). And to make matters worse, they demand (or their neo-liberal apologists do) that government not use their spending powers to compensate citizens for the depredations of tax avoidance. Although the conventional view that taxes fund government spending is inaccurate (see chapter 10), the fact that the tax avoiders believe it gives us an insight into the mentality of the culprits—the wealthy individuals, the CEOs and managers of multinational corporations, the law firms and tax agents who work within and help maintain the system of gross inequality (i.e. domination). Not only are they fully aware their actions deprive millions of basic necessities (although not for the reasons they think), their multinational organisations convince governments to impose 'structural adjustment' and 'austerity' programs that make matters worse by cutting funding for the common good. This is the mindset of the dominator—his own prerogatives at any cost, heedless of the pain he causes.

But if Modern Money Theory is correct in saying that taxes are not revenue (see chapter 10), the problem with tax havens may be more complex than that they siphon off money that the government could have used for public purposes. If taxes are not revenue, 'in principle large multinationals could be allowed to get away with not paying taxes'.[91] If the private sector takes its money out of the country where it earned it, then 'the public sector [can] fill... the investment void and create... public investment goods'. That would simply mean that 'the "offshoring" ... would see a decline in private sector activity and a rise in public sector activity' (Mitchell, 2012).

But to suggest that 'a rise in public sector activity' (i.e. government spending) could compensate for tax avoidance/evasion by the private sector, is to ignore current political realities. Under the domination of neo-liberalism,

---

91. https://www.facebook.com/green.modernmoneytheoryandpractice/ posts/897976880285456 – viewed 9.8.2018.

governments are prohibited from spending on public goods by the global ruling class that demands 'fiscal restraint' from governments as a condition for loans or for a high credit rating. Neo-liberalism demands adherence to the belief that government spending causes inflation, that 'budgets' must always be balanced, that 'deficits' are bad and 'surpluses' good, that 'taxpayers' fund government spending. Such beliefs are solidly entrenched in a public opinion formed by a mass media owned by the powerful, and in our so-called 'democratic' governments whose elections are engineered by big money. Mythical though they might be (see chapter 10), these are the beliefs behind the fiscal policies of the last several decades. To a mindset formed by these beliefs, public sector activity is anathema.

The consequences of tax avoidance/evasion

But if we accept the Modern Money Theory proposition that taxes 'drive money', that is, that taxation ensures that money is in demand (i.e. valuable, trusted and negotiable, rather than being simply pieces of metal or paper, bookkeeping entries or computer keystrokes), then it is possible that the tax avoidance/evasion on the scale exposed by the release of the Panama Papers (among other sources) (Escobar, 2016; Quiggin, 2016) threatens to kill the goose that lays the golden eggs. If money depends on taxation, then treating tax laws with contempt threatens to bring money into disrepute. If taxation is necessary to maintain the value of money by maintaining the demand for it, what is the effect on money of government failure to collect taxes on such a grand scale? What does it do to the value of money? Widespread tax avoidance/evasion is intended to accumulate wealth in the hands of the few, but it defeats its own purpose if that 'wealth' eventually becomes worthless because it undermines the foundation on which money is based.

As far as I have been able to discover, no economic framework (including Modern Money Theory) suggests that the depreciation of money might be a consequence of widespread tax avoidance/evasion, or of 'inequality' (i.e. domination) more generally. However, there are indications that excessive wealth accumulation does have deleterious effects on the economy. One of those indications is the 'business cycle', the periodic booms and busts to which capitalism is notoriously prone. To attribute the boom/bust cycle to excessive wealth accumulation is not, of course, the orthodox, or even the Marxist, approach to the question, both of which explain it in terms of the expansion and contraction of industrial capitalism (except when the right wing explains it in terms of government interference in the economy).

For one mainstream source (Investopedia), for example, the problem is 'overinvestment': 'when credit is too easy to obtain and interest rates are too low, people will overinvest … [and] [t]hings that have been overinvested in … decline in value'. For Marx, the problem was 'over-production': 'In these crises, there breaks out an epidemic … the epidemic of over-production … too much civilisation, too much means of subsistence, too much industry, too much commerce' (*Communist Manifesto*). But the bubble that preceded the 2008 global financial crisis was not caused by 'too much industry, too much commerce', but by hyper-speculation and massive levels of fraud in the financial sector. In the bust that followed that particular boom, a great deal of money became so worthless it vanished altogether (although it was not primarily the wealth of the speculators that vanished, but of small-scale investors who were tricked into putting their savings into speculative 'investments' they knew nothing about). Tax avoidance/evasion was not the primary cause of the crisis (for the implication of tax havens in the GFC, see: TJN, 2016), but it is part of the same system of inequality.

The usual name for the depreciation of money is 'inflation': money comes to be worth less because prices rise. However, the problem with the world's economies in these days of rampant inequality is not inflation but deflation.[92] As early as 2002, Alan Greenspan said: 'recent experience understandably has stimulated policymakers worldwide to refocus on deflation and its consequences, decades after dismissing it as a possibility so remote that it no longer warranted serious attention (Greenspan, 2002).[93]

Investopedia defines deflation as 'a general decline in prices'. That makes money more valuable (it can buy more things), and so does the rise in unemployment that accompanies it. Unemployment means that the demand for money is greater than the supply, or rather, that a large proportion of the population can't get access to enough money, however much of it there actually is. Investopedia tells us that deflation is 'often caused by a reduction in the supply of money or credit … [and] also by a decrease in government, personal or investment spending'. But this tells us nothing about the causes of deflation. What is meant by 'a reduction in the supply of money'? To whom? There has been no reduction in the supply of money to the rich throughout this unprecedented period of deflation, on the contrary, as the massive and

---

92. https://touchstoneblog.org.uk/2016/09/imf-warn-global-deflation/ – viewed 9.8.2018.

93. He also said that the US didn't have to worry: 'the United States is nowhere close to sliding into a pernicious deflation'. But prediction is a dangerous practice: in August 2015, three of the four US Census regions 'experienced deflation' (https://www.cnbc.com/2015/10/13/the-us-is-closer-to-deflation-than-you-think.html – viewed 9.8.2018).

increasing levels of inequality show. There has, however, been a reduction for most people, for those now unemployed or underemployed, and for those who lost their life savings in the global financial crisis. A reduction in the supply of money to government? But government is the issuer of money and it can always make more by increasing government spending or crediting the relevant bank accounts. Well, perhaps not always, but certainly as long as there is un- and underemployment. But inequality does reduce the money supply available to the rest of the population, and so it is possible that it is inequality that is responsible for the current period of deflation.

However that may be, if it is the case that taxes do not provide the money to fund government spending, then the problem with tax havens is not that they deprive governments of revenue. Mitchell argues that the problem is prior to and much wider than tax havens, and the solution is to prevent inequality developing in the first place (Mitchell, 2012). There would be no tax havens if there were no hyper-accumulation of surplus wealth to put in them.

The problem is an economic system that allows wealth to be accumulated at the expense of most of the world's population, and eventually of the whole of humanity, including the dominators. While the existence of tax havens is part of the problem, it is a symptom rather than a cause. The cause is to be found in the legacies of past colonialism and present corruption, looting by multinational corporations, and a world economy that grabs resources without compensation and heedlessly devours them without thought for the future.

So demands for 'austerity' and 'structural adjustment' forbid governments to use their spending powers to increase 'public sector activity' to compensate for the money taken out of the economy by multinational tax avoidance. It is this prohibition, together with government corruption and the theft of natural resources, abuse of humankind and biosystems by multinationals (i.e. 'inequality'), that is responsible for the denial of basic medical care to people in the Third World, and not because the tax revenues are not there to pay for it. Moreover, the money poured into tax havens is not the currency issued by the governments of the Third World. As Wray has pointed out, when the governments of developing nations cannot impose and collect sufficient taxes, their spending is constrained by the population's willingness to sell for domestic currency. 'And that, in turn,' he continued, 'is caused by a preference for use of foreign currency for domestic purposes other than paying taxes. While this is not a big problem in developed countries, it can be a serious problem in developing nations' (Wray, 2011-12: Blog #9). The governments of the nations beggared by multinational tax avoidance are not the sovereign issuers of the currency stashed in tax havens. It is not the Angolan *Kwanza*, the Ethiopian *birr*, the Congolese *franc*, the Zambian *kwacha*, the Ugandan *shilling* or the Nigerian *naira* the tax avoiders are amassing, but US dollars above all, British pounds, Euros or South African rands. Multinational corporations steal the wealth of Third World nations with the connivance of corrupt governments, sell it elsewhere for prices paid in more valued currency, and stash it in tax havens rather than returning it to the countries they stole it from.

The reason Third World governments can't use their own currency to provide basic services is that an economy does not consist only of money, but also of concrete resources: 'government spending is only constrained by what real goods and services are offered in return for it' (Mitchell and Mosler, 2002). There are economic constraints on government spending, but while the political constraints are mythical, or more precisely, ideological, the economic constraints are real. Government spending ought not to go beyond of the productive capacity of the nation. If the productive capacity of the nation is being siphoned off by powerful foreigners without compensation, it is not available for the government to buy. Moreover, Third World countries are heavily indebted to those same powerful foreigners, who impose austerity conditions that demand government spending service the loans advanced by wealthy rent-seekers, not serve the people. Endemic government corruption (which is not confined to Third World countries) doesn't help either.

On this account, tax havens are one of the symptoms of 'inequality' (or domination, as I would prefer to call it), not one of its causes. They are symptomatic of the dissociated arrogance and unwarranted entitlement characteristic of the male supremacist economic system, but they are not the basic problem. Rather, the basic problem is an economic system that functions, not for the common good, but in the interests of male power without end.

Chapter Eight: Capitalism and Poverty

Poverty is not the same thing as inequality, but inequality does not enable people to 'pull themselves up from poverty', despite the right-wing insistence that it does (Watson, 2015: 12). Indeed, there is a worldwide consensus that there is a connection between 'inequality' and poverty, at least to the extent that 'increasing income inequality has slowed the pace of poverty reduction' (UNDP, 2013: 78). This is hardly surprising if, as I argue, 'inequality' is simply a euphemism for domination.

Poverty decreasing?

However, despite the widespread agreement about the connection between 'inequality' and poverty, the general consensus is that poverty has been decreasing (even if the rate of decrease has slowed), even as inequality has reached unprecedented levels. This purported decrease in poverty is, at least in part, attributed to the UN's Millennium Development Goals. There were eight MDGs, set by the UN General Assembly in 2000, progress towards which was to be assessed in 2015 (UNDP, 2002: 16-17). In 2015 they were replaced by 17 Sustainable Development Goals, with ending poverty still in first place, and ending hunger in second place (Ford, 2015). The SDGs[94] are intended to 'finish the job that the Millennium Development Goals started, and leave no one behind'.[95]

The job that the Millennium Development Goals started, according to the UN Secretary General, Ban Ki-Moon, in the Foreword to the 2015 Millennium Development Goals report, involved a 'global mobilization ... [which] has produced the most successful anti-poverty movement in history' (United Nations, 2015). The UN had announced in 2013 that the first Millennium

---

94   http://www.undp.org/content/undp/en/home/sustainable-development-goals.html – viewed 9.8.2018.

95.   This statement no longer appears on the UNDP website. For a good discussion of both the MDGs and the SDGs, see Pritchett, 2015.

Development Goal of halving the proportion of people in extreme poverty by 2015 had already been met: 'the proportion of people living in extreme poverty fell from 43.1% in 1990 to 22.4% in 2008' (UNDP, 2013: 12). But, the report went on, '[a]n estimated 1.57 billion people, or more than 30% of the population of the 104 countries studied for this Report, [still] live in multidimensional poverty', that is, poverty measured not by income but by health, and levels of education and living standards. Moreover, 'the population living in multidimensional poverty exceeds that living in income poverty' (pp.13-14), that is, even when people were not defined as 'poor' (or rather, as 'extremely poor'), they still suffered from poverty-related disadvantages. This is hardly surprising, given that 'extreme income poverty' is defined in global poverty measurements as less than $US1.25 a day.[96] So what the UN and the World Bank appeal to as evidence of 'the most successful anti-poverty movement in history' is a halving of the proportion of people whose income is $1.25 a day or less. But how valid is that measurement criterion?

Measurement—$1.25

This International Poverty Line of $1.25 was chosen by the World Bank as a 'representative, absolute poverty line for low income countries'. It was based on the domestic poverty lines of eight of the poorest countries in a sample of 33 countries during the mid-1980s (Reddy and Pogge, 2003: 37n8). According to Lant Pritchett, it was set so low so that there could be no doubt that people at that level of income were indeed poor. '[T]here was a fear', he said, 'that using a high poverty line would lead to accusations that the World Bank was "overstating" poverty in order to expand its mandate or funding, thus detracting from effective advocacy' (Pritchett, 2006: 5). Whatever the accuracy of that assessment of the Bank's motivations (and the author worked for the World Bank so he should know) (Pritchett, 2003: 6), setting an International Poverty Line this low, with the implication that those whose incomes are above the line are not extremely poor, is hardly an accurate mapping of world poverty.

Here are some comparisons with income levels in the US. They are not strict comparisons because the $1.25 amount is 'purchasing power parity'. This is the amount of the local currency required to buy a certain 'basket' of commodities at local prices stated in $US. Local prices in the US are

---

96. $1.25 is the cut-off figure used in the reports of decreasing global poverty since 2008. It was originally $1 a day or $370 a year in 1985 prices (World Bank, 1990), and was updated to $1.90 at the beginning of October 2015 (http://www.un.org/millenniumgoals/pdf/Goal_1_fs.pdf – viewed 9.8.2018).

not the same as local prices in the Third World (and there would seem to be an assumption that the latter are much, much lower), and commodities American people buy are not the same as commodities bought by people in other countries. Nonetheless, there is some comparability, given that the reference currency is $US.

In 1990 (the year the World Bank first published its approach to assessing worldwide poverty), the minimum wage for employees in the US was $3.80 an hour.[97] In other words, the law said that US employees had to be paid at least $30.40 for an eight-hour day, over 30 times the $1-a-day amount estimated as a poverty line for people in the poorest countries. The US poverty guideline[98] for a single person in 1990 was $6,280 a year, or $17.20 a day ($12,700 a year or $34.80 a day for a family of four). By the World Bank's $1.25 standard it would seem as though no one was poor in the US, but that of course is not true. The US federal government has long waged a 'war on poverty', and the fight is not over yet (Matthews, 2014). Many US citizens live on incomes below the exiguous official poverty line, 14.8% of the population or 46.7 million people in 2014 (DeNavas-Walt and Proctor, 2015: 12); and even the minimum wage was (and remains) inadequate for a decent standard of living in the US. The Center for Economic and Policy Research found that, in 2010, the jobs held by just over 75% of workers in the US didn't pay decent wages or provide adequate benefits (Schmitt and Jones, 2012).

Even people working full-time can be eligible for some form of poverty alleviation (even food stamps), so low are the wages paid by some of America's largest employers (e.g. Walmart, McDonalds):

> More than half (52 percent) of the families of front-line fast-food workers are enrolled in one or more public programs, compared to 25 percent of the workforce as a whole … People working in fast-food jobs are more likely to live in or near poverty. One in five families with a member holding a fast-food job has an income below the poverty line, and 43 percent have an income two times the federal poverty level or less. Even full-time hours are not enough to compensate for low wages. The families of more than half of the fast-food workers employed 40 or more hours per week are enrolled in public assistance programs (Allegretto et al, 2013: 1).

---

97. http://www.dol.gov/whd/minwage/chart.htm – viewed 9.8.2018.

98. This is the 'poverty line' used to assess someone's eligibility for financial assistance from the federal government. It is not the figure used by the Census Bureau to calculate the number of poor persons (https://aspe.hhs.gov/prior-hhs-poverty-guidelines-and-federal-register-references – viewed 9.8.2018).

Quite apart from the poverty of those employed in the fast-food industry, the fact that a quarter of the US workforce is 'enrolled in one or more public programs' is a disgrace, a telling indictment of the power of corporations to dictate government policy at public expense. The authors have estimated that this subsidy to the fast-food industry was $7 billion a year (and subsidising the wage costs of big business overall was $243 billion a year from 2007 to 2011) (Allegretto et al, 2013). Clearly, there is poverty in the US. The US federal government is not renowned for its generosity towards its poorest citizens, so the situation must be dire indeed if it underwrites the cost of living for people who are already employed. But low as the pay of many workers in the US is (not to mention the poverty line, which is even lower), $1.25 is a tiny fraction of that. As Anand et al (2010) put it:

> All of the poverty lines used to measure global poverty represent living standards that are hard to fathom by those in advanced industrial countries. What would it be like to live on $1 a day, or $2 a day—on an annual income of $365 to $730? For most of us, it is beyond conception. The poverty standards in the US are closer to $15 a day, and a visit to the slums of Detroit or New York provides a picture of what life is like for those with incomes at this low level (Anand et al, 2010: 2).

So despite the fact that the World Bank's pronouncements on the extent of and trends in global poverty have been widely cited and lauded as evidence that the world's economy is benefiting everyone (if slowly), that conclusion is based on measurement criteria that, as Sanjay Reddy and Thomas Pogge (2005) argue, are neither 'meaningful nor reliable'. The World Bank's method of estimating global income poverty, they say, is meaningless because an International Poverty Line of $1.25 bears no relation to the real requirements of human beings; and it is unreliable because the Bank's Purchasing Power Parity calculations do not make local currencies equivalent for a number of reasons (e.g. estimates can vary markedly depending on which base year is chosen), and the information available, especially from some of the poorest countries on earth, is too limited to justify any conclusions about the extent of poverty or any trends either up or down. As a consequence, the Bank may be both understating the extent of global income poverty, and mistaken in asserting that it has recently declined. The authors are not adamant in stating this conclusion. They do not say that the Bank is wrong to say that poverty has declined. They merely say that the methods used and the evidence available are not sufficient to decide one way or the other.[99]

---

99. For other critiques of the World Bank's approach to global poverty, see also: Deaton, 2002; Deeming and Gubhaju, 2014; Reddy, 2008; Reddy and Minoiu, 2007; Reddy and

WB reply

One of the World Bank's researchers has replied to Reddy and Pogge's criticisms (Ravallion, 2010), but his defence of the Bank and its methods is not very convincing, both because he interprets the criticism as an attack on the personal integrity of the Bank's researchers, and because he doesn't really address the substance of the criticism. 'A lay reader of the Reddy and Pogge chapter in this volume',[100] he said, 'might be forgiven for suspecting that the World Bank's data producers and researchers are real scoundrels'. But appealing to hurt feelings is not only an inadequate response to criticism, it also points to the weakness of his own argument.

To take just a single example: To counter Reddy and Pogge's argument about the inadequacy of the $1.25-a-day for meeting basic human needs, Ravallion simply asserts that it is adequate: 'The national poverty lines we use are all founded on reasonably well-specified "basic needs," and in this respect they are no more "questionable" than (say) the official poverty line of the US' (Ravallion, 2010: 97-8). But assertion is not argument and he presents no evidence to show that $1.25 a day is sufficiently adequate that people living on more than that amount are no longer in extreme poverty. Moreover, the official poverty line of the US is indeed questionable, and for the same reason: the sum specified doesn't allow for a decent standard of living (Greenberg, 2009), even though it is many times the $1.25-a-day standard. Again, there is evidence to suggest that people whose income is above $1.25 a day, even well above, are indeed in extreme poverty in the sense that they lack the resources to provide themselves with basic necessities. For example, Pritchett said that, on the basis of four widely-used indicators of well-being—child health, malnutrition, education, and the proportion of income spent on food—the *richest* 20% of households in poor countries are much worse off than the poor in rich countries (Pritchett, 2003: 14).

Measurement—$10 to $20

Reddy and Pogge are right to say that $1.25 is a meaningless global poverty line, because it makes no sense to say that people who earn $1.25 a day (or even $1.90 a day) are not in extreme poverty, even in the Third World where the standard of living is so much lower than in the West (although there is also the question of whether that should continue to be the case—

Pogge, 2002, 2003, 2010.

100. i.e. Anand et al, eds, 2010. The version of Reddy and Pogge's argument cited above (dated 2005) is an expanded version of the same arguments.

see below). Moreover, not everyone uses this figure of $1.25 as a way of estimating poverty. Pritchett has suggested more realistic income levels for measuring world poverty, either $15 a day (in his 2003 publication) or $10 a day (in 2006). He acknowledged that the $15-a-day standard would mean that more than 80% of the population of most poor countries would be counted as poor. But he pointed out that people whose incomes were less than $15 had lower standards of living than the poor in rich countries, suffered higher levels of malnutrition and child mortality, spent very high proportions of their income on food, and had inadequate access to education.

Environmental activists (Baer et al, 2008) have suggested $20 per person per day ($7,500 per person per year) as a 'development threshold' below which people cannot be expected to contribute resources towards combating climate warming. (Their point is that, because the primary responsibility for the problem lies with the rich nations, they should bear most of the cost of the solution, especially the US who should contribute one-third of the resources necessary, with the European Union contributing a quarter). The $20-a-day figure was 25% above a global poverty line of $16 a day. The authors estimate that this cut-off point of $20 a day would mean that only around a third of the world's population would count as not poor (p.61). But, they say, this is the level 'where poor people begin to enter the lower levels of the global consuming class ... [and] begin to have some small amount of discretionary income' (p.10). It is also the level 'at which the classic plagues of poverty – malnutrition, high infant mortality, low educational attainment, high relative food expenditures – begin to disappear' (p.16). But even these much higher cut-off points are unrealistic when applied to incomes in the West.

Not only income

But income is not the only source of information the World Bank (and others) use as evidence that poverty had reduced. There are other indicators which, according to Reddy and Pogge (2005: 37), are not subject to the same objections as the income measure. The 1997 Human Development report from the UN Development Programme (UNDP, 1997) introduced a 'human poverty index' which used 'indicators of the most basic dimensions of deprivation: a short life, lack of basic education and lack of access to public and private resources' (p.5). The 2015 report on the MDGs (UN, 2015) doesn't mention the human poverty index, but its multidimensional poverty is similar: levels of malnutrition, maternal and infant mortality, health, education and literacy, and access to sanitation and clean drinkable water—the multiple dimensions that go to make up a decent standard of living.

According to the MDG report, it would seem as though there has been some success in all these areas: the mortality rate for women in pregnancy and childbirth fell by 45% worldwide between 1990 and 2015; the mortality rate for children under five worldwide fell from 90 births per 1,000 live births to 43 in the same period; the proportion of undernourished people in 'the developing regions' almost halved; the proportion of people worldwide 'using an improved drinking water source' increased from 76% in 1990 to 91% in 2015,[101] and so did access to sanitation with a decrease in the proportion of people 'practising open defecation'; the proportion of children in 'the developing regions' enrolled in primary school increased (from 83% in 2000 to 91% in 2015), and the literacy rate among young adults aged 15 to 24 also increased (from 83% in 1990 to 91% in 2015); and the situation of women improved on a number of dimensions—school attendance, employment, parliamentary representation (UN, 2015: 4-7 for a summary). So it would seem that poverty has indeed decreased despite the inadequacy of the $1.25 measure. The overall message is one of continued improvement.

Reliability

But again, this conclusion depends on the reliability of the information used to measure it, and the reliability of the World Bank's information is questionable, largely because the data are simply not there. The World Bank itself acknowledges that there are 'huge gaps in the collection of poverty data'. Seventy-eight of the poorest nations did not hold the three-yearly household surveys that would show whether or not conditions had improved, including 29 countries that had 'no poverty data' for the years between 2002 and 2011, and another 28 with just one survey that collected the relevant information (World Bank, 2015). So the information was unreliable for 78 countries where the need was most urgent, while for 57 countries it was impossible to say anything at all about changing levels of poverty.

---

101. The 'improvement' referred to the fact that more people were able to use piped water rather than 'unprotected wells and springs and surface water' although, given that only 58% of the global population had 'access to piped water on premises' (UN, 2015: 58), this would still mean trips to the water source and back home carrying full containers, a task traditionally allocated to women and children. The report does not say what the 'wells and springs and surface water' needed to be protected from, presumably that 'open defecation', but also industry, especially mining. In the latter case, not even piped water sources would protect people since mining pollutes the rivers and ground water from which the piped water is sourced.

Seventy-eight countries is a high proportion of the world's countries, although the exact proportion is unknown because there are a number of different ways of estimating how many countries there are in the world. The UN recognises 195 sovereign states,[102] but the Millennium Development Goals are not relevant for the so-called 'developed' nations. According to the World Bank, in the 2016 fiscal year there were 80 high-income economies (those with average incomes of $12,736 or more, across the whole population, not just wage and salary earners).[103] Excluding those 80 economies from the world poverty statistics leaves 115 countries (although it is well to remember that the International Poverty Line is based on the domestic poverty lines of just eight of the poorest countries in the world). So 78 countries represents around 68% of the 115 countries where it is claimed there has been 'the most successful anti-poverty movement in history'. In other words, in over two-thirds of those countries the data are not reliable enough to judge the extent of poverty, much less whether or not it has decreased. The World Bank says they are going to 'address' those huge gaps in data, but until they're addressed, any claims about poverty reduction are premature. As Reddy and Pogge said:

> Statements that global income poverty is decreasing have no evidential justification in light of the uncertainties associated with present and past estimates of its extent … the monitoring of world poverty, necessary to assess whether the Millennium Development Goals are being achieved, cannot reliably be undertaken at present (Reddy and Pogge, 2003: 19).

Comparisons

Debate about worldwide poverty raises the question of the extent to which living standards in the Third World should (and could) be raised to the level of living standards in the West. Pritchett argues that it should:

> [t]he reasonable and fair definition of a poverty line to be used in the World Bank's poverty reduction objective is that the level of human deprivation that is unacceptable for the citizens of industrialized countries should also be unacceptable for all other countries of the world (Pritchett, 2003: 30).

---

102. http://www.polgeonow.com/2011/04/how-many-countries-are-there-in-world.html – viewed 9.8.2018.

103. This information on countries by GNI per capita income was no longer available at May 2017. Instead, the information is for the 2017 fiscal year—79 high-income countries with a per capita income of $12,476 or more ('World Bank country and lending groups').

But if the pronouncements of multinational organisations like the UN and the World Bank are any guide, the answer to that question is 'no'. Using income of $1.25 a day to assess whether or not someone counts as poor, simply makes no sense as a cut-off point beyond which one is not counted as 'extremely poor', certainly in the West, but elsewhere as well. It is hard to imagine anywhere in the world where $1.25 a day would even buy enough food for one person, much less a family, not to mention other necessities such as clothing, shelter and utilities.

The attitude of the World Bank towards 'the developing regions' was inadvertently exposed by a brief remark in its 1990 report on poverty to the effect that 'in some countries indoor plumbing is a luxury, but in others it is a "necessity"' (World Bank, 1990: 27). Note the Bank's use of quotation marks around "necessity". Does that mean that indoor plumbing is never necessary, and that anyone who insists it is is mistaken? But good sanitation is vital for maintaining the health of populations everywhere and indoor plumbing is part of that. Indeed, halving the proportion of the population without access to basic sanitation was Target C of Millennium Development Goal No. 7 (along with access to safe drinking water). It is likely that those who see it as a luxury are either people who are so used to being poor that they cannot even conceive that they might ever have access to it, or they are people who are quite happy with levels of poverty rare in the West. Indoor plumbing should be a human right. Providing it along with the infrastructure for re-cycling the waste, especially the water, should be not only a vital part of any program for alleviating poverty, but also a vital part of any country's economy. But it would require the kind of 'government spending' anathematised by the powerful interests who dictate government policy.

Causes

Even if the World Bank is right and poverty is diminishing worldwide, it is not at all clear that that diminution is due to capitalism, or 'growth' as it is usually termed in this context. After all, the MDGs[104] themselves were initiated by governments—'all the world's countries and all the world's leading development institutions'—and most could only be implemented through government action, e.g. universal primary education, 'gender' equality, reductions in child and maternal mortality, combating HIV/AIDS and malaria, ensuring everyone is adequately nourished, providing sanitation and clean water, 'access to public goods or common-property resources'

---

104. http://www.un.org/millenniumgoals/bkgd.shtml – viewed 9.8.2018.

(World Bank, 1990: 26). The UN does see a poverty-reduction role for capitalism through partnerships with individual firms in specific projects. For example, the UN Development Programme partnered with the Ikea Foundation to help dairy workers in Utter Pradesh to become independent producers, and with a Brazilian company, Natura Cosméticos, to train 74,300 women as 'beauty advisers', i.e. sales representatives for cosmetics firms.[105] (This would be no help for women who strongly object to the cosmetics industry on the grounds that it demeans women). But for the most part, those with the responsibility for reducing poverty are national governments, not 'the market'.

Indeed, 'the market' and its 'growth' have frequently made people poorer. It is well-known that poor people in poor countries are the worst affected by global warming with its rising sea levels and diminishing water resources caused by the fossil fuel industry. As the UN put it in its final report on the MDGs: 'Climate change and environmental degradation undermine progress achieved, and poor people suffer the most' (UN, 2015: 8). Moreover, unprotected water resources are constantly being threatened, and often destroyed, by the mining industry (although this is not confined to 'the poor' or the Third World). In the US it is clear that much of the poverty is due to the influence of major corporations whose money and lobbyists successfully pressure government to cave in to the short-term interests of big business (see the example above of the wages paid by the fast-food industry).

Indeed, it has been argued that capitalism requires poverty as an essential aspect of its standard operating procedures. The best known of these arguments is Marx's 'industrial reserve army of labour' thesis. The argument does not meet with general agreement, even on the political left (Beechey and Perkins, 1987: 123-33), but it is echoed from a surprising direction—by neo-liberal accounts of what is necessary for the healthy workings of 'the economy'.

Talk of 'social exclusion' notwithstanding, the 'reserve army of labour' thesis suggests that the unemployed have a very precise role to play inside the capitalist economy, that they provide a resource which can be called upon in times of economic growth and discarded when the need for labour power diminishes (in Marx's version), or that they serve to keep down the cost of labour power and hence curb inflation (in more recent versions).

Marx argued that the process of capital accumulation 'constantly produces … a relatively redundant working population … a surplus population …

---

105. http://www.un.org/millenniumgoals/pdf/Goal_1_fs.pdf – viewed 9.8.2018.

[which] forms a disposable industrial reserve army ... a mass of human material always ready for exploitation by capital'. There were, in Marx's view, a number of reasons why capitalism needs 'a population surplus in relation to capital's average requirements for valorization'. Not all industries develop at the same rate, and wherever industry was expanding, 'there must be the possibility of suddenly throwing great masses of men into the decisive areas without doing any damage to the scale of production in other spheres' by withdrawing labour from them. Moreover, capitalism's characteristic cycles of 'alternate expansion and contraction', whereby 'periods of average activity' are succeeded by 'production at high pressure, crisis, and stagnation', give rise to different labour requirements—high demand during times of accelerated production, low demand during downturns and stagnation, and average demand in between. These cycles are managed by alternately drawing people into the labour force during the booms, and throwing them out of work—'setting them free'—in times of bust. In between, maintaining a level of unemployment guarantees a pool of workers available at a moment's notice. It is achieved partly through labour-saving technology, partly through over-working the employed segment of the working-class. But unemployment also has another function—that of pacifying the working population by keeping them insecure and in competition with each other. In times of average or low productivity it 'weighs down the active army of workers'; while in boom times it 'puts a curb on their pretensions' (Marx, 1976: 781-94).

More recently a further element has been added to the 'reserve army of labour' thesis—that maintaining a level of permanent unemployment serves to keep down inflation. This involves the construct of 'NAIRU'—'non-accelerating inflation rate of unemployment'. In true ideological fashion, this level is termed 'natural'. A *Dictionary of Economics* tells us: 'Because unemployment cannot be held below the natural rate without accelerating inflation ... the natural rate of unemployment ... is often called ... NAIRU' (Bannock et al, 1992).

But despite the unequivocal tone of this dictionary entry, the truth of the theory is by no means obvious. One of the chief stumbling blocks is the lack of agreement on the actual size of this 'natural' level of unemployment and hence the lack of any way of empirically establishing a connection between it (since there is no way of knowing what 'it' is) and the rate of inflation. Indeed, if history is any guide it would seem there is no connection. Barry Hughes pointed out in 1980 that estimates of the NAIRU in Australia had varied from between 1.5% and 2% at the beginning of the 1970s to 8% or more in 1979 and 1980, since even 6% to 7% unemployment was having no effect on the inflation rate (Hughes, 1980: 219). Far from it being the case that a high unemployment rate was bringing down the inflation rate, both were at unprecedented high levels, and not only in Australia. As the above-mentioned *Dictionary of Economics* phrased it: 'high unemployment … re-emerged as a worsening phenomenon in Western economies after the oil-crisis of 1973, for the first time simultaneously appearing with high inflation' (Bannock et al, 1992). This should have falsified the theory but it did not. Facts are never allowed to contradict ideological positions, and economists still assert a connection as though it were self-evident.

The NAIRU model does not meet with universal acceptance. As L. Randall Wray put it:

> If you want to produce psychopaths, beat the crap out of them when they are young, convince them that the world is dog-eat-dog, make them fight for every scrap of food, and eliminate all protection in the work place[,] [m]ake life as precarious as possible, with workers fearing they could be replaced by the unemployed—losing their jobs and joining the ranks of the starving masses. Richly reward the strong and punish the weak. (I think I just described an entire sector of the modern economy, where the psychopaths rise to the top …). That is the idea behind NAIRU, which is so dear to the hearts of most economists (Wray, 2011-12: Blog #50). (See also: Mitchell, 2001; Mitchell and Mosler, 2002; Singh, 1995).

Nonetheless, it is seriously and widely discussed among the orthodox and occupies a respected place in the canon (as evidenced by its unproblematic appearance in dictionaries of economics). But it has even more radical implications than the 'reserve army' thesis. While the latter argues only that unemployment is necessary in order to keep down the cost of labour power, the NAIRU thesis says that unemployment is necessary to keep down the cost of everything, 'inflation' being a term covering the price of commodities in general. Hence not only does the discipline of economics hold the unemployed responsible for their own unemployment and poverty, it holds them responsible for undermining the very wealth of nations itself. That such an outright absurdity could continue to be maintained speaks volumes for the power of ideology and the dominant interests it purveys.

Some commentators see high unemployment as a recent development, as a consequence of the inflation-inducing 'oil shocks' of the early 1970s coming after a post-war period of 'full employment'. Mitchell (2001) expands on that theme by arguing that, since the early 1970s, governments, and Australian governments in particular, have been focused on fighting inflation by accepting the 'natural' unemployment thesis and by cutting back on public employment. But it is not at all clear that there was in fact a period of full employment after the Second World War. Official statistics are unreliable in this regard, given how many people were excluded from the category of 'unemployed' (and still are), the discouraged and demoralised, for example, and the disabled and the underemployed. Then there are the married women, at that time directly debarred from the labour market by explicit regulations against their employment, and indirectly debarred by lack of child care and cultural imperatives about what was necessary for good mothering.

For both Marxism and orthodox economic theory, then, keeping down the costs of labour power by maintaining a pool of unemployed is not a recent development at all, but a structural feature of the capitalist labour market. Both perceive the same reality—the maintenance of a certain level of unemployment, and hence of poverty, as a prerequisite for the normal functioning of the capitalist economy. But whereas Marxism deplored this fact, perceiving the human misery it causes, capitalist ideology regards it as natural and inevitable.

Another name for 'reserve army of labour' is 'churning', the process whereby periods of employment alternate with periods of unemployment at the lower end of the labour market. People are moved in and out of work according to the demands of the labour market, demands that are set by employers, not by employees (Byrne, 1997: 39). Nonetheless, this movement in and out of the workforce is seen by capitalism's right-wing apologists, not surprisingly, as voluntary behaviour or personal deficiencies on the part of the workers. Lawrence Mead, for example, one of the main architects of 'welfare reform' in the US and of the neo-liberal attack on 'welfare' everywhere (Ramesh, 2010), located churning in a 'fall in capability' on the part of workers. Instead of seeing the increasing casualisation and de-skilling of the workforce as a requirement of the economic system, he saw it as a characteristic of 'the American workforce' which 'may be less skilled and motivated than it once was' (Mead, 1986: 24-5).

But although this is a necessary assumption if the worldwide orthodoxy on unemployment policy is to be maintained, it makes no more sense to attribute this churning to the behaviour and motivations of the unemployed, than it does to attribute rising levels of unemployment to them. It is hardly conceivable that such major economic and social changes could be caused by the most powerless members of the community. As Frances Fox Piven has pointed out, the main actors in the right-wing drama of 'welfare reform' in the US were 'poor women, especially poor women of color ... [who were being held] to blame for poverty, for social disorganization, for family breakdown, for the weakening of morality in America, and for all the economic anxieties Americans feel' (Piven, 2001: 35). In contrast, the reserve army of labour thesis places the onus where it belongs, with those who have the power to make a difference, those whose interest it is to create and accumulate wealth by whatever means at whatever cost. It avoids the irrationality of locating the causes with those most harmed by the system, and refuses to justify poverty by making the poor responsible for it themselves.

Under the worldwide consensus around 'active labour market' policies and 'welfare reform', the unemployed are humiliated twice, once by the poverty and then by being blamed for it with coerced workfare. But this very degradation is their function within the system. It is the extent to which they are literally deprived of value, first of money and then of the common courtesies available to other citizens, that they provide the greatest service to the capitalist economy. They are of the greatest use to capitalism to the extent that they can be defined as being of least value. Their lack of access to money, capitalist society's only measure of value, means both that they serve to keep down the price of labour power and that they are undeserving of the considerations normally regarded as available to citizens. As Piven and Cloward commented, the work-test obligation placed on the unemployed 'is designed to spur people to offer themselves to any employer on any terms. And it does this by making pariahs of those who cannot support themselves' (Piven and Cloward 1987a: 39). Neo-liberal unemployment policies make a mockery of any notion of a 'free world'. For the poor there is no freedom, not only in the indirect sense that inadequate resources place constraints on action, but also in the direct sense of permission for those in authority to exert overt compulsion on the impoverished. Hence participation on the part of liberal democratic governments in the worldwide consensus on coercive and punitive measures to 'assist' the unemployed, aided by the discipline of economics, transgresses their own professed beliefs. This is a grave threat to all that social democracy purportedly holds dear.

And finally, it has been argued that poverty is caused by overpopulation. Poverty would be overcome if there were fewer people, either globally or within any particular country. But in the first place poverty is not necessarily a consequence of scarcity, of too many people and too few resources, but rather of the accumulation of what resources there are in the hands of the few. As Ingham said: 'It should be noted that it is the institution of property rights that produces a socially created, not a natural, scarcity' (Ingham,

2008).[106] For example, enough food is produced to feed the present world population of around 7.3 billion,[107] but it is not distributed equitably because it is a commodity and must be paid for. If people can't afford it they can't have it. As well, a large proportion of it is wasted—an estimated 40% of food in the US, and around one-third of food worldwide[108]—because it can't be sold and its commodity-form means it can't be given away.

Moreover, any causal connection between poverty and over-population is the other way round, that is, it is the poverty that causes the overpopulation. People have a lot of children when there is a high death rate among children for poverty-related reasons (malnutrition, homelessness, filthy living conditions, no access to sanitation, clean water, vaccinations or adequate health care), and when women are powerless to say 'no'. With improved financial conditions and more female control, people have fewer children because those they do have are likely to survive and women have a say in how many children they have (or don't have).[109] The best way of reducing the world's population is to abolish poverty, especially among women.

Conclusion

It would seem that poverty is an ineradicable part of the capitalist system, at least as it is currently constituted and has been throughout its history. Attempts on the part of its apologists at the World Bank (and elsewhere) to deny that are unconvincing. Whether or not we can know that poverty is decreasing (or increasing) depends on the validity and reliability of the measures being used to estimate it, and they are not sufficiently robust to justify claims about decreases in poverty worldwide. The data supposedly measuring levels and trends in health, mortality, malnutrition, education, etc., are hardly adequate to support the conclusions drawn from them; and the $1.25-a-day criterion hardly justifies the conclusion that extreme poverty has been reduced. Given the evidence showing that extreme poverty continues even when people earn well above that limit (which should be obvious anyway), the criterion is indeed meaningless.

But even if poverty or some of its worst effects were decreasing, that improvement is not the result of any improvement in the standard operations

---

106. My Kindle version has no page numbers. The sentence quoted occurs in chapter 5, footnote 4.

107. http://www.oxfam.ca/there-enough-food-feed-world – viewed 9.8.2018.

108. http://www.gracelinks.org/2244/food-waste – viewed 9.8.2018.

109. http://borgenproject.org/poverty-and-overpopulation/ – viewed 9.8.2018.

of capitalism. On the contrary, it comes from that 'government spending' so excoriated by capitalism's apologists. Not only is capitalism not at the centre of any amelioration of the lot of the poor worldwide, it does its best to ensure that that will not happen. Although tax avoidance/evasion does not directly deprive governments of funding, everyone (with the exception of heterodox economists like the Modern Money Theorists) believes that it does. So those multinational corporations making such liberal use of tax havens believe that they are depriving governments of the wherewithal to spend for public purposes, including relieving poverty through public employment and adequate levels of social security. The fact that they are wrong about that—government obeisance to neo-liberal demands to rein in spending and balance budgets is the effective method here—does not detract from their callousness. But it is not simply a matter of personal character deficiencies. The system structured to create endless, unconstrained wealth is also structured to create poverty. It is not possible to have one without the other.

Chapter Nine: Finance Capital

> Modern finance, at least what is practiced at the biggest banks, is about fraud ... finance is not even a zero sum game—it largely makes a negative economic contribution ... the imbalance is one of power. The disease is money manager capitalism (Wray, 2011).

> The world is in the hands of these guys (Michel Camdessus, chief executive of the IMF, justifying the $50 billion bailout of the super-rich investors in Mexico in early 1995—Haseler, 2000: 25).

> The parasites have won the battle. The bondholders and the central bankers rule the world (Harvey, 2014: 139).

> Steve Eisman ... calls ... the executive mind-set that led to the market crack-up ... "hedge fund disease" and says "it should be in the DSM-V [the fifth edition of the American Psychiatric Association's Diagnostic and Statistical Manual of Mental Disorders]. It used to be suffered only by kings and dictators. The symptoms are megalomania, plus narcissism, plus solipsism". If you're worth $500 million, he asks, "how could you be wrong about anything? To think something is to make it happen. You're God" (Ehrenreich, 2010: 190-1).[110]

> Today's financial analogue [for primitive accumulation] occurs when banks create credit freely and supply it to corporate raiders for leveraged buyouts or to buy the public domain being privatized (Hudson, 2010).

For most people most of the time, capitalism is industrial capitalism, where profit is generated for firms and their CEOs and major shareholders through the production of goods and services by people paid to do the work. But another important aspect of capitalism is the finance industry. As suggested by the quotes at the beginning of this chapter, this industry is central to present-day capitalism.

---

110. Steve Eisman is reported in Wikipedia (18.11.2011) to be 'a money manager famous for shorting securitized subprime home mortgages'. Whatever that means, it is clear that he knows what he is talking about on this issue of who has 'hedge fund disease', as long as he includes himself among them.

Again, most people most of the time assume the finance industry has a fundamental role in financing productivity and thus contributing to social purposes. But the finance sector has never been interested in financing industry (Ingham, 1984). Its focus on short-term profit rather than the long-term investments required by industry too often means that it operates in the interests of speculation like that which led to the recent global financial crisis (the 'hedge fund disease'). This speculation is still continuing, and not only has no one been brought to account,[111] many of those who created the crisis were bailed out with public money. Instead of being punished for the destruction they wreaked, they were rewarded. This is an example of what economists call 'moral hazard', defined by one commentator in the context of financial deregulation in the US as 'a strong disincentive for people to behave ethically' (O'Hehir, 2010). In other (less euphemistic) words, the absence of any risk for the perpetrators behind the proliferation of financial commodities was a strong *incentive* to *criminal* behaviour, as should be obvious, but the drive for male power overrides any ethical considerations. The global financial crisis and the subsequent failure of the authorities to bring the perpetrators to account is an exemplary illustration of that arrogant masculinist dissociation that knows no bounds: entitlement at the expense of others (those who lost their homes and life savings, people dependent on the social services subject to spending cuts because the money supposedly wasn't there to pay for them), and dissociation, not only from common decency and humanity, but also from any genuine economic rationality.

As is the case with economics more generally, I find the finance industry difficult to understand. In part this is because of how hard it is to sort out fact from ideology (or the genuinely human functions of the economy from the interests of domination). As is usually the case with 'arcane language' (Pixley, 2004: 104), it serves a purpose: to mask what is actually going on and maintain the public's consent to policies and practices that undermine well-being (although this is never entirely successful). But it would seem that I am not alone in my bemusement. For example, Robert Peston, BBC business editor and author of a book about the global financial crisis called *How Do We Fix This Mess?* said in an interview that he found it 'incredibly difficult to understand' a banker's explanation of credit default swaps and collateralised debt obligations. He also said he believed that most other people didn't understand either, including finance industry insiders such as people who

---

111. except in Iceland—see: Bedard, 2016; Motroc, 2016; Scrutton and Sigurdardottir, 2015.

sit on the boards of banks, finance ministers, central bankers and regulators (Anonymous, 2012).

But again, as in the case of economics more generally, if I'm talking about forms of male power I have to say something about the finance industry. The havoc wreaked on the economy by the finance sector provides an excellent example of the consequences of that dissociated masculine entitlement that enables men to accumulate wealth endlessly while the devil takes the hindmost.

I do know that the finance industry has waxed fat under the neo-liberal hegemony, reaching over $600 trillion or ten times world GDP at the time of the global financial crisis (Brown, 2008; Kapoor, 2010: 94-5), and that little has been done since to stop it happening again. Finance capital is exactly what Hannah Arendt called the 'ugly dream' of the bourgeoisie whereby 'money beget[s] money' without 'go[ing] the long way of investment in production':

> The secret of the new happy fulfilment was precisely that economic laws no longer stood in the way of the greed of the owning classes. Money could finally beget money because power, with complete disregard for all laws—economic as well as ethical—could appropriate wealth ... The owners of superfluous capital were the first section of the class to want profits without fulfilling some real social function—even if it was the function of an exploiting producer (Arendt, 1951: 37, 150).

Arendt was talking about imperialism, but the description fits the finance industry as well. Its only commodity is money. As Michael Hudson put it: 'Today's financial engineering aims not at industrial engineering to increase output or cut the costs of production, but at the disembodied M-M^1 – making money from money itself in a sterile "zero-sum" transfer payment' (Hudson, 2010).[112] Money begetting money, that 'ugly dream of the bourgeoisie', has been more than adequately realised by a finance industry bloated by the decades of neo-liberal deregulation.

Fictitious capital

For a number of reasons, Marx (among others) called the finance sector 'fictitious capital': because the profit it generated did not come from the production and sale of real commodities, because the 'commodities' it did

---

112. M-M^1 is a reference to Marx's discussion in Volume 1 of *Capital* of 'the general formula for capital' (Chapter 4), which he notated as 'M-C-M^{1}': money (which buys a) commodity (which is sold for) 'the original sum plus an increment ... "surplus value"' (Marx, 1976[1867]: 251). In finance capitalism, the commodity is deleted. The sequence goes from money to more money without the intermediation of any commodities, or at least, of any concrete goods and services.

'produce' (i.e. interest and gain from successful risk-taking) had no existence except as book-keeping entries, and because it led inevitably to economic crises. As Marx put it: 'interest-bearing capital, in general, is the fountainhead of all manner of insane forms, so that debts, for instance, can appear to the banker as commodities' (Marx, 2010: 319).

The term did not originate with Marx. It had been in common usage for around a century before Marx wrote about it (in the writings included in volume III of *Capital*). It was used as early as 1755 by Richard Cantillon in his posthumously published book, *Essai sur la nature du commerce en général*, to refer to the Mississippi Bubble of 1719-20 and the South Sea Bubble of 1720, from both of which he made money.[113] Adam Smith used the term 'fictitious' to refer to repayments of loans that had already been discounted numerous times before the due date for re-payment: 'The stream [of money] which, by means of those circulating bills of exchange, had once been made to run out from the coffers of the banks, was never replaced by any stream which really run into them' (Smith, 2007: 242-3). It was used by Ricardo in the British parliament in 1819 in the context of the debate on the expediency of the resumption of cash payments by the Bank of England.[114] Thomas Jefferson used the term in a letter written at the end of 1820: 'The flood of paper money, as you well know, had produced an exaggeration of nominal prices and at the same time a facility of obtaining money, which not only encouraged speculations on fictitious capital, but seduced those of real capital, even in private life, to contract debts too freely'.[115]

There is a sense in which money itself could be called 'fictitious' because it is abstract. There is nothing concrete behind it that makes it valuable. It is valueless in the sense that it has no use (apart from buying useful things with it). You can't eat it, wear it, live in it, etc. And yet it is the source of all value (you can acquire the material things you want with it), although where its value comes from is not immediately obvious. As Ingham said 'economic value is not "natural" like the relatively constant properties of, say, distance and weight' (Ingham, 2002: 130). What gives it an anchor in the real world is a social relation such as the power of sovereign currency-issuing governments to collect taxes (see chapter 10).

---

113. http://www.socialiststudies.org.uk/cinc%20fictitious.shtml – viewed 9.8.2018.

114. http://bthp23.com/PerelmanFictCap.pdf – viewed 9.8.2018.

115. http://www.let.rug.nl/usa/presidents/thomas-jefferson/letters-of-thomas-jefferson/jefl264.php – viewed 9.8.2018.

Nonetheless, there is a kind of disjunction between the finance industry and what might be called a real economy. The governor of the Reserve Bank of Australia, Glen Stevens, for example, took this disjunction for granted in a speech he gave in 2014 (Stevens, 2014; Maiden, 2014). He was talking about the global financial crisis and the need for entrepreneurs to take risks in order to get the economy working again. He said that risk-taking in the financial sector was probably 'a trade-off worth making', if it meant that *'more genuine entrepreneurs in the economy ... were more prepared to take a risk* [too] – on a new product, a new factory or process, an innovation, a new market or a new employee' (emphasis added). However, he went on,

> if some years from now we find ourselves looking back and concluding that such "real economy" entrepreneurial risk-taking has not really taken place, and all that has happened is that financial risk-taking and leverage have risen, we would be disappointed [in our expectations] (Stevens, 2014).

He said that it was 'very difficult, at this stage, to evaluate how well the trade-off is operating ... the evidence is hard to read ... it always takes time for an economy to heal after a financial crisis'.

But if it's not possible to tell how well the real economy is operating six or seven years after the crisis, how long do we have to wait? And what would count as evidence if what has already happened does not? This is a classic way in which ideologies, in this case the neo-liberal consensus, evade acknowledging the consequences—we're always at a stage where it's 'very difficult to evaluate how well [this or that policy or consequence] is operating'. Moreover, the RBA governor ignored the fact that it was 'financial risk-taking and leverage' that caused the crisis in the first place at the expense of the real economy, and hence it was hardly likely to provide a solution. But because central banks are part of the problem, their CEOs cannot afford to be too open about capitalism's standard operating procedures: 'the myth of the supposed independence of the modern central bank ... is but a smokescreen to hide the fact that monetary policy is run for the benefit of Wall Street and London and Frankfurt and Paris' (Wray, 2011).

In another sense, however, financial assets are not at all fictitious. Ingham has argued against referring to 'capitalist money' as 'fictitious' because the production of money is a social reality: 'all forms of money have their own "social relations" that consist in credit-debt relations' (Ingham, 2013: 320n1). Moreover, the finance industry has real effects in the real world. Nonetheless, there is something dissociated about a finance industry that buys and sells nothing but ever more attenuated forms of debt.

Commodities

'Debt' is the most general term for the commodities produced by the finance industry, but the recently invented debts typical of the modern version have other names too: derivatives, structured financial products, credit default swaps, collateralised debt obligations, junk bonds, private label securities. These debts are commodities in the sense that they are bought and sold and they generate profit, but they have no real economic value. They are not anchored in any real-world goods or services, and as a consequence they are prone to 'debt-leveraged asset-price inflation' (Hudson, 2010). In other words, they create 'bubbles' because there are no limits to expansion—until the debts are called in and the economy crashes because there is nothing with which to honour those debts.

Derivatives (to go straight to the horse's mouth) are defined by the IMF as 'financial instruments that are linked to a specific financial instrument or indicator or commodity, and through which specific financial risks can be traded in financial markets in their own right … The value of a financial derivative derives from the price of an underlying item, such as an asset or index' (IMF, 1998: 2). But this definition does not clarify matters. How are derivatives 'linked to a specific financial instrument or indicator or commodity'? It isn't through ownership: the owner of the derivative is not the owner of the 'underlying item'. It seems to me that the IMF has confused 'value' and 'price' ('the value of a financial derivative'). As the global financial crisis demonstrated, derivatives have no value, in the sense that they are not in fact 'linked' to any 'specific financial instrument or indicator or commodity', only their price is. When the debts are called in, they don't even have a price because they had no value in the first place.

The most comprehensible form of derivative is 'futures', contracts whereby the seller and purchaser of an actual commodity fix the price for a specified length of time, and hence avoid the risk of price falls (the seller) or rises (the buyer) over that period. In either case, both have security of income. For example, a farmer enters into a futures contract when a crop is planted so that he[116] knows what his income will be when the crop is harvested. In the case of the purchaser, if the price is fixed at the beginning of the season, he is protected against any rise in prices during the season, although he stands to lose money if the price falls. In order to protect himself against

---

116. This is far too individualistic a way of describing the issue. In fact, these 'farmers' are likely to be multinational agribusinesses at the top of the food chain when it comes to the finance industry. However, I will stay with the individualistic terminology, despite the

that possibility, he can take out an 'option', whereby he pays the original price if prices rise over the time of the contract, but the new price if prices have fallen since the contract was signed: 'Options were invented because people liked the security of knowing they could buy or sell at a certain price, but wanted the chance to profit if the market price suited them better at the time of delivery' (BBC, 2003). The seller of the option benefits from the premiums paid while the buyer loses the money he paid in premiums but saves money by not having to pay the eventual increased price, or by paying the eventual lower price.

I can understand this kind of derivative (at least I think I do—although options sound to me like the 'free lunch' orthodox economics says you can't have). I can see that their purpose is to give certainty about income, and that one of the parties will benefit further over and above that certainty—the seller if prices fall, the buyer if prices rise. But when it comes to the more recent forms of derivative, comprehension flees. I suspect, however, that the problem lies, not in my flawed understanding, but in the nature of the finance industry. Too much clarity would expose what is really going on as (perfectly legal) scams.

According to the experts, derivatives play an important role in the economy, or at least in the finance industry. The IMF again:

> Financial derivatives are used for a number of purposes including risk management, hedging, arbitrage between markets, and speculation. Financial derivatives enable parties to trade specific financial risks— such as interest rate risk, currency, equity and commodity price risk, and credit risk, etc.—to other entities who are more willing, or better suited, to take or manage these risks, typically, but not always, without trading in a primary asset or commodity (IMF, 1998: 2).

My incomprehension in this case revolves around the question of why 'entities' might be 'more willing, or better suited, to take or manage these risks' and what's in it for them (i.e. their profit), and why anyone would engage in trading when there are no 'primary assets or commodities'. Clearly, there is profit to be made, but again I don't know where the profit comes from. Who is charged what for what? Given that it all eventually went pear-shaped in the GFC, perhaps these are questions the finance industry should have been asking themselves all along.

---

fact that much of the action I describe is done by institutional investors, both because it makes for easier expression and because the decisions are made by individuals, mostly men, in accordance with the character structure required by male supremacy.

To give just one more example of a (to me) incomprehensible statement about the benefits of derivatives:

> if "properly" handled, [they] can bring substantial economic benefits. These instruments help economic agents to improve their management of market and credit risks. They also foster financial innovation and market developments, increasing the market resilience to shocks (Chui, 2012: 3).

But far from 'increasing the market resilience to shocks', derivatives were the prime cause of the 2008 global financial crisis.

Credit default swaps

The most common form of financial derivative is a credit default swap. To quote another expert source, this is 'designed to transfer the credit exposure of fixed income products between two or more parties'.[117] The BBC's 'simple guide' to derivatives said that they are 'basically a way of allowing traders to hedge their bets'. This is 'a good thing' because

> [it] can protect companies and banks against unexpected developments, for example sudden falls or rises in the value of currencies or commodities … In simple terms, an investor can buy a derivative which bets that the market will move against them so that they win either way (BBC, 2003).

Or as one commentator put it: 'the basic idea is that you can insure an investment you want to go *up* by betting it will go *down*' (Brown, 2008— original emphasis), 'shorting' it, in other words. This seems to me like another free lunch. But someone has to pay for it and, as it turned out, it was paid for by the whole world economy.

Examples given in the literature only increase my confusion. 'You can bet on next Wednesday's weather, if a counterparty wants to take the other side' (Harris, 2009). While I can understand that someone addicted to gambling might want to bet on anything and everything, I can't understand why this might be a supposedly reputable aspect of the finance industry.

Or to take another example: two authors at the Federal Reserve Bank of St Louis (Noeth and Sengupta, 2012) likened what happens with a credit default swap to 'an individual insuring his neighbor's car and getting paid if the neighbor is involved in a car accident … even though he may have no financial stake in his neighbor's car'. Another commentator (Harris, 2009) also used the analogy of car insurance. 'Imagine', she said, 'being able to

---

117. http://www.investopedia.com/terms/c/creditdefaultswap.asp – viewed 9.8.2018.

insure a car ... your neighbors will let their [reckless] teenage son drive'. In other words, it's highly likely that the car will be written-off in an accident. It is possible, she goes on, to buy 'as many insurance policies on this car as you can afford to pay premiums on ... by using financial derivatives called swaps'. When the car is inevitably written-off, 'you—and any friends you clued in on the deal—might collect millions, even billions, of dollars', while paying the owner only the depreciated price of the vehicle. This author did not say from whom 'you' collected all this money (the insurance company? the CDS seller?). I can see that such an arrangement would lead to a financial crisis for whoever it was who had to pay up, but I can't understand why anyone would take the risk.

In another example (Clark, 2008), an individual (also addressed as 'you') has bought 'your friend Jimmy's health insurance policy from the company that issued it'. The reason 'you' bought it, the source says, was so that you could collect the monthly premiums. But the source says nothing about why the insurance company sold it. After all, if the company no longer owned the policy it could no longer collect the premiums. On the other hand, of course, neither would the company be liable for the payout in the event of a 'credit event'. This kind of spreading of the risk is common in the insurance industry. Warren Buffet (2003)[118] acknowledged that 'the derivatives business' was similar to reinsurance. 'Like Hell, both are easy to enter and almost impossible to exit', he said. Both require large payments many years after the original contract is signed, sometimes decades later; and both 'generate reported earnings that are often wildly overstated', and their complexity means that even 'expert auditors could easily and honestly have widely varying opinions' (as indeed they did in the case of the companies that crashed during the global financial crisis). The insurance industry is regulated while CDSs are not, but the regulations don't prevent disaster. After all, one of the biggest failures of the global financial crisis was an insurance company (AIG).[119]

---

118. Buffet is one of the richest men in the world and CEO of Berkshire Hathaway Inc., a US multinational conglomerate with a major interest in insurance. He is one of the more personable of America's super-wealthy, or at least his public persona is, and his chairman's speech to the company in its 2002 annual report (Buffett, 2003) is a delightful read. His comments on the differential tax rates he paid in comparison with his office staff and cleaner were widely reported. "'There wasn't anyone in the office, from the receptionist up, who paid as low a tax rate and I have no tax planning; I don't have an accountant or use tax shelters. I just follow what the US Congress tells me to do'", he said (Clark, 2007).

119. 'insurance giant AIG was saved from collapse by an $85 billion infusion of government cash. The bailout also saved those holding the bag on credit default swaps on the company's bonds; a credit event was averted by government intervention' (Clark, 2008).

Subprime mortgages

At the centre of the derivatives market (and the global financial crisis) was the US subprime mortgage industry. 'Subprime' mortgages are housing loans given to people whose credit ratings are so low they are unlikely to be able to service the mortgage. Because there is a high risk of default on these loans, borrowers are charged a higher rate of interest, even though this increases the risk of default. This risk was supposedly avoided by 'collateralized debt obligations' ('the credit exposure ... [was transferred] between two or more parties'). CDOs involved pooling these mortgages and creating 'securities' ('securitisation') that were sold to unsuspecting 'investors' around the world. 'Securitisation' supposedly spread the risk by packaging mortgages together so that 'investors' bought a percentage of multiple mortgages rather than any single one (although it's not clear to me why a hundred risky mortgages should be any more secure than a single risky mortgage). CDOs were also partitioned into tranches according to degree of entitlement. Those with the highest level of entitlement had first claim on the mortgage payments, the next level was paid only after the first level had been paid, and so on down the line. The last in line carried the most risk. There was evidently much mirth in the industry at the success of this strategy. These last-in-line 'securities' were jocularly known as 'toxic waste'—proof that these men were well aware that what they were selling was worse than worthless.

Further proof is supplied by the common name for subprime mortgages: they were referred to as 'NINJA' loans: 'No income, no job or assets'. At the same time this knowledge co-existed with the belief that the 'securitisation' process was beneficial. According to one expert, 'credit default swaps based on subprime mortgages provided investors with several valuable benefits, including improved price discovery and an ability to hedge the risks of subprime mortgages' (Stulz, 2010: 77). But the risks weren't hedged, as it turned out, when the global financial crisis hit. Or at least, the risks weren't hedged for the people who trusted the banks and other financial institutions who advised them, and who believed the credit agencies who gave the credit default swaps and other derivatives the highest credit ratings. Those who were in a position to take advantage of the 'improved price discovery' (whatever that is) and pass the risks on to someone else, having collected their fees and bonuses along the way, were the only ones to savour the 'valuable benefits' when the crunch came.

The risk of default on subprime mortgages is extremely high. It is highly unlikely that people with too little income to service the mortgage would be able to do so, not to mention pay the higher interest rates charged because of that likelihood. It is because of that risk, indeed, that near certainty, of default by the poor that banks have regulations (to the extent that they do) requiring them to lend only to people who can afford to service the loan. It is incomprehensible why anyone would buy a credit default swap whose underlying asset is subprime mortgages with their near certainty of default. But, of course, nobody knew. Or rather, nobody but the insiders knew. As Robert Peston commented in his book, *How Do We Fix this Mess?*: "'So this terrifyingly vast and seriously dangerous global industry grows up with really only the participants—who are pocketing enormous bonuses—knowing about it or understanding it'" (Anonymous, 2012).

Subprime mortgages are the way US officialdom has tried to house the poor: 'It was in the late 1990's … under the urging of the Clinton Administration that Fannie Mae and Freddie Mac began to operate as social welfare agencies instead of financial institutions' (Watkins, 2008). Whereas other countries provide public housing which is rented so that it stays in the public housing stock and is available for the next generation (although never in sufficient quantities), the US subprime system embraces the principle of home-ownership among people who would qualify for public housing in most other countries. The US is more averse to providing public housing than any other country in the world (although no government under the influence of the neo-liberal agenda likes it—there is too much wealth at stake to be giving it away free). There is public housing in the US,[120] occupied by approximately 1.2 million households, but it is a drop in the ocean of need and it is not available for single people (unless they are elderly or disabled).

The US is notorious for its neo-liberal ideological aversion to anything that hints at 'socialism' in the form of government initiatives to support those of its citizens who fail to thrive under capitalism. Consequently, the US federal government does little to directly help 'the poor', but instead channels that 'help' through 'the market'. This is the case with mortgages for 'the poor' (otherwise known as 'low- to middle-income earners'). The two largest mortgage finance lenders in the US are the 'government-sponsored' enterprises, Fannie Mae[121] (the Federal National Mortgage Association) and Freddie Mac (the Federal Home Mortgage Corporation). Both companies

---

120. http://portal.hud.gov/hudportal/HUD?src=/topics/rental_assistance/phprog — viewed 9.8.2018.

121. The nickname comes from the sound of its initials, FNMA (Watkins, 2008). Freddie Mac was so-called as a complement to 'Fannie Mae', and presumably because the last two initials of the acronym are 'MC'

are privately owned, but they are guaranteed by the federal government with a line of credit through the US Treasury, and by exemption from state and local income taxes and from oversight by the Securities and Exchange Commission. This is a classic neo-liberal version of 'the market' whereby the profits are privatised and the losses socialised via a government guarantee.

Fannie Mae was originally established in 1938 as part of Franklin Delano Roosevelt's New Deal response to the Great Depression, as a way of increasing home ownership and the availability of affordable housing. But rather than building public housing or making housing loans directly to 'the poor', Fannie Mae channelled federal money through local banks by buying their mortgages and thus freeing up capital for them to make more loans. This is known as a 'secondary mortgage market'. In 1968, Fannie Mae was 'privatised' by Lyndon B. Johnson supposedly in order to release more money for the Vietnam War. It was at this point that it became the first-ever 'government-sponsored enterprise', with profits paid to shareholders (the 'enterprise') while being guaranteed by government backing and exempted from taxation and oversight ('government-sponsored'). Freddie Mac was created in 1970, supposedly in order to provide some competition for Fannie Mae and break up the latter's monopolisation of the market, and to expand the secondary mortgage market. Freddie Mac's function was to buy loans from Savings and Loan Associations, while Fannie Mae focused on banks and other mortgage finance companies (Alford, 2003; Fowler et al, 2008).

These two organisations were at the forefront of those directly responsible for the global financial crisis.[122] Under changes introduced in the 1990s by the Clinton Administration, Fannie Mae required banks to lower their lending standards in relation to down payments and income, in order to fulfil a quota of mortgages lent to people who would not be eligible for loans under the previous criteria. When the inevitable happened and the subprime borrowers defaulted on their mortgage payments, the real estate market in the US was flooded with houses for sale and house prices dropped catastrophically. This decline meant that many mortgage debts came to exceed what people could sell the property for, and many people defaulted on their loans rather than continuing to pay the banks. Fannie Mae and Freddie Mac were inundated with claims on the mortgage default insurance they had provided, and they couldn't pay it. They were declared bankrupt and there was an instantaneous loss in value for all the mortgages they covered, not only the subprime ones.

---

122. The following discussion of Fannie Mae and Freddie Mac is largely based on Watkins, 2008.

They had provided default insurance for around half of the home mortgages in the US (Watkins, 2008).

So the US 'solution' to the social problem of the homelessness caused by leaving the provision of basic necessities to 'the market', is to involve 'the market' by allowing it free rein with the government stepping in to bail out any problems. As might have been expected (and was),[123] this was a recipe for economic disaster, especially as the derivatives based on US subprime mortgages were sold to 'foreign investors', i.e. to institutions in other countries. It would have been far cheaper and far less damaging for the global economy, if the US government had provided public rental accommodation for those of its citizens who were never going to be able to afford housing in any capitalist 'market'. Adequate supplies of public housing might also dampen down or even prevent housing price bubbles, by ensuring that there is enough affordable housing for those who need it.

But the ideologues, avatars and beneficiaries of capitalism never learn. In 2015, President Obama is reported to be 'trying to encourage private equity to return to the mortgage financing market, thus reducing the government's involvement' (Phillips, 2015). The President's plan is reported to be particularly reliant on 'a healthy secondary mortgage market'. This is despite the fact that the involvement of 'private equity' in the 'secondary mortgage market' was what caused 'the meltdown in the subprime mortgage market in 2007-2008', when 'private equity' withdrew from the mortgage market after its depredations had wreaked such havoc. It was at that point that the US federal government stepped in with a bailout through Fannie Mae, Freddie Mac, Federal Housing Administration and Veterans Affairs, and in 2015 was the investor in over 90% of the nation's mortgages. Even the ideologues can see that a federal government intervention of 90% into the mortgage market contradicts their 'small government' credo. But rather than acknowledging that government has a role to play in the economy, they cling to their belief in the beneficence of 'the market' in the teeth of the evidence.

Some of the finance industry's leading players have been highly critical of derivatives. George Soros, for example, referred to them as 'toxic instruments' and 'a destructive force', and called for them to be 'strictly regulated': 'Only those who own the underlying bonds ought to be allowed to buy them', he said (Soros, 2009). Warren Buffet said that there is 'an extraordinarily wide range' of derivatives, 'limited only by the imagination of man (or sometimes,

---

123. See the jocular remarks quoted above. Robert E. Marks (2013, 2015) mentioned a number of 'Cassandras' who warned of the dire consequences of such financial practices, and were ignored. For a warning written just before the crisis, see: Henwood, 2006.

so it seems, madmen)'. They all require 'money to change hands at some future date', sometimes 20 or more years in the future (Buffet, 2003). Buffet did famously warn against them in 2003, describing them as 'dangerous', 'time bombs, both for the parties that deal in them and the economic system' and 'financial weapons of mass destruction, carrying dangers that, while now latent, are potentially lethal'. They are 'prone to mischief' because they can be used to give a falsely inflated impression of a company's worth, as happened with Enron. He himself was trying to offload the derivatives his company had acquired when they bought out another company, but it was proving to be 'easier said than done' (Buffet, 2003: 13-15). But again, such criticism has had no influence on the male supremacist mindset that worships the power gained through wealth and destruction.

It is no accident that these financial 'commodities' were only recently invented during the hegemony of neo-liberalism. It is true that there were precedents at least as early as the eighteenth century, when the term 'fictitious capital' was in general use. But the latest version of male power has been relentless in its invention of more and more ways to amass wealth. There was money to be made for the sellers in bonuses, commissions and enormous salaries based on volume, and for the buyers as long as they kept the debt moving and didn't end up holding it when it had finally crashed and became worthless. The participants either ignored the destructiveness of this process of wealth creation, or they revelled in it as yet another indication of how powerful they were (as long as the destruction happened to someone else).

Chapter Ten: On Money

Money is paradoxical: it is the measure of all material value and yet the material of which it is made is valueless; all money is debt and yet the repayment of debt extinguishes money; government spending both is and is not dependent on taxation; sovereign governments are the issuers of currency and yet most money is created by private banks; money displays all the arrogance and dissociation of the male supremacist mindset and yet no economy is possible without it. In what follows I make an attempt to resolve these paradoxes, at least in part.

Money is at the heart of capitalism. Profit is money, wealth is money accumulated in the hands of the few, and poverty is its lack or insufficiency. Money is the measure of all material value in capitalist society, and too often, the measure of such non-material values as human rights, dignity, comfort and security as well. Everyone knows what money is, how to get it, what to do with it, and how important it is to have access to enough of it. And yet money is a very peculiar thing, and there is no agreement among the experts about what money is or where its value comes from. As Keynes expressed it with his usual dry wit: "'I know of only three people who really understand money. A professor at another university; one of my students; and a rather junior clerk at the Bank of England'" (Ingham, 2004a: 3).

Certainly, orthodox economics has little to say about money. As Ingham has noted, economists 'have had great difficulty in actually finding a place for money in their scheme' (Ingham, 1996: 508). Ingham attributes this obliviousness to '[t]wo basic methodological tenets in mainstream economics': the assumption that an economy is 'essentially barter exchange' of 'real' commodities with money merely as a neutral medium facilitating these exchanges; and the assumption that these exchanges happen between individuals for whom money is simply a means for satisfying their desires, i.e. 'the methodological individualism of the rational utility maximization model'

(Ingham, 2000). The upshot is 'the startling paradox' that 'the mainstream, or orthodox, tradition of modern economics does not attach much theoretical importance to money' (Ingham, 2004a: 7). But then, as Modern Many theorist, Ellis Winningham, noted, 'The challenge for those who wish to see progress, is to erase from their minds all traces of orthodox economic thought'. (This is the masthead statement on the website).[124]

This silence about money on the part of mainstream economics is not surprising. If capitalism is male power and money is central to that power, then one of the best ways to disguise the interests it serves is to refuse to discuss it. As L. Randall Wray put it:

> The purpose of reducing money to "arithmetic", then, is to hide the social relations behind a "natural veil" of asocial market exchange. To be sure, the veil is transparent to the over-indebted borrower, to the hungry who lacks money for food, or to the unemployed without money wages. For the committed ideologue, however, or for the professional economist, that veil completely obscures the sociological nature of money in a quite "useful" way' (Wray, 2004: 237).

Wray does not, of course, mention male power. In his account, it is 'the committed ideologue' and 'the professional economist' who find a use for the refusal to discuss money within the dominant economic discourse. Nonetheless, he does recognise that this obscurity around money is ideological, and that however 'useful' it might be, there are classes of people—the hungry, the unemployed and the over-indebted—who are disadvantaged by it.

Modern Money Theory

Modern Money Theory[125] not only promises to fill in the peculiar lacuna around money within orthodox economic theory, it makes more sense than mainstream economics' 'rational economic man' construct, its obsession with ever more sophisticated statistical models, its reliance on the beneficence of 'markets', and its insistence that governments must make 'savings' if they spend beyond their 'budgets'. It doesn't have anything to say about the role money plays in domination (of course), and I extrapolate from it in ways that those with more knowledge than I might not agree with. However, there are

---

124. http://elliswinningham.net/ – viewed 9.8.2018.

125. See, for example: Galbraith, 2012, 2014a; Ingham 2004a, b; Innes, 2004a, b; Kadmos and O'Hara, 2000; Mosler, 2010a, b; Pierce, 2013; Pixley and Harcourt, eds, 2013; Tymoigne and Wray, 2013; Wray, 2004, 2011-12, 2013, 2014; Wray, ed., 2004; and websites of the following: Bill Mitchell; Modern Monetary Theory: Real Economics; New Economic Perspectives; Levy Economics Institute; Ellis Winningham.

aspects of MMT that depict the ways in which an economy could be used for the common good. It accords with Francis Bacon's advice: 'Money is like muck: not good unless it be spread'. The way it suggests the money should be spread is primarily through full employment, backed by a governmental Job Guarantee whereby the government provides employment for all those who want to work but who are not provided for by the private sector. It also argues for adequate income-support systems for those unable to work, either temporarily or permanently. In answer to the neo-liberal question, 'Who's going to pay for it?' MMT says that a government can afford to pay for anything that can be bought in its own currency. If this kind of policy were ever to be put into practice, money could be used in the interests of all, not just for the wealthy few.

For the orthodox, there is no possibility of putting it into practice because, in their view, this is not the way an economy works. Modern Money Theory says, however, that it is not a theory but a depiction of the way an economy does actually work, and that the neo-liberal policies and practices that refuse to operate in this way are economically damaging. And certainly, the evidence is all on the MMT side, given that it is the orthodox agenda that produces boom and bust 'business cycles', depressions, recessions and global financial crises, desperate worldwide poverty, a never-ending stream of money poured into weapons of mass destruction, a refugee crisis worse than that caused by WWII, and historically unprecedented levels of wealth inequality.

Modern Money Theory is largely an extension and renewal of the work of John Maynard Keynes (among others). It is a heterodox economic framework (as opposed to the orthodoxy of mainstream economics), and a counterweight to the neo-liberal hegemony of the last several decades (Pierce, 2013). It has had little influence on government policy or public opinion, although one proponent, Stephanie Kelton, was an advisor to presidential candidate, Bernie Sanders (Wade, 2016); and it is starting to be favourably reported in the mainstream media as an alternative to the neo-classical economic theory that currently dominates government policy (Jamrisko, 2016; Mosler, 2010b; Wade, 2016). Although the mainstream view is that Keynesianism was shown to be irrelevant during the 1970s and subsequently, I have not been able to find any satisfactory reason why that might be so (notwithstanding oil price shocks, falling rates of profit, inflation and the need for surplus capital to find new markets). Rather, the repudiation of Keynesian economics would appear to be an ideological ploy justifying the resurgence of the unfettered capitalism (so-called 'inequality') we have been witnessing since the 1970s. Keynesianism fell into disrepute (in certain powerful circles), not because it had been found to be irrelevant or false, but because powerful men decided (for whatever reason) that they no longer needed to share the wealth. If that is the case, then Keynesianism, as it is developed within Modern Money Theory, might still be relevant as an account of the way an economy works. Whether that economy would still be capitalist is debatable, given the link between orthodoxy and capitalism, and given too the lack of success of Keynesian attempts to retain capitalism while ameliorating its worst effects.

Value and social relations

To start with, there is the question of where money gets its value from. The forms it takes—coins, paper, computer keystrokes—are valueless and yet it is the most valuable substance in the world. Even when the value of money was supposedly linked to gold (the 'gold standard'), the link was always more theoretical than real. As J. K. Galbraith said, 'It was an arrangement that operated with more precision in the textbooks than in the real world' (Galbraith, 1975: 156). It was not true that it was gold that gave money its value. The 'standard' was a convention set by those with the power to make the decisions about how much gold a currency was worth: 'Money of account may be linked to some material standard of value [e.g. gold] – but this is always first established *authoritatively*' (Ingham, 2002: 127—original emphasis). The exact weight of gold it took to equal the British pound sterling, for example, was a consequence of Britain's financial power: 'the gold standard was actually a gold-sterling standard, based on the credit-creating capacity of the City of London – which, in essence, was an expression of Great Britain's hegemony' (Ingham, 2002: 141n6). There are good reasons why the gold standard was only a short chapter in the history of money (Wray, 2004: 244). J. K. Galbraith dates it from 1879 to 1971 (when 'the final attenuated version' was cancelled by Richard Nixon), although most of the countries involved in World War I had abandoned it by the end of the war (Galbraith, 1975: 57, 157). Using gold to value money is not in fact the way an economy works, and Britain's return to the gold standard in 1925 was 'perhaps the most decisively damaging action involving money in modern times' (p.178). So the gold standard didn't work as a guarantee of the value of money.

The most general answer to the question of where money gets its value is 'society'—money is a social relation.[126] It is not a substance or a thing, but a 'socially constructed abstract value' (Ingham, 2002: 127). In one sense this is obvious because money is not something that occurs naturally (Ingham,

---

126. Ingham, 1996, 2000, 2002, 2004a, b, 2005; Pixley and Harcourt, eds, 2013; Wray, ed., 2004.

1996: 510). Its existence depends on certain 'social structural conditions', 'a monetary system' consisting of 'an institutionalized banking practice and constitutional legitimacy of the political authority in which the promises of banks and the states to pay [are] currency' (Ingham, 1996: 510, 515, 523). But there is more to it than that.

The commonsense view of money's value is that it comes from employment and production. People work and are given money for their time, energy and skills (or rather, they are given money if their time, energy and skills are recognised as 'employment'—there is a great deal of work that is unpaid, e.g. work that is traditionally allocated to women, work done by creative artists); and goods and services are produced and people pay to buy them, thus providing firms with the money to stay in business (paying employees and creditors, buying resources, etc.) and make a profit. It is true that, as Wray put it, 'the "real" value of money (what it can purchase domestically) is determined by what must be done to obtain it … [i.e.] by providing labour services or goods or promises to pay to the markets … [and] "transfers" provided mainly by government (welfare, subsidies … pensions and so on)' (Wray, 2004: 250). And as Geoff Harcourt said: 'Though money and financial factors are integrated in complex ways in the workings of the economy, ultimately it is real resources – work forces (sizes and skills), capital goods and natural resources – that set the upper limit at any moment of time on the size of the community's standard of living' (Harcourt, 2014). But the organisations that pay people do not produce the currency themselves (except for the government), they circulate currency that has been produced elsewhere. Employment and the production of goods and services are part of the circulation of value that makes up an economy, but the money that serves as the circulating medium gets its imprimatur from the authority of the state.

Money and the state

As Ingham (among others) has pointed out, money needs an authority to make it count as money: 'the standardisation of the [monetary] unit of account in relation to any standard of value has to be established by an authority' (Ingham, 2002: 130). The authority that establishes the value of money is the modern nation state:[127] 'the production of trust in money and

---

127. This only applies to national/federal governments, not to state, provincial or local governments because the latter do not produce their own money. They do raise revenue from the charges they levy, e.g. 'stamp duty' on property transactions in the case of the Australian states and territories, 'rates' in the case of local councils. But then, neither

modern credit money in particular has been inextricably bound up with the rise of the modern constitutional state' (Ingham, 2000). There is, according to Ingham (and Keynes), 'overwhelming historical evidence that money is indeed a "creation of the state"' (Ingham, 2002: 132). Just as government has a monopoly on the use of legitimate force, so also it has a monopoly on establishing what is to count as money. So the original source of money is government. '*[A]ll money*', says Ingham, '*is, in a very important sense, "fiat" money*' (2002, p.128—original emphasis). The Latin word 'fiat' means 'let it be done', and it refers to an official order given by someone who has the authority to make sure it is carried out.[128] In this case, the authority belongs to the nation state. It is nation states that have the sovereign power to issue their own currency. It is only nation states that have the legitimacy to ensure that money is accepted.[129]

Modern nation states are the ultimate source of money. Money only counts as money with a government imprimatur. It is true that the economy is global, that it reaches across nation states to all the countries in the world. But the currencies with which the global economy operates are national, there is no global currency. And some national currencies are more powerful than others, with the $US the most powerful of all, reflecting its domination of the world economy.

While governments are the ultimate arbiters of what counts as money, most of the money in circulation is produced by banks making loans. The unit of account is specified by the government, but its amount is largely generated by banking. Banks, as one commentator put it, play an 'active role … in the emergence and continuous renewal of capitalism' (Hayes, 2013: 41). They do this by issuing loans which become credits elsewhere in the system and are spent. Banks literally create money with these loans. The money lent out does not come from the savings of the banks' depositors. At

---

of these is called a 'tax'. Some of the revenue of this level of government comes from federal funding (Mitchell, 2010b).

128. The original authoritative 'someone' was God. The phrase, 'fiat lux'—'let there be light'— comes from the Book of Genesis account of the Creation in the Latin Vulgate bible: 'And God said, Let there be light: and there was light'. Given the arrogant entitlement of men of power, the connection is unlikely to be accidental, although it is of course as unconscious as Jung's 'huge thing'.

129. The existence of Bitcoin and the euro might seem to disprove this assertion. But e-money has yet to show that it is a serious alternative to national currencies (Ingham, 2002); and the parlous state of the economies of some of the members of the European Union would seem to indicate that there is still a connection between national sovereignty and a healthy national economy.

any one time the loans outstanding are many multiples of the amount kept as deposits in banks. So money is a creation of nation states channelled through the banking system: 'banks create money through lending with a state licence to do so' (Pixley and Harcourt, 2013: 2).

Taxation and government spending

Taxation is invariably interpreted as government revenue (except within Modern Money Theory). As one conventional source says: 'Where does the government get all of the money it spends? From taxpayers. The government does not have its own money'.[130] (This latter statement is nonsense because sovereign currency-issuing governments are the ultimate source of money). And criticism of tax havens is based on the assumption that the non-payment of taxes on the money that is hidden offshore means there is less money for public purposes.

But according to Modern Money Theory, taxation does not fund government spending:[131] 'Taxpayers don't fund anything' (Mitchell, 2010a). Money must be created in the first place before it can be paid in taxes (although in practice the creation of money and its destruction in taxation is a continuous process with no beginning or end):

> government spending (by the Treasury or spending and lending by the central bank) must come first, i.e. it must come before taxes or bond offerings [i.e. government debt]. Spending is done through monetary creation ex-nihilo [out of nothing][132] in the same way a bank lends (buying financial assets) by crediting bank accounts; taxes and bond offerings lead to monetary destruction … in the same way that loan repayments destroy bank deposits (Tymoigne and Wray, 2013: 9, 30).

So money must exist before it can be paid in tax. It is true that taxation enables governments to get access to economic resources, but not by providing the money with which to buy them. Rather, the need to pay tax underlies economic activity and is an important reason why goods and services are produced. (See the next section).

---

130. http://www.investopedia.com/ask/answers/13/government-spend-taxes.asp – viewed 9.8.2018.

131. Again, this doesn't apply to state, provincial or local governments.

132. Strictly speaking, this statement is false, given that authority discussed above. However, it means that there is no material basis for money, such as gold: 'Money is not in fact created out of nothing, but out of the kinds of social relations necessary for its existence' (Ingham, 2002: 141n3).

Moreover, actual government practice shows that tax revenue is not necessary to fund government spending, at least for some purposes. There is spending on so-called 'defence', especially the US government's perennial waging of war in other people's lands. This kind of spending[133] never seems to be restricted by any considerations that it might be unaffordable because there isn't sufficient tax revenue to fund it. Then there is the 'quantitative easing' whereby governments bailed out the 'too-big-to-fail' financial institutions in the wake of the global financial crisis. That money did not come from increased taxes, nor from spending cuts to health, education and welfare. Although subsequent cuts to spending in these areas are justified by the size of the 'budget deficit' caused by the bailouts, the money for them came from the government's issuing of its own fiat money of account. Cutting government spending is always justified by the size of the 'budget deficits' that result from such bailouts (and from the destruction caused by military spending). But the spending happens before such 'savings' are made, and 'deficits'—the amount of money the government has spent over and above its receipts—are standard operating procedures in modern economies. The US government, for example, has run a deficit in almost all years since 1960.[134]

It is not only the Modern Money Theorists (who tend towards the left-wing of the political spectrum) who say that governments can always decide to spend more than they collect in taxes. Alan Greenspan, for example, has no left-wing tendencies whatsoever but he has been known to present the same argument. He was Chairman of the US Federal Reserve Bank from 1987 to 2006 and one of the chief defenders of the financial system until the global financial crisis hit. He has been widely quoted saying: "'The United States can pay any debt it has because we can always print money to do that. So there is zero probability of default'" (Harvey, 2012). Harvey also quotes a number of other sources 'from across the political spectrum' all saying the same thing. So it would appear that, despite the inordinate influence on government policy of the mainstream view, there is general agreement that governments can afford to pay for whatever they can buy in their own currency. As long as the nation's currency is in good standing, as long as its productive capacity is underutilised (including labour that is unemployed), and as long as government spending is directed towards real wealth (rather

---

133. http://theaimn.com/wondering-cant-afford-schools-hospitals/ – viewed 9.8.2018.

134. http://www.usgovernmentspending.com/federal_deficit_chart.html – viewed 9.8.2018.

than engaging in war, propping up shonky financial empires, or motivated by the greed of the politicians), governments can spend what they like.

Thomas Piketty (2016) also seems at one point to be arguing that governments do not need tax revenues to fund their spending, at least in the short term and for certain purposes. He attributed government failure to curb the use of tax havens to the fact that '[t]heir central banks had printed enough currency to avoid the complete collapse of the financial system'. This printing of money 'avoided a widespread depression', although it was not a long-term solution to the problem of 'financial opacity' because it meant that 'the necessary structural, regulatory and fiscal reforms' had not been implemented. These reforms were necessary because 'the persistent hypertrophy of private-sector balance sheets [i.e. the massive accumulation of wealth in the hands of the few] and the extreme fragility of the system as a whole' meant that there would be further crises, and 'the economic outlook in the wealthy countries remains gloomy' (Piketty, 2013: 384 of 452). In fact, though, he subscribes to the conventional mainstream view. 'There are two main ways for a government to finance its expenses: taxes and debt' (Piketty, 2013: 377 of 452). His 'printing money' comment is a reference to the function of central banks as lenders of last resort.

Nonetheless, if central banks can 'print money' to keep the financial system from collapsing, they can also print money to fund other important economic resources like health care, aged care and the 'ageing population', women's refuges, unemployment benefits, job creation, public housing, etc. They don't need to worry about balancing the budget or going into deficit because there is no such thing as a government 'budget' (see below). Jeremy Corbyn (2015) called this a 'people's quantitative easing', that is, fiscal stimulus to invest in such productive ventures as 'new large scale housing, energy, transport and digital projects'. Writing in response to the UK conservative government's Budget, he argued that such investment 'would give our economy a huge boost: upgrading our outdated infrastructure and creating over a million skilled jobs and genuine apprenticeships. Businesses large and small would benefit from the knock-on effects to the supply chain—and again from the advantages that the upgraded infrastructure would bring'.

Government refusal to spend for the public good is a political decision, not a matter of economic necessity. Neo-liberal governments do not like spending for the common good. When Greenspan said that the US can pay any debt he was not, of course, thinking of government spending for health, education and welfare, those public goods so hated by the right wing. (It was in the context of the US debt-ceiling crisis of 2011). Nonetheless, his statement does mean that governments do not use taxes to fund their spending because their spending does not need funding apart from their capacity to issue their own sovereign currency.

The functions of taxation

So the function of taxation is not to raise government revenue. As Beardsley Ruml, a former Chairman of the Federal Reserve Bank of New York[135] (Mosler, 2010b), put it in the title of his 1946 article, 'Taxes for revenue are obsolete' (Ruml, 1946). Whatever revenue-raising role taxation might have played historically, by 1946 at least that was no longer its purpose. Ruml attributed this change to '[t]wo changes of the greatest consequence [that] have occurred in the last twenty-five years' (i.e. since 1920): improvements in the management of central banks; and the elimination of the gold standard,[136] both of which meant, he said, that the federal government was finally freed from the domestic money market. But the fact that taxation no longer counts as government revenue does not mean that taxation itself is obsolete. On the contrary, it has a number of functions, the most important of which is maintaining the value of money.

The main function of taxation is to maintain the sovereignty of the designated money of account and ensure that it is not challenged by any other currency. The primary function of taxation is to give nation states the authority to get their currency accepted as legal tender: 'in the case of a sovereign government, there is a special power—the ability to tax—that virtually guarantees that households and firms will want to accumulate the government's debt [i.e. money]' (Wray, 2011-12: Blog #4. See also the other references in footnote 2). As Ingham put it: 'the state doesn't actually need the taxpayers' money … it is the taxpayers who need the states' money to meet their tax debt' (Ingham, 2004a: 79). It is not only Modern Money Theory that says that the demand for money depends on taxation. Take, for example, the following statement from the Bank of England: '[The government has] to make sure that there will always be demand for the currency by accepting it as tax payments' (McLeay et al, 2014: 7); and many theorists throughout

---

135. The US Federal Reserve Bank ('the Fed') is the central bank of the US. It is not a single entity, however, but consists of 12 regional banks, each with a certain amount of autonomy 'based on economic considerations' but under the supervision of the Federal Reserve Board of Governors ('Structure of the Federal Reserve System') (https://www.federalreserve.gov/aboutthefed/structure-federal-reserve-system.htm – viewed 9.8.2018).

136. The US had effectively abandoned the gold standard by 1933, although the connection between gold and the $US was not finally severed until 1971.

the history of economic thought, including Adam Smith, Keynes, Marx and John Stuart Mill, also accepted versions of the 'tax-driven money' thesis (Forstater, 2004).

So the primary purpose of taxation is to ensure that the money of account designated by a nation state will be in demand because it is needed to pay taxes, as well as any other payments required by governments (fees, fines). As Wray puts it, 'Taxes drive money … there really is something standing behind the money things: the promise of the issuer to take them back' (Wray, 2011-12: Blogs #8, #52). The reason why a government's fiat money is acceptable is because 'the government's currency is the main (and usually the only) thing accepted by government in payment of taxes' (Wray, 2011-12: Blog #8). The governmental authority to designate what counts as money within each nation state is the government power to demand the payment of taxes and impose sanctions, including imprisonment, on those who do not pay. Of course, these things have a momentum and a life of their own. National currencies have continued to hold their value (more or less) despite widespread tax avoidance/evasion by multinational corporations. There have been incidents of inflation, and currently deflation is a worldwide problem, although whether tax avoidance/evasion is implicated is not clear (largely because the question is not asked, as far as I have been able to find out).

Taxation has other functions besides its role in giving authority to money. It is also instrumental in enabling governments to get access to goods and services, not by providing the money to buy them, but by requiring people to engage in productive activities in order to earn money to pay their taxes. As Mitchell put it: 'taxation is a way that the government can elicit productive resources and final goods and services from the non-government sector … [by] promot[ing] offers from private individuals to government of goods and services in return for the necessary funds to extinguish the tax liabilities' (Mitchell, 2014). And Wray said,

> While it would be incorrect … to argue that taxes "pay for" government spending, it is true that inability to impose and enforce tax liabilities will limit the amount of resources government can command. The problem is not really one of government "affordability" but rather of limited government ability to mobilize resources because it cannot impose and enforce taxes at a sufficient level to achieve the desired result. Government can always "afford" to spend more (in the sense that it can issue more currency), but if it cannot enforce and collect taxes it will not find sufficient willingness to accept its domestic currency in sales to government (Wray, 2011-12: #Blog 9).

For Ruml (who did not mention the money-driving function of taxation) there were four principal purposes served by federal taxes: to stabilise the currency (otherwise known as 'the avoidance of inflation'); to redistribute wealth and income in the interests of reducing inequality; to subsidise or penalise various industries (e.g. tariffs on imported goods so that they are not cheaper than the same goods produced locally, taxes on cigarettes and alcohol); and to expose the costs of public goods (e.g. highways, social security) (Ruml, 1946). In the most general terms, Ruml's argument is that a tax program is not an end in itself, but a means towards attaining other goals. Decisions about what those other goals might be are not a matter of tax policy, but of 'basic national policy which should be established, in the first instance, independently of any national tax program'. They are, said Ruml, 'questions as to the kind of country we want and the kind of life we want to lead'. The tax system exists to serve whatever solutions to these questions are arrived at through the democratic process of policy-making. 'The public purpose which is served', he said, 'should never be obscured in a tax program under the mask of raising revenue'.

The myth of the balanced budget[137]

However, this is not the view that has influenced government policy in relation to money in the last several decades of neo-liberalism. Neo-liberal governments insist they have 'budgets' which they are expected to 'balance' by not spending more than they collect in taxes and certainly by avoiding 'running a deficit', or even better, by generating a 'surplus' of taxes over spending.

American economist and Nobel Prize winner, Paul A. Samuelson, called the belief in balanced budgets (i.e. no spending beyond what is collected in taxes) a 'myth'. The social purpose of this myth, according to Samuelson, was similar to that of '"old fashioned religion"', that is, '"to scare people … into behaving in a way that the long-run civilized life requires"'. Civilised life required '"discipline in the allocation of resources or you will have anarchistic chaos and inefficiency"', and the belief that '"the budget must be balanced at all times"', superstition though it was, served that purpose (quoted in Wray, 2011-12: Blog #31). Wray argues that, however functional the myth was historically, it eventually became 'harmful' because it 'came to be believed as the truth'. But myth is always believed as the truth and as common sense,

---

137. Bill Mitchell referred to this as 'the neo-liberal myth-making machine', and castigated the Australian press for its ignorant, unquestioning acceptance of it (http://bilbo. economicoutlook.net/blog/?p=26512 – viewed 9.8.2018).

otherwise it would have no influence; and it was always harmful. So it cannot be that the truth status of the balanced budgets myth changed from myth to truth. It must always have been seen as truth if it was to serve its purpose, i.e. to restrain government spending (supposedly): 'it is necessary to constrain government spending with the "myth" precisely because it does not really face a budget constraint' (Blog #32).

But if governments do *not* 'really face a budget constraint', why is there any need for a myth that says they do? Samuelson said the need was for 'discipline in the allocation of resources' and a shield against 'anarchistic chaos and inefficiency', and hence a requirement of 'civilised life'. But as Wray said, 'We don't need myths. We need more democracy, more understanding, and more transparency. We do need to constrain our leaders—but not through dysfunctional superstitions' (Wray, 2010). Moreover, it is not everyone who is expected to exercise 'discipline in the allocation of resources'. When it is a question of something wanted by powerful men, whether funding for the destruction they need to bolster their delusions of grandeur ('defence') or resources to rectify their mistakes, there is no question of balancing the budget by constraining this kind of spending. As Wray put it, 'There are plenty of "keystrokes" to buy financial assets [i.e. 'quantitative easing'], but no "keystrokes" to pay wages' (Wray, 2011-12: Blog #31).

Another popular reason given for curbing government spending is that too much of it supposedly causes inflation. The Wikipedia entry on 'Government debt' grudgingly acknowledged[138] that governments did not need to go into debt in order to fund their spending because they 'can also create money'. They can 'monetize their debt' and thus remove the need to pay the interest on loans. However (the entry went on), this does not 'truly cancel ... government debt', and it 'can result in hyperinflation if used unsparingly'. At this point, the Wikipedia editors demand a citation '[citation needed]', but presumably the author(s) felt that it was sufficiently 'well-known' (within the terms of the myth) that government spending 'causes inflation' not to need any further citation.

In fact, even highly respectable segments of the mainstream are these days prepared to acknowledge that that government spending does not cause inflation. The Assistant Vice President of the Federal Reserve Bank of St Louis, for example, said he had 'found almost no effect of government spending on inflation' in a research study he conducted with Rong Li of Renmin University of China (Dupor, 2016). An economist writing in *The New*

---

138. Wikipedia entry, 'Government debt' (viewed 13.7.2016)

York Times (Mulligan, 2009) said that he had found that 'inflation rates and government spending are weakly correlated, if correlated at all'. Although he did make a bow towards orthodoxy by saying that 'it is easy to imagine high inflation as a consequence of excessive government spending', his own research study 'found significant positive correlations between inflation and government spending only in cases when military spending grew'. In other words, government spending was only inflationary when it was used for unproductive, indeed destructive, purposes. This article attracted a flurry of disagreement in the comments section, although little in the way of argument or evidence. The following restatement of orthodoxy is a typical example: 'They always taught us in school, Inflation is too much money chasing too few goods. Is the government NOT printing money to accomplish their spending agenda? If not, could you please explain how they are paying. And if they are, could you please explain how this is not an example of that adage we memorized in economics 101'.

There are genuine limits on government spending: it must be productive spending (i.e. not on warmongering or on extreme luxury goods for politicians' personal consumption), and the productive capacity must be there (i.e. not siphoned off by multinational corporations). But the purpose of a budgeting process is not to 'balance the budget', but to disclose what the government is spending on what and how much, and to hold them accountable (insofar as that is possible given the undemocratic nature of neo-liberal governance). But governments are not limited in their spending by the size of their 'budgets' because they do not operate with budgets. They are the sovereign producers of their own currency and, within these limits, they can spend what they like.

Government debt and the Memorable Alliance

'[The Australian government] are playing right into the hands of the super-rich who want a permanent pool of unemployment, a low paid workforce and less government interference in corporate oversight (Kelly, 2016)

One of the things that supposedly unbalances budgets is government debt. In accordance with the myth, budgets get unbalanced because governments need to go into debt to finance their spending (as well as collecting taxes). But if we accept the thesis that governments 'can always print money' to pay off their debts (as Greenspan put it), why do they need to go into debt in the first place? The short answer is that government debt is an important support for private profit.

The function government debt plays in the modern money system originated in a pact between the two arms of the modern ruling class, capital and the nation state. Max Weber called this a 'memorable alliance', and it was exemplified by the founding of the Bank of England in 1694.[139] For Weber, the modern economy was a consequence of this alliance, which was originally for the purposes of waging war. The capitalist class agreed to lend the nation states money to finance their wars:

> at the beginning of modern history, the various countries engaged in the struggle for power needed ever more capital for political reasons and because of the expanding money economy. This resulted in that memorable alliance between the rising states and the sought-after and privileged capitalist powers that was a major factor in creating modern capitalism (Weber, 1978: 353).

The alliance had been preceded by a struggle for dominance between the nation state and those 'privileged capitalist powers'. At the time these were largely merchants who used private credit for their transactions ('bills of exchange', etc.), thus setting them in competition with the monarchs who were issuing their own sovereign currency (Ingham, 2004a: 78-9). The eventual solution was to share the production of money between banks and the state. As Geoff Mann put it:

> The alliance made sense for both parties. The state recognised the importance of the fact that the banking system can create an elastic supply of credit-money, fuelling economic growth. Capital recognised that money could only do the work it was supposed to do across space and time if it was secured by a strong territorial state (Mann, 2013: 202).

This solution ensured that the wealthy would lend to government because it put an end to the arbitrary refusal of monarchs to repay loans. The wealthy knew their loans would be repaid because they were managed through the Bank of England (and later central banks in other countries), over which they themselves had control.

Taxation was part of the settlement: wealthy money-holders would lend to the state and the state would levy taxes in order to make the interest payments. Thus the dividends of the state's creditors were '*believed* to be secured by taxes' (Ingham, 2004: 79—original emphasis). This is the purpose of Samuelson's 'myth of the balanced budget': to reassure the government's creditors that their money is safe and that the state is doing its best to make sure it is. So an important function of taxation in the eyes of 'this brood of

---

139. Ingham, 2004: 115; Mann, 2013: 201-2; Pixley, 2013: 273; Rose and Spiegel, 2015: 45n31.

bankocrats, financiers, *rentiers*, brokers, stock-jobbers, etc.' (Marx, 1976: 919) is its role in securing their money.

The real reason governments go into debt is not to finance their spending, but to service that long-standing alliance between the nation state and that brood so eloquently described by Marx. These currently consist of corporations and wealthy individuals who own the bonds, securities, etc, issued by governments. As one commentator put it:

> Public borrowing provides corporate welfare in the form of risk-free income flows to the rich. It allows them to safely keep their funds in bonds during uncertain times and provides a risk-free benchmark on which to price other, riskier financial products (Kelly—comment on Kelly, 2016).

So the beneficiaries of government debt are the rich,[140] many of them foreigners.[141] Mitchell calls the issuing of public debt 'corporate welfare', and asks, 'Why would we want to provide government annuities to private profit-seeking investors?' All the arguments justifying public debt, he said, 'can be reduced to special pleading by speculators for risk free assets' (Mitchell, 2015).

This is not the way it is presented to the general public. There is little mention of the fact that government debt is largely owned by the wealthy. Instead, discourses on public debt engage in the spurious equality of individualism: 'Governments issue debt whenever they borrow from *the public* ... *people* are interested in how many goods they can buy with the wealth their bonds represent ' (Seater, 2008—emphases added). It is still widely believed that those who are liable for the repayment of government debt are 'the taxpayers': 'When the government borrows, it promises to repay the lender. To make those repayments the government ultimately will have to raise extra taxes' (Seater, 2008). Again: 'As a government draws in much its income from its population, government debt is an indirect debt of the taxpayers'.[142]

---

140. Strictly speaking, not all of those who hold government debt are rich. Much of it is held by such financial institutions as superannuation funds and pension funds, which invest on behalf of middle- and even low-income earners. However, it is only the rich who have sufficient clout to influence government policy, e.g. the 'bond vigilantes' who 'protest ... monetary or fiscal policies [they] consider ... inflationary by selling bonds' (Wikipedia entry, 'Bond vigilante' -- viewed 8.6.2016).

141. In early 2004, foreigners held nearly half ($1.7 trillion) of the $3.5 trillion of US debt held by private investors (http://www.econlib.org/library/Enc/GovernmentDebtandDeficits. html – viewed 9.8.2018.

142. https://www.statista.com/statistics/268177/countries-with-the-highest-public-debt/ – viewed 9.8.2018.

The theory of fiat currency exposes these statements as false. Governments do not draw their income from the population. Sovereign governments that issue their own currency with the power of taxation to command resources do not have 'income'.

But the belief that government debt must be repaid by 'the taxpayers' is all part of the myth. If governments do not fund their spending through taxation, they do not need to go into debt either. As the above-mentioned Wikipedia entry acknowledged. 'Government debt is not the only method … of financing government operations … Governments can also create money'. Wikipedia immediately slips into the ideological excuse that forbids governments to 'create money' to fund their operations, i.e. that it would cause, not just inflation, but 'hyperinflation'. But governments 'create money' all the time. It is true that they licence banks to do most of the creation through loans. But the money in which the loans and their repayments are made is that which is stipulated by the nation state. It is not up to the banks to say what currency constitutes a loan and its repayment. They have to use the already-existing currency.

But ideology is impervious to argument and evidence. Its function is to justify the power of might-makes-right. In this case, the belief that taxes fund the repayment of government debt is consonant with our current system of domination whereby the rich profit from government debt and the rest of us pay for it when governments are prevented from spending for the public good by the myth of the 'balanced budget'. It is the same logic that informed government policy after the global financial crisis—the wealthy profited from the crisis and the rest of us paid the price. The fact that taxes cannot be used to repay government debt doesn't fit with the ideological embrace of a hierarchical social order where wealth accumulation by the favoured (or ruthless) few is the highest good that must be served by everybody. It is a social order of exploitation and appropriation in every sphere and the social arrangements of money are no exception.

Money and domination

Nonetheless, false though it might be, the myth is powerfully influential because it services the society of domination. The nation states that do the bidding of the wealthy operate *as if* governments needed to go into debt to fund their spending because government debt benefits the wealthy. They operate *as if* government revenue were dependent on taxation because wealth is created by appropriation from the non-wealthy and the wealthy can (and do) avoid paying taxes. Nation states operate *as if* governments had budgets (just like households) and hence could run out of money if they spend too much. The function of this latter belief is to prevent governments from spending for the common good and thereby reducing inequality and impeding the progress of wealth creation. This is the logic behind the neo-liberal austerity programs (and the 'structural adjustment' imposed on the Third World) that have decimated national economies and created massive levels of inequality while the global wealthy grow richer and richer. These are the 'strong vested interests that militate against governments using their fiscal capacity' for the common good, including full employment (Mitchell, 2017).

Because of money's centrality to capitalism, its social relations are those of domination. As Geoff Mann put it: 'modern capitalist money … is non-democratic by definition' (Mann, 2013: 198). The 'political constraints' (Wray, 2011-12: Blog #5) on government spending involve the expectation that governments will operate in the interests of the powerful. Claims to democracy, the protests of citizens, and periodic flashes of decency within government itself, will sometimes push them in the direction of the common good. But domination rules (by definition) and will have its way (unless that is recognised and resisted). The social purpose served by Samuelson's myth is not a 'civilising' discipline for everyone, but a discipline demanded of governments in the interests of wealth accumulation, and an imposition on the powerless by the powerful.

Conclusion

Given how central money is to male power, it is hardly surprising that it is propped up by ideological justifications serving to establish and maintain that power. Part of this is the peculiar silence about money on the part of orthodox economics although, given its role as the ideological justification for the capitalist economy, that is hardly surprising. Other ideological justifications are: the insistence on the need for balanced budgets; the belief that government spending causes inflation; and the belief that governments need taxes and debt to fund their spending. Whether or not a government can afford to spend money depends, not on the amount of tax it can raise (or at least not directly), but on its political commitment. It is the right-wing political commitment of neo-liberal governments that cries poor when it is a question of funding for the common good, and slavishly obeys the funding demands of powerful men. Assertions that certain projects are unaffordable because the tax revenue is not there to pay for them are spurious. The way money currently operates, and is seen to operate, is consonant with the economic system of capitalism which enables the accumulation of wealth in the hands of the ruthless few, but generates powerlessness in large proportions of the population. These are the social relations of money as it is currently constituted.

To the extent that government serves the interests of powerful elites, money becomes an instrument of domination, accumulated in the hands of the few and inadequately supplied to the rest of the population. To the extent that government serves the public interest though, money as a social institution belongs to all of us. The idea that money might belong to the whole citizenry is entailed by the very notion of a democracy that allows people control over their own lives. It is also enshrined in the welfare state, however meanly.

But the social institution of money is still constituted by male power, privilege and prestige, which appear to need helplessness and a stark contrast between wealth and poverty. Domination (justified by neo-liberal ideology) demands that governments not alleviate that poverty by spending that would benefit everyone. (And let us not forget the cruelty that is a crucial aspect of domination). Of course the powerful are not omnipotent, and every self-styled 'democratic' government must use some of its spending capability to provide important public goods. But even that democratic principle is being eroded by privatisation as wealthy men grab every resource they can with the collusion of so-called 'democratic' governments. Driven by their arrogant sense of entitlement they take what they can, while their dissociation leads them to disregard, not only the rights and needs of others, but also their own immersion in the human condition. Unless it is recognised that the problem is not 'inequality' but domination, and domination by men created by a monstrous system that they themselves create, we have not identified the root of the problem.

Chapter Eleven: Capitalism Redeemed?

Would it be possible to separate the technical aspects of capitalism out from its ethically reprehensible aspects, so that it operates for and not against human well-being? Could we have the employment, the wealth creation and the 'sustained dynamism' without male domination? Is it possible that some of its technical aspects might be reclaimable for the benefit of everyone (rather than simply for the ruthless few), that capitalism could be revamped with the male supremacist aspects removed while retaining the mechanisms for producing and distributing resources?

It has been (fairly) plausibly argued that capitalism is a good thing, even by those who reject its worst aspects. For example, David Simon, creator of the social commentary television drama, *The Wire*, and a speaker at the Festival of Dangerous Ideas in Sydney in 2013, is highly critical of capitalism, while at the same time arguing that it has its good points. In an article published in *The Guardian* (Simon, 2013), he did hold capitalism accountable for 'the mess we've dug for ourselves'. This mess involves a nation divided into haves and have-nots (the US), with falling family incomes, with around 10% to 15% of the population 'no longer necessary to the operation of the economy', and with a diminution of labour which means 'in human terms ... [that] human beings are worth less'. It is characterised by 'the abandonment of basic services, such as ... functional public education', by the highest rate of imprisonment 'in the history of mankind' fuelled by 'an alleged war on dangerous drugs that is in fact merely a war on the poor', and by a corruption of the electoral process to serve the interests of the rich.

At the same time, Simon said that capitalism 'provided a lot more freedom', and that it turned a working class 'that had no discretionary income at the beginning of the [twentieth] century ... into a consumer class ... [with] money to buy all the stuff that they needed to live'. 'Capitalism', he said, 'is a remarkable engine ... for producing wealth ... if you're trying to build a society and have that society advance. You wouldn't want to go forward at this point without it'. He was not arguing for capitalism unalloyed, but for a capitalism reined in by socialist values such as 'collective bargaining and union wages', by the kinds of values expressed in the New Deal and Great Society initiatives of the 1930s and 1960s in the US. What he was arguing for was a society that 'includes the best aspects of socialistic thought and of free-market capitalism', and that 'every stratum … has a stake in, that they all share'.

However, his defence of capitalism is unconvincing. The notion that capitalism is somehow connected to freedom is pure ideology. Right-wing apologists for capitalism are hugely enamoured of 'freedom'/'liberty', but not for everyone. Bertrand Russell put it well: 'Advocates of capitalism are very apt to appeal to the sacred principles of liberty, which are embodied in one maxim: the fortunate must not be restrained in the exercise of tyranny over the unfortunate' (*Sceptical Essays* Chapter 13). As for that working class with 'money to buy all the stuff that they needed to live', under the neo-liberal hegemony of the last few decades, capitalism has abandoned it in the rich nations in favour of the hyper-exploitation of people in the Third World, who are certainly not paid enough money to buy what they need to live. And, yes, capitalism does create wealth, but not for everyone, as current levels of inequality demonstrate all too clearly.

Nonetheless, it may be that humanising capitalism is within the bounds of possibility, despite the failure of the Keynesian experiment. Small and medium-sized businesses, for example, are capitalist—they require capital in order to exist, they generate profit, they benefit from the legal system of property relations, they employ people who are paid wages and salaries—but their size means that they are less prone to the unlimited entitlement and dehumanised dissociation characteristic of a male supremacist, masculinised culture. By definition, the extent of their entitlement is limited and they tend to produce real goods and services. It is true that small businesses cannot avoid participating in the process of turning everything into commodities, including people, or being tied into the global economy in one way or another; but then, neither can individuals. But they engage in human-sized economic activities and hence promise to add to, rather than detract from, human well-being.

Even large-scale enterprises can perhaps counteract capitalism's inherent tendency to dehumanise. To the extent that enterprises are ethically managed, pay their employees a living wage, pay their taxes, don't pollute or otherwise damage the environment, produce commodities that contribute to human well-being, and take responsibility for disposing of those commodities once they have reached the end of their useful life, it is possible that there could be an economy that acknowledged our common humanity. However, it is unlikely that that economy would be recognisably capitalist.

We have the economic system we have because male domination breeds the kind of men we have, and the kinds of men it breeds maintain the system that gives them power, violently if necessary. Unless the problem is tackled at its root—the belief that only men count as 'human' and the social arrangements based on that belief—nothing much will change. Many of the methods by which wealth was (and still is) concentrated in the hands of the few—through violence and the expropriation of those powerless to resist, and through financial bubbles that eventually burst taking ordinary people's money with it—display that typical arrogant entitlement and utter disregard for the needs and rights of others characteristic of male supremacy.

The capitalist economy is one of the chief domains within which a masculine sense of entitlement that knows no bounds exerts itself. Capitalism creates the wealth that breeds both the rich men and their conviction that they can get away with anything. Its dissociation from any genuine humanity is shown by its exclusive focus on wealth-creation, its heedlessness to the destruction it causes—to the environment, to those it employs to do its dirty work, and to those it will not employ at all—its rapacity that knows no bounds, its demands that the world bow to its will—governments and populations alike—and its creation of a finance industry utterly disconnected from any real productive activity whatsoever. Capitalism is male supremacy gone mad, only marginally less crazy than fascism, war and mass violence (to which it periodically resorts). The only saving grace for the human race is that its worst depredations meet with resistance, and it doesn't always have everything its own way. But (to vary a well-known saying) power over others corrupts and domination corrupts absolutely.[143] Being in a position to have all your wants satisfied without regard for the rights of others, or (more to the point) benefiting from a system where some prosper at the expense of the many, even at the expense of the whole of humanity, is destructive; and to make matters worse, given the power and reach of the capitalist economy we are all made complicit, whether we will it or not. Capitalism is the historically new form of male rule, the bourgeois or 'modern' form that appeared once the 'traditional', feudal form had been overcome. To vary a saying of Marx

---

143. The phrase, 'Power tends to corrupt, and absolute power corrupts absolutely', appeared in a letter written in 1887 by the first Baron Lord Acton (1834-1902). He was not the originator of the idea, which was primarily a critique of the absolute monarchies (hence

and Engels: the history of all societies is the history of domination,[144] and capitalist society is no exception.

Capitalism is another ruse of male supremacy, a system of economic and social organisation whose primary reason for existence is the accumulation of wealth for a few powerful men (along with those women who benefit materially from their connections to men or from willing participation in institutions established for the aggrandisement of men). In that sense its purpose is not, as the jargon goes, 'the efficient allocation of scarce resources' (Rochon and Rossi, 2003: xx), still less the satisfaction of human needs and a contribution to genuine human well-being. This is not to deny that some people have benefited materially from capitalism, and not all of them could be called rich and powerful. However, there are crucial aspects of capitalism which are inherently dehumanising because they feed a voracious appetite for entitlement without limits and serve no genuinely human purpose (such as material comfort and security for all).

Perhaps capitalism could be redeemed for genuinely human purposes. It has been responsible for some important developments in human well-being, and it would seem that we are stuck with it after all. However, in order for that redemption to happen, the functions it serves for male domination must be acknowledged and resisted; and given how difficult it is to acknowledge, much less challenge, its nature as a system of domination (still less the arrogant masculinity that drives its worst depredations), that happy outcome is a long way off.

The odds in favour of humanising capitalism look vanishingly small. The power that enormous wealth brings tends to corrupt and dehumanise both its owners and its worshippers (who are not necessarily wealthy themselves), and to make the rest of us accessories through lack of alternative ways of supplying ourselves with the basic necessities of life. Not only does enormous size give rise to dissociated arrogance, capitalism's reason for existence—its profit—depends on commodification. This is dehumanising in at least two ways. It puts a price on everything, including basic necessities, while failing to provide everyone with the income necessary to buy those necessities; and its labour market puts a price on people, while excluding from its sphere of value, and hence from the resources necessary for maintaining life itself, those whose labour power is unwanted.

---

the repetition of the word 'absolute') (http://www.phrases.org.uk/meanings/absolute-power-corrupts-absolutely.html – viewed 9.8.2018).

144. What Marx and Engels actually said in *The Communist Manifesto* was: 'The history of all hitherto existing society is the history of class struggles'.

None of this is absolute, and it is possible that it could be managed to obviate the worst consequences, e.g. through tax and welfare systems that prevent the hyper-accumulation of wealth and redistribute it. But if capitalism is to be transformed into a humanised form, the problem has to be acknowledged first. Its dehumanising tendencies must be recognised in order to be counteracted. That would mean challenging and reining in those aspects of the system that enable masculinist arrogance and dissociation, along with the wealth and power to rule the world at the expense of large segments of the earth's population, and ultimately of everyone. First and foremost, it means recognising the masculinity of capitalism, admitting that a driven need for wealth and power is something that a male supremacist culture breeds in (some) men. What follows from that as a program for action, I don't know; and neither do I know where the power to do the reining in might come from. However, it seems to me that the fact that the masculinity of capitalism is never mentioned is significant factor in maintaining the system. If that is so, then saying it aloud is a small step towards challenging its legitimacy.

For there is an end. Converting the world's resources into money can continue only as long as there are resources to convert. Once they are gone, money too will become valueless. As Claudia von Werlhof argued:

> the abstract wealth created for accumulation implies the destruction of nature as concrete wealth. The result is a "hole in the ground" and next to it a garbage dump with used commodities, outdated machinery and money without value. However, once all concrete wealth (which today consists mainly of the last natural resources) will be gone, abstract wealth will disappear as well. It will, in Marx's words, "evaporate". The fact that abstract wealth is not real wealth will become obvious, and so will the answer to the question of [what kind of] wealth modern economic activity has really created. In the end it is nothing but monetary wealth (and even this mainly exists virtually or on accounts) that constitutes a monoculture controlled by a tiny minority (Werlhof, 2015).

Capitalism and the male supremacy it upholds currently make life a misery for billions while the rich get richer and richer. But once it has destroyed the earth, there will be nowhere for anyone to hide. Once there is nothing left to buy, money won't save you, no matter how much of it you might have. The solution is simple: spread the money around (as Francis Bacon advised 500 years ago), so that everyone can buy basic necessities. This is the only kind of economy that can justifiably be called healthy. Part of that spreading would involve government spending for the common good, including providing paid employment for those the private sector won't employ and adequate benefit payments for those who can't work. It would also involve collecting taxes from the wealthy so that they can't stockpile money elsewhere than the economy that produced it. These suggestions are wildly unrealistic, given the overriding hegemony of the right wing worldwide. But the impossibilities are political and hence within the sphere of human action. The problem is that those with the power choose not to exercise it in the interests of the common good, and it may be too late anyway.

Chapter Twelve: Fascism

the SS was the ideal incarnation of fascism's overt assertion of the righteousness of violence, the right to have total power over others and to treat them as absolutely inferior. It was in the SS that this assertion seemed most complete, because they acted it out in a singularly brutal and efficient manner; and because they dramatized it by linking themselves to certain aesthetic standards. The SS was designed as an elite military community that would be not only supremely violent but also supremely beautiful (Sontag, 1974: 321).

Capitalism and fascism

Hannah Arendt argued that capitalism was responsible for fascism because it produced the social conditions that gave rise to it, especially during its imperialist phase, which Arendt located in the forty years from 1884 to the beginning of the First World War. 'Some of the fundamental aspects of this time', she said, 'appear so close to totalitarian phenomena of the twentieth century that it may be justifiable to consider the whole period a preparatory stage for coming catastrophes' (Arendt, 1951: 123). Strictly speaking, Arendt was talking about totalitarianism, not fascism, and she made a distinction between the two. 'Mussolini's Fascism', she said, 'up to 1938 was not totalitarian but just an ordinary nationalist dictatorship developed logically from a multiparty democracy' (p.257). Nonetheless, her prime example of totalitarianism was Nazism, which has come to be regarded as the exemplar of fascism and its most extreme form (e.g. Theweleit, 1987, 1989).

So capitalism's imperialist phase prepared the ground for Nazism. Capitalism needed imperialism, she argued, in order to find investment opportunities for its surplus wealth. The tremendously increased wealth produced by capitalist production under a social system based on maldistribution, she argued, had resulted in 'oversaving'—that is, an accumulation of capital condemned to idleness if it couldn't find opportunities beyond 'the existing national capacity for production and consumption':

> This money was actually superfluous, needed by nobody though owned by a growing class of somebodies. The ensuing crises and depressions during the decades preceding the era of imperialism ... forced the bourgeoisie to realize for the first time that the original sin of simple robbery, which centuries ago had made possible the "original accumulation of capital" (Marx) ... had eventually to be repeated lest the motor of accumulation suddenly die down. In the face of this danger, which threatened not only the bourgeoisie but the whole nation with a catastrophic breakdown in production, capitalist producers understood that the forms and laws of their production system "from the beginning had been calculated for the whole earth" [quoting Rosa Luxemburg] (Arendt, 1951: 147-8).

For this notion of superfluous capital and its role in imperialism, Arendt referenced J. A. Hobson, *Imperialism* (London, 1905, 1938), who 'gave a masterly analysis of the driving economic forces and motives [of imperialism] as well as some of its political implications' (Arendt, 1951: 147n41). Subsequent research has found that Hobson was wrong to suggest that imperialism was motivated by a need to find investment for surplus capital, for the simple reason that the colonies received very little of the capital exported by the chief capital-exporting countries up to 1914 (Ingham, 1984: 121-6).

Nonetheless, whether or not imperialism was necessary to put surplus capital to work, it was certainly a capitalist enterprise; and just as capitalism has always done, it operated through brute force. In Arendt's view, however, imperialism heightened capitalism's brutality beyond previous levels. It taught the capitalist ruling class that it could get away with anything, it created racism, and it found a use for the alienated masses capitalism had already produced, in the 'completely unprincipled power politics' (Arendt, 1951: 156) imperialism visited on its overseas 'dominions'.

Imperialism showed capitalism that in foreign lands it could exercise power to the utmost level of ferocity and never be called to account. The imperialist phase of the capitalist ruling class made violence and power for its own sake into deliberate policy:

> Here, in backward regions without industries and political organization, where violence was given more latitude than in any Western country, the so-called laws of capitalism were actually allowed to create realities ... Only when exported money succeeded in stimulating the export of power could it accomplish its owners' designs. Only the unlimited

accumulation of power could bring about the unlimited accumulation of capital (Arendt, 1951: 136-7).

While violence has always been implicit in political action and power is its ultimate rationale, under imperialism violence and power unrestrained by law became 'a destructive principle that will not stop until there is nothing left to violate' (pp.137-8).

Imperialism also exacerbated racism, the most familiar public face of fascism.[145] Racism, or at least xenophobia, preceded the imperialist era, but imperialist capitalism had a peculiar affinity for racism, 'the main ideological weapon of imperialistic politics' (Arendt. 1951: 160). Arendt found an account of that affinity in Hobbes' *Leviathan*. Hobbes was writing in the seventeenth century, long before the period Arendt was describing, but at a time when the English capitalist class had already been making its economic power felt for around a century. He argued that a body politic serving the interests of this new class required 'the exclusion in principle of the idea of [a common] humanity' (Arendt, 1951: 157), because the 'social contract' that was the basis for society was possible only within a nation state. Foreigners, therefore, were 'necessarily outside of the human contract', and relations with them were still at 'the perpetual war of all against all' stage that the social contract within each nation state had managed to rein in (at least, according to Hobbes). Once the notion of a common humanity has been abolished, Arendt said,

> then nothing is more plausible than a theory according to which brown, yellow, or black races are descended from some other species of apes than the white race, and that all together are predestined by nature to war against each other until they have disappeared from the face of the earth ... race is, politically speaking, not the beginning of humanity but its end, not the origin of peoples but their decay, not the natural birth of man but his unnatural death (Arendt, 1951: 157).

But while imperialism may have exacerbated capitalism's brutality, that brutality is inherent in an economic system that benefits the ruthless few and excludes so much of humanity. Already throughout the nineteenth century, capitalism's 'unending process of property accumulation' had created massive

---

145. As I argue at length below, fascism is the most extreme expression of a masculinity of entitlement and dissociation, its central organising principle first and foremost the fear and hatred of women.

inequality (Arendt, 1951: 142). Whatever it did with its 'superfluous capital', it also created 'superfluous' people[146]—those for whom capital had no use:

> Older than the superfluous wealth was another by-product of capitalist production: the human debris that every crisis, following invariably upon each period of industrial growth, eliminated permanently from producing society (Arendt, 1951: 150).

This 'mob, begotten by the monstrous accumulation of capital' (Arendt, 1951: 151), owed no allegiance to a society that had nothing to offer them. They were 'free of all principles' (p.156) and utterly without care or concern for other human beings, because state and society had no care or concern for them. Because imperialism was also devoid of ethical principles, it found this quality of the mob useful for what it needed to do in foreign lands. The massive accumulation of wealth led the bourgeoisie to the conclusion that 'the "original sin" of "original accumulation of capital" would need additional sins to keep the system going … superfluous wealth created by overaccumulation … needed the mob's help to find safe and profitable investment' (Arendt, 1951: 156).

But while the other European nations, especially Great Britain, managed by and large to keep the 'alliance between capital and mob' (Arendt, 1951: 155) confined to their overseas 'possessions', the German bourgeoisie finally 'threw off the mask of hypocrisy and openly confess[ed] its relationship to the mob, calling on it expressly to champion its property interests' (p.156). The reason this happened in Germany, rather than in England, Holland or France, was because the German bourgeoisie was less secure than in other countries. It did not fully develop until the latter half of the nineteenth century, and that development was accompanied by the growth of a strong, revolutionary working-class movement:

> the German bourgeoisie staked everything on the Hitler movement and aspired to rule with the help of the mob, but then it turned out to be too late. The bourgeoisie succeeded in destroying the nation-state but won a Pyrrhic victory; the mob proved quite capable of taking care of politics

---

146. This notion of 'superfluous' people was addressed more recently by Zygmunt Bauman with his concept of 'wasted lives' (Bauman, 2004) (although he did not reference Arendt). The chief culprit in this wasting of human potential Bauman named 'modernity'. He did acknowledge that capitalism ('globalization', 'economic progress') had something to do with 'horrors of exclusion' (p.128), but only as one aspect of 'modernity', not as the prime cause. The other aspect was 'that of life politics'. However, he connected life politics to the 'forces of globalization', which 'blends with similar fears reeking from perishing inter-human bonds and disintegrating group solidarities' (p.129). But it is not clear where the stench pervading 'life politics' comes from, if not from capitalism, especially as his prime exemplar of a culture of disposability is consumer society.

by itself and liquidated the bourgeoisie along with all other classes and institutions (Arendt, 1951: 123-4).

Arendt's argument is similar to Marx's argument that capitalism creates the means for its own destruction. In Arendt's words: 'the mob is not only the refuse but also the by-product of bourgeois society, directly produced by it and therefore never quite separable from it' (Arendt, 1951: 155). It differs from Marx's account, however, in that Arendt had none of Marx's optimism. In her account, there was no proletariat potentially able to lead us all to the better world of the classless society. Instead, capitalism produced masses of alienated people whose enraged resentment at their deprivations gave rise to a nihilism that produced nothing but violence and more violence, death and more death.

What Arendt did not fully investigate was the role of scapegoats in deflecting the attention of 'superfluous' populations away from the real cause of their ills and towards innocent targets. Her focus was on anti-Semitism and the historical situation of the Jews, and she objected to the theory of the scapegoat because it implied that the Jews were simply helpless victims of circumstances outside their control, rather than active historical participants. But by keeping her focus solely on the historically specific situation of the Jews, she failed to see the wider implications of scapegoating and its perennial function for domination, whether totalitarian or 'democratic'. She failed to see that scapegoating is the central defining characteristic of fascism. The dehumanisation of certain categories of people and their exclusion from human rights, even the right to life itself, is what motivates fascist brutality. But that dehumanisation is part of capitalism's standard operating procedure of producing 'superfluous' populations—those who have no right to basic necessities and hence to the means for living in material comfort and security. Masculinity reacts with enraged entitlement to such deprivations ('the mob'), but domination requires that the rage be directed elsewhere than the true source of the deprivations. Women are perennial scapegoats for male rage, but 'other' categories of men serve a similar purpose—to deflect the rage away from the system of domination that deprives people of their human capabilities.

Nonetheless, in connecting capitalism and totalitarian fascism, Arendt was sounding a warning. She was saying that capitalism's standard operating procedures, if unchecked, can lead to humanity's worst nightmare, and she was showing us that we have already been provided with an example of just that eventuality. She argued that accumulating massive wealth and degrading people by treating them as superfluous is an evil that just keeps getting worse. Today's version of the same male arrogance and crazed dissociation is heading in the same direction. While the details might differ, much of what is happening in the world today is fascistic in the sense that people are being treated as less than human by capitalism's unchecked standard operating procedures, e.g. the land grabs that deprive people of their traditional ways of life and wreck their environments; the taking of industry 'off-shore' that destroys workforce opportunities in the rich nations in order to cheapen labour power by creating unsafe, degrading, badly-paid working conditions elsewhere. And when people are not even needed by capital they are treated as less than human, whether deprived of basic necessities, or treated as nothing but impediments to wealth-creation.

The period Arendt was talking about culminated in Nazism and other forms of totalitarianism, accompanied by the Great Depression and bracketed by two world wars. Since then there hasn't been another world war (yet), but there has always been war somewhere in the world; and with the rise of murderous radical islamism, the West (and the US in particular) has been presented with another excuse to intensify its own murderous regime. US warmongering has created yet more generations of 'superfluous' populations. Arendt argued that even slavery was preferable to the statelessness of people forced out of their countries of origin. At least slaves 'still belonged to some sort of human community; their labor was needed, used, and exploited, and this kept them within the pale of humanity' (Arendt, 1951: 297). She was speaking about the refugees flooding the world to escape the horrors of the two world wars and the genocidal policies of Nazism, who were outside 'the pale of humanity', as least as far as the powers-that-be are concerned. Again today, there are people fleeing their homelands in their millions, banished by war, massacres, bombings, drone strikes and planned exterminations, largely orchestrated or aided by the US and its allies. And again today, they are welcomed nowhere, subjected to policies and practices excluding them from humanity by violating their human rights (e.g. the indefinite detention of asylum seekers perpetrated by recent successive Australian governments). This is fascism.

There hasn't been a Great Depression either, but there have been numerous recessions, the latest and greatest (so far) being the 2008 global financial crisis, often referred to as 'the Great Recession'. The perpetrators are still in power, still doing exactly what they were doing to bring about the crisis. It would seem that the lessons of the twentieth century are still to be learnt, and the dissociated arrogance of men hasn't diminished. There was an interregnum during the twentieth century after the Second World War, with the introduction of the welfare state and Keynesian curbs on capital. But by the 1970s, the system of domination had started to expand again, justified ideologically by what has come to be known as neo-liberalism.

In the case of the 'superfluous' people, what Arendt is describing is the mindset of the populations in the grip of the totalitarian regimes (specifically Nazism), but she could also be describing many of the more recent examples of crazed dissociation: the seemingly endless, murderous involvement of the US and its allies in the Middle East in order to control the supplies of oil that fuel the capitalist economy;[147] the gamblers in the finance industry who brought on the global financial crisis; Tea Party Republicans in the US House of Representatives, who held the nation to ransom because they objected to legislation that made health care more affordable for more people; and the rise and rise of Donald Trump and his henchmen to the US presidency. Arendt called this nihilism and regarded it as 'unexpected and unpredicted' (Arendt, 1951: 316), but it has clearly persisted. This is only to be expected if, as I argue, dissociation is central to male supremacy's culture of masculinity. Nihilism is another name for that dissociation.

The centrality of masculinity

The historical experience of fascism, of which Nazism is the most extreme example, provides an object lesson for what can happen when the violent dehumanisation engendered by masculinity's dissociated arrogance is bolstered by official sanction and comes to prevail across a whole nation. Fascism is what society looks like when the arrogant entitlement and crazed dissociation of male supremacy is unleashed. Fascism is the most glaring public example of the physical brutality aspect of male supremacist masculinity,[148] and men who embrace fascism are among the most glaring exemplars of the character structure of male supremacy. Fascism is what male supremacy looks like when it no longer bothers to disguise itself as something other than it is. But

---

147. 'Not only does [the US invasion of Iraq] constitute an attempt to control the global oil spigot and hence the global economy through domination over the Middle East. It also constitutes a powerful US military bridgehead on the Eurasian land mass which, when taken together with its gathering alliances from Poland down through the Balkans, yields it a powerful geostrategic position in Eurasia with at least the potentiality to disrupt any consolidation of a Eurasian power that could indeed be the next step in that endless accumulation of political power that must always accompany the equally endless accumulation of capital' (Harvey, 2003: 85).

148. The most obvious examples in the private sphere are what is euphemistically called (with characteristic agent-deletion) 'domestic violence' or 'violence against women', and male sexual abuse of children.

while there is an academic literature on the masculinity of fascism, and even on the continuities between fascism and 'normative' masculinity, there is little awareness of the relevance of male domination to fascism. There is little recognition of the fact that any understanding of the connections between fascism and masculinity must come from an understanding of the nature of male domination, that the type of masculinity that lends itself to fascism is a male supremacist masculinity, not something inherent in men.

For example, Klaus Theweleit, whose sprawling two-volume work on masculinity and fascism, *Male Fantasies*, is the definitive work on the subject, frequently couches his argument in individualist terms, as though the issue were about types of men:

> Is there a true *boundary* separating "fascists" from "nonfascist" men? Is it useful to apply the term "fascist" only to ardent party members and functionaries, and to regard the remainder as deluded, opportunistic, or forced into compliance? Or is it true, as many feminists claim, that fascism is simply the norm for males living under capitalist-patriarchal conditions? (vol.1, p.27—original emphasis).

His answer to the latter question (which is in the affirmative) continues this individualist emphasis. '[A]ny male reading the texts of these soldier males— and not taking immediate refuge in repression', he said, 'might find in them a whole series of traits he recognizes from his own past or present behavior, from his own fantasies. (Any man who categorically denies this might want to verify it by asking the present, or past, women in his life.)' (vol.1, p.89).

Jessica Benjamin and Anson Rabinbach, in their introduction to the second volume of *Male Fantasies*, also put the question in terms of different types of men. Theweleit assumes, they said, 'a continuum between ordinary male fantasy and its violent counterpart', in the sense that the 'soldier males' of Weimar Germany 'were enacting the fantasies that everyone [male] keeps under wraps'. For these authors, the 'natural' question was: 'what distinguishes these *Freikorpsmen* from other men?' (Benjamin and Rabinbach, 1989: xiv).

But asking the question in this way, that is, by assuming that what we are talking about are types of men, is to focus attention on something inherent in men, rather than starting with the cultural imperatives of domination that 'make'[149] male supremacist men. While it is true that those imperatives structure personality characteristics and make them meaningful, the breeding ground for fascism is the system of male supremacy. Fascism is the brutally naked expression of male supremacist dehumanisation, firstly of women,

---

149. This is a reference to Beauvoir's famous remark that 'women are made not born'.

but also of other categories of people already singled out by the prevailing historical conditions of oppression: 'Jews', gypsies, Slavs, homosexuals and the disabled (and women) in the case of Nazi Germany; 'Muslims', 'Mexicans', 'blacks',[150] Native Americans and 'Jews' (and women), in the case of Donald Trump's America; and 'Muslims', 'boat people', 'illegals' (and women, especially if she becomes Prime Minister) in the case of successive recent Australian governments. That dehumanisation licences the brutality that is fascism's chief defining characteristic. These are the people who can be harmed with impunity, up to and including murder, because they are not 'human' as male supremacy defines it. Thus fascism is the expression of the deathliness at the heart of male supremacy, unleavened by any genuine humanity. Theweleit does get there eventually, but in a roundabout way and without saying very much at all about the social arrangements of capitalist male supremacy which breed the kind of character structure historically identified as 'fascist'.

Moreover, there is a failure in the literature to draw out the implications of the crucial importance of masculinity to fascism. If fascism is characterised by male supremacist meanings and values based on the dehumanising premise that only men count as 'human', if it is peculiarly suited to (certain) men and comes into being in what they perceive to be their own interests and is avidly embraced by them, and if it excludes women from everything fascism values, in other words, if it is essentially masculine, then to speak of fascism in general terms without acknowledging that, is to misperceive the nature of fascism.

If theories of fascism fail to acknowledge masculinity, it is not surprising that there is little agreement about exactly what fascism is, and that the received opinion within the literature on fascism is that the phenomenon is notoriously difficult to define. One of the leading scholars in the area has referred to it as a 'conundrum' (Roger Griffin, quoted in Mangan, 1999f: 4), while another said that the struggle to place it historically made her feel 'way over [her] head'. 'When I am not nauseated by descriptions of fascist oppression', she said, 'I am dizzy from all the effort of organizing a definition of fascism. The movement that appeals to all people … feels like an ocean' (Kaplan, 1986: 7).

---

150. 'Laziness is a trait in blacks. It really is, I believe that. It's not anything they can control', he is reported to have said (http://www.huffingtonpost.com.au/entry/donald-trump-racist-examples_us_56d47177e4b03260bf777e83 – viewed 9.8.2018). This belief in the 'laziness' of blacks is widespread throughout the US population, and a major 'reason' why Americans hate 'welfare' (Gilens, 1999).

There are scholars who agree that masculinity is somehow involved (see below), but that agreement is clearly not universal, since many an influential study of fascism makes no mention of masculinity. Take, for example, the following list from one such study, of the defining characteristics of fascism:

> extreme chauvinistic nationalism with pronounced imperialistic, expansionist tendencies; an anti-socialist, anti-Marxist thrust aimed at the destruction of working-class organizations and their Marxist political philosophy; the basis in a mass party drawing from all sectors of society, though with pronounced support in the middle class and proving attractive to the peasantry and to various uprooted or highly unstable sectors of the population; fixation on a charismatic, plebiscitarily legitimized leader; extreme intolerance towards all oppositional and presumed oppositional groups, expressed through vicious terror, open violence, and ruthless repression; glorification of militarism and war ... dependence upon an "alliance" with existing elites – industrial, agrarian, military, and bureaucratic – for their political breakthrough; and at least an initial function – despite a populist-revolutionary, anti-establishment rhetoric – in the stabilization or restoration of social order and capitalist structures (quoted from Ian Kershaw, 1993, *The Nazi Dictatorship*, in Mangan, 1999f: 5).

All these factors are indeed characteristic of fascism: the ultra-nationalism and imperialism; the demonisation of 'communism'; the seemingly unaffiliated politics (opposed to both working-class organisation and big business, at least rhetorically in the latter case); the worship of the leader; terror and violence as standard political practice; the glorification of war; and the actual support given to the powers-that-be despite the anti-establishment rhetoric. But failing to mention the masculinity of fascism is to leave out its central defining characteristic and ignore the key to understanding it. Fascism was created by, for and about men, dehumanised by its exclusion of women from any participation in what counted as its most valued activities—politics and war. Indeed, not only did fascism exclude women, it even preferred their total obliteration, as Klaus Theweleit found (see below).

Among those who do address the issue of masculinity and fascism, there is general agreement that masculinity is somehow central. There is, of course, the horse's mouth himself, Joseph Goebbels, Nazi Minister of Propaganda, who was reported to have said[151] in 1934:

> The National Socialist movement is in its nature a masculine movement
> ... While man must give to life the great lines and forms, it is the task

---

151. In a publication called *Der Nationalsozialistische Staat* edited by Walter Gehl.

of woman out of her inner fullness and inner eagerness to fill these lines and forms with colour. The realms of directing and shaping are not hard to find in public life. To such realms belong for one thing the tremendously great sphere of politics. This sphere without qualification must be claimed by man ... The outstanding and highest calling of woman is always that of wife and mother ... so will woman find her personal happiness in family and child (quoted in Kirkpatrick, 1939: 107).[152]

In this passage Goebbels states clearly the values of male supremacist masculinity: the male entitlement to 'greatness' at women's expense; and the dissociation involved in stubbornly believing, both in the 'greatness' of (some) men, and in women's subordination to men and obliviousness to the fact that men live their lives in 'family and child', too.

The US researcher who quoted Goebbels' statement elaborated on it by quoting an interview with Goebbels's wife, Magda, reported in the London *Daily Mail*, where she was reported to have said that 'marriage ... is undoubtedly best for a woman'. He commented that 'one gathers the impression that the master propagandist has succeeded in imposing upon his wife at least outward conformity to his point of view'. As things turned out, however, her agreement with her husband (or perhaps with her husband's boss, Hitler) was not only 'outward' but wholehearted and unto death; and marriage was far from being 'best' for Magda, or for the six children she and Goebbels had together. When it became clear that German defeat was inevitable, she killed her children in the Führerbunker in Berlin on 1 May 1945, after which she and her husband committed suicide.[153]

Often, the connection between fascism and masculinity is simply asserted without any further development of exactly what that connection might be. Barbara Spackman (1996), for example, notes that 'an obsession with virility is one of the distinctive traits of fascist discourse, a commonplace that is ... sometimes simply taken for granted as a sort of linguistic tic' (p.3). Fascism's masculinity is taken as self-evident, 'a kind of verbal campaign button', with no discussion of the interrelationships between masculinity and any other of the traits attributed to fascism.

---

152. At the time Kirkpatrick wrote this book, *Woman in Nazi Germany*, he was Professor of Sociology at the University of Minnesota. The university had given him leave, and the Guggenheim Foundation had given him a grant, to spend a year in Nazi Germany studying 'the status of women and family life in present-day Germany' (Kirkpatrick, 1939: 7).

153. For fictionalised accounts of these events, see: Craigie, 2010; Rosenberg, 2011; Ziervogel, 2013.

To give just one example: Gigliola Gori's article (1999) about masculinity in fascist Italy contains numerous mentions of masculinity and emphasises its importance in that context, including the article's title, 'Model of masculinity'. But there is no account of how Italian fascist masculinity—'the shaping of the New Man', 'the model of the Superman'—might be implicated in the other aspects of fascism the author discusses. What is the significance of masculinity, for example, for fascism 'as a political totalitarian movement of the right', or as 'the passion for nationalism' (p.27), or as 'a civic religion which soon became a political religion, whereby belief in myths, rites and symbols was joined to faith in the Duce' (p.28)? The author does not tell us how totalitarianism or nationalism or faith in the Duce might be masculine.

Moreover, this article illustrates another common tendency: to forget that, if we are talking about masculinity, we are only talking about men, not about people. To give just one of a myriad of examples: if the Italian fascist program was to create 'an élite race of Supermen', it was not 'the Italian people' who were to be transformed, only the men (Gori, 1999: 28).[154] The assumption here is that transforming the men is to transform the people, oblivious to the exclusion of women and what that might mean for the kind of 'people' referred to. While this might be regarded as a fine point—men, after all, are people too—the tendency to slide into 'people' when it is only men under discussion is also a tendency to take the male as the 'human' norm. The solution is not to include women in institutions created to exclude them. In the case of male supremacist masculinity women can't be included anyway. The solution is to keep the focus on men with full awareness of the possible dehumanisation involved in social arrangements based on the exclusion of women.

In an article in an edited volume dedicated to the work of Klaus Theweleit, called *The Attractions of Fascism*, John Milfull (1990) did fill in some of the connections between masculinity and fascism. He said that, even though we know fascism was attractive to women, it was without doubt 'male business … in an almost absolute sense' (p.178), both because it excluded women from any important role, and because it liberated 'repressed wishes and phantasies'

---

154. 'This essay is concerned with the educational scheme to fascisticize, that is to transform the Italian people – traditionally individualist and lazy – into an elite race of Supermen' (Gori, 1999: 28). This attempt on the part of the fascist regime to change the character of Italian men was unsuccessful: 'Perhaps because of an intelligently critical attitude or perhaps due to bored cynicism or even perhaps because of an atavistic idleness, men did not conform perfectly to the virile ideal of the New Italian. In fact, beyond appearances, the Italian male did not completely change – unlike men in Nazi Germany – into the strong, sculptured and obedient warrior ready to die for the cause' (p.52).

(p.183) peculiar to men. Among those wishes and fantasies was a 'subtle equation between male role, revolver and penis'. For the fascist male, '[t] he revolver-penis [was] the sign of manhood, ready to subdue the "enemy" (and) woman' (p.182). Milfull also said that fascism was characterised by fear of female sexuality, and that 'the construction of a male myth of power and dominance' was the fascist male's way of compensating for his sense of inadequacy (p.181).

But in the first place, it was not female sexuality the fascist male was afraid of, but sexual intercourse *with* women. This doesn't always involve female sexuality—prostitution and rape, for example, are forms of male sexuality with women but more or less forcibly imposed on women; neither is motivated by women's own sexual desire. Moreover, in the case of 'a male myth of power and dominance' and fascist fear of women, Milfull has it the wrong way round. The sense of dominance is not a consequence of male fear but a cause of it. The fascist male fears women because their very existence gives the lie to his male supremacist character armour constructed around a world without women. What those men feared was not 'female sexuality' but, as Theweleit discovered, the threat that women posed to the dehumanisation of the fascist worldview. They feared what they felt was 'total annihilation and dismemberment' (Theweleit, 1987: 205). Why they should have felt as though they would be annihilated and dismembered by women, and not just sexually, is discussed below.

The male body

A concern, even an obsession, with the male body has also been identified in some of the literature as that aspect of masculinity of most relevance to fascism.[155] J. A. Mangan (1999f), who quoted the above passage from Kershaw's *Nazi Dictatorship*, added to Kershaw's list 'the projection of the martial male body as a symbol of state power' (p.5), and commented on the 'remarkable congruence' worldwide on the centrality of 'the male body' to fascism. Mangan even connected this preoccupation with the male body with 'supremacy': 'Virtually everywhere, [the male body] was superordinate because it was superior in purpose – the achievement of supremacy' (p.23).

---

155. Mosse, 1996; two issues of *The International Journal of the History of Sport* (1999, volume 16, nos. 2 and 4), 'Shaping the Superman' (no.2), and 'Superman Supreme' (no.4). 'The concern [in these issues of the journal] is a modern male icon – the Aryan Man as Prometheus Unbound, the Superman of German Fascism. The book is, therefore, a study of masculinity as a metaphor and especially of the muscular male body as a moral symbol – inviolable, invulnerable, dominant' (Mangan, 1999a: 1). See also: Mangan, 1999b, c, d, e, f.

But it's not clear how a concern with the male body leads to 'supremacy'. Indeed, in Mangan's description of the functions the male body served for fascism, it seemed more like a victim than a conqueror. It 'symbolized self-sacrifice', he said, 'it was expendable ... it was a dispensable icon' (p.23). There is nothing in a preoccupation with the male body in itself, no matter how obsessed, that would lead to the dehumanised brutality that is fascism. That there was in fact a connection between a fascination with the male body and physical brutality is beyond doubt. But something else was necessary to turn such a fascination into 'supremacy'.

One suggestion that appears in the literature is a connection between worship of the male body and racism. Gigliola Gori (1999) said that Italian fascism contrasted '[t]he beauty of the Fascist as an eternally young and powerful male ... with the ugliness of the non-Fascist male typified by the flabby, aged liberal bourgeois: the Jewish profiteer with his prominent nose, the Negro from Abyssinia with his too prominent features' (p.39).[156] The implication is that certain categories of (male) persons—Jews in particular—were regarded as inferior because they were seen to be ugly, and that that lack of physical beauty justified the murderous violence visited on them. However, the fascists didn't only kill men ('ugly' or not); and the fascist leaders themselves were hardly models of male beauty. Although Mussolini did tend to parade around bare-chested and provide numerous demonstrations of his sporting prowess, he had a 'rather stumpy figure' (p.37) which bore no resemblance to the statues of classical Greek and Roman athletes; not to mention the Nazi leaders. Of course, inconsistencies within an ideological discourse are irrelevant if its beneficiaries are powerful enough, and a ruling class prepared to murder people on a mass scale does not need to concern itself with illogicality and absurdity in its justificatory discourse. But Gori also pointed out that '[t]he cult of the male body as a symbol of ruthless, sacrificial Aryan beauty characteristic of Germany ... did not occur in Italy' (p.54). So a linking of fascism and masculinity through obsession with the male body does not in and of itself explain fascism's brutality.

G. L. Mosse (1996) also argued that it was racism that turned the fascist fascination with the male body into brutality. He said that '[i]t was racism that pushed National Socialism over the edge, it was the race war that led to the [Nazi program of] extermination' and allowed the 'possibilities ... [that] were only latent in the construction of modern masculinity ... [to] become reality'. Those latent possibilities were 'the warrior qualities of masculinity' which

---

156. Citing Mosse, 1995.

fascism 'heightened', he said. It was racism that 'brutalized [those qualities] and transformed theory and rhetoric into reality' (p.155). But again, it is not clear what the male body had to do with it, even though it is true that fascist brutality was racist (although as Mosse pointed out, 'Italian fascism did not go in for mass murder') (p.180). Mosse refers to 'warrior qualities' which were brutalised by racism. But 'warrior qualities' are already brutal whether they are racist or not. They are inherently violent because they assume the existence of an enemy who needs to be killed, and they require training in ways to defeat that enemy and the provision of weapons with which to do it. Racism identifies 'an enemy', but 'warriors' will find an enemy anywhere because that's what they do. If Mosse is saying that dehumanised violence is 'latent' within 'modern masculinity', then I agree with him. But that potential is not confined to racism, and its source is not the male body. Rather, the potential for male violence is immersion within a culture of male supremacy which dissociates men from the real world and the existence of women, and gives them a sense of entitlement unfettered by the rights of others.

'Male Fantasies'

I have used Klaus Theweleit's two-volume, *Male Fantasies*, as the main source for what I have to say about fascism and masculinity in what follows. It is the best known and most exhaustive of the texts discussing the connections between masculinity and fascism,[157] and comes closest to identifying what it is about masculinity that might lead to fascism. It is a detailed account of the mindset of certain fascist 'soldier males', most of them proto-Nazis and members of Freikorps, as exposed in their writings. These writings consist of over 250 texts comprising novels, biographies, memoirs, journals, battle descriptions, eyewitness reports, reflections, and poems and songs about the era. The culture laid bare in these writings expressed clearly the brutal type of masculinity so appropriate for the Nazi program of mass murder, together with the crazed hatred of women which accompanied it.

The Freikorps were 'private armies of former imperial soldiers, anti-Communist youth, adventurers, and sundry drifters organized in the volatile atmosphere of post-World War I Germany' (Benjamin and Rabinbach, 1989: ix-x). These men were thugs and murderers but they were not pariahs.

---

157. The historical period Theweleit writes about—the period in Germany and Central Europe between the two world wars—is more accurately identified as 'Nazi' rather than fascist, since the latter term covers far more, both geographically and historically than the former. However, not all the 'soldier males' whose writings Theweleit examines were Nazis, and some of them were critical of the Nazi movement, but all of them subscribed to a fascist belief-system.

Rather, they were initially paid by the Weimar government to suppress the revolutionary working class in Germany and in other parts of central Europe, which they did by hunting down and killing 'communists'. As Theweleit said, 'Without the *Freikorps*, the workers would never have been crushed so absolutely' (vol.2, p.382). They were officially disbanded in early 1920, but many of them formed the Nazi party's first group of enforcers, the SA. One Freikorps, the Marinebrigade Erhardt, formed of former naval personnel, was the first to use the swastika as its symbol.[158]

Attitudes to women

One of Theweleit's main findings, and one that surprised him because he hadn't been expecting it, related to 'the peculiarities' of the ways in which the Freikorpsmen wrote about women, and hence the implications of that for how they and the Nazi regime felt about women behind the pro-family rhetoric. In the most general terms, these men wanted to annihilate women. They had no use for women, not as wives, sexual partners, comrades, or even fellow creatures existing on the earth. They didn't want any women left alive at all:

> Representations of murders committed against women [in these writings] frequently end on [a] peculiar note of satisfaction ("—and there was peace again in the land") … Once she … is reduced to a pulp, a shapeless, bloody mass, the man can breathe a sigh of relief (vol.1, p.191, 196).

That there were any positive female characters at all in their writings was due to the thin thread still connecting them to reality. They managed their hatred of women in the usual way by embracing the common or garden type misogyny of the 'good'/'bad' woman dichotomy. But that left them with the dilemma of what to do with the 'good' women, given their detestation of women altogether. So their writings justified the beating or killing of 'bad' women, but while they reluctantly allowed the existence of the 'good' women (wives, mothers, 'white nurses', virgin sisters), they rendered them lifeless— killed off by 'the Reds' or just simply dying.

The Freikorps writings rarely mention women at all, but when they do they speak of women, they use a limited number of stereotypical categories: wives, sisters (siblings and nursing sisters), mothers (even more rarely), and a phantasmagoria of murdering harpies variously identified as 'Red nurses', 'whores' and 'proletarian women'.

---

158. Wikipedia, 'Nazism' (viewed 11.4.2014)

Wives

Theweleit began the first volume of *Male Fantasies* with a brief review of seven marriages in Freikorps circles, in order to illustrate 'the peculiarities' of the ways in which these men spoke of women (vol.1, pp.3-18). In fact, there were more than seven marriages because some of the men had been married more than once. Theweleit found that, with a single exception (discussed below), none of the wives were named. For example, Hermann Ehrhardt, commander of the Freikorps Ehrhardt brigade, said of his marriage:[159]

> "I got married when I was a young naval lieutenant. Because I belonged to the North Sea Fleet, I felt confident I'd be stationed in Wilhelmshaven. Naturally I was very happy when my father-in-law … had a little cottage built for me" (vol.1, p.3).

Even beyond the fact that that Ehrhardt did not name his wife, what is said here about his 'marriage' is peculiar in other ways too. In this particular example the wife doesn't appear in the passage at all. He isn't married to anyone—his naval rank and place of abode are more worthy of mention than his bride. 'Father-in-law' is mentioned but no 'wife'; and the cottage he acquires as a consequence of 'getting married' is his alone ('built for me'), even though her father built it.

Another example: In his memoirs,[160] a Freikorps commander, Gerhard Rossbach, attributed his survival of the purge of the SA in 1934 to the fact that the door to his study was hidden (where he kept his correspondence with the SA leader, Ernst Röhm), because his wife had placed a wall-hanging over it. But he didn't give her a name, and what he said about her death was brief and dismissive. When he came home after spending time in jail, he said, he 'found his wife suffering from a nervous disorder. She died soon afterward'. That was it; he never mentioned her again. He had 'a second wife', he said, whom he described as 'an actress with Heinrich George's Schiller Theater'. She was also unnamed but, as Theweleit noted, the sentence which introduces her is dominated by the name of a man. The only other thing he said about this second wife was that their honeymoon 'gave me the opportunity I needed' to travel outside the country (vol.1, p.4-5).

---

159. The publication Theweleit took this quote from is *Kapitän Ehrhardt: Abenteuer und Schicksal* (1924) by Friedrich Freksa.

160. *Mein Weg durch die Zeit: Erinnerungen unt Bekenntnisse* (My Path through the Era: Recollections and Confessions) Vereinigte Weiburger Buchdruckverein, Weiburg an der Lahn, 1950. Rossbach reworked his memoirs after the war, and published them in 1950.

The single wife who is named in these stories of Freikorps marriages ('Gertrud') was married to naval lieutenant Manfred von Killinger, a member of the Erhardt Marine Brigade.[161] She is described in some detail and given words of her own to say (unlike the other, nameless wives). However, the words she is given are the kind of thing the Freikorpsmen themselves say. "'I know what you're thinking'", she is recorded saying at the end of the First World War by her husband, "'You're thinking about the Freikorps that are being set up everywhere against the Spartacists[162] … The bitter truth is that … the decent soldier has to fight again now … now is the time to grit your teeth and save Germany from the Red flood'" (vol.1, p.16). Perhaps it is not so much the wife who is being named here, but rather, the speaker of such ideologically sound sentiments that they deserve a name because they are usually uttered by, for and about men. In contrast, when it's a question of what belongs unequivocally to women, i.e. the birth of children, the same wife is not even mentioned (much less named), not even when the child is a boy: "'Tiny Peter opened his [eyes] to the world on the Lindendorf'" (vol.1, p.17).

Another way of denying wives any reality is to kill them off, for example, Rossbach's wife who 'died soon afterward' when he came home from prison (vol.1, p.4). One of Dwinger's Freikorps novels[163] contains at least two accounts of the death of a wife. The first is so brief it hardly merits being called 'an account'. On being asked whether he had ever been in love, one

---

161. In his memoirs, *Der Klabautermann: Eine Lebensgeschichte* Munich, 1936. A 'Klabautermann' is a mythical water spirit from the Baltic and the North Sea supposedly responsible for keeping a ship in good running order. Killinger was a Nazi politician in Saxony, a member of the SA (and survived the purge), Nazi Consul-General in San Francisco from 1936 to 1939, and ambassador to Romania from 1941 to 1944, where he played a major role in implementing Romania's policy of extermination. He committed suicide on 2 September 1944 in order to avoid capture by the Russian army.

162. The Spartacus League (named after a slave, Spartacus, who led a revolt of slaves against the Romans in 73BC) was a revolutionary left-wing organisation formed at the beginning of the First World War by Rosa Luxemburg and Karl Liebknecht (among others), both of whom were murdered after they were arrested. In January 1919, the Spartacists were the leaders of an unsuccessful attempt to overthrow the government, which was put down by the Freikorps and what was left of the German army

163. Edwin Erich Dwinger (1898-1981) was one of the most popular authors in Nazi Germany. His books sold around two million copies and made him very rich (Fritzsche, 2009). This novel, *Auf halbem Wege* (Halfway) deals with the Kapp Putsch (a failed attempt to overthrow the Weimar government) and the suppression of the left-wing Ruhr revolt of 1920 (with the connivance of the Weimar government). Both of these involved Freikorps members although the troops had been officially disbanded in early 1920. The other Freikorps novel is *Die letzten Reiter* (The Last Riders) (1935), which deals with the efforts of a mounted Freikorps troop to secure Courtland against the Bolsheviks.

character "'finally whispered: 'Yes … but she died—as my bride'"" (vol.1, p.33). In the second one, not only is the wife killed off, her death is used as the excuse for what the soldier really wants to do, that is, to massacre as many of his perceived enemies ('the Reds') as possible : "'I had such a beautiful young wife … the Reds beat her to death while I was off at the front. But I've avenged her already and will keep avenging her. I'll send thousands after her to their graves, like kings of olden times'" (vol.1, p.34).

Dwinger's novels expose very clearly the men's aversion to marriage. These men don't want wives at all. None of Dwinger's Freikorps officers is married or connected to a woman in any way. The reason given is the men's loyalty to each other and the higher ideals they are fighting for. He has one character say of his commander that he is not married because "'he believes in the old saying: 'Swear an oath to the black flag alone, and you'll have nothing else to call your own!' … Freikorps men aren't almost all bachelors for nothing'" (vol.1, p.33).

Apart from wives, any occurrence of sexual relations with women is either understated or denied outright in these men's writings. For example, when the hero of Ernst von Salomon's novel,[164] gets out of prison, he visits a (nameless) woman he had fallen in love with, but nothing happens. She was "'visibly startled'" to see him but she didn't say anything and neither did he: "'When she glanced over at me, I staunchly held back any feelings of sympathy'" (vol.1, p.9). Again, on a one-day leave Ernst Jünger[165] goes home with a woman, and '[f]or that hour I am her husband'. But what he says they did has no sexual connotations at all: "'I … sit in peace with her before the

---

164. *Die Geächteten* (The Outlaws), a fictionalised account of his adventures as a Freikorps member. Salomon was involved in the murder of Walther Rathenau, Germany's Foreign Minister, in 1922, and served a five-year prison sentence for his part in the murder. (He provided the assassins with a car). He was also involved in an attempted 'Feme' murder, but served only a short term in prison because he spared the life of the victim when he pleaded for mercy. He kept his distance from the Nazis, but he managed to live fairly comfortably in the Third Reich, working as a film maker. 'Feme' murders were committed by right-wing vigilante groups against political opponents in Weimar Germany, whom they suspected of disclosing their stockpiling of arms to the allied forces. The term 'Feme' is a reference to 'a kind of frontier justice practiced in medieval Germany', whereby criminals were 'tried' and executed outside the official judicial system (Brenner, 2001: 84ff).

165. Ernst Jünger was a much-decorated soldier, and neither a Freikorps member nor a Nazi. He refused to be publicly associated with them and was critical of much of what they did, especially their anti-Semitism and the SS atrocities committed in occupied Europe. However, his writings contained many of the same themes as the Freikorps writings, 'particularly in relation to the construction of a male type who finds life without war and weapons unimaginable' (vol.1, p.24).

fireplace, hand in hand'" (vol.1, p.38). Another example: Captain Berthold[166] turns down the opportunity for a vaguely hinted-at sexual encounter with a serving girl at the inn he is staying at: 'The girl steps up to him ... He remains where he is ... but still he feels this young woman who asks every evening whether he wants anything else ... "No, thank you. Everything is in order!" ... Then she is gone from the room' (vol.1, p.40).

Mothers

Mothers are among the women whom the soldier-male authors view positively. But '[e]ven the "good mother" is ... a split figure', as Theweleit noted (vol.1, p.103). On the one hand mothers are revered figures: '"good angels," "the best of all women," "homes" that can be loved "infinitely" and "above all else" (as only Germany can otherwise be loved)' (vol.1, p.104). On the other hand they never live happy, fulfilled peaceful lives. Only suffering is worthy of reverence, and the worst suffering these men can think of to inflict on their mothers is the loss of their sons (although their husbands get killed, too). Of course, their own mothers can't lose their sons—a man can't write anything after his own death. So the suffering mothers are the mothers of their comrades: '"I had a comrade", goes the song ... "and he had a mother"' (vol.1, p.103). These mothers are portrayed as heroic, as 'mothers-of-iron' who refuse to break down and give way to tears at the deaths of their sons.

There are also hints of a covert aggression against mothers: in Salomon's assumption that a preacher's admonitions against mothers who 'perform[ed] indecent acts with the lodger' referred to his own mother; in the attitude of the husband towards his wife and mother of his two children in Rudolf Herzog's novel, *Wieland the Blacksmith*: 'he knew that she would die a slow death. From that time on, his eyes became brighter and clearer whenever he looked at her [etc.]', a passage that reads as though her dying delighted him. Theweleit comments: 'Are the only good mothers dead mothers?' (vol.1, p.104-6) But then, even less is said about mothers than about wives in these men's writings.

---

166. Rudolf Berthold was a pioneer aviator of World War I and a war hero who shot down 44 enemy planes and kept returning to battle before his wounds from the last engagement had healed. He organised a Freikorps and fought the Bolsheviks in Latvia. He was killed in street fighting in 1920. At least two of the texts Theweleit cites relate to him: Gengler, Ludwig F. (1934) *Rudolf Berthold: Sieger in 44 Luftschlachten, erschlagen im Bruderkampf für Deutschlands Freiheit* (Rudolf Berthold: Victor of 44 Air Battles, Slain in the Brotherhood Struggle for Germany's Freedom), which contains large portions from Berthold's diary; and Thor Goote's (Johannes M. Berg) (1937) *Kamerad Berthold der 'unvergleichliche Franke': Bild eines deutschen Soldaten* (Comrade Berthold the 'Incomparable Frankonian': Picture of a German Soldier). The quote is taken from the second one.

Sisters

Sisters are also portrayed positively, or at least, their own sisters and the virgin sisters of comrades are, together with what Theweleit calls 'white sisters',[167] the nurses who look after the men when they are wounded. However, the fact that a woman is a 'sister' means that she is sexually taboo, and hence can be viewed positively because there is no possibility of any intimacy. 'What this all comes down to', Theweleit says, 'is that no object seems attainable and no object relations seem capable of being formed' (vol.1, p.125).

Stranger women—those who don't fall into the conventional categories of mother, wife, sister—are also a kind of 'sister'. They are 'Red sisters', also variously identified as 'proletarian women', 'rifle women' and (unsurprisingly) 'whores'. With these stranger women, the murderous hatred the soldier males feel towards all women is given free rein, although often projected onto the women themselves.[168] One piece of Nazi propaganda described them thus:

> "It is well known that there were rifle-women behind the Red lines who were under orders to stop the troops from falling back, or if the retreat could not be stopped, to shoot at their own people. The rifle-women were the sort of cruel furies only Bolshevism could devise … these women were bestialized and devoid of all feeling" (vol.1, p.76).

Here 'rifle-women' are portrayed as fearsome to their own troops, but on most occasions in these writings, they are portrayed as fearsome to their enemies, the soldier males. In the men's eyes these women supposedly want to torture and mutilate the men, castrate them and tear them into little pieces. They therefore deserve to be wiped out in a 'bloody mass' whenever and wherever they are encountered. 'Red sisters' are proletarian women and 'prostitutes', and they sometimes masquerade as 'white sisters' in order to fool the men into letting them get close enough so that they (the 'rifle women') can kill and mutilate them.

---

167. 'White' means right-wing. Its usual usage is in the phrase 'White terror', which designates the murderous rampages of right-wing, counter-revolutionary forces, in contrast to the 'Red terror' those right-wing forces insisted they were fighting.

168. Theweleit argues that the term 'projection' is inadequate to describe the way these men interpret the world, because it doesn't capture the enormity of their destructiveness. It is, he said, 'an inadequate term to describe a process in which perceived reality is annihilated in order to preserve the life of an ideational representation' (vol.1, p.87). But while projection might be inadequate as the only description of the way these men saw the world, it certainly describes the way they wrote about women. It was not the women who tortured, murdered and mutilated people, but the soldier males themselves. These men were paranoid, terrified of being annihilated by a threat that didn't exist, and projection is the chief psychic mechanism of paranoia.

The Freikorps soldier's fantasy of 'Red nurses'/'rifle women' did have some minimal grounding in reality. There actually were women to be found near the front lines of the workers' ranks in the Ruhr uprising in March 1920 (which was brutally crushed by the German army aided by the Freikorps). But these women had no weapons and they certainly did not behave in the way they were described in the men's writings. The soldiers knew of only two kinds of women at the front lines—nurses and prostitutes. Since these front-line women were 'communists' (they were on the side of the workers), they must be prostitutes, even though they might also be nurses.

Reports and newsletters provided the 'evidence':

> The mobilization of so-called Red Cross nurses is characteristic of the moral turpitude of the Red troops. These medical detachments are recruited exclusively from the ranks of prostitutes, especially from Oberhausen.

> Brothel inmates are put into service as Red Cross nurses.

> the countless women and prostitutes in the battle sectors and behind the front—most of them disguised as nurses—made for completely impossible conditions.[169]

The women must be 'whores' because they were proletarian women and there was nothing the soldier males hated more than 'female communists'. How the soldier males saw women was expressed by Ernst von Salomon describing a demonstration against the Berthold Freikorps in Hamburg:

> "Shaking their fists, the women shriek at us. Stones, pots, fragments begin to fly … They hammer into us, hefty women … their aprons soaked and skirts muddied, red and wrinkled faces hissing beneath wind-whipped hair … They spit, swear, shriek … Women are the worst. Men fight with fists, but the women also spit and swear—you can't just plant your fist into their ugly pusses" (vol.1, p.65).

And indeed, the Freikorpsmen did far more than punch women in the face. They set out to exterminate them, justifying their brutality by insisting that the women had weapons and were the aggressors. For example, two women were shot supposedly because they had revolvers hidden in their clothing, one with the gun sewn into her slip, the other with a gun in her stockings,

---

169. Vol.1, pp.83-4. The first passage is from a press report on a visit to the staff of the Schulz Freikorps in Wesel, quoted in Lucas, Erhard (1970) *Märzrevolution im Ruhrgebiet 1920* (The March 1920 Revolution in the Ruhr Region), volume 2, p.83; the second is from an official report to the Defense Ministry on 17 March 1920, quoted in Roden, Hans, ed. (1935) *Deutsche Soldaten*, p.139; the third is from *Die deutschen Freikorps 1918 to 1923* (1936), p.411, by the Nazi historian, Wilhelm von Oertzen.

although the husband of the first woman denied on oath that she had had a gun; while ten Red Cross nurses were shot because they supposedly had a weapon each (vol.1, pp.447-8n6).

The writings contain a number of examples of females so horrific (according to the soldiers) that the men could hardly be blamed if they killed such dreadful creatures:

> "the women and girls of the industrial population … who practiced such cruelties … [as] the mutilations of our wounded in … the first weeks of the war" (vol.1, p.61);

> "a young factory girl … [who] pulled a pistol from under her apron" with which she shot the cavalry officer, Count Truchs, after which she "jumped onto his face, grinding his monocle, that accursed symbol [of aristocracy], over and over again into his eyes with the heels of her rough shoes" (vol.1, pp.70-2);

> "Spartacist women riding shaggy horses, hair flying, two pistols in each hand" (vol.1, pp.72);

> "a hand grenade under a woman's skirt" (vol.1, pp.73);

> "the worst thing is … to be captured by this bestial enemy, to suffer the most drawn-out, bitter, and tortured death imaginable at the hands of sadistically grinning rifle-women" (vol.1, pp.74);

> "the dead … will continue to scream into eternity, those twelve savaged men of the Iron Legion, each drenched in black blood between hips and thighs, each with that terrible wound with which the bestial [female] foe has desecrated defenceless wounded men" (vol.1, pp.74).

As Theweleit points out, where the soldiers said they found these weapons on the women is significant. The weapons invariably appeared from under the women's skirts, exactly where a penis would be if the woman had one. The stranger women in the soldier males' writings were always depicted with weapons ('rifle-women'). That was the men's excuse for killing them. But, in the fantastical imaginings of these men's psyches, if these women had weapons they must also have had penises, since as Milfull (1990) pointed out, a revolver was another kind of penis for fascist men. The 'rifle-women's' behaviour was also that of penis-bearers. Theweleit illustrates this with the way the 'Spartacist women' were depicted. Their flying hair, shaggy horses and two pistols in each hand were clearly mythical. The women had no horses, shaggy or otherwise; their hair was unlikely to be flying around in the strait-laced fashions of the early twentieth-century; and two pistols in each hand is an inefficient way to carry weapons—presumably the author got so carried away in his portrayal of these mythical women that he failed to notice the absurdity. As Theweleit argues, this hyper-activity is a phallic potency that has nothing to do with women's behaviour.

Even more to this point of phallic potency, some of the 'rifle-women' were given names: "'The commissar addressed her by her first name, Marja'" (vol.1, p.74); "'Wearing her stained, silk morning-gown, Katja came over to join the men'" (vol.1, p.75); "'Rosa Luxemburg is a she-devil'" (vol.1, p.76); "'There, in a ditch … sat Red Marie" (vol.1, p.184). Theweleit suggests that the refusal to give wives names is motivated by a desire to deny them any reality: 'Married women remain nameless so that they do not take on the contours of figures in concrete reality' (vol.1, p.74). A name, he says, 'functions … as a penis-attribute', and hence '[t]he lack of a name … seems to guarantee [that there is] no penis [present]'. He points out that '[t]here isn't a single named female in any of those novels and biographies who doesn't turn out to be a "whore"', a 'rifle-woman, the woman with the castrating penis'. 'Leaving one's own wife nameless', he says, 'is a powerful piece of magic' (vol.1, p.75).

However, this account confuses a number of separate issues, or rather, and more precisely, it conflates a number of moves in the logic of dehumanising women. The first move is the equation of penis-possession and reality or, more accurately, 'human' status—only those who have penises are real because only penis-bearers are 'human'. The next move equates name and penis-possession—only those who have penises have names because only they are 'human beings'. The reason why names are denied to women then becomes obvious—names are not appropriate for women because women are not human beings because they don't have penises. But there is a further move beyond that, a move that is necessitated by the fact that women continue to exist. If women continue to exist, they must have penises (because only penis-possession defines who is real). But if they have penises, they must be as belligerent and murderously violent as the soldier males themselves and must therefore be exterminated before they can do to the men what the men want to do to them. As Theweleit put it: *'terror against a woman who isn't identified with the mother/sister image is essentially self-defense* … It looks very much as if the killings are conceived as corrective measures, which alter the false appearances of the women so that their "true natures" can become visible' (vol.1, pp.183, 196—original emphasis). These men felt entitled to kill women because they 'knew' with utter certainty that the women would annihilate them if they didn't kill the women first, and women weren't human anyway so killing them was justified.

Of course, the men knew no such thing. These men's lives were not threatened by women in any recognisable sense of the words 'life' and 'threaten'. What women did threaten, however, was the soldier male's sense of reality. Their very existence threatened that reality because in the soldier male's world there were no women. If one's sense of reality is based on the 'knowledge' that women don't exist, their continued existence, or worse, intimacy with them, threatens the very foundations of one's world. Only violence, preferably violence that exterminates women, can re-establish the 'truth' of the 'knowledge' of women's non-existence.

Sex and violence/murder

Often, the very thought of sexual intimacy with a woman gives rise to thoughts of violence and death:

> Ernst von Salomon: "I fell in love. I plunged into a bottomless chasm of savage longing for death, and at the same moment I was hurled toward the burning sun of an intense affirmation of life. One nod from her and I'd have been ready to blow myself, my house, the city, or the world sky-high" (vol.1, p.9).

> Jünger: "I ... sit in peace with her before the fireplace. Tomorrow, yes, tomorrow my brain will be shot to flames" (vol.1, p.38).

> Jünger again: "I plunge my gaze into the eyes of passing women, fleeting and penetrating as a pistol shot, and rejoice when they are forced to smile" (vol.1, p.38).

> "Her nakedness assaults him with a sudden glowing shudder, a gust of wind across a placid lake. He says nothing, but with a jolt his breath rushes into his blood, filling it with pearls, quivering bubbles, a gushing froth, just as the blood of men shot in the lungs leaves them lying yellow and silent like corpses, while the blood spurts endlessly, gurgling and seething at every breath—breath which they heave up, groaning, as if by a block and tackle, the air is so heavy and laden" (vol.1, p.43).[170]

Theweleit tentatively interprets this connection between sex and violent death as the consequence of 'the fear of dissolution through union with a woman', which 'causes desire to flee from its object, then transform itself into a representation of violence' (vol.1, p.45) (tentatively, because he couches it as a question). But although I agree that these men were terrified of 'dissolution through union with a woman', I would suggest that the object of their desire

---

170. Quoted from Franz Schauwecker's novel of the First World War, *Aufbruch der Nation* (The Nation Awakes), 1929. Eric J. Leed says of him: 'In the 1920s and 1930s Franz Schauwecker was one of the leading spokesmen of *Soldatischer Nationalismus*, one of the most important fictionalizers and ideologizers of the war experience' (Leed, 1978: 687). This was despite the fact that his personal war experience was one of vicious bullying at the hands of the working-class men in his unit.

was not women at all but violence. Theweleit sums up this attitude thus: 'You couldn't be a man without fighting, and being a man was the only way of being alive' (vol.1, p.395). What terrified them about women was the threat women posed to the only reality they allowed themselves to know. Their desire was not 'fleeing from its object', but rather, fleeing from what threatened its object—the existence and closeness of a woman—and towards its real erotic object—violence. For these men only violence was erotic, especially violence against women. They described it lovingly, in sensuous detail, wallowing in its voluptuousness. In violence they came alive—cold, hard, erect and invincible. The continued existence of women and what they stood for, especially in intimate encounters—love, compassion, caring, recognition, respect, in short, life and genuine humanity—threatened to take that away from them, to falsify it and dissolve it into nothingness. Only violence enabled them to maintain their reality in the face of those women whose very existence they feared would shatter it irretrievably.

Obliteration

Violence was not the only way the men managed to obliterate women in their writings. Theweleit gave a number of examples of their defenses against women. For example, the writer immediately switches from talking about a woman to talking about other men (as in Ehrhardt's remark about his marriage). Again, in an intimate encounter with a woman, the man is struck with paralysis ("he cannot even lift a finger"), or rendered lifeless by thoughts of his mother ("'As if I were long dead'"—a song sung to him by his mother). One writer is even bold enough to doubt the existence of women altogether, while instantly moving to what he considers more important: "'Women? … Are there such things? 'Swear an oath to the black flag alone, and you'll have nothing to call your own!'"'. As Theweleit puts it: 'Relationships with women are dissolved and transformed into new male attitudes, into political stances, revelations of the true path, etc.' (vol.1, p.35).

One of the more peculiar examples of this literary treatment of women is supplied by von Lettow-Vorbeck[171] in his autobiography. He is talking about a stop-over he made in Italy on his way home from Africa, where he visited a museum:

---

171. Paul von Lettow-Vorbeck was a general in the Imperial German army and commander of its forces in the East African campaign. He was the only undefeated German commander of the First World War. He was not a Nazi, in fact he loathed Hitler and refused an offer the Nazis made him of an ambassadorship in London (Whitaker, 2013). However, he was a 'soldier male' with many of the same attitudes towards women, although without the violence. He did not marry until he was nearly 50.

"In Rome, I was struck by the charming sculpture of Mars in repose … Cupid strokes his knee, eyeing him impishly. Colonel Trench has told me … how overwhelming it would be to see white women after years of colonial warfare. Mythology had captured the ancient relationship between Mars and Venus with complete psychological accuracy" (vol.1, p.36).

As Theweleit points out, not only does the author substitute a statue for an actual 'white woman', it's a statue of a two males, a man and a boy. For the soldier male, 'complete psychological accuracy' in sexual relations between the sexes can proceed without any involvement of women at all. And no, this particular man was neither homosexual nor a paedophile; he was simply used to living in a world without women.

Commenting on Dwinger's *Auf halbem Wege* (Halfway) (1939), Theweleit noted that the message about women conveyed by these novels was that

[r]eal men lack nothing when women are lacking … Denial of women is only natural, and therefore worthy … anyone who wants to join the troops should leave women behind. The men one meets there don't need women (vol.1, pp.33-4).

'Communism'

The hatred and fear the soldier males felt for 'communism' matched their hatred and fear of women. Indeed, they would seem to be one and the same thing, as evidenced by their insistence that 'proletarian women' were at the forefront of those forces threatening to inundate them with a 'Red flood'.

According to Theweleit, what these men feared in the women was the women's sexual experience, and this fear, he said, 'is brought into association with the word "communist"'. '"In women", wrote one soldier male, "the first theoretical realization of communist ideals always has to do with the sexual drive"' (vol.1, p.68).[172] At the same time, Theweleit also said that the horror elicited in these men by what they called 'proletarian women' was in fact unnameable, at least by the men themselves. In other words, 'proletarian women' was not an accurate description of what these men feared.

I would suggest that what these men hated about 'communism' was the promise it held out of a society of caring, sharing, equality and mutual

---

172. Delmar, Maximilian (1925) *Französische Frauen: Erlebnisse und Beobachten, Reflexionen, Paradoxe* (French Women: Life Experience and Observations, Reflections, Paradoxes). Delmar was a major in the imperial German army and not a Freikorps member. But, says Theweleit, '[h]e did write about women' (vol.1, p.447n14), or rather, he wrote down his fantasies about women, and expressed more clearly than any of the other soldier males the fear and loathing these men felt about women.

respect, in other words, a society of genuine humanity. I am not suggesting that that is what communism is, either theoretically or in practice. The 'communism' the soldier males feared was a myth anyway. But given that it was so threatening, it must have been utterly opposed (in their imaginations) to the world the soldier males themselves embraced, a world populated with enemies managed through violence, hatred, terror and death. The soldier male's world was a dehumanised one, barricaded against his own humanity and waging endless war against the humanity of others, including their right to life. Anything that suggested human beings might cooperate rather than kill each other would be anathema to a psyche whose sense of reality would crumble if he were to accept that as true. The demonisation of 'communism' was readily available to fend off that eventuality. Characteristic of the crudest form of capitalistic scare-mongering, it serves the ideological purpose of demonstrating that there is no alternative to capitalism, and that any attempt to provide an alternative can only lead to disaster. But these men were not defending capitalism (even though they were used by the Weimar government for that purpose), and their devotion to war and violence had nothing to do with money-making. Their motives were different from those of capitalist ideologues.

Theweleit's explanation for the soldier male's hatred of communism suggests that 'communism' poses three kinds of threat. Its insistence that society is riven by conflict (in other words, its class analysis) threatens his wholeness; its championing of the lower classes ('the masses') threatens his power; and its appearance (to the eyes of the soldier males) as a revolt of 'younger' sons seeking to take on the mantle of father/dictator threatens his status as 'elder'—or only—son by virtue of his incorporation into the fascist totality formation under a Führer:

> Conflicts of interest among the members of a society or contradictions fought out between diverse social organizations and groupings split the wholeness of the soldier male, his totality. When the Left argues for capitalist society to be seen in terms of class analysis, the fascist is robbed of his bodily unity, ripped in half … the bellicose Communist … is an agent of the lower orders—and he threatens to deprive the fascist of power … The fascists see [the] demand for a "dictatorship of the proletariat" as formulated by the younger sons of the father, whom they presume to be in league with all manner of scum and rabble. Their pretensions to "dictatorship" are seen to indicate aspirations to the status of father (vol.2, p.102, 378, 375).

I think Theweleit is correct in identifying social disruption and the rise to power of the 'lower orders' (whether or not they are experienced as younger brothers), as aspects of the supposed threat communism poses to the psychic reality of the fascist male. Communism can be seen as a promise to disrupt the fascist status quo of hierarchy and domination, and to do so in the name of those most oppressed (whatever the feasibility of such a project). But this does not address what is even more explicit in the soldier males' texts—the close connection between 'communism' and women. Both would seem to represent the same thing: a humanity diametrically opposed to the soldier males' reality of violence and death, and hence, one that promises cooperation not competition, connection not conflict, caring and nurturing not violence, love not terror, life not death. Such a reality would radically bring into question the soldier male's own. Of course, neither women nor communism (however construed) necessarily promise any such thing. But what is at issue here is not how 'women' or 'communism' might be interpreted in other contexts. What is at issue is how 'women' and 'communism' might be perceived by a psyche consumed by a murderous hatred for something they named 'proletarian women', and what that 'something' might be (since there was no such thing as 'proletarian women' except in the soldier males' imagination). It is because the soldier male's world was so dehumanised, that I have suggested that that 'something' is what I have called 'genuine humanity'.

Although he does not dwell on this point at any length, Theweleit would seem to agree. An ego like the soldier male's, he said, 'derives … from [these] men's compulsion to subjugate and repulse what is specifically human within them' (vol.2, p.162), constantly faced with 'the danger of immediate fragmentation on contact with living life'. That fragmentation is avoided, he said, by being 'inserted into some larger social formation that guarantees and maintains its boundaries' (vol.2, p.222). But that does not solve the problem of being threatened by 'living life', it merely provides a larger barricade against it. And the problem of being threatened by 'living life', as that problem was manifested in the psyches of the soldier males, had horrendous consequences for many millions of people, just because men like that were 'inserted into some larger social formation' with a culture that mirrored the dehumanisation they carried within. Theweleit was not suggesting that a larger social formation was any solution to the destruction wreaked by the soldier males, he was simply describing what happened. As he himself pointed out, the 'revenge' the soldier males say they are seeking 'is exacted on any being who continues to live life as such; on individuals whose "desire to desire" has never been transformed into the urge to murder' (vol.2, p.367).

And this was not simply a matter of the way they expressed themselves, but the way they acted:

> We should beware ... of seeing this in terms of expression alone ... [It] takes place not on the level of representation alone but on that of action. Fascist revenge is vast and expansive; it devastates the earth and annihilates human beings by the millions ... While it may be possible to classify certain of the party congresses as expressive theatre or representation, the same terms can never be applied to war or civil war, and certainly not to the concentration camp (vol.2, p.367).

Characteristics of the soldier males

What was the character structure demanded by the fascist lifeworld embraced by these soldier males, as shown in their writings? What kinds of human beings were these soldier males? The first thing that must be said about these men is their propensity for violence. They worshipped violence, especially in its condoned form—war: "'War was in his blood ... He was born for war; it was the only state in which he had ever been able to live life to the full ... we were both the executors of war and its creations, men whose life led inexorably to warfare'"[173] (vol.2, p.385).

This is the violence Theweleit refers to throughout Volume 2 as 'the White Terror', those counter-revolutionary forces that suppressed the left-wing uprisings in the Baltic states and Germany itself between the two world wars: 'these men ... went flying across the landscape like shrapnel from a machine blown apart at the seams, ripping to pieces whatever they encountered' (vol.2, p.207). The soldier males were quite clear about their propensity for violence: "'I had always taken particular pleasure in destruction ... Our men felt the original human desire beating and screaming for justice inside them—the desire for destruction'" (Salomon, *Die Geächteten*); "'Deep in his eyes, there glows a cold and merciless will to destruction'"[174] (vol.2, p.383).

Nevertheless despite the pleasure, their violence was driven by fear, Theweleit argued, even though in actual fact they were not the victims of atrocities but the ones perpetrating them: 'these men's only resource is their compulsion for revenge (though they speak as victims reduced to this state

---

173. Ernst Jünger (1922) *Des Kampf als innerres Erlebnis* (Battle as Inner Experience).

174. Friedrich Wilhelm Heinz (1930) *Sprengstoff* (Explosive). Heinz was a right-wing monarchist and a member of the Freikorps Ehrhardt, and he belonged to the Nazi party. But he was also a member of the anti-Hitler resistance that tried to prevent the outbreak of the Second World War and plotted unsuccessfully to assassinate Hitler in 1944. Surprisingly, he survived the discovery of the plot and died in 1968 (http://sculptinghistory.blogspot.com/2011/09/friedrich-wilhelm-heinz.html – viewed 9.8.2018).

by others on whom vengeance *can no longer be wrought*)' (vol.2, p.367—original emphasis). But there was something real they were afraid of. Theweleit saw this in terms of irruptions of the soldier males' own unconscious, of streams of terror and desire seemingly elicited by 'outside' forces—'the Red flood', 'proletarian women', 'the mass'—but in fact coming from areas of the soldier males' own psyches that threatened to inundate them with feelings they had not learned to manage: 'As we saw in our analysis of some of the most widespread acts of fascist terror, the tormentor derives his triumph from his success in divesting himself of his "unconscious"—which he destroys in the person of the tormented' (vol.2, p.384).

Theweleit suggested that the soldier males be seen 'as human beings born in a state of incompletion, or as human beings who are not-yet-fully-born' (vol.2, p.212). In other words, these men were infantile (although Theweleit did not use this term). Others have also argued that the fascist mentality is infantile. Silke Hesse (1990), for example, saw fascist society as 'a gang of adolescent youths' because bonds between young men were the only social relationships it validated. Whatever its propaganda said about 'the family' and women's positive role therein, Nazi society in fact repudiated any form of human relationship, including fatherhood, except for a male brotherhood of youth. As Theweleit also discovered, the fascist gang was not even interested in subordinating women; they obliterated them instead. Hesse argued that the adolescent male gang model had a number of political functions for any dictatorship. The adolescent male is no longer attached to his family of origin (and is also probably in rebellion against it), and he hasn't formed any other attachments. He is therefore available for attachment to the leader through whatever cause the leader uses to bind the immature psyche to him. Moreover, adolescents are still at a formative stage when they're looking for role models to identify with. Hesse commented that all armies exploit these characteristics to some extent, but in Germany at this historical period it came to dominate the entire society.

For Theweleit, the soldier males' infantilism showed in their need to be 'inserted into some larger social formation that guarantees and maintains [the ego's] boundaries' (vol.2, p.222), 'total' social organisations such as the fatherland, the German 'volk', homeland, the uniform, the exclusive company of men prepared to die for honour, glory and each other ('der Männerbund') (etc.). The most immediate of these were their militaristic organisations: 'The soldier carries a boundary with him, in the shape of the uniform, and the belt and crossbelt in particular' (vol.2, p.223). Theweleit described this as 'the totality-armor of the troop formation' (vol.2, p.207), and referred to the desire to be part of a totality as a lifelong yearning for 'unification with maternal bodies, within which [the man] can become "whole," born to completion' (vol.2, p.213).

Leaving aside the oxymoron of describing blatantly male supremacist organisations like the Freikorps as 'maternal bodies', Theweleit's point was that these were men who were still immersed in what Margaret Mahler has called the 'symbiotic phase' of the mother-infant relationship characteristic of the first four to five months of life (Mahler, 1967, 1974; Mahler et al, 2000). As a consequence, Theweleit argued, they had not developed the normal kind of ego that results from the resolution of the Oedipus complex: 'the "ego" arises through identifications within Oedipus' (vol.2, p.212). According to the theory of the Oedipus complex, it is identification with the father's social power—'the agent of socially defined power within the family' (vol.2, p.213)—that ensures the development of an ego, that sense of self that comes into being when the child comes to awareness of a self separate from other objects in the world, including other people. Instead of an integral ego and a healthy sense of self, these men had developed an ego like a suit of armour, hard and rigid but also fragile because it was imposed on a psyche incapable of assimilating it. This 'external' kind of ego was what resulted from 'the pain they have experienced in physical punishment and … their possible inundation as children by a mother's intermittent or sometimes constant and intense emotional involvement'; and its consequence was 'the damming in and negativization of the men's bodily flows … the expulsion of all pleasurable sensation from their body surface … a skin gripped by hard and stringent hands' (vol.2, p.212).

Theweleit found parallels between the psychic reality of the soldier males and that of the psychotic and severely disturbed children Mahler worked with: 'There seems to me to be a very striking correspondence between what Mahler identifies as features of "psychosis" in children and the behavioral traits of the soldier male as I have attempted to reconstruct them from his writings and actions' (vol.2, p.220). He was not arguing that these men were psychotic, but because they hadn't developed a fully integrated ego, they had 'never attained the security of body boundaries libidinally invested from within' (vol.2, p.211). They feared their own unconscious with its 'streams of desire', which they could not manage, or even let themselves be aware of, because they hadn't developed a sufficiently strong sense of self to enable them to accept these 'streams' as part of themselves. Their fear of being inundated and overwhelmed was a fear of their own inner life: 'For the soldier male [who is a] dam [holding back the floods], none of the streams

… can be allowed to flow. He is out to prevent all of them from flowing: "imaginary" and real streams, streams of sperm and desire'. In contrast, Theweleit continues, human life needs to keep flowing like a nourishing stream: 'human beings live in, and on, flows. They die when streams dry up' (vol.1, p.266).

But these totalities, far from controlling them and keeping them in check, in fact encouraged the 'savage torrents' of their violence. As Theweleit pointed out, some of their worst atrocities were committed as part of the troop formation, egged on by the officers who knew that the men needed practice in shedding blood if they were to be of any use in stemming the 'Red tide': 'it was indeed on such occasional infringements that "normal" military discipline was founded. If the machine does not drink blood from time to time it creaks, grinds, and becomes defective' (vol.2, p.209). So while it may be the case that the soldier males were infantile in their need to immerse themselves in a larger totality as an escape from facing their own 'streams of desire', Theweleit's account of how they failed to develop a genuinely human sense of self is less than satisfactory.

Mother-blaming

The first unsatisfactory aspect is a tendency towards mother-blaming. Theweleit himself is aware that this is a danger but he doesn't always avoid it, vide his statement quoted above regarding 'possible inundation as children by a mother's intermittent or sometimes constant and intense emotional involvement' (vol.2, p.212). He says that '[t]here is admittedly a danger' in saying that mothers play a crucial part in the installation of the 'crazed order of half-born destructiveness' that is fascism. Any such statement, he says, 'could be used to reconstruct women as sources of evil'. Nonetheless, he does say that 'that order would have been *unthinkable* without the effective support of mothers'; and that there were 'crucial maternal influences … on sons who were only too eager to insert themselves into the deadly macromachines of fascism' (vol.2, p.384—original emphasis). And his attempt to mend matters doesn't help. He says that 'the mother-child relationship could equally well become the basis for a revolutionary perception of women as producers of nonmurderous human beings … given the importance ascribed by Balint, Mahler, and others to [the symbiotic phase]'. But given that his book is not concerned with the maternal production of *non*-murderous human beings and that he has nothing to say about such a process, we are left with mothers as the original source of the child-rearing practices that lead to the fascist mindset. He does attribute the development of the rigid 'body-armour' of the soldier male to the brutal training he received during adolescence as an officer cadet in the military academy (vol.2, pp.143-53). But adolescence occurs many years after the infantile 'symbiotic' phase when, Theweleit argues, the 'not-yet-fully-born' fascist psyche is inculcated; and only 'mother' is around then.

Moreover, his account of the aetiology of autism suggests that he does tend to hold mothers responsible for how their children turn out. 'Autistic children', he said, 'are generally unplanned and emotionally starved; they are often rejected from birth by the mother and have had either negative or nonexistent early breast and eye contact: or they are children who have been neglected and "left out in the cold" by both parents' (vol.2, p.222). But perhaps he doesn't believe that any more. Certainly, the experts have stopped blaming mothers for their children's autism:[175]

> The exact causes of autism spectrum disorder (ASD) are unknown, although it is thought that several complex genetic and environmental factors are involved.[176]

> recent research suggests that Autism may result when a child with a genetic susceptibility and/or abnormal Omega-3 fatty acid profile in cell membranes is exposed to one or more environmental insults (heavy metal exposure, virus or bacteria) resulting in malfunctioning cells (often in the gut and brain). This can happen "in utero" (during pregnancy) or after birth (post-partum).[177]

To give Theweleit his due, he doesn't often talk about mothers in connection with the symbiotic phase. His primary concern is with the psyche of the sons. It wasn't mothers, after all, who formed themselves into Freikorps brigades of 'spinning fragments whose chaoticized "id" sought escape in savage torrents' (vol.2, p.207), no matter how encouraging German mothers might have been, wittingly or unwittingly. And he is right to see the period of early infancy as crucial to the formation of the male supremacist psyche, not because of the behaviour of mothers, but because it is a period of utter helplessness, and there is nothing the supremacist mind hates, fears and denies more than his own helplessness. Theweleit is also right to see the need to belong body, mind and soul to a totalising collectivity as a form of

---

175. For a refutation of the medical profession's erroneous conviction that autism was caused by cold, unloving mothers, see: Park, 1967.

176. http://www.nhs.uk/Conditions/Autistic-spectrum-disorder/Pages/Causes.aspx – viewed 9.8.2018.

177. http://www.autism.net.au/Autism_causes.htm – viewed 9.8.2018.

infantilism. It allows the true believer to participate in the omnipotence of the totality so much larger than his own puny self, and absolves him of the responsibility for his own actions that belongs to normal adulthood.

Oedipus complex

Another problem concerns his appeal to an Oedipus complex as a necessary process in developing a sense of self. Margaret Mahler's writings had nothing to say about it, despite Theweleit's constant references to her work as the source of his concept of the 'not-yet-fully-born'. She didn't repudiate the notion of an Oedipus complex. Because she saw herself writing within the Freudian tradition, she continued to make approving references to it, as well as to 'castration anxiety'. She called the developmental process she was talking about 'preoedipal', for example, and suggested that what happened to the child during this time could cause difficulties for 'the resolution of the complex object-related conflicts of the oedipal period' (Mahler et al, 1975: 230). But in her account, infants in the first three years of life develop a sense of themselves through a separation-individuation process primarily and importantly in relation to their mothers (as long as the mothering is 'good enough'—to use Winnicott's term).[178] Indeed, the foundation for the later development of the ego is laid down even before the separation-individuation process begins, i.e. during the symbiotic phase[179] itself (Theweleit's reference point in his account of fascist men as 'not-yet-fully-born'): 'It is within this matrix of physiological and sociobiological dependency on the mother that the structural differentiation takes place which lead to the individual's organization for adaptation: the functioning ego' (Mahler et al, 1975: 45).

In Mahler's account a symbiotic phase does precede the separation-individuation process, but the infant's journey of separation-individuation subsequent to the initial symbiotic unity with the mother doesn't need fathers, Oedipally speaking. It takes place in four sub-phases in the life of the infant: 'differentiation, practicing, rapprochement, and "on the way to libidinal object constancy"' (Mahler et al, 1975: 39-40), in each of which the mother's involvement is central. To give one example:

---

178. For example: 'Infant development [is] facilitated by good-enough maternal care' (Winnicott, 1960: 595).

179. Mahler said she wasn't using the term 'symbiosis' in the usual sense, it was a metaphor: 'Unlike the biological concept of symbiosis, it does not describe what actually happens in a mutually beneficial relationship between two separate individuals of different species (Mahler et al, 1975: 44).

> During the entire practicing subphase, the child has evoked the delighted and automatic admiration of the adult world, specifically of his average "ordinary devoted mother" [citing Winnicott, 1960]. Her admiration, when it is forthcoming, augments the practicing toddler's sound narcissism, his love of himself. Every new achievement, every new feat of the fledgling elicits admiration, at first unsolicited, later more or less exhibitionistically provoked by him from the entire adult object world around him (Mahler, 1974: 99).

In this account fathers are not necessary for infants' normal, healthy ego development, even though they might be important as loving parents, mothers' partners and part of the adult world. What the Oedipus theory adds to this is that, as *fathers* (rather than nurturing adult human beings), they are necessary for the inculcation of the chief value of male supremacy—penis-possession and its lack (i.e. masculinity and femininity). Or rather, because the issue is one of meanings and values and not personality characteristics (or not in the first place), the Oedipal theory is an ideology of 'father'—popularly couched in terms of reverence for 'the family', aversion to 'single mothers', and panegyrics about the importance of 'both parents'. As an ideology, the Oedipus complex needs no actual father present to make its influence felt. It can be channelled through the child's mother, other adults and the child's peers, or more likely, through the ubiquitous television industry. But however it happens, the ego that develops under the influence of the Oedipus complex is a male supremacist one, not a genuinely human one (in the sense in which I am using the term).

The clearest indication of this is that the Oedipus complex doesn't apply to females (or to males to the extent that they are to grow into genuinely human adults). In Freud's theory of the Oedipus complex, the ego of the child develops through fear of the father's power to castrate, then renunciation of the mother, and then eventual identification with the father. But obviously this just-so story applies only to males. As Freud himself remarked perfunctorily: 'We have an impression here that what we have said about the Oedipus complex applies with complete strictness to the male child only' (Freud, 1931: 375). The Oedipal phase starts with the threat of castration (supposedly) and females don't have penises to be cut off; neither can they eventually identify with the father because they're the wrong sex (well anyway, a different one). So girls don't go through the Oedipal phase. Does that mean that women therefore have fragile egos? Indeed it could mean exactly that. In a world made in the image and likeness of men, women do have a hard time developing a sense of self. (So do men to the extent that they want a genuinely human sense of self, something that male supremacy denies them). But that fragile female ego (always supposing that that is the case) does not lead women to commit acts of violence. That is a male prerogative; most of the violence in the world is perpetrated by men.

So there is something else going on here. I would argue that, far from it being the case that the soldier males lacked an Oedipal ego, they were only too well socialised into the ethos of the Oedipus complex, with its hyper-valuation of penis-possession, its standard operating procedures of fear and loss, and its obliteration of female humanity. Adherence to the theory of the Oedipus complex meant that it was common among the early Freudians (and Freud himself) to see femaleness (always called 'femininity') in terms of lack: females lacked the only bodily organ that conferred 'human' status. But read from a genuinely human standpoint, successful resolution of the Oedipus complex means it is males who lack something. To the extent that they are successfully inculcated with the meanings and values of male supremacist penis-possession, they lack a healthy, integrated sense of self capable of recognising and respecting others and being able to accept recognition in return. What domination requires, if its male children are to be socialised into a culture of dominance and violence, is a psychic structure characterised by this kind of absence.

In the soldier males it had been replaced with an ego more like 'fragmented armor' (vol.2, pp.106-10), which tended to disintegrate when its own infantile fear and rage ('instincts') were elicited under conditions of stress. Because this ego is not self-aware enough to be able to acknowledge those 'instincts' as its own, it locates the source of its fear and rage elsewhere ('the Red flood', 'proletarian whores', or anyone not belonging to the totality of the troop-formation); and because the rage and fear feel like annihilation, the perceived source of the threat must be killed before it can carry it out: 'the soldiers … beat and shot to death whatever they met in their vicinity, enemy and nonenemy' (vol.2, p.207—original emphasis). Murder was essential to the ego of the soldier male: 'In his lethal penetration of other human beings, the soldier male "distances" himself, "differentiates" himself in opposition to them, and thus once again escapes death by apportioning it to others' (vol.2, p.208). Killing makes him feel safe: 'After the blood bath is over and thirst is quenched … when the man feels content in the knowledge that every limb is in its place; he transforms himself with relative rapidity into the unfeeling but satisfied pig he once was' (vol.2, p.209).

Theweleit is partly correct in identifying the unconscious urges of the soldier males as the source of their fear. Clinically speaking, these men were paranoid. They felt themselves menaced by outside forces while the feeling of menace really came from within, from the threatened collapse of the too-rigid defences they had built up to maintain the reality of their dehumanised male supremacist world. Characteristic of a paranoid reality is a sense of justification rendered impregnable by the fact that there are indeed outside forces threatening to demolish their world. Those forces are the resistance the men encounter as they attempt to impose their own reality on the world around them. The resistance belongs to that genuine humanity which I have suggested contains the alternative to male supremacy. In the case of the soldier males, the threat from the 'outside' is a consequence of their own prior commitment to a death-dealing, dehumanised world, and of the violence they wreak in their efforts to maintain that world.

These men were indeed threatened by their own 'streams of desire', but those urges were not erotic impulses towards women which became violent as the result of repression. This is Theweleit's argument: 'the *concrete* form of the struggle against the flowing-machine productive force of the unconscious had been (and still is) a battle against women, against female sexuality' (vol.1, p.258—original emphasis). But it was not female sexuality these men were fighting, although that was the way in which they portrayed what they were fighting against ('Red nurses', 'whores'). Male sex with women is not female sexuality, as rape and prostitution show only too clearly. Prostitution has nothing to do with female sexuality; it is an institution established to service *male* sexuality. Women supply the service more or less willingly, and sometimes children too, always unwillingly. But the women who supply the service are not motivated by sexual desire, but by the need for money or by coercion; and the children are always coerced. The sexual desire and the demand belong to men. Prostitution exists because there is something wrong with men, not because women sell a sexuality that can in any way be seen as their own.

Moreover, the men weren't acting on their own sexual desire either. Their writings contain no accounts of sex: 'Whenever the possibility of sexual relations with women arises in these accounts, the writer takes pains to point out that nothing actually happens' (vol.1, p.37). Indeed, so averse were these men to any form of sexual intercourse with women, that they didn't even rape them: 'It would seem "logical" for the soldiers to react to being sexually aroused by the Red nurses by deciding to rape them on the spot. Yet that *hardly ever* occurred, either in novels or in fact' (vol.1, p.155—original emphasis).

So the desires streaming out of the soldier male unconscious were not sexual. Rather, I would suggest, they were streams of a desire for life, of genuine humanity in other words, which the men could not afford to acknowledge because that streaming threatened to demolish their male supremacist reality. Women were so threatening because their very existence gave the lie to the worldview of these men, a world consisting only of men where women did not exist; and 'communism' was so threatening because it seemed to promise social relations of mutual respect and equality that would overthrow the relations of domination and subordination the soldier males needed if they were to maintain their identity. The violence served to defend the armoured self from the importuning of their own humanity, against which the armour had been originally erected. For the soldier male, whose self-awareness was structured around the glorification of war, violence, fighting and death, any hint of genuine humanity felt like his own annihilation. In that sense, Theweleit is wrong when he argues that it is 'difficult to conceptualize the behavior of the soldier male in Oedipal terms' (vol.2, p.210). On the contrary, these men were only too fully-born into egos structured by the phallic requirements of the Oedipus complex, and into the reality of male supremacy. What they lacked was a sense of common humanity, as their brutality demonstrated only too clearly.

Dissociation

The worldview of the fascist male is obviously dissociated. Theweleit put this in terms of 'the fascist process of appropriating and transmuting reality' in the writings of the soldier males. This process took the form of appeals to overarching transpersonal entities which provided the justification for holding everyday life in contempt:

> That preoccupation with large-scale politics, with the destinies of the race and humanity, implies a negation of the small, the close-at-hand, of microhistory. By moving outward to broad horizons, to the public and the social, they attempt to avoid the private, the intimate, the individual' (vol.1, p.88).

As Theweleit put it, '[t]hey feel closer in spirit to the mythical Nibelungs than to afternoon teatime' (vol.1, p.88). However, Theweleit's account understates the problem involved in the fascist 'transmutation' of reality. As he himself frequently pointed out, the fascist mentality didn't just want to change reality, he wanted to destroy it. As Salomon so aptly phrased it, they took 'particular pleasure in destruction'. While it is true that they held in contempt 'the private, the intimate, the individual', they wanted to destroy the ordinary

227

desire of ordinary people to live lives of peace, security and contentment, because such lives had no place for the soldier males' grandiose desires for glory.

But the primary form dissociation takes in the writings of the soldier males is the obliteration of women. A world without women cannot be a genuinely human world. Conventional malestream media thrive on the obliteration of women too (this is one of the continuities between fascism and everyday male supremacy everywhere); but the dissociation displayed in the language of the soldier males is peculiarly blatant. Theweleit identified two ways in which that language obliterated reality. The first involved their treatment of everyday life. Whenever they wrote about such commonplace things as their physical relations to other people, to themselves, to their work, and to their feelings, their language became, Theweleit says, 'meaningless, apparently voided, "aborted"'. The second way involved things where their feelings were fiercely engaged, what Theweleit referred to as 'configurations of "living intensity"'. Examples included descriptions of battles, their 'world-historical missions', and their feelings about 'inferior' others—the proletariat, blacks, Jews, women. In these cases, says Theweleit, 'their language … usurp[s] its objects, it becomes the parasite that penetrates them and dissolves their boundaries; the force that strips them of their "object-ness" and drains them of life' (vol.2, p.347-8).

But the soldier males also recorded experiences that would qualify as dissociation even on clinical criteria: descriptions of trance-like fugue states and blackouts, where the retreat from reality is total, even if it lasts only a short time. One example comes from Salomon's 1933 novel, *Kadetten* (Cadets). Salomon writes about being in a town square full of people just before the outbreak of the First World War. Reality dims around him even though the sun is shining brightly, he loses sight and hearing, and his perception of the person standing next to him fades away:

> "The whole square was suddenly filled with a great black mass [of people]. I began to wonder why the mass should be black – the sun was shining in all its glory … I listened but could hear nothing … For a moment the mass seemed simply to disappear … even the man at my side … started to swim before my eyes, to lose his fleshy reality" (vol.1, p.41).

What brings him back to himself is the announcement from the man standing next to him that "'the war is coming at last'".

Another example of dissociated perception comes from Dwinger's *Auf halbem Wege*. The author describes an incident where the soldiers fire one round into a crowd they perceive as a 'mass' threatening to 'surge and engulf them in a single movement'. After that single shot:

> "[a] scream (exploded into the sky) … incomprehensibly, the square emptied within seconds! A few dozen, a handful of dark stains still lay scattered, trampled underfoot by the mass's own senseless flight; but the roaring, raging human wave had been magically obliterated" (vol.2, p.33-4).

The dissociation here can be seen, firstly, in the ease with which the soldier males dispersed the crowd and the instantaneous rapidity with which it happened ('magically obliterated … within seconds'). Then there is the description of the people who had been killed by the soldier males themselves as 'dark stains', and attributing those 'dark stains' to the people who had run away from the soldiers—'trampled underfoot by the mass'. And then there is the reference to the crowd's flight as 'senseless', when there is nothing at all senseless about running away from danger.

Another example comes from Jünger's *Über den Schmerz* (On Pain). It is similar to Dwinger's example in that this 'mass', too, is 'magically obliterated'. This time the crowd was fired upon by a three-man machine-gun detachment, and "'vanished without trace from the scene … one minute after the order to fire'". The author continues: "'There was something magical about the image [of the empty scene]; it evoked the profound joy that holds us irresistibly in its grasp at the unmasking of some odious demon'" (vol.2, p.34).

Another example comes from a different context—listening to a speech. The example comes from Joseph Goebbels' novel, *Michael*.[180] The eponymous first-person narrator is in a hall with a lot of other men, "'all poor and downtrodden'", when one of the men gets up and starts speaking. Very soon, Michael is "'captivated'". He is also swept away by what the man is saying and taken out of himself: "'I had no knowledge of what was happening inside me … I no longer knew what I was doing. I was almost out of my mind … By now I could hear nothing; I was intoxicated … What happened then I cannot say'" (vol.2, p.121-2). Neither does he tell his readers what it was that the speaker said, apart from the exclamation: "'Honor? Work? The flag?'" (vol.2, p.121). Theweleit points out that this 'reticence on the explicit content of fascist speeches' was typical of the writings of the soldier males (vol.2, p.127).

According to Theweleit, trance-like states were brought on by 'any contact between "inner" and "outer" realms—any boundary transgression' (vol.1,

---

180 Yes, *that* Goebbels, Nazi Minister for Propaganda, who committed suicide with Hitler in the bunker in 1945, along with his wife, Magda, after killing their six children.

p.263). He refers to this as a form of "'satisfaction'" involving "'unification [which] can be achieved only *in opposition to* consciousness'" (vol.2, p.127—original emphasis). In other words, the man needs to lose consciousness because his defences have been breached:

> Whenever the thresholds are crossed—the ubiquitous thresholds of prohibitions across the body, thresholds of defense and control, thresholds of fear before the regions of the unknown—the transition takes place in a state of trance, intoxication, or miracle. This applies both to killing and to participation (for this is more than mere listening) in the speeches of the leader (vol.2, p.127).

Theweleit's account is less than clear at this point. He says that this has something to do with 'redemption': 'both [killing and participation in the speeches] represent forms of external contact through which the fascist male receives redemption … and redemption includes loss of consciousness' (vol.2, p.127—original ellipsis). But it is unlikely that what is involved here is 'redemption'. Clearly, both killing people and fascist speechifying arouse in the soldier male something he doesn't want to face; but it doesn't make sense to suggest that he is redeemed when he successfully manages to avoid facing it. I would suggest (again) that what he is avoiding facing is his own loss of humanity. He loses consciousness as a way of managing the protests of humanity against the dehumanisation of the fascist worldview. If he remained conscious he would be faced with what he has been denying and he can't afford to allow that to happen.

It is not immediately obvious why participating in the over-blown rhetoric of the fascist speech should threaten to remind the soldier male of his lost humanity. After all, those speeches were intended to reinforce the dehumanised fascist worldview and they were extraordinarily successful in doing just that, if the evidence of the soldier males' writings is any guide (together with what we know historically about Nazi rallies). For the same reason—because they were so successful—it's not clear why the speeches would have crossed the soldier males' 'thresholds' of defence against 'regions of the unknown' either, because the speeches were meant to reinforce their defences: '[t]he external form of the speech appears to function as part of the fascist body-armor' (vol.2, p.128).

I would suggest that the reason why fascist speeches threatened to remind the hearers of the humanity they were denying by their participation, was precisely because they were so successful. They reduced people to mindless particles in a dehumanised whole and turned the assembled crowd into a mob—'the mass in totality-formation'. The fascist speech—indeed, any form of demagoguery—is a form of dehumanisation. To the extent that people participate in it, it strips them of their ability to think, and hence of their ability to give reasons, to make decisions, to behave decently and to act responsibly. As Theweleit said, 'the assembled crowd does not assemble in order to think or to be enlightened'; and neither does the speaker intend to enlighten them. He 'simply produces twenty or thirty versions of a statement that is in any case already familiar to and applauded by everyone present'. The speech has no factual or conceptual content, a necessary omission if the speaker is to succeed in his aim of 'speak[ing] the inexpressible … rous[ing] the imprisoned desire of the masses … to form it into a … longed-for "unity" and "wholeness"' (vol.2, p.129). It is the very enormity of the dehumanisation that rouses the hearers' humanity in protest, a genuinely human response that must be defeated by a deliberate dulling of awareness if participation in the dehumanised 'wholeness' is to be maintained.

An even more extreme form of dehumanisation is killing people, and many of the trance-like accounts occurred in this context. For example, in the incidents described above, the square empties 'incomprehensibly', the 'mass' is 'magically obliterated', even though it was the soldier males themselves who had fired into the crowd. This evasion of responsibility for killing people occurs many times. One example involved a 'Red nurse'/'rifle woman' who '"lay behind the bushes, in the most tender embrace with her lover. A grenade had caught her off guard in the practice of her true profession"' (i.e. prostitution) (vol.1, p.82).[181] It was presumably the author himself who threw the grenade, but he does not say so. There is also the peculiarity of coupling 'most tender embrace' with the act of blowing someone to pieces, and neglecting to mention that there were two people who were killed by the grenade.

Another example involved what the author called '"a regrettable accident"' whereby '"nurse Ida Sode of the Marienberg convent was shot in the head while observing the battle from the bell tower of the convent church"' (vol.1, p.174).[182] The information is firmly couched in the passive voice and no one is said to be responsible.

In another example the murders happen offstage. They are committed by members of the author's own troop, but the author himself is not involved.

---

181. Adolf Schultz (1922) *Ein Freikorps im Industriegebiet* (A Freikorps in the Industrial Area). Schultz was a Freikorps commander.

182. From the memoirs of Georg Ludwig Rudolf Maercker (1921 *Vom Kaiserheer zur Reichswehr*. Maercker (1865-1924) was a General in the German army in the First World War and organised the first Freikorps unit.

He doesn't even witness them. The author is a member of a Freikorps troop in Latvia, who are conducting a house-to-house search when they come upon the "'horribly mutilated corpses'" of their comrades in the cellar of a building where two women are living. The author describes what happens next: "'two or three men storm upstairs. The dull thudding of clubs is heard. Both women lie dead on the floor of their room'". He comments: "'the act was sudden but unjust. The women ... hadn't carried out the evil deed'", that is, it wasn't the women who murdered the men in the cellar. In fact, "'they can prove that they took in, and even patched up, a wounded German soldier'". This man is with the women when his comrades arrive, and it is he who tells them to go and look in the cellar (vol.1, p.183-4).[183] The dissociated tone of this narrative is shown in the 'noises off' nature of the murder, the feeble reaction ('unjust'), the eventual conclusion that the women deserved to be clubbed to death—"'The women were aware of the horrors in the cellar, of course, and had probably even given complete assent to the fate that befell the poor wounded men'"—and that they were only peasants anyway—they wore "'heavy sheepskins and bast shoes'".[184]

Entitlement

The fascist sense of entitlement of the soldier male is well-known. To take just one soldier male's view, Wilhelm Weigand in *Die Rote Flut* 1935:

> "Shall I tell you what is the scourge of our being as Germans? It is the depth of the tension between the mass and those towering individuals in whom the German essence lives and grows creative ... precisely because the German individual towers so high above men of other countries, the German mass is all the more dreadful" (vol.2, p.48).

Theirs was the mentality of men who believed absolutely in their 'right' to kill those they deemed inferior beings, a 'right' bestowed on them by their superiority over ordinary people ('the mass') and their membership in the larger entity to which they owed allegiance. That larger entity was always Germany whatever else it was as well. Salomon, in *Die Geächteten*:

> "I knew we could never have been wrong; we had lived our lives in accordance with the urgent will of the epoch, and had indeed been increasingly applauded for our actions ... We were haunted by our time,

---

183. Erich Balla (1932) *Landsknechte wurden wir: Abenteur aus dem Baltikum* (Fighting Men: Adventure in the Baltic). Balla was a Freikorps commander in the Baltic

184. According to Wikipedia (9.4.2014), bast shoes are a kind of basket woven and fitted to the shape of a foot, and made from tree bark. They were the traditional footwear of poor people who lived in the forest areas of Northern Europe.

haunted by its destruction, haunted too by the pain we would have to suffer if destruction was to be made fruitful" (vol.2, p.382).

For Captain Berthold, 'the German' was surrounded by inferior beings envious of his superiority and threatening to drag him back into the mire from which he had so valiantly extracted himself:

"The man who heaves himself out of the mass and sets larger goals for his life is universally ostracized; only a very few understand him … The whole enemy alliance against us is built on hatred and envy of the tirelessly forward-striving, restlessly toiling German" (vol.2, p.50).

The sense of entitlement conveyed by this passage from Berthold's diary arises not only from the fact that he is German, but also from feelings of injury and victimisation. He and his fellows are being held back by 'the mass' and by enemies who hate them and who are sufficiently well-organised to be able to halt the progress of those who have risen above the masses. 'Destruction' was necessary to fend off the 'hatred and envy'. But, as Theweleit pointed out, these men were 'the most powerful of the fighting forces available to big business, the bourgeoisie and the peasantry, in their various struggles against the revolutionary proletariat' after the First World War (vol.2, p.382). These men created victims, they were not among the victimised.

The overweening sense of entitlement of the fascist worldview was also expressed in a statement attributed to Hermann Goering by Rush Rhees: 'Recht ist das, was uns gefällt' ('Right is whatever we want it to be') (Rhees, 1970: 101). Ludwig Wittgenstein's famous response to this when Rhees quoted it to him, was to say: 'even that is a kind of ethics. It is helpful in silencing objections to a certain attitude. And it should be considered along with other ethical judgements and discussions, in the anthropological discussions which we may have to conduct' (pp.101-2). What that means in anybody's guess, but according to Paul Johnston, there is a sense in which this statement of Goering's 'constitutes precisely a rejection of the ethical' (Johnston, 1989: 114) (and perhaps Goering intended exactly that). Ethics, i.e. judgements about what it morally right and wrong, has its own logic that has nothing to do with likes and dislikes (pace Wittgenstein). Liking something does not make it morally right, just as disliking it does not make it morally wrong. That this fascist worldview is inherently masculine (in the male supremacist sense) is shown by the fact that only men had access to the resources necessary to impose this particular 'ethical' stance, whether it was the power of 'great sphere of politics' (which was available only to the leaders) or the power of physical brutality (available to any man who cared to exercise it).

Both

It is in this sense of entitlement that the soldier male's dissociation from reality is most clearly shown. For example, in *Michael*, Goebbels provides a statement of the fascist belief in their mission to re-make the world. He distinguishes between 'expressionists' (the powerful who make the world in their own image and likeness) and 'impressionists' (weaklings who are nothing but a reflection of what the world imposes on them):

> "All of us today are expressionists, men who wish to form the external world out of our own inner selves. The expressionist builds a new world in himself. His inner ardor is his secret and his power; but his conceptual world is repeatedly shattered on contact with reality. The soul of the impressionist is a microcosmic image of the macrocosmos. But the soul of the expressionist is a new macrocosmos, a world in and of itself. The expressionist's perception of the world derives from his sense of his own autocratic selfhood; both he and the world are explosive" (vol.2, p.368).

Again, Jünger, in his novel *Feuer und Blut* (Fire and Blood), provides a statement of the overarching importance of war in fashioning a reality where Germany is dominant:

> "We were the God of War incarnate ... we rose up with a Germanic fury that brooked no resistance. Only terror could counter the hatred of the men we confronted, yet allow us to retain our dignity. And so we stand here today as the terrible executors of an absolute justice—a justice that follows its own laws, a justice asserted against even the strongest will in a hostile world" (vol.2, p.368).

In *Die Geächteten*, Salomon provides an explicit statement of this fascist ethic of arrogant entitlement, together with the way in which it is dissociated from any genuine humanity. For Salomon, the soldier males were entitled to fight any 'ruler' whose power they regarded as 'illegitimate', because they were uniquely connected to an 'infinite and deep-rooted force', which was nothing less than a mandate from God. This same mandate also entitled them to determine the future, presumably for the whole human race, since he did not specify whose future he was talking about. But the dissociation from any genuine humanity is most clearly expressed in the distinction he makes between 'illegitimate' and 'legitimate' power. The former is explicitly identified as power that responds to human needs; the latter is power that supposedly arises out of the mythical 'infinite and deep-rooted force':

> "It was, and will always remain, our duty to fight rulers whose power is illegitimate. The order of values of illegitimate power is dictated by

human needs; that of legitimate power is defined by the infinite and deep-rooted force out of which needs are first created. This force was our unique and constant point of reference ... Not content with deliberating the possible meaning of the future, we set about determining the criteria of judgement. Such was the task entrusted to us; and the only crime we could commit was failure. We were fighting God's fight with the demons" (vol.2, p.377).

What is so terrifying about the dissociated reality of these men is the fact that they gained sufficient power and credibility to make it a reality for millions of people. Yes, there was resistance, both from individuals who retained their connection to their own humanity and saw the fascist reality for the dehumanised horror that it was, and from other powers-that-be (than Germany)—the 'Second World War'. But fascism became a reality for millions, and not always reluctantly. So it is important to be clear that what Theweleit's soldier males were dissociated from was not reality in a factual sense, but the reality of a genuine humanity that embraces life and love instead of hatred, violence and death.

Continuities

There is a general consensus that fascism didn't arise out of nowhere and that it hasn't gone away, in other words, that there is a continuity between fascism and social life more generally. But as in the case of definitions of fascism, there are different views about what it is that preceded its historical appearance and gave rise to it, and what it is that persists despite its defeat as a form of nationhood. While many of these views express the continuity in terms of masculinity—a brutal male supremacist form of what is still recognisably normative—others find the continuity elsewhere.

Susan Sontag, for example, saw the continuity in terms of 'fascination'. Fascism still appealed to people (and presumably always would), because it involved what she referred to as 'ideas' that still existed under other names. Her article, 'Fascinating fascism' (1974), made no mention of masculinity, and it was also not concerned with fascism's violence. '[I]t is generally thought', she said, 'that National Socialism ... more broadly, fascism ... stands only for brutishness and terror. But this is not true' (p.319). Or rather, it wasn't the whole truth. Fascism, she insisted, also exercised an ongoing fascination, because it appealed to

ideals that are persistent today under other banners: the ideal of life as art; the cult of beauty; the fetishism of courage; the dissolution of alienation in ecstatic feelings of community; the repudiation of the intellect; the family of man (under the parenthood of leaders) (Sontag, 1974: 319-20).

There is nothing particularly masculine about these 'ideals' and neither are they necessarily violent. But while attempts to understand fascism as something other than 'brutishness and terror' might be an interesting intellectual exercise, the driving need to understand it comes from precisely its brutality. The important question in this context is: what is the connection between brutality and those persistent 'ideas'?

And in fact, Sontag did not move very far away from 'brutishness and terror' in her account of the ongoing fascination of fascism. That fascination is sexual, she said. It consists of 'powerful and growing currents of sexual feeling, those that generally go by the name of sadomasochism' (p.324). Sontag appeared to believe that the fascination of sadomasochism was its theatricality; it was an exciting contrast to sex as practised by 'ordinary people'. But as she herself acknowledges, the central defining characteristic of sadomasochism is 'domination and enslavement' (p.325), and it is the fascination with 'domination and enslavement' that provides the link with fascism.

This, of course, is the reason for its brutality. A culture of domination and enslavement provides the dehumanised justification for violence and murder, for crazed entitlement on the part of the powerful, and disentitlement, even to a right to life, imposed on the helpless. That such meanings and values persist, despite fascism's historical defeat, is due to the continued existence of male supremacy. Sontag had nothing to say about this. She didn't criticise fascism, perhaps because that had already been done, perhaps because she wanted to say something new about it. For her, the historical occurrence of fascism supplied a resource for what is now only innocent fun and pleasure: 'Of course, most people who are turned on by SS uniforms are not signifying approval of what the Nazis did, if indeed they have more than the sketchiest idea of what that might be' (Sontag, 1974: 323-4). But this is a failure of the moral responsibility we all have to fight the evil that men do to the best of our ability. A desire that involves pleasurable acting out of any aspect of Nazism (as opposed to a moral stance of horror and outright condemnation) is complicit with it. It is that complicity that is the continuity between 'what the Nazis did' and present-day society, especially those elements of society whose sexual desire involves a 'fad for Nazi regalia' (p.325). Even though such faddishness does not involve the same degree of violence historical fascism visited on the helpless, it does involve a weakening, if not the complete absence, of any genuinely human ethical sensibility on the part of the sadomasochist play-actors who do not know 'what the Nazis did'.

There are other suggestions about the ways in which the meanings and values of historical fascism might still be relevant now. Writing in the 1990 volume dedicated to the work of Klaus Theweleit, Bernd Hüppauf (1990) saw the continuity in terms of a 'technological vision of man as raw material with no core, who must therefore be moulded according to the perceived needs of the modern age'. This vision took a particularly 'primitive and violent' form under fascism, he said, but it did not end with the defeat of the fascist regimes, and 'its threatening consequences are still virulent' (p.76). His use of the word 'man' can be taken literally, since he was only talking about men. However, he did not acknowledge that; and he made no attempt to analyse the ways in which the 'technological vision of man as raw material with no core' might be connected to masculinity of 'the modern age'.

Allen Guttmann (1999) found a similarity between 'the Fascisms that spread like a virus through European culture in the 1920s and 1930s' and certain themes in D. H. Lawrence's novels, *Aaron's Rod*, *Kangaroo* and *The Plumed Serpent*. That similarity involved 'an authoritarian irrationality [and] a belief in charismatic leadership on the basis of "blood knowledge"' (p.170). Guttmann pointed out that Lawrence was not a supporter of fascism. He 'disliked the bureaucratic brutality of Italian Fascism as it was actually institutionalized' (p.170), and he didn't live to see the Nazis come to power (he died in 1930). But Guttmann didn't say how authoritarianism, irrationality, leadership and 'blood knowledge' might structure masculinity (or vice versa); nor did he make any connections between these phenomena and the politically condoned violence of fascism.

Other commentators did see the continuity between fascism and everyday life in terms of masculinity. Mosse (1996) argued that worship of the male body was not only central to fascism, it was also central to what he referred to as 'modern masculinity … a stereotype that became normative' throughout all Western societies from the beginning of the nineteenth century, and not just those conventionally recognised as fascist. 'Modern masculinity', he said, 'was to define itself through an ideal of manly beauty that symbolized virtue. That is why we shall deal so extensively with both the ideal male body and its attributes' (p.5). But as I have already pointed out, a fascination with the male body is not sufficient to explain the dehumanised violence that is fascism, 'warrior qualities' notwithstanding.

Once again, it is Klaus Theweleit who gives us one of the more interesting and relevant accounts of the continuities between fascism and male supremacist masculinity more generally. Fascism, in his view, was simply an extreme version of a cultural milieu that had existed throughout Europe for centuries:

> In the preceding section we traced the ways in which a particular conception of culture had emerged during the course of European history, one framed in terms of a centralistic subjection of nature, of femininity [i.e. women], and, finally, of the individual unconscious, all of which have been banished from the male ego. Under fascism, this labor of destruction gradually extended to everything living: the fascist quality of "soldierliness" was simply an extension of existing definitions of culture (vol.2, p.49).

Fascism can take over the hearts and minds of men (and of women, too, to the extent that they support those men) because the desires and realities of the male supremacist obliteration of women already exist. As Theweleit put it towards the end of his second volume:

> '[Hitler's] final speech to the party conference … highlights his capacity to speak expertly of states and desires that were indeed massively present in the assembled blocks of his listeners—a capacity that would in fact have been wasted, had those states and desires not already been existent … What he expressed quite explicitly was the whole configuration of existence as a "man among men," in a form appropriate to his time, namely fascism (vol.2, p.413).

His account of the soldier males as 'not-yet-fully-born' attributed their failure to develop into mature adults largely to child-rearing practices in Wilhelmine Germany that led male children to develop the kind of ego that needed violence to shore it up:

> My suspicion is that only a handful of men in Wilhelmine Germany had the good fortune to be in some sense fully born—and not many more in the rest of Europe. This seems to be borne out by the numerous parallels I have been able to trace between the behavior of the soldier males and that of the "average man." What I am suggesting, in other words, is that a psychic type whose basic structure was more or less "psychotic" may have been the norm in Germany … Men in Wilhelmine society were actively prevented from developing an ego capable of integrating their negativized unconscious into more or less peaceable social forms (vol.2, pp.213, 384).

In the context of a reading of Theweleit's work, John Milfull (1990) also argued that the continuity between fascist masculinity and masculinity more generally was to be found in the way boys were socialised (although in less detail than Theweleit). It was 'a socialization process which produced the aggressions thus liberated' by fascism, and that socialisation process wasn't confined to the fascist historical period but predated it (p.185):

> A society which transmits patterns of behaviour based on dominance and violence to its male children can scarcely be surprised if they show themselves susceptible to these viruses in later life, however "rational" and "humane" [that society's] explicit values may seem (Milfull, 1990: 177).

Theweleit also saw a continuity between the historical period of Wilhelmine Germany and 'bourgeois history' more generally. 'I consider it unjustified', he said, 'to see the "fascist" male as an isolated case. His development is part of a wider history ... The problem of fascism has to be seen as a problem of the "normal" organization of our lived relations' (vol.2, p.384, 358). Like Hannah Arendt (although without referencing her work), he argued that the seeds of fascism could be found in the imperialist phase of capitalism, not for any economic reasons, but because it created the kind of character structure that reached its most extreme form under fascism. In a section in volume 1 called 'Origins of the Anti-Female Armor' (vol.1, p.300-63), he briefly traced the origins of 'the "civilized" [bourgeois, male] ego' (vol.1, p.301) using two texts illustrating 'the ways the European male ego develops in opposition to woman' (vol.2, p.384).[185] This 'civilised' ego of the developing bourgeois ruling class was the character structure of the men who carried out 'the expansion of Europe throughout the rest of the world', in other words, to imperialism:

> The man who initiates and implements processes of expansion ("*deterritorialization*") is converted by these processes into a sharply defined entity; a kernel of energy and enterprising spirit; a tough, armoured ship that can be sent out to seize and "order" the world according to the European perspective. The man puts on a coat of "armor" (a key word for Elias). A lengthy process of "self-distancing," "self-control," and "self-scrutiny" ensues—a "subduing of affect," an opposition of "interior" and "exterior," of near and far; an ego to which everything else becomes subordinate (vol.1, p.302—original emphasis).

Imperialism, the world domination by the European powers which started towards the end of the fifteenth century but reached its height towards the end of the nineteenth century, in no way differed in its arrogant entitlement and inhumanity from the worldview of the fascist male. Both saw other

---

185. The two texts are *The Process of Civilization* (Der Prozess der Zivilisaton) (1936) by Norbert Elias and *Mastery of Nature in Humans* (Naturbeherrschung am Menschen) (1974) by Rudolf zur Lippe.

human beings as less than fully human and hence as undeserving of even a right to survival, 'natives' in the case of the imperialist mindset, 'Jews' (principally) in the case of fascism. Both systematically exterminated people, for plunder, 'glory', wealth and profit in the case of imperialism, for some supposed 'higher' collectivity ('race', 'nation', 'fatherland', 'volk') in the case of fascism. And both required a character structure rigidly closed off to genuine humanity, barricaded against self and other in the interests of power, including the most crude form, physical violence.

This 'civilised' bourgeois ego is exclusively male: 'the new human being who emerges from that process ... of development of the bourgeois individual ... is, first and foremost, a new *man*' (vol.1, p.300—original emphasis). It is a character structured not only by the requirements of the new form of domination emerging out of the disintegration of feudalism, but also by the kinds of 'lived relations' between the sexes that maintained men's dominion over women, even as those relations lost their traditional, feudal justifications.

Theweleit has little to say about how and why that happened. For example, in a section in volume 1 called 'Streams: All that Flows', supposedly devoted to 'historical changes in function to which women have been subjected in patriarchal male-female relations' (vol.1, p.272), his main focus is on 'writers who haven't closed themselves off to feeling "the lava and the water in the streams of their desire," and letting them flow' (vol.1, p.258). In other words, the focus is on writings which depict what for Theweleit is the opposite of fascism, at least as far as 'streams of desire' are concerned. Nonetheless, this section does contain a succinct account of what might constitute a connection between 'patriarchy' and capitalism, and of the functions women's subordination might serve for capitalism. Not only does women's subordination provide men with goods and services women are not paid for, he says, it also maintains hierarchies of entitlement among men:

> Under patriarchy, the productive force of women has been effectively excluded from participating in male public and social productions. What has happened to that force? For one thing, it must have trickled away in direct slave labor for men. But I don't think that form of absorption explains everything, or that the function of women is confined to being portable power packs for men ... It seems to me that women were subjugated and exploited in more than simply the direct fashion. They were put to worse use, namely, by themselves having to absorb the productive force of men belonging to the subjugated classes of their eras—all to the benefit of the dominant class ... desire, if it flows at all,

flows in a certain sense through women. In some way or other, it always flows in relation to the image of woman. (It is never allowed to flow aimlessly as a desire for freedom …) (vol.1, p.272—original emphases).

What Theweleit is saying here is that, by keeping male energies focused on sexual access to women, the system of domination pacifies the men of the subordinate classes and keeps them under control.[186] The subordination of women serves a purpose for capitalist society, and it is this that provided a fertile ground for the dehumanised ethos of fascism.

Virginia Woolf

But Klaus Theweleit was not the first or the only writer to draw a parallel between fascism and masculinity more generally. Virginia Woolf also located the origin of fascism in the familiar 'lived relations' of the male domination of women (although she didn't use that terminology). In 1938, on the eve of the Second World War, five years after the Nazi Party's accession to power and 16 years into the reign of the Italian fascist government, Virginia Woolf argued in her essay, *Three Guineas*, that there were similarities between the Nazi and fascist dictatorships on the one hand, and the rest of the Western world on the other. The connection was the male domination of women. Quoting from the sayings and writings of a plethora of male pundits— newspaper correspondents, politicians, archbishops and other dignitaries, not to mention St Paul—and comparing them with Hitler's and Mussolini's own statements, she built up a picture not only of the socially subordinate position of women, but also of the kind of character structure domination required of men.

It is true that things have changed since 1938. In particular, her two major concerns—women's exclusion from institutions of higher learning (Oxford and Cambridge) and the paltriness of their salaries in comparison with men's—have largely improved (although women are still paid less than men). But her hope that women's admission to higher education and their financial independence might end male domination has not been realised. This is not surprising. Not only did subsequent events not happen in the way she envisaged (at least in the case of women's admission to higher education), she herself underestimated the power, the reach and the seductiveness of the male supremacist system.

---

186. This argument is based on the work of Wilhelm Reich. There is plenty of evidence from the colonial history of Australia, for example, for the truth of Reich's insight into the ruling-class belief that men could be pacified by being given access to women (Summers, 1975).

In the case of higher education, she was not arguing that women be admitted to universities as they had been traditionally set up for men. '[T] he old education of the old colleges', she said, 'breeds neither a particular respect for liberty nor a particular hatred of war' (Woolf, 1938: 131). Rather, she was arguing that women needed to establish educational institutions of their own that would not, she said, be teaching 'the arts of dominating other people … the arts of ruling, of acquiring land and capital' (p.132). For that reason they must be prepared to remain poor because they would not be eligible for any of the 'very handsome bequests and donations' from industry that the men's institutions relied on. But colleges for women that were poor in monetary terms while rich in liberty and peaceableness, and independent from the traditionally male institutions, did not eventuate.

Moreover, she placed too much faith in education and financial independence. She assumed that women's acquisition of these would be sufficient to bring about equality between the sexes, and perhaps even bring an end to war (the main theme of her essay). But while there have been some improvements in those two areas in the 70-odd years since she wrote, male supremacy and its propensity for violence and destruction has not come to an end. The sexes may now be less unequal than they were in Virginia Woolf's time, but at least part of that lessening of inequality has been brought about by making women more like men, not by lessening the power and influence of male supremacy.

Nonetheless, some of what she had to say about the male supremacist character structure is still relevant. The main reason she drew a parallel between the fascist regimes and the England of her own day was the fact that both favoured the subordination of women to men. But she also had a vision of the kind of human being domination created. He was

> a monstrous male, loud of voice, hard of fist, childishly intent upon scoring the floor of the earth with chalk marks, within whose mystic boundaries human beings are penned, rigidly, separately, artificially; where, daubed red and gold, decorated like a savage with feathers he goes through mystic rites and enjoys the dubious pleasures of power and dominion while we, "his" women, are locked in the private house without share in the many societies of which his society is composed (Woolf, 1938: 203).

Woolf did not use the word 'domination', she said 'society' instead. Here she seemed to believe that it was 'society' that was the problem, and that there was a private sphere somewhere other than 'society' where men treated women as fellow human beings: 'we look upon societies as conspiracies that sink the private brother, whom many of us have reason to respect' (p.203). At another point she clearly believed no such thing—'the public and the private worlds are inseparably connected … the tyrannies and servilities of the one are the tyrannies and servilities of the other' (p.240)—and it is that view which largely prevailed throughout her essay. But private or public, what makes a man a man, 'the essence of manhood', is fighting. Citing the 'Italian and German dictators' alongside a certain Lord Knebworth, Woolf describes the fighting man as

> the quintessence of virility, the perfect type of which all the others are imperfect adumbrations. He is a man certainly. His eyes are glazed; his eyes glare. His body, which is braced in an unnatural position, is tightly cased in a uniform. Upon the breast of that uniform are sewn several medals and other mystic symbols. His hand is upon a sword. He is called in German and Italian Führer and Duce; in our own language Tyrant or Dictator (Woolf, 1938: 240, 292).

Woolf was insightful about what domination did to the men who embraced it. In the above two quotations she is describing both that sense of entitlement that justifies its bearer in the use of violence, and the dissociation from common humanity involved in the conviction that fighting is somehow the essence of what it is to be human. Although she did not make any explicit connection between women's subordination and male violence (for example, that male violence becomes less restrained the more men are detached and estranged from women), she was perfectly clear that the problem was not confined to countries known to be ruled by dictators, but existed in England, too, despite its reputation for democracy and fair play.

Fascism and the US

And with a Trump administration in charge in the US, the spectre of an unleashed fascism raises its ugly head once again. The circumstances that gave rise to the Nazis are similar to the circumstances that have given rise to the Trump phenomenon. There is the beggaring of large proportions of the population—through war, government debt and massive inflation in Germany in the early 1920s, and after decades of neo-liberal rule currently in the US. There is the destruction of any political alternative to the ruling class—by murdering the socialist/communist opposition in Germany after the First World War, and by the gerrymandering of electorates in the US (and elsewhere), electoral rules which ensure that votes for candidates from parties other than the two ruling-class parties do not count, and in the case of the immediate precursor to the election of Donald Trump, the refusal of the Democratic Party to select Bernie Sanders as their presidential candidate. And violence is endemic in US society, far more so than in any other developed nation: with its obsession with gun ownership ('my sex the revolver', the character structure Milfull identified in fascist men); its mass murderers whose aggrieved entitlement has killed thousands of people; its waging of war against countries that pose no threat to the US; the murder of its black citizens by those who are rarely if ever brought to justice; and its 'border control' forces and the use of militarised police against protestors like the water protectors in North Dakota trying to stop the oil pipeline threatening to pollute the land and water resources.

There are differences between Nazi Germany and the US of the present day. The Trump administration has not so far closed down the media outlets criticising their activities, simply countered them with lies and refused them access to the White House. The US has not established the kinds of death camps that existed in Nazi Germany (although the Nazis didn't have them to start with, either). But the US does have the highest rate of prison incarceration of its own population in the world (737 people per 100,0000; Australia's rate is 125 per 100,000).[187] The US is also the owner of the prison at Guantánamo Bay, whose inmates have been tortured and deprived of the most basic of legal rights.[188] While the inmates are supposedly 'terrorists', the vast majority have not been convicted of any crime and hence are innocent in the sense that they have not yet been proven guilty. Nine detainees have died in this prison, more than the number of those who have been convicted (one man by a civilian court and six men by the military in Guantánamo). Moreover, 86 men have been cleared for release, that is, they have been formally found to be not guilty, but are still being held in the prison.[189] These are the characteristics of the concentration camp—the arbitrary arrests, the indefinite length of detention, the scant regard for the lives and well-being of the inmates including torture, in a word, the dehumanisation, deliberate, condoned, extra-legal and yet sanctioned at the highest level of the nation state.

Moreover, concentration camps were part of US polity long before Guantánamo Bay. In fact, the US was the first modern state to use them. That

---

187. http://news.bbc.co.uk/2/shared/spl/hi/uk/06/prisons/html/nn2page1.stm – viewed 9.8.'18.

188. http://www.reuters.com/article/2013/10/22/us-usa-guantanamo-idUSBRE99L15220131022 – viewed 9.8.'18.

189. http://www.nytimes.com/2012/09/14/opinion/life-and-death-at-guantanamo-bay.html?_r=0 – viewed 9.8.'18.

distinction (if that is the right word) is usually attributed to the British,[190] who herded people together under inhumane conditions with little or no concern for their well-being, or even their lives, during the Boer war in the first years of the twentieth century. The purpose of the camps was supposedly to cut the Boer fighters off from their support among the population. But most of those who died in the camps were children under the age of 16, among both the whites and the black Africans (the latter of whom were kept in separate camps from the whites, and under even worse conditions).

But the use of concentration camps in the US was earlier.[191] As part of the forced removal of the Cherokee Nation in 1838, people were rounded up by soldiers and placed in detention camps in Tennessee where they were held until they could be forcibly removed to the west from their homes in Georgia, Alabama, North Carolina, and Tennessee. Although the commander in charge of the removal had instructed his soldiers to treat the people humanely, conditions were horrendous. The camps quickly became overcrowded and no provision was made for the extra numbers. Sanitary arrangements were inadequate and there were outbreaks of dysentery and typhus, as well as measles, cholera and whooping cough. Not enough food and water had been provided, people had to live and sleep out in the open with little protection from the summer heat, and many people died. The reason why Indian populations had to be 'removed' in the first place reflected the typical interests of capitalist accumulation by dispossession: the white settlers whose numbers were rapidly expanding wanted the land, especially the big cotton farmers, and no sense of a common humanity was going to be allowed to stand in their way.

A more notorious example of a nineteenth-century concentration camp in the US (more notorious, because this time it involved 'white men') was the camp at Andersonville in Georgia.[192] It was built early in 1864 by Confederate officials to house Union prisoners of war captured during the Civil War. During the 14 months of its existence, it held more than 45,000 soldiers, between 26,000 and 33,000 at any one time in an area designed to hold 10,000. Almost 13,000 died. When the war ended, the camp commandant was tried and found guilty of murder by a military tribunal convened by the

---

190. https://mrdivis.wordpress.com/2012/01/11/worlds-first-concentration-camps/ –
viewed 9.8.'18.

191. http://www.encyclopediaofalabama.org/article/h-1433 – viewed 9.8.'18.

192. http://www.civilwar.org/education/history/warfare-and-logistics/warfare/
andersonville.html – viewed 9.8.'18.

Northern victors, and hanged.[193] There was no such retribution for those responsible for the death toll among the 'removed' Cherokee people in the camp in Tennessee.

These are examples of that masculinist dissociation and arrogant entitlement characteristic of fascism, of male domination more generally, and of capitalism. In the case of the Indian 'removal', the white settlers needed more land so they took it, with no regard for the entitlements of the original inhabitants. Like colonised people the world over, these people were treated, not only as though they had no rights, but as though they were worthless. They were provided with no food with which to satisfy the common human condition of hunger, no water to drink and to keep themselves clean, no sanitation to dispose of their waste, and no shelter from the elements. They were not even the 'raw material' for making something. In the arrogant eyes of the colonisers, they were 'superfluous' people whose lives were of no value even for exploitation. And the same thing happened wherever the European nations colonised the rest of the world.

It is true that, both in these cases and in the case of the British camps during the Boer War, the lethal conditions were largely the result of inadvertence rather than deliberate policies of extermination (in contrast to the Nazi camps and the Soviet Gulags). In that sense, the West is different from the totalitarian regimes. But that inadvertence partakes of the same dissociation and unwarranted entitlement as the deliberate malice (although on a less obvious scale). The dissociation is the failure to recognise the humanity of those incarcerated by failing to supply them with the necessities of life, a failure that is never excusable, however inadvertent. The entitlement is shown through its opposite, the disentitlement of those whose needs need not be taken into account because they are deemed unworthy even of a right to life. Although there was no deliberate attempt at extermination, the dehumanisation evident in the failure to organise basic necessities for those forcibly prevented from providing for themselves, differs only in degree from the Nazi death camps. With that history to build on, the Trump administration is fully primed for fascism.

Conclusion

Both capitalism and fascism operate as though there were 'superfluous' people, people who have no right to anything, including the right to life, and who are therefore treated as though they were less than human. Fascism's

---

193. For a fictionalised account of the Andersonville camp, see: Kantor, 1955.

denial of human rights is direct—through thuggery and murder. Capitalism's denial is usually indirect—through depriving people of the material resources necessary to maintain life. But through its military arm, capitalism is as brutal as fascism, and as heedless of human life. It is also more technologically sophisticated, since it is the source of the wealth needed for waging war, and hence far more murderously competent. Fascism motivates individuals in a mob, but capitalism is destroying the earth in its pursuit of profit and power.

But the first people made superfluous under conditions of male supremacy are women. Klaus Theweleit has exposed the mentality of fascist men, the most extreme exemplars of the culture of male supremacy. These men want to exterminate women and their mentality has not vanished from the earth, despite the military defeat of Nazism. A version can be found in the transsexual agenda. Insisting that men can be women abolishes the category of women. If there is no special category of women, there is no basis on which to defend women from male encroachment or to claim rights as women. While the transsexual repetition of the fascist attitude to women might seem to be more farcical than tragic, it does have serious repercussions. It eliminates any possibility for redressing the harms done to women by men under male supremacist conditions.

Already, women's lives matter less than men's. To take just one Australian example, a comparison of the New South Wales government's response to the deaths of two men, with the non-response of government to the deaths of dozens of women at the hands of men. After two young men were punched to the ground and killed by other men in 2012 and 2014, the NSW government passed legislation providing for a mandatory eight-year sentence for anyone who fatally punched someone while under the influence of drugs or alcohol. As well, the government mandated strict restrictions on the trading hours of bars and clubs (the 'lock out' laws).[194] But nothing was done in response to the information provided in the August 2014 submission to the Australian Senate's inquiry into 'domestic violence', by the feminist online community organisation, Destroy the Joint. That submission informed the inquiry of the number of domestic violence murders of women by men in 2012 (46), 2013 (50) and to date in 2014 (43). Neither was there any government response to the information that 73 women were killed in 2016,[195] most of them by a man

---

194. http://www.abc.net.au/news/2014-01-30/one-punch-alcohol-laws-pass-in-nsw-lower-house/5227078 – viewed 9.8.'18.

195. https://www.facebook.com/notes/destroy-the-joint/counting-dead-women-australia-2016-we-count-every-known-death-due-to-violence-ag/1258375197543555 – viewed 9.8.'18

or men. Instead, the federal government cut $29 million from the funding for the homelessness services (Hill and Cohen, 2015) needed to save women's lives. At the same time, the NSW government's Going Home Staying Home 'overhaul' of homelessness services abolished specialist women's refuges from 14 September 2014,[196] making their funding dependent on providing general homelessness services and hence accepting men. This reduced the number of women's refuges in Sydney from 20 to one, and thrust desperate women into the hands of faith-based charity organisations with none of the expertise of the refuge movement and, in many cases, with an inbuilt misogyny that bodes ill for women's safety. Two male deaths, and Sydney's night life is closed down to prevent any further recurrence (presumably); 71 female deaths, and services that might save women's lives are abolished. Such contempt for women is the same mindset as that of Theweleit's fascist soldier males. It is true that the brutality is not overt or personal, at least on the part of the responsible governmental apparatuses. But these government actions have left women at the mercy of men whose brutality differs not at all from fascist thuggery.

Fascism is characterised by outright physical brutality against categories of persons defined as non-human. The foundational category is women, for both fascism and male supremacy, but there is also an affinity between fascism and capitalism. Both violate the human rights of certain of categories of people, fascism in order to justify its brutality, capitalism by creating 'superfluous' populations deprived of basic material necessities. On Arendt's account, capitalism created the social conditions and the mindset that paved the way for fascism. The destruction that imperialism visited on the colonised countries was imported back into Europe by the totalitarian regimes, specifically Nazi Germany. Like the imperialists, these regimes embraced without shame or subterfuge the principle of 'permanently increasing power' which underlies capitalism's bourgeois society. With the advent of a Donald Trump US presidency, the mob is again 'taking care of politics by itself'. Whether or not it will lead to the liquidation of 'all classes and institutions', including the ruling class, remains to be seen. But the German bourgeoisie thought they could control the Nazis and they were wrong.

---

196. http://weaveinc.org.au/Index%20Page%20Papers/SOS%20Women's%20Refuges.pdf – viewed 9.8.'18.

Chapter Thirteen: Surrogacy

> I suggest we call out this cruel business for what it is: trafficking in babies; reproductive slavery; a violation of the human rights of both the birth mother and her offspring … The first order of business would be to lower the demand for all forms of surrogacy, including so-called altruistic surrogacy. There is no right to a child. A deep desire for a child does not justify the narcissistic exploitation of another woman's body and soul, as well as her health – two women, in fact, if an egg donor is also needed (Klein, 2015).
>
> Commercial surrogacy should not be permitted in Sweden and society should discourage this type of surrogacy, even when it is done in other countries. According to the investigation, we want to emphasize that commercial surrogacy is contrary to UN conventions on women's and children's rights, both of which prohibit the trafficking of women and children (Stockholm UN Association, 2016)

Introduction

In a capitalist economy everything is for sale, and to the extent that the economy is allowed to dictate the ways people should live, a capitalist *society* is a society where everything is for sale. There is nothing intrinsically wrong with selling things, but commodification is not just about selling things. Rather, in a capitalist economy it is the chief engine for the ceaseless accumulation of wealth in the hands of the few. As such, it creates a society where non-commodities, including people (workers, prostituted women, and 'surrogate' mothers and the babies they bear), are turned into things to be bought and sold, or things to be used and discarded.

One of the most grievous examples of the commodification of human beings is the practice that has come to be called 'surrogacy', that is, the use of a woman's body to produce a baby for someone else, most often a man, who pays for it. I say 'grievous' because it is such a blatant use of women's bodies in the interests of men, and because it dehumanises the very roots of human existence—the birthing of new human beings. Its wide acceptance is also an excellent example of the domination of social life by the meanings and values of both capitalism ('the market') and masculine entitlement and dissociation. The creation of new human beings as a commercial transaction becomes 'right and good', no different in kind from any other commercial transaction.

As a critic of surrogacy, I am tempted to say it is 'against nature', except that being against nature is not necessarily a bad thing, given that a great deal of what human beings do is against nature, and given, too, nature's tendency to operate 'red in tooth and claw'.[197] Nature is not always benign, and controlling nature in the form of disease, famine, maternal and infant mortality, ignorance, etc. can only add to the sum total of human happiness. So I am not arguing that surrogacy is wrong because it is 'against nature'. I am arguing that it violates an ethics of genuine humanity in even the best-managed case, that it is wrong and ought not to be condoned. I am arguing that it is harmful, exploitative and dehumanising, and that it serves the arrogant and dissociated purposes of men at the expense of women and children, and that it should be legally prohibited. I have no power to make that happen, of course, but I do insist that I have the right to say it.

I recognise that people (mainly men) have been doing it despite the already-existing prohibitions, and that they will continue to do so. The technology is there, some areas of officialdom are onside and the opinion-makers in the malestream media are so enthusiastic about it, and the culture of masculinity that requires that men be given what they want is so dominant. So the babies are born (and will continue to be). The section below on law has some suggestions about how governments might deal with the issue, and I have nothing to add to those suggestions. My purpose here is to clarify an ethical stance of feminist resistance to surrogacy within a context that spells out the masculinist interests involved.[198]

---

197 The origin of this phrase is Tennyson's poem, *In Memoriam A. H .H.* (1850). A. H .H. was his friend, Arthur Henry Hallam: 'Who trusted God was love indeed / And love Creation's final law / Tho' Nature, red in tooth and claw / With ravine, shriek'd against his creed'. Here, Tennyson sees nature as the mortal enemy of divine love, whereas it's more likely to be the case that, if there are any mortal enemies of love around, they're probably men, not nature (http://www.phrases.org.uk/meanings/red-in-tooth-and-claw.html).

198. For feminist resistance to the surrogacy industry, see: FINRRAGE (Feminist International Network of Resistance to Reproductive and Genetic Engineering); Stop Surrogacy Now; as well as many of the references cited in this chapter.

Terminology

Before going any further, I should clarify the terms used in discussions of surrogacy. What is called 'commercial surrogacy' is, of course, the backbone of the industry. It involves payment, not only to the woman or women whose body parts and services are used to produce the child to be relinquished, but also to the middlemen—the brokers, lawyers, doctors, clinics, agencies and others who organise the arrangements and make the profits. Then there is so-called 'altruistic surrogacy', where the woman is not paid and presumably neither is anyone else apart from the medical personnel involved in pregnancy, birth and the necessary IVF technology. The terminology ('altruistic') implies that her motive for producing a child for someone else is purely to help others, with no thought of any benefit to herself. It is not clear why someone would do this—put herself through invasive medical procedures and the pain of bearing a child she cannot raise, especially for strangers; but there is every indication that even in 'altruistic' surrogacy there can be some degree of coercion involved (see below). In the case of commercial surrogacy, the coercion is poverty, racism and the latest neo-liberal version of colonialism exploiting destitution in Third World.

Then there is a distinction made between two different ways in which the ova are sourced: 'traditional' and 'gestational' surrogacy. In the former, the ovum is the surrogacy woman's own and presumably it is not extracted from her body but fertilised by artificial insemination.[199] In 'gestational' surrogacy, the ovum comes from one woman and is implanted after fertilisation in the womb of another woman altogether, who becomes the birth mother. In that case, two women are used to produce a single child. This is the 'preferred' form of surrogacy in the industry (preferred by the brokers, the medical profession and the surrogacy customers—what the women themselves prefer is not mentioned). It is regarded as a guarantee that the woman will be more willing to relinquish the baby, since it is not genetically related to her. Here, genetics becomes a fetish, both symbolising and denying the actual social relations of male domination, giving absolute priority to the sperm at the expense of the woman's experience of birth following on from nine months of pregnancy.

I have used the singular term, 'ovum', because I am talking about a single child, and each child is produced from a single ovum (and sperm). In actuality, however, surrogacy never involves just a single ovum. The process

---

199. I haven't been able to find out whether this is the case, or whether her ova are extracted and fertilised *in vitro*. It is the case, though, that the woman who is to carry the child to term is dosed with 'fertility' drugs, whether the ova are her own or someone else's.

of 'egg collection' via ovarian hyperstimulation (or superovulation), and their *in vitro* fertilisation (IVF) to make the embryos, involve many ova; and sometimes more than one embryo is implanted in the uterus of the birth mother. Because there is such a high failure rate even after implantation of the fertilised embryo(s) into the uterus (not to mention the earlier stages of the IVF treatment cycle),[200] there is more chance of a live birth with multiple embryos. And I use the technical term, 'ovum' (plural, 'ova'), instead of 'egg', because the word 'egg' implies something easily accessible, like hens' eggs.

The word 'surrogacy' doesn't appear in my 1978 edition of the Shorter Oxford English Dictionary. 'Surrogate' does though, and it is defined as: '1. A person appointed by authority to act in place of another ... 2. A person or (usu[ally]) a thing that acts for or takes the place of another'. It comes from a Latin word, 'subrogare', meaning 'to put in another's place'. There is no mention in this edition of the OED of women bearing children for someone else. This might be because IVF technology was only just getting started in the late 1970s. According to an internet article on 'surrogate motherhood':

> The first recognized surrogate mother arrangement was made in 1976. Between 1976 and 1988, roughly 600 children were born in the United States to surrogate mothers. Since the late 1980s, surrogacy has been more common: between 1987 and 1992, an estimated 5,000 surrogate births occurred in the United States.[201]

But the principle—using a woman other than a wife to bear a man's child—has been known at least since biblical times. As many a commentary on the issue has pointed out, the Book of Genesis in the Old Testament tells the stories of the servant girl, Hagar, who was made pregnant by Abraham and bore him a son when his wife, Sarah, couldn't; and of the servant girls, Bilha and Zilpa, who bore additional sons for Jacob (as well as the ones he already had with his other two wives, Leah and Rachel) (Ber, 2000: 156. See also: Haberman, 2014; Ketchum, 1989: 117). So the IVF technology is not strictly necessary for surrogacy arrangements, although it does democratise the procedure. It makes it available for any man at all (as long as he has enough money), and not just for tyrannical biblical patriarchs.

---

200. Each IVF treatment cycle involves five stages: 1. 'controlled ovarian hyperstimulation' (i.e. superovulation); 2. 'oocyte pick-up (OPU) where mature oocytes [i.e. ova] are aspirated from [i.e. sucked out of] ovarian follicles under anaesthesia'; 3. fertilisation; 4. embryo maturation; and 5. 'transfer of one or more embryos into the uterus' of the birth mother (Macaldowie et al, 2012: 1)

201. http://legal-dictionary.thefreedictionary.com/Surrogate+Motherhood.

But if the 1978 OED definition of 'surrogate' didn't mention childbirth, the word's meaning has now been wholly taken over, even to the extent of coining a new word, 'surrogacy', by an industry whose production machinery consists of women's bodies.

Feminists have argued that 'surrogate' is the wrong word for the woman who gives birth to the baby, that she isn't a substitute mother but the real one. For example, Robyn Rowland said:

> "Surrogate" means "substitute" (not a *real* mother), yet the woman is actually the *birth mother* and has a relationship with the child born based on the intimacy of its development inside her body and the relationship she has formed with the fetus and with the imagined child. Men tend to negate this experience, make it invisible and unimportant, because it is so unfamiliar to them (Rowland, 1992: 157—original emphases. See also: Ewing and Rowland, 1990; Nelson and Nelson, 1989: 86; Rowland, 1987, 1990).

Again, as Sara Ann Ketchum argued:

> [The 'surrogate mother' and 'renting a womb' terminology] allows the defenders of paternal rights to argue for the importance of biological (genetic) connection when it comes to the father's rights, but bury the greater physical connection between the mother and the child in talk that suggests that mothers are mere receptacles (shades of Aristotle's biology) or that the mother has a more artificial relationship to the child than does the father or the potential adoptive mother. But, at the time of birth, the natural relationship is between the mother and child (Ketchum, 1989: 125n2).

However, that is not a reason for feminism to abandon the words 'surrogate' and 'surrogacy'. There are other interpretations of the term that accord with the feminist project of exposing the male supremacist interests served by the new surrogacy industry. Although the term 'surrogate' is usually coupled with the word 'mother', in fact the woman who gives birth to the child is not a substitute *mother* (just as Robyn Rowland and others have argued), but a substitute *wife*.[202] As Margaret Jane Radin has pointed out, 'the very label we now give the birth mother reflects the father's ownership: she is a "surrogate" for "his" wife in her role of bearing "his" child' (Radin, 1987: 1929n276). The man's wife is not able to bear him a child, or he doesn't have a wife, so he substitutes another woman either to give him the child his own

---

202. The Australian government's National Bioethics Consultative Committee also noted that 'the "surrogate" role is in fact that of surrogate wife rather than surrogate mother', although the authors attributed this view to someone else ('It has also been argued that'), and did not place any great significance on it (NBCC, 1990: 3).

wife cannot, or to give him a child even though he doesn't have a wife. It is true that there are also women who use surrogacy services (see below). But women nowadays (under the neo-liberal, postmodern hegemony) are permitted, indeed required, to participate in social arrangements organised in the interests of men. That's what 'equality' means under conditions of male supremacy. But the participation of women makes the system no less male supremacist in its exploitation of the bodies of women.

There is another interpretation of 'surrogate' which exposes more clearly the dehumanisation inherent in the industry. What is involved in surrogacy arrangements is not only the substitution of one woman for another, but also the substitution of a purely genetic connection between a man and a child, for a genuinely human relationship. The 'genuinely human' I am referring to here is the relationship between the woman who gives birth and the child she bears. That is the core of the relationship at the beginning of every human life, whatever else may be added to it, and even though there are times when it is not possible (e.g. when mother and child are separated for reasons outside anyone's control, or because she is incapable or might harm the child). Surrogacy arrangements are very much within someone's control, and have nothing to do with the competence or otherwise of the birth mother. To deliberately organise a system based on such separations is to deliberately distort a central aspect of what it is to be human.

For these reasons I will retain the terms 'surrogacy' and 'surrogate'. I will not be using the term 'surrogate mother' since I agree with other feminists that the birth mother is not a substitute but the real mother. To refer to the woman whose body is used to produce the child(ren) to be relinquished, I use the terms 'birth mother', 'relinquishing mother' and 'surrogacy woman' (as a shorthand way of referring to the woman who participates in surrogacy arrangements).

Positive spin

One of the most disturbing aspects of this surrogacy thing is how socially acceptable it is. While commercial surrogacy is illegal in many countries and in all Australian jurisdictions (except for the Northern Territory), 'infertility' clinics and other agencies offering surrogacy 'services' are proliferating and advertising openly. The malestream—whether popular media, academe or officialdom—is predominantly either approving or morally neutral. The more sober literature on surrogacy (as opposed to the popular press) adopts a stance of objectivity. As one academic source put it: 'My approach to transnational surrogacy is not to deem these practices "good" or "bad," but to examine how surrogacy markets emerge through a focus on individuals who participate in such markets' (Rudrappa, 2010: 255). But to refuse to condemn surrogacy is to implicitly condone it.

Media presentations of the issue, in contrast, are wild with enthusiasm, with photos of cute kids and beaming 'parents' and the word 'love' liberally scattered throughout. To give just one example from the Australian media in the wake of the Gammy case (see below):

> [The term 'selfishness'] should not apply to individuals or couples, whether gay or straight, driven by the primal longing to hold a tiny baby in their arms, to nurture a child to adulthood, to give and receive the boundless, heartbreaking love that makes the world go round (Szego, 2014).

Again, 'Children are our future, our hope', trumpets Surrogacy Australia on its website,[203] as though having children were all that was at stake and the exploitation of women of so little consequence it is not mentioned. Criticism, when there is any, is played down and stands no chance of being heard against the cacophony of joyful shouts of congratulation for the 'parents' who now have children they would have had to do without if they hadn't had access to surrogacy.

The Akanksha clinic

Surrogacy has received the ultimate media accolade—endorsement on the Oprah Winfrey Show.[204] The Akanksha Infertility Clinic in Anand, Gujarat, was featured on Oprah in October 2007, together with its director and founder, Doctor Nayna Patel. In 2013, the Akanksha clinic was just one of around 150 infertility clinics in India, about 60 percent of which offered commercial surrogacy (Lee, 2013), but it became especially famous as 'the place they raved about on Oprah' (Carney, 2010). Between 2004 and 2013, there were 684 babies produced at the Akanksha clinic, by 500 women (Lee, 2013, citing the clinic as the source of this information).

The show featured an American couple who commissioned a baby at the Akanksha clinic using their own ovum and sperm. The tone of the piece was wholly positive, even to the extent that surrogacy was presented as some kind of high-level friendly diplomatic understanding between the US and India. According to the reporter on the story, '"Now this baby and this couple will have this bond with this country. And in a way, become these sort of

---

203. http://www.surrogacyaustralia.org/.

204. Brooks, 2007. For a text version of what was depicted on the show, see: Ling, 2006.

ambassadors, these cultural ambassadors … It's confirmation of how close our countries can really be"' (Ling, 2006). The focus was almost exclusively on the commissioning parents. The possibility that the birth mothers might be being exploited was raised, only to be firmly rejected: 'some worry these women are being exploited. According to Lisa [the reporter on the story], this is absolutely not the case. "This is so transformative," Lisa says' (Ling, 2006). The American intended mother saw the arrangement as one of mutual benefit: '"we were able to come together, [the birth mother] and I, and give each other a life that neither of us could achieve on our own. And I just don't see what's wrong with that"' (Ling, 2006).

What's wrong with that is well documented. One of the two residential units the Akanksha clinic provided for the women was a squat concrete bungalow surrounded by concrete walls, barbed wire and an iron gate. It was once a storehouse for the bootleg liquor seized by police. The women told a journalist that the clinic's other hostel wasn't as nice (Carney, 2010). Published photos of the Akanksha clinic accommodation graphically illustrate the lack of respect with which the women who bear the children are treated (see: Carney, 2010; Lee, 2014). The photos show the women in dormitories, sitting or lying on thin mattresses on metal cots, with no privacy, not even curtains between the beds. The photos were taken in daylight, hence it might be assumed that the women spend all or most of the daylight hours shut up in these dormitories. One set of photos shows a woman writhing in pain three days after the cesarean delivery of the baby she bore for an American couple: 'Even eating and sitting hurt' (Lee, 2014, Part 3). Why she was not given adequate pain relief is not explained.

The Akansha Clinic was still going strong in October 2015, when it delivered its 1000th baby (Kumar, 2015). Indeed, it would appear to be going from strength to strength. In 2010, it was a pink three-storey building tucked into a narrow alley, with pockmarked exterior walls and a stark interior (Carney, 2010). By January 2017, it was called the Akanksha Hospital and Research Institute,[205] featuring a modern multi-storey building faced with blue glass and surrounded by neat gardens. By that time it had produced 1162 'surrogate babies'. Presumably it was the beneficiary of the Indian government's 'free-market' policies and the private money that has flowed into health care catering for rich foreigners (Carney, 2010). Surrogacy is not mentioned as one of its services (despite its boast about 'surrogate babies' and the fact that 'surrogate' still appears in its domain address).

---

205. http://www.ivf-surrogate.com/.

What will happen now that the law has changed to make commercial surrogacy illegal is unclear. While the law might prohibit commercial surrogacy, it has little or no enforcement provisions, and the Akanksha is a powerful institution.

Officialdom

Although commercial surrogacy remains illegal in Australia, areas of officialdom are onside. For example, the Australian Institute for Family Studies (the 'Australian Government's key research body in the area of family wellbeing') invited surrogacy advocate, Sam Everingham, to write its chapter on surrogacy in its publication on families, policy and the law (Hayes and Higgs, eds, 2014). Everingham is the founder and CEO of Families through Surrogacy,[206] 'Australia's go-to resource for media, government and intended parents'. He and his male partner employed Indian surrogates to bear children for them. His views extolling the benefits of surrogacy were widely reported in the media in the wake of the Gammy case (see below).

The AIFS publication (Hayes and Higgs, eds, 2014) contains no criticism of surrogacy. It is acknowledged to be 'a market' but the editors show no disquiet at this. The authors of the commentary preceding Everingham's article (Cuthbert and Fronek, 2014) said that they were led by their work on adoption 'to characterise the … commercial production of children for the purposes of family formation as a "market" for children that adapts in response to pressures of supply and demand' (p.56). This was not seen as a cause for concern, nor as a reason to reject commercial surrogacy out-of-hand. On the contrary, they saw it as a good thing because it 'may be empowering for consumers':

> The exchange of money … brings clarity to the transaction and helps obviate potential emotional complications that may exist in altruistic surrogacy arrangements. Especially when brokered through an agency, commercial offshore surrogacy appears to offer both a market model and a surety of possession that are not available through other means (Cuthbert and Fronek, 2014: 61).

Although they do not mention it, the authors must have been worried about being accused of supporting baby trafficking, because they said that the market was 'not for the child per se, but for the reproductive labour and associated medical services that produce the child' (p.61). But saying it does not make it so, and the customers certainly see it as a transaction 'for the child

---

206. http://www.familiesthrusurrogacy.com/about-us/.

per se'. True, they also have to pay for the 'reproductive services' that don't result in a baby—the IVF failure rate is high and the 'clinics' are commercial enterprises, after all. But the customers are paying for a child, just as the customers of child traffickers are.

The authors also acknowledge that there are 'inequalities in wealth and power', but payment, it would seem, reassures all parties: 'Narratives of the liberating effects of the money earned through surrogacy … may … assist in soothing consciences and persuading all concerned that the mother and the commissioning parents are well and truly square' (Cuthbert and Fronek, 2014: 63). And again, this official publication of the Australian Institute of Family Studies fails to condemn those who use their comparative wealth and power to exploit the bodies of women. In fact, the authors discussed surrogacy as a kind of 'intercountry adoption'. But while there are issues of wealth and power involved in intercountry adoption, surrogacy is not like adoption. In adoption, no woman has been coerced by poverty to bear a child she is forced to relinquish. Moreover, surrogacy is not only about children, it's about women and what they can be coerced into providing for men—the money in the case of their husbands ('the family'), the children in the case of the well-heeled customers.

Earlier, The Australian government's National Bioethics Consultative Committee[207] had taken the same ethically neutral stance on surrogacy, arguing that it was a form of personal service, no different in kind from any other type of personal service. (For a similar argument, see: Belliotti, 1988). As the Committee put it:

> The fact … that a surrogate mother performs a service for another for payment does not of itself make the arrangement "commercial" in the pejorative sense, nor does it imply that the surrogate mother is necessarily being "exploited" or used merely as a means to the ends of others (NBCC, 1990: 10).

---

207. This was established in 1988 to advise the state and federal governments on surrogacy (as well as on IVF, genetic engineering and euthanasia). It released its first report in 1990, and its second report, on implementation and the drafting of model legislation, a year later. It was not typical of the official position on surrogacy in Australia. It was the only one of 10 Australian committees of inquiry into surrogacy to that date that did not either recommend that it be legally prohibited altogether, or at least express 'grave reservations about the practice' (Stuhmcke, 1995). However, its stance of 'objectivity' was taken seriously as a valid approach to the issue.

But, again, saying it does not make it so. The Committee quoted with approval the comments about the Warnock Report[208] by the British moral philosopher, R. M. Hare. The Warnock Report had rejected surrogacy 'on the ground that it involved people using others as means to their own ends'. Hare was quoted saying, "'It may be that surrogacy is different ... from other forms of personal service [where people are used as a means and not treated as ends in themselves] but we are not told in what respect'".

The ethical stance appealed to by the Warnock committee as a reason for rejecting surrogacy was verbalised by Immanuel Kant over two centuries ago: 'Act so that you treat humanity, whether of your own person or that of another, always as an end and never as a means only' (Kant, 1990: 46). Surrogacy treats the women who give birth as a mere means to an end—a child—and not as ends in themselves. Some customers are aware of the problem (without, of course, citing Kant). For example, the American woman quoted above in the context of the Oprah Winfrey show about the Akansha clinic, who said that she and the birth mother 'were able to come together' to influence each other's life for the better, was clearly struggling with this means/ends conflict. It is highly likely, however, that the conflict was resolved in favour of simply treating the Indian surrogacy woman as a mere means. It is unlikely that there was any further contact between the Americans and the woman in India. The contact is through agencies and clinics, with little or no direct contact between customer and baby-producer.

In her discussion of the Kantian argument in the context of the 'free market' in babies and women's bodies, Sara Ann Ketchum says:

> On this argument, selling people is objectionable because it is treating them as means rather than as ends, as objects rather than as persons. People who can be bought and sold are being treated as being of less moral significance than are those who buy and sell. Allowing babies to be bought and sold adds an extra legal wedge between the status of children and that of adults, and allowing women's bodies to be bought and sold (or "rented" if you prefer) adds to the inequality between men and women. Moreover, making babies and women's bodies available for sale raises specters of the rich "harvesting" the babies of the poor ... The most straightforward argument for prohibiting baby-selling is that it is selling a human being and that any selling of a human being should be prohibited because it devalues human life and human individuals. This argument gains moral force from its analogy with slavery (Ketchum, 1989: 118).

208. The 1984 report of the Committee of Inquiry into Human Fertilisation and Embryology, chaired by Dame Mary Warnock.

Philosopher Hare believed he had an answer to the use of the Kantian imperative as an argument against surrogacy. He pointed out that Kant's stricture against using others as a means towards one's own ends was qualified, not absolute. It warned against using people *only* as a means, without also treating them as ends in themselves. It was acceptable to do both, for example, as in the case of employing 'a steeplejack' (Hare's example), who is used as a means by his employer to do whatever it is steeplejacks do, but also as an end in himself because he is paid (NBCC, 1990: 10).

This argument—that surrogacy is no different from any other form of personal service, that it is just a job like any other—is one of the main forms of justification for surrogacy (another justification is that the woman hired for surrogacy purposes is acting from her own free will, or 'personal autonomy', as the NBCC put it—see below). It is true that people are constantly being used as means towards the ends of others, and that those uses are often unexceptionable. In the case of shop assistants, for example, all that is required to avoid using them *only* as a means, is adequate payment for their time and energy on the part of their employer, and politeness and respect for the humanity shared by both parties to the face-to-face transaction. But surrogacy is not like that; or rather, it is not like that from a standpoint concerned about what surrogacy implies for what it is to be human. As I said above, surrogacy involves the very roots of human existence, and treating the production of new human beings as a commercial transaction distorts that basic relationship into something inhuman.

It is no surprise that Hare (among so many others) could not see that. What is at stake are first and foremost the interests women have in being recognised as full human beings. But men do not give birth, and the dominant ethos of male supremacy elides the interests of women whenever they come into conflict with what men want. An ethical standpoint in the interests of women was clearly not shared by Professor Hare. He *was* told how surrogacy was different from 'other forms of personal service' (indeed, that it was not a 'form of personal service' at all and hence not an 'other' one), but he chose not to believe what he was told. He was told that using a woman's body to produce a child for someone else is a grossly unacceptable use of another human being, but he didn't agree. He was a devotee of male supremacy's foundational form of dissociation: what men want overrides any need women have for safety and personal autonomy.

The majority of the Australian National Bioethics Consultative Committee also subscribed to this foundational premise. It did not condemn surrogacy outright, although its recommendations still hedged surrogacy about with severe restrictions that sit oddly with its stance of objectivity. There were two opinions dissenting from the Committee's recommendation that surrogacy be legally permitted, as well as from its overall libertarian approach towards surrogacy. One was by Sister Regis Mary Dunne, who had a background in microbiology and genetics and was Director of the Provincial Bioethics Centre for the Queensland Catholic Dioceses. The other dissenting opinion was by Heather Dietrich, lecturer and researcher in science and technology at the University of Technology, Sydney. Both agreed that the Committee's reliance on the principle of personal autonomy was unconvincing, that surrogacy did indeed treat women and children as commodities, that it ought not to be defined as medical treatment, and that it had deleterious consequences for public policy (NBCC, 1990: 47-64). But their arguments did not sway the rest of the committee.

The Committee's discussion was based on three principles: 'personal autonomy', 'justice' and 'the common good', with priority given to 'the principle of personal autonomy': 'namely that people should be free to make their own life decisions for themselves so long as those decisions do not involve harm to others' (NBCC, 1990: 47). But as Sister Dunne pointed out, this principle gives undue weight to the desires of the commissioning couple at the expense of the birth mother; and it conflicts with any notion of the common good (or 'public good'):

> The argument that the persons involved are acting freely and exercising their liberty does not take into account whether in the overall public good they are entitled to do this, as the consequences of their action will not be contained with them, nor does it address the moral question of whether they ought to do this (NBCC, 1990: 47).

While the Committee said that their personal autonomy principle excluded 'harm to others', in fact they either ignored, or were inexcusably ignorant of, the well-documented harms involved in even the best regulated surrogacy arrangements (see below). As Robyn Rowland (1990) pointed out, the Committee summarily dismissed women's accounts of their negative experiences of surrogacy (i.e. Klein, ed., 1989). The Committee insisted that those accounts did 'not *prove* anything about the ethical status of surrogacy', they were simply '[v]arious statements made by some American surrogate mothers' about 'emotional and ill-considered attempts at surrogate motherhood' (NBCC, 1990: 10—original emphasis). The Committee was also less than truthful when they said that there were '600 cases of surrogacy reported in the U.S. over some years' and that 'very few have raised serious problems' (NBCC, 1990: 39n20). The source cited in support of this supposed finding about 600 cases (Rachels, 1987) gives no reference for it; and the author even suggests that it is impossible to know how many cases there have been: '(Exact figures are hard to come by, because there are no central records)' (Rachels, 1987: 358). Thus the Bioethics Committee was able to deny the harm caused by the surrogacy industry by lying about the evidence.

There is a widely-held and influential belief that the conflict between the critical stance against surrogacy, and the view that there is nothing wrong with it, can be resolved by more research. For example, the reviewer of a book called *The Birth of Surrogacy in Israel* (Tovino, 2005/2006) said that the author believed 'that many of the arguments against surrogacy (including the argument that surrogacy is degrading to women and exploitive of women and children) are not grounded in research' (p.257). This research, it would seem, would show that the arguments against surrogacy, the author went on to say, are 'inconsistent with the views of Israelis who have participated in the surrogacy process'.

But if the research was properly conducted it would be unlikely to discover only views favourable to surrogacy; and by uncovering unfavourable views it would simply reproduce the conflict. It might be argued that those who have gone through the process are best qualified to know what is involved. But it could also be said that they are the least qualified because they have a vested interest in not seeing surrogacy in an unfavourable light—the parents because they have got their heart's desire, the birth mother because she cannot allow herself to feel the pain of relinquishment or the fear of the future consequences for her health of the superovulation regime.

No amount of research, no matter how carefully designed, can definitively settle the question of who is right—the supporters of surrogacy or its critics. These are ethical positions *about* facts, not conclusions arrived at on the basis of better or worse evidence. Supporters and critics have equal access to the facts, they simply react differently to those facts. Those reactions are partly emotional, partly moral and political. The emotional reactions on the part of the supporters of surrogacy are warm feelings about the beautiful babies and happy parents, and at a more subterranean level, a commitment to the male supremacist mandate that women exist to serve and service men. Its critics are concerned about the implications for what it means to be human (although this is often couched in the more anodyne terms of 'public policy'). The opposing moral positions are, of course, obvious. Supporting surrogacy is to approve of it and regard it as complying with 'the right and the good', while criticising it is to condemn it as 'wrong and bad'. The political implications of each of those opposite positions, however, can only be seen from the critical side. In order to support surrogacy it is necessary to see it as wholly innocent—to view all parties as already equal and see it as nothing but the exercise of 'personal autonomy'. In other words, it is necessary to ignore relations of power and questions of who benefits to the detriment of whom. In contrast, the critique of surrogacy questions that innocence, exposes the masculinist interests involved, and gives priority to the harm done to women over giving men what they want.

Choice?

As well as the insistence that surrogacy is just a job like any other, defending it involves seeing it as a free choice on the part of the women hired for surrogacy purposes. This insistence is usually coupled with an emotional defence of women's right to choose, combined with an attack on the critics of surrogacy who are seen as impediments to the exercise of that right. For example, in the context of an argument in favour of 'egg donation' for stem cell research (and surrogacy), Leslie Cannold (2006) said in an article on *On Line Opinion* that women have a 'right … to be treated as rational citizens, deserving of the same rights and opportunities as men', that they can 'give informed consent to egg donation', and that any woman who doesn't want to donate her 'eggs' 'can still say "no"'. No one, she said, 'deserve[s] … the freedom to stop me, or any other women, making my own risk-benefit calculation, and my own choice'. Arguments disagreeing with this position, she said, are 'infantilising', 'patronising' and 'offensively sexist'.

The feminist response to this is to point out that it is not a question of women's choice, but rather of the power and influence of the biotechnology industry to ensure that women are not given a choice in any real sense. As Renate Klein pointed out (2006) in response to Cannold's *On Line Opinion* article, women are not adequately informed about the dangers. 'Egg extraction is an invasive process', she said, and women are not always given sufficient information about the known, short-term risks, much less the long-term risks. No one knows what these risks are because women who have been subjected to ova extraction are not being systematically followed up. Moreover, the way the information is presented is deceptive. Klein (2006) tells us that a survey by the Australian National Health and Medical Research Council, of the information in the brochures given to women in IVF clinics, found that not all of them pointed out the main dangers of IVF, and that the information they did contain was presented 'in an overly positive manner'. The information conveyed to women downplayed the dangers (or ignored them altogether in the case of the long-term risks), and the procedures are described in terms of their benefits—although in the case of both surrogacy and stem-cell research, those benefits accrue to others, not to the woman herself. This is where the notion of 'altruism' comes in. The only conceivable benefit a woman can expect from undergoing a surrogate pregnancy is doing good for others.

To insist (as Cannold does) that women are capable of informed consent when the relevant information is systematically withheld, is to participate in the dissociation typical of the masculinist culture of male supremacy. Cannold accused the feminist position of 'factual sloppiness', but it is her own position that is divorced from reality. Couching her argument in terms of 'equality' with men is a bizarre distortion of what is at stake. There is nothing in men's experience that bears the slightest resemblance to ova extraction. While sperm donation is the closest approximation (because both sperm and ova are gametes), it simply involves ordinary ejaculation, requiring no drugs, surgical procedures or adverse consequences. Men's need for information about how their sex cells are harvested, and what the physiological consequences might be, is nothing like women's need. To the extent that that information is lacking or inadequate, there can be no question of 'informed consent', and hence of choice.

The feminist argument against surrogacy also refers to the social pressures on women to be altruistic, even self-sacrificing (see below). As Janice Raymond put it: 'Any valorizing of altruistic surrogacy and reproductive gift-giving must be assessed within the wider context of women's political inequality' (Raymond, 1990). Jocelyn Scutt adds to this point by saying that the pressures on the surrogate are even greater than the usual pressures on women because, in giving away the child she gives birth to, she could be perceived as a 'bad mother'. If she is to resist that judgement, she must insist on the moral worth of what she is doing:

> [B]ecause she fulfills, ultimately, the role of the "bad" mother— the mother who gives her child away, the "surrogate" is required to live up to the vision of altruistic woman even more rigidly than any other pregnant woman. Her original position of altruism—I wish to give myself to others, for their use—locks her into a position where, whatever her wishes, she must continue to give herself for others, for their use (Scutt, 1991).

This kind of argument is often interpreted for anti-feminist purposes as saying that women are dupes or, to use alternative terminology, that they are suffering from 'bad faith' or 'false consciousness'.

It is true that feminist arguments are saying that volunteering to undergo a surrogacy pregnancy is willingly doing something that is against one's own best interests, although they do not use the terminology of 'bad faith'/'false consciousness'. But such arguments are frequently interpreted in terms of arguing for the existence of false consciousness; and the accuser (who disagrees that there is any such thing) does use the terminology. For example, a certain Raymond Belliotti (1988) (who concludes that arguments against surrogacy 'do not establish [its] moral impermissibility') uses the terminology of 'false consciousness' to challenge what he sees as arguments dismissing women's own accounts of their experiences:[209]

> if a woman reported satisfaction or fulfillment after completing her functions as a surrogate, such reports would be dismissed by Marxists [and feminism] as ideological distortions because they would be viewed as parasitic upon past capitalist exploitation, role indoctrination, and training … surrogate mothers are not the victims of false consciousness because … the joys of reproductive activity correspond truly to their experiences … [and] Marxists must respect the actual reports of the surrogates (Belliotti, 1988: 401, 402).

For this commentator, respecting the actual reports of the surrogates trumps accounts of surrogacy that interpret it as 'exploitation, role indoctrination, and training', as long, that is, as they are reports of women's 'satisfaction or fulfillment'. But not all women who have undergone surrogacy experiences report being satisfied or fulfilled. Take the example of Gammy's mother, who said, "'I would like to tell Thai women – don't get into this business as a surrogate. Don't just think only for money … if something goes wrong no one will help us and the baby will be abandoned from society, then we have to take responsibility for that'" (Murdoch, 2014a).[210]

Or take the example of a woman in India, who was quite clear that her experience of surrogacy was coerced, although not by any one person in particular, but by the sheer need for survival. She said:

---

209. Belliotti ascribes these supposed dismissals of 'the actual reports of the surrogates' to 'Marxists', not to feminism, probably because the notion of false consciousness and the theory behind it originated with Marxism.

210. On the other hand, the Thai surrogacy broker, Ms Kamonthip, was reported to say that Gammy's mother 'encouraged other women to become surrogate mothers'. "'If you have had sad experience about being surrogate'", this woman is reported to have said to Gammy's mother, "'why did you recruit surrogate mothers for some agencies just two months ago?'" (Paddenburg et al, 2014). Perhaps Gammy's mother had changed her mind, although the broker was not a very reliable witness: 'Before she disappeared last week, Ms Kamonthip also gave conflicting accounts of dealings between her, the birth

"Who would choose to do this? I have had a lifetime's worth of injections pumped into me. Some big ones in my hips hurt so much. In the beginning I had about 20-25 pills almost every day. I feel bloated all the time. But I know I have to do it for my children's future.

This is not work, this is *majboori* (a compulsion). Where we are now, it can't possibly get any worse … In our village we don't have a hut to live in or crops in our farm. This work is not ethical—it's just something we have to do to survive. When we heard of this surrogacy business, we didn't have any clothes to wear after the rains—just one pair that used to get wet—and our house had fallen down. What were we to do? Let me tell you something, there are many families like ours who want to do it, but either the husband doesn't approve or the wife doesn't agree to do it. These people are jealous. These are the kind of people who call it immoral. And if everyone in the family agrees, society disapproves. But I say, if your family is starving what will you do with respect? Prestige won't fill an empty stomach" (Pande 2009: 160-1. See also: Barlass, 2014; Klein, ed., 1989).

It is true that Belliotti says that he is not talking about 'the Anglo-American exportation of surrogacy to Third World countries' (i.e. Thailand or India). He acknowledged the exportation of surrogacy to the Third World as a problem, saying that it 'parallels in several respects the exploitation of colonies or other impoverished areas by capitalist countries seeking cheaper labor forces, lessened public scrutiny, and fewer governmental regulations' (Belliotti, 1988: 410n1). So these women's reports do not count as a counter-example to other (Anglo-American) women's reports of satisfaction and fulfilment, because he would agree that they were exploited, although by neo-colonialism not by surrogacy.

But their exploitation is a peculiarly female one—only women (and the children they bear) can be exploited by the surrogacy industry. Perhaps the fact that they share the sex of women everywhere means that the exploitation they suffer is also shared by women elsewhere. How is it that the same experience can be exploitative in one place but not in another? Belliotti does have an answer to this: surrogacy is exploitative in the Third World because of the poverty, but not in developed countries like the US because women are not (so) poor. In the US, he says, 'as an empirical matter few candidates for surrogate motherhood are drawn from the lowest economic and educational strata' (Belliotti, 1988: 398). But this is simply not true. Rosalie Ber (2000) cites two 1983 studies of what she refers to as 'gestational surrogate mothers',

mother, and the biological parents. Police and welfare authorities want to interview Ms Kamonthip' (Alford and Taylor, 2014). For an account of the Gammy case, see below.

both of which found that '[m]ost of these women were from the working class, with low educational backgrounds and almost all expected to be paid for their service'.[211]

And poverty is not the only form of compulsion. Take, for example, a middle-class American woman's account of the reasons why she volunteered for surrogacy:

> At the [information] meeting [arranged by the surrogacy firm], hearing about all these desperate people who want a baby and have unsuccessfully tried everything to have children, you're made to feel you're a saint and that this is the gift of life, the most unselfish thing a human being could give another human being ... You are told that this is the couple's child, not yours. Some women like me think we can do this wonderful thing and save these people from this heartache (Patricia Foster in Klein, ed., 1989: 151).

While this is not compulsion in the same way as the desperate poverty of the Indian woman, it is not informed consent either. In particular, she was not told of the crucial factor that subsequently opened her eyes to the exploitative nature of surrogacy—her grief at losing the baby she was told was 'not yours', and her powerlessness to prevent that happening.

Moreover, there are some women who might have been satisfied at one point, but who later change their minds and view the experience in a thoroughly negative light. Elizabeth Kane's report (1989) is one such example. She was the first woman in the US to undergo a surrogacy pregnancy under contract, in 1980, and her initial feelings about surrogacy were wholly positive. Her main motive, she said, 'seemed to be altruistic'. She was personally acquainted with a number of women suffering from infertility—'a favorite aunt', 'a close friend in high school', 'four or five [other] friends', her sister and sister-in-law. She 'strongly felt that infertile women needed a solution to their problems' and that 'having a baby for a friend' was 'an act of sisterhood'. So she contacted 'an infertility specialist' and volunteered 'to have a baby for a woman [she] had never met'.

She also spent a year travelling around the country appearing on talk shows promoting surrogacy. She said that, early in the pregnancy during her first television appearance, she 'glowed with warm feelings for the expectant couple and the entire concept of surrogate parenting'. She 'told sceptical audiences [she] had the RIGHT to do as [she] wished with [her] body'. But

---

211. The references for the two studies are: Parker, P. J. (1983) 'Motivation of surrogate mothers – initial findings' *American Journal of Psychiatry* 140: 117-18; and Ragone, H. (1994) *Surrogate Motherhood – Conception in the Heart.* Boulder and Oxford: Westview Press

by the time the boy she gave birth to was six months old, she was starting to realise that the experience was having deleterious effects on her life, and on the lives of her husband and her other three children. She also started to realise that she had been demeaned by the way she was treated by the infertility specialist and the broker. It took her another six years to acknowledge this publicly, but eventually she joined the National Coalition against Surrogacy working to raise women's awareness of, yes, the exploitative nature of surrogacy and of how the indoctrination worked in her own case. 'Today', she said, 'I am protesting the breeding of American women as though they were bovine'. What would respecting the report of a surrogate mean in this case? Should we have believed her first report and then changed our minds when she changed hers?

There are a number of problems with Belliotti's assumption that the only reliable reports of something, surrogacy in this case, are those given by someone with personal experience. It doesn't account for the fact people can give conflicting reports of the same experience. So some women report positive experiences with surrogacy (although Belliotti does not quote any, the media does), others report negative ones. Which is the reliable report, given they contradict each other? For Belliotti, the positive reports are the true ones, and he copes with the negative reports by ignoring their existence. He castigates feminists for (supposedly) dismissing women's reports of 'satisfaction or fulfillment' with surrogacy, and yet that is exactly what he does. He doesn't go so far as to accuse women who have had negative experiences of surrogacy of 'false consciousness'. He manages the contradiction between two conflicting reports of surrogacy experiences by simply not mentioning the negative reports.

Another problem is that, if the only people who can know about anything are those who have experienced it, what happens to the rest of us? It excludes those who have not had the experience, and that includes Belliotti himself. By his own argument, he has no right to an opinion.

'Altruistic' surrogacy

It might be assumed that, because so-called 'altruistic' surrogacy does not involve payment and there is therefore no question of women being coerced into it by poverty, it is not subject to the same ethical condemnation as commercial surrogacy. Indeed, that seems to be the assumption behind explicit exclusions of 'altruistic' surrogacy from the scope of the law in jurisdictions where there are laws prohibiting commercial surrogacy, including Australia. But as feminists have pointed out, so-called 'altruistic' surrogacy is subject to the same dissociation as commercial surrogacy. The physically harmful procedures are the same, the grief of relinquishing is the same, and there is still the possibility of coercion, even if it takes the form of guilt and emotional blackmail rather than destitution. As Robyn Rowland pointed out:

> There are three assumptions in the arguments of advocates of altruistic surrogacy. They assume that power dynamics do not operate within families, that a woman is less connected to a child which is not from her own egg, and that genetics determine the most important relationships (Rowland, 1990).

All three assumptions are false. In the case of the first one, even though there might be no contract or financial inducement, there are pressures arising from family loyalty and the possibility of emotional blackmail. The second assumption has been empirically falsified by the grief of the women at having to relinquish the baby. To quote just one woman:

> afterwards it was terrible. As soon as I delivered him they took him away. And the first thing I did was to tell [my husband] to do something so that they would not take him away. I ... wanted to have him, I wanted to keep him (Arditti, 1990: 39).

There is also the effect on the surrogacy woman's other children, the (non) siblings of the baby-to-be:

> The older one did not have any problem, but the little one would cry when they would tell him that the one that would be born was not his brother (Arditti, 1990: 39).

> After her brother Andrew [the surrogacy baby] was born last March, my twelve-year-old daughter kept having nightmares (Patricia Foster in Klein, ed., 1989: 153).

> The "surrogacy" arrangement has disrupted my family forever. I did not realize the effect it would have on my daughter. When I came home from the hospital, my daughter, aged eight at the time, asked: "Mommy, if I am a bad girl, are you going to give me away too?" (Nancy Barrass in Klein, ed., 1989: 158).

As Robin Rowland has pointed out, surrogacy can cause personal problems for everyone concerned: 'for the couples involved ... the children born, the relinquishing mothers, and the brothers and sisters of children who are given away' (Rowland, 1990). This is hardly surprising, given that it violates genuine humanity.

The third of the above assumptions—'genetics determine the most important relationship'—could be more accurately re-worded as 'the sperm determines the most important relationship', since it is the sperm that determines where the child belongs, not the ovum. (See the discussion below of the male domination of the industry).

A story about some of the things that can go wrong with 'altruistic' surrogacy appeared in the *Sydney Morning Herald* in August 2014, around the time the Gammy story was big news around the world (Barlass, 2014). A 40-year-old woman 'offered to help out a couple' (as the author put it) by agreeing 'to carry their child'. She had been friends with these people for 20 years, they were her children's godparents, and before the surrogacy experience she had trusted them enough to give them power of attorney over her affairs should she become incompetent. The trouble started when the support that had been promised throughout the pregnancy did not eventuate: "'I thought I was going to be supported'", the woman was reported saying, but the friend for whom she was carrying the baby did not keep her promise to help: "'I think my friend came over twice during the whole pregnancy to cook me and the kids dinner'". The friend did offer to pay for a cleaner, but the surrogate woman was worried that that might be defined as payment for the baby and hence would be illegal. She also had trouble getting reimbursed for the legitimate expenses she incurred as a result of the pregnancy. Of course, one case doesn't prove anything, but it does suggest that 'altruistic' surrogacy might have its own forms of exploitation.

'A few disgusting cases'

My condemnation of surrogacy is not based on what an editorial in the *Sydney Morning Herald* referred to as 'a few disgusting cases' (SMH, 2014). Even the best-case scenario is morally wrong. Expecting a woman to carry a child to term and then give it up to someone else is inherently wrong—even the best managed procedures are abusive because they are exploitative and dehumanising. Only the boundless male entitlement and dissociation from genuine humanity of the male supremacist mindset could fail to see that. It is hardly surprising, then, that surrogacy can lead to such extremes of evil that even that male supremacist mind can see it.

For example, there was the case reported in media around the world of two Australian men who bought a male child from a Russian woman for $8,000. They not only sexually abused the child themselves, but also passed him around to other men they met through an international organisation called the Boy Lovers Network. The evidence for what these men did to the boy came from videos showing him being sexually abused by at least eight other men, and included a video of one of the men sexually abusing him when he was less than two weeks old. The boy was six when he was taken away from the men and placed with extended family in the US. One of the men was sentenced to 40 years in jail in the US where they were living when they was arrested, the other to 30 years. His sentence was reduced because he had supplied the passwords enabling the authorities to identify and arrest the other men in the paedophile ring.[212] Strictly speaking, the men hadn't acquired the boy through a surrogacy arrangement, although most of the media sources said they did. Rather, '[t]hey located a pregnant woman in Russia who did not want the child because the father had left her'. However, they had tried to have a child through a surrogate, and presumably the only thing that stopped them was the high rate of failure of IVF (SBS, 2013).

There is no way of telling how widespread is the practice of men commissioning children in order to use them as sex toys (or even if it occurs at all). But given the prevalence of child sexual abuse among men, the lack of oversight of the surrogacy industry, and the inherent nature of an industry whose only commodity is human beings, it is unlikely that these two men are the only ones who have tried.

There are other instances of children born of surrogacy arrangements who have ended up in the hands of convicted paedophiles, although it is not known if the children were deliberately commissioned to feed the infantile sexual appetites of these men. There was the Israeli man who had served eighteen months in prison for sexually abusing children, and who acquired a daughter born to an Indian woman. The case was exposed by a reporter for the *Jewish Chronicle* (Rubin, 2013) when the girl was four years old. The reporter said that the 'Israeli authorities [were] at a legal standstill over the [child's] adoption' because 'under current legislation [they] [did] not have the power to remove the girl from him'. (See also: First Post, 2013; Kumar and Chopra, 2013).

The Israeli law, the Surrogate Mother Agreements (Approval of the Agreement and Status of the Child) Law, 1996, allows for commercial surrogacy, but only between a heterosexual couple and the surrogate woman (i.e. without any paid middlemen), and only with the permission of 'statutory committee composed of relevant professionals (physicians, a social worker, a psychologist and a lawyer) and a cleric of the parties' religion', and only within Israel (Shalev, 1998: 59-61). However, it would appear that there are no sanctions when these conditions are breached. 'The authorities [are] helpless' (Nair, 2013) to do anything to stop this man adopting a small girl. Supposedly, he 'has been kept under observation', but such a reassurance

212. Anna Maria, 2014; Dean and Piotrowski, 2014; Ralston, 2013; US Attorney's Office, 2013.

is worthless. It is unlikely he is observed 24/7. The same helplessness was evident in relation to the Australian 'father' in the Gammy case, and the same feeble reassurances were given (see below). These are men who would not pass any legal requirement for 'working with children', and yet they are allowed to live with a small child. It would seem that men can get away with anything.

Then there was the Japanese man whose sperm fathered 16 babies through surrogacy arrangements (Rawlinson, 2014). The case was investigated by Interpol as an instance of a 'baby factory'. (What happened to the Japanese man, not to mention the babies, was not clear at the time of writing [late October, 2014]). The case came to light as a result of the publicity given to the Gammy case, although one surrogacy clinic owner said she had 'warned Interpol about him even before the first baby [of two at this clinic] was born in June 2013'. She said that "'[a]s soon as they got pregnant, he requested more. He said he wanted 10 to 15 babies a year, and that he wanted to continue the baby-making process until he's dead'". She also said that he had told the clinic manager 'that "he wanted to win elections and could use his big family for voting", and that "the best thing I can do for the world is to leave many children"'. His lawyer said that the man 'simply wants a large family and has the means to support it'. The lawyer also said: "'There are assets purchased under these babies' names. There are savings accounts for these babies, and investments. If he were to sell these babies, why would he give them these benefits?'" The arrogance is breathtaking in its dissociation from the realities of human existence. There is the glorification of his sperm—'the best thing I can do for the world'—the blind belief that only money counts, and the obliteration of any notion of the importance for infants of love, care, nurture and genuine human recognition. This is the kind of dehumanised, delusional masculinity created by male supremacy, not only as a personality characteristic of this particular man and his lawyer, but also of a surrogacy industry that allows such things to happen.

There was also the case of a man who commissioned a baby conceived with his sperm, who killed the baby when he was barely a month old.

> In 1993 ... James A. Austin, a single twenty-six year old male, contacted ICA [Infertility Center of America, Noel Keane's business] for assistance in becoming a father ... on December 8, 1994, a baby boy, Jonathan, was born to Appellant in the state of Indiana. On December 9, 1994, Austin, together with an ICA representative, arrived in Appellant's hospital room to take physical custody of Jonathan. At that time, Appellant transferred Jonathan to his sperm-donor father, Austin. Austin took his

newborn son to his residence in Bethlehem, Pennsylvania, where he repeatedly abused Jonathan, causing him to suffer severe head and brain injuries, including "shaken baby syndrome." One month after his birth, on January 8, 1995, Jonathan was admitted to Muhlenberg Hospital, and was transferred shortly thereafter to Children's Hospital in Philadelphia. Jonathan died as a consequence of these injuries on January 17, 1995.[213]

Gammy[214]

And then there was Gammy. This is the name of a boy with Down syndrome born in December 2013 to a Thai woman who had been paid by an 'Australian couple' to bear him and his twin sister for them. She had agreed to the surrogacy arrangement because of her family's poverty: 'Because of poverty and debts and the money that was offered was a lot for me, in my mind, with that money, we can educate my children, we can repay our debt, we can help our mother and we still have some funds to start a small business selling things', she was reported to say in translation (Ferguson, 2014a).[215]

The initial newsworthy aspect of the case was that baby boy had been 'abandoned by his Australian biological parents',[216] who had refused to accept him because he had Down syndrome (Murdoch, 2014a). The babies' birth mother discovered she was having twins three months after the insemination procedure. The inseminating medical staff presumably knew all along, since they were the ones who placed the fertilised ova in her uterus and, it would seem, didn't even tell her, much less ask her permission. Gammy's Down syndrome condition was discovered four months into the pregnancy. According to 'a source familiar with the case', when 'the Australian parents' were told that he had Down syndrome, they said they did not want the boy. The babies' birth mother was quoted saying, "'They told me to have an abortion

---

213. http://caselaw.findlaw.com/pa-superior-court/1190217.html.

214. I haven't used any names in this account of the Gammy case (apart from the baby boy himself), although most of them are freely available in the mainstream media references I give. I am concerned with the system, not the individual actors within it.

215. There were varying reports of the amount she was said to have received. It was also reported that she wasn't paid a final instalment: "'the agent never paid the rest of the 70,000 baht ($2341) owed to me'" (Murdoch, 2014a, b).

216. In fact, only the man was a 'biological parent'. The twins' genetic make-up comprised ova from a woman/women other than the babies' birth mother, fertilised with the man's sperm: '[The babies' mother] told Fairfax Media that [the man's wife] was not the twin's biological mother, saying she did not supply the egg that was implanted in her ... She said the egg came from a Thai woman through a surrogacy agency' (Murdoch and Browne, 2014).

but I didn't agree because I am afraid of sin'", referring to her Buddhist beliefs. It was reported that, when the babies were born, the girl was taken away by the surrogacy broker (the agent paid to make the arrangements), who left the boy behind. It was reported that the babies' mother never saw 'the Australian couple' (Murdoch, 2014a), but she was also reported to have said that 'the children's biological father' had visited her after the birth, and 'only bought milk for the girl'. She also said that "'the father never looked at Gammy ... could say he never touched Gammy at all'", and that 'the pair had cried on the day they collected their daughter from hospital but left their son behind' (Dean and Piotrowski, 2014).

In an interview on the ABC's *7.30 Report* program on 6 August (reported in Murdoch, 2014c), the Thai surrogacy broker said that the babies' mother and the Australian 'couple' 'could not reach agreement in the late stage of the pregnancy and for one month after the births as the premature and unwell babies remained together in a Bangkok public hospital'. It was the babies' mother who "'came up with a solution'", she said, and that was that she would take the boy. The report did not say what the disagreement was about, but given that the 'solution' involved the babies' mother keeping Gammy, it was presumably disagreement about the fate of the baby boy once 'the Australian couple' had refused to take him.

The first reports at the end of July and the beginning of August 2014, said that the 'parents' were anonymous, but by Monday 4 August, the media had tracked them down to a house in Bunbury, Western Australia. The house was empty when the media arrived, but by the next day, 5 August, their names had been revealed. It was also revealed that the man's wife was Chinese, and he had met her through a 'dating agency' called 'QPid Success' (Dean and Piotrowski, 2014).[217]

What was also revealed was the fact that the father had been convicted in the 1990s of sex offences against small girls: '[The father] was jailed in the late 1990s for sexually molesting two girls under the age of 10 and was sentenced to three years behind bars. While serving time for that crime, in 1998 he was charged with six counts of indecently dealing with a child under the age of 13 and was convicted and sentenced again' (Dean et al, 2014). At least one of the girls was as young as five, and 'some of the offences involved penetration' (according to an ABC television reporter who was quoting information from the Western Australian District Court). The father had committed the offences over a 10-year period, from his mid-20s to his

---

217. or 'Chinese dating agency website Zhanjiang Happy Marriage Agency' (Paddenburg et al, 2014).

mid-30s, when he had 'a stable home life' and three children of his own (Ferguson, 2014c). A certain Mr Page, a surrogacy lawyer, was reported to have said that the girl twin 'may be able to continue to live with her Australian father if child protection authorities deem he is no longer a risk' (Dean et al, 2014). How the authorities were going to ensure that, he did not say; and given the lamentable past record of 'child protection' authorities everywhere, it is not clear how they might do it. Indeed, it would seem as though the Department had been aware that the father had a baby in his 'care' (for want of a better word) as early as 15 May, but did not begin any investigations until the issue was exposed in the media at the beginning of August (Bickers, 2014).

On 5 August the *Bunbury Mail* reported a staunch defence of 'the couple' by a friend. They had 'never wanted to give him up', the friend said, and neither did they leave him behind because he had Down syndrome. They had left Thailand because they were afraid they would lose the girl if they stayed, given that 'the government in Bangkok collapsed'. The friend also said that the boy was very sick when he was born, and that 'the couple' were told he would die within a day and that they should say goodbye to him (Dean and Piotrowski, 2014). The ABC's *7.30 Report* said that they had been in contact with 'the couple' identified as the boy's 'biological parents', but that they had refused to be interviewed and denied any knowledge of the boy (Ferguson, 2014a).

On Sunday 10 August, 'the couple' were interviewed on Channel Nine's *60 Minutes* program.[218] During the interview, they said that they had not agreed with Gammy's mother's offer to take the boy. The father said that he was going to reclaim Gammy, that they had wanted to take both babies but that they had left with only the girl when they became worried that they would lose both of them when the birth mother threatened to report them to the police. 'The couple' also said they had left Thailand because their visas were about to expire. However, the authors of the SMH article pointed out that they had not tried to renew them; nor had they sought advice from the Australian Embassy about how to get Gammy back to Australia. They denied that they had demanded an abortion. However, the father did admit that he was angry when he heard the foetus had Down syndrome, and said he had asked the agency for a refund because '"This is your fault"'. He also admitted that, had he known about the disability earlier, he would have insisted on an abortion because no '"parent wants a son with a disability"'.

---

218. The quotes below were taken from the report of the program next day in the *Sydney Morning Herald* (Murdoch and Browne, 2014).

However, the information about the father's demand for an abortion did not only come from Gammy's mother. A former employee of the surrogacy agency was reported on 17 September to say: "'He did not want the baby, he just wanted to do anything so he would not have to have that baby'" (Sales, 2014). She said that, when the babies' mother refused to abort the Down syndrome foetus, the father suggested that the baby be left outside a temple for the monks to look after. The agency refused to do this because they wouldn't do it to a baby, but also because he wasn't Thai. This employee's story was confirmed by the agency's owner (who lived in California). "'Those Australian people are so bad'", he was reported to have said, "'They beg me to drop baby Gammy at the temple at night and run away. They told me don't worry … the monk will take care of the baby. These are very ugly people'". He also said that both husband and wife had requested abortion, the wife having begged the owner's Chinese wife in a phone conversation "'to get rid of the baby'" (Sales, 2014).

This was not the story the father's wife told during the *60 Minutes* interview on 10 August (Murdoch and Browne, 2014). At one point she said, "'We asked her [Gammy's birth mother] can you please give us back our baby boy … She got very, very angry. She said if she cannot take (the) boy, she will keep both of them'". The father agreed with this, saying that Gammy's mother had "'said if we tried to take the baby boy she was going to get the police and she was going to keep both of them'". In the article reporting the interview, the babies' mother was quoted denying this: "'I never said I would keep both babies and would go to the police … I only talked to the police when the (surrogacy) agent would not give me the money I was owed'".[219]

In response to the interviewer's question about whether or not the baby girl 'would be safe in his care', the father was reported to have replied that 'he no longer had sexual urges towards young girls after undergoing counselling in prison'. "'I don't have this urge to do anything anymore'", he said. "'She will be 100 per cent safe. I will do everything in the world to protect my little girl. I have been convicted of child sex offences and I hang my head in shame for that and I am deeply regretful and I am so sorry to those people'". He was also reported to have said that 'he realised he had done the wrong thing after thinking how devastated he would be if someone sexually abused his children' (Murdoch and Browne, 2014).

He already had three adult children, to whom he was reported to be very close. Two of them, a son and a daughter, defended their father in the media.

---

219. The article does not give the source of the quotes from the babies' mother.

Two days after the news of his father's sexual offences against small girls was released to the media, the son ('who did not wish to be named') was reported to have said: "'I can tell you how good of a father my dad was towards us. He's amazing. He's brought the best out of all of us kids … He's just got a massive heart'". He insisted the family were all very close, "'even my mother, his ex-wife'", and that his father had worked hard to rehabilitate himself and 'get his life back on track': "'He's made mistakes, we've accepted it … he's made up for them. For everything to be brought back up (is) pretty heartbreaking to be honest'".

A week later his adult daughter also defended him in the media. She said that he 'will be a wonderful father to [the] baby [girl]', and that she herself is "'one of the luckiest people in the world" to have grown up with a loving father'. She denied that he would have left Gammy behind on purpose. They had been to so much trouble and spent so much money to get a baby, including many years of unsuccessful IVF treatment, that they "'wouldn't be able to leave it behind on purpose … no matter how [the] child had been born or what disability they were born with'". She said she was the source of the story that Gammy had died, not her father and his wife. She knew it wasn't true, but "I thought it would be easier to say he had passed away and then have to explain it later on if he came home". About her father's convictions for sexual offences, she said that it 'had devastated her family, along with his victims', but that she 'believe[d] in the system – they wouldn't have let him out or let him see me again if they thought he was a risk'", she said. "'His past has absolutely nothing to do with this'" (Miller, 2014).

The media furore about the father's convictions for child sexual offences spurred the Western Australian Department of Child Protection and Family Support into action for the first time on 5 August, although (as mentioned above) they had known about it since 15 May. It would seem that they had been told by a 'younger family member' (Bickers, 2014). Neither the name of this family member nor their relationship to the baby's father were revealed in the media (other than to say that they were 'a close relative') (Wahlquist, 2014), although the relative was named in state parliament (Wahlquist and Spagnolo, 2014). On 5 August the Department 'left a note at the couple's home asking for a meeting' and started an investigation, while on 7 August, the Minister was reported to have said that "'there was nothing to suggest the seven-month-old [sister] was at any risk, but a full assessment was under way'" (Partridge, 2014). The investigation was put on hold when the man's wife went to China for her mother's funeral, taking the baby girl with her, although it was resumed towards the end of September when she returned home (Bickers, 2014). In early November, it was reported in the media that the Department had allowed the West Australian couple to retain custody of the baby girl 'under strict conditions' (AAP, 2014).

On 14 April 2016, the Chief Judge of the Family Court of Western Australian ruled that Gammy's sister would continue to live with the Australian 'couple', rather than being returned to her Thai birth mother, who had asked that the baby be returned to her when she heard that the Australian man was a convicted paedophile. The judge ruled in favour of the Australians because 'He found the three-year-old, who has been raised by the [couple] since birth, lived a happy and content life, and would be traumatised if removed from the only parents she's ever known' (McNeill, 2016).

It is, of course, difficult to know who to believe from the media reports. The babies' Thai mother said the Australian couple rejected the baby and they did so because he had Down syndrome. The couple have both denied it, but then, they would, wouldn't they? Certainly, if surrogacy arrangements had been legal in his home state of Western Australia, this man would not have been able to take advantage of them, given his convictions for sexual abuse of children. But then he would simply have gone overseas in that case too. Even laws against overseas surrogacy arrangements would not have stopped him, as it has presumably not stopped the citizens of New South Wales, Queensland and the Australian Capital Territory, where there are laws against overseas surrogacy but where no one has yet been charged.

The law

Australia

Commercial surrogacy is illegal in Australia, as it is in most other Western countries with the exception of Israel and some states in the US. There is no national legislation in Australia in relation to surrogacy arrangements, but all the states and territories with the exception of the Northern Territory have laws prohibiting commercial surrogacy within Australia, although so-called 'altruistic' surrogacy is not unlawful. In the absence of any specific legislation, surrogacy is not illegal in the Northern Territory, i.e. no one is threatened with fines or gaol, but neither is there any way of establishing legal parentage. Most other Australian jurisdictions have legislated to regulate lawful surrogacy arrangements (those where no payment is involved except for expenses), and provide for the transfer of legal parentage[220] from the birth

---

220. Australian Government Department of Immigration and Border Control (http://www. immi.gov.au/media/fact-sheets/36a_surrogacy.htm). The new name of this department

mother to the surrogacy customers. Queensland, NSW and the Australian Capital Territory have also passed legislation making overseas commercial surrogacy arrangements a criminal offence, with penalties involving both fines and gaol sentences. However, no one has ever been charged, much less convicted under this legislation and it hasn't deterred the surrogacy customers. For example, there was the case of 'a couple' from NSW who had commissioned and paid for twins—a boy and a girl—born to an Indian woman in 2012 (Ireland, 2015). This 'couple' (only the husband was cited in the newspaper article) had violated two aspects of the NSW legislation—that prohibiting commercial surrogacy, and that prohibiting overseas surrogacy. To make matters worse, the 'couple' had refused to take the boy, not because he was disabled (as in the case of Gammy), but because they said (or the husband did) that they couldn't afford two children.

Israel

Israel is one of the few developed countries in the world where commercial surrogacy is legal.[221] The Israeli law, the Surrogate Mother Agreements (Approval of the Agreement and Status of the Child) Law, 1996, originally allowed only heterosexual couples to enter into surrogacy arrangements. (That was changed in June 2014—see below). It specifies that what it calls the 'carrying mother' must be unmarried, unrelated to either of the 'intended parents', and of the same religion as the 'intended' mother, i.e. the woman who will be raising the child. It also specifies that the sperm used for the IVF must be the intended father's, and that the ovum must come from a woman other than the 'carrying mother'. All these specifications are meant to ensure that the surrogacy legislation complies with Jewish religious law. As Carmel Shalev (1998) points out, these religious requirements have 'patriarchal' implications, in that they put 'the genetic continuity of the man at the center of attention' (p.70), and involve 'a reproduction of the male model of parenthood (genetic) and a depreciation of what is unique to the female model of parenthood (gestation)' (p.71).

---

is shocking. It used to be called the Department of Immigration and Citizenship, and before that the Department of Immigration and Multicultural Affairs, and before that, simply the Department of Immigration. I don't know when the phrase 'border control' became part of the name, but it is most likely yet another aspect of the demonising of asylum seekers on the part of the current right-wing federal government (sworn in on 18 September, 2013). Australia has no need for 'border control'. No one is threatening to invade us, and the numbers of asylum seekers reaching our shores are miniscule in comparison with the numbers pouring into Europe.

221. It is also legal in some US states.

The secular law also requires surrogacy arrangements to be approved by a statutory committee consisting of relevant professionals (physicians, a social worker, a psychologist and a lawyer) and a cleric of the parties' religion. The application to the Committee must include written evidence of the suitability of the parties, including psychological evaluations together with documentation showing that the intended mother is unable to become pregnant or carry a child to term or that pregnancy would endanger her health. The law also provides for a register of all the surrogacy orders issued, to which children born of surrogacy arrangements can have access once they reach 18 years of age (Shalev, 1998: 60-4).

The commercial aspect of surrogacy is strictly regulated by the Israeli law. The amount of the payment must be approved by the statutory committee, and it is not a payment for work or for services rendered. The terminology refers to 'covering actual expenses' and 'compensating for loss of time, suffering, loss of income or temporary loss of earning capacity'. Moreover, if the 'carrying mother' receives payment beyond that which the committee has approved, she can be charged with a criminal offence with a maximum penalty of one year in gaol (Shalev, 1998: 72). There are also criminal penalties for 'persons acting "on behalf" of the parties to the agreement' (p.72).

On 1 June, 2014, the Israeli parliament voted to expand legal access to surrogacy arrangements, both in Israel and overseas, to single people and 'same-sex couples' (Times of Israel, 2014).

Elsewhere

India legalised commercial surrogacy in 2001 but left it unregulated.[222] The Law Commission of India submitted a report on the need for legislation,[223] recommending that 'such an arrangement should not be for commercial purposes'. Until January 2013, there were no restrictions on who could enter into surrogacy arrangements to acquire babies, but at that time the Indian Home Ministry tightened visa requirements, restricting visas to couples who had been married for at least two years and those whose countries recognised surrogacy (Bishop, 2013; Brewster, 2013; Lee, 2013). This was in response to the baby Manji case. This baby was commissioned by a Japanese couple who abandoned her because they divorced and neither wanted her. She was cared for in hospital for six months and was finally allowed to go to Japan with her

---

222. http://www.india.embassy.gov.au/ndli/vm_surrogacy.html.

223. http://www.surrogacylawsindia.com/legality.php?id= 7&menu_id=71.

grandmother on a one-year humanitarian visa, although this didn't resolve the question of her citizenship status (Bishop, 2013).

In 2016, India announced the passage of a new law on surrogacy, which bans commercial and international surrogacy, and restricts its use to infertile Indian couples who have been married for at least five years, and who are close relatives of the woman hired to give birth. It thus excludes gay men. It also explicitly prohibits commissioning couples from abandoning children produced under the surrogacy arrangement. However, the law contains no enforcement provision, no criminal penalties, and no mechanism or funding for implementing and monitoring it. It is unclear what the effect of the legislation will be on the notorious Akanksha Clinic; and in a country like India, with its long history of 'dowry deaths' and 'sati', it is unlikely that the prohibition on commercial surrogacy will abolish coercion (Sloan, 2016).

In response to the Gammy case, as well as the case of the Japanese man who fathered 16 children, Thailand has imposed restrictions on surrogacy opportunities. In November 2014, a bill banning commercial surrogacy and specifying a penalty of up to 10 years in prison passed its first reading in the Thai parliament, with a final reading expected within a month. The medical council of Thailand did have a regulation penalising doctors with loss of their licence if they performed surrogacy for pay. But that regulation was rarely, if ever, enforced, and surrogacy was entirely unregulated (Associated Press, 2014).

The push for legalisation

Legalisation is the most commonly suggested solution for extreme cases like those described above. In the wake of the Gammy case, there was a concerted effort on the part of the media and interested parties such as doctors, lawyers, brokers and other fertility industry participants, to push for the legalisation of commercial surrogacy within Australia. The rationale given for this drive is that it is the lack of regulation that is causing all the problems. As one commentator put it, it is the 'unregulated environment that is exposing babies and the women who carry them to a higher risk of bad health outcomes' (Alexander, 2014). A certain Stephen Page, widely quoted and described in the press as 'one of Australia's most eminent surrogacy lawyers', was reported to have said: '"Have [legalised] commercial surrogacy, and have it consistent … Australian clinics are highly regarded, we had the first IVF baby born in Melbourne. If we did it properly here, as they do in the US, we'll avoid exploitation of anybody – intended parents, surrogates, surrogates' partners, donors, donors' partners and above all the children"'

(Snow and Murdoch, 2014). But there is no way to 'do it properly' because surrogacy is inherently harmful.

Another argument for legalising commercial surrogacy arrangements is that people will simply go elsewhere if they can't get what they want legally here in Australia. For example, in an article on the website of the Law Research Centre at UTS, law academic Professor Isabel Karpin, was reported to say, "'The restrictions in Australia are forcing people overseas. Instead of making commercial surrogacy illegal we should regulate it so that these kinds of things don't occur'" (Brediceanu, 2014). But the fact that people will do it anyway is not a good reason to make it legal. People will always commit murder, but no one is arguing that murder be legalised. If something violates the common good, there should be laws against it, no matter how ineffectual. Law is an assertion of community acceptance and non-acceptability (whatever else it may as well), and surrogacy is unacceptable if women are to be accorded full human status.

Arguments in favour of legalisation give absolute priority to the desire to have children (without acknowledging that that desire is predominantly men's). Take, for example, one journalist's reference to 'desperate Australians renting wombs' (Szego, 2014). 'A carefully designed [legislative] system', she said, could be seen 'as a gentle nudge for a woman already inclined to help out'. Yet another journalist (Percy, 2014) stated categorically that 'there is clearly a high demand for the service', and referred to surrogacy arrangements as an 'aspect of recurring human conduct'. But the demand for surrogacy is not 'recurring human conduct', any more than the consumption of Coca Cola is. It's a desire elicited by the industry, and it did not exist before the industry did. A desire for children on the part of those who cannot conceive them may be perennial, but surrogacy as a way of satisfying that desire is not. There would be no demand for the 'service' if there were no provision of it. As an anonymous *Sydney Morning Herald* letter writer put it: 'In life we cannot always have what we want … Sadly some of us are destined to be childless … Just because a woman desperately wants a baby does not give her the right to have one at any cost, personal or financial'.

Moreover, regulating the 'industry' will not make the extreme cases go away, as the example of Israel shows. No law would allow convicted pedophiles to commission babies, so they will always go elsewhere, however accommodating towards commercial surrogacy the domestic laws might be. Elsewhere—Mexico, Ukraine, Panama, etc.—would still be available for those who did not qualify under whatever guidelines the legislation required.

There are prominent legal authorities who have come out in favour of surrogacy. Chief Judge John Pascoe of the Federal Circuit Court of Australia said that it was 'futile to continue a prohibition on commercial surrogacy' because the laws were an 'evident failure' and the criminal sanctions were not enforced. Moreover, children already existed and the courts had to decide what was in their best interests, and it was hardly in the children's best interests to have the only parents they knew jailed. He quoted from a 2012 decision in the Family Court of Australia, saying: '"it's probably too late to ask whether – or to inquire into the legality of the arrangements that had been made. The court really needs to take children as it finds them"' (Pascoe, 2013: 4-5).[224]

Chief Justice Diana Bryant, head of the Family Court of Australia, is also pro-surrogacy. She is reported to have said that she was 'confident Australia will legalise commercial surrogacy', and that this would be a good thing because it 'will help defeat the "dark side" of an international trade that leads to exploitation and the tragic rejection of children such baby Gammy in Thailand' (Feneley, 2015). But then, the Family Court does not have a good record when it comes to protecting the safety of women and children. With the help of changes to family law introduced by an Australian Labor government (Hill, 2015), it has been hijacked by the self-styled 'men's rights' activists, violent men whose sense of aggrieved entitlement extends to what they seem to regard as their inalienable right to abuse their children. Time and again the Court has handed down decisions awarding custody to the abusing father, ignoring evidence from social workers, the children's mothers and the children themselves (Hill, 2015; Olding, 2016).

This is despite the fact that these men were probably responsible for a series of murderous attacks on judges of the Family Court in the early 1980s, one of which involved a bomb that killed the wife of one of the judges (ABC News, 2015). Or is it because of that very fact? The mainstream media blamed the Family Court itself for the attacks. An editorial in the *Sydney Morning Herald* opined that '"there must be something seriously wrong with the Family Court system for such an outrage to occur"', while the *Bulletin* was of the view that 'the attacks "exposed serious flaws in our divorce machinery"'. The government of the day respectfully consulted 'fathers' rights groups' about what was to be done, and eventually introduced a new guiding principle into the Family Law Act: that children were to have regular contact with both parents. The principle that children had a right to

---

224. This publication can no longer be found on the internet.

be safe from 'family violence' (note the agent deletion) was also included in the legislation (Hill 2015), but it has been subsequently honoured more in the breach than the observance (Laing, 2010). Thus did the government capitulate to violent men, demonstrating once again that what men want trumps the basic human rights of women and children.

So far, however, commercial surrogacy remains illegal in all Australian jurisdictions, and the official position remains firmly opposed to legalisation. In 2016, the Australian House of Representatives Standing Committee on Social Policy and Legal Affairs released a report recommending that 'the practice of commercial surrogacy remain illegal in Australia'. The main reason given was that, 'even with the best of regulatory intentions, there is still significant potential for the exploitation of surrogates and children to occur' (Australian House of Representatives, 2016: v). Also in 2016, the Social Affairs Committee of the Parliamentary Assembly of the Council of Europe voted against all forms of surrogacy, 'altruistic' as well as commercial (Lahl, 2016). The European Parliament had already passed a resolution condemning surrogacy on 17 December 2015. In a report on human rights, it states that it

> [c]ondemns the practice of surrogacy, which undermines the human dignity of the woman since her body and its reproductive functions are used as a commodity; considers that the practice of gestational surrogacy which involves reproductive exploitation and use of the human body for financial or other gain, in particular in the case of vulnerable women in developing countries, shall be prohibited and treated as a matter of urgency in human rights instruments.[225]

These are hopeful signs, but the practice continues nonetheless with no end in sight.

Suggestions

There have been suggestions made about what the law might do. There were several put forward in February 1991 at a conference in Melbourne called 'Surrogacy—in whose interest?' aiming 'to examine the ethical, social, legal, and policy issues arising in surrogacy' (Salomone, 1992).[226] At the

---

225. http://europeanpost.co/the-european-parliament-condemned-all-forms-of-surrogacy/.

226. The conference was organised by a community welfare organisation, the Mission of St. James and St. John (one of Anglicare's precursors), together with the Australian Institute of Family Studies, the Australian Council of Social Services, the Victorian Council of Social Services, and the Social Work Department of the Phillip Institute of Technology. FINRRAGE members were among the attendees (Salomone, 1992).

final plenary session, the conference issued a unanimous statement which 'reject[ed] the institutionalisation and regulatory system contained in the proposals of the National Bioethics Consultative Committee', and gave a number of suggestions about how Australian law might deal with the issue. It recommended that 'surrogacy arrangements should be null, void and illegal—and unenforceable'. It was 'contrary to public policy', because it treated children as commodities, exploited women's bodies, and was destructive of the surrogacy woman's family. While supporting the existing legislation prohibiting surrogacy in Victoria, South Australia and Queensland, the conference statement recommended that that legislation be strengthened by making surrogacy contracts/agreements unenforceable in a court of law, and by prohibiting and penalising the activities of the middlemen such as doctors, lawyers and IVF clinics. It also stated explicitly that no penalties should be imposed on the surrogacy woman herself, nor on 'the couple', that 'paramount consideration' should be given to 'the welfare and interests of the child born from the arrangement', and that 'any dispute which arises should be dealt with in the Family Court under the Family Law Act' (Salomone, 1992). Clearly, these recommendations recognise that surrogacy arrangements will continue to happen and children will continue to be born, just as they have already, despite the illegality.

Although the conference statement did not mention it, British surrogacy law is similar to the statement's own suggestions.[227] Commercial surrogacy is illegal in Britain, although not unpaid arrangements, and legal parentage is not automatically granted on the basis of a contract, but can only be established through a family court or an adoption agency after the child's birth. Moreover, the birth mother's right to keep the child is absolute, even when she's not genetically related to the child. It can't be signed away through a pre-birth contract, although she can sign a parental order after the birth transferring her right to the surrogacy consumers (Ketchum, 1989: 124).

Despite the objections raised against the NBCC at the 1991 conference, the recommendations of the NBCC were not so very different from the conference's own (apart from the Bioethics Committee's refusal to condemn surrogacy). The NBCC did recommend that surrogacy 'should not be totally prohibited', but they also said that it shouldn't be 'freely allowed' either, and that it should be restricted to 'non-contractual or voluntary [i.e. non-commercial] arrangements'. It 'should be strictly controlled by uniform legislation' across Australia, and legislation should make 'all surrogacy arrangements

---

227. https://www.gov.uk/rights-for-surrogate-mothers.

unenforceable'. In other words, if the birth mother wants to keep the child, her wishes should have priority over those of the commissioning person(s). The Committee had also recommended that legislation specify 'controlling mechanisms for agencies' and place controls on advertising (NBCC, 1990: 36). The agencies regulating surrogacy should be state-run and non-profit, records should be kept and counselling provided. The birth mother should have a one-month cooling-off period but after she had relinquished the child the commissioning person(s) would automatically become the child's parents (instead of having to go through an adoption process). The Committee also recommended that there be no criminal penalties for any of the parties (Emmerson, 1996: 10).

For men at women's expense

The feminist case against surrogacy focuses on the harm to women, the damage to the bodies, hearts, minds and souls of women subjected to dangerous medical procedures and heart-breaking separations. But it also exposes the male domination of the industry, the fact that surrogacy is an industry run in the interests of men at the expense of women (Klein, ed., 1989; Scutt, 1990).

Surrogacy arrangements exist to supply men with children conceived with their own sperm. Whether or not most of the users are men (I know of no research that addresses the question), their 'needs' are paramount. Any potential risks to the women whose bodies are used are either downplayed or completely ignored, while the women who will bring the children up are either given a minimal secondary role, or (in the case of gay and single men) absent altogether. Most surrogacy consumers are probably heterosexual couples, but the surrogate-born child is almost invariably a product of the commissioning man's sperm, whoever's ova are used (sometimes the man's female partner via IVF, often an anonymous 'egg donor' who is not the woman who bears the child to term). Women are not prevented from using surrogacy services, and the advertising explicitly encourages them (see below). But the vast majority of the users of surrogacy are men, either alone or with a female partner. As Janice Raymond put it: 'Surrogacy is about two women doing for one man, both of whom provide mere maternal environments. It is a reproductive *menage à trois*, again with the man at the center' (Raymond, 1988a).

Sometimes there are three women—in the case of a man in a heterosexual couple whose genetic child is the result of an ovum from one woman carried in the womb of another woman and raised by yet another woman. There are also (at least) three women servicing gay male couples when each man wants a child fathered by his own sperm—one woman (or more) supplies the ova, and two women carry the babies to term.

In her participant observation research into one particular commercial surrogacy agency in the US, Susan Ince found that it was quite clear from the contract she had to sign, and from the actual practice of the company, 'that the purchasing father is the key figure of the industry'. She had applied to the agency to be a 'surrogate' although she didn't intend to follow through with her application. It was intended for research purposes only, to find out how the company treated the child-bearers and the women who would have the major responsibility for bringing up the children, what provision there was for medical and psychological safeguards, and how the surrogates stood legally and financially. In the very first phone call she was told that "'the child is the child of the natural parents. That means the father'"; the contract specified that the child was to be delivered to the father; and every effort was made to include him in the progress of the pregnancy. In contrast, the woman who would eventually be caring for the child was rarely mentioned and there were no plans to include her at any stage (Ince, 1984: 112).

It might be argued that it is only to be expected that the surrogacy industry would be dominated by men. A fertile man always needs a woman if he's to have a baby, whereas fertile women can have their own babies, and artificial insemination (if needed) is comparatively easy to get access to. But that is not the reason for the male domination of the surrogacy industry. Rather, it partakes of the same arrogant entitlement and dissociation from genuine humanity that characterises male supremacy more generally. Men feel themselves entitled to get what they want. They want ownership of the process that their sperm initiates (as they see it), and ownership of the enduring end result of that process, the child.

The insight that surrogacy really exists only for men (with women allowed the usual token admittance) is not based on research. There is no research on the question of whose interests are driving the growth of the industry. But a careful reading of the language used exposes the male interests involved, even while it seems deliberately engineered to hide them (along with all those other interests that cluster around any perceived opportunity for profit-making). As Janice Raymond said:

> the term *surrogate mother* … mask[s] the male demand for genetic progeny, the professionals who carry out the procedures, and the brokers who mediate the contracts and benefit most by this enterprise.

She quotes Louise Vandelac, who said:

"No expression specifically designates the sires; the initiators and principal beneficiaries of birth contracts float in the carefree realm of the unnamed … Safely hidden by the discourse, as if they themselves were 'carried' by the bearing mothers, these men vanish from the linguistic context, and their motivations, their interests, and their roles are thereby easily concealed" (Raymond, 1994: 139).

To call a woman who gives birth to a baby a 'surrogate mother' is a splendid example of male supremacist dissociation. It obliterates everything women experience in pregnancy and birth, and severs the genuinely human connection between birth mother and the child she bears. It is not just the language that severs that connection, of course; the language simply follows the practice and precisely identifies the male supremacist culture within which the practice is embedded. Within the meanings and values of that culture, the woman who gives birth is a 'substitute' because, once she has fulfilled her function, the man has no further use for her. She is dispensable and the child becomes wholly his. He doesn't even need a wife, as the 'gay dads' have found; even if he does have a wife, the child is not genetically hers, and the spermatic relationship is the only one recognised by the male supremacist mindset and the law. Awareness and recognition of the woman who contributed the ovum, and the woman who contributed the nine-month gestation period, is excised from the child's life; the child is his and his alone because he contributed the sperm.

This, of course, describes the most extreme cases. Some people have tried to humanise the process by getting to know the woman with whom they make the surrogacy arrangements. But the extreme cases are the norm, especially (although not always) when the arrangements happen overseas; and while the comparatively wealthy 'couples' might show concern for the woman who is bearing 'their' child, I have yet to see any mention of a relationship with the woman who undergoes the superovulation procedure to produce the ova that get fertilised with his sperm.

The male domination of the industry is a well-kept secret. Most definitions of surrogacy are gender-neutral in their depictions of who the buyers are, referring to 'couples' or 'persons' or 'parents' rather than men. For example, the Australian government's report on assisted reproductive technology in Australia (Macaldowie et al, 2012: 2) defined 'surrogacy arrangements' as those 'where a woman, known as the gestational carrier, agrees to carry a child for another person or couple, known as the intended parent(s), with the intention that the child will be raised by the intended parent(s)'.

Others, however, are quite explicit about the male interests involved without, however, seeing anything wrong with it. As the author of the obituary of Noel Keane, 'father' of the surrogacy industry (Winkler, 1988), put it: 'In a typical agreement, a woman is artificially inseminated with sperm from a man whose wife cannot conceive. At term, the surrogate mother surrenders her parental rights, receives a fee and *turns over the baby to its biological father*, whose wife may then become its adoptive mother' (Van Gelder, 1997—emphasis added). One of surrogacy's chief advocates, psychiatrist Philip J. Parker,[228] defined a 'surrogate mother' as 'a woman who contracts to be impregnated through artificial insemination of the semen provided by *a man who will take custody of the newborn* after delivery' (Parker, 1982: 341—emphasis added). As a staunch defender of surrogacy, Parker did not intend this as a criticism and he gave it no particular importance since elsewhere he used the term 'couple'. "'I believe"', he is reported to have said, "'that a married couple's use of a surrogate mother to bear the husband's biologic child falls into the category of a fundamental right'" (quoted in Corea, 1985: 234-5).

Noel Keane, too, was a great believer in this 'fundamental right'. He was reported to have said: "'I don't have any ethical problems with what I'm doing. I think everyone's got a right to have a biological child – at least, we do in the United States. I think it [surrogacy] is absolutely right'" (Kirsten Kozolanka in Klein, ed., 1989: 126). This is yet another splendid example of speaking from a masculinist standpoint. The only 'right' allowed is the man's. The right of women to base their decisions on their own knowledge and experience of pregnancy and childbirth is inconceivable from this standpoint. He doesn't have any ethical problems because he can't see the world from a standpoint based on the humanity of women. Only men matter. And it is this standpoint that has prevailed over and over again in the brave new world of surrogacy, as women are dosed with dangerous chemicals, implanted with embryos they will (hopefully) eventually give birth to but must relinquish, and lose their children to a male-defined legal system.

---

228. Author of 'Motivation of surrogate mothers: initial findings' *American Journal of Psychiatry* 140(1), 1983. Parker attributed the fact that Michigan was 'one of the primary centers of activity for surrogate motherhood in the United States' largely to 'the efforts of attorney Noel Keane' (Parker, 1982: 341). Keane, said Parker, had been bringing surrogates and intending parents together 'for over five years', and had initiated several widely publicised lawsuits involving surrogacy. According to Wikipedia, Keane wrote the first surrogacy contract in 1980, and was responsible for the contract in the Baby M case (see below).

Baby M

A particularly blatant example of the workings of the male-defined legal system is the ruling of New Jersey Superior Court judge, Harvey R. Sorkow, in the first of two legal decisions on the Baby M case in 1987. He upheld the validity of the surrogacy contract, awarded custody of the child to the man who commissioned it, and allowed his wife to adopt the baby (Raymond, 1994: 31). In his 'Opinion' he was quite open and unapologetic about the reason for his decision, and about the masculinist interests involved: "'The biological father pays the surrogate for her willingness to be impregnated and carry *his* child to term. At birth, the father does not purchase the child. *He cannot purchase what is already his*'" (Raymond, 1988a, quoting from Sorkow's 31 March 'Opinion'—Raymond's emphases).

The naming of the case also exposed the masculinist interests at stake, as did the interested parties named in the contract.[229] The birth mother had called the baby 'Sarah', but 'Baby M' referred to the name the genetic father had given her, 'Melissa'; and the parties to the contract included the birth mother's husband (as well as the birth mother herself and the commissioning man), but not the commissioning man's wife, despite the fact that it was she who would have primary responsibility for caring for the child. Sorkow's decision, however, did allow her to adopt the child.

That decision was later partly overturned by a higher court, the New Jersey Supreme Court, at least in principle, although the actual outcome was the same. The Supreme Court's judgement said:

> "We invalidate the surrogacy contract because it conflicts with the law and public policy of this State. While we recognize the depth of the yearning of infertile couples to have their own children, we find payment of money to a 'surrogate' mother illegal, perhaps criminal, and potentially degrading to women" (Oliver, 1989: 95, quoting from the court decision).

But despite this ruling and the statement that commercial surrogacy was 'illegal, perhaps criminal', not only did the court not recommend that the genetic father be prosecuted, it awarded him custody on the grounds of 'the best interests of the child'.

Gena Corea said, quite rightly, that this view belonged to a patriarchal (or as I would prefer to name it, male supremacist) value system, since it saw 'no harm in using a woman for the purpose for which she is intended:

---

229. http://www.casebriefs.com/blog/law/family-law/family-law-keyed-to-weisberg/adoption-and-alternatives-to-adoption/in-re-baby-m/.

reproduction'. But we could also look at that term 'fundamental right' and see it as yet another example of that arrogant masculine sense of entitlement. Clearly, this supposed 'fundamental right' is the man's, masked by the use of the term 'couple'. It is he who wants a 'biologic child'. Robyn Rowland (1990) cited research with couples using IVF, that found that "'men usually appear to be the driving force behind the preference for a biological child. Many women told us they would be happy to adopt, but their husbands wanted a genetic connection. The men agreed'".

There is also research that seemingly comes to the opposite conclusion, that it is *women* whose desire for a child is so great that they turn to surrogacy. One author (Rudrappa, 2010), for example, cited evidence indicating that it was usually the wife who brought up the issue of surrogacy. One of those pieces of evidence was the story of one woman's use of surrogacy to procure a child for herself. The husband in this case was not especially keen on the surrogacy idea and would have been quite happy to adopt a child. The other piece of evidence was a study investigating how women and men viewed the new reproductive technologies. Many of the women interviewed for this study wanted to "'maintain … the biological lineage through a child that is not only biologically related but that visibly resembles the father'". In this case, too, it was not the men who wanted to see themselves in their children. The author of the study was quoted saying that this desire for a genetic connection between the man and the child "'may reinforce patriarchy'" (Rudrappa, 2010: 263), as indeed it does, even though the desire is the woman's, not the man's.[230] In these cases it is the wife who wants a child genetically related to her husband, rather than the man himself. But she wants it for him. The 'fundamental right' remains the man's, whether or not he cares to avail himself of it.

Some women

Like all male supremacist institutions in these days of 'equal opportunity', women are permitted to take advantage of other women in surrogacy arrangements. Certainly, the companies that sell the product and the medical experts who provide the technology are equal-opportunity suppliers. For

---

230. These two texts are: Griswold, Zara (2005) *Surrogacy was the Way: Twenty Intended Mothers Tell Their Stories* Gurnee, Il: Nightengale [sic] Press; and Becker, Gay (2000) *The Elusive Embryo: How Women and Men Approach New Reproductive Technologies* Berkeley, CA: University of California Press.

example, Genea,[231] one of the largest and most reputable IVF companies in Australia, uses non-sex-specific language to refer to surrogacy customers, who could be either women or men, or both: 'Surrogacy is a form of assisted reproductive treatment (ART) in which one woman carries a child in her uterus and delivers it for *another person or couple*'. Surrogacy Australia's list of 'what sort of Australians use surrogacy' includes everyone: 'heterosexual women … single women or lesbian couples … single or same-sex partnered men'.[232] Again, potential surrogacy clients were identified by a Swedish author[233] as: 'infertile women, single men, homosexual couples, female athletes who don't want to lose years of their careers but still desire a child who is genetically related to them—not to mention those women who have aesthetic reasons for not wanting their bodies to be compromised by a pregnancy' (Ekman, 2013: 151). Note, however, that these were not actual clients, but imaginary ones suggested by someone with a vested interest in surrogacy.

It is true that women who take advantage of surrogacy arrangements can behave as badly as any man convinced of the rightness of his cause. One example concerns an American woman, a client of the Akanksha clinic, who was using a surrogate in India rather in the US for a number of reasons. Not only was it cheaper, the Indian women had fewer (if any) legal rights to the children than women in the US (or so the American woman believed). Moreover, the women bearing the children were under closer surveillance in India than they were in the US, where, the American woman was reported to say,

> [y]ou have no idea if your surrogate mother is smoking, drinking alcohol, doing drugs. You don't know what she's doing. You have a third-party agency as a mediator between the two of you [in the US], but there's no one policing her in the sense that you don't know what's going on (Scott, 2007).

---

231. http://www.genea.com.au/my-fertility/i-need-help/fertility-alternatives/surrogacy. One of its founders was Professor Alan Trounson, a leading IVF pioneer in Australia. He owns shares in the company. It is not the largest IVF company, or it wasn't in June 2013. That honour belonged to Virtus, 'the first fertility group in the world to float on the stock market' (Medew, 2014; Medew and Baker, 2013).

232. Well, perhaps not everyone—there are no transgendered folk there (http://www.surrogacyaustralia.org/about-us/general-info-on-overseas-surrogacy).

233. A man called Kutte Jönsson, philosopher and member of the Swedish Association for Surrogacy, in (2003) *Det förbjudna mödraskapet* (Forbidden Motherhood). This list omits heterosexual couples, who would be the primary users of surrogacy, especially as many jurisdictions where surrogacy is legal restrict it to heterosexual couples. But perhaps that was why the author omitted them—it was too obvious to need saying.

In India, in contrast, at least at the Akanksha clinic, the women live in the clinic or in accommodation where they are constantly supervised. The rationale for this is that their diet and health can be monitored, and indeed, many women undergoing surrogacy receive better nutrition and health care than they would if they had remained in their own homes. But they are also allowed little control over their lives during the time they are pregnant with the commissioned child.

Another example of a female surrogacy consumer thoroughly embedded in male supremacist values was the American woman who, at the age of 49, decided she wanted to have children but found she couldn't. Her doctor suggested she avail herself of 'fertility assistance', but instead she decided to hire another woman to bear a child for her because she didn't want to personally undergo the required treatment. She was reported to be 'highly skeptical of the hormonal regimens that form the basis of such treatment and worried about the long-term effects of taking such drugs' (Rudrappa, 2010: 260). She had no concern, presumably, about the long-term effects on the other woman or women.

The fact that women can be surrogacy consumers too does not mean that therefore surrogacy is not male dominated. In these days of neo-liberal 'equality', women are allowed to behave like men. Indeed, the participation of women is one way of disguising the masculine interests involved.

Gay men
Gay men have taken to the surrogacy industry with great enthusiasm. The media love them. Story after story extols the joys of 'gay dads' and 'their' children, born from the bodies of women hired for that purpose.

For example, in a 2011 article on the 'Care2' website,[234] the author waxed lyrical about 'a new family' comprising 'two dads' and a new born baby: 'Welcome to the world, Caspian', the author enthused 'I ... know ... how much you were longed for and how much you are loved'. The author

---

234. 'Care2' is 'a social network website ... founded ... in 1998 to help connect activists from around the world'. Its championing of many categories of the oppressed makes it predominantly left-wing in political orientation, although its leftist orientation is never acknowledged and would probably be hotly denied, based as it is in the US: 'We pride ourselves on being a different kind of company ... we're committed to using the power of business to make a positive social and earth-friendly impact on the world'. But like the political left-wing everywhere, it is oblivious to the more deeply radical of feminist insights. For example, it has embraced the cause of 'same-sex marriage' (as well as the gay male exploitation of women's bodies), ignoring the feminist critique that marriage originated in the oppression of women and is therefore irredeemable for feminist purposes.

admitted she had never met the baby's 'fathers', but somehow she 'knows' that the baby 'entered the world deeply and completely loved'.

Again, here in Australia a gay male couple each fathered (in the sperm donor sense) a child, both of whom were born of surrogacy arrangements in Thailand. The reporting was wholly positive: 'Cuddled in the arms of doting parents Mark and Matt, newborns Tate and Estelle are the contented faces of a unique Australian modern family', enthuses the text of the news item on the internet (Crouch, 2014). Both children were 'conceived from eggs harvested from a single donor woman' and born 'by caesarean section' to two women in Thailand. The 'single donor woman' was not either of the Thai women who carried the children to term. She was anonymous, her participation arranged by 'an agent' in Thailand, 'offering a choice of ethnicities'. Not surprisingly, '[t]he men chose caucasian'. (The woman was probably eastern European, eastern Europe being another part of the world where women are sufficiently poverty-stricken to offer themselves for the hyper-ovulation procedures). So these men exploited the bodies of three women, all of whom underwent major medical procedures to provide them with babies. The donor woman's procedure to have her eggs harvested would perhaps have been less invasive than a caesarean delivery because it would (probably) have been laproscopic, i.e. through a small incision in the abdomen. But she would have had to undergo a general anaesthetic; and she would have been subjected to superovulation with the known risky side-effects of ovarian hyper-stimulation syndrome (see below).

The news report did not say whether or not these men knew what they were putting women through in order to acquire their 'unique Australian modern family'. But if the media reports and the existence of websites such as 'gaydadsaustralia.com' are any guide, there's nothing 'unique' about it. 'Same-sex couples', or inevitably 'LGBTQ',[235] are ubiquitous in the surrogacy domain. One 'fertility specialist' in India was quoted saying that more than one third of her clients were Australian gay men (Brewster, 2013). Neither is there anything unique about 'choosing caucasian' as the source of the ova.

---

235. 'lesbian, gay, bisexual, transgender or queer' (Stechyson, 2013a). But lesbians would have little or no call for surrogacy, although they are listed by Surrogacy Australia as one of the types of people 'who choose surrogacy': 'single women or lesbian couples who can't or don't want to go through pregnancy or artificial insemination'. They are presumably included in the interests of 'gender equality'. I haven't seen this difference mentioned anywhere. The story Natalie Stechyson (2013b) tells about two lesbians in Canada was not about surrogacy, but about the problems the women had with the donor of the sperm one of the women was inseminated with. Having originally said in writing that he waived all parental rights, he not only changed his mind, he served the women with a writ demanding custody 'on all the special occasions' (Christmas, birthdays, etc.).

The founder and CEO of the Los Angeles-based medical tourism company, PlanetHospital, a certain Rudy Rupak Acharya, was reported to have said in 2009 that, 'because of growing demand from his clients for eggs from Caucasian women, he's started to fly donors to India from the former Soviet republic of Georgia' (Cohen, 2009).[236]

I am not arguing that gay men ought not to be fathers, either in the relational sense that they have a loving connection with a child, or in the sperm donor sense. There is no reason why gay man can't be as good fathers as straight men. However, I am appalled at the exploitation of women and the glorification of that exploitation in the name of 'love'. There is an utter disregard of the physical danger of ovarian hyperstimulation, and of what it is like for a woman to give birth and have the child taken away from her. In a world where women had a say, this cavalier approach to childbirth and to women's health would not happen.

I am also worried about children being raised without mothers, and not only that, children who will never know their mothers because in the ordinary human relational sense, they have none. The assertion by one of the South Australian men that 'There is not a part of parenting that is gender specific', is not true. There is a difference between mothering and fathering. This is expressed in the different meanings of these two terms. Mothering a child implies on-going care and nurturing, whereas fathering a child implies simply a biological contribution. I am not suggesting that being a woman invariably means that someone is nurturing, and being a man invariably means that someone is not. I'm sure there are men who are more caring and considerate people than some women. But the gay male surrogacy-users have already exploited women; and their obliviousness to that fact, together with their arrogant insistence that what they want they should have, and their dissociation from the realities of women's bodies and lives, does not bode well for their mothering abilities. The same could be said of women who use other women in surrogacy arrangements, of course; they, too, have exploited women and shown scant regard for the women used in the process, especially the 'egg donors'. But male supremacy's arrogance and dissociation manifest more clearly in men who are, after all, its rightful bearers within

---

236. PlanetHospital no longer lists surrogacy as a procedure on its website. According to media reports in May 2014 (Cooper et al, 2014; Darnovsky, 2014a), it was accused of 'deceiving its clients and stealing their money'. It would seem that it couldn't honour its contracts, especially with gay men, when it tried to move its surrogacy operations to Mexico when India closed its doors to everyone but long-term heterosexual couples.

male supremacy's masculinist culture; and arrogance and dissociation are not appropriate character traits for the raising of children.

'Infertility'

The surrogacy literature frequently expresses sympathy for those people (usually referred to as 'couples' or women) who cannot have children the usual way, who are 'infertile'. Indeed, aid for the infertile is a major ideological justification for surrogacy (and the IVF industry more generally). As one source put it:

> Is it any wonder ... that women and men who have experienced the agonizing frustration of remaining childless despite all their best efforts should turn to medical technology for control over their infertility? (Nelson and Nelson, 1989: 85).

This is followed by a warmly sympathetic account of some suggested reasons why 'women and men' might 'go to considerable lengths to have children of their own' (p.86).

The feminist response to this is to refer to the patriarchal ideology of motherhood that influences women to want children by making them feel that they are not 'real' women if they can't have children. For example, Janice Raymond said: '[In patriarchal ideology] [a] woman is fulfilled through breeding. She enters reality only as a mother, and any woman who rejects that role is suspect, disorderly, and out of place' (Raymond, 1988a).

However, while this might be true in the case of women who are prepared to use the body of another woman to produce a child for themselves, in the case of the birth and relinquishing mother herself, surrogacy is not a reinforcement of women's role in motherhood, but a denial of it. The connection between a woman and the child she has given birth to is broken, and what is left in the malestream view is the genetic connection to a man (with sometimes the man's wife as the child's adoptive mother). 'Infertility' in this sense is a male supremacist code word disguising what is really going on—a technological, and hence dissociated, way of re-asserting the male control over childbirth that the demise of marriage has undermined. It is not, of course, the main way—even at its most popular, surrogacy would probably always comprise a numerically small proportion of the babies who are born (the prescience of Margaret Atwood's Handmaid's Tale notwithstanding). But it is a way of managing childbirth in a world governed by the prevalence of the male supremacist values of male entitlement and dissociation.

Harmful medicine and the IVF industry

Surrogacy these days would not be possible without the IVF industry, and so all the problems belonging to IVF can be found in surrogacy too.[237] Because IVF relies on medical interventions, used mainly on the bodies of women, so does surrogacy. It has been said that men, too, can undergo painful procedures in the course of infertility diagnoses. As one source put it: 'Men can be subjected to painful testicular biopsies for sperm' (Medew and Baker, 2013); and a website for Sentara Norfolk General Hospital in Virginia in the US, advertising infertility treatments for men, mentions surgery 'to repair dilated scrotal veins', correct obstructions and reverse vasectomy.[238] But these are not typical treatments for infertility, whereas procedures subjecting a healthy female body to medical interventions are standard in the surrogacy industry (and the 'infertility' industry more generally).

'Egg harvesting'

Surrogacy is not possible without a supply of women's ova available for the necessary IVF procedures. But women, unlike hens, do not lay their 'eggs' and leave them lying around. 'Eggs' need to be 'harvested', and that involves, not only getting ova out of a woman's body, but doses of artificial hormones that to make the woman produce multiple ova. In the words of one impeccably scientific article:

> Since the pioneering days of *in vitro* fertilization (IVF), ovarian stimulation has been an integral part of assisted reproductive techniques (ARTs). The goal of ovarian stimulation is to induce ongoing development of multiple dominant follicles and to mature many oocytes [ova] to improve chances for conception ... This approach of *interfering* with physiological mechanisms underlying single dominant follicle selection is usually applied in normo-ovulatory women (Macklon et al, 2006: 170—emphasis added).

---

237. Arditti, 1990; Ber, 2000; Corea, 1985; Ekman, 2013; Ewing and Rowland, 1990; FINRRAGE, 1989; Gallagher, 2014; Gupta, 2006, 2012; Hawthorne, 2008; Hawthorne and Klein, eds, 1991; Ince, 1984; Kane, 1989; Ketchum, 1989; Klein, 1991, 2006, 2008, 2009; Klein, ed., 1989; Mies, 1988; Raymond, 1988a, b, 1989, 1994; Rowland, 1987, 1990, 1992; Salomone, 1992; Scutt, 1991; Scutt, ed., 1988; Spallone, 1989; Spallone and Steinberg, 1987; Spar, 2006; Sussex, 1991; Winkler, 1988; and the Feminist International Network of Resistance to Reproductive and Genetic Engineering (FINRRAGE).

238 .http://www.sentara.com/Services/Urology/UrologyServicesatSentara/Pages/ treatment_male_infertility.aspx. Sentara Norfolk General Hospital no longer offers these services.

In other words, the drugs stimulating the ovaries to produce multiple ova-bearing follicles instead of the usual single one, are given to women who ovulate normally. The doses of hormones are necessary for two reasons. The healthy female body normally produces only one ovum each time it ovulates, and one ovum is not enough for IVF procedures (still experimental after many decades); so it must be made to produce multiple ova to allow for wastage in the subsequent stages of the IVF procedure: '[ovarian stimulation] allows for inefficiencies in subsequent oocyte maturation, fertilization *in vitro*, embryo culture, embryo selection for transfer, and implantation' (Macklon et al, 2006: 170-1). In the second place, the timing of natural ovulation cannot be controlled or even known with any certainty. Artificially stimulating ovulation gives the doctors control over the timing of the ovulation process, what one of the early researchers called 'ovulation to order' (Corea, 1985: 108-10).

The surgical intrusion into the female body to collect the ova is via a small incision (laproscopy) through the vaginal wall and into the follicles, but it does require a general anaesthetic. Surgery is necessary because ovulation occurs inside a woman's body and the 'egg collector' (i.e. doctor) has to penetrate the woman's body to get to the ova. This might seem too obvious to need saying, but the language used in the industry—'multiple dominant follicles … to mature many oocytes', for example—does tend to disguise the fact that all this is happening inside a woman's body.

Then there are the hormones used to dose women in order to get them to over-produce ova. There is some evidence that these procedures could have detrimental effects on women's health, both in the short term and in the long term. For example, a newspaper article mentioned a recent case in India involving a 21-year-old woman who was injected with a follicle-stimulation hormone and who produced 40 ova in a single cycle. The article said that the UK Human Fertilisation and Embryology Authority described this as 'potentially life-threatening for the egg donor' (Johnston, 2007). The article did not say whether or not the young woman did in fact die, nor whether she was given any follow-up care, nor for how long that care lasted, nor whether she would be monitored for the rest of her life, nor whether her case was part of an ongoing research project. But the latter is highly unlikely, given the paucity of research in developed countries, much less in Third World countries.

In another example, the authors of the above-mentioned scientific article (Macklon et al, 2006) said of clomiphene citrate ('still the most applied drug for infertility therapies worldwide'), that it 'does not appear to be associated with preterm birth and congenital abnormalities', but that 'data from well-designed prospective studies are lacking'. At the same time, they acknowledged that there was some evidence of a 'putative increased risk of ovarian cancer reported to be associated with the use of CC for more than 12 months', and that as a result, it was 'licensed for just 6 months of use in some countries' (Macklon et al, 2006: 176).

Again, a certain P. M. Bolton, writing to the British medical journal, *The Lancet*, in 1977 from the Department of Surgery at the University of Queensland, said that she/he had seen cases of 'synchronous bilateral breast cancer' (i.e. cancer in both breasts at the same time) in two young women 'who had taken clomiphene because of infertility'. One of the women, who was 28 at the time she took the clomiphene in 1968, had died by the time of writing (in 1974). The other woman was still alive, but her 'treatment' had started later (in 1972 when she was 29), and the most recent medical update of her condition at the time of writing was 'a bone scan [which] has revealed an area in the lumbar spine suggestive of a metastatic disease' (i.e. it was likely that the cancer had spread to her lower spine). The writer said that it 'may have been fortuitous' that these two young women developed cancer after taking clomiphene, but both the fact that they were so young and the nature of the cancer were 'unusual' (Bolton, 1977).

The most immediate of the nasty short-term effects of ovarian stimulation drugs is what is called 'ovarian hyperstimulation syndrome' (OHSS). This has been known to have effects ranging from 'mild forms' such as 'nausea, vomiting, diarrhoea, and abdominal distention', to more serious forms such as '[t]hromboembolism, renal failure, adult respiratory distress, and haemorrhage from ovarian rupture' (Beeson and Lippman, 2006: 574).[239] One woman described the effects thus: 'The day after an increased dosage [of Pergonal] my waist size increased one inch every hour. Breathing asthmatically and with my legs swelling perceptibly I was admitted to the casualty ward'.[240]

Because of the side-effects, around a quarter of those who enroll in an IVF program leave after a first unsuccessful attempt, 'even in countries

---

239. For more details of the symptoms of OHSS, graded into levels of severity, see: Aboulgar and Mansour, 2003.

240. Maggie Humm in Klein, ed., 1989: 42. 'Pergonal is obtained from the urine of menopausal women. The intention of Pergonal therapy is to bypass the hypothalamus/pituitary part of the [ovulation] pathway and to stimulate the ovaries direct using the same hormones [that would have been produced in the hypothalamus/pituitary]' (from a letter to Maggie written by one of the doctors—Klein, ed., 1989: 39).

where costs are covered by health insurance companies' (Macklon et al, 2006: 187). Reports differ on how often the side effects occur. According to the American Society of Reproductive Medicine (quoted in Beeson and Lippman, 2006: 574), the mild forms occur in 10% to 20% of IVF cycles, although Macklon et al (2006: 187) said that they occurred in 20% to 35% of IVF cycles, and Aboulgar and Mansour (2003: 277) said that 'mild forms [of OHSS] can occur in most patients after ovarian stimulation'. These authors go on to say that, because these symptoms can occur in most patients, they do 'not require special treatment'. Macklon et al (2006: 187) also said that 'moderate forms' of OHSS (i.e. forms that are stronger than 'mild') occurred in 3% to 6% of cycles, while severe forms occurred in 0.1% to 0.2%. They also said that 'moderate to critical OHSS is very rare' after treatment with clomiphene citrate, but that it is 'an important complication of gonadotropin use', and that '[t]he risk is further increased when adjuvant GnRH agonist treatment is employed'.

These are percentages of IVF cycles. They do not tell us what proportion of women are affected, because women usually go through multiple cycles. However, instances of women requiring hospitalisation after ovarian hyperstimulation are '"by no means rare"' according to the American Society of Reproductive Medicine; and in Australia in 2010, 200 women were hospitalised for OHSS (Medew and Baker, 2013). There have also been some deaths reported. In 1988, an article in an Israeli magazine reported that a woman had died after being dosed with Pergonal. Based on an interview with her husband, the article did not say she died because she took the drug; rather, it contained allegations of medical negligence, that the doctor did not follow the correct procedures in treating his wife, and it was that negligence that killed her. Nonetheless, the article did say that the drug was 'treacherous', that any woman taking it should have an ultrasound every two days, and that '[o]verstimulation of the ovaries can create a change in blood-clotting ... is always a dramatic condition and sets off a chain of reactions as a result of Pergonal' (Alison Solomon, in Klein, ed., 1989b: 46-50).

In the UK there were reports of five women who had died by June 2005 (Beeson and Lippman, 2006: 574); and researchers have noted that OHSS can lead to thrombosis, primarily in the jugular vein, which 'may have fatal consequences' (Macklon et al, 2006: 187-8). In fact, there is general agreement that OHSS can be life-threatening (Rizk and Smitz, 1992: 320; Aboulgar and Mansour, 2003: 285; Delvigne et al, 2002: 1994). Researchers in Israel (Mozes et al, 1965) reported that 12 women had developed 'hyperstimulation syndrome' after being dosed with human menopausal gonadotrophin and human chorionic gonadotrophin combined. Two of these women developed embolisms, one in the femoral artery and one in the carotid artery. The woman with the embolism in her leg had to have her right leg amputated, while the one with the embolism in her neck died. The researchers do not tell us how many women were in the overall sample, so it is not possible to say what proportion of that sample the 12 women were. They simply say, 'During 158 courses of … [the] treatment, we observed the hyperstimulation syndrome in twelve cases'. The 158 does not refer to the number of women because one woman can have a number of courses. The two women whose cases the authors discuss had received five courses between them.

But whatever the effects of the drugs used to stimulate the ovaries to over-produce—mild, moderate, severe or lethal—OHSS is a 'syndrome' that didn't exist before IVF. It is a new iatrogenic disease peculiar to the IVF industry, and a risk run by any woman who undergoes hyper-ovulation, whether she is a woman doing it for herself (or her male partner) or a surrogate doing it for someone else, whether for money or just out of the goodness of her heart.

Not surprisingly, given the masculinist standpoint of the industry, the cause of this new 'syndrome' is located with women's bodies, rather than with the drugs they are dosed with. As one official statement put it: 'Ovarian hyperstimulation syndrome (OHSS) happens when *your ovaries overreact* to the fertility drugs you're taking. Your ovaries may quickly swell to several times their normal size. They may also leak fluid into your abdomen' (emphasis added).[241] This is despite the fact that the source acknowledges that the severity of symptoms depends on the dosage level: 'Procedures which use lower doses of fertility drugs, such as egg donation, tend to have lower rates of severe OHSS than those that use higher doses'. A more accurate account of the agency involved would be to say that 'ovarian hyperstimulation syndrome (OHSS) happens when the fertility drugs you're taking make your ovaries overreact'. Left to themselves, the ovaries would not swell quickly to several times their normal size, nor leak fluid into the woman's abdomen. This source says that '[a]bout one in three women having IVF develop mild OHSS', which it describes as 'tummy [sic] swelling or bloating', 'mild tummy pain' and 'nausea'. It does not give any incidence for severe effects, although it does warn that '[s]erious complications can put your life at risk'.

There is little reliable data on the long-term health risks of ovarian hyperstimulation (Mackon et al, 2006: 189). Two members of Hands Off

---

241. http://www.babycenter.com.au/x1014381/what-is-ovarian-hyperstimulation-syndrome.

Our Ovaries[242] quoted Suzanne Parisian, a former Chief Medical Officer of the United States Food and Drug Administration, who said:

> "Pharmaceutical firms have not been required by either the government or physicians to collect safety data for IVF drugs regarding risk of cancer or other serious health conditions despite the drugs having been available in the United States for several decades" (Beeson and Lippman, 2006: 574)

In her critique of the use of women's ova for cloning research, Katrina George quoted the 2007 report of a committee in the US for Assessing the Medical Risks of Human Oocyte Donation for Stem Cell Research, which 'concluded that one of the "most striking facts ... is just how little is known with certainty about the long-term health outcomes for the women who undergo the procedure"' (George, 2008: 286). The report quoted a submission from a Dr. Ness to a review conducted by the US Institute of Medicine and the National Research Council, which said that there did appear to be an increase over time in the incidence of ovarian, breast and endometrial cancers among women who had been dosed with clomiphene citrate (one of the most commonly-used hormonal drugs to stimulate egg production). He also said, however, that it was not possible to tell, because of "'the possibility that many studies have missed the increased cancer risk because they haven't followed their subjects for enough years'".

There was one large-scale, long-term study—of 12,000 women who had received ovulation-stimulating drugs between 1965 and 1988—which found that the women were no more likely to develop breast or ovarian cancer than the general population, although they were around 1.8 times more likely to develop uterine cancer (Pearson, 2006). But the study covered mainly clomiphene citrate, and there was little information about the effects of other, newer drugs introduced in the 1980s. Large cohort follow-up studies linked to National Cancer Registries have not uncovered any link between ovarian hyperstimulation with gonadotropins and increased risk of ovarian disease, either cancerous or non-malignant. But the findings of some smaller studies suggest that ovarian hyperstimulation with gonadotropins may be responsible for higher levels of precancerous conditions (Macklon et al, 2006:189).

---

242. http://handsoffourovaries.com/. This is an organisation devoted primarily to working for 'a moratorium on [human] egg extraction for research purposes'. Their concern for the medical profession's experimentation on women is relevant to surrogacy and IVF more generally.

Moreover, higher rates of cancer and other detrimental effects might not appear until the women are in their 50s or 60s, or even in the next generation. A case in point is what happened with the synthetic oestrogen, DES (Diethylstilbestrol). Prescribed during the late 1940s and the 1950s to prevent miscarriage and other pregnancy complications, it was subsequently found to have caused reproductive problems for the children of the women who took it. Their daughters have higher risks of 'clear cell adenocarcinoma of the vagina/cervix, structural abnormalities in the reproductive tract, miscarriage, tubal (ectopic) pregnancy, infertility and premature birth'. If those daughters are over 40 years of age they have a higher risk of breast cancer than the general population. Men who are the sons of the women who took DES while they were pregnant are more likely than the general population of men to have abnormally small testes, undescended testes, and non-cancerous cysts on the testes. The research continues into the third generation, the grandchildren of the women originally prescribed the drug.[243]

But there is little research being conducted into the effects of the drugs for ovarian hyperstimulation. If the health of American women who have undergone IVF is not being followed up, it is highly unlikely that there is any monitoring of the subsequent health of those women from Eastern Europe (and elsewhere) who provide such a plentiful supply of 'eggs' for the surrogacy industry, and especially for well-off gay men (if the stories in the malestream media are any guide). As Helen Pearson has commented: 'it's unclear who will drive the effort [for research], particularly when private fertility clinics may have little interest in finding out the potential risks of the drugs they use' (Pearson, 2006: 608). (See also: Klein and Rowland, 1988; Klein, 1991).

Harmful procedures specific to surrogacy

It must be remembered that women who agree to surrogacy arrangements are perfectly healthy, indeed, good health is often stated as a requirement. And yet they are subjected to medical interventions that could have deleterious effects on their health in the future. But even if there are no long-term detrimental effects, the medical procedures are invasive and painful, and they are not done for the sake of the woman's own health.

Firstly, the woman's body must be prepared to receive the embryo. This involves hormones to suppress her own ovulatory cycle and then injections of oestrogen to build the lining of the uterus. Then, after the embryo has been

---

243. http://www.cancercouncil.com.au/880/news-media/get-the-facts/cancer-prevention-get-the-facts/cancer-council-new-south-wales-diethylstilbestrol-des-and-cancer/.

transferred she is given daily injections of progesterone to ensure that her body retains the pregnancy. Amrita Pande (2009), reporting on her research with surrogacy women in India, said that the women she spoke to often didn't know what the procedures were that they were being subjected to, but they did know about the pain. As one woman said: "'In the beginning I used to get ten-ten injections that hurt so much'" (Pande, 2009: 147). Kajsa Ekis Ekman (2013) said that these multiple drug treatments are given to women in gestational surrogacy (where the ovum is not the woman's own, it has been taken from another woman and fertilised by the surrogacy consumer's sperm). 'They have to inject themselves with hormones 2 to 3 times a day for 3 to 4 months', she said (p.165).

Then there is the use of caesarean deliveries in surrogacy arrangements. There is no information on just how prevalent that use is. Representatives of the reproductive technology industry (Stafford-Bell at al, 2014: 330),[244] investigating 'the outcomes of surrogacy among Australian intended parents who engage in compensated surrogacy overseas', were unable to find out whether the babies were born naturally or by caesarean. The authors commented, however, that it was 'common practice in India and Thailand to use elective caesarean section for surrogacy pregnancies' (p.332).

Caesareans are not minor surgical procedures. They are major operations that lead to far more medical complications than normal birth; and the best medical practice recommends that they not be performed if there are no medical indications that they are needed. A WHO survey of nine Asian countries in 2007 and 2008 found that women who had a cesarean when there was no medical need for it, were 10 times more likely to be admitted to an intensive care unit than those who gave birth normally; and women whose labour had already started when they had a caesarean despite not needing it, were 67 times more likely to be admitted to intensive care than those who had had a natural birth (Ajeet and Nandkishore, 2013: 514-15). The authors of the report commented that "'the most important finding of the survey is the increased risk of maternal mortality and severe morbidity ... in women who undergo cesarean section with no indication'" (p.515).

In 2010 it was reported (Carney, 2010) that a young woman in India died after giving birth by caesarean in a fertility clinic. In the words of the journalist who investigated and wrote up the story:

> Last May ... a young surrogate named Easwari died after giving birth at the Ishwarya Fertility Clinic in the city of Coimbatore. A year earlier, her

---

244. Those representatives were: Surrogacy Australia, Reproduction and Collaborative Trials in Australia and New Zealand, and Victorian Assisted Reproductive Treatment Authority.

husband, Murugan, had seen an ad calling for surrogates and asked her to sign up to earn the family extra money. As a second wife, Easwari was hard-pressed to refuse. The pregnancy went smoothly and she gave birth to a healthy child. But Easwari began bleeding heavily afterward, and the clinic was unprepared for complications. Unable to stop Easwari's hemorrhaging, clinic officials told Murugan to book his own ambulance to a nearby hospital. Easwari died en route. The child was delivered to the customer according to contract, and the fertility clinic denied any wrongdoing. But in a police complaint the husband suggested that the clinic had essentially dumped responsibility for his dying wife. The official investigation was perfunctory. (The clinic did not respond to emailed questions for this story.) (Carney, 2010).

It would appear that the clinic, a place where women are constantly giving birth, had no access to obstetrical specialists. The author said that no woman he interviewed in any of the clinics he visited expected to give birth naturally, that they all expected that the babies they were carrying would be delivered by caesarean (Carney, 2010).

A story (Lee, 2013) told about the experiences of an American couple who entered into surrogacy arrangements with the famous Akanksha clinic in India, suggests that the clinics prefer to hide the extent to which women are subjected to caesarean sections (or at least the most famous one does). When the American couple first arrived at the clinic Dr. Patel told them that the woman carrying the baby they had commissioned had "'gone into spontaneous labor right now'", and that the baby should be born by the afternoon of the next day. But the doctor also said, "'We may induce her tomorrow if she doesn't go into spontaneous labor'". The couple were confused by this explanation. Why would labour need to be induced if she had gone into spontaneous labour? Nonetheless they were amazed at the coincidence, and delighted that they had arrived just in time. As it turned out, though, the baby was delivered by caesarean. Dr. Patel's explanation was that the caesarean had been necessary because the baby was too big. But the nursing staff said that they had been readying the woman for surgery from the beginning, and at seven pounds two ounces (3.2 kilograms), the baby was not large at all.

Moreover, according to the author of the story, around three-quarters of the babies born at the clinic were delivered by caesarean (although she gave no source for this information). Dr. Patel was quoted insisting that she didn't perform caesareans for reasons of convenience, and that the safety of the baby was her only concern. She said her clinic's high rate was the result of complications resulting from the IVF procedures including higher than normal numbers of twins and triplets, and of the fact that many of the women giving birth in her clinic had already had caesareans. But these 'explanations' don't really explain the Akanksha clinic's high rate. In the first place, whether or not a woman is implanted with more than one embryo is wholly under the control of the fertility experts. She doesn't spontaneously generate them. If the clinic wanted to reduce the high caesarean rate out of a concern for the subsequent health of the women who produce the babies, the solution lies in their own hands. They can stop implanting women with more than one embryo. Moreover, on the clinic's own figures, multiple births do not comprise three-quarters of the births that occur there. If 500 women gave birth to 684 babies (Lee, 2013) only 184 births were multiples, i.e. 27%, not three-quarters.

In the second place, it is the original caesarean that needs explaining, not those that follow on from the original one. Did the original caesarean occur at an infertility clinic? Perhaps even this one? If so, why? Given that the good doctor's own explanations for her clinic's high rate of caesareans do not hold up under close examination, there must be reasons other than concern for the health of mother and child. Perhaps those reasons *do* relate to convenience, notwithstanding the doctor's disclaimers, at least the convenience of the clinic and their clients, and ignoring the convenience of the women who give birth. These are the kinds of reasons suggested in the literature. Commentators have pointed out that caesareans are quicker than normal labour and enable the clinic to schedule deliveries at times convenient for the clinic and for the paying customers (Carney, 2010; Rotabi and Bromfield, 2012: 133). One commentator said that some clinics charged extra for them (Carney, 2010), in which case they would be a source of extra revenue for the clinic. But whether benign or exploitative (and beneficence towards poor, uneducated women on the part of unregulated, profit-making enterprises is beyond the bounds of belief), there are undoubtedly detrimental effects on the health of the women operated upon.

'Success' rates

The 'success' rates of IVF treatment are woeful, although they have certainly improved since the first 'test tube' baby, Louise Brown, was born in Britain in July 1978. According to Gena Corea (1985: 116), only three of the women who had participated in IVF experiments up to 1980 had given birth to babies, a percentage she said was 0.04%. Corea's figures are rather obscure. In the text she says that there were 278 women who had participated in IVF up to that time, but a footnote says '287'. On my calculations, three is 1.04%

of 287, not 0.04% (and 1.07% of 278). However, whatever the precise figure, it is clear that IVF was not a successful procedure in its early days.

Things have been improving, although not by much, and the 'success' rates quoted indicate that the procedures remain experimental. In 1988, Klein and Rowland (1988) quoted 'take-home baby rates' of 8.5% for Britain for the year 1985, of 6.8% for France for 1986, and 7.4% for Australia for 1986/87. Actually, they quoted them as failure rates of 91.5%, 93.2% and 92.6% respectively, since calling these figures 'success' rates was misleading. This, they said, is 'basically a failed technology with some clinics having a zero take-home baby rate' (Klein and Rowland, 1988).

More recent figures from Australia show still more improvement although again, hardly to a level that justifies the huge amount of experimentation on women. According to the figures published by the National Perinatal Epidemiology and Statistics Unit at the University of New South Wales (Macaldowie et al, 2013: vi, 4),[245] only 17.5% of assisted reproductive technology treatment cycles in Australia and New Zealand in 2011 resulted in live births.

But counting treatment cycles is not counting numbers of women, since many women undergo more than one cycle (the average for Australian women in 2011 was 1.9); and once we look at the percentage of women undergoing treatment cycles who had given birth, the figures look somewhat better. Between 2009 and 2011, Australian Institute of Health and Welfare followed up a cohort of women through a number of cycles (an average of 2.3 cycles per woman). The report said that

> the cumulative live delivery rate [in this cohort of women] was 21.1% after the first cycle, increasing to 31.1% after two cycles, 36.0% after three cycles, 38.6% after four cycles, and 40.0% after five cycles. The cumulative live delivery rate did not increase markedly with additional treatments after five cycles (Macaldowie et al, 2013: vi).

However, this is still a less-than-fifty-percent chance of getting a baby after five cycles of IVF, and very few women persisted to that point: 'More than 90% of women had less [sic] than five cycles during the three year period' (Macaldowie et al, 2013: 55). Over two-fifths of this cohort of women (44.3%) had only one cycle of treatment (Macaldowie et al, 2013: 55, Table 48), although 21.1% of those who had only one cycle did not continue with the treatment because they gave birth after that single cycle. The remainder of the 44.3% who gave up after one cycle (i.e. 23.2%) must have

---

245. Previous publications under this authorship were produced by Australian Government's Institute of Health and Welfare (e.g. Macaldowie et al, 2012).

left without giving birth: 'A treatment can be discontinued for a variety of reasons, including inadequate response of ovaries to medication, excessive ovarian stimulation, failure to obtain oocytes, failure of oocyte fertilisation, inadequate embryo growth or patient choice' (Macaldowie et al, 2013: 10). Indeed, this attrition rate of just over 23% after (or during) the first treatment cycle is similar to the 25% rate uncovered by a 25-year review of the science behind ovarian stimulation for IVF (Macklon et al, 2006: 187). The authors attribute this high rate of withdrawal to the painful and debilitating effects of the treatment:

> Complications related to invasive IVF procedures such as oocyte retrieval and embryo transfer, predominantly involve infection and bleeding along with anesthesia problems. The drawbacks associated with profound ovarian stimulation for IVF include considerable patient discomfort such as weight gain, headache, mood swings, breast tenderness, abdominal pain, and sometimes diarrhea and nausea. In this respect, it is important to appreciate that after a first unsuccessful IVF attempt, around 25% of patients refrain from a second cycle, even in countries where costs are covered by health insurance companies (Macklon et al, 2006: 187).

The industry's advertising tends towards the misleading. For many years 'success' was defined in terms of pregnancy rates instead of rates of live births (Brigitte Oberauer in Klein, ed., 1989b: 120n7). This was the finding of a survey of IVF clinics in the US in the late 1980s (Klein, 2008: 159, citing Corea and Ince, 1987). Although live birth rates are reported now, there is still a tendency to quote pregnancy rates as an indication of success as well, despite the fact that a miscarriage is probably even more heart-wrenching than failure at an earlier stage. Pregnancy rates are higher than live birth rates, but they are deceptive because of the incidence of miscarriage. In 2011 in Australia and New Zealand, 20.1% of pregnancies 'resulted in early pregnancy loss', i.e. miscarried earlier than 20 weeks, and another 1.3% did not result in a live birth (Macaldowie et al, 2013: 34). There is a difference between becoming pregnant and actually giving birth to a healthy full-term baby, and it is the latter information that prospective parents want, i.e. what are their chances of giving birth to a live, healthy baby.

Genea does give their success rate in terms of live births, but the bar chart comparing their own rates with those of other clinics gives the 'clinical pregnancy rate' first (Genea, 37%; other clinics, 27.1%) and then the 'live birth rate' (Genea, 28.7%; other clinics, 20.5%).[246] But this information looks nothing like the official published statistics: 17.5% of treatment cycles resulting in live births across all centres in Australia and New Zealand, and 21.1% of the 2009-2011 cohort (Macaldowie et al, 2013). However, the discrepancy might be explained by the fact that the official rates (Macaldowie et al, 2013) are quoted in terms of 'initiated cycles', i.e. the percentage of live deliveries is a percentage of all five stages of the treatment cycle, whereas Genea quotes rates in terms of 'embryo transfers', i.e. the number of live deliveries resulting from the fifth stage of the cycle. But there are many women who start IVF treatment who do not get to the embryo-transfer stage for any of the reasons suggested above. In the case of the cycles where women's own ova were used, there were 23.7% fewer treatment cycles at the embryo-transfer stage than at the beginning (40,696 initiated cycles and 31,053 that proceeded to embryo-transfer stage) (Macaldowie et al, 2013: 10, Figure 1). So live-birth figures notwithstanding, Genea is still inflating its 'success' rate, since many of its customers would not even get to the stage where their chances of a live baby reached 28.7%.

But this is not the information Genea highlights on their homepage. Instead, what is emphasised is the claim that their '25 years of world leading fertility expertise, research and results have created a 40% greater chance of taking home a baby when assisted by Genea than the average of other clinics combined throughout Australia and New Zealand'. Now, 40% sounds pretty impressive, until you realise that it is not the chance of getting a baby, but simply the difference between Genea's 'success' rates and those of other IVF clinics. Whether or not the claim is accurate is not clear. It can't be checked because the published sources don't provide results for individual fertility centres,[247] and 28.7% is not 40% more than 20.5% (the 8.2 percentage-point difference is 28.6%, not 40%). And it could be that a less-than-careful reading might interpret the 40% as a success rate. One journalist, for example, said that '[m]ost clinics say these cycles have a 30 to 40 per cent success rate of a live birth, depending on the woman's age and circumstances' (Medew, 2014).

But anyway, a comparison between Genea and other clinics is not what intending parents want to know. They want to know what their chances are

---

246. The success rates quoted on the Genea website in May 2017 were greater than those quoted here (viewed October, 2014). However, they are still given in terms of 'embryo transfer' (i.e. the 5th stage), not in terms of 'initiated cycles' (i.e. they exclude all the failures that happen during the 1st four stages of the cycle of treatment).

247. https://npesu.unsw.edu.au/data-collection/australian-new-zealand-assisted-reproduction-database-anzard.

of having a baby. According to the best available research, in Australia it's not even 50% even after five very expensive attempts.

The surrogacy industry, however, claims otherwise. The following statements appeared on US surrogacy clinic websites on 10 February 2017:

'Over half of all gestational carriers get pregnant after the first IVF attempt ... 90 percent of surrogates achieve pregnancy by the second or third try' (Attain Fertility, clinics in 37 US states);[248]

'Some programs are reporting delivery rates of over 50% per transfer for gestational surrogacy cases (using eggs from women under about age 37)' (Advanced Fertility Center of Chicago);[249]

'our IVF clinic has a surrogacy success rate of about 65% ... where the sperm donor has had thorough medical evaluations, the egg donor is young and has a positive fertility history, and where the surrogate is also young and has met rigorous fertility criteria ... which is quite good for international agencies. Overall success rates for Fresh Embryo Transfers are around 65%, and 45% with Frozen Embryo Transfer. The rate of a successful birth is 95% once the surrogate is pregnant' (Sensible Surrogacy, Las Vegas, 'with client support in Europe and North America');[250]

'High Pregnancy Success Rate – our high surrogate/egg donor pregnancy rate – over 80% surrogacy pregnancy for 10+ years* and over 87% egg donor pregnancy rate for 10+ years*' (San Diego).[251] [The asterisks indicate a footnote at the bottom of the page in font so small (6pt) it is impossible to read. Once enlarged, the note tells us that] 'The pregnancy success rate for surrogacy and egg donation cycles are not SART reported', that is, they are not the figures reported to the Society for Assisted Reproductive Technology,[252] 'the primary organization of professionals dedicated to the practice of assisted reproductive technologies (ART) in the United States'.

Like the Australian research, the US research tells a different story from these claims on the part of the industry. According to the Center for Disease Control within the US Department of Health and Human Services, only 26.9% of ART cycles using fresh non-donor 'eggs' or embryos in 2014

---

248. http://attainfertility.com/topic/treatments-options-surrogacy-success-rates.

249. http://www.advancedfertility.com/surrogacy.htm.

250. http://www.sensiblesurrogacy.com/surrogacy-success-rates/.

251. http://fertile.com/san-diego-ivf-and-infertility-treatment-clinic/gestational-surrogacy/.

252. http://www.sart.org/.

resulted in live births, and live births resulted from only 37.3% of transfers (i.e. implanting the fertilised embryo(s) in the woman's uterus) (US CDC, 2014: 14, Table 8). These figures relate to women who were not using surrogates, but were undergoing IVF on their own behalf. What the report called 'gestational carriers' comprised less than 1% of ART cycles using fresh non-donor[253] 'eggs' or embryos (p.5), but it did seem as though 'using a gestational carrier' improved the chances of a live birth, if only slightly. Percentages of live births after an embryo had been implanted in a surrogate uterus varied between 0% and 11% higher than when the woman herself gestated the foetus (p.41). Still, even the highest percentage difference – 11% (+37.3% = 48.3%) – does not bring the success rates up to the percentages claimed by the industry; and there is no discernable reason for the percentage differences. For example, the highest difference (11%) occurred among ART patients aged 41 to 42 (i.e. the age of the woman whose ova were used, not of the surrogate), whereas the 0% occurred among women who were only one or two years older (43-44), the next age group (>44) had a surrogacy success rate that was 4.1% higher than the women who bore their own children, and women under 35 had a surrogacy success rate 7.2% higher than own birth (US CDC, 2014: 41, Figure 35). Either the surrogacy industry are not reporting their phenomenal success rates to the relevant statistical authorities, or they are lying.

Conclusion

To see surrogacy as just another kind of job, or as some kind of 'choice' on women's part, makes perfect sense within a mindset complicit with male domination's major premise that women are not valuable ends in themselves but a means for men's gratification. The women's experiences of nine-months gestation, of grief at having to relinquish a child carried in one's own body, of breasts preparing themselves to feed the baby, are obliterated, given no weight at all in favour of the almighty sperm buttressed by the equally mighty money.

Concern for the women used in the industry is non-existent. The bodies of 'egg donors' are subjected to doses of drugs in order to increase the rate of ova production from the normal one a month. It is not known whether

---

253. The 'non-donor' terminology is inaccurate in the case of 'gestational carriers'. It refers to the fact that the ova used for the pregnancy are sourced from the woman who will raise the child: 'A gestational carrier or gestational surrogate is a woman who agrees to carry a developing embryo *created from another woman's egg* for others' (US CDC, 2014: 41— emphasis added). In fact, from the standpoint of the 'gestational carrier', the embryo she is carrying is donated because it is not sourced from her body.

these drugs will have long-term adverse effects on the women. They are not medically followed up once they have fulfilled the surrogacy contract by giving birth to a baby and handing it over to the man (usually) who paid the money. No one cares enough to find out.

As well as being administered the drugs, 'donors' have their ova 'harvested' through incisions in the abdominal wall. The incisions are small—laproscopic—but they are intrusions into a healthy body involving general anaesthesia for a purpose other than the woman's own well-being. The extent to which these procedures have any deleterious consequences for the women is not known. No one cares enough to find out.

The body of the woman who gives birth will most likely be subjected to a caesarean section. How many of these surrogacy children are delivered by caesarean is not known. No one cares enough to find out.

What is known is that a caesarean section involves major abdominal surgery. What happens to the health of these women subsequently is not known. No one cares enough to find out.

It is no accident that the commodified objects are women and children. Denying women's humanity by treating them as objects is male supremacy's standard operating procedure, as feminism has long pointed out. And male supremacy has no concern for children's humanity either; they are valuable simply as the product of sperm, whose own value rests on the fact that it emanates from the male body via the hyper-valued penis. In the male supremacist worldview, women are simply part of the furniture of a world created for men, to be used for men's pleasure and convenience (the old phrase, 'wine, women and song', is a neat expression of this attitude); and children are men's possessions, being nothing but a product of men's ejaculate.

I am not suggesting that men inevitably regard children in this way simply because they are men. What I am talking about is the ideology of male supremacy and its effects on the social world. I am talking about the culture of (male supremacist) masculinity which permeates social life and hearts and minds but not inevitably. There is always the possibility, and often the actuality, that it is counteracted by genuine humanity, and there is a worldwide resistance to surrogacy as well as its malestream acceptance. In that sense, men can relate to children as genuine human beings. I am suggesting, however, that surrogacy arrangements are wholly male supremacist in the values they espouse and the meanings they impose on the people caught up in them. Surrogacy displays that arrogant male entitlement and dissociation that characterises male supremacy wherever it appears. In that sense, men who use surrogacy arrangements have already shown their commitment to these dehumanised values by using the bodies of women with no consideration for those women's feelings or for the consequences for their health and well-being. And yes, women have too, but often—how often it is impossible to say—women who use surrogacy arrangements are doing it for the man in their life; or if they are doing it for their own purposes, they are taking advantage of a system devised in the first place by men for men.

With Jyotsna Agnihotri Gupta, I, too, would assert that 'using the bodies of others as tools for self-actualization, is contrary to basic moral principles and human dignity' (Gupta, 2012: 47). I would add that, the reason why using the bodies of others is commonplace and so staunchly defended, is that it owes its existence to a basic tenet of the male supremacist system. That this so-called 'surrogacy' is even conceivable (much less a thriving industry and applauded and validated in the malestream media) is testimony to the powerful influence of male supremacy's f oundational premise that only men count as 'human' and that women exist only to serve and service men. From this foundational premise flow the male sense of entitlement at any cost, and the dissociation from any sense of a common humanity.

Chapter Fourteen: Transsexualism

Introduction

On the face of it, the rise and rise of male transsexualism would appear to falsify my earlier account of the origins of the male supremacist character structure in terms of glorification of the penis and repudiation of the female. Transsexual men want to be 'women' and they repudiate their penises, or at least, the original pioneers did. However, transsexualism is still a male supremacist character structure and the male remains the 'human' norm. If men can be 'women' and women can insist they are 'men' even while they are giving birth (MacDonald, 2015),[254] there can be no real women. If women are 'non-male' (Rea, 2016),[255] mothers are 'gestational parents',[256] and what is specific to women is something superficial that can be obliterated by changing the terminology, the 'real' female is the one that men have made. At one point it even seemed as though the transsexual agenda had coopted menstruation. An internet article said that transsexual men (referred to as 'trans women') could also have this aspect of the 'full female experience' if they bought the right product to insert into their 'post-op canals' (Mason, 2015). The article was 'fake news',[257] a bit of satire not meant to be taken literally. Nonetheless, given how dissociated transsexualism is, it was not much more bizarre than many of its other claims.

---

254. Wikipedia: 'Transgender pregnancy'.

255. This example was not literally a demand made by transsexual men. It was a request on a Young Greens Women Twitter account for 'non-male' members to 'follow' them. However, it does indicate the power of the transsexual agenda, that it could be embraced as a radical stance by young women for whom it should have been an insult.

256. Enter 'transgender gestational parent' into any internet search engine.

257. http://www.snopes.com/transgender-tampons/.

Still, it might seem as though transsexualism does not belong in this present work because it does not appear to harm anyone but the one who is doing the transgendering, the one who chooses to undergo the medical and surgical procedures. But the harm done by transsexualism is not confined to transsexual individuals harming themselves. As Sheila Jeffreys has pointed out (2014), there are numerous ways in which the transsexual project hurts others. There is the surgical and hormonal mutilation of healthy bodies, even those of children, by the medical profession; there is the pain of the partners, children and other loved ones of the 'transitioner'; there are the changes transsexual men are demanding to legislation, regulations, human rights documents, etc., some of which are eroding the rights of women; there are the demands transsexual men are making to be allowed inclusion into women-only spaces (toilets, prisons, feminist spaces, refuges, rape crisis centres); and there is the damage done to women when men claim prerogatives at women's expense.

More importantly for this present project, transsexualism qualifies for inclusion because it partakes of the same masculine dissociation and unwarranted sense of entitlement as the rest of male supremacist reality. When men claim they are 'women', they are claiming access to a status they cannot have (the dissociation), and in so doing, their sense of entitlement drives them to throw away common sense, declare black is white (or male is female), insist that everyone else believe it too, and bully those who will not comply. Not all transsexual men behave in the ways described below; some of them do not even call themselves 'women'. As Julie Bindel has pointed out, it's only a tiny minority of transsexual people who agitate to shut down any debate and who abuse critics like her. They're 'a small, nasty crowd', she said (Bindel, 2015). But this is the public face of transsexualism, the loudest noise that gets the most attention and has had the most influence across the malestream.

I am using the term 'transsexualism', rather than 'transgenderism' (or 'trans') which is more commonly used nowadays, for two reasons: because 'transsexualism' was the original term (Raymond, 1980) and I see no reason to change it; and because I regard the term 'gender' as meaningless (Thompson, 1989, 1991, 2001), a signifier whose squishiness seems deliberately designed to euphemise what is really going on.

Since I do not agree with the theory behind the practice of transsexualism (i.e. that it is possible to change one's sex), I do not agree with the terminology which relies on that theory. So I do not say 'women' when I am referring to those whom Janice Raymond called 'male-to-constructed-females'. I call them transsexual men because the transsexual agenda is typical of male supremacist reality more generally. Its insistence that men are 'women' is dissociated from any genuine human reality where men do not make unreasonable demands on women; and the behaviour of transsexual men is still masculine, despite their supposed repudiation of the 'role', in their sense of entitlement to be recognised as 'women' and referred to by the 'correct' pronouns despite what anyone else might think, and in their use of bullying tactics to get what they want.

In the 'transgender' literature the term 'transsexual men' invariably refers to *women* who purport to have 'transitioned' to become 'men'. But I insist on identifying people by their original sex because of my conviction that it is not possible to change it. Men who claim to be 'women' are still men (and women who claim to be 'men' are still women). So I say 'transsexual men' where the advocates of transsexualism would say 'transsexual *women*' (or trans, or transgender). R. W. Connell, for example, consistently uses the terminology of 'transsexual women' to refer to men who have 'transitioned', defining them as 'women [that is, men] who have been through a process of transition between locations in the gender order, from earlier definition as a boy or man toward the embodiment and social position of a woman' (Connell, 2012: 857-8).[258]

Sheila Jeffreys uses the term 'male-bodied transgenders' to refer to 'persons of the male sex who transgender' (Jeffreys, 2014). She is making the same point I am making, that male-to-female constructed transsexuals remain men whatever they might say they are. But I prefer to keep calling them men. I also use masculine pronouns to refer to them.

These usages of mine (and Jeffreys', among others) are in defiance of the demands of transsexual activist men that they be referred to as 'she'. But when I say 'transsexual men', I mean men, whether their bodies are intact or not (and it would seem that most men who claim they are 'women' are now retaining their male genitalia).[259] Such usages attract accusations of

---

258. Connell is Australia's leading sociologist, and yet his references to 'transsexual women' constantly individualise his account. This is especially noticeable when 'transsexual women' are contrasted with 'feminism', e.g. the heading, *Encounters of feminism and transsexual women* (p.858). Here he allows that feminism might be political discourse, but its opponent is a set of unfairly treated individuals—the issue is personal not political.

259. 'According to the National Center [for Transgender Equality and the National Gay and Lesbian Task Force] survey, most trans women [sic] have taken female hormones, but only about a quarter of them have had genital surgery' (Goldberg, 2014). Most transsexual women are not taking the final step either. Even when they undergo mastectomy and hysterectomy, most do not undergo phalloplasty, and they tend to retain their vaginas and vulvas (Bockting et al, 2009). Some government instrumentalities are falling into line

'transphobia' and 'hate speech', but such accusations are not genuine attempts at clarification. Rather, they are silencing tactics, a kind of bullying intended to fend off criticism without actually engaging with it (see 'Language' section below), and as such to be resisted.

Before going any further, it is worth looking at the possibility that there may be different types of male transsexualism, since the behaviour described below might be typical of only one type. The DSM IV discussion of 'Gender Identity Disorder'[260] suggests there are four types, when it says that 'substantial proportions' of men with GID can be found in all four of the categories of sexual attraction, namely, 'Sexually Attracted to Males, Sexually Attracted to Females, Sexually Attracted to Both, and Sexually Attracted to Neither'. However, there is some evidence that there are in fact only two main types of male transsexualism, one homosexual and one heterosexual (Bailey, 2003; Blanchard, 1985, 1989a, b; Freund et al, 1982).

A researcher at the Gender Identity Clinic at the Clarke Institute of Psychiatry in Toronto (Blanchard, 1989a) has suggested on the basis of a review of 'cross-gender taxonomies', that three of the conventional four types be classified together into a 'nonhomosexual' category, because they share certain characteristics which distinguish them from the homosexual category. The author referred to this category as 'nonhomosexual' rather than heterosexual, because it included an 'asexual' sub-type who had no sexual feelings towards either sex. The 'heterosexual' sub-group in the non-homosexual category comprised those men whose sexual experience followed the conventional pattern, most of them married with children, although some could perform sexually with women only by fantasising that they themselves were 'women'. The 'bisexual' sub-group comprised those whose erotic interest in men was not elicited by the partner's male body (as is the case in true homosexual attraction), but by fantasies of being a 'woman' penetrated by a man. In the case of the 'asexual' sub-group, the 'gender dysphoria' overrode any possible erotic attraction to women. As the author put it (quoting Hirschfeld),[261] '"the woman within" completely supplants her fleshly rivals' (Blanchard, 1989a: 324). All three of these non-homosexual types were distinguished from the homosexual type in the same

---

with the transsexual agenda by not requiring 'sex-reassignment' surgery as a prerequisite for changing one's 'gender' in official documents (Blake, 2015).

260. http://www.mental-health-today.com/gender/dsm.htm.

261. Magnus Hirschfeld was German sexologist and early advocate for sexual minorities (he died in 1935). He founded an Institute for Sexual Research in Berlin in 1919, which was looted by the Nazis who burned its library when they came to power.

way. They were sexually oriented towards themselves (as 'women'), while the homosexual type was sexually oriented towards male partners, with the idea of themselves as 'women' a means for attracting heterosexual men. All three engaged in fetishistic cross-dressing, i.e. being sexually aroused by the wearing of female apparel, whereas cross-dressing was not sexually arousing for the homosexual type; and whereas the homosexual type tended to be very feminine in looks and behaviour, both as children and as adults, the non-homosexual types were not. The non-homosexual types also tended to be older when they first presented as a 'gender identity' clinic.

The author (Blanchard, 1989a: 323) has suggested using the term 'autogynephilia ("love of oneself as a woman")' as a way of describing the three non-homosexual categories of male transsexualism. However, rather than introducing an unfamiliar and tongue-twisting term, it is possible to see these categories simply as heterosexual (in contrast to the homosexuality of the other category). They all fit the definition of male heterosexuality as sexual attraction of a man for a woman, even though the 'woman' in all three cases is a fantasy. Moreover, once I learned that transsexual men could be either homosexual or heterosexual, I began to wonder whether the men who have been making such importunate demands on women might be the heterosexual men, not the homosexual men. If it were so, then it would not be because homosexual men are more respectful of women's right to say 'no' to male encroachment, but because they don't care what women think. Their energies are all directed towards other men. I can't imagine any way of finding out if homosexual transsexual men are different from the heterosexual men in this way. The research literature shows no interest in the demands (some) transsexual men are making of women, much less whom those demands are coming from.

Female-to-'male'

Most of this chapter on transsexualism focuses on men who claim they are 'women', both because transsexualism is a predominantly male phenomenon, something (some) men do, and because those who are exercising typically masculine aggrieved entitlement in their encroachments on women are male-to-'female' transsexual men. There are women who claim to be 'men' and who undergo medical procedures in pursuit of that aim. But although transsexuality in women is also a consequence of the meanings and values of male supremacy, it is also different from the transsexual urge in men.

Transsexualism is not an equal opportunity phenomenon. It was started by men, there are far more men than women who insist they are the opposite sex, and most of the 'transgender' activists are men, as are most of those who demand that aspects of the public sphere—birth certificates, passports, human rights legislation—change to reflect their wishes. Moreover, while the men who 'transition' are clearly either homosexual or heterosexual (although most are heterosexual), how to characterise the sexual orientation of transsexual women is unclear. The DSM IV entry for 'Gender Identity Disorder' says: 'Virtually all the females with gender identity disorder will receive the same specifier—Sexually Attracted to Female—although there are exceptional cases involving females who are sexually Attracted to Males'. In other words nearly all the women who become 'men' are lesbians, although there might be some heterosexual women among them.

But things are rather more complicated than that. Transsexual women typically find their attempts to live as lesbians unsatisfactory; they feel that they are 'men', and hence that any sexual relationships they have with women are 'heterosexual' although with themselves as the 'man' (Cameron, 1996; Devor, 1999; Rottnek, ed., 1999). Moreover, although some transsexual women are sexually attracted to and have sexual relations with men both before and after 'transition', sexual relations with heterosexual men beforehand tend to be unsatisfactory, even aversive (because the men treat them as women), while afterwards, they identify as 'gay men' with gay men (Bockting et al, 2009; Coleman et al, 1993). So transsexual women's sexual relations with women would be called lesbian in more conventional terms, but they insist they are 'heterosexual', while their sexual relations with men, which would be seen conventionally as heterosexual, are 'gay'. Their conviction that they are 'men' defines everything else: men are not the appropriate sex objects for heterosexual men, but they are appropriate sex objects for homosexual men. So transsexual women can enjoy sex with homosexual men, even vaginal penetration (since most retain their female genitalia) (Bockting et al, 2009), but not with heterosexual men.

Sheila Jeffreys believes, following the DSM IV specification, that most transsexual women were originally lesbians, and that the transsexual phenomenon has meant the fracturing of lesbian communities and the disappearing of lesbians themselves in the rejection of their female selves. This has had the effect of weakening feminism, she argues, because of the crucial role lesbian feminist politics played in second wave feminism. Not only were lesbians at the forefront in establishing services for women—rape crisis centres, refuges from men's domestic violence, health centres, bookshops, conferences, etc.—they 'provided … the ethical core of feminist politics on sexuality and relationships' (Jeffreys, 2014: 46). Moreover, lesbian feminism's strategy of separatism opened up spaces for women where men could not go and enabled women to relate to each other without male interference. The notion of women wanting respite from men is a bizarre one within a male supremacist culture saturated with messages about women's need for men. But lesbian feminism was at the centre of the resistance to that culture, and provided women with opportunities to come together simply as women out of the physical presence of men. In other words, the 'transgendering' of lesbians is part of the male supremacist backlash against feminism (Mantilla, 2000).

If this analysis is correct, the disappearing of lesbians, combined with what Jeffreys (2014) refers to as the 'entryism' of transsexual men (i.e. men who insist they be allowed entry to women-only spaces, and heterosexual men whose sexual desire after their 'transition' remains directed towards women and who therefore call themselves 'lesbians'—see below), the suspicion arises that male supremacy took the threat of lesbian separatism very seriously indeed, despite the fact that it is barely thinkable within male supremacist terms, and reacted accordingly. Lesbians insisting they are 'men', and men insisting they are 'lesbians', looks like the death of separatism. Or it would be, were it not for two cogent facts: the lesbians insisting they are 'men' were probably not committed to separatism anyway; and radical feminism continues to refuse to accept men as women.

However, once again the issue is rather more complicated. For many transsexual women, it is not possible to say that they were heterosexual before their 'transition', but neither is it possible to say they were lesbians. In both cases they found the sex at the very least unenjoyable, at most unpleasant, because they were treated like women. As the authors of one study commented in the case of one woman they interviewed: 'as with heterosexual men, in relationships with lesbian women she was perceived and treated as a woman. This was intolerable due to her gender dysphoria' (Coleman et al, 1993: 43). Lesbianism did not allow them to escape from their female condition, it reinforced it. As one woman said, "'My mother suggested I was lesbian. I reacted very upset. There isn't anything more female than that!'" (Coleman et al, 1993: 43). So in addition to wanting to be 'men' (or believing they are), transsexual women hate their own femaleness; and if they retain their external genitalia, they refer to themselves as 'men' with a vagina, just as transsexual men refer to themselves as 'women' with a penis. This is precisely the basic premise and nightmarish logic of male supremacy: the destruction of everything genuinely female. Like the desire of transsexual men, transsexual women's desire too is structured in accordance with the meanings and values of male supremacy.

The transsexual enterprise in relation to women can be summed up as a desire to be 'fully human'. Rather than interpreting the feeling as wanting to be a 'man', I would suggest, given what feminism has uncovered about male supremacy, that it is more accurately interpreted as wanting to be recognised as a human being. The findings of a study by Kristen Schilt (2006) support the notion that what women want from being perceived as 'men' is recognition as fully human. Schilt interviewed 29 transsexual women who worked in blue-collar jobs such a forklift truck driving, who had found that they were treated much better as 'men' than they had been as women. They were seen to be more competent and have more authority, they gained more respect and recognition for their work, they were no longer subjected to groping and sexualised comments, and they had more economic opportunities and higher status than they had had as women (Schilt, 2006: 475).

It is not surprising that a woman might want to be a man, given the male supremacist equation of being a man with being human, and given the ways in which male supremacy demeans and diminishes women. What a woman who wants to be a man wants is to be recognised as fully human. But by interpreting her feelings as 'wanting to be a man' rather than finding her own way of being a human female, she is complicit with the male supremacist ideology which reserves 'full humanity' only for men. Despite the differences, both transsexual sexes uphold the meanings and values of male supremacy, the women by destroying their own femaleness and reinforcing the belief that only men count as 'human', and the men by intruding on women yet again, demanding to be accepted as 'women', demanding access to women's spaces.

Male entitlement

Australian of the Year finalist and transgender military officer Catherine McGregor … told the prominent gay and lesbian magazine the *Star Observer* that the National Australia Day Council board did "not have the courage to go with an LGBTI person". "I thought it was time … It was a weak and conventional choice," she said. "I think I'll die without seeing a trans Australian of the Year and I think that's terribly sad." (Wroe, 2016).

One of the clearest indications that transsexual men remain men whatever they do to their bodies and however they dress, is their sense of entitlement, the demands they make on society in general and women in particular. In pursuit of what they feel they are entitled to, they take their claims into the law courts, demand inclusion into women's spaces, abuse and censor those who do not agree with them, and make sexual demands of the lesbians whose ranks they insist they have joined. They have also introduced new terminology designed to show how oppressed they are and to express contempt for those who refuse to see the world their way.

Terminology

Of course transsexualism does require inventiveness with language, given that its meaning runs so radically counter to commonly-understood usages. Nothing could be more inventive than calling men 'women', insisting that penis-bearing bodies are female, and referring to them with feminine pronouns.

One transsexual neologism is the prefix 'cis', as in 'ciswomen' (i.e. women who were born female) or 'cisgender' ('individuals who have a match between the gender they were assigned at birth, their bodies, and their personal identity', as opposed to 'transgender' where there is purportedly no such match) (Schilt and Westbrook, 2009). In its original meaning, 'cis' is a Latin prefix meaning 'here' or 'on this side of', as in 'Cisalpine Gaul' meaning 'Gaul on this side of the Alps', i.e. on the same side as Rome and hence close to the ruling power. The contrast to Cisalpine Gaul is 'Transalpine Gaul', meaning Gaul across the Alps from Rome. The use of 'cis' in transsexual discourse has nothing to do with ancient Roman history, of course; rather, it is a punning reference to it, given that the prefix that means its opposite is 'trans'. (Clearly, someone in the transsexual empire had a classical bent). It refers to people whose 'gender' identity is the conventional one, who are on 'this side' of the 'gender binary' as part of the mainstream. It is the opposite of 'trans' (transsexual/transgender), those who are on the further side, 'across' the divide from everyone else. The important point about the distinction for transsexual activism is that being on the 'cis' side supposedly endows people with all the privileges that come with social validation.

Another neologism is the word 'transphobia', meaning hostility towards transsexualism, or rather, towards transsexuals (since the debates are invariably individualised). It is an extrapolation from 'homophobia' or hostility towards homosexuals, and it is subject to the same objection: that it individualises the opposition to homosexuality and hence obliterates the political dimension (Plummer, 1981). Celia Kitzinger (1987) argued that the way in which 'homophobia' is defined in the scales used in psychological research into the phenomenon leaves no room for a standpoint such as lesbian feminism that rejects the liberal humanist framework of the research. Liberal humanism, Kitzinger argued, 'postulates the existence of a private atomized "inner self" ... [and] perpetuates the salvationist notion of the person saving herself regardless of society' (p.62). In contrast, lesbian feminism 'offers a theory central to which is an analysis of lesbianism and heterosexuality as political institutions ... [i.e.] the belief that patriarchy ... is the root of all forms of oppression ... [and] heterosexuality [is] ... a socially constructed and institutionalized structure which is instrumental in the perpetuation of male supremacy' (pp.63-4). Coming from that framework, a research participant would disagree (at least in part) with some of the statements scored as 'non-homophobic' (and hence be scored as 'homophobic'). For example, one is meant to agree with the statement that 'homosexuals should be given social equality'. And yet, a lesbian feminist perspective would disagree with some forms of equality (same-sex marriage, for example,[262] or sexual behaviour that demeans women), and hence register as 'homophobic' as a result.

But then, transsexualism is not radical; on the contrary, it embraces many conventional norms. It is not worried about individualism either, because it is embedded in it. On the one side, there is a set of unjustly treated transsexual individuals whose desire originates only in themselves; on the other side, there is another set of individuals, unpleasant and mostly radical feminists, who are the ones treating the transsexual individuals unfairly by refusing to recognise them as women. The epithet, 'transphobia', is an accusation that some individuals are doing harm to other individuals, and yet most if not all of what is included under the ambit of 'transphobia' is simply disagreement, whether deliberate or inadvertent, with the transsexual enterprise. As such, 'transphobia' is being used as a form of intimidation, a tactic to silence criticism.

The 'Transphobia' Wikipedia site, for example, includes as manifestations of this syndrome, not only such obviously detrimental practices as harassment and violence, restricted access to health care, workplace discrimination, and 'political disenfranchisement', but also something called 'misgendering and exclusion'. This latter includes any form of disagreement with the way the world is interpreted by the transsexual agenda. Examples include using the 'wrong' pronouns, calling a transsexual man 'sir' when he's presenting as a 'woman', using someone's masculine name when he's got a new feminine one, and refusing transsexual men access to women's toilets, homeless shelters, refuges, prisons. The Wikipedia entry interprets all these things as

---

262. This is my example, not Kitzinger's.

harmful, even going so far as to connect the use of the 'wrong' pronouns with murder. The murderer of a 'Colorado transgender teenager' referred to him as 'it', while a '21-year-old New York trans woman' was referred to as 'he' at his memorial service, a language usage that was interpreted as 'part of the violence that led to [his] death'.[263]

So my use of the 'wrong' pronouns throughout this section is, according to the transsexual viewpoint, a form of 'transphobia', motivated at worst by murderous hatred, at the very least by 'antagonistic attitudes and feelings against transsexuality and transsexual or transgender people' (as the definition of 'transphobia' puts it). But in fact my use of the pronouns is not motivated by antagonism towards individuals, much less by 'emotional disgust, fear, anger or discomfort' (as the definition goes on to say). Rather, it is motivated by disagreement with the notion that men can be women. This disagreement brings one into conflict not just with transsexual individuals, but with such powerful malestream institutions as the medical profession, anti-discrimination and human rights legislation, the mass media, and the academic publishing industry, including many respectable peer-reviewed journals. The social acceptance of transsexualism is one example of the way in which the individualism of liberal tolerance (Marcuse, 1971; Thompson, 2002a, b) provides good service for loud male voices. (The tolerance of surrogacy, prostitution and pornography are other examples).

My approach to transsexualism is not individualistic. What I *feel* has nothing to do with my argument. While I might indeed be irritated at men once again intruding upon women, and in such a bizarre way, I am not arguing that transsexualism is wrong because of the way I feel. I am arguing that it is wrong because it is yet another ruse of male supremacy, another way in which men exercise their sense of entitlement at women's expense, enabled by that dissociated approach to the world peculiar to the character structure of masculinity.

---

263. The Wikipedia entry on 'Feminist views on transgenderism and transsexualism' (viewed 5.5.'15) is in fact anti-feminist. It is the transsexual lobby's version of a 'feminist' view of transsexualism. While radical feminists (Janice Raymond, Sheila Jeffreys) are quoted accurately, what they say is immediately undermined with the transsexual viewpoint, and given no credence in its own terms. The same criticism applies to the work of Julie Bindel, who is traduced and grossly misrepresented by the transsexual lobby. The latter appear to have taken over Google, as well as Wikipedia. The first page of hits from entering 'Julie Bindel' and 'transgender' into the search engine is wholly devoted to the transsexual lobby. For examples of the genuine radical feminist view of transsexualism (apart from Raymond and Jeffreys), see: Gallus Mag, 2013a, b; Vigo, 2013; and the following websites: Gender Trender; Feminist Current.

Another neologism is the acronym, TERF, standing for 'Trans-exclusionary radical feminist'. This, too, is a silencing tactic. A telling example of the transsexual position on this is provided by a website called 'RationalWiki'. Below, I present excerpts from this text with very little comment. There would be no point since, clearly, the writer(s) have heard all the feminist arguments and not only do they disagree with them, they cannot afford to engage with them in any (dare I say?) rational way. There is no meeting ground or halfway point between the insistence that men can be women and the insistence that they can't. If the radical feminist position on transsexualism is correct, the transsexual position is wrong and defending it is defending the indefensible. That this may indeed be the case is suggested by the tactics transsexualism's advocates use to counter the feminist position, i.e. by distorting the radical feminist message into a grotesque parody, and by personally attacking and censoring those radical feminists who are most out-spoken in their disagreement. 'Trans-exclusionary radical feminism (or TERF)', says this RationalWiki entry,

> is a subgroup of radical feminism characterized by transphobia, especially transmisogyny, and hostility to the third wave of feminism. They believe that the only real women™[264] are those born with a vagina and XX chromosomes. They wish to completely enforce the classic gender binary, supporting gender essentialism … They are, in short, a hate group that by no means represents mainstream feminism … Transphobic radfems seem to almost universally reject the concept of cisgender privilege, and even the term "cisgender" itself, as somehow demeaning to "women born women" (another controversial term in LGBTQ+ circles that is usually understood as a transphobic shibboleth). In other words, TERFs go so far as to reject any terminology models (for words such as "woman" or "man") that are not based on biological organs, gametes, or chromosome.[265]

In fact this website, 'RationalWiki', is not rational at all if one refuses to accept the idea that men can become women (a refusal that is much wider than radical feminism). It claims to be 'documenting the full range of crank ideas … [and] the finest lunacy the internet has to offer'. It portrays radical feminism and the insistence that men can't be women as a 'crank idea' and

---

264. The 'Trade Mark' superscript is a link to a RationalWiki entry called 'No True Scotsman'. This refers to a logical fallacy involving exclusion from a particular category of persons (Scotsmen, in this case) of those with undesirable characteristics (committing sex crimes): 'No true Scotsman would do such a thing'. The implication is that radical feminism has copyrighted the word 'woman' in order to exclude transsexual men from the category.

265. http://rationalwiki.org/wiki/Trans-exclusionary_radical_feminism.

'lunacy', while presenting transsexualism as the 'rational' alternative. But from a radical feminist (and common sense) standpoint, it is the insistence that men are 'women' that is the crank idea; and the lunacy is the insistence that biological organs, gametes, or chromosomes have nothing to do with sex. The website also contains a vicious attack on Cathy Brennan, a well-known critic of transsexualism in the US, which starts with a quote from a certain Natalie Reed: '[Cathy] Brennan, in case the name isn't met by you with immediate, horrified recognition and a shiver down your spine … is one of the most vocal, adamant and bitter of the transphobic wing of radical feminism'. RationalWiki accuses radical feminism of 'hate', but the approving use of language like this is far more hateful than anything radical feminism has ever said about transsexualism (or transsexuals).

As well as demanding the use of new terminology, the transsexual lobby demands the abolition of conventional terminology for referring to females and female anatomy (their reason being that transsexual men are 'women' even though they don't have female anatomy). Writing in the *New York Times*, Elinor Burkett (2015) gave a number of examples. In January 2014, when an abortion-rights campaigner sent out a tweet about a benefit for abortion funding called 'A Night of a Thousand Vaginas', she was inundated with criticism for using the word 'vagina'. A tweet by a 'Dr Jane Chi', for example, said, '"Given the constant genital policing, you can't expect trans folks to feel included by an event title focused on a policed, binary genital"'. A blogger said, '"So you're really committed to doubling down on using a term that you've been told many times is exclusionary & harmful?"'. And, of course, she got called a 'TERF'. But 'trans folks' without vaginas don't need abortions, so it's not clear why they should have been included (except that, as men, they feel entitled to go wherever they please, no matter how irrational, oppressive or just plain silly).

Another example of transsexuals' objections to the word 'vagina' involved Eve Ensler's play 'The Vagina Monologues', which was to be performed at a liberal arts college for women in January 2015. The performance was cancelled because, according to the chairwoman of the student group who were to perform the play, it was an '"extremely narrow perspective on what it means to be a woman"'.

Other examples involved the use of the word 'woman'. The hashtags #StandWithTexasWomen and #WeTrustWomen were attacked as 'exclusionary'. Burkett quoted one blogger saying, '"Abortion rights and reproductive justice is not a women's issue … [it's] a uterus owner's issue"'. The blogger was referring to women identifying as 'men', who still had a uterus and hence could become pregnant and need an abortion, but who called themselves 'men', not women.

As Burkett commented, '[t]he landscape that's being mapped and the language that comes with it are impossible to understand and just as hard to navigate' (if one takes any notice of these demands). On the one hand, these objections demand that the word 'woman' not be used, while on the other hand, transsexual men demand that they be called 'women'. So it is forbidden to use the word 'women' when referring to real women, but it is mandatory to use it when referring to transsexual men. This is not simply 'a binary view of gender that's hopelessly antiquated' as transsexual activists would have us believe. It is more sinister than that. As Burkett asks, 'are those who have transitioned from men the only "legitimate" women left?' And the answer from within the meanings and values of the transsexual empire would appear to be 'yes'. While this is seldom acknowledged explicitly, there are those who are quite open about it. For example, Raymond quotes from a letter written by one transsexual man to a journal in 1977, which said:

> "Genetic women cannot possess the very special courage, brilliance, sensitivity and compassion—and overview—that derives from the [male] transsexual experience. Free from the chains of menstruation and child-bearing, transsexual women [i.e. men] are obviously far superior to Gennys [i.e. genetic females] in many ways. Genetic women are becoming quite obsolete, which is obvious, and the future belongs to transsexual women [i.e. men]" (Raymond, 1980: 117).

While this letter writer is just one individual, his is not an isolated view. Again, this is the logic of male supremacy: the extermination of everything genuinely female. Not all transsexual men feel this way to the extent that their genuine humanity forbids it. But it is the logic of the transsexual project.

'Entryism'

The transsexual assertion of self is not confined to language. Transsexual men have been known to insist that, because they are 'women', they have the right to enter women-only spaces, even (especially?) if the women don't want them there. For example, a women's health centre worker reported that, when one transsexual man was asked why they didn't set up their own transsexual support groups instead of demanding entry to women's centres, his reply referred to "'wanting to be accepted as a woman and wanting to be among women … to see his identity confirmed by being among women'" (Gottschalk, 2009: 175).

The earliest recorded instance of this male demand to be allowed entry into women-only spaces happened at the West Coast Feminist Conference in Los Angeles in 1973. A man wearing a dress turned up at the conference saying he had been invited (he had been) and that he was really a woman and a lesbian—'(he was easily identifiable, at least—he was the only person there wearing a skirt)' (Morgan, 1978: 171). Many of the lesbians were outraged at his presence at a woman-only conference, and this brought them into conflict with those whose spirit of liberal tolerance supported his presence. The same spirit had presumably inspired the conference organisers; they had invited him despite the well-known fact that his presence had already caused dissension and disruption among lesbians: he was known to have pressured at least one lesbian to have sex with him; and his attempt to join a lesbian organisation, the San Francisco Daughters of Bilitis Chapter, had nearly destroyed it by setting lesbians against each other, as some supported him in his self-identification while others refused to. Moreover, his sense of male entitlement was clearly shown in his response when women begged him not to attend the conference. He replied that 'if he were kept out he would bring federal suit against these women on the charges of "discrimination and criminal conspiracy to discriminate"' (Morgan, 1978: 171). This is his masculine sense of grandiose entitlement—he will use the law to get what he wants because it exists for him.

Connell (Connell, 2012: 860) gave an account of this same incident, although he was of course on the side of the intruder, not of the lesbians; and he interpreted the incident as a conflict between individuals rather than sociologically, as a conflict between two unequal worldviews: masculine entitlement on the one hand, and women's right to freedom from male interference on the other. He said that Morgan's above account was 'a public attack in quite violent language against a transsexual woman [i.e. man] … invited to perform as a musician at a lesbian-feminist conference in California'. On one side there was only Robin Morgan, thus disappearing the feminist politics, not to mention the many other lesbians who also objected to the man's presence. On the other side was 'a transsexual woman' whom Connell named as 'Beth Elliott', who was at the conference because he 'had been invited to perform as a musician', not because he was exercising his masculine sense of entitlement to ride roughshod over what women want, or because the organisers were exercising repressive tolerance (Marcuse, 1971).

A better-known example involved the Michigan Womyn's Music Festival, an explicitly women-only event when it started in 1976 and for many years thereafter. The first recorded instance of an attempt by a transsexual man to attend the Festival occurred in 1991. He was asked to leave 'after several women recognized her [sic] as a trans woman [sic] and expressed discomfort with her [sic] presence in the space'.[266] In 1994, a 'Camp Trans' was set up outside the front gate of the Festival as a protest against this exclusion, with the 'original mission [of] fighting for trans women's [i.e. men's] inclusion in queer women's [i.e. lesbians'] communities'.[267] Five years later, a second 'Camp Trans' was set up. Its name, 'Son of Trans', inadvertently exposes the fact that its creators were well aware that they remained men, no matter how vehemently they might insist they were women. After all, they didn't call it 'Daughter of Trans'. It was maintained until 2010, when 'allegations of violence and vandalism at the Festival, and … a confrontation between attendees of Camp Trans and a tow-truck driver near the gates … [led to] the National Forest revok[ing] the permit for camping at the site' and it ceased to exist (Morris, 2005: 624).

During the time Camp Trans was in existence there were numerous occasions on which men calling themselves 'women' disrupted the Festival: in 1999, a naked man with intact genitalia insisted on his right to bathe with naked women by stripping off and entering the showers; in 2005, Camp Trans broadcast loud male singing near the Festival's quiet-camping area on a Saturday night; and throughout the life of the Camp Trans, its 'annual vigil at MichFest gates' (Trans Women, 2010) badgered attendees, workers and performers to get them to boycott the Festival.

The violence between the tow-truck driver and some of the Trans campers in 2010 was an unintended consequence of this 'annual vigil'. The driver was parked outside the Festival entrance with his engine running while he waited. Because Camp Trans was crowded up against the Festival area, he was also near the Camp Trans gate where a speaker was telling people about its history. There are conflicting accounts of how the tow-truck driver was asked to turn off his engine. According to the account written by those 'Trans' campers who had challenged the tow-truck driver, he was 'approached to turn his engine off' (Trans Women, 2010). Another commentator (Dirt, 2010),[268] however, said that that approach was 'vitriolic' and 'insulting' and involved his being asked to 'turn his "fucking" truck off'. At this point, the tow truck

---

266. http://www.michfestmatters.com/myths-and-truths-about-the-michigan-womyns-music-festival/.

267. http://en.wikipedia.org/wiki/Camp_Trans.

268. This can no longer be found on the internet (August, 2018). Entering the title into a search engine retrieves only pro-trans indeology.

driver's response was polite—he called those who had approached him 'sir'. He was not to know how provocative this was to men who insist they are 'women' and who demand that everyone believe that. Those who had been thus 'misgendered' then called over a number of Camp Trans members who rushed towards the driver as though to physically attack him. The driver jumped down from his truck holding a tow chain to defend himself, and at that point a number of women from the Festival came to his aid.

Those who had confronted the driver gave a different, and less believable, account of the same events. They said that the driver had responded by 'threaten[ing] two trans people's lives, aggressively misgender[ing] a trans woman [sic], and ultimately wield[ing] a large tow chain threatening to kill all of the trans people who had surfaced to protect their friends' (Trans Women, 2010). But for a number of reasons this account is unbelievable, e.g. it omits to mention the aggressive way in which the driver was initially approached, and it assumes it is reasonable to expect that an ordinary member of the public would know that transsexual men wanted to be addressed as women. Moreover, the violence continued throughout the week, including the sound of gunshots (although no one appeared to know who was doing the shooting or where the shots were coming from). This ongoing violence was driven in part, according to the critical commentator mentioned above (Dirt, 2010), by the presence of large numbers of transsexual women who were taking synthetic forms of testosterone. Not only was the Festival faced with 'men who insist they're women [though] acting like men', there were also greater numbers than usual of 'women insisting they're men [though] acting like teenage boys', and who were as aggressive and disruptive as the men.

The vandalism within the Festival area itself during the 2010 season, together with the message of a leaflet distributed at the same time, involved a particularly egregious piece of nastiness that exposed a transsexual misogyny so vicious it yearned for the extermination of women altogether. The vandalism consisted of the words 'Real Womyn Have Cocks' painted on a wall of one of the Festival kitchens; the leaflet read:

> Second-Wave "Feminists", A hot load from my monstrous tranny-cock embodies womanhood more than the pieces of menstral (sic) art your transphobic cunts could ever hope to create. (Love, Womyn-born-Monsters, *Pink and Black Attack*, 2010: 8).[269]

---

269. This 'zine can no longer be found on the internet. However, the Wikipedia entry for 'Camp Trans' contained the same information, including this quote, on 3 March 2017 (although it also expressed doubt that the incident had occurred).

The editors of the 'queer anarchist' publication in which this appeared included it without comment and without condemning it. They saw the issue simply as one of 'identity': men identifying as 'women; the tow-truck driver's challengers questioning their 'identity' as members of a community because their fellow campers did not support them unreservedly. Such dissociation obliterates not only women's right to live in safety free from virulent hatred, it also obliterates any genuinely human response to it. There is nothing about being a man that would prevent someone from taking a stand against views like these, but the magazine's editors did not do so.

Despite (or perhaps because of) the years of harassment from 'Camp Trans' and affiliated individuals, the organisers of the Michigan Women's Music Festival were at one point remarkably conciliatory towards the transsexual agenda (although the publications documenting that conciliatory attitude can no longer be found on the internet). They said that they accepted transsexual men as 'women': 'The Festival recognizes the identity of trans women as women' (*Pink and Black Attack*, 2010: 8); and that no one was excluded on the grounds that he wasn't a woman. Again: 'When someone buys a Festival ticket, no one questions their sex, nor does the Festival question anyone's sex at either the Front Gate or on the Land during the Festival' (*Pink and Black Attack*, 2010: 8). Lisa Vogel, one of the Festival's founders, was reported to say, 'Trans womyn and transmen have always attended this gathering', and that since the incident in 1991, 'Festival organizers have never asked a trans womon to leave the Festival'.[270] Nonetheless, transsexuals continued to complain that the Festival 'remains committed to admitting "womyn-born-womyn" only', which we know translates to "none of you gendertrash scum allowed"'.[271] Leaving aside the 'gendertrash scum' comment, and despite the sometimes conciliatory approach of the Michfest organisers, it would seem that the transsexual claim was correct: Michfest was restricted to 'womyn-born-womyn' only. A 2006 statement by Lisa Vogel said that quite clearly. Michfest, she said, was 'intended for womyn who were born as and have lived their entire life experience as womyn', and she asked 'the transwomen's

---

270 .http://en.wikipedia.org/wiki/Michigan_Womyn%27s_Music_Festival_and_transgender_people#cite_note-6. These statements no longer appear in this Wikipedia entry. It does contain a 2014 statement by Lisa, supposedly apologising for asking the 'trans womon' to leave the festival grounds in 1991. But the source this statement was taken from has been deleted.

271. http://legalminds.lp.findlaw.com/list/queerlaw-edit/msg03071.html. This publication has also vanished from the internet. Not only is it unavailable at the original URL, entering the phrase 'none of you gendertrash scum allowed' into a search engine brings up no hits at all.

community' to respect 'womon-born womon ... as a valid gender identity'. She was still conciliatory in that she accepted 'transwomen' as 'women'. She referred to them as 'sisters in struggle', and said that 'we stand shoulder to shoulder as women'.[272] But there was no longer any doubt that Michfest did not include 'transwomen'. However, their insistence that it should include them is a typical example of dissociated male entitlement.

Here in Australia in 1993, the Sydney Lesbian Space project came to grief in conflict over the admission of transsexual men. The project had raised around $250,000 to buy a property that could be used as a lesbian community centre. Some of the contributors to the fund were transsexual men, on the understanding that they would be included as 'lesbians'. But after an incident in Brisbane, where a lesbian event was disrupted by transsexual men demanding entrance, some members of the Sydney collective decided to exclude transsexual men from the space. Other collective members objected to this, and because the conflict was irreconcilable, the project was abandoned (Jeffreys, 2014: 168-9).

Transsexual men are now being accepted as clients at women's health centres, despite the fact that their health problems are not women's health problems. For example, the Lyon Martin Women's Health Services in San Francisco has dropped the word 'Women's' from its name and now provides 'transgender' services alongside traditional health services for women. Deleting the word 'Women's' would appear to indicate some ambivalence about the female status of transsexual men; or perhaps it's simply an accommodation with the claim by transsexual women that they are 'men'. Whatever the case, it is clear that the focus on women's health as it is traditionally understood has been shifted by the transsexual agenda.

Whether or not the inclusion of transsexual men in what were originally women's services has had a negative impact on *women's* access to those services, given that that was a primary reason for establishing women's services in the first place, it is not possible to say. But if the experience of one women's refuge in Australia is any guide, it is a possibility. Workers at the refuge, interviewed by Lorene Gottschalk (2009) for her study exploring the implications of 'transgenderism' for women's services, told what happened when they accepted one 'transgender' client. He was brought to the refuge as a 'woman' because he said he was and he was wearing a dress, even though it was clear from his mannerisms and his Adam's apple that he was a man. The staff initially accommodated him with the women and children, but

---

272. http://eminism.org/michigan/20060822-mwmf.txt.

the women objected: 'they "did not want someone with a penis with them … I'm not going in there, he's got a penis" (Gottschalk, 2009: 176). He was accommodated on his own for six weeks, which meant that that space was not available for women and children during that time. The refuge had a policy of 'not discriminating' against 'transgender' people, both because their clients came to them through mainstream services (including the police) and they felt they had no choice but to accept whoever was referred, and because they were afraid of breaking the law if they 'discriminated'. As Australian anti-discrimination law stands at the moment, it would not have required the refuge to accommodate this man, because he was not a recognised transgender person, that is, he had not had 'sex reassignment (gender affirmation) surgery' (NSW ADB, nd1).

Sex-reassignment surgery is a prerequisite for most of the government concessions to the transsexual agenda in Australia. It is not a requirement for making a claim of discrimination to an anti-discrimination board, but someone who hasn't had sex reassignment surgery cannot legally require people to recognise them as their 'preferred gender' (NSW ADB, nd1). So when the NSW Anti-Discrimination Board says that 'a male to female recognised transgender person generally [has] the right to be considered for a job that is for women only, and to receive a service for women only, for example to attend a women-only gym' (NSW ADB, nd1), this refers only to someone who has had surgery. Given that the man described above still had his penis, he was not 'a recognised transgender person' within the terms of the Act, and hence the refuge would have been legally within their rights to refuse to accommodate him.

However, this is changing. (See the discussion below of the law changes enabling men to claim they are 'women' without having had surgery to remove their genitals).

'Cotton ceiling'

Perhaps the most bizarre demand for inclusion made by transsexual men is that lesbians welcome them as sexual partners. Not surprisingly, lesbians tend to resist this demand. The men, however, do not take 'no' for an answer. To express their sense of outrage at being denied what they believe is rightfully theirs, they have coined yet another neologism: 'the cotton ceiling'. A transsexual activist explains what this means:

> The cotton ceiling is a theory proposed by trans porn star and activist Drew DeVeaux to explain the experiences queer trans women [i.e. men] have with simultaneous social inclusion and sexual exclusion within the

broader queer women's [i.e. lesbian] communities. Basically, it means that cis queer women will be friends with us and talk day and night about trans rights and ending transmisogyny, but will still not consider us viable sexual partners. The term cotton ceiling is a reference to the "glass ceiling" that second wave feminist [sic] identified in the workforce, wherein women could only advance so high in the workforce but could not break through into positions of power and authority. The cotton represents underwear, signifying sex.[273]

Lesbians' refusal to allow men sexual access is, said one transsexual supporter, 'abusive' (of men). The tenth of 10 examples of supposed 'abusive behaviour on the part of some friends, family, lovers and partners' towards 'trans people', listed by an 'ex-lesbian mental health counselor', reads as follows: 'Refusing to date trans women [i.e. men], especially those who identify with having cocks, or who haven't had "bottom surgery" – particularly if you identify as lesbian'.[274]

To add to the bizarre incongruity, the 'cotton ceiling' author quoted above also says that he does not 'consider trans women with penises [i.e. men] to be male-bodied, unless that is how they identify … Trans women's [i.e. men's] bodies are female bodies, whether or not we have penises'. So these men demanding sex with lesbians have intact genitalia. They have not had 'sex-reassignment' surgery, and yet they call themselves 'women' and 'lesbians' (and even if they had had surgery, this 'self-identification' is open to question). So what they are demanding of lesbians is that they engage in the heterosexual, penis-in-vagina sex that the word 'lesbian' excludes (and probably just because it is excluded). Despite the incongruity, these men are not joking. What they are doing is expressing the oldest and most entrenched form of male entitlement—unimpeded sexual access to women. It takes an unconventional form but its meaning is the same; and women who refuse to acquiesce in this male demand are violating the most basic of the rights granted to men under male supremacy. (See also: Vigo, 2013) .

Malestream recognition

The transsexual agenda has had remarkable success at getting recognition from the malestream. As one (approving) commentator put it, 'the trans-rights movement is growing in power and cachet' (Goldberg, 2014). Another (critical) commentator agreed:

---

273. https://factcheckme.wordpress.com/2012/03/13/the-cotton-ceiling-really/.

274. http://www.thescavenger.net/sex-gender-sexual-diversity/158-sgd-diversity/879-what-transphobia-looks-like-a-primer-for-family-friends-and-loved-ones.html.

> It's ... remarkable how quickly and easily trans people were added to the list of groups who are legally protected against discrimination, and even more remarkable that what was written into equality law was their own principle of self-definition—if you identify as a man/woman then you are entitled to be recognized as a man/woman. In a very short time, this tiny and previously marginal minority has managed to make trans equality a high profile issue, and support for it part of the liberal consensus (Campbell, 2013).

This is nowhere more obvious than in their influence on the law. Transsexual activists and supporters have been pushing, successfully in many cases, to get the surgery prerequisite abolished: 'No one should be pressured into having sex reassignment surgery in order to gain acceptance as a trans person'.[275] A number of jurisdictions have passed legislation enabling transsexuals to gain official recognition of their 'new gender' without undergoing 'sex-reassignment' surgery or even hormone treatment.

Since 2014, three Canadian provinces, British Colombia, Alberta and Manitoba, have all passed legislation allowing transsexuals to change their 'gender' on official documents without having undergone 'sex-reassignment' surgery; and from April 2015, the Canadian federal government no longer requires someone to have undergone surgery before changing their 'gender' on citizenship documents (Blake, 2015).

In the UK, there is the 2004 Gender Recognition Act (Jeffreys, 2008b), proposed and passed under a Labour government. Julie Bindel describes the Act and its possible consequences:

> Since 2004, it has been possible for those diagnosed with GD [gender dysphoria] to be assigned the sex of their choice, providing that the person has lived as the opposite sex for two years, has no plans to change back again and can provide evidence of the above. It is not necessary to have undergone hormone treatment or surgery. In other words, a pre-operative man could apply for a job in a women-only rape counselling service and, if refused on grounds of his sex, could take the employer to court on the grounds that "he" is legally a "she" (Bindel, 2009)

And yet, transsexual activists are still not satisfied, despite the fact that British law already supports men with fully intact male genitals in their 'identification' as 'women'. The activists have convinced the UK Tory government to reconsider the GRA to make it even 'easier for trans people to achieve legal recognition' (UK Government, 2018: 2). Throughout 2018,

---

275. http://www.gaychristian101.com/can-you-explain-transsexualism.html.

the UK government held a GRA Consultation with that aim in mind. 'This consultation', the authors said,

> does not consider the question of whether trans people exist, whether they have the right to legally change their gender, or whether it is right for a person of any age to identify with another gender, or with no gender. Trans and non-binary people are members of our society and should be treated with respect (UK Government, 2018: 4).

This leaves no room for insisting that men can't be women (or women, men), and that male transsexualism is yet another male encroachment on women (and female transsexualism yet another example of the male as the 'human' norm). This is not the same as 'the question of whether trans people exist'. It is not a question of people at all, but of meanings and values. Whatever transsexual people feel when they say they feel like the opposite sex (all right, 'gender'), they are misnaming those feelings. In the world in which I live and understand reality, men cannot be women. This is not to disrespect 'trans and non-binary people'. It is to disagree with them, a stance that is far more respectful than craven capitulation or ignoring them.

The Minister's introduction to the GRA Consultation document did say that they wanted 'to hear from women's groups who we know have expressed some concerns about the implications of our proposals'. The government, she said, was 'not proposing to amend the Equality Act 2010 and the protections contained within it', and she acknowledged that 'there are concerns about interactions between the two Acts'. A number of times throughout the Consultation document women's refuges were mentioned along with the possibility that 'single or same sex services exceptions' in the 2010 Equality Act 'might allow, for example, a domestic violence refuge for women to refuse entry to a trans person' [i.e. a transsexual man]. It would appear, however, that this exemption is not absolute (as it was before the law came down on the side of men who claim they're 'women'). It can only operate 'provided it is proportionate to do so [i.e. to exclude men] and the purpose is legitimate'. But if men are legally 'women', there can be no legitimate reason for refusing a man entry. What would count as 'a legitimate purpose' for excluding a transsexual man from a women's refuge?—that he attacks the women and/or the children; that the women don't want to share intimate spaces with a man? This may lead to his being evicted from the refuge, but by that time the women and children have already been traumatised. The truth of the matter is that, once men claim to be 'women' and important social institutions like the British government agree, there is no possibility of reconciling women's rights with transsexual demands. Once men are 'women' in the eyes of the law and influential arenas of public opinion, there is no longer any women's space that can't be penetrated by men.

In Australia, the Australian Human Rights Commission has recommended that '[t]he definition of sex affirmation treatment should be broadened so that surgery is not the only criteria [sic] for a change in legal sex' (AHRC, 2009: 31); and on 20 March 2014, the ACT Legislative Assembly passed the Births, Deaths and Marriages Registration Amendment Act[276] so that people who wish to change their sex on their ACT birth certificate no longer need 'sex reassignment' surgery, although they do have to provide evidence that they have received clinical treatment to change their sex. This means that fully intact transsexual men have a legally enforceable right to enter women's spaces in the Australian Capital Territory simply because they say they're 'women'. Given that most of the men who are calling themselves 'women' these days are not undergoing surgery (see footnote 6), and given, too, that women's services staff already believe that they have to accept transsexual men, this is a very real possibility.

However, the complaints brought to the NSW Anti-Discrimination Board of discrimination on the grounds of 'transgender' by September 2015 did not include any examples of transsexual men claiming entry to women's services.[277] There was one complaint from a transsexual man about being told to use the men's toilets at a golf club. The Board (and the legislation) required the club management to acquiesce in the transsexual man's demand and 'to allow her [sic] to use the female toilets without restriction'. As things stand at the moment, transsexual men do not need to claim entry to women's services, because right-wing governments are doing their best to abolish them. In 2012, for example, the NSW Baird government introduced its 'Going Home Staying Home' policy (or in other words, if women want a home they'd better stay where they are—not the sort of advice that women whose 'home' includes a violent man need to hear). This has led to the closure of many women's refuges, with women shunted into general, faith-based homelessness services with none of the expertise gained over the years by the feminist women's refuge movement (Bacon and Dalley, 2015). However, while the abolition of women-only services might thwart transsexual men's demands for inclusion, there are other public entities where those demands

---

276. http://www.legislation.act.gov.au/a/2014-8/20140426-57511/pdf/2014-8.pdf.

277 .http://www.antidiscrimination.justice.nsw.gov.au/Pages/adb1_resources/adb1_equaltimeconciliation/conciliations_transgender.aspx

can be made, e.g. prisons, hospitals, women's toilets.[278] The malestream still gives no recognition to women's right to freedom from encroachment by men.

Another powerful malestream opinion-maker is Google. As far as Google is concerned, transsexual men deserve more attention as 'women' than real women do. On 19 January 2017, I typed into the Google search engine 'How many women were killed in 2016', and the first hit, the one right at the top of the first page listing of 10, was 'These are the trans people killed in 2016'. Moreover, five out of the 10 hits on the first page were about 'transgender people', only three were about women and one of these was a 'pro-life' website which was actually about 'babies' (and women) dying in abortions. The remaining two were about police killing and being killed. The UK 'Counting dead women' organisation, which keeps track of women killed by men, was listed seventh on the second page. For Google, 'trans' has greater priority as 'women' than women do.

The transsexual agenda is not only supported by 'the liberal consensus', it is also embraced in self-styled left-wing circles. This was pointed out by one commentator in the context of the Radfems Respond conference in Portland OR (see below). She said that radical feminists' insistence 'on regarding transgender women as men' was one of two positions that had 'made radical feminism anathema to much of the left' (Goldberg, 2014). (The other was the radical feminist position on prostitution). But then, the male left doesn't have a good track-record in embracing feminist issues, and its validation of prostitution, pornography and surrogacy means that they continue to miss the point about male entitlement at women's expense.

Despite transsexual activists' belief that they are not accepted by the mainstream, in fact their success in changing mainstream attitudes has been phenomenal. As yet one more male-defined issue, transsexualism is welcomed by the malestream. The media publish favourable reports, the publishing industry produces volume after volume, academe pours out articles in the 'scholarly' journals, the medical profession bows to their wishes, legal systems change laws and regulations in their favour, and the courts provide them with precedents.

By 2007 all Australian jurisdictions had included 'transgender'/'transsexuality' in their anti-discrimination legislation (Maddison and Partridge, 2007: 14). At the federal level, transsexuality (as 'gender identity') was included as a ground

---

278. Private groups are outside the scope of anti-discrimination law, although what counts as 'private' varies depending on who's asking. See the discussion below of the decision of the South Australian Equal Opportunity Tribunal in relation to Sappho's Party.

of unlawful discrimination in the Sex Discrimination Amendment (Sexual Orientation, Gender Identity and Intersex Status) Act 2013 (Cth);[279] and the Act's previous definition of 'woman' was repealed (Section 14, Subsection 4(1) (definition of *woman*) Repeal the definition).[280] I don't know what the Act's previous definition of 'woman' was, but its deletion presumably means that men can now claim discrimination under the 'gender identity' of 'women'. The transsexual agenda has also had an influence internationally on human rights documents, courts and other bodies. For example, after an initial period of reluctance to make any findings in relation to the laws and practices of European states (in cases against the UK government brought to the Court from 1986 to 1998), the European Court of Human Rights eventually agreed (in 2002) that laws that did not recognise a person's 'change of gender' were a 'serious interference with private life' (AHRC, 2009: 12).

All Australian states and territories now allow people to get a new birth certificate saying they are the sex they want to be (or 'affirm'), Victoria being the last jurisdiction to do so, in 2004. At present (June 2015) a new birth certificate will only be issued to 'a recognised transgender person', i.e. someone who has undergone the relevant surgery, or is undergoing medical treatment to make the 'transition' (Grenfell and Hewitt, 2012). But given the strong push to abolish this requirement, that may change in the future. At the federal level, transsexual people can also get passports issued in their 'new gender' but again, they must be a recognised transgender person.[281] The sex on the passport does not have to be confined to 'male' and 'female': 'A passport may be issued to sex and gender diverse applicants in M (male), F (female) or X (indeterminate/unspecified/intersex)'.

The Department of Foreign Affairs and Trade (DFAT), which issues passports, is a federal government department. So it would seem that the Australian government has taken on board, not only the notion that people can change their sex, but also the notion that someone can choose to be neither sex. By June 2015, most of the state and territory jurisdictions had not yet followed suit by allowing a 'no sexual identity' option on birth certificates, although it is probably only a matter of time. Both NSW and the Australian Capital Territory (where both the federal government and DFAT

---

279. https://www.humanrights.gov.au/our-work/sexual-orientation-sex-gender-identity/projects/new-protection.

280 .http://parlinfo.aph.gov.au/parlInfo/download/legislation/bills/r5026_aspassed/toc_pdf/13090b01.pdf;fileType=application%2Fpdf.

281. https://www.passports.gov.au/forms/Documents/B14.pdf.

reside) allow this option on birth and 'Change of sex' certificates. The ACT Registry of Births, Deaths and Marriages has the same wording as DFAT (i.e. 'indeterminate/unspecified/intersex'), while the wording on the form in NSW is 'non-specific'.

This wording is the largely work of one man, Norrie, who was born male in Scotland and underwent a 'sex affirmation procedure' in 1989 that 'did not resolve [his] sexual ambiguity'. He instigated a series of hearings and court cases culminating in a ruling in 2014 by all five High Court of Australia judges in the case of NSW Registrar of Births, Deaths and Marriages v Norrie (HCA 11, 2 April),[282] that residents of NSW could have their sex officially registered as 'non-specific':

> The question in this appeal is whether it was within the Registrar's power to record in the [NSW] Register that the sex of the respondent, Norrie, was, as she said in her application, "non-specific". That question should be answered in the affirmative.

Although Norrie did not 'identify' as a 'woman', or even as female, he did expect to be referred to by feminine pronouns. As the judges commented: 'The respondent uses, and [for] these reasons [we also] use, the personal pronouns "she" and "her" to refer to the respondent'.

In November 2009, Norrie had applied for his sex to be registered at the NSW Registry of Births, Deaths and Marriages as 'non-specific' (rather than as 'male' or 'female'). Initially the Registrar agreed to this request, and in February 2010 Norrie received a 'Recognised Details (Change of Sex) Certificate' and a Change of Name Certificate, both of which recorded his sex as 'not specified'. Later however, it was decided that the certificate was invalid and a new one was issued saying that his sex was 'not stated'. Norrie then lodged an application with the NSW Administrative Decisions Tribunal requesting a review of the Registrar's decision. The Tribunal concluded that the Registrar could not legally change someone's sex to 'non-specific', even though they agreed that Norrie identified as 'non-specific' and that he would be making a false declaration if he said he was either 'male' or 'female'.[283] The Tribunal said that the Act intended to address the situation of people not born in NSW was 'predicated on an assumption that all people can be classified into two distinct and plainly identifiable sexes, male and female'. Norrie appealed to the Tribunal's appeal panel but his application was

---

282. http://www6.austlii.edu.au/cgi-bin/viewdoc/au/cases/cth/HCA/2014/11.html

283. The 'change of sex' applicant is required to sign the application form certifying that they have understood that 'it is a punishable offence to give false information in this application'.

rejected. In 2013, he appealed to the NSW Court of Appeal, which allowed his appeal and ordered that the Tribunal's decision be set aside and that the Registrar pay Norrie's court costs. In November 2013, the NSW Registrar appealed to the High Court of Australia which granted their application on condition that they pay Norrie's costs in that court too, as well as in the NSW Court of Appeal. As noted above, the High Court found in favour of Norrie and his claim to 'non-specific' sex, commenting that the relevant Act 'recognises that a person's sex may be neither male nor female', and that 'the Registrar's initial determination of Norrie's application was right'.

Human rights tribunals are common venues for transsexual claims to recognition. One such claim was brought by a post-operative transsexual, Kimberly Nixon, to the British Columbia Human Rights Tribunal against the Vancouver Rape Relief and Women's Shelter in 1995. The claim was that his human rights were violated by the Shelter's refusal to permit him to participate in a training session for rape counselling at the Shelter. When the collective were told of the complaint, they tried to make amends by offering a formal written apology as well as an apology in person, suggesting other ways he could help the work of the Shelter (e.g. by joining a fundraising committee), and offering him $500 in acknowledgement of his hurt feelings. They also requested mediation. He rejected all these offers.

The Tribunal released its decision in January 2002, ruling that life experience as a girl and woman was not a necessary pre-requisite to be a counsellor of raped and battered women, upholding Nixon's complaint, and awarding him $7,500. In the meantime, in 1996 Nixon had left another organisation, Battered Women's Support Services, over a dispute regarding the role of transsexual men (called 'women') in the organisation. In December 2003, the British Columbia Supreme Court set aside the Human Rights Tribunal's decision, and declined to send it back to the Tribunal to be reheard. In April 2005, Nixon appealed to the British Columbia Court of Appeal, and in December of that year, that Court also ruled in favour of the Shelter and upheld the decision of the BC Supreme Court. In February 2007, the Supreme Court of Canada dismissed Nixon's request to appeal the Court of Appeal's decision, and ordered him to pay the costs of Vancouver Rape Relief,[284] although he had not done so by June 2009. In this case the feminist organisation fought back and eventually won, but at enormous expense of time and money (Boyle, 2011: 494-5).

---

284. http://www.rapereliefshelter.bc.ca/learn/resources/chronology-events-kimberly-nixon-vs-vancouver-rape-relief-society.

Another man who used the notion of human rights to try and force women to accept him was Susan Amy Mamela. He had not divested himself of his male genitals but still identified as a transsexual 'lesbian female', although not as a 'woman' on the grounds that the term was a socio-political construct. In 1999, he brought a complaint of discrimination to the same Human Rights Tribunal against the Vancouver Lesbian Connection, originally formed in 1985. Initially, the collective running the Centre had refused to accept him as a member because he had been raised male and still had his male genitals. But he wouldn't take 'no' for an answer and persisted in his demands to be included, until finally they changed their policy to include him (and any other man who was 'transitioning' to become a 'lesbian'), by describing their membership as 'self-identified lesbian, bisexual, and transsexual queer womyn'. However, after a time he began behaving disruptively, harassing staff and volunteers, using resources without clearing it with anyone else, answering the crisis line without training or permission, and demanding the women have sex with him because he was a 'lesbian' too. Eventually the Centre suspended him for a year on the grounds of aggressive and sexually offensive behaviour. The Human Rights Tribunal upheld his complaint, not because they found it justified, but because the Lesbian Connection failed to appear to put its case, not having the money to defend themselves. The Centre was ordered to pay him $3,000 to compensate him for the hurt to his 'dignity, feelings and self-respect'. But by that time the Centre had disbanded, having neither time, energy nor money to fight. According to Jeffreys, it was the behaviour of this man that caused the demise of this first lesbian centre in Canada (Jeffreys, 2014: 169; Boyle, 2011: 193-4).

An Australian example eventually had a happier outcome for the lesbian organisation, but again at great trouble and expense, and without any acknowledgement that lesbians might have a right to exclude men from their gatherings. In December 2005, a transsexual man contacted the South Australian Commissioner of Equal Opportunity to lodge a complaint that he had been discriminated against because a lesbian association, Sappho's Party Inc, had refused to sell him a ticket to a party to be held in the Adelaide Hills in January, 2006.[285] The case was eventually dismissed in 2009 on the grounds that the party was a private affair (private events are not covered by anti-discrimination legislation). However, although the Tribunal had found for the lesbians and against the transsexual man, the finding was only based on a technicality. There was no suggestion that lesbians had a right to get together

---

285. The following is taken from Overell, 2009, and the Tribunal's official Judgment (http://www.austlii.edu.au/au/cases/sa/SAEOT/2009/50.html).

without the intrusion of men calling themselves 'women'. In fact, all three members of the Tribunal were agreed that the transsexual man (referred to as 'she' in the Tribunal report of the case) 'was excluded, or discriminated against, by reason of her [sic] transsexuality'.

Moreover, only two of the three Tribunal members agreed that the party was private. The third member of the Tribunal argued that a private function could still be defined as 'public' if it was publicly advertised (as this one had been, through the distribution of flyers). The implication is that lesbian-only events will have to restrict their advertising to personal invitation only and not distribute flyers or advertise in any public media, in case any subsequent equal opportunity, human rights or anti-discrimination tribunal happens to agree with this third member, defines them as a 'public' organisation, and fines them for refusing to accept transsexual men. The other two members also discussed a number of other reasons why the event might have been defined as 'public'—Sappho's Party Inc was an incorporated association (because the organisers wanted public liability insurance coverage); the venue for the party was a commercial one; and there were entry fees. Even though the Tribunal members eventually rejected these arguments, another Tribunal with different members might decide differently.

The behaviour of the transsexual activists, both the complainant himself and his supporters, displayed the usual male entitlement. During the mediation proceedings prior to the Tribunal hearing, transsexual activists insulted and threatened members of Sappho's Party Inc, while the court staff looked on without intervening (Erinyes, 2010: 16-17). One official report of the matter (Overell, 2009) simply referred to the mediation proceedings as having 'failed', with no reference to the activists' behaviour. Moreover, during the Tribunal proceedings the transsexual man presented what some lesbians referred to as 'pornographic self-portraits' (presumably pictures of his reconstructed genitalia), to prove his 'femaleness' (Erinyes, 2010: 16-17). And after all this, the transsexual man had no intention of attending Sappho's Party. The third, dissenting Tribunal member noted in his judgement that 'Ms [sic] O'Keefe gave evidence that she [sic] had no intention of attending the event even had Sappho's Party invited her [sic] to do so. I also note that she [sic] received considerable publicity for her [sic] cause through the prosecution of this matter'. So it would seem that the complaint was at the very least, nothing but a publicity stunt, at worst, an attempt to punish women for daring to exclude men. It was not a genuine attempt to redress a perceived wrong, or even to claim a perceived entitlement. It was a vexatious complaint, wasting the Tribunal's time and resources, and harassing and frightening the lesbians who spent years worrying about the outcome. On those grounds alone, it should have been thrown out by the Tribunal.

The transsexual agenda is also distorting crime statistics. Crimes committed by transsexual men are reported as crimes committed by women. For example, an article in a local paper in the UK said that a judge had 'criticised the lack of treatment programmes for women who download child porn after learning there were only courses set up for men' (Hunt, 2016). The clue that the perpetrator was not a woman at all was contained in a quoted comment by the defence lawyer, who said that the accused 'lived in a rural area where there was not a very good understanding of identity and transgender matters'. Consequently, 'she' was reduced to downloading child pornography because 'she' was 'feeling excluded from the local community' (Hunt, 2016). But this 'transgender' person was engaging in male behaviour, and hence the courses set up for men would have been entirely appropriate for him (always supposing such courses are appropriate for anyone). However that may be, the crime statistics now contain one 'female' child pornography offender who was not actually female.

Censorship

Transsexuals' complaints that they are not accepted by the mainstream need to be taken with a grain of salt. Their influence has been extensive: the legal profession treats them seriously, the medical profession has long been acquiescent, and the media are on side (for two examples, see: Bibby, 2013; Farrelly, 2013). So influential is the transsexual agenda that its aggrieved entitlement and cries of 'hate speech' are taken seriously and any criticism is censored by organisations caving in to the transsexuals' demands. The chief target of transsexual wrath is radical feminism, or rather, radical *feminists*, since the issue is individualised and the attacks are personal, directed against particular radical feminist critics. Chief among those individuals attacked and vilified by name are: Professor Sheila Jeffreys (formerly Professor of Political Science at the University of Melbourne), journalists Julie Burchill and Julie Bindel in the UK, and in the US, Cathy Brennan and Lierre Keith and her colleagues at Deep Green Resistance. These women are primary targets of transsexual rage, even death threats, and they are constantly being subjected to the 'transphobic' slur.

For example, in 2012, *The Observer* newspaper censored an article by journalist Julie Burchill in response to complaints from transsexual activists. The article, called 'Transsexuals should cut it out', was partly a defence of her friend Suzanne Moore, who was receiving abuse and threats from transsexual activists on Twitter. Moore had commented in a book chapter on women's anger, that 'women were angry about "not having the ideal body shape – that of a Brazilian transsexual"' (Burchill, 2013),[286] and the transsexual lobby found this offensive. Moore herself was responding to an Associated Press report about transsexual fashion models in Brazil, whom the report presented as better 'women' than real women, or at least better at femininity: '"The trans-models have a proverbial leg up on their female colleagues. Unlike even the thinnest of women, without cellulite and stretch marks ... once they've lasered away facial and body hair, they can look more feminine than models who were born female"' (Moore, 2013). The transsexual lobby had nothing to say about this report, with its implication that transsexual men make better 'women' than women themselves.

It is true that Burchill's article contained some intemperate language: she said that she imagined that 'being monstered [by transsexuals] ... [might] be something akin to being savaged by a dead sheep'; she said that transsexual men were '[e]ducated beyond all common sense and honesty, [and] it was a hoot to see the screaming-mimis accuse Suze of white feminist privilege'; and she referred to them as 'a bunch of dicks in chick's clothing ... of bed-wetters in bad wigs ... [and] [s]hims, shemales, whatever you're calling yourselves these days'. But she didn't threaten anyone with violence and death, unlike the transsexual lobby—Moore said that one of the tweets she received threatened her with decapitation (Moore, 2013). As one commentator pointed out, '[i]f what you want is balanced commentary on the issues of the day, you don't commission Julie Burchill' (Campbell, 2013). She was responding with over-the-top humour from a position at least as valid as the transsexual one (and in my view, the only valid viewpoint on transsexualism), to Twitter attacks so vicious that her friend was 'driven from her chosen mode of time-wasting' (Moore had cancelled her Twitter account) (Burchill, 2012). But management caved in to the transsexual agenda, deleted Burchill's article from the ironically named 'commentisfree' segment of their website, and posted an apology instead. This act of censorship deleted not only Burchill's article, but also the supportive feminist comments that had followed it. As one feminist said:

---

286. Originally published in *The Observer* but withdrawn from publication in response to complaints from transsexuals. It was republished in *The Telegraph* and then on GenderTrender. The original URL for the article on the *Guardian* website redirected readers to an abject, pro-transsexualism statement from John Mulholland, editor of *The Observer*.

The decision to remove Julie Burchill's article means that the comments many of us made, where we explained that being subjected to vicious and disproportionate abuse online, simply for critiquing gender, is a daily experience of radical feminists, have also been removed (rubyfruit2, 2013).

Feminist conferences are a prime target for transsexual activists' wrath. For example, they were successful in getting the Radfem conference in London in 2012 expelled from its original venue, Conway Hall, the Ethical Society's HQ. The venue owners cancelled the conference booking when transsexual activists objected on the grounds that the conference was women-only and transsexual men were excluded, and that one of the keynote speakers was Sheila Jeffreys. She was to be speaking about prostitution not transsexualism, but because she disagrees with the idea that men can be 'women', the transsexual lobby does its best to stop her speaking on anything at all. The Conway Hall officials said that they were cancelling the Radfem conference booking because the ideas presented at the conference "'conflict with our ethos, principles, and culture'" (Goldberg, 2014). One wonders whether they even bothered to look at the conference program or read the speakers' already published work. The conference did go ahead, but at a venue that could not be publicly advertised and to which attendees had to escorted from a nearby meeting place.

As for the Ethical Society's ethos, etc., it was founded in 1787 'in rebellion against the doctrine of eternal hell'. Today its aim is 'the advancement of study, research and education in humanist ethical principles', of which there appear to be two main ones: a refusal to believe in God and in such religious beliefs as life after death; and a commitment to living the best ethical life one can inspired by the Golden Rule, 'Treat other people in a way you would like to be treated yourself' and 'Do not treat others as you would not like to be treated yourself'.[287] There is nothing in those two principles that conflicts with radical feminism or with anything Sheila Jeffreys might say. But in fact the Conway Hall officials broke their own Rule: they wouldn't like to be condemned without a hearing, and yet that is exactly what they did to the 2012 Radfem conference.

The Conway Hall officials were prevented from seeing that because of the limitations of 'humanism', with its exclusive focus on individuals and consequent obliviousness to male domination (not to mention their failure to investigate what the conference was actually about). So they interpreted the transsexual men complaining about their exclusion from the Radfem

---

287. http://www.simpleguidetohumanism.org.uk/.

conference as individuals who were not being treated according to the Golden Rule—radical feminists wouldn't like to be excluded, so they shouldn't exclude anyone else. The Ethical Society and other 'humanist' organisations aspire to what I have called genuine humanity, but their Golden Rule assumes that everybody is already equal, that everybody has the same power to decide to treat others fairly. This individualism blinds them to the systematic ways in which male power operates. They cannot see that treating unequals equally simply reproduces the current system of inequality (or rather, domination). Their statement that the Radfem conference conflicted with their ethos was false; there is no conflict between feminism and the 'Golden Rule'. But there is a conflict between insisting that men can be 'women' and insisting that they can't. For radical feminism, men insisting they are 'women' is yet one more male encroachment.

The Radfems Respond event in Portland, Oregon, in May 2014, was organised by Lierre Keith and her colleagues at Deep Green Resistance. It, too, was forced to change its venue because of pressure from the transsexual lobby (Goldberg, 2014). The event was an open meeting intended to answer questions from the general public about the radical feminist position on prostitution and 'gender'. The original venue was a Quaker Meeting House, but the Friends cancelled the booking in response to a change.org petition from the transsexual lobby. The reason given for the cancellation was that the Radfems Respond speakers had engaged in 'abusive language and behavior'.[288] But not only was no evidence provided to support this allegation, the abusive language was all on the transsexuals' side.

The Quaker Meeting's decision to cancel the booking is incomprehensible. Not only did they receive a number of well-argued, heartfelt letters, including some from Quakers, respectfully requesting that the decision be reversed,[289] the petition itself (Profitt, 2014) reads like the most irrational of conspiracy theories. 'Radical Feminists', it said, 'are a hateful group, increasingly defining themselves by their hatred of trans people … [and their claim to dialogue is] hate speech'. The repetition of the word 'hate' alone should have been a warning signal that this was not a communication to be trusted. As well, the petition told silly lies that could have been easily checked. For example, its statement that 'Sheila Jefferies [sic] convinced congress to cancel a plan to cover gender-related healthcare for those suffering from gender dysphoria' could not possibly be true because Jeffreys is not a US citizen and has never

---

288. https://radfemsrespond.wordpress.com/backlash/.

289. https://radfemsrespond.wordpress.com/60-2/.

testified before Congress. Again, the statement that 'Cathy Brennan posts naked pictures of trans women online in order to shame them' was not only a lie, it is the kind of lie that doesn't even make sense (and again, is easily checkable). And to give a final example from this influential petition, there is the statement that 'Cathy Brennan … wrote to the UN asking them not to extend human rights to transgender people'. But far from objecting to human rights for transsexuals, Brennan explicitly supported them in her letter to the UN: 'we recognize the legitimate needs of transgender and transsexual women [i.e. men] to operate in the world free from irrational discrimination'. Her concern was that, in abolishing sex-segregated facilities for women, 'gender identity' legislation increased the danger of women being subjected to male sexual violence, and hence eroded the human rights of women.[290] That such dishonesty, distortion and irrationality could have been taken seriously is beyond belief. But such is the influence of the transsexual lobby that their demands take precedence over any needs women might have, not to mention reasonableness. What, after all, could be more unreasonable than insisting that men are 'women'?

There was also another attempt by the transsexual lobby to get Radfems Respond excluded from the next venue they found, the Central Library. An article posted on the Portland Independent Media Center[291] displayed the same frenetic extremism as the change.org petition. The organisers of the event, the text of the article screamed, 'are people who want trans folks to be outlawed and be executed in prison unless they go back to their birth sex because to them genital is destiny … These hateful FASCISTS do not belong in Oregon!'. However, the library refused to cancel the event, on the grounds of free speech.

Other feminist conferences forced to change venues because of transsexual harassment include a gathering in Toronto in 2013, called Radfems Rise Up (Goldberg, 2014), and the 2013 Radfem conference in London (as well as the 2012 conference). In the case of the 2013 Radfem conference, the original venue, the Irish Centre, didn't have the resources to deal with the harassment by the transsexual activists, who yelled at staff, threatened them, and published their personal information on the internet. The Centre was sympathetic to the feminists, however, and helped them get another venue (Vigo, 2013). Another conference, the Women Up North Conference in

---

290. https://gendertrender.files.wordpress.com/2012/08/hungerford_csw_communication_2012_8-28-2012.pdf.

291. http://portland.indymedia.org/en/2014/05/427239.shtml?discuss. This post can no longer be found on the internet.

Manchester in 2012, was also harassed by transsexual activists, not because they were excluded from the conference (they weren't), but because they were excluded from a single session, 'Female Survivors of Sexual Abuse'.[292]

The ire of transsexual activists is not directed only towards radical feminists. They do their best to silence other critics, too. In May 2011, a conference in London organised by the Royal College of Psychiatrists' Gay and Lesbian Special Interest Group, called 'Transgenderism: Time to Change', was cancelled because of pressure from the transsexual lobby (Jeffreys, 2014: 2). One of these speakers was a Consultant Psychiatrist and Psychotherapist, Dr Az Hakeem. His invitation to speak was one of the reasons why the Charing Cross Gender Identity Clinic withdrew from the conference because he supposedly engaged in '"pathologising" trans people' (Green, 2011). However, those making this accusation must have been ignorant of what the man actually said. Far from 'pathologising' transsexualism, he is very supportive; he is not opposed to transsexualism or even to sex-reassignment surgery. He has simply said that 'gender reassignment may not be helpful' for everyone with 'gender identity conditions'.[293] Since most transsexual men are not themselves undergoing sex reassignment surgery these days, it is puzzling why this should arouse transsexual activists' ire.

Another man who has aroused the ire of the transsexual activists protesting the conference was J. Michael Bailey, whose book, *The Man Who Would Be Queen*, was published in 2003. Bailey became a target because of the book's popularising of the theory that there are two distinct types of transsexualism (see above), especially the notion of 'autogynephilia', 'the erotic orientation of a male toward the fantasy that he is female' (Bailey, 2005).

The attacks, which started soon after the book was published, were initially orchestrated by Lynn Conway, a transsexual activist who had lived for decades as a 'woman' (he 'transitioned' in 1968), but whose behaviour displayed that extreme form of aggrieved entitlement so typical of men. Conway not only devoted a large section of his website to damning Bailey's book, he contacted everyone who wrote the positive blurbs on the book's cover, got the book removed from the National Academy of Sciences' website (but only for a few hours), and likened the book to '"the Nazi propaganda films about Jews in WWII"' (Bailey, 2005). However, Conway's reactions were subdued in comparison with those of another transsexual man, Andrea James, whose

---

292. https://gendertrender.wordpress.com/2012/05/30/women-up-north-feminist-conference-protested-no-platformed-for-scheduling-a-female-only-survivor-of-sex-abuse-workshop/.

293. http://www.drazhakeem.com/specialist-psychotherapy-for-gender-dysphoria/.

website was linked with Conway's. James took pictures of Bailey's children from his website and posted them on his own with obscene messages, including the libel that Bailey had sodomised them; he also threatened people whom Bailey had thanked for help on his book. Under Conway's influence, one of the people Bailey had referred to extensively in the book filed a complaint against him with the Institutional Review Board, the body responsible for research ethics approval at Northwestern University, alleging that Bailey had not gained his consent. Bailey's defence was that he was not doing academic research, but rather the kind of research that journalists do. Moreover, he and this person had been friends for years, and he had had no problem with the book until he came into contact with Conway. There was also a vexatious and untrue complaint by a transsexual prostitute, also discussed extensively in the book, that Bailey had had sex with him. Bailey denied it and the Review Board refused to consider it.

One of the reasons given for cancelling the conference was the withdrawal of the Gender Identity Clinic, who had said that there was '"disquiet" in the trans community' about the presence of some of the other invited speakers (Green, 2011). Chief among those other speakers was journalist Julie Bindel, whose public criticism of transsexualism has made her persona non grata with the transsexual lobby. Her views on 'trans issues', said one outraged, pro-trans commentator, were '"offensive" and "outdated"': she had 'once called gender reassignment surgery "modern-day aversion therapy for gays and lesbians"' (Green, 2011). This statement can be found in Bindel's 2009 article, 'The operation that can ruin your life'. It followed on from a comment about Iran, the country with the second highest number of sex-change operations in the world (after Thailand), where homosexuality is illegal and punishable by death. Sex-change surgery performed on gay men is seen by the Iranian authorities to turn them into heterosexual women and thus exterminate their homosexuality, just as hanging them would. Calling transsexual surgery aversion therapy seems a mild understatement in the face of such a reality.

Ironically, one of the reasons the Gender Identity clinic gave for its withdrawal was that the conference was 'one-sided', and that the organisers hadn't 'talked to the trans community and included people' (Green, 2011). And yet the clinic had been invited; if the conference had gone ahead any 'one-sidedness' would have been its own fault. But the actions of the transsexual lobby were not directed towards providing an alternative voice, but towards closing down the conference altogether. Their aim was not to contest views they disagreed with, but to silence them.

Julie Bindel came to the attention of the transsexual lobby with her 2004 article in *The Guardian*, 'Gender benders, beware'. In it she stated her approval of the British Columbia Supreme Court's decision to reverse the earlier human rights tribunal decision in favour of Kimberly Nixon; referred to Nixon as 'a man in a dress'; and said: 'Think about a world inhabited just by transsexuals. It would look like the set of Grease'. The then readers' editor of *The Guardian* received around 200 letters of complaint about the article, and apologised: "'[This column] abused an already abused minority that *The Guardian* might have been expected to protect'". Bindel also later apologised for the language she had used, saying, 'In hindsight, the sarcasm I used in my column was misplaced and insensitive' (Bindel, 2007). But this did not placate the transsexual lobby, given that she did not change her mind about her objections to transsexualism. She said that she had been banned from speaking by the National Union of Students Women's Campaign (the only other people ever banned by the National Union of Students were fascist groups like the British National Party). She also said that a number of self-styled 'feminist' organisations had been frightened into banning her from speaking at public events for fear of protests by transsexual lobbyists (Bindel, 2009).

In 2007, she was invited by the producer of the Radio 4 debating series, 'Hecklers', to speak about transsexualism on the program. She chose the title, 'Sex change surgery is unnecessary mutilation'. The opposition was formidable, with four transsexual experts on the panel opposed to her single dissenting voice and an audience stacked with transsexual activists. One blogger on a transsexual activist website wrote: "'The debate is a thinly veiled opportunity to allow the dreadfully transphobic Julie Bindel a platform for her odious views'". She was of course outvoted, but she felt she had done her job in putting a case that was so seldom allowed to be heard. The debate seems to have been polite and non-confrontational. She referred to it as 'one of the most challenging and stimulating debates I have taken part in', not because she managed to convince anyone—she didn't—but because she was able to put her point of view, if briefly, without being howled down (Bindel, 2007).

'No-platforming'

Transsexual activists do their best to silence the voices of their critics by getting their speaking engagements cancelled, even when the topic under discussion is not transsexualism. The transsexual agenda sees the issues only in terms of individuals. Not only does it reinterpret criticism of transsexualism as 'attacks' on 'transgenders', it also targets its critics personally. Everything they say is rejected just because they are the ones who said it. Bindel says she has sometimes been prevented by the transsexual lobby from speaking about her main interest, which is sexual violence (Bindel, 2015). Lierre Keith said that, in May 2014, she needed a police escort in order to attend the Public Interest Environmental Law Conference at the University of Oregon to speak about environmental issues. The university administration hired six police officers to protect her after they had received a relentless stream of threats against her from transsexual supporters. Earlier, in 2010 at the Bay Area Anarchist Bookfair, she had had pies heavily laced with chilli thrown at her and was hit in the face.[294]

In 2013, Janice Raymond, author of *The Transsexual Empire*, had an invitation to speak cancelled by a Norwegian government agency because a letter to the editor of a major Norwegian newspaper had accused her of 'transphobia'. This was despite the fact that she hadn't written or spoken on transsexual issues since 1994 when she wrote a new introduction to the book, and also despite the fact that she wasn't doing so this time either. Instead, she was to advise the government agency on prostitution legislation as part of her work on sex trafficking. She told the journalist interviewing her that this kind of thing had been happening "'much more frequently within the last couple of years'" (Goldberg, 2014).

In 1995, Sheila Jeffreys was asked to speak at a conference in Melbourne called 'Have Your Say', which was organised around issues of youth and sexuality. But the invitation was withdrawn when Jeffreys said that she would have to say something about transsexualism as a human rights violation because she felt she had a responsibility to warn any young people who might be contemplating it. She was told that no criticism of transgenderism was allowed because the conference was intended to be supportive of 'transgenders' (Jeffreys, 1997: 70). This is typical of alphabet-soup (LGBT-whatever) and so-called 'feminist' circles, where banning criticism of transsexualism is often simply an automatic knee-jerk reaction beyond challenge or debate. Jeffreys was also not allowed to speak at least one a Reclaim the Night event in Melbourne, and in 2011, a conference in Brisbane was cancelled because she was one of the advertised speakers. She also said that a reading group that had discussed her work online was called 'transphobic' and told that they shouldn't be reading her work (Jeffreys, 2011). She describes her own experiences of transsexual vilification and silencing:

---

294. https://radfemsrespond.wordpress.com/60-2/.

For several years there has been a concerted campaign via the internet and on the ground, to ensure that I, and any other persons who have criticised transgenderism, from any academic discipline, are not given opportunities to speak in public … Whatever the topic of my presentation, and whether in Australia, the UK or the US, transgender activists bombard the organising group and the venue with emails accusing me of transhate, transphobia, hate speech, and seek to have me banned. On blogs, Facebook and Twitter they accuse me of wanting to "eliminate" transgendered persons, and they wish me dead … These activists threaten demonstrations and placards against me at any venue where I speak. What is clear is that transgender activists do not want any criticism of the practice to be made (Jeffreys, 2012).

She has suggested that the reason transsexual activists are so virulent in their resistance to any criticism is because they are defending the indefensible: 'The degree of vituperation and the energy expended by the activists may suggest that they fear the practice of transgenderism could justifiably be subjected to criticism, and might not stand up to rigorous research and debate, if critics were allowed to speak out' (Jeffreys, 2012).

Abuse

Transsexual activists are frequently abusive, their behaviour typical of that aggrieved entitlement that drives so much male violence, including death threats. For example, Jeffreys mentioned that one transsexual man created an image consisting of an aerosol can of pesticide with a photo of her on it and a slogan saying "'kills rad fems instantly'" (Jeffreys, 2012).

In another example, when Bindel arrived at the entrance to a Stonewall function where she was a nominee for a Stonewall Journalist of the Year award, she was met with a huge demonstration of transsexuals and their supporters, shouting 'Bindel the Bigot'; and again, she needed a police escort. Her nomination had called forth scores of blogs and message boards filled with attacks on her. On one, called 'Genocide and Julie Bindel', someone wrote, "'She is an active oppressor of trans people. I hope she dies an agonising and premature death of cancer in the very near future. It would make the world a better place'" (Bindel, 2009).

Samantha Berg, one of Lierre Keith's colleagues in Deep Green Resistance, was personally harassed by transsexual activists while she was organising the Radfem Reboot Conference in Portland. She received threats of violence, including bomb threats, which became more than just threats when a molotov cocktail was thrown into a local bank (Vigo, 2013).

Even apart from the bomb threats and the Molotov cocktail, the threats around the Radfem Reboot Conference were particularly frightening. Abusive posts proliferated on social media, many of them outright death threats saying 'kill terfs'.[295] Given the frequency of mass shootings in the US, fuelled by the kind of male rage the transsexual activists were displaying, the women had good reasons for being very worried indeed.

Transsexual activists frequently accuse radical feminists of 'hate speech' and abusiveness, but those accusations can only be projection (in the psychoanalytic sense). It is the transsexual activists who are abusive and who advocate hatred, not radical feminists. As Lierre Keith pointed out (see above), 'You will not find a single example—not anywhere—of a transgender person needing a police escort to stay safe from feminists … feminists have never attempted to shut down a transgender event, violently or otherwise'.

Explanations

The phenomenon of transsexualism does need to be explained, especially in the case of men. How is it that a member of the dominant sex wants to be a member of the subordinate sex? Or to put it another way, how can it be that men want to divest themselves of their penises, that precious symbol of 'human' status so valorised within the culture of male supremacy? These questions are couched in a feminist idiom, but the malestream would have its own version of the same question couched in terms of contempt for women and inspired by that castration anxiety exposed by Freud. Men are usually horrified, even terrified, at the thought of losing their penises. How, then, is it possible that some men not only lack that fear of castration, but actively desire it?

Explanation is also called for because the transsexual meaning— the feeling of being 'a woman in a man's body', or a man's claim to be 'a woman'—makes no sense. Of course, a transsexual man's response to that would be that it makes sense to him (and he would insist on being referred by feminine pronouns). But it makes no sense within the commonsense universe of meaning where there are two sexes. Theorists of transsexualism would most likely agree with this latter statement, given that they explicitly repudiate commonsense with their insistence that transsexualism involves a radical questioning of 'gender' (which means in this instance the fact that there are two sexes). As Connell put it: 'gender reassignment is a subversive process. It dramatically expresses the mutability and historicity of gender …

---

295. https://radfemsrespond.wordpress.com/recent-anti-feminist-hate-speech/.

Transsexuality involves deep gender disruption and reconstitution' (Connell, 2010: 17-18). Clearly, transsexualism is meant to challenge and demolish the commonsense meaning, and hence not to make sense within its terms. But when we ask why the common understanding that there are two sexes needs to be 'mutated', 'disrupted' and 'reconstituted', the only explanation available refers to the men's feelings: the commonsense reality that there are two sexes needs to be abolished because there are men who feel they are 'women'. But some people's feelings are not sufficient reason to question commonsense understandings, and the feelings are what needs to be explained in the first place.

There are a number of different kinds of explanations available: those preferred by transsexuals themselves; psychological/psychoanalytic explanations; and feminist explanations. On the whole, transsexuals themselves prefer not to explain it because a demand for explanation implies that transsexualism is pathological and they are insistent that it's not. If there's nothing wrong there's nothing to explain. Psychological explanations refer to the ways in which transsexual men are socialised in early childhood, and these explanations do tend to interpret transsexualism as pathological, as evidenced by terminology such as 'abnormality', 'psychologically harmful influences', 'malignant personality disorder', 'borderline', 'primitive defenses and defective ego functions'. Feminist explanations refer to the culture of male supremacy, in particular to 'sex roles', the part they play in the subordination of women, and transsexualism's reinforcement of those roles in the attempts to 'change gender'.

The transsexual agenda explains it primarily in terms of feelings. To give just one example:

> When we strip away all our big words, I feel what's left as an essential "core" of my transsexualism is my feelings. I feel what makes me happy and what makes me unhappy are my "ultimate true description of being transsexual" ... Even if there was a transsexual gene or something, it's my emotional experiences which make me who I am. So, to me, emotions are at the center of what describes transsexuality.[296]

But this is a description, not an explanation. It says that transsexualism manifests itself as certain feelings, but it doesn't explain where the feelings come from, nor how they might fit into any wider cultural context. However, as the reference to 'a transsexual gene or something' indicates, transsexuals also explain the phenomenon in terms of biology:

---

296. http://www.genderpsychology.org/transsexual/meaning.html.

It is almost universally believed that during the formation of the fetus in utero, a hormonal imbalance affects the development of the body sex characteristics in a way that is misaligned with the core gender brain wiring.[297]

But whether couched in terms of emotions or biology, transsexual explanations are individualistic. As the framers of the Yogyakarta Principles[298] put it, 'gender identity' involves "'each person's deeply felt internal and individual experience of gender, which may or may not correspond with the sex assigned at birth, including the personal sense of the body (which may involve, if freely chosen, modification of bodily appearance or function by medical, surgical or other means) and other expressions of gender, including dress, speech and mannerisms'" (quoted in Jeffreys, 2014: 147).

It is no accident that these justificatory 'explanations' are individualistic, referring only to something within each individual, something that is assumed to originate there and nowhere else. Individualism is one of the chief discursive mechanisms of domination, one of the main ways of hiding its existence (Thompson, 2001: 43-50). If only individuals exist, there can be no overarching system of domination, just a series of autonomous, self-engendered and most importantly, equal, entities who come together only after they have recognised they might have something in common because they feel the same way. On this account, the source of transsexualism is the individual psyche. Feelings are the explanatory bedrock; their existence is regarded as a sufficient reason for all that follows—the medical and surgical interventions, the demands for changes to identity documents and pronouns. Once the feelings have been identified there is no need to seek any further explanation.

But in fact the transsexual empire is not based on feelings but on interpretations of what those feelings mean, and interpretations are cultural. They originate in a shared universe of meaning that is not confined to any particular individual or individuals, even though it feels like one's own deepest reality. Interpretations of what feelings mean are shared. It is true that we all react differently to the shared meanings of the cultural milieu we are born into, and that the source of the feelings can be brought into consciousness and evaluated instead of being blindly acted upon. Even among transsexual

---

297. https://answers.yahoo.com/question/index?qid=20080621160042AAOV85Y.

298. Advice to the UN from 'an international panel of experts', 'on the application of international human rights law in relation to sexual orientation and gender identity', formalised in 2007 (although not incorporated into any Conventions or Declarations) (Jeffreys, 2014: 146; AHRC, 2009: 11-12).

men themselves there are differences. Not all of them make the demands described here; some do not even claim to be women. But although feelings are experienced as peculiarly one's own, arising from deep within the self, interpretations of those feelings come from the shared cultural environment.

The experts' explanations (psychological, psychoanalytic, psychotherapeutic and medical) tentatively agree that biological factors might have a role to play, although they also note that no evidence of any biological influence has ever been found; but they prefer to explain it in terms of the individual's life history. Harry Benjamin (1999), for example, suggested some form of 'imprinting' might be at work, or alternatively, 'psychologically harmful influences in childhood, so-called "conditioning"', along with 'an inherited predisposition'. Robert J. Stoller was convinced that transsexualism was, unsurprisingly, caused by their mothers: 'the inability of [the boys'] mothers to permit their sons to separate from their mothers' bodies' (Stoller, 1968: 200). Psychoanalyst Ethel Spector Person also explained transsexualism in terms of the mother-son relationship, although she insisted that, rather than holding the boys too close, their mother were 'excessively distant' and 'insensitive to the child's emotional needs' (Person, 1999: 120). Conditioning into transsexualism was still their mothers' fault, though. However, the main consensus among the experts is that the direct cause (the 'etiology') is unknown. Transsexual activists reject explanations such as these, which interpret transsexualism as a personality disorder. They regard it instead as the expression of their true selves, hence the insistence on a biological origin for their feelings. But experts and transsexuals are in agreement that the explanation for transsexualism can only be found within the individual, either his biology or his life history.

Feminist explanations are couched in terms of 'sex roles'. Sex roles, Raymond said, are 'the fabric by which a sexist society is held together' (Raymond, 1980: xviii-xix), and transsexualism is an expression of the 'sex-role stereotyping' characteristic of 'the patriarchy'. 'I would suggest', she said, 'that a patriarchal society and its social currents of masculinity and femininity is the *First Cause* of transsexualism' (Raymond, 1980: xviii—original emphasis). Sheila Jeffreys expands on this insight thus:

> Transsexualism … is deeply reactionary, a way of preventing the disruption and elimination of gender roles which lies at the basis of the feminist project. Transsexualism opposes feminism by maintaining and reinforcing false and constructed notions of correct femininity and masculinity. The vast majority of transsexuals still subscribe to the

traditional stereotype of women and seek to become "real" feminine women (Jeffreys, 1997: 56-7).

So transsexualism contributes to women's subordination by reinforcing sex roles, the masculinity and femininity that are responsible for that subordination.

At first sight it might seem that the critique of sex roles is where transsexualism and feminism are in agreement. Connell certainly believes that transsexualism and feminism belong together: 'Because transsexual women's [sic] lives are shaped by the intransigence of gender, there is necessarily common ground with feminism' (Connell 2012: 872). But Connell's view of feminism is flawed, confined as it is to the work of Judith Butler, liberal feminism,[299] and queer theory (which is arguably anti-feminist in its 'questioning' of the category of 'women'). At best, these discourses ignore feminism's central problematic, male supremacy; at worst, they are actively hostile towards it.

Moreover, feminism's challenge to conventional forms of masculinity and femininity is very different from transsexualism's. It involves no bodily changes and no switching of 'sex roles', but rather a change in consciousness, away from belief in the principle that only men count as 'human' (however that might manifest itself), and towards acceptance of the full humanity of women and genuine humanity for all.

But although the feminist explanation in terms of sex roles is not individualistic—sex roles are produced by a patriarchal society, not by the individual psyche or physiology—it is not entirely adequate as an explanation either for women's oppression or for transsexualism. It is true that most transsexual men are required to present themselves in stereotypically feminine ways, but some do not, especially those who insist they are 'lesbians' (and who behave no less imperialistically in their demands to be recognised as 'women' than their feminine counterparts). Moreover, the terminology of 'sex roles' gives no hint of the real problem, i.e. male supremacy with its subordination of women, its dissociated approach to the world, and its arrogant sense of entitlement. The feminist theorists who use that terminology do connect 'sex roles' to male supremacy, but the terminology itself does not.

---

299. 'Much of what transsexual women [sic] need is already contained in feminist agendas: equity in education, adequate child care, equal employment conditions and wage justice, prevention of gender-based violence, resistance to sexist culture, and what Scandinavian feminists have called a "women-friendly" state' (Connell, 2012: 872). It is unclear what use transsexual men would have for child care; and the violence women are subjected to is more clearly acknowledged as male violence, rather than disguised with the mealy-mouthed 'gender-based'.

Raymond (1980: xvi) suggested that male transsexualism 'may be one way by which men attempt to possess females' creative energies', an attempt doomed to failure because all they can manage is 'artifactual femaleness'. But while I agree with Raymond that male transsexualism involves envy of femaleness and the desire to possess it, that also requires explaining. Why would men envy and desire something so belittled and demeaned under male supremacist conditions?

As should be clear from my discussion of feminist object relations (see chapter 4), I would agree with at least some aspects of the psychoanalytic explanation for transsexualism. The intensity of the transsexual male's desire for femininity indicates that it originates in infancy and early childhood, with the infant's progress towards separation and individuation from mother and the beginnings of the development of awareness, memory, personality and language. So early are those beginnings that it is not surprising that transsexuals feel they are born that way. Psychoanalyst Ethel Spector Person locates the genesis of male transsexualism in

> [the child's] reparative fantasy of symbiotic fusion with the mother to counter separation anxiety. In this way, mother and child become one and the anxiety is allayed, but the cost is an ambiguous core gender identity (sense of maleness) (Person, 1999: 111).

She also said that the fantasy is established even before the child is three years old. Strictly speaking, the fantasy of symbiotic fusion occurs only in what she called 'primary transsexualism'. There is a secondary from of male transsexualism, which comes later. Here, the separation anxiety is managed 'not by symbiotic fusion with the mother but by resort to transitional and part-objects', e.g. feminine clothing and other accoutrements.

But whenever in life it manifests itself, the intensity of the feelings indicates that its roots lie in infancy, at that time of life when awareness is just starting to develop. This is the reason why the desire feels as though it is innate. It happens during the time when self, memory and language are just developing, and hence before there is a fully developed consciousness that can understand what is going on and make choices. In this, transsexual men are no different from anyone else. Everyone is born a helpless infant who must become a separate individual and learn the ways of the world. Each of us does it in our own way, and we all have to manage the conflict between the demands of male supremacy and a need to be genuinely human. Transsexualism is one way of doing this, but it is still complicit with the meanings and values of male supremacy. The enthusiasm with which it has been embraced by major malestream institutions provides some evidence of that complicity.

Male transsexualism is best explained in terms of the culture of male supremacy, 'sex roles' certainly, but more importantly in terms of a conflict between the demands made of males within a male supremacist reality on the one hand, and what I have called the genuinely human on the other. The starting point is a genuinely human desire to escape from the burden of masculinity, its demands to participate in or be subjected to bullying, contempt, degradation and violence, and the emptiness of its dissociated existence. But the solution to the dilemma is a male supremacist one—take over the only other persona offered, the feminine one. Because this strategy is male supremacist it has male supremacist effects. From a feminist standpoint, these are men who are attempting to storm the last bastion to hold out against masculine intrusion: femaleness. Femaleness is the one space men cannot occupy, but the dissociation characteristic of male supremacy enables that knowledge to be repressed and to resurface as aggrieved entitlement. The genuinely human alternative would be to accept the body one was born with while rejecting the demands the male supremacist culture makes of it.

And it is important to remember that most 'transsexual' men nowadays are not divesting themselves of their penises. Instead, they are insisting that they are 'women' despite their male genitalia, and demanding that women recognise them as such, and that society does too—by allowing them to change the 'gender' on their birth certificates, by including them in anti-discrimination legislation, etc. In the light of this recent development, perhaps the psychoanalytic explanations are out of date. These men are not all that different from other (male supremacist) men after all. They make unwarranted demands on women, they bully when they can't get their own way, and they insist that the world change to suit them—all this and keeping their penises as well.

Conclusion

A culture that makes possible the assertion that transsexual men are 'women', displays both the dissociation and the arrogant entitlement typical of male supremacist masculinity. The dissociation is shown in its divorce from reality, while the entitlement is shown in the behaviour, in the demands that women recognise them as women and that everyone see the world their way (including governments, bureaucracies, human rights organisations, etc.), and in their insistence that they be allowed to occupy the social space of women whether or not the women want them there. The cultural phenomenon of transsexualism is as imperialistic as any of the other demands male supremacy imposes.

Much is made in the transsexual literature of deconstructing the 'gender binary' (i.e. the fact that there are two sexes). But transsexualism undermines only the female half of the male-female dichotomy. It leaves maleness untouched because most men are not transsexual and the maintenance of masculinity can safely be left with them. But the phenomenon of transsexual men claiming to be women brings femaleness radically into question. If men can be 'women', where does that leave women? As just another kind of man, still inferior because she was not born with a penis and so has not made any momentous decision to become a 'woman'? If men can be 'women', even leaving aside the claim some transsexual men make that they are superior 'women' to the ones who were born female, the meaning of women as their own sex, unique, inviolable, irreplaceable, ceases to exist. That is what radical feminism is resisting: the reality of a transsexual world where 'women' have become just one more male fantasy, 'a figment of men's imagination' (as Sheila Jeffreys put it) (Jeffreys, 2014: 6). In the case of transsexual women (so-called 'trans men'), embracing the male as the 'human' norm reinforces both the male entitlement and the dissociation.

The bedrock of the feminist stance on transsexualism is that men are not women (nor women men). Everyone shares a common humanity, and in that sense women and men are the same (including those who see themselves as 'transgender'). But until the many and shifting guises of male supremacy have been exposed for what they are, any claims made by men to get access to women must be at the least very carefully evaluated, and repudiated if they are found to benefit masculinity at women's expense. Despite their claims to femininity and their embrace of its more superficial trappings, transsexual men remain masculine in their dissociation from ordinary life and their aggravated sense of entitlement that leads them to demand that the world change to suit them.

Transsexualism is one version of the dissociation from humanity demanded by male supremacy and that originates in the repudiation of the devalued female. It originates in maleness. All transsexual men were born with penises and most are now choosing to keep them, while transsexual women (called 'trans men') embrace the male as the 'human' norm. That origin inculcates in men the dissociation and unwarranted entitlement of male supremacist masculinity. Transsexualism displays the same arrogance as any other aspect of the male supremacist character structure. It demands that the world acquiesce in its version of reality—by changing legislation, regulations, human rights documents, patterns of speech, etc., in its favour, and allowing self-identified transsexual men inclusion into women-only spaces (toilets, prisons, hospital wards, feminist spaces, refuges, rape crisis centres)—and reacts with enraged aggrieved entitlement when the demands are not met. Transsexualism is still repudiation of the female driven by penis-possession. It obliterates women, it does not recognise them as fully human, and in doing do it participates in the symbolic violence that is male supremacy.

Chapter Fifteen: US 'Welfare Reform'

> Social policy has to promote inclusion—ensuring nondiscrimination and equal treatment is critical for political and social stability—and provide basic social services, which can underpin long-term economic growth by supporting the emergence of a healthy, educated labour force. Not all such services need be provided publically. But the state should ensure that all citizens have secure access to the basic requirements of human development (UNDP, 2013: 5).

> Am researching poverty & hunger in the US after Bill Clinton's 1996 destruction of the welfare system—a destruction endorsed & shilled by Hillary Clinton. That so-called reform massively increased starvation in the US among children, women, disabled, elderly, & weighs heaviest on Blacks, Latinos, Native Americans, & undocumented immigrants because racism is built into the reformed system. That post is forthcoming & isn't just a condemnation of the Clinton candidacy but of the whole damn system where official, & certainly conservative, estimates of chronic hunger in the US are 16% of the population—about 50 million people (Scully, 2016).

A particularly stark example of the culture of masculinity in action is US 'welfare reform',[300] a piece of vicious thuggery involving some of the most powerful men in the nation bullying the most helpless citizens already victimised by the system that made those men so powerful. These are the changes in the US federal government's involvement in 'welfare' provision signed into law by President Bill Clinton in 1996.[301] Called the Personal

---

300. I put 'welfare reform' in quotation marks because the changes involved neither reform (in the sense of improvement) nor welfare (in the sense of genuine aid for the poor).

301. Mary Scully's words were written in the context of the 2016 presidential campaign, hence the reference to Hillary Clinton. When she was First Lady during Bill Clinton's presidency, Hillary supported PRWORA although she did not officially have any power to influence the outcome. She unequivocally came out in support of it in her 2003 memoir, *Living History*, saying that she agreed that her husband should sign it into law, and that she had

Responsibility and Work Opportunities Reconciliation Act (commonly known as PRWORA), it abolished the previous program, Aid to Families with Dependent Children (AFDC—originally called Aid to Dependent Children) established under the Social Security Act of 1935, and substituted instead a program called Temporary Assistance to Needy Families (TANF). TANF is just one of a number of US 'welfare' programs that provide cash and other meagre resources for people who have little or no access to income from employment (see below). But 'welfare reform' refers specifically to the PRWORA legislation and the TANF program it instituted.

Clinton's original 'welfare reform' bill, proposed in 1994, was somewhat less harsh than PRWORA, in that it supposedly guaranteed a public sector job (albeit low-paid) or a government-subsidised one in the private sector, and allowed for a number of exemptions from the time limits. But in 1994 the Republicans gained control of both Houses of Congress. As one commentator put it: 'a cohesive Republican majority stormed into the Congress and effectively set the national social policy agenda' (Butz, 2012). They demanded changes more in line with their more punitive vision of 'welfare' as set out in their *Contract With America* document (Weissmann, 2016). This document, released during the 1994 Congressional election campaign, proposed many of the same policies as PRWORA (e.g. devolution to the States and five-year time limits). But their view of 'welfare' was even harsher: 'Discourage illegitimacy and teen pregnancy by prohibiting welfare to minor mothers and denying increased AFDC for additional children while on welfare, cut spending for welfare programs, and enact a tough two-years-and-out provision with work requirements to promote individual responsibility'.[302] The right wing's detestation of the weakest and most helpless victims of the system that made these powerful men so rich is unmistakable. Still, the Republicans were not solely responsible for the form the legislation finally took. It did have bipartisan support (although there were objections) (see below).

'worked hard to round up votes for its passage'. She has also since commented favourably on the 'reform' a number of times in public, while ignoring the mounting evidence of poverty and distress. Her 2016 presidential campaign was conspicuously silent on the issue: 'Hillary constantly positions herself as the best advocate for women and children, but does not feel politically or morally compelled to call for fixing the broken TANF system she helped to create' (Marchevsky and Theoharis, 2016).

302. http://media.mcclatchydc.com/static/pdf/1994-contract-with-america.pdf.

'An unqualified success'?

'Welfare reform' has been hailed by the right wing (and by many media pundits and 'objective', hard-headed, quantitative academic researchers) as an undoubted success. A 2006 editorial in *The New Republic*, widely quoted throughout the internet, asserted that '[a] broad consensus now holds that welfare reform was certainly not a disaster—and that it may, in fact, have worked much as its designers had hoped',[303] as indeed it had, given that the massive reductions in the 'welfare' rolls brought the 'welfare' system to an end.

A Professor of Economics agreed that 'welfare reform' had been a success: 'That the 1996 welfare reform was a success, in overall terms and on average, is almost universally accepted by policy analysts and researchers' (Moffitt, 2008: 31). The reason for its success, in the professor's view, was that it 'imposed credible and enforceable work requirements into [sic] the program for the first time, as well as establishing time limits on lifetime receipt ... reduced the program caseload and governmental expenditures on the program ... [and] had generally positive average effects on employment, earnings, and income, and generally negative effects on poverty rates'. He did acknowledge that 'a small fraction of the single mother population was made worse off by the reform'. But it would seem that they only had themselves to blame: 'it is possible that families who are in turmoil or who cannot organize their lives sufficiently to comply with the rules are the same ones who are forced off welfare, and are likely to be worse off as a result' (Moffitt, 2008: 3, 22).

The co-director of the National Poverty Center and Visiting Fellow at the Brookings Institution, Rebecca M. Blank, also believed 'welfare reform' was a 'success'. The reason she gave was that 'low-income women want to work and provide better futures for their children' (Blank and Kovak, 2008). Earlier (in 2000) she had been quoted saying:

> So far, the evidence suggests that welfare reform is proceeding as well as or better than most analysts had expected. In terms of declining caseloads and increasing work effort among single mothers, welfare reform has been an astonishing success ... The research in this book suggests we are on the right track with many policy efforts (in an edited

---

303. 'Fared well' *The New Republic* 235(10): 7, 4 September, 2006. I have been unable to get access to this publication. The editorial was quoted favourably on two Wikipedia sites, the *New World Encyclopedia* 'Great Society' site, and a right-wing blog (http://www.avikroy. net/).

volume called *Finding Jobs: Work and Welfare Reform*, quoted in Albelda, 2001: 76n2).

More recently, in the context of the introduction of the Welfare Reform Act of 2011 (one of many right-wing attempts to 'reform' the 'reform' in an even more punitive direction), the Republican Committee on Education and Labor called it 'one of the most successful social policies ever enacted'. Its effects, they said, 'have been nothing short of dramatic: millions of Americans have moved from welfare to work; caseloads are down more than 50 percent; incomes are up; and child poverty has decreased'.[304]

Pundits congratulate PRWORA for the increase in employment rates among 'welfare mothers' (ignoring the fact that employment in a low-wage economy does not lift people out of poverty). '[I]n fact millions of families have since moved off the TANF rolls and begun to provide for themselves', the Republicans also said in 2011, this time in the Republican Study Committee.[305] Not surprisingly, the right-wing Heritage Foundation agreed: 'The immediate results [of PRWORA] clearly vindicated the conservative hypothesis about "workfare," as droves of former (and potential future) welfare dependents became productive employees in the private economy'. Even objective academic researchers agree that PRWORA had been successful in getting women jobs:

> In retrospect, it is clear that the critics were too pessimistic about the employment prospects of welfare mothers, as employment among single mothers increased substantially after welfare reform (Turner et al, 2006: 228).

To be fair, these authors did acknowledge, at least in part, that not all the news on 'welfare' mothers' employment was positive:

> PRWORA's critics were correct, however, when they suggested that some welfare recipients would fail to secure stable employment … a small, but growing, proportion of former recipients have failed to make a successful transition from cash assistance to work (Turner et al, 2006: 228).

However, the authors made a point of saying that it was only 'a small proportion' of former 'welfare' recipients who failed to get work (although they did acknowledge that that proportion was growing). But the proportion may not have been so small if poverty had been their focus rather than

---

304. http://archives.republicans.edlabor.house.gov/showissue.aspx?IID=15.

305. http://www.heritage.org/research/reports/2013/01/the-unfinished-work-of-welfare-reform

employment, especially if the poverty measure was more realistic than the official thresholds (see below).

Despite the evidence of continued widespread poverty (see below), it is still being asserted that PRWORA has improved matters for the poor. For example:

> By the numbers, welfare reform is an unqualified success. Caseloads that were bulging at more than 5 million back in 1996 have been cut in half. The child poverty rate, which peaked at more than 22 percent, has plummeted to 16 percent, allowing more than 2.9 million children to move out of poverty (Marks, 2003).[306]

Leaving aside the question of whether 16% of children in poverty constitutes anything like a 'plummet', the numbers eight years later (in 2011) told a different story. In that year, 23% of America's children were living in households with incomes below the official poverty thresholds.[307] By 2015, 22% of children still lived in families with incomes below the poverty threshold, although almost 40% of US children had lived below that threshold for at least one year before the age of 18, three-quarters of black children and 30% of white children (Picchi, 2015; Ratcliffe, 2015). But the official poverty threshold used to measure these proportions is grossly inadequate at measuring the proportion of the population who are destitute (see below). An income above this line does not mean that someone has left poverty behind if that income is still not enough to buy basic necessities. So the official figures grossly understate the proportion of the population in poverty. However, even on the official figures, 'welfare reform' can hardly be counted a success, much less an unqualified one.

Dissenting voices

Others are not so sanguine about the success of 'welfare reform'. TANF has been described as AFDC's 'bitterly worse successor' (Albelda and Withorn 2001: 9), and as, 'in human terms, a catastrophic mistake' (Ehrenreich, 2010:

---

306. The focus on 'child poverty' (rather than poverty more generally) is one of the triumphs of the right-wing, neo-liberal approach to social policy. I once asked a well-known poverty researcher (who shall remain nameless) the reason for this focus, and he said it was because we know that children are not to blame for their own poverty, and hence (presumably) helping them is justified. The implication here is that adults are to blame for their own poverty, and hence helping them is not justified. My response was that most people are not to blame for their own poverty, that poverty was a consequence of the way the economy was organised. (I think he had walked away by that time). I don't know whether he actually believed this himself, or whether he was simply telling me what was generally believed to be the reason for the focus on 'child' poverty.

307. http://datacenter.kidscount.org/data/acrossstates/Rankings.aspx?ind=43.

217). Another commentator said: 'Despite claims by politicians and policy makers that the 50% reduction in the welfare rolls is proof of its resounding success, many women are in fact barely surviving' (Roschelle, 2008: 195). A Health and Human Services official, Peter Edelman, referred to PRWORA as 'the worst thing [Bill Clinton] has ever done', and resigned in protest, as did Mary Jo Bane, another Department of Health and Human Services official (Kennedy, 1998: 254n). Three members of Clinton's own party were outraged. 'How, how can any person of faith, of conscience, vote for a bill that will put a million more kids into poverty?' said one. 'The Republicans will throw two million people, children, into poverty, and my President will only throw one million into poverty', said another. And another one called the legislation '[t]his deadly and Draconian piece of garbage' that 'will do nothing to reform the conditions of poverty and unemployment suffered by our Nation's most vulnerable' (Kennedy, 1998: 255n101). To no avail. The legislation was supported by a majority in both Houses and Clinton was unmoved.

Even staunch 'welfare reformers' thought that PRWORA had gone too far. Daniel Patrick Moynihan, Democratic Senator for New York at the time, was opposed to the legislation from the outset, both because of the time limits and because removing federal responsibility for the poor was, he said, '"the most brutal act of social policy since Reconstruction"' (Butz, 2012: 55). He called PRWORA 'a truly awful welfare bill—one that cuts off benefits to millions of poor children' (Moynihan, 1996: 40); he referred to 'millions of infants [being] put to the sword' (p.41); and he said in a letter to Clinton: 'To drop 2,414,000 black and Hispanic dependent children from our federal life support system would surely be the most brutal act of social policy since Reconstruction' (p.58).

And yet, his own position was not so very far removed from that of the 'reformers'. As author of *The Negro Family: The Case for National Action* (1965), he believed that single motherhood and their reliance on 'welfare' was the ruination of the African-American segment of the population; and as a supporter of the 1988 Family Support Act (Baum, 1991; Oliker, 1994; Szanton, 1991) (see below) he was a staunch believer in the existence of 'welfare dependency' and not at all averse to 'put[ting] welfare mothers to work' (Moynihan, 1996: 40). As a member of his staff put it:

> our intent [in the Family Support Act] was to increase parental responsibility for children. We wanted to obligate absent parents (usually fathers) to pay court-ordered child support. We wanted to obligate custodial parents (usually mothers) to try to become self-sufficient by

preparing for and taking jobs. Toward that end, we wanted to establish new state-designed education, training, and work-experience programs in which able-bodied AFDC adults would be required to participate. When AFDC families worked their way off welfare, we wanted them to have some transitional assistance with medical care and child care, so that they could afford to take entry-level jobs and still remain independent of welfare. Finally, we wanted to extend the AFDC program to all poor families, including those with both parents in the home (Baum, 1991: 607).

Like the architects of PRWORA, Moynihan and the other earlier 'welfare reformers' displayed a dissociated obliviousness to the social importance of the work the women were already doing in raising their children, and to the social structural causes of the poverty of women and children without an adult male wage. Still, he seemed to feel that PRWORA went too far.

Fine words from the United Nations notwithstanding, 'secure access to the basic requirements of human development' is not what 'welfare reform' provided, nor what it was intended to provide. The most that can be said about PRWORA's 'success' is that it was an unprecedented success in reducing the welfare rolls, and an unmitigated failure in reducing poverty.

Frances Fox Piven

Another dissenting voice was Frances Fox Piven. She referred to PRWORA as 'the logic of unfettered greed', and attributed it to 'a business class on a roll as it moves to use public policy to shore up private profits' (Piven, 2001: 28-9). She argued that the dramatic decreases in the welfare rolls did not mean the end of extreme poverty. On the contrary, poverty had increased since the passing of PRWORA, although little attention had been paid to this consequence of 'welfare reform'. She said that it was 'adding several million desperately poor women' to a the bottom of a labour market of already insecure jobs, while the workfare provisions were 'creating a virtually indentured labor force' (p.33). 'The propelling force behind the campaign against welfare', she said,

arises not from some quasi-mystical economic globalization but from business politics and from the political ideas and political strategies conceived by business and the political Right (Piven, 2001: 35).

Piven is a long-time social activist,[308] who has been protesting for many years against 'welfare' policies in the US (along with her husband, Richard Cloward, who died in 2001). Their early work was a major influence on the

_____
308. http://asteria.fivecolleges.edu/findaids/sophiasmith/mnsss52_bioghist.html.

National Welfare Rights Organization, of which she was a founder, the first in a long line of grass-roots organisations Piven was involved with. In the 1960s, she worked with welfare-rights groups encouraging people to apply for the benefits they were entitled to under the legislation, and legally challenging the most unjust aspects of 'welfare' policy. During the 1980s and 1990s, she continued to campaign against welfare cutbacks, including PRWORA. In 2016, she was still a Distinguished Professor of Political Science and Sociology in the Graduate School and University Center at the City University of New York, where she continued to teach;[309] and she continued to serve on the boards of many advocacy groups like Community Voices Heard, where she shared not only her knowledge, but also the funds she raised through speaking engagements. Perhaps her best known work, co-written with Cloward, is *Regulating the Poor*, first published in 1971 and updated in 1993.

One of the earliest of their joint publications, a 1966 article called 'The weight of the poor: a strategy to end poverty' (Piven and Cloward, 1966), managed to arouse the ire of a spokesman for the rabid right-wing, a TV shock jock called Glenn Beck (although not until 2010). In January of that year, Beck verbally attacked Piven and her late husband, Richard Cloward, on his television program on Fox News Channel, accusing them of being 'an enemy of the constitution' and of being responsible 'for a plan to "intentionally collapse our economic system"' (Stelter, 2011). As a consequence of Beck's attacks, Piven received death threats from his thuggish followers, both on his website and via her own email account.

'The weight of the poor' argued that, if everyone who was eligible for welfare enrolled to make valid claims for assistance, the system would become overloaded and be forced to change. The problems it caused might even lead to a guaranteed minimum income. According to the Fox News shock-jock, this was '"economic sabotage"'. It was a plan '"to overwhelm the system and bring about the fall of capitalism by overloading the government bureaucracy with impossible demands and bring on economic collapse"' (Stelter, 2011). Piven continued to be targeted by Beck throughout the following year, culminating in a reaction to another of Piven's articles, this time recommending that unemployed people stage mass protests '"something like the strikes and riots that have spread across Greece"'. Beck's reaction was to accuse her of inciting violence. She answered that the massing of people was not in itself violent, and that Beck was trying to frighten his viewers.

---

309. https://www.gc.cuny.edu/Page-Elements/Academics-Research-Centers-Initiatives/
    Doctoral-Programs/Political-Science/Faculty-Bios/Frances-Fox-Piven.

Fox News Channel is owned by Rupert Murdoch and not surprisingly, management refused to censure Beck or order him to stop his vilification, saying that Beck personally was not recommending violence on his program and that they had no control over what was posted on his website. The Center for Constitutional Rights, who had requested the Channel to stop Beck making inflammatory allegations against Piven, pointed out that '"there comes a point when constant intentional repetition of provocative, incendiary, emotional misinformation and falsehoods about a person can put that person in actual physical danger of a violent response"'.

As far as I know, no commentator has noted what is really interesting about Beck's diatribes, and that is his conviction that poverty is essential for the continued existence of the capitalist economy, and that without poverty the system would collapse. In this he is in complete agreement with Marx. But Marx deplored the connection between capitalism and poverty and saw the end of capitalism as a good thing. Beck on the other hand, as a faithful scion of the right wing, deplored any threat to capital whatsoever, including attempts to ameliorate its worst effects.

PRWORA and the culture of masculinity

As Piven said, PRWORA is a capitulation to the demands of rich, powerful men whose dissociated arrogance is interested only in the development of their own wealth and influence. Its framers and supporters are convinced they are entitled to their own great wealth while enforcing harsh forms of destitution both on those they employ to generate their profits, and those they won't employ when doing so might impinge on their profits. 'Welfare reform' is only one aspect of an economy dehumanised by the arrogant entitlement of powerful men, and the capitalist economy is only one aspect (although a major one) of a society organised around the limitless rapacity of the US ruling class. But 'welfare reform' is a particularly egregious example of male domination. It was devised by men and imposed on women, and touted as a 'success' despite its dehumanised brutality and its imperviousness to rational criticism. The fact that it is still in existence so many years after the legislation was first passed (in 1996) is a telling indictment of a nation that, while it sells itself as 'the leader of the free world', is really a 'land of misery and plutocracy' (Anelauskas, 1999)[310] (as has become abundantly clear with the

---

310. This book is an excellent resource for evidence about the parlous state of US society, including the military and economic havoc the US has wreaked on the rest of the world in defence of its corporate interests. Anelauskas does not identify the dissociation and

take-over of the US government by the rabid right wing headed by Donald Trump). Male domination is not confined to the US, but US 'welfare reform' provides a stark template for the neo-liberal demolition of the welfare state in the rest of the world.

In saying that 'welfare reform' is the product of a culture of masculinity I am also saying that it is the product of the mentality of the right wing. It was largely orchestrated by the Republicans who controlled both Houses in Congress at the time, even though it was signed into law by a Democratic president. Right-wing meanings and values are structured around fear and hatred of women (see chapters 2 and 12), which can be allayed only by ensuring that women are under the control of men either individually or institutionally, especially their child-bearing capacity. This need of the policy-makers for women to be under the control of men is demonstrated by their panic about 'out-of-wedlock births', described in the Act as 'a crisis in our Nation', and the emphasis on marriage as 'the foundation of a successful society'.

In calling US 'welfare reform' a culture of masculinity I am not suggesting that only men are responsible for the US 'welfare' system. Although there appear to be few (if any) women among the architects of PRWORA, women have always been involved in 'welfare' policy in the US. As Linda Gordon has pointed out:

> [o]ne of the ironies of welfare state development is that in the United States, where women exerted more influence on domestic social policy than in most other countries, female welfare clients (and children) were treated worse than in most other countries (Gordon, 1994: 8).

Women have exerted some influence on 'welfare' policy in the US, at least in relation to the 1935 Social Security Act, Gordon's main focus of attention in her history of single mothers and welfare (Gordon, 1994). But influential though they might have been, these women were working within a system whose meanings and values were already set in train by the principle that only (some) men count as 'human' and women are tolerated only as long as they subscribe to the system. The women did subscribe to some of these values—the belief that only some single mothers were 'deserving', for example. But whatever the values they held most dear, they were powerless in the face of masculinist interests. Gordon referred to these as 'powerful minorities ... southern Congressmen and the economic interests they represented, who demanded protection of their low-wage labor force [strictly speaking,

---

arrogant entitlement of Corporate America as masculine, however. No malestream theorist does.

protection of their right to exploit a low-wage labour force]; and politicians who benefited from patronage power at the state level' (Gordon, 1994: 254, 266). It was these masculinist interests that prevailed in the design of the US 'welfare' system, and the system remains male supremacist, however many women work in it.

Racism

'Welfare reform' is also racist,[311] its chief target being young black women and their children. Young black men are targeted by the criminal 'justice' system. Loïc Wacquant argued that the conflation of young, male blackness with crime 're-activates "race" by giving a legitimate outlet to the expression of anti-black animus in the form of the public vituperation of criminals and prisoners' (Wacquant, 2002: 56). In much the same way, the conflation of young, female blackness with 'welfare' gives a legitimised outlet to the public vituperation of 'welfare'. Indeed, it has been persuasively argued that racism is the reason why the malicious parsimoniousness of 'welfare' is so acceptable to the US population: '[t]he primary reason the American welfare state denies even to white people some of the privileges of citizenship is its reluctance to establish programs that will grant these privileges to Blacks' (Roberts, 1996: 1576n88).

Often the racism is not expressed overtly. The police violence towards black Americans is, of course, about as overt as racism gets. Also overt was Trump's 'executive order' of 27 January 2017 'suspend[ing] entry' to the US of 'for 90 days… of aliens from countries referred to in … the Immigration and Nationality Act … [whether] immigrants and nonimmigrants'. In true Trumpian fashion, the title of this order was a lie screaming in 28pt bold: **PROTECTING THE NATION FROM FOREIGN TERRORIST ENTRY INTO THE UNITED STATES**.[312] It was a lie because it had nothing to say about the real sources of terrorism in the US: the infantile male obsession with guns; the aggrieved entitlement of men and boys at the bottom of the male supremacist pecking order; and the euphemistically named 'domestic violence' perpetrated by men against women because they can. But then it is the function of racism to provide scapegoats to deflect attention from the real culprits. These are not only rich men and their corporations and acolytes who have wrecked the economy, but also the gun-

---

311. Baldwin, 2010; Burnham, 2001, 2002; Flanders et al, 1996; Gordon, 1994; Hancock, 2003; Orloff, 2002; Quadagno, 1994.

312. https://www.whitehouse.gov/the-press-office/2017/01/27/executive-order-protecting-nation-foreign-terrorist-entry-united-states.

toting men and the aggrieved men responsible for the terrible violence of US society. These are the real terrorists, but Trump's order made no mention of them.

But there is also a form of racism that is not acknowledged as such openly. Instead it is coded (Desmond-Harris, 2014; López, 2015), especially in the case of African-Americans. (In the Trump era, there are no holds barred in relation to 'Muslims' or 'Mexicans'). In this form of coding, African-Americans are not mentioned explicitly, but there is a subliminal recognition that that is who is being referred to in pejorative statements about 'welfare' or 'crime'. The mainstream media have made sure of that, to the extent that they are owned and controlled by powerful men who need scapegoats in order to deflect attention from their own depredations.[313]

While I agree that racism is a primary reason why 'welfare reform' is so vicious, the US 'welfare' system is also a creation of arrogant, dissociated masculine entitlement. As I have argued elsewhere (Thompson, 2001: 133-45), the dehumanisation inherent in racism mimics male supremacy's dehumanisation of women. Having already dehumanised women, the world of men is not one of equality and respect; rather, it is a hierarchical realm of worth and worthlessness, worship and contempt, sycophancy and arrogant entitlement, and 'race' is one of the categories used to mark the difference. US society certainly hates its black population, as is demonstrated by the murder of black people by white police who usually escape scot free. But that hatred is part of the masculinity I am talking about. My focus on masculine entitlement and dissociation is an emphasis, not an absolute. Yes, the US 'welfare' system is racist, and behind the racism lies a lethal masculinity to whom black lives matter only as scapegoats for white men's aggrieved entitlement. Murder and mass incarceration (and poverty) are the ways in which US society treats black men, 'welfare' (and poverty) is the way it treats black women. 'Welfare' is so mean, both because it is seen to be something black people need and because it is seen to be something women need.

'Welfare queen'

One of the best known uses of a racially-coded image is that of the 'welfare queen'. As one commentator put it:

---

313. As another liberal 'democracy', Australia has scapegoats too. 'Muslims' and 'asylum seekers' are favourites at the moment (2016), but Aboriginal people are a constant target for right-wing invective, as are the 'unemployed'. 'Asians' seem to have gone out of fashion, although at one time they were vilified as threatening 'hordes'. Although the Australian government has introduced mandatory work requirements for single mothers in emulation of the US pattern, the legislation is not quite as vicious as PRWORA.

the notion of the welfare queen [has] taken on the status of common knowledge, or what is known as a "narrative script". The welfare queen script has two key components: welfare recipients are disproportionately women; and women on welfare are disproportionately African-American (Gilliam, 1999).

Neither of these components is true: most 'welfare' recipients are children; and African-Americans comprise only a minority of the families on 'welfare'. It is true that a woman in Chicago was arrested for 'welfare' fraud, as well as being suspected of numerous offenses she was never charged with. But the image of a 'welfare queen' served purposes far beyond the misdeeds of one woman. She provided the occasion for attacks on 'welfare' across the board, and she has been used ever since as an exemplary instance of a black 'welfare chiseler' to demonise 'welfare' claimants, and as part of the justification for abolishing 'welfare as we know it'. Invariably portrayed as a single black woman, the 'welfare queen' image not only framed the debates on welfare reform, it also had a powerful influence on the formation of official 'welfare' policy (Baldwin, 2010: 37).

The most famous usage was that of Ronald Reagan during his 1976 presidential campaign. "'There's a woman in Chicago'", Reagan is reported to have said, who "'has 80 names, 30 addresses, 12 Social Security cards and is collecting veterans' benefits on four nonexisting deceased husbands … And she's collecting Social Security on her cards. She's got Medicaid, getting food stamps and she is collecting welfare under each of her names. Her tax-free cash income alone is over $150,000'" (Fialka, 1976; Zucchino, 1997: 64-5). The 'welfare queen' terminology was not originally Reagan's, having been first used in an article in the African-American magazine, Jet (1974). The *Chicago Tribune* picked up the story (and the terminology) as part of its reporting on waste, fraud and mismanagement in the Illinois Department of Public Aid. It was also the *Tribune* that exposed her ownership of jewellery, furs and a Cadillac. It was strongly implied that these had been bought with the proceeds of her 'welfare' fraud, although it is more likely that they were stolen or bought with the proceeds of her other criminal activities. According to the journalist who later investigated the woman's career, the *Tribune* focused on this woman in order to make the story more exciting. Simply reporting on bureaucratic mismanagement, he said, 'didn't make for an engaging read … "State orders probe of Medicaid" is not a headline that provokes shock and anger' (Levin, 2013). The 'welfare queen' story was more useful for evoking 'shock and anger' than simply reporting the facts, appealing as it did to already entrenched prejudices about women, 'welfare' and African-Americans. But by focusing the 'shock and anger' on a single, wildly atypical individual, the newspaper diverted attention away from the real problem—the waste, fraud and mismanagement—which was not perpetrated by 'welfare' claimants but by corrupt providers or over-worked caseworkers.

The woman did exist and her exploits were common knowledge, thanks to the *Chicago Tribune*'s campaign. She was referred to as 'Linda Taylor', although her original name was probably Martha Miller and she did have 80 or more aliases. But the woman in Chicago was not a genuine 'welfare' claimant, but a career criminal for whom 'welfare' fraud was just one of her many crimes, and probably not even the worst. Far from being typical of 'welfare' claimants, she was psychopathic and/or psychotic menace who 'destroyed lives' (Levin, 2013). She was 'far more depraved than even Ronald Reagan could have imagined'. There were suspicions (reported in the *Tribune*) that she was a murderer and a kidnapper, and that she stole babies and either sold them or simply left them behind if she couldn't get rid of them in any other way. 'Welfare' fraud was the least of her crimes.

Moreover, despite the prevalent belief that she was African-American,[314] and the widespread use of 'welfare queen' to demonise black women (and the fact that her 'welfare'-fraud case was first reported in *Jet*), she was probably not black, although she did pose as a black woman in order to claim 'welfare'. She was recorded as 'white' in the 1940 census and on her son's birth certificate (Levin, 2013).

Interestingly, the 'welfare queen' article appeared in a section of the *Jet* magazine titled 'The Sexes'. This is most likely a code for 'women', but it is not clear why the sex of the fraudster was highlighted in this way. Surely such categories as, say, 'welfare fraud' or 'crime in Chicago' or 'the Illinois criminal justice system' or 'police investigations' would be more relevant to the story than the sex of the accused. A 'welfare queen' can only be a woman, but she was hardly so typical of women in general that her story could be placed under a heading that included all women. Except, of course, subliminally. Perhaps the very real monstrosity of this woman awakened that infantile misogynist fear of the 'monstrous feminine' (Creed, 1993), that archetype of male dread that locates monstrosity with all women because any woman can take away his power. Creed puts this in terms of a male fear of castration and the 'vagina dentata', and while I see this as partly correct, I prefer to see it in terms of power. In male supremacist terms, the penis is the symbol of 'human' status and hence the symbol of his power over women. He fears

---

314. 'The woman Reagan was talking about was African-American' (Gilliam, 1999).

women because he fears that women will do to him what he does to them, i.e. render him powerless. In the infantile psyche nurtured by male supremacist imaginings, that happens by taking away his penis. That women can indeed make him powerless is seen to be obvious, given that a woman once had the power of life and death over him, when he was an infant and, more importantly (given the murderous rage evoked in the right-wing mind by abortion), when he was a foetus in utero. A truly monstrous woman such as this 'Linda Taylor' is not seen as a single, atypical individual, but as a representative of what men unconsciously fear most—the destroying female who lurks within every woman.

These are the subliminal fears motivating 'welfare reform' (and not just one African-American writing in a popular magazine). Women applying for 'welfare' are women who are not under the control of men, especially their child-bearing capacity. They must be brought back under control and rendered powerless through marriage and bureaucratic disentitlement. These are the fears aroused by the 'welfare queen' lie spread by Reagan, aided and abetted by a mass media more interested in appealing to ignorance and prejudice than in telling the truth. They did not invent the woman or her exploits, but they did lie by implying that this woman was representative of 'welfare' claimants in general. They also lied by implying that the problem of fraud was largely committed by claimants, rather than by the providers, e.g. 'doctors who billed Medicaid for fictitious procedures', or over-worked caseworkers deprived of the resources to do their jobs properly (Levin, 2013). Combined with the fear and loathing of the descendants of slaves that permeates US culture, this makes for a lethal social reality.

These misogynist and racist codes operate to keep the 'welfare' system small and mean, and to enable politicians to win votes by doing so, although it would seem that it is not 'welfare' per se that Americans hate. According to Martin Gilens, survey after survey shows that they strongly support it, and believe that the government is not doing enough for education, health care, child care, the elderly, the homeless or the poor (Gilens, 1999: 2). What the American public hate, he says, is 'welfare' being given to the 'undeserving' poor, those perceived as 'lazy'. And the undeserving poor, those who 'would rather sit at home and collect benefits than work hard to support themselves' (p.3), are invariably perceived by 'the American public' as black. Farcical though the 'welfare queen' image might be, it appeals to the race hatred that festers in the American psyche and, not incidentally, serves a function for the less eligibility principle necessary for maintaining a low-wage economy (see below). If 'welfare' recipients can use their benefits to ride around in Cadillacs and buy jewellery and fur coats, it justifies keeping benefits low.

'Welfare reform' and the slave-owner mentality

Racism is not peculiar to the US. Rather, it is a worldwide phenomenon. The details vary from place to place—the treatment of African-Americans is different from the treatment of indigenous Australians, for example, and both are different from anti-Semitism, and from the internecine conflicts between the Serbs and Croats, and from the massacres of the Tutsis by the Hutus in Rwanda. What they all have in common is a denial of the humanity of some category of persons and the power to violate these people's basic human rights, even their right to life.

What is peculiar to the US version of racism is the nation's history of slavery and the compromises made with slave-owners and the wealthy white men who are their ideological descendants. The very existence of African-American people is a constant reproach for the atrocities of slavery. But those who profit from it and its modern derivatives will not acknowledge their own complicity and instead project the problem of race onto its victims by portraying them as responsible for their own poverty. And rich white men and their media representatives have the power to win a significant proportion of the US population to their point of view through a mass media that purvey the interests of the powerful as the interests of all, and create and shape people's attitudes towards 'welfare', poverty and the poor (among other things) (Chomsky and Herman, 1988).

Slavery and 'welfare reform' are 'genealogically linked', just as slavery is linked to the mass imprisonment of black men (Wacquant, 2002). Loïc Wacquant has argued that it is not possible to understand the US prison system—'its timing, composition, and smooth onset as well as the quiet ignorance or acceptance of its deleterious effects on those it affects' (Wacquant, 2002: 41)—without first understanding slavery 'as historic starting point and functional analogue'. In the same way, it is not possible to understand 'welfare reform' without linking it to the nation's heritage of slavery. The stereotype of blacks as lazy, for example, 'grew out of, and was used to defend, slavery' (Gilens, 1999: 3). For that reason I prefer the terminology 'slave-owner mentality' to 'racism', because it more precisely describes in the US context. As researchers have noted:

> the congressional/presidential embrace of the principles embodied in
> PRWORA makes perfect sense: ... they represented the interests of
> the people who put them in power, people whose class interests pursue

the logic of global capital. The premises of that logic include a flexible, contingent—and terrified—workforce and the substitution for real jobs of mandatory work activity. That arrangement is terribly like what was once called slavery in America, an arrangement also protected and promoted by the state (Baptist and Bricker-Jenkins, 2001: 148).

'Workfare' displays this modern version of the slave-owner mentality particularly clearly. It has always been an aspect of supposed 'welfare' systems, but PRWORA embraced it even more enthusiastically than its predecessors did. While workfare is not chattel slavery where the master owns the slave outright, it is a form of slavery, both because it is coerced and because the workers are not paid a living wage; nor are they even paid the going rate in the low-wage economy. As one commentator noted,

[p]rograms that force recipients to perform menial labor for subsistence benefits resemble involuntary servitude more than the creation of meaningful work. Work programs cannot possibly enable untrained and poorly educated women to achieve financial self-sufficiency, especially in an economy structured against women and with diminishing demand for unskilled workers (Roberts, 1996: 1583).

The reason the women don't get work, she said, was because the jobs paid poverty wages and the women lost their benefits and the child care and health cover when they took those jobs. Workfare is even worse than what Marxists used to call 'wage slavery', i.e. working in demeaning or dangerous jobs coerced by the whip of hunger, since there is no pretence that the jobs 'welfare' recipients are forced to take pay any wages at all. 'Welfare's' callous disregard for the lives and human dignity of those who fail to thrive under the capitalist mode of production stems from the logic of workfare: the demand for a large pool of readily available, ever cheaper labour, both on the part of capital and on the part of a corporatised state doing capital's bidding.

PRWORA's 'work participation' requirement was (and is) more often used as a tool of bureaucratic disentitlement (see below) than as a variant of slave labour. However, the mentality that produced workfare and 'welfare reform' is the same slave-owner mentality that feels itself entitled to exploit human beings for profit, or, in the case of corporatised public organisations, for reducing the supposed 'budget deficit' while cutting taxes for the rich.

Frances Fox Piven gave a number of examples of workfare being used as what she referred to as 'a virtually indentured labor force':

In Baltimore, for example, welfare recipients were used to break a strike of housekeepers in the Baltimore Omni Hotel. In New York City, some 45,000 welfare recipients are now cleaning the streets and the subways, doing jobs previously held by unionized public workers. In Mississippi, welfare recipients are assigned to chicken-processing and catfish plants, and one manager told the press cheerfully that he had been assured by welfare officials that women who did not work out at the plant would not be given welfare again (Piven, 2001: 29).

Another example involved the use of 'workfare labor' by the New York City Department of Parks and Recreation as part of New York's Work Experience Program (WEP). This program, which was touted as the largest workfare program in the US when it was initiated in 1995 by the then mayor, Rudolph Giuliani, involved 'public assistance recipients work[ing] off their benefits in government and nonprofit agencies' (Cohen, 1999: 4). WEP was still operative in 2012, when the New York City's Human Resources Administration website said: 'The Work Experience Program (WEP) is designed to provide a simulated work experience to individuals receiving cash assistance. Through this program, an employable individual is assigned to work for his/her cash assistance and food stamp benefits at NYC government agencies or private, not-for-profit agencies throughout the five boroughs'.[315] At around the same time (2012), New York City mayor, Michael Bloomberg, was quoted in an UNDP publication saying: 'In New York City, we are working to better the lives of our residents in many ways', although WEP was not mentioned as one of these ways (UNDP, 2013: 9, Box 3). By 2016, twenty years after PRWORA became law, WEP was still in existence, although now it was being administered by the City's Department of Sanitation. Public Assistance recipients were referred to this Department by the Human Resources Administration, 'to be placed in clerical, custodial and street cleaning assignments'.[316]

The early days of this program were described in a report by a Columbia University academic (Cohen, 1999) who, however, was hardly an unbiased observer. His research was paid for 'with the generous support of the PricewaterhouseCoopers Endowment on the Business of Government'. The ethical status of PwC (as it is familiarly known) is somewhat dubious (to put it mildly). It is one of the four biggest accounting firms in the world, and it kept signing off on the toxic financial products produced by the banking

---

315. http://www.nyc.gov/html/hra/html/programs/employment_services.shtml.   This statement can no longer be found on the internet, probably because of the change in departments. In other states WEP is often euphemistically termed 'internship' (http://www.opportunityjobnetwork.com/delaware/work-experience-rev1.html).

316. http://www1.nyc.gov/assets/dsny/about/inside-dsny/work-enrichment-program.shtml.

industry, that were directly responsible for the 2008 global financial crisis. In August 2016, PwC settled a $5.5 billion lawsuit over its failure to expose the massive fraud at one of the mortgage lenders it was supposedly auditing (Fitzgerald, 2016).

Not surprisingly, this author said he 'takes no position on the policy issue of workfare' (and he certainly wouldn't use the terms like 'slavery' or 'indentured labour' to describe it). Nonetheless, the 'people', most of them women, were not paid wages by the Department for whom they worked 'picking up trash in parks' and cleaning 'bathrooms' (i.e. public toilet blocks). But if they refused to do it, they lost their benefits. In full accord with the values of his paymaster, the author referred to this particular instance of workfare as 'cutting edge business practices'. Such a business practice, he said, was very useful 'during a time of continued budget stringency'. It resulted in an undoubted good—it kept the parks clean. The City saved money by not having to pay wages while still getting the work done. If it weren't for the labour of 'welfare' recipients, New York's parks would have been in a bad way because the Department had been cutting back on paid staff for years.

The stance taken by this intrepid researcher is not surprising, given who paid for his research. But there are important ethical issues involved that this author ignores. Not to pay people even the minimum wage, while coercing them to work by threatening to take away the pittance 'welfare' pays, is similar to employing slave labour. As Wisconsin State Senator, Gwen Moore, said to business leaders at a forum on Wisconsin's workfare program, W-2 ('Wisconsin Works'): '"This is just a way of delivering low-wage workers to your businesses … We've already done that. We've had a civil war over it"' (Bauer, 1996). Forgetting history as a prerequisite for continued exploitation verges on social dementia; and not to take a stand against this modern form of slavery is to take academic 'objectivity' to the point of dissociation.

PRWORA's meanness

The Act overall is small-minded and mean, but there are particular clauses which display such hostility towards the most powerless members of society, it is hard to believe that the US can still call itself a democracy.

Medicaid

People can have their Medicaid coverage terminated for any perceived 'failure to meet work requirements' (although their children can still be covered). Given that 'work requirements' are largely the occasion for bureaucratic disentitlement, it is not hard to imagine that, for some people, this would be a death sentence. And the US already has the highest rate of deaths from treatable conditions in the developed world (Nolte and McKee, 2008).

Food stamps

PRWORA made access to food stamps more difficult by also tying it to 'work participation'. Not only does the 'welfare' recipient herself become ineligible for food stamps, so do her children. Single people, i.e. anyone who is not 'a parent or other member of a household with responsibility for a dependent child … [or] pregnant', cannot get food stamps for any longer than three months in each three-year period unless they work or 'participate in a work program' for 20 hours a week.

Child support

Then there is PRWORA's position on child support. Women who are receiving 'welfare' must sign over to the State their right to any money collected from fathers as child support. The State must then forward this money to the federal government to reimburse it for the federal component of the 'welfare' payment. The State can pay whatever is left to the family but it can also keep it to reimburse itself for its own component of the 'welfare' payment. This is one reason why men resent paying child support—it doesn't go to the children and their mother, it goes to the government.

Responsibility for the behaviour of others

The Act makes people responsible for the behaviour of others. Recipients can be sanctioned, for example, if their children truant, and if the father is a minor and doesn't pay child support, his parents can be made to pay it.

'Aliens'

PRWORA denies supplemental security income (SSI, the disability support program) and food stamps to non-citizens, called 'aliens' in the wording of the Act, even those who are 'qualified', i.e. who are in the country legally. They can receive TANF and Medicaid after they have lived in the US for five years, but only if the State they are living in decides to grant it. Illegal immigrants cannot receive federal benefits at all, and PRWORA explicitly forbids State and local programs from giving them benefits as well.

According to one source (Harvard Law Review, 2005: 2247), Congress was 'address[ing] voter outrage' towards immigrants with these changes to immigrant eligibility for public benefits. Polls had found that 72% of respondents wanted a reduction in immigration, while 58% agreed 'that immigrants took "more from the U.S. economy through social services and unemployment than they contribute[d] through taxes and productivity'". However, Congress is highly selective about what kind of 'voter outrage' it will address. It has so far been reluctant, for example, to address the outrage expressed at the absence of a universal health-care system, or that expressed against its wars in the Middle East, or at the issues of inequality and injustice raised by the Occupy Movement. Voter outrage against immigration is whipped up by the mass media and the pollsters. Migrants, especially if they can be identified as 'Muslims' or 'Mexicans', do tend to provide handy scapegoats for diverting attention from the real cause of the poverty and degradation afflicting so many US citizens.[317]

SSI

Perhaps the most mean-spirited part of an Act replete with niggardliness was its narrowing of eligibility standards for children with disabilities. PRWORA introduced a more restrictive definition of eligibility that applied only to child cases, and required redetermination of eligibility based on adult criteria when an SSI child turned 18. There is little information about the consequences of these changes, but it has been estimated that, by 2001, there were 250,000 eligible cases (22%) fewer than there would have been without the PRWORA changes (Schmidt, 2004).

Children and their mothers

PRWORA allows for children to be eligible for TANF cash assistance (as long as they remain 'children', i.e. under the age of 18) while their mothers[318] receive nothing on their own behalf. Children can also be eligible for food stamps and Medicaid[319] even though their mothers are not. There are a

---

317. From a 2007 research report from the State of Connecticut General Assembly: 'The 1996 federal PRWORA legislation generally barred new legal immigrants from federally funded assistance programs for their first five years in the U.S. It made exceptions for certain groups, including political asylees and refugees. (Subsequent enactments eased some of PROWRA's restrictions.) In response, the legislature established state-funded programs to ensure that this assistance remained available. These programs continue to operate [in 2007], despite attempts by the Executive Branch to eliminate them' (http://www.cga.ct.gov/2007/rpt/2007-R-0705.htm).

318. Since they are mainly mothers, I refuse to use the euphemising term, 'parents'.

319. Under Obama's 2010 Affordable Care Act, from January 2014 'parents of children will be eligible at a uniform income level across all states'. Adults are eligible if they have incomes 'below 133 percent of the federal poverty level' (http://www.medicaid.gov/AffordableCareAct/Provisions/Eligibility.html). This will probably change with the advent of the Trump administration, who are determined to repeal the Affordable Care Act.

number of reasons why a mother might not be eligible for TANF: she is already receiving a disability pension (Supplemental Security Income or SSI); she is a recent immigrant; the child is not living with their mother; she has been subjected to a sanction which has withdrawn the assistance she had been receiving (Zedlewski, 2002: 7n2); or she has reached the lifetime limit on 'welfare' receipt. The US Office of Family Assistance gave the following percentages for each reason for child-only assistance. In over two-fifths of the child-only cases (43%), the children were not living with their mothers ('No Parent in Assistance Unit'). In just over a quarter of the cases (25.4%), the mother was not receiving assistance because she was a recent immigrant, while just under a quarter of the mothers (22.9%) were in receipt of disability benefits (SSI). Nearly eight percent (7.6%) of the mothers were not receiving benefits because they had been sanctioned, while another 1.1% were not receiving them for 'Other' reasons (US OFA, 2016a: Table 8). The money is supposedly earmarked for the child although it is, of course, paid to the relevant adult, the child by definition not being a responsible adult.

Child-only cases are a significant proportion of the post-PRWORA 'welfare' population. In some states (Florida, Georgia, Idaho, Illinois and Louisiana) three-quarters or more of the TANF caseload is child-only assistance (Zedlewski and Golden, 2010: 3). Nationwide in 2000, the mother was not eligible for assistance in just over a quarter (26%) of TANF families (Zedlewski, 2002: 7n2). Between 2000-2005 the number of child-only cases grew (Danielson and Klerman, 2008: 710), and in 2009 the average number per month of child-only cases where no adult received benefits was nearly half of the 1.8 million families receiving cash assistance under TANF (Lower-Basch, 2011b: 1). In Fiscal Year 2015, child-only receipt of TANF still comprised nearly half the TANF families (48.6% or 648,669 families out of a total of 1,333,707 families) (US OFA, 2016a: Table 5).

The notion that the children's welfare is separate from their mothers' well-being is bizarre. It is typical of masculinist dissociation from the realities of the lives of women and children, not to mention the policy-makers' own humanity. Is the mother to whom the money is paid not to use it for herself? What if that is the only income coming into the household? Is she expected to feed, clothe and provide accommodation for her children but not for herself? Do her children live in the house while she doesn't? Do they eat while she starves? Are they clothed while she is dressed in rags and tatters?

It is true that these questions are not realistic. Given how meagre the benefit payments are, they pay for hardly anything anyway. But such questions do point to the crazed assumptions that must lie behind the US 'welfare' system. And crazed assumptions have crazed effects. Reducing payments to mothers breaks up families. Low 'welfare' benefits have been found to be related to higher rates of foster care. Foster care payments are higher than TANF payments (especially reduced or cancelled TANF payments), and they are paid to the whole family. But a woman cannot foster her own children, so she must give them over to someone else if they are to have access to more income than she is allowed:

> foster care may serve as a substitute for welfare … foster families may receive payments as foster families that exceed the welfare benefits the mother could have qualified for had she retained the child in her own care—providing families in states with low welfare benefits with incentives to place children in foster care … [and in fact,] children living in states with low welfare benefits are more likely to be living away from their parents (Paxson and Waldfogel, 1999: 21).

States are required to give priority to foster care with relatives, but foster care is still detrimental for children: 'Children in foster care are at high risk for emotional, behavioral, developmental, and physical health problems' (Barbell and Freundlich, 2001: 6). But then, the architects of PRWORA were not really concerned about children's well-being, and the Trump administration is likely to be even less concerned.

Reauthorisation

PRWORA was due to expire in September 2002 and to be reauthorised that same year. However, disagreements between the House of Representatives and the Senate on what changes to make, meant that reauthorisation was delayed, and PRWORA remained in force as originally intended by way of a series of extensions passed by Congress (King and Mueser, 2005: 4; Lower-Basch, 2011a: 3). Reauthorisation was finally achieved in the Deficit Reduction Act (DRA) of 2005 (passed in February 2006). Despite research indicating the need for relaxing some of the harsher requirements imposed on 'welfare' claimants (Paxson and Waldfogel, 1999), the DRA actually increased their severity. TANF was scheduled for reauthorisation again five years later in 2010, but again it was postponed and the 2005 modifications were simply extended multiple times (CLASP).[320] It was extended again to September 2016 as part of the 2016 fiscal year appropriations package.[321]

Other social-assistance programs

The majority of 'welfare' recipients are single mothers and their children (Acs et al, 2003: 7). Some of the families who are so poor they require 'welfare' if they are to survive are two-parent families, and the federal government does provide some funding for them. Called AFDC-UP (Unemployed Parent), it was established in 1961 and continued under TANF. Until the 1988 Family Support Act extended UP benefits to two-parent families across all the States (to take effect by 1990), the States did not have to provide it, and at that time (1988), 22 States did not have a UP program. UP has stricter work requirements for eligibility than AFDC/TANF. The principal earner has to have had a recent work history and must not be currently working too many hours, no matter how low paid the job (Winkler, 1993). It has always been a very small program. Two-parent families comprise only 5% of TANF families (Zedlewski, 2002: 7n2; Hahn et al, 2012b: 18). Their numbers are limited by the workforce restrictions (Epstein, 1997: 23), as well as by the fact that people don't know of its existence (Winkler, 1993).

Consequently, 'welfare reform' is directed at only part of the poor population, while large numbers of people—childless adults, childless families and immigrants—are ignored, or explicitly excluded in the case of immigrants (Handler, 2008: 25). In 2000, single parents (mainly women) made up 66% of the 'welfare' caseload, while 26% of families did not have an eligible parent, i.e. they were children only. So the TANF program instituted by 'welfare reform' is, by and large, only for women and children. There are no federally-funded poverty-alleviation programs for childless men who have never worked or whose employment history is intermittent: 'poor, able-bodied, single males ... are expected to be self-sufficient without government assistance ... They are ineligible for any federally subsidized form of public assistance, and must rely on state-funded general assistance programs' (Schram, 1995: 126). Or, as another commentator put it: 'Able-bodied men without dependents have been consigned to the institutional oblivion of state general assistance' (Backer, 1995: 387n236) (And presumably this is also true

320. The Center for Law and Social Policy. This is a public-interest law organisation, started in 1969 by four lawyers inspired by the Civil Rights Movement (http://www.clasp.org/federal-policy/legislation-and-reauthorizations/tanf-reauthorization).

321. http://www.naco.org/resources/reauthorize-temporary-assistance-needy-families-tanf-block-grant-0.

for poor, able-bodied, single females). Those US citizens who are poor and childless and have no recent employment history, receive no cash assistance from the federal government at all (although they can receive food stamps and Medicaid), but are dependent on state programs of General Assistance, which States are not obliged to provide.

There is provision for unemployment benefits for those who have been employed but who are now 'unemployed through no fault of their own (as determined under State law)'.[322] These are 'intended to provide temporary financial assistance to unemployed workers who meet the requirements of State law'. The unemployment scheme is administered by each State with oversight by the Employment and Training Administration of the federal Department of Labor. Each State has different requirements and conditions for receipt of unemployment benefits, although in most States the maximum length of time for which benefits can be paid is 26 weeks. It is largely funded by payroll taxes (although in three States, applicants are required to have contributed something themselves to be eligible). There is provision for Extended Benefits,[323] a further benefit-period of up to 13 weeks 'during periods of high unemployment', and some States have provision for an extra seven weeks 'during periods of extremely high unemployment'. However, 'not everyone who qualified for regular benefits will qualify for Extended Benefits'.[324]

Unsurprisingly, this is a program with a number of bureaucratic disentitlements (see below), not least of which is the fact that it is temporary. Once the 26-week period has come to an end, that is the end of the social safety net for that person. It is true that there is provision to extend that period, but whether or not it is extended depends on official decisions at the State level about the state of the economy, not on the situation of the individual unemployed person. The American Recovery and Reinvestment Act, which was passed in February 2009 as a response to the global financial crisis, provided federal money to the States to enable them to extend unemployment benefits beyond the usual limits, but that was a temporary measure. That money was no longer being provided by the 2012 fiscal year (US CBO, 2015: 2, Table 1). Moreover, even the 26-week period can be reduced whenever a State administration so decides, as can the amount of the benefits received. The *Denver Post* reported at the beginning of 2016 that,

---

322. https://workforcesecurity.doleta.gov/unemploy/uifactsheet.asp.

323. https://workforcesecurity.doleta.gov/unemploy/extenben.asp.

324. https://eligibility.com/unemployment.

'since the end of the Great Recession, eight States have reduced the number of weeks that people can draw benefits, while others have cut the amount of money the unemployed can collect'. Missouri, for example, halved the time period from 26 to 13 weeks (Associated Press, 2016). Moreover, casual, part-time and self-employed workers are not eligible for unemployment benefits. The US 'welfare' system more generally is no kinder to the men who fail to thrive under capitalism than it is to women.

There is also the government-funded Supplemental Security Income (SSI) program for the aged, blind, and disabled, and Social Security. The latter consists of retirement, survivors, and disability insurance programs drawn upon in the event of illness, accident or death of the wage-earner, and as an old-age pension. It is not funded by the federal government, but rather by FICA taxes (Federal Insurance Contributions Act). Employers and employees each pay 6.2 percent of wages up to $118,000 (in 2014). Both of these are administered by the Social Security Administration (SSA).

Then there are the federal non-cash programs: food stamps (the name was changed to Supplemental Nutrition Assistance Program or SNAP on 1 October 2008); the Women, Infant and Children Food Program (WIC); food programs for schools and for the elderly; Medicare (for those over 65 and people with disabilities) and Medicaid (for people on low incomes); some public housing; and an Earned Income Tax Credit for the working poor. Receipt of these programs, however, does not add up to a living wage. The existence of SNAP and other food programs means that there is less starvation in the US than would have been the case if people's access to food was wholly dependent on the capitalist economy. But having to use food stamps to keep one's self and family from starvation is degrading because it broadcasts the fact of one's poverty. And it is never enough. Receipt of food stamps is intermittent—there are limits on how many food stamps a family can get in any one month. No one could escape starvation on food stamps alone. And yet US politicians, especially Republicans, constantly seek to reduce people's entitlements even further (see below).

The principle of 'less eligibility'

This has been described as 'the oldest principle in the provision of relief to the poor', one that demands 'that the system of public assistance and benefit levels should in no way interfere with the (moral and economic) imperative to work' (Peck, 1998a: 546). 'Welfare' serves important functions for capitalist societies (by subsidising the low-wage economy), but that cannot be acknowledged because capitalist societies are 'democracies' and must be seen to operate in the interests of all including the disadvantaged. So 'welfare' must give the appearance of helping the disadvantaged while not threatening the system of wealth and power that causes the disadvantage. While purporting to provide assistance to those who cannot provide for themselves, 'welfare' must not intrude upon the prerogatives of the powerful by impeding the generation of profit. As the editors of *The Mean Season* put it:

> the American welfare state is in many way a flawed and fragmented creation … [its] programs represent an uneasy compromise between the demands of the economically vulnerable and the resistance of the economically powerful (Block et al, 1987: xi).

All 'welfare' systems must adhere to what is known as 'the principle of less eligibility', which is actually a principle of less desirability. This is the rule, stated explicitly in the English Poor Law Commissioners' report of 1834, that the situation of 'welfare' recipients must be less desirable than that of the lowest paid wage-earners:

> "The first and most essential of all conditions, a principle which we find universally admitted, even by those whose practice is at variance with it, is, that his [the relief recipient's] situation on the whole shall not be made really or apparently so eligible [i.e., desirable] as the situation of the independent laborer of the lowest class" (quoted in Piven and Cloward, 1993: 35).

The principle ordains that there must be no viable alternative to wage labour, for if there were, it is believed, people would not want to work in the kinds of jobs capitalism provides. So no 'welfare' system provides an income sufficient to live on, even at the most frugal level.

The 'eligibility principle' was reiterated in the US in the early 1990s by a Panel on Poverty and Family Assistance established by the Committee on National Statistics of the National Research Council. The Panel was formed in response to a request from Congress that they investigate the possibility of a new poverty measure to replace the one currently in use (Blank, 2008). Their report is commonly referred to as the National Academy of Science or NAS report (Citro and Michael, eds, 1995). The authors argued in favour of keeping 'welfare' benefits not only lower than the lowest wages, but also lower than the poverty level, itself a fraction of those same low wages. (Official figures grossly understate the level of poverty in the US. Even people with income twice the poverty level are still poor enough to qualify for social assistance) (see below).

The authors of the NAS report gave several reasons why 'welfare' benefits should be kept lower than the poverty level, although only one of those reasons made any reference to the 'less eligibility' principle (and not under that name). The panel members made what they said was the 'obvious' point that 'measuring need ... is different from determining the proper societal response to that need' (Citro and Michael, eds, 1995: 94-6). '[A] benefit standard could differ from a poverty standard', they said, and 'the design of an assistance program could deviate from the goal of helping everyone who is classified as poor'. But it is not at all obvious that measuring need ought to be different from responding to that need. Indeed, if the aim is to abolish poverty, then 'the proper societal response' ought to be to address the full extent of the need uncovered by the measurement. There are operational difficulties, both with measuring need accurately and with what to do about addressing the problem. But to assert that there are some aspects of poverty that will not be addressed, is to abandon any fight against it.

The first of the reasons the NAS report gave for designing 'an assistance program ... [that] deviate[d] from the goal of helping everyone who is classified as poor' (Citro and Michael, eds, 1995: 95) was 'scarce budget resources'. This 'scarcity' meant that there was a need 'to target payments on particular groups', e.g. poor families with children, or the poorest families. But 'budget resources' for 'welfare' are scarce, not because the money is scarce, but because of political decisions about where the government's priorities lie. Federal governments that are the sovereign issuers of their own currency, like the US federal government (although not State, local or city governments), can spend what they like on anything that can be bought in their own currency (see chapter 10). It would seem that there is no scarcity of resources for the 'war on terrorism' or for bailing out corporations caught in a trap of their own making by their crazed financial behaviour. The reason why 'budget resources' for 'welfare' are scarce is because governments of liberal so-called democracies place so much importance on wealth accumulation in the hands of the few (not to mention macho posturing). From this standpoint, the possibility of an economy that might nurture the population, rather than exploit and degrade it, is inconceivable, literally unthinkable. The fiscal resources of federal governments are rarely scarce. The only scarcity around is that of the policy-makers' humanity.

Another reason given by the NAS report for the paucity of 'welfare' benefits involved 'the existence of multiple assistance programs [which] can affect the level of the benefit standard that makes sense for any one of them'. As an example the authors gave the interaction of AFDC[325] with

---

325. Aid the Families with Dependent Children. The report preceded the passing of PRWORA and the establishment of TANF.

food stamps and housing assistance. 'It makes little sense', they said, 'to think of an AFDC benefit standard in isolation from other programs' (Citro and Michael, eds, 1995: 95). The argument is that it would not be feasible to raise the AFDC benefit to lift people out of poverty, because then they wouldn't be eligible for food stamps or housing assistance. Of course, if they were genuinely lifted out of poverty they wouldn't need such degrading 'assistance' as food stamps. If people cannot afford to buy their own food, they are still poor, no matter how far above that stringent official poverty line their income might be.

The NAS report's (oblique) reference to the less eligibility principle comes with their third and final reason for keeping benefits low. They refer to the 'incentive effects'[326] of any attempt to alleviate need through 'welfare'. Those whose 'incentives' might be affected by a level of 'welfare' benefits that raised them out of poverty are 'families'; and the incentives that might be aroused in them are negative ones, at least from the point of view that maintaining a low-wage economy is a good thing: '[F]amilies who are provided [with] benefits designed to raise them above the poverty line may reduce their work effort so that the net effect is to leave them in poverty' (Citro and Michael, eds, 1995: 95). The authors do not mention either the less eligibility principle or the advantages for wealth and power of a low-wage economy. Instead, they write as though it were to the advantage of 'welfare' recipients themselves to keep them in direst poverty because it gives them a (positive) incentive to keep up their work effort as 'the best way out of poverty'. But in a low-wage economy, this is simply not true.

The principle of less eligibility gives the lie to the familiar right-wing excuse for 'welfare reform', i.e. that it was necessary because 'welfare' as we had come to know it had not abolished poverty. It was never intended to, but rather to maintain it (see chapter 8). 'Welfare reform' is not different. Far from reducing poverty, it was only intended to reduce 'dependency', defined solely in term of 'welfare' receipt. So if the numbers of people 'dependent' on 'welfare' dropped, PRWORA was judged to be successful whatever the means used to achieve the reductions and whatever the consequences. However, although

---

326. This is a typical example of the way in which the discipline of economics uses language. It is both agent-deleted (whose incentives?) and value neutral. The agent deletion allows economics to remove people from its account of the world, both those who prosper from the capitalist system that it serves, and those who are harmed by it. The value-neutrality serves the same purpose in a context where one of the most important issues of the day—widespread poverty in the wealthiest nation on earth—cries out for a principled stance of moral outrage if poverty is to be abolished. Outrage will not in itself abolish poverty, but without it there is not even any motivation to begin the process.

the framers of PRWORA showed a cavalier disregard for the effects of the legislation on poverty levels, poverty cannot be entirely ignored in even the most dissociated debates around 'welfare'. The 'welfare reformers' addressed the issue through the job mantra underpinning workfare: 'the best way out of poverty is a job'. But PRWORA did not fulfil its lying, ideological promise to get people into work that paid a living wage.

The problem with the US 'welfare' system is not only that it is the meanest in the Western World, but that it has made greater concessions to the powerful. 'Welfare' must not intrude upon the business of profit-making, and the lower paid and more docile the workforce, the greater the profits. The US 'welfare' system exists in the context of the lowest wage economy in the developed world. The poor in the US—those whose income is insufficient to get them secure continuous access to food, housing and other necessities—even include people who work in full-time, year-round jobs, so any 'welfare' the system provides must be designed to keep people extremely poor. It is true that poverty in the developed countries would have been worse without a welfare state, even in the US. Food stamps, free medical care and a small amount of income are preferable to nothing at all. But even if the poverty has been less severe than it might have been, it is still poverty with all its insults to health and human dignity. A 'welfare' system can only exist to the extent that it maintains poverty, and the US system has taken that message to heart with a callous enthusiasm unmatched in the Western world. PRWORA continues that dishonourable tradition.

Truth, the first casualty of 'welfare reform'

'Welfare reform' is based on a series of lies. There is the lie that women's childbearing should be under the control of men, expressed in the extolling of marriage as 'the foundation of a successful society' and assertions that 'out-of-wedlock birth' is 'the crisis in our Nation' (see below). There is the lie that PRWORA would lead to employment, when the Act contained no provision for creating employment nor for sanctioning States that did not help women find jobs. There is also the lie that getting a job was the way out of poverty, when the low-wage economy ensures that many people, even in full-time employment cannot earn enough to feed themselves and their families. There is the lie that only 'dependence' on 'welfare' matters, while ignoring dependence on poorly paid, degrading jobs, and women's financial dependence on violent men. There is the lie that PRWORA would 'empower' women—'Most Democrats and Republicans wanted to pass welfare legislation shifting the emphasis from dependence to empowerment'

(Clinton, 2006)—when it only impoverished them further. There is the purveying of these lies to the American public, with corporation-controlled media manufacturing consent to the lie that 'welfare reform' was 'successful'. And above all, there is the lie that federal governments cannot afford to pay for welfare. They can (see chapter 10).

The dissociation characteristic of the culture of masculinity is displayed in the very name of the Act, the inappropriateness of which has been noted by a number of commentators. The historian, Tony Judt, for example, referred to the name of the Act as 'a revealingly Orwellian label' for 'legislation that sought to gut welfare provision'. The legislation, he said, corrupted 'our moral sentiments' and showed that '[w]e have become insensible to the human costs of apparently rational social policies' (Judt, 2010: 23). Jane L. Collins remarked that the legislation was named 'without shame or irony' (Collins, 2008), while another commentator referred to the language which characterised the debate which led up to PRWORA as 'cloak, sword, and shield' (Backer, 1995: 342). In other words, it was warlike language, designed to cover up what was actually going on, and to attack and defend against an enemy. The author does not say what it might be that the 'welfare reform' proselytisers were covering up, nor who the enemy was. (He discusses 'the imagery of moral worthiness and sin' that has always characterised debates about poor relief, but does not connect that to his original warlike imagery). I would suggest that what was (and still is) being covered up is the fact that 'welfare' recipients were being used as scapegoats to deflect attention from the real source of the nation's problems—power and wealth and the role of the US government in obeying the bidding of the men who own it. Poor single mothers, especially if they are African-American, that is, the most powerless members of society, are defined as the enemy.

This is the chief of the egregious lies behind 'welfare reform'—that poor women and their children are such a threat to the American way of life that they are not entitled to adequate help from the federal government ('the taxpayers') or, in many cases, any help at all. This is expressed in assertions that 'welfare reform' is in the interests of all. There are bountiful examples of this speaking-in-the-interests-of-all, all of them characterised by relentless use of the first person plural pronoun ('we', 'our', 'us'). But to illustrate, take this example from Bill Clinton's address at a 'welfare reform' conference in Kansas in 1994:

> I came out here to the heart of America ... to talk about the values that sustain us all as citizens and as Americans: faith and family, work and responsibility, community and opportunity (Clinton, 1994).

He even had the temerity to include 'welfare' recipients in 'us all', and worse, to quote them in support of his own agenda and against their own interests:

> work is preferable to welfare. And it must be enforced … And let me say, one of the most rewarding things that happened today in our little meeting before I came down was I asked all these fine ladies who are here … who used to be on welfare … I said, now, if we were able to provide these services … in getting people back to work … do you believe that it should be mandatory to participate in this program? Every one of them said, absolutely. Absolutely. (Applause.) (Clinton, 1994).[327]

Clinton's concern (i.e. lack of it) for these women who supposedly agreed 'absolutely' with him is demonstrated by what happened to one of them.[328] When she had a stoke in 2002, she couldn't get her health care funded by Medicaid because she was no longer on 'welfare', and the job that Clinton insisted was 'preferable to welfare' didn't provide health care. She wrote to Clinton and asked him to help. He didn't. She died in March 2014 aged 59 (Jilani, 2016; Marchevsky and Theoharis, 2016).

But there are a number of categories of citizens this self-congratulatory encomium to the benefits of 'welfare reform' does not include. One category constitutes those who are perceptive enough and have enough integrity not to be fooled by the unctuous demagoguery of the politicians' trade. The most obvious category, however, consists of the 'welfare' recipients themselves and the wider constituency of the poor, fewer and fewer of whom were ever going to be able to qualify for 'welfare' as the 'reforms' were rolled out. The Act Clinton was proposing to pass did not improve matters for them but in fact made them worse. He may have got some former recipients to agree with him 'absolutely'. What young woman would not be flattered to be singled out by the President of the United States? But that does not make his assertions true. Most of the millions who left the 'welfare' rolls (or never joined them), actively discouraged by the bureaucratic disentitlement built into the Act, remain poor. The information that this was in fact what would happen was freely available to the legislators before the legislation was passed. They chose to ignore it.

Moreover, given 'welfare reform's' function in cheapening already disastrously cheap labour, another category who cannot be included in the 'us all' are workers in the low-wage economy. Their wages and conditions were eroded even further by the influx of millions of extra workers competing

---

327. The type of 'work' this is is discussed below in the 'Workfare' section.

328. http://www.arkansasonline.com/obituaries/2014/mar/19/lillie-harden-ar/.

for their jobs. Or rather, their wages and conditions would have been further eroded, if it were true that 'welfare' recipients were unemployed prior to PRWORA and subsequently forced into the workforce. In fact, however, 'welfare' recipients and low-wage workers are the same constituency, churned between 'welfare' and low-wage employment with little or no possibility of being paid a living wage. And 'welfare' recipients are frequently employed at the same time as they are registered on the rolls, because the low-wage economy doesn't pay enough to make them ineligible for benefits. The message that 'welfare' recipients are not in paid employment is another lie.

It is quite possible that the impression Clinton wanted to convey that 'welfare reform' would benefit those subjected to it was an outright lie in the sense that the lawmakers knew it was false but callously went ahead anyway (see the last section of chapter 19). It is hard to credit that the Act's framers really believed that 'welfare reform' benefited poor women, given how punitive the Act is. But whether or not they believed it, they had the power to get most of the rest of the population ('the voters') to believe it too.

In one sense, however, Clinton was right when he implied that 'welfare reform' was relevant to 'us all as citizens and as Americans', although not because it expresses 'values that sustain us'. It emphatically does not—vindictive bullying of the weak sustains nobody. PRWORA is relevant to all US citizens because the nation's economy creates high levels of poverty, and anyone could find that they need to avail themselves of the social safety net. If it is grossly inadequate, anyone could find themselves free-falling through the bottom of the economy with no firm landing anywhere in sight. It is 'welfare reform' that threatens American society because, together with the low-wage economy it feeds, it exacerbates poverty and degradation.

The only constituency to benefit from 'welfare reform' are the wealthy men who profit from the low-wage economy that causes the poverty. The US system of 'welfare' subsidises big business in the sense that it partly pays for the reproduction of the workforce. Firms can keep wages low because government picks up the tab to keep some of those people some of the time from starvation. Government is reluctant to do this when it is a question of helping the poor, hence the niggardliness of the system; but it is not at all reluctant to subsidise the rich. This presents government with a dilemma: how to keep helping the rich without doing too much to help the poor. PRWORA's resolution of this dilemma tipped the balance in favour of the rich far more than any previous 'welfare' arrangements.

It also involved Clinton (and all the 'welfare reformers') in another lie, this time of omission rather than commission—the failure to acknowledge where the real interests lie. A low-wage economy comprises commercial enterprises which use people to produce goods and services (usually the latter) without adequately compensating them for their time and energy. Someone is not being adequately compensated, either if they cannot get full-time work but must be constantly prepared to take whatever work is available, or if what they are being paid for working full-time is not sufficient to buy basic necessities. The US economy is the worst low-wage economy in the Western world in that sense. Its wealthy men get rich by exploiting the very people they blame for being poor. This leads to another lie—that there is well-paying work available for former 'welfare' recipients. It is assumed without question that the reason women are on 'welfare' is because they are wilfully refusing to take up paid employment and so have to be coerced to do so. In fact, 'welfare' recipients have always worked in paid employment. It just doesn't pay enough to make them independent of 'welfare'.

There are problems with the pseudo-inclusiveness of the first person plural ('we', 'us', 'our'), whoever uses it. Judt, for example, referred to the corruption of 'our' moral sentiments and said that 'we' are insensible to the human costs of legislation like PRWORA. But he surely does not include himself among those with corrupt moral sentiments. If he can see a social policy as corrupt and condemn it, he is part of the solution, not part of the problem. Presumably the nod towards inclusiveness by the well-intentioned (as opposed to the shonky ideologues propping up wealth and power) is intended to indicate that society has some responsibility for bad social policy (i.e. all of us), not just those who actually framed the legislation. There is some truth in that—the problem is wider than those particular individuals, and everyone has a responsibility to see the legislation for what it really is and resist being taken in by the justificatory ideology. But 'society' is not monolithic. There is room for resistance and that resistance is not well captured by making all of 'us' responsible for the problems, especially those of us who have placed ourselves among the resisters. Nonetheless, Judt's description of the Act's title as 'Orwellian' and his recognition of its dehumanising consequences is accurate. As part of the opposition to the niggardliness of the US 'welfare' system, it stands in stark contrast to the official line about how successful 'welfare' reform has been.

The term 'Orwellian' is much favoured by the right wing. For example, Ric Perry, governor of Texas, referred to President Obama's Affordable Care Act as 'Orwellian', because it would 'make Texas a mere appendage of the federal government when it comes to health care' (Webster, 2012).[329] There is some justification in Orwell's own writings for this right-wing usage. One of the names Orwell gave to the totalitarian regime he was depicting was 'Ingsoc', short for 'English socialism', with the implication that tyrannical intrusions by the state into private life were characteristic of socialism. But calling something 'socialism' does not make it so. Nazism, for example, called itself 'National Socialism'. And totalitarianism—state rule which dictates to people what they should do in their personal lives with severe sanctions if they do not comply—is characteristic of the right-wing's deflecting of attention from the depredations of the ruling class by blaming the victims. It is certainly characteristic of 'welfare' (and not only in the US).

The US is generally regarded as the opposite of totalitarian, as the epitome of freedom and democracy and the staunch enemy of big government. But this is right-wing ideology. 'Welfare' systems established by the right wing are clearly totalitarian. They mandate interference in and monitoring of people's private lives by 'welfare' bureaucracy supposedly for their own good. Typical is the attitude of the director of the Department of Public Social Services in Riverside County in California, who justified his department's 'work first' approach in testimony before the US Senate in 1995:

> "Employment, however modest, teaches and reinforces very basic, yet essential, skills necessary for acquiring and retaining employment that many people take for granted but not all of us have, such as: setting the alarm clock; getting to work on time; accepting supervision; learning to complete tasks reliably; getting along with co-workers; and, dressing appropriately for work" (quoted in Peck, 1998a: 536).

Right-wing (i.e. neo-liberal) 'welfare' systems make bureaucratic demands on people (but only if they are poor) that no self-respecting liberal democracy ought to countenance, and punishes them by depriving them of their income when they do not obey (even when they cannot). The US 'welfare' state even has a history of trying to control poor women's sexual behaviour. PRWORA goes one step further than any previous 'welfare' legislation by limiting the period of time any one person can receive 'welfare' to five years over a whole lifetime. Depriving people of income of the last resort, while doing nothing to ensure that there are jobs for all and that those jobs pay a living wage, has horrendous consequences for the personal lives of a considerable proportion of the US population.

---

329. In fact, state governments are always 'appendages of the federal government', fiscally speaking, since they are not the sovereign issuers of their own currency (see chapter 10).

Or rather, it would have horrendous consequences if 'welfare' benefits paid anything near what people need to live on. Since they do not, and 'welfare' recipients have always had to find other ways of ensuring survival for themselves and their children, withdrawing them probably makes little difference. However, even that little difference matters at the income level of eligibility for 'welfare'.

The totalitarian implications of the term 'Orwellian', as they are elucidated in Orwell's notion of 'Newspeak', the invented language of domination which he described in an Appendix to *Nineteen Eighty-Four*, are relevant to the institution of 'welfare reform'. It is true that much of what he said about Newspeak is not politically relevant. It throws little light on the functions Newspeak played for his fictional ruling class, variously named Ingsoc, Big Brother and the Party. For example, it is not clear how useful for the business of ruling are Newspeak's two grammatical peculiarities, namely the inter-changeability of different parts of speech, and the use of 'un-' attached to a word to indicate a negative and 'plus-' to indicate a positive (e.g. 'uncold' to mean 'warm and 'pluscold' to mean 'very cold'). However, other aspects of his characterisation of Newspeak are apt descriptions of language used in the service of domination, where denial is the norm and awareness of what is really going on must be suppressed. The 'special function' of Newspeak, he said,

> was not so much to express meanings as to destroy them … In Newspeak it was seldom possible to follow a heretical thought further than the perception that it *was* heretical … Newspeak was designed not to extend but to *diminish* the range of thought (Orwell, 2000: 318, 319, 313—original emphases).

But one of the characteristics of Newspeak that runs throughout the novel is not addressed in Orwell's Appendix, that is, that it is used to tell flagrant lies by baldly asserting that certain crucial words mean the opposite of what they really mean. This is illustrated in the novel by the slogans of the Party inscribed on the face of the 'Ministry of Truth' building: WAR IS PEACE. FREEDOM IS SLAVERY. IGNORANCE IS STRENGTH. It is also illustrated by the names and functions of the four Ministries: the Ministry of Truth tells lies; the Ministry of Peace wages war; the Ministry of Love tortures and kills people; and the Ministry of Plenty is responsible for managing the economy so that all but a small elite live under conditions of scarcity and deprivation.

The title of the US 'welfare reform' Act, 'Personal Responsibility and Work Opportunities Reconciliation', is Orwellian Newspeak in this sense. It lies about who is really responsible for poverty and for providing employment; it also lies about the existence of work opportunities. As for 'reconciliation', this is one of those destroyed words. Signifying nothing, it appears to have no function whatsoever, at least in conveying meaning.

The effrontery of the title of this legislation is breathtaking. In saying that women have to take responsibility for their children it assumes, not only that they do not already do that, but that they have access to the means for doing it—sufficient income to provide themselves and their children with the necessities of life. Neither 'welfare' nor the low-wage labour market provides that income, but these are the only two alternatives US society can offer. In fact, the only 'responsibility' mandated by 'welfare reform' is to comply with whatever degrading and futile activity the bureaucratic mind can devise.

But if PRWORA holds the poor responsible for doing something about their poverty, it fails even to mention those who do have the power to create jobs and pay living wages. Business and government have no responsibilities, personal or otherwise, under PRWORA. The Act is silent on the responsibility of business to provide jobs that pay a living wage, or the responsibility of government to provide its citizens with sufficient income to live in dignity and comfort, given that 'the market' cannot provide everyone with a good job. The Act does not require the powerful to take responsibility; nor is there any responsibility on the part of the rich and powerful to provide work opportunities in return for their massive wealth; nor do they lose their incomes if they fail to comply with some trifling bureaucratic requirement. Indeed, even outright fraud on the part of the for-profit private firms providing 'welfare services' does not lead to their contracts being cancelled (See the 'Privatisation' section below).

As for those 'work opportunities'—the Act does not create any. In defiance of the actual state of affairs, the Act assumes that there is work enough for everyone and that it pays a living wage. But PRWORA does not mandate a living wage. Employers do not have a responsibility under the Act to pay decent wages. It has nothing whatsoever to say about poverty. Some of the supporters of 'welfare reform' do mention poverty, but they exhibit the same dissociation as the legislation. They refuse to see past the myth that employment is the way out of poverty, by wilfully ignoring the reality of wages and conditions at the bottom of the US labour market.

And then there is the 'welfare' program established by PRWORA—TANF, the 'temporary assistance to needy families'. No one must be under any illusion that the state might provide a basic open-ended minimum income for those for whom the economy has no use. The Orwellian nature of the wording is indicated by the fact that even the right-wing[330] know that poverty need not be temporary. Not only can it last a lifetime, it can even be intergenerational. Indeed, the right-wing uses the supposed existence of an intergenerational 'culture of poverty' as one of their arguments for 'doing something about the welfare mess'. The right-wing sees this as the fault of poor individuals, and the economy which causes the poverty is never mentioned. As a result their 'solutions'—'educationandtraining' and punishment, i.e. the withdrawal of income support as a way of making people get jobs—are individualistic and ultimately futile because they don't address the real causes of poverty.

The 'educationandtraining' available in the 'manpower training programs' is unlikely to prepare anyone for well-paid employment before the five-year time limit expires. It is invariably short-term, usually a matter of weeks, and it does not provide people with high-level skills. As Epstein (1997) said:

> the training programs provided little opportunity to overcome personal, subcultural, or structural obstacles to employment. Their meager provisions were seemingly intended more as a sop to participants and a symbol of charitability ... than as a serious attempt to transmit skills. It takes more than a few months of cursory training to prepare a productive worker. Moreover, the training itself seems cruel and futile unless it leads to employment that can provide a livable wage (Epstein, 1997: 180).

And then there are the acronyms. While PRWORA and TANF are ugly neologisms, many of the State 'welfare' programs have titles whose initials spell out ordinary words designed to convey the 'welfare reform' ideology at a glance. There's WIN, the 1967 federal Work Incentive Program, and GAIN, Greater Avenues for Independence which began operating in California in 1986, and JOBS, the federal Job Opportunities and Basic Skills program established under the 1988 Family Support Act, and Florida's WAGES (Work And Gain Economic Self-Sufficiency), and New York City's BEGIN (Begin Employment, Gain Independence Now) (Youdelman and Getsos, 2005: 15). Such up-beat names give the lie to the reality of failed programs, unlearnt lessons and an exploitative labour market.

A national crisis: 'born out of wedlock'

The wording of the PRWORA starts with the heading, 'TITLE I—BLOCK GRANTS FOR TEMPORARY ASSISTANCE FOR NEEDY FAMILIES', but in fact the first three pages of this section have nothing to say about

---

330. I include Bill Clinton and his administration in this. 'Right-wing' designates support for the interests of domination, and support for PRWORA is certainly that.

block grants. Instead, they detail what are called 'findings', the first of which is that '(1) Marriage is the foundation of a successful society'. This is a proposition as empty of meaning as the employment mantra 'the best way out of poverty is a job'. If it is taken literally there can't be much marriage in the US. America is hardly a successful society. Americans are in poorer health and die younger than people in other high-income countries (US Institute of Medicine, 2013a, b), with a much higher rate of maternal mortality—US women are ten times more likely than women in Poland or Norway to die in childbirth (Morris, 2015). The nation has vast inequalities in wealth, high levels of poverty including the highest rate of child poverty in the developed world, nearly 30 million people still without health insurance,[331] and over 43 million receiving food stamps in May 2016.[332] Its economic practices include shonky financial dealings that cause global economic crises, mortgage foreclosures by banks who have already been recompensed by the federal government, and a system of industry that is a primary (although by no means the sole) contributor to global warming. Violence is endemic, including massacres by domestic male terrorists (high-school boys and white supremacists), an inability to control the proliferation of gun ownership, the killing of black people by police who are not even charged much less convicted, and wars on foreign soil which massacre untold numbers of the civilian population as well as sending American soldiers home in body bags.

The driving force of US society is not marriage but the rapacity of the US ruling class. To quote Anelauskas again on the appalling state of US society (from a chapter called 'Socialism for the rich'):

> the environment of misery, greed, and crime Americans live in today is caused first of all by the permeation throughout American society of a perverted corporate ethic which distorts human nature, discourages compassion and cooperation amongst people, and encourages

---

331. The proportion of the population without health insurance dropped with the introduction of the Affordable Care Act ('Obamacare') in 2010 (http://obamacarefacts.com/uninsured-rates/). Before the introduction of the Act, 15.7% of the US population were without health insurance, whereas a National Health Interview Survey in the first three months of 2015 found that the proportion was 9.2%, or 29 million people. This is the lowest recorded rate of uninsured people in over 50 years, but it is still a long way from coverage for the whole population. A large part of the problem is that Republican state administrations are refusing to introduce the program, thus depriving eligible citizens of health care. But another part of the problem lies with the limitations of the Act itself, which does not guarantee universal coverage. And even that improvement will be reversed by the Trump administration if they have their way.

332. http://frac.org/reports-and-resources/snapfood-stamp-monthly-participation-data/. The food stamp program was renamed the Supplemental Nutrition Assistance Program or SNAP on 1 October 2008.

competition and ultimately, violence. Giant American corporations are today major causes of poverty, exploitation, community destabilization, discrimination, ill health and environmental destruction in the United States and even around the world. People here, all of them, are locked into an economic, social, and political system dominated by Corporate America. It directly and indirectly affects their mentality, their livelihood, their well-being and their prospects for the future (Anelauskas, 1999: 282).

However, none of this constitutes 'the crisis in our Nation' which so concerned PRWORA's framers. Rather, the national 'crisis' supposedly addressed by the Act is unwed motherhood. PRWORA says:

> The negative consequences of an out-of-wedlock birth on the mother, the child, the family, and society are well documented … in light of this demonstration of the crisis in our Nation, it is the sense of the Congress that prevention of out-of-wedlock pregnancy and reduction in out-of-wedlock birth are very important Government interests and the policy contained in [this Act] is intended to address the crisis (SEC. 101(8), (10), pp.7, 8).

But it is not clear on the face of it why unwed motherhood should cause such anxiety in the minds of rich powerful men that they have come to perceive it as a national crisis. The Act does document a number of negative consequences: teenage mothers 'go on public assistance' earlier and stay longer; and children 'born out-of-wedlock' have lower birth weights, suffer more abuse and neglect, do less well in school, are more likely to become 'teenage parents', less likely to have 'an intact marriage', and are 'are 3 times more likely to be on welfare when they grow up' (SEC. 101(8)(A-F). But all these outcomes are the consequences of poverty, and women's poverty in particular. If there is a national crisis around these issues, it is women's poverty, and (because it is hard to imagine that women's poverty could be rectified without also rectifying the poverty of children and men) poverty across the board.

But this is something the framers of the Act, right-wing ideologues to a man (and woman), do not acknowledge. They cannot acknowledge the real sources of poverty either because they themselves profit from the system that causes it, or because they idealise those who do and represent their interests. US lawmakers,[333] their wealthy patrons and their ideological cheer squad feel the need to dissociate themselves from that truth because they

---

333. This is not peculiar to the US. It is common to liberal democracies everywhere.

need to purvey the notion that they are speaking in the interests of all ('the voters'), and not just in the interests of the powerful few.

The Act does acknowledge some culpability on the part of men, although not the men who benefit most from 'welfare reform' (or think they do). It states that '[t]he increase of teenage pregnancies among the youngest girls … is linked to predatory sexual practices by men who are significantly older' (SEC. 101(7), p.7); and the Senate emphasised the need for States and local jurisdictions to 'aggressively enforce statutory rape laws' (SEC. 906, pp.245-6). But the rape of children by predatory men is not characterised as a national crisis, only the girls' pregnancies are. Moreover, the Act does not allow the fact that these girls have been raped to excuse them from the workfare requirements or the punitive financial sanctions of the Act; and combating the rape of children does not appear among the aims of the Act.

Single mothers, particularly single mothers who are black, are the scapegoats of the US economy. The right-wing mind is so keen to attribute poverty to mothers' non-marital status because it deflects attention from their own culpability in prospering from a system which drives others into destitution. The pity of it is that millions who are not wealthy men believe them. The belief that poor young women are responsible for their own poverty and that of their children is the dominant belief about 'welfare' in the US.

Of course mothers who are not married are likely to be poor. They do not have access to a male wage, and they have restricted access to a full-time female wage (81% of the male wage at the median)[334] because young children have to be cared for full-time and women are not paid for raising children. But the poverty is a consequence of the way the US economy is structured, not of the parenting arrangements into which children are born.

There is an odour of hatred permeating PRWORA. The men who drafted and passed the legislation must hate their victims—those people, especially women, especially black women, whose life chances are diminished by an economic system that exploits and then discards them. The right-wing mind hates women, and it especially hates women it has exploited, and even more so, if they are the descendants of the slaves the right-wing mind still thinks he owns. It is this hatred that lies behind the punitiveness of PRWORA. The right-wing mind also fears women's power to bear and raise children, and needs to see that they are under the control of men. Hence the emphasis on 'marriage as the foundation of a successful society' (and the murderous hatred of abortion). They cannot abide the thought of women and children

---

334. Based on 2010 data from the US Bureau of Labor Statistics (http://www.forbes.com/sites/realspin/2012/05/21/mind-the-malefemale-income-gap-but-dont-exaggerate-it/).

without men, and PRWORA is motivated by their need to bring women with children back under male control by depriving them of any reasonable alternative.

Chapter Sixteen: PRWORA's Innovations

PRWORA is usually regarded as a marked change in the US 'welfare' system. The Wikipedia entry for PRWORA,[335] for example, states that it is 'considered to be a fundamental shift in both the method and goal of federal cash assistance to the poor'. One commentator believed that the 1996 'welfare reform has reconfigured both the policy and political landscape' (Brodkin, 2003: 29). Joel Handler (2008: 4) delineated four ways in which he believed PRWORA changed the income maintenance program for poor families: it 'dramatically' expanded permission for the States to develop their own welfare programs; it explicitly stated that income support was no longer an entitlement but conditional on 'employment'-related requirements; it expanded the sanctions States were permitted to impose for recipients' non-compliance; and it imposed a five-year lifetime limit on 'welfare' receipt.[336] Similarly, Mary-Jo Bane, the former assistant secretary for children and families in the US Department of Health and Human Services (Bane, 1997: 49) believed that block grants to the States and the five-year limits on 'welfare' receipt 'abdicate[d] federal responsibility for needy children by abolishing any entitlement to benefits or services'.

As I argue below (in chapter 17), PRWORA did retain the substance of what went before in the sense that all the old right-wing resistances to 'welfare' triumphed. Still, there were changes. In the first place, there is no longer even a pretence that the federal government has a responsibility to tackle poverty, given that the Act explicitly withdraws people's entitlement.

---

335. Viewed 19 April 2012.

336. Handler also believed that there were fundamental assumptions which remained unchanged throughout all instances of 'welfare reform': "'social welfare programs reflect fundamental attitudes towards the category of the poor to be served'" (quoted in Backer, 1995: 341n15).

Bad as the old 'welfare' was, PRWORA has made things worse. As one commentator remarked:

> The demise of the old welfare [with the enactment of PRWORA in 1996] ... marked the end of welfare *politics* as we knew it. In the tepid debate over reauthorization in the fall of 2002, the bitter conflicts of earlier years over government's role in addressing poverty were replaced by half-hearted tinkering ... The old welfare acknowledged, in principle, a political commitment to relieve poverty and lessen inequality, even if, in practice, that commitment was limited, benefits were ungenerous, and access uneven ... As bad as the old welfare may have been, there is reason to lament its demise after all (Brodkin, 2003: 35-6—original emphasis).

Time limits

PRWORA introduced a mandatory lifetime time-limit of five years for receipt of 'welfare' payments:

> NO ASSISTANCE FOR MORE THAN 5 YEARS.—IN GENERAL.—A State to which a grant is made under section 403 shall not use any part of the grant to provide assistance to a family that includes an adult who has received assistance under any State program funded under this part attributable to funds provided by the Federal Government, for 60 months (whether or not consecutive) (SEC.408 (a) (7)(A), p.33).

Children were exempted from the five-year limit, and provision was also made for exemptions from the five-year limit for families in hardship or escaping from what is elsewhere in the Act identified as 'domestic violence':[337]

> HARDSHIP EXCEPTION.—IN GENERAL.—The State may exempt a family from the application of subparagraph (A) by reason of hardship or if the family includes an individual who has been battered or subjected to extreme cruelty (Sec.408 (a)(7)(C)(i), pp.33-4).

But only a portion of a State's caseload of 'welfare' recipients could be exempted from the five-year time limit in any one year:

> LIMITATION.—The number of families with respect to which an exemption made by a State under clause (i) is in effect for a fiscal year

---

337. 'DOMESTIC VIOLENCE DEFINED.—For purposes of this paragraph, the term "domestic violence" has the same meaning as the term "battered or subjected to extreme cruelty"' (SEC. 402 (a)(7)(B), p.11).

shall not exceed 20 percent of the average monthly number of families to which assistance is provided (Sec.408 (a)(7)(C)(ii), p.34).

And although PRWORA set the lifetime limit at five years, States could set shorter time limits, and many of them had been doing so even before 1996. The threat of time limits was already being used by State administrations before 1996 'as a means of destabilizing clients' (Peck, 1998a: 546).

As things turned out, however, time limits were not necessary to 'end welfare as we know it'. Ten years after the passing of PRWORA, few families had had benefits terminated because they'd reached the five-year time limit (Acs and Loprest, 2007: 114). This was not because the States were exercising their right to exempt people from the time limit. Eighteen States offered no exemptions at all, and there were nearly 60,000 families who had their benefits terminated when they reached the time limit in States with time limits shorter than five years (Cheeseborough, 2002: 4). The main reason why people left 'welfare' was the bureaucratic disentitlement built into the Act and the enthusiasm with which it was exercised by State administrations (see below).

Block grants and devolution to the States

The first of PRWORA's innovations detailed in the Act (TITLE I) restricted federal funding for 'welfare' to fixed annual sums—'block grants'—and the authority to operate welfare programs was devolved from the federal government to the States (Kennedy, 1998: 252). As well, PRWORA contained a Maintenance of Effort (MOE) requirement whereby each State was to contribute at least 80% of the funding it had contributed to AFDC in 1994. In 2011, the total MOE contribution from states was $15 billion.

One commentator (Stoesz, 1997: 68) referred to PRWORA's use of the block grant system for 'welfare' as 'ironic' (although a stronger term of opprobrium might have been more appropriate), because the block grant system had already been shown to be a tragic failure in achieving the aims it supposedly set out to achieve. Stoesz pointed out that the last social program that was devolved to the states through block grants, the Title XX Social Services Block Grant to State children's agencies, had failed to have any impact on the numbers of children who died of abuse and neglect annually.

The block grant system under TANF is one of the ways in which PWRORA's expressed intention of disentitling citizens is carried out. There was no provision in the Act for increasing the funding if the need increased, for example, if unemployment and poverty levels rose during a recession:

the federal grant is unconnected to changing levels of need. During a period of recession, if welfare caseloads rise and a state runs out of block grant funds, eligible applicants for public aid could be denied assistance, unless the state had the fiscal resources and political will to provide supplementary funding (Gilbert, 1998: 105).

The original TANF block grant funding in 1996 was $16.5 billion (Pavetti and Schott, 2011: 5). That was still the nominal sum in 2016, 20 years later, and in the meantime it had decreased in value by more than a third (Pavetti and Schott, 2016: 5; US OFA, 2016b). The federal government did provide additional TANF funding of up to $5 billion through the 2009 American Recovery and Reinvestment Act, as a response to the global financial crisis. But it was only provided for one fiscal year—1 October 2009 to 30 September 2010—and the time was too short to enable all the money to be spent (Hahn et al, 2012b: 3). The President's Budget for Fiscal Year 2017 also promised a further $10 billion in new funding over five years (US OFA, 2016b). But if TANF is to be funded to the original level, given that it has lost a third of its value through inflation, it would need an extra $5.5 billion in the first year, indexed for inflation for each subsequent year. But that is hardly likely, given the precipitous drop in the 'welfare' caseloads (see below), which 'ended welfare as we know it' (although not poverty).

The block grant system was part of the process of decentralising control over 'welfare' by devolving responsibility away from the federal level of government to the individual States. The federal government still funds such programs as food stamps (SNAP) and other food programs, Medicaid and Medicare, SSI/Old Age Assistance and public housing. But the passing on to the States of the responsibility for the management of the cash assistance aspect of 'welfare' was part of PRWORA's disentitlement process: 'The secret triumph of devolution lay, not in the opportunities for innovation, but in the opportunity for a quiet unravelling of the safety net' (Brodkin, 2003: 31). It is also the latest victory in the ruling class' persistent fight against 'welfare'.

American society's attempts to aid the poor have all emanated from the federal government, in 1935 when President Franklin D. Roosevelt introduced the Social Security Act as part of his New Deal, and again during the 1960s when the Kennedy and Johnson administrations liberalised and expanded the programs initiated in the 1930s in response to massive civil unrest especially among African-Americans in the inner cities. 'Welfare' was a national issue. Initiatives and directives poured out of Washington, or that was how it seemed to the right-wing mind, and that was where the

'War on Poverty' was declared (Peck, 2001; Piven and Cloward, 1987). This was the 'Big Government' of right-wing ideology—federally-sponsored initiatives directed at the inner city, intentionally designed to bypass State administrations (Handler and Hasenfeld, 1991).

PRWORA's devolution of responsibility for 'welfare' to the states disrupted this trajectory of genuine, if largely half-hearted and compromised, attempts at 'welfare reform', and consigned them to the historical past. It did indeed 'end welfare as we have come to know it'. It did not, however, end poverty. As the manager of a non-profit human services agency in Worcester, MA, put it:

> "[the 'welfare reform' program in Massachusetts] is not just mean-spirited, it's also ill-conceived, and not well implemented … It's not as though the low-income population hasn't been scrutinized to death for ten to fifteen years. Study after study after study … There really isn't any rationale. This is mostly a value-based, emotional argument that has won over that says that people that are poor, it's their fault, that's about it. It's really contrary to just about every study, if the goal is to lift people out of poverty. But they've used all the rhetoric, skillfully, to say, this will be the jump-start, to lift people out of poverty. And it couldn't be more contrary in practice. I don't think the general public, however, in any way shape or form, has a full understanding of that" (interviewed by Jamie Peck, February, 1996) (Peck, 2001: 162).

PRWORA's devolution to the States is part of the culture of decentralisation that predominates in the US political system, whereby 'States' rights' are given precedence over the authority of the federal government. The decentralisation of governmental powers was incorporated into the Constitution as a compromise with the slave-owning States of the South and the business-owning northern States whose power was State-based. As Piven and Cloward pointed out, '[d]ecentralization … had its roots in sectional economic differences which have always marked American politics (particularly the distinctive economy and society of the Southern section)' (Piven and Cloward, 1993: 437). The call for 'States' rights' and decentralisation was originally a thinly-disguised defence of an economy based on slavery, and later, of the power base of economic domination in the US:

> the decentralization built into the system of national representation by the privileging of regions over population, particularly in the Senate and the electoral college, gave the oligarchical Southern section a strong grip on the national government. And a system of divided powers in the national government meant that grip could become a stranglehold

on national policy, especially as powerful Southern Democrats in the Congress allied themselves with Northern Republicans beginning in the late 1930s (Piven and Cloward, 1993: 442-3).

PRWORA's devolution of responsibility for 'welfare' to the States (along with all the other forms of disentitlement) was the merely the latest skirmish in the war against the poor. If the descendants of slave-owners can't return to their former slave-owning ways, their political system at least allows them to establish and maintain a similar system. Federal responsibility for needy children, and people's entitlement to assistance, have never been allowed to override 'States' rights' and the powerful economic and racist interests they support. As Jamie Peck put it:

> Southern conservatives opposed the expansion and federalization of welfare from the New Deal onward, repeatedly insisting on state autonomy and "flexibility", local control over benefit levels, and local discretion in administration as a means of maintaining the region's regressive labor-market norms. The truncated and distorted state of the U.S. welfare system is testimony to the strength of these political forces (Peck, 2001: 66).

From the beginning it was obvious that devolving responsibility for 'welfare' to the States would worsen the situation of America's poor. In the first place, many of the State administrations had shown themselves to be eager advocates of the kind of 'welfare reform' culminating in PRWORA. Devolution to the States meant the end of even the most minimal restrictions on a 'race to the bottom' competition to reduce 'welfare' provision to the lowest possible level (Brodkin, 1997: 2; Kennedy, 1998: 255). As one commentator put it a year before PRWORA was passed: 'While Clinton and the Republican Congress contemplate the end of welfare, states are ending welfare on their own by slashing benefits, tightening regulations, and introducing punitive behavioral requirements' (Schram, 1995: 166).

Yet another reason why transferring administrative responsibility to the states was a bad thing for the poor, was that decentralisation dissipated the political opposition to 'welfare reform'. It bypassed the well-established advocacy system focused on Washington, and made the policy-making process far more difficult to track, much less respond to. It made the lobbying and campaigning machinery that had been constructed around the federal system largely redundant, and left the responsibility for exerting pressure on policy-making with state- and local-level organisations with vastly less capacity for political influence than those organised nationally. This dissipation of welfare-rights activism was deliberate. As Peck pointed out, 'Such a fragmentation of political opposition was an explicit objective of right-wing advocates of welfare downloading and the block-grant mechanism' (Peck, 2001: 71).

But the main reason why PRWORA gave the States control over the disbursement of 'welfare' funds, and worsened the situation of the poor, concerns the powerful influence of business interests over state administrations. As Piven (2001: 30) has pointed out, State governments are more vulnerable than the federal government to business threats to leave the State if the administration doesn't do what business wants. She also said that State politics were 'even murkier than the politics of Washington' and that there was less scrutiny from the press. As a consequence of the connections between the labor market interests of business and State governments, she said, the new State-run welfare programs were likely to be even less responsive to the interests of the poor than under the federal regime.

Peck (2001) also argued that State (and local) administrations were particularly vulnerable to the threat by business lobby groups, whether made explicit or not, that industry would go elsewhere if the administration spent 'too much' on public goods, especially welfare. The state governors through the National Governors' Association had had a significant influence on the framing of the precursor to PRWORA, the 1988 Family Support Act, which set up the JOBS 'training' program. They helped to establish the political foundations for the consensus around 'workfare' and to codify the language of 'mutual obligation' and welfare 'contract'. Channelling the funding for 'welfare' through each individual State placed its recipients directly at the mercy of those whose interests lay in maintaining poverty, not in ending it. As Peck said: 'Stripped down to its labor-regulatory essence, workfare is not about creating jobs for people that don't have them; it is about creating workers for jobs that nobody wants' (Peck, 2001: 6).

The interest business has in 'welfare reform' is its effect in cheapening even further the already bad pay and conditions at the bottom of the US labour market, by taking away even the most minimal alternative to participation in the labour force. As has been pointed out by any number of commentators I have cited in this context, cheapening labour was in fact the main reason for 'welfare reform' both in the US and elsewhere, although it was carried to its greatest extremes in the US. Those who pushed the 'reforms' most strongly and who had the power to make their interests prevail were business interests committed to cheapening labour power (capitalism, in other words), their organised political structure (both the Republican and the Democrat parties) and their right-wing apologists. As one commentator put it:

Perhaps the most powerful of these groups ... promoting restrictive welfare policies ... were low-wage employers [i.e. employers who paid low wages] and ideologically conservative corporations and wealthy families.[338] The interests of those groups were represented by corporate-sponsored think tanks, such as the American Enterprise Institute, the Heritage Foundation, and the Hudson Institute, as well as the U.S. Chamber of Commerce, all of which actively promoted welfare reform ... By 2000, all of these organizations supported time limits, strict work requirements, and the elimination of welfare entitlements (Reese, 2007: 50-1).

Collectively, these are called 'conservatives' in the US—'ideologically conservative corporations'—but it is more accurate to call their interests 'right wing' in the sense in which I have outlined it (in chapter 2). It would be even more accurate to call those interests 'masculinist', characterised as they are by entitlement for the rich and a pathological dissociation from any sense of a common humanity.

Disentitlement

The overriding purpose of PRWORA was, as Bill Clinton said so clearly (and so often), 'to end welfare as we know it'. As one commentator put it:

> With grand ceremonial splendor, President Clinton, in a speech delivered in Kansas City, Missouri on June 14, 1994, announced his intention to deliver to Congress a "plan to change the welfare system." The President assured his audience that this plan would "end welfare as we know it ... to change it from a system based on dependence to a system that works toward independence ... to change it so that the focus is clearly on work" (Backer, 1995: 339).

Clinton had been saying the same thing for years. Earlier, in an address to students at Georgetown University in October, 1991, he said, 'In my

---

338. This terminology of 'families' is a common usage, but it is inaccurate. The influential individuals belonging to those 'wealthy families', the ones who accumulated the wealth and who were lobbying so successfully to maintain and even increase their privileges, would be men. Any women belonging to these 'families' would either be passively enjoying the wealth accumulated by the men, or (like Hillary Clinton) actively working in support of an agenda set by men in the interests of male domination. Perhaps the usage is an unthinking acceptance of the notion of 'family trusts', the legal entities wealthy men use to hide their wealth and avoid paying taxes. If so, such a euphemistic usage sits uneasily in a text whose analysis is highly critical of 'welfare reform' and its consequences for the poor.

administration we're going to put an end to welfare as we have come to know it'.[339]

What he did not say was that ending 'welfare' was to be accomplished by abolishing citizens' entitlement to it. The Act says so explicitly:

> NO INDIVIDUAL ENTITLEMENT.—This part shall not be interpreted to entitle any individual or family to assistance under any State program funded under this part (SEC. 401(a), (b), p.9).

Under the previous AFDC funding arrangements anyone who qualified for 'welfare' and applied for it was entitled, as long as they fulfilled the increasingly onerous requirements. If the need for 'welfare' rose (because unemployment or poverty increased), the federal government would increase the funding. Under the PRWORA block-grant system, that no longer happens.

PRWORA also disentitles citizens by giving the States more power to dream up ever more vindictive ways of doing so:

> The purpose of this part is to increase the flexibility of States in operating a program designed to—(1) provide assistance to needy families ... (2) end the dependence of needy parents on government benefits by promoting job preparation, work, and marriage; (3) prevent and reduce the incidence of out-of-wedlock pregnancies and establish annual numerical goals for preventing and reducing the incidence of these pregnancies; and (4) encourage the formation and maintenance of two-parent families (SEC. 401(a), (b), p.9).

PRWORA calls this 'flexibility', but the states have interpreted it only one way—to be even more punitive than the Act itself. They have displayed no flexibility in the direction of less punishment and more generosity.

Bureaucratic disentitlement

> In fact, it takes little in the way of policy innovation to drive the welfare rolls down and coerce women into low-wage work. All that is required are regulations and administrative practices that make benefits exceedingly difficult to get, which is what the 1996 legislation accomplished (Piven, 2006: xix).

Not only does PRWORA explicitly disentitle US citizens from access to 'welfare', it also further entrenches punitive rules and regulations which deny people benefits even though their destitution makes them eligible. One of the reasons bureaucratic requirements are so successful as a method of disentitlement is because showing compliance requires documentation, and people in dire circumstances have great difficulty in keeping documents. Many

---

339. https://www.ibiblio.org/pub/academic/political-science/speeches/clinton.dir/c24.txtp.

would be homeless, others would have had so many changes of address it would be impossible for them to know what they had done with the relevant papers, or even if they had had any papers in the first place.

Michael Lipsky's 1984 definition of bureaucratic disentitlement, devised long before PRWORA, describes it as

> a mode of fiscal and programmatic retrenchment that takes place through obscure and routine actions of public authorities, and through failures to take action, that result in distributive consequences ... Bureaucratic disentitlement takes place in the hidden recesses of routine or obscure decision making, or the unobtrusive nondecisions of policymakers. Therefore, it tends to allocate entitlements without the accountability that normally restrains government excesses or allows full discussion of critical distributive issues (Lipsky, 1984: 3).

Lipsky's account is not entirely satisfactory. It implies that governments cut back on public services only intermittently ('in periods of retrenchment') (p.12). But cutbacks are standard operating procedures in the bureaucracy of 'welfare', fuelled as it is by perceptions of 'welfare' recipients as 'undeserving' and, more to the point, black (Gilens, 1999). Government is always trying to retrench 'welfare' and to end it as we have come to know it, and so the procedures to ensure this and to demean the recipients are always with us.

Still, Lipsky's account did provide an analysis of the ways in which bureaucratic disentitlement operates. He suggested four ways in which eligible people are denied essential goods and services they cannot buy for themselves, by 'welfare' organisations which supposedly exist to provide them. The first method is rationing people's access to benefits by making it stressful and costly in terms of trust and human dignity. Examples include: inadequate staffing levels and staff unhelpfulness; inefficient record-keeping (e.g. 'losing' people's verification documents); regimentation and surveillance of recipients; intimidating letters making threatening demands; and burdensome verification requirements for cash assistance (e.g. photo id for cashing cheques, proof that children have been vaccinated, a requirement that children succeed in school) (pp.8-9).

The second method involves rationing the benefits, i.e. never having enough material assistance available to satisfy the full extent of the need. Housing, legal aid and child care are well-known examples. As Lipsky comments: 'It is not that public policy has failed to recognize the need; there is no policy to meet the need ... [and] people realize that, although their needs have been recognized, no resources are available to help them' (pp.9-10).

The third method Lipsky characterises as 'letting "natural" forces have their way', or in other words, 'regarding problems as beyond the ability of society to solve them'. The two examples he gives are inflation, where cash benefit levels are not increased with increases in the cost of living, and the housing market, where housing becomes more and more expensive but housing policy does not increase the supply of affordable housing. This method is another example of rationing, and like the others, it maintains the form of the policy while reducing benefits in practice (pp.10-12).

The fourth method of direct bureaucratic disentitlement involves procedures which reduce the ability of staff to help recipients. Examples include time studies, excessive reporting requirements and under-staffing. Especially noteworthy are government drives 'to reduce the error rate', which invariably focus only on 'errors' that might be seen as excessively lenient towards recipients, and never on errors that lead to recipients or applicants being denied benefits. As Lipsky said, this 'weights the tenuous balance between helpfulness and distrust in favor of distrust' (Lipsky, 1984: 13).

However, while all four methods (and more) are still in existence, Lipsky's account has not kept up with the times. In the post-PRWORA 'welfare' climate, the underhandedness that he saw as the main characteristic of bureaucratic disentitlement ('obscure and routine actions', 'failures to take action', 'hidden recesses', 'unobtrusive nondecisions') is far less in evidence. When Lipsky was writing, there was still the pretence that 'welfare' systems were democratic institutions. As such, they were supposed to be motivated by justice, fairness, equality and respect for human dignity, although because they had to compromise with domination, they were always unjust, unfair and degrading in the process of maintaining the gross inequalities that domination creates. That contradiction has traditionally been managed through deceitfulness—the superficial appearance of a helping hand, which is contradicted by the actual operations of the system. Such deviousness was characteristic of the political motivation to hobble the 'welfare' system without actually saying so overtly. With PRWORA and the shamelessness of the disentitlement clause, there is less need for any pretence that 'welfare' is a democratic institution (not that that has diminished the incidence of the lying).

Disentitlement is built into the system. Researchers from the Urban Institute[340] (Hahn et al, 2012b: 15-17) described two types of practices

---

340. The Urban Institute was established in 1968 'to understand the problems facing America's cities and assess the programs of the War on Poverty' (http://www.urban.org/about). Their approach is sympathetic to the plight of the poor, but the obligation to 'not take

intended to deter people from receiving ongoing cash assistance. The first practice they referred to as 'formal diversion' because it is explicitly acknowledged as such. It involves providing applicants with a lump sum payment which both disqualifies them from receiving any more assistance for an extended period of time, and ensures that they are not counted on the rolls. The other practice they refer to as 'informal diversion'. It involves all the old tried and true methods described above (and more), 'whether intentionally or not', the authors say. Examples include 'encourag[ing] [sic] applicants to consider alternatives to cash assistance' and 'policies require[ing] applicants to participate in work-related activities before their applications are completed'. The authors refer to informal diversion as 'the "hassle factor," whereby receiving TANF assistance may not be worth the hassle for some potential applicants'. But such a description trivialises the reality. Receiving TANF assistance could make the difference between being homeless and being housed, being well-fed and being ill-fed (or not at all), clothing the children properly and letting their clothing deteriorate into rags, and so on. Desperation is not well described as 'hassle', when what is at stake is the choice between acknowledging someone's human dignity and humiliating them.

Examples

There are many, many examples in the literature of experiences of bureaucratic disentitlement and the contemptuous treatment of poor women and children. A number of these examples are listed in the report of a study in Chicago (Brodkin et al, 2005). The study investigated calls to the Public Benefits Hotline at the Legal Assistance Foundation, and analysed the kinds of difficulties people had in getting access to 'welfare' benefits. It took place between August 2000 and July 2001, three or more years after 'welfare reform' had supposedly begun 'moving families from welfare to work'. Among the difficulties people called the hotline about were: misinterpretations of work requirements penalising those who should have been exempt (i.e. those caring for young children or family members with disabilities); routine sanctioning of people for missing appointments even when they did not receive notice; routine sanctioning of people for not attending job-training programs even though they had jobs; frequent erroneous cut-offs caused by the agency losing the paperwork; frequent redeterminations of eligibility necessitated by those cut-offs; requirements that people take low-wage, dead-end jobs and drop

---

positions on issues' means that they cannot be too explicit in exposing the right-wing moral and political foundations of the form 'welfare' takes in the US.

out of programs to improve their job skills; and phones unanswered, voice mailboxes full, fax lines busy, caseworkers unavailable, and offices where it was not possible to drop off documents or fill out application forms. And caller after caller told the hotline of experiences where the system could not correct administrative mistakes, or even acknowledge they had happened.

Another, thankfully short-lived, example occurred in Florida. In 2011, Florida passed a law requiring all TANF applicants to take a drug test when applying for benefits. Not only was this a gross invasion of people's privacy, it was also a shameless attempt at bureaucratic disentitlement, since the law required applicants to pay for the tests themselves. Those testing negative would be reimbursed later, but TANF applicants are unlikely to have the money in the first place, and hence were debarred from applying for assistance. However, in October 2011, a federal judge issued a temporary injunction blocking Florida's drug-testing law (Hahn et al, 2012b: 16-17n15), on the grounds that it could be violating the Constitution's Fourth Amendment which protects citizens from unlawful searches and seizures; and in December 2013, a district judge made that injunction permanent (Fader, 2015).

Another egregious example of PRWORA's bureaucratic disentitlement concerns Texas' full-family sanction whereby the whole family, mother and children, lose benefits (Hahn et al, 2012b: 37). Called 'pay for performance' and introduced in 2003, this sanction is imposed if the 'parent' fails to carry out certain 'personal responsibility requirements'. These requirements are not only 'work'-related, they also involve children's school attendance and immunisations, and cooperation with the State's attempts to collect child support from absent fathers. This had the effect of drastically reducing the 'welfare' caseload. For several years before 2003, the caseload in Texas had been around 130,000 families. In 2004, it had fallen to just over 100,000, and by 2005 it had dropped further to around 80,000. Moreover, by that time more than two-thirds of those remaining on the rolls were child-only cases. Officialdom continued to maintain the fiction that the bureaucratic requirements were just another way of helping 'clients'. One official was reported to say that the reason why the proportion of full-family sanctions had declined was because 'clients' were complying with the requirements (Hahn et al, 2012b: 37). There is, however, another, more likely explanation. Full-family sanctions declined because those who could not comply had been excluded from the 'welfare' rolls and hence no longer counted as 'clients', even though they remained as destitute as before. But such an explanation does not fit within the fact-free realm that is 'welfare' ideology.[341]

Another of PRWORA's disentitlements is Wisconsin's 'job ready' scheme. According to the Wisconsin W-2[342] Monitoring Task Force (2002), 'job ready' was the name for W-2's Case Management Services. 'Welfare' agencies (both private and public) could decide that applicants for TANF benefits had had some work experience (i.e. were 'employable'), and assign them to 30 days of unpaid 'job search', supposedly with the help of 'case management'. But contractors were found to be applying this criterion even to women with limited education and little or no work experience (IWF, 1998; Rotker et al, 2002). This is hardly surprising, since it allowed the agencies to deny cash assistance to applicants for those 30 days (and longer, if the applicant was found to be non-compliant), and thus keep the money for themselves.

The Institute for Wisconsin's Future, a non-profit public policy research and community-outreach organisation, investigated the impact of W-2 during its implementation period from September 1997 to June 1998. They found that, of those AFDC cases that transferred to TANF in the W-2 program, about 30% were classified as 'job ready'. According to the Wisconsin W-2 Monitoring Task Force, by 2001 the proportion of those who were determined to be 'job ready' or were denied assistance for other reasons had risen to 64% (IWF, 1998: 12). The 'job ready' category was a boon for the contractors with responsibility for managing W-2's 'welfare' program. The fewer people who received cash assistance, the more money was available for the 'welfare' providers.

The stories of what happens to people subjected to callous, arbitrary disentitlement for reasons that make no sense, are heart-rending. The following is taken from a report written by a community activist in the District of Columbia, who was part of a group helping homeless families in a local office of the Office of Emergency Shelter and Support Services (OESSS), the department that administered the publicly-funded DC overnight-shelter system from 1984 to 1994. The women and children are homeless and are waiting to see whether or not they can get a bed for the night:

> "The waiting area is a stark, oppressively stuffy room with dim lights and pale walls. A yellowed map of the United States hangs conspicuously in one corner, while the remaining walls are bare, except for the black

---

341. Full-family sanctions were still being imposed in 2016, when a senior academic recommended to the US House Ways and Means Committee that they be abolished (King, 2016).

342. Short for 'Wisconsin Works'.

and white flyers dot[ting] them, commanding 'NO EATING IN THIS WAITING AREA.' The gray floor is strewn with broken crayons, pencils, and scraps of paper filled with child[ren's] scrawl perhaps representative of their own innocent frustration in the waiting. There is no clock on the wall—a fitting omission in a room where time stands still ... By 2:00 p.m. children who have been at OESSS since 8:00 a.m. are either crying from hunger or falling asleep. Women cannot feed their children in the building, nor can they leave to get food for fear that they will be called for their intake interview and miss it. One woman fed her children sandwiches in the bathroom so they would not starve while waiting to be called" (Bennett, 1995: 2157-8, quoting from Kira Finkler & Patricia Kennedy 'Monitoring OESSS and the Intake Process 16', Jan. 8, 1992).

The horror and pity of being subjected to this humiliating treatment surpasses belief, and yet it is standard operating procedure in a land where rich men's hatred of 'welfare' infests the whole population via the mass media. But horrifying though this was, things got even worse. The text quoted was written by one of a group of community activists and law students who spent time in this waiting room in order to observe what went on during the application process, and to help applicants if they needed it. This project came to an end when one of the lawyers was threatened with arrest and handcuffed while he was trying to advise applicants, and the waiting room was subsequently closed to outsiders (Bennett, 1995: 2158n3).

This next example is taken from a list of seven such examples gathered from interviews with people who responded to the 2002 National Survey of America's Families (Zedlewski and Nelson, 2003: 28). The examples are presented by the authors as 'coping strategies' on the part of the families, but they are also examples of the consequences of bureaucratic disentitlement:

> Single mother with three children living in Georgia. Laid off from her job at a fast-food restaurant in January 2002, the mother says that her diabetes makes her feel ill and that she is often unable to work. She left welfare because she could not meet the work requirements and is uninsured. Her food stamps recently ended because she did not bring in the proper paperwork documenting the absent father's child support ... Family has Section 8 housing assistance, which pays the entire rent. The absent father pays $300 per month (one-quarter of the poverty level), which, according to the respondent, is "as much as he can." When asked how the family will eat (considering it did not receive food stamps), the mother said she hoped that her ex-husband would buy the family food. She has a brother and sister who live nearby and provide moral support.

Barbara Ehrenreich quoted one of her informants, Kaaryn Gustafson of the University of Connecticut Law School saying, "'applying for welfare is a lot like being booked by the police'":

> There may be a mug shot, fingerprinting, and lengthy interrogations as to one's children's true paternity. The ostensible goal is to prevent welfare fraud, but the psychological impact is to turn poverty itself into a kind of crime (Ehrenreich, 2011).

That these methods are successful in getting people off the 'welfare' rolls is beyond doubt, but the extent of it is unknown given the chaotic nature of the record-keeping. To give just one example: the Wisconsin W-2 Monitoring Task Force (2002: 12-13) asked YW Works[343] for their records on what had happened to the families who had applied for assistance in their administrative region. The Task Force found it 'troubling' that fewer than half the people who did get an appointment ever received cash assistance (48% in 2001 and 43% in the first half of 2002). They attributed this to the W-2 policy requiring staff to try and get people to apply elsewhere. This meant that staff actively discouraged people from applying, e.g. they portrayed the work requirements of the program in such a negative light that people were frightened away, or they put administrative roadblocks in the way (such as requiring repeat appointments for verifying documentation). The Task Force also found that these diverted applicants were never followed up to make sure that they did find jobs. They also said that they were 'dismayed' when they found that no information was kept on the numbers of people who came to the YW office to inquire about receiving services but who left or were sent away without being given an appointment. Hence the figures that were kept understated the problem of bureaucratic disentitlement, although to what extent it was impossible to know. Not only do the policy-makers ignore research findings that do not suit their welfare-hating agenda, the information is frequently not even available to be researched.

Declining 'welfare' rolls

As it turned out, PRWORA's bureaucratic disentitlement had exactly the effect intended: it dramatically reduced the numbers of people on the 'welfare' rolls. The size and speed of the reductions in the welfare rolls was the one change that was unprecedented. Never before in the history of 'welfare', even in the US, have the numbers of people registered for income support gone down so far so fast. Neither the block grants nor the time limits were

---

343. Originally a for-profit subsidiary of the YWCA. The 'YW', then, stands for 'young women'.

necessary to achieve these reductions. The numbers plummeted long before the time limits came due or the money ran out, engineered through the same forms of bureaucratic disentitlement that have always been used to keep people off the rolls and get them off once they were on (Brodkin, 2006; Brodkin and Majmundar, 2010; Lipsky, 1984). PRWORA did not end such practices, it entrenched them.

As any number of interested observers have noted, the numbers of TANF recipients have dropped precipitously, from 12.24 million recipients nationally in August 1996 to 6.28 million recipients in June 2000 (Schram and Soss, 2001: 50), and subsequently from 2.3 million families in 2000 to 1.9 million in the first part of 2006 (Acs and Loprest, 2007: 21). By March 2015, the numbers of recipients had declined even further, to 1.6 million families (4.1 million people), despite population increases and the global financial crisis. Most of the recipients (2.9 million) were children (Falk, 2015).

In some states the rolls had diminished by less than 20% by 2008, but in others the decline was more than 75% (Zedlewski and Golden, 2010: 1). By 2008 in the midst of the global financial crisis, the numbers of welfare recipients nationally had fallen by about 72% from the high point before the passage of PRWORA.[344] In New York City between 1994 and 2010, the welfare rolls declined by 69.6% (Bach, 2011: 547). Descriptions of the decreases as 'dramatic' and 'astounding' are scattered throughout the 'welfare reform' literature.

Much of the discussion of decline in numbers on the 'welfare' rolls locates the responsibility for the decreases with the poor women themselves, rather than with a system deliberately devised to expel people from the rolls and deter them from applying for 'welfare' in the first place. Or rather, when the relevant authorities are mentioned, the fact that 'welfare' has been deliberately designed to prevent people from making claims is seen as a good thing, or at least as morally neutral. It is assumed that the women have some power to decide whether or not to apply for 'welfare', and that after PRWORA became law they decided that applying for 'welfare' wasn't worth the hassle. But in fact they have no choice. The bureaucratic requirements are impossible, and no one could fulfil them. And yet the declines in the 'welfare' caseloads are attributed to the behaviour of the poor themselves.

Sometimes that attribution of responsibility is inadvertent. For example, a researcher with the Urban Institute said:

---

344. Schram et al, 2010: 744, quoting the US Department of Health and Human Services' 2009 figures on 'welfare' caseloads.

> The declining participation rate tells us that something in welfare programs has changed: either more families are eligible for small cash benefits (which *families see as too minimal to pursue*, depressing the average participation rate) or more families with real needs are *staying away* from the welfare office (Zedlewski, 2002: 2—emphases added).

To be fair, it should be pointed out that this particular author is fully aware of what happens in 'welfare' offices. But to talk about the declines in the 'welfare' rolls in terms of women deciding not to pursue cash benefits or staying away from 'welfare' offices, is to attribute an agency to women they do not have. Women are disqualified by procedures and strategies outside their control. The reality is that the system is deliberately stacked against them, and officials send people away for arbitrary bureaucratic reasons that 'welfare' claimants have no control over.

Sometimes, however, attributing the declines in the 'welfare' rolls to women themselves is not at all inadvertent, but rather, the result of an unashamed commitment to the right-wing belief that the way to solve the problem of poverty is to change the behaviour of the poor. In reviewing 'the research literature on the effects of the reform', the above-quoted Professor of Economics, for example, discussed 'the decline in welfare use and caseloads' in terms of what the women might have done (Moffitt, 2008: 20). 'Many women', he said, 'who would ordinarily have gone onto welfare when faced with a decline in income or earnings—possibly a temporary one—instead stayed off welfare after the reform'. He did acknowledge that there might be understandable reasons why many women 'stayed off welfare'. 'Reform', he said, 'would naturally be thought to make welfare less attractive' with its 'increased work requirements, sanctions, and time limits'. These requirements, however, were 'credible' (p.3), he said, and so if women 'stayed off welfare' they only had themselves to blame. The only cause of the diminishing enrolments he mentions is the behaviour and 'motivations' of the women. Against all reason and reality, he speaks as though the women are self-sufficient individuals whose preference is not to participate—they 'choose not to apply' they 'fail to meet the requirements' (p.25). Such an approach '"imputes to the poor the identity of self-interested, utility maximizing individuals who need to be given the right incentives so that they will change their behavior and enable the state better to manage the problems of poverty and welfare dependency"' (Schram, 1995: 4, quoted in Peck, 2001: 93-4). The task of 'welfare reform', according to the right-wing ideologues, was to change women's behaviour, but in fact the real task was to design a 'welfare' system that made it almost impossible to comply, to allow 'welfare' officials to refuse people assistance for bureaucratic reasons, and to pander to State administrations eager to reduce the 'welfare' rolls by any means whatsoever.

A particularly galling piece of right-wing mystification is the argument put forward by a self-identified strong supporter of tougher welfare policies and his colleague (Besharov and Germanis, 2007: 44-5). 'Why', they ask, 'would mothers leave welfare without having jobs?' After all, '[t]he burdens placed on them [i.e. the bureaucratic disentitlements described above] hardly seem a sufficient reason for them to abandon the only means of support for themselves and their children'. The answer, they said, as shown by studies of women who had left 'welfare', was that '[t]hese mothers have other sources of support besides welfare'. While some of those sources of support were other government programs (SSI, Social Security), others involved 'help (such as transportation assistance, a place to stay, or food) from family or friends'. So it didn't matter that women were refused 'welfare' assistance even though they didn't have jobs, their 'family or friends' would keep them from homelessness and starvation. These authors ignored the possibility that the 'family or friends' might be as poor as the women themselves, and hence not in a position to help much. Nor did they remark on the fact that refusing the women 'welfare' did not make them independent. They were no longer dependent on 'welfare', and that was all that mattered.

Reasons for the declines

The PRWORA-instigated decline in the 'welfare' caseloads is largely due to that bureaucratic disentitlement described above. While this certainly has an effect on women's behaviour, it is a form of coercion, not of choice. It operates in two ways: through the forcible removal of women from the rolls mainly through sanctions for infractions (real or perceived) of the rules; and through the refusal to register people in the first place:

> States have utilized two major strategies to reduce their rolls so much. One is to deny people access to the rolls when they come in to apply … The other is to make use of strong sanctioning policies that remove people from the rolls, temporarily and sometimes permanently, for sometimes minor infractions of various rules governing recipients (Edelman, 2010: 2).

The above-mentioned Professor of Economics made the same point:

These reductions were no doubt a result of families who were sanctioned off welfare as well as eligible families who choose [sic][345] not to apply for the program because of the new work requirements, or attempted to apply and were rejected because of failure to meet those requirements (Moffitt, 2008: 25).

Sanctions

Although 'welfare' has always been administered through sanctions, their importance increased with the passage of PRWORA, along with the numbers of things for which people could be sanctioned (Handler, 2008: 12). The Californian CalWORKs program is a typical example of how sanctions are applied. There are three levels: the first reduction in or abolition of cash benefits applies until the recipient complies; the second applies for three months, whether or not she complies; and the third and subsequent sanctions are applied for six months (Hasenfeld et al, 2004: 308). These sanctions are not only punitive in themselves, the way they are administered is extra punitive. People are often not informed when they apply for 'welfare' about the fact that they can be sanctioned; nor are they given the reasons why they might be. They are not even told that they have been sanctioned. They are expected to know from the fact that their cash assistance has reduced or ceased. And it frequently happens that the sanctions are wrongly applied (Hasenfeld et al, 2004: 317). But however they are administered, sanctions provide a splendid way to reduce the rolls, and there are indications that this is not only what sanctions were used for, this is the way their framers intended them to be used.

Sanctioning has become pervasive under TANF. Surveys of 'welfare' recipients in Cleveland, Philadelphia, Miami, and Los Angeles found sanction rates varying from 20% in Los Angeles to 50% in Miami. Other studies following recipients over time showed even higher estimates, ranging from 45% to 60% (Handler, 2008: 12).

The states where the 'welfare' rolls have decreased the most are those states which have imposed immediate, full-family sanctions, i.e. where a woman's first failure to comply with a program rule is met with withdrawal of aid for their entire family (Schram and Soss, 2001: 59). By 2012, 22 states were eliminating the family's entire benefit for the first infringement of the

---

345. There is a problem with the present tense here because the rest of the sentence is in the past tense. But there is also a problem with the notion of 'choice' in this context. This is the self-sufficient individual of neo-liberal economics, who has access to everything he needs and only has himself to blame if he willfully chooses not to avail himself of it. Applied to America's poor it is grotesque.

program requirements. This is another of PRWORA's innovations. It was not permitted under the previous AFDC program (Zedlewski et al, 2012: 2).

Entry denied

The other way in which PRWORA reduces the numbers on the 'welfare' rolls through declining rates of entry. It is not clear whether the declining entries or the increased exits contributed more to the decreases. Some researchers say that the higher numbers of people exiting played a larger role than the declining numbers of people entering, even though 'changes in entry were an important part of caseload decline' (Acs and Loprest, 2007: v). Others have found that 'decreasing … entry explained roughly half of the decline in the caseload' (Grogger et al, 2003: 291). The above-quoted Professor of Economics believed that 'much of the decline in welfare use and caseloads arose because of decreased entry instead of increased exit' (Moffitt, 2008: 20).

But if 'welfare' agencies keep no records of those who are turned away,[346] there is no way of finding out the extent the refusal of entry to eligible claimants. One commentator (Stoesz, 1997: 71) estimated that outright denial of benefits to those who were eligible possibly reached one quarter of the applicants in some 'welfare' offices at the beginning of the 'welfare reform' regime, although he admitted that the prevalence was unknown. He predicted that the States would lose no time in excluding families from their caseloads, squeezed as they were between the static resources of the block grants, and increasingly impossible demands from the federal government to place people in jobs.

PRWORA mandated a 'work participation rate' of 30 hours a week for 25% of all families in the caseload in the first year (1997), increasing by 5% a year to 50% in 2002 'or thereafter'; and 75% of two-parent families increasing to 90% by 1999 (SEC. 407(a)(1)(2), p.25). States could meet their quotas by reducing the rolls instead of enrolling more people in 'work participation' activities (Hahn et al, 2012a: 4). So the most efficient way the States could fulfil these quotas was by screening out those least likely to be employed.

> The work participation rate is simply the ratio of the number of adult TANF recipients who are working or in specified work-related activities to the number of families with adults receiving cash assistance through TANF-related programs. Georgia's work participation rate has increased dramatically in recent years – from 11 percent in 2003 to over 65 percent

---

346. YW Works, for example, was found to keep no information on the numbers of people who were sent away without being given an appointment.

in 2006. But the increased work participation rate is primarily a factor of fewer families receiving assistance (Schott, 2007: 1).

These practices defeated the stated purpose of the legislation, i.e. to get people into jobs, but they did serve the real purpose, i.e. to reduce the numbers of people on 'welfare'. This was clearly stated by the US Office of Child Support Enforcement (1996) under the heading 'Making welfare a transition to work':

> recipients must work after two years on assistance, with few exceptions. Twenty-five percent of all families in each state must be engaged in work activities or have left the rolls in fiscal year … 1997, rising to 50 percent in … 2002 (US CSE, 1996—emphasis added).

Workfare

Another of PRWORA's innovations was the introduction of work requirements across the board as a condition for receiving benefits (although this aspect of PRWORA has a long history preceding this particular piece of legislation—see below). States must

> [r]equire a parent or caretaker receiving assistance under the program to engage in work (as defined by the State) once the State determines the parent or caretaker is ready to engage in work, or once the parent or caretaker has received assistance under the program for 24 months (whether or not consecutive), whichever is earlier (SEC. 402(a)(1)(A) (ii), p.9).

PRWORA created 12 'work activities', participation in any one of which counted as 'engaging in work':

(1) unsubsidized employment;

(2) subsidized private sector employment;

(3) subsidized public sector employment;

(4) work experience (including work associated with the refurbishing of publicly assisted housing) if sufficient private sector employment is not available;

(5) on-the-job training;

(6) job search and job readiness assistance;

(7) community service programs;

(8) vocational educational training (not to exceed 12 months with respect to any individual);

(9) job skills training directly related to employment;

(10) education directly related to employment, in the case of a recipient who has not received a high school diploma or a certificate of high school equivalency;

(11) satisfactory attendance at secondary school or in a course of study leading to a certificate of general equivalence, in the case of a recipient who has not completed secondary school or received such a certificate; and

(12) the provision of child care services to an individual who is participating in a community service program (SEC. 407. Mandatory Work Requirements, (d) Work Activities Defined (1)-(12).

The Deficit Reduction Act of 2005 divided these into nine core activities and three non-core activities, the latter all relating to the educational activities (9, 10 and 11). The 'non-core' activities only counted towards 'engaging in work' if the 'welfare' recipient was already participating in core activities for at least 20 hours a week. Thus, those activities that the ideology insists are most important for getting people into work (i.e. more education) were reduced in importance and made more difficult.

The onus was on the States—either they met these goals or they lost their funding. But there was also a positive incentive, for the States, although not for the recipients—the PRWORA legislation set aside $1 billion dollars for 'performance bonuses to reward states for moving welfare recipients into jobs' by 2003. The source doesn't say whether that also included moving recipients off the rolls even if they weren't in jobs. Nor does it comment on the fact that, if the person was still on the 'welfare' rolls while being 'engaged in work activities', those activities clearly did not to end poverty or 'dependence' on 'welfare'.

The following examples of the activities that counted as 'work participation' give some idea of how 'work participation' operated in practice. The first two are taken from a report on research by an advocacy organisation, Community Voices Heard, into New York City's Employment Services and Placement (ESP) program (see below) (Youdelman and Getsos, 2005), the third from California's GAIN program (Greater Avenues for Independence), established in 1985 under the Family Support Act of 1988:

"We did nothing all day. There wasn't a single workshop or class. There would just be sixty or seventy of us crammed into a small room … doing nothing for eight hours—a lot of people left because it was such a waste of time." ESP Client #6'.

"You do resumé writing—you write your own and then they help you edit it. After that you take classes on interview skills, how to fill out an application, you do a personality self-assessment, and sometimes they show videos about how to behave on a job site or how to talk on the phone. The workshops are helpful but they dragged them out—they made people sit there while they repeated information just so you would stay all day." ESP Client #4.

When participants enter the job club … they are issued with a terse set of "Job Club Rules": 1. Be on time—8.30 to 12.30;   2. Dress for success; 3. Full class participation; 4. No criticisms; 5. No food; 6. No drink; 7. No gum; 8. Daily job search … Participants are required to cold call employers from the GAIN office, each being stationed (for several hours per day) in a booth containing a telephone and a telephone directory which is backed by a mirror so as to permit the self-monitoring of poise and telephone manner … participants are expected to make at least 25 calls per day to new employer contacts, at least three days a week, while making at least 15 personal visits to employers' premises each week. Each participant is expected to generate at least five positive job leads per day' (Peck, 1998a: 541, 545).

Such non-activities, not surprisingly, utterly failed to get people into work. One example of this failure was the ESP program in New York City, investigated in 2004 by Community Voices Heard (Youdelman and Getsos, 2005). The authors described the service as 'a comprehensive work-first policy' which operated by

transforming welfare centers into job centers, expanding the local unpaid Work Experience Program … to cover tens of thousands of single mothers, instituting intensive job search activities for people on welfare, and aggressively sanctioning non-participating welfare recipients (Youdelman and Getsos, 2005: 1).

This failed to move people into jobs, although its sanctioning procedures were highly successful in moving people off 'welfare'. The study found that, according to the Human Resources Administration's (HRA) statistics for six months in 2004, 82% of the 2,305 people registered as 'seen by the system' had been sanctioned ('Failed to Comply'—FTC). The report of the study defined sanctions as:

[d]enial of or reduction in welfare benefits … The length of time over which benefits are reduced depends on whether or not a household contains a dependent child and the number of times the individual has Failed to Comply (Youdelman and Getsos, 2005: 16).

The researchers said that the service providers (called 'vendors') had told them that they felt that they didn't have much choice but to sanction people en masse because the emphasis on sanctioning was written into the structure of the program. The system gave the vendors no resources for working with people over time to address the problems they had in finding and keeping jobs, or to help them avoid non-compliance; the referral process persisted in assigning people to the wrong ESP site because they were not properly assessed or not assessed at all; and the administrative tracking process was inadequate and led to people being wrongly sanctioned. As one ESP provider said, 'It's crazy. People get FTCed [Failure to Comply] for not attending … even though they were [attending] at an interview!' (p.4). And the system offered people so few options that they were sent back to the same type of program over and over again. As another ESP provider said,

> Why continue to send people to the same program if it's not working? … HRA [the Human Resources Administration] tells us to FTC them, but why? They are just sent to another ESP Site. We're known for keeping people on our roster for too long. But, if we FTC everyone, we wouldn't have anyone. The whole system is a recycling process (Youdelman and Getsos, 2005: 7).

As for getting people into jobs, according to the 2004 HRA statistics only 8% of those who had been referred to the ESPs were placed in jobs, and only just over a third of those still had their jobs at the end of the six months (i.e. 35% of that 8%). Of the other two-thirds (of the 8% employed six months earlier), just under half had returned to public assistance, and just over half were 'unaccounted for', i.e. they were neither in employment nor receiving 'welfare' (Youdelman and Getsos, 2005: 3). If the program could only get 8% of its caseload into jobs, and just a fraction of that 8% into jobs that lasted six months, it was an utter failure at what was supposed to be its primary purpose, i.e. 'job placement'. Such results suggest that the reason for the New York ESP program (and 'welfare reform' in general) is not getting people jobs, much less reducing poverty. The 2006 re-authorisation process took absolutely no notice of this report nor of others like it, and the subsequent legislation reinforced the problems the report identified.

Not about work

If these 'work activities' are typical, then 'welfare reform' is clearly not an 'imperative to work'. Such exercises in futility cannot possibly get people work, as indeed they do not. They're a form of harassment, and intended as such in order to comply with PRWORA's demand for disentitlement. Under PRWORA, the States must ensure that a certain percentage of 'families' are 'engaged in work activities' (as the Office of Child Support Enforcement put it)—25% by 1997, 50% by 2002, etc. There are two ways of achieving those percentages. One is to get people into jobs, but the other is to ensure that those people who are *not* engaged in work activities 'have left the rolls', so that those who *are* so engaged become a larger proportion of the whole. This was the option invariably chosen. For example, examination of data on Georgia's TANF program (Schott, 2007) found that the state's recent increased workforce participation rate among TANF recipients was the result of fewer families receiving assistance, and not the result of more families in work or work-related activities. The work-participation rate of Georgia's TANF recipients increased dramatically from 2003 to 2006—from 11% in 2003 to over 65% in 2006—but the *numbers* in the adult caseloads declined even more dramatically—by more than 88% between 2004 and 2006. The data also showed that most of the families who left the rolls were not working; that the proportion of those who were working at the time they had left the rolls had fallen since 2001; and that there had been a sharp rise in the numbers of applications that were denied for bureaucratic reasons.

As one commentator noted:

> no matter what the particular "work test" each state and county implement, it has clearly become a major tool, coupled with sanctions, in denying aid and reducing the welfare rolls (Hasenfeld, 2010: 152).

Citing the findings of the Community Voices Heard research (Youdelman and Getsos, 2004, 2005), one commentator wrote that there was 'something quite disturbing' about the fact that the overwhelming majority of people in the ESP program were sanctioned and not employed at all, and that the same private contractors got their contracts renewed on similar terms despite their massive failure to place people in jobs. She quoted the executive director of the non-profit Women's Housing and Economic Development Corporation (WHEDCO), Nancy Biberman, speaking about her organisation's experience as a partner in the ESP program with the for-profit organisation, America Works:

> The ESP program and contracts were never intended to result in viable jobs for welfare recipients. The rapid reduction of the welfare caseload was the public policy mandate out of which the ESP program was created ... The contracts were structured to provide financial incentives for "rapid labor market attachment" (the expressly stated goal of HRA commissioner Jason Turner). Consequently at best they provided quick job placements and woefully unsatisfactory job retention outcomes (Bach, 2009: 289n55).

Biberman was also quoted saying that '[t]he ESP contracts were children of short-sighted social policy and privatization ideology, which have proven both costly and inappropriate in the human services sector'. She described the policy as 'egregiously myopic', and said that 'the payment milestones in these "performance-based" contracts … forced even the most mission-driven providers into unconscionable work' (Sanger, 2003: 56). For this reason, WHEDCO's partnership with America Works was short-lived. They found that America Works' services to the women were inadequate, that the need to make a profit short-changed the women they were supposed to be serving, and that WHEDCO itself was having to use extra resources to subsidise the work it was doing with America Works. To make matters worse, America Works took the credit for the significant investment WHEDCO had made in supplementing services. As Biberman said, '"We barely broke even on the arrangement because we provided layer upon layer of solid support services. But it was our investment that made America Works's performance so good"' (Sanger, 2003: 83).

A job paying a living wage is the least likely outcome for a 'welfare' leaver; and the 2005 TANF reauthorisation simply made matters worse.

> The 2005 TANF reauthorization, which applied work requirements to state-funded programs and focused on documenting participation in countable work activities, has primarily had the effect of increasing the paperwork burden on clients, caseworkers, and administrators, and reducing state flexibility, with no evidence that it has caused states to develop more effective programs … One study of employment counselors in Minnesota found that they spent 53 percent of their TANF time on documentation activities, such as verifying, collecting, and reporting information for work participation rates, and only 47 percent on direct service activities, such as creating employment plans, identifying barriers to work, and assisting with job search (Lower-Basch, 2011a: 2).

In the light of policies like these, it is clear that the real purpose of 'welfare reform' lies elsewhere than helping people get employment. The real purpose is to end 'welfare', just as Clinton said it was, not, however, by ending the *need* for 'welfare' by ending poverty, but by reducing the 'welfare' rolls through savage forms of disentitlement. This has been so extraordinarily successful in reducing the 'welfare' rolls, that it must have been the intention all along.

'A job as the best way out of poverty' is the ideological mantra which disguises the real purpose behind 'welfare reform'. If the policy-makers cared about whether or not people got jobs, much less jobs that paid a living wage, they would acknowledge the true state of the labour market—no possibility of employment for everyone, a low-wage economy which ought to be the scandal of the western world but is not, and sending employment 'off-shore' where people are paid a minute fraction of even the low wages available domestically. They would also acknowledge that the fate of 'welfare leavers' is not self-sufficiency through employment, but high levels of sanctions, being churned through jobs paying starvation wages, or having no visible means of support at all. They would recognise too that PRWORA's disentitlement means that a significant proportion of America's poor are refused permission to apply for 'welfare' in the first place, despite their eligibility. Given that the policy-makers acknowledge none of this, that the policies of 'welfare reform' do not lead to employment, and in the light of that explicit disentitlement clause and the glee with which the right-wing have heralded the reductions in the 'welfare' rolls, it is obvious that the purpose of the emphasis on 'work participation' is not to find people jobs, but to provide the occasion for disentitlement.

Bill Clinton's legacy was summed up by David Harvey:

> one of the effects of President Clinton's reform of the welfare system in the United States and the introduction of 'workfare' requirements in 1995 ... [was] that wage levels throughout the whole labour force diminish[ed] without necessarily generating much new employment, thus contributing to the rising rate of exploitation of labour and ... higher profits for capital and widening income disparities ... The far more punitive conditions of welfare for the unemployed end up, of course, increasing the vast pool of poverty-ridden unemployed who cannot find a job because none are being generated in the face of the twin forces of globalisation (and competition with massive latent reserves) and labour-saving technological changes. Clinton has been handsomely rewarded since by business organisations, earning some $17 million in 2012 from speaker's fees mainly from business groups (Harvey, 2014: 100-1).

Oblivious to the actual effects of his 'ending welfare', Clinton is still congratulating himself on PRWORA's 'success' (Clinton, 2006).

Whether workfare has been a success or a failure depends on its purpose. The manifest purpose of 'welfare reform'—'alleviating poverty' and 'creat[ing] effective pathways to economic opportunity' (as one advocacy organisation put it)[347]—is not in fact its real purpose. Its real purpose is to abolish entitlement to welfare and to deflect attention away from the real cause of poverty by blaming the victims. For decades it has been known that workfare is not successful at getting people jobs. In 1962, for example, the federal Bureau of Family Services reported in relation to the work programs

---

347. http://www.clasp.org/.

for men in the 1950s, that "'work relief cannot reduce the public assistance rolls [by getting people into jobs] unless the economy produces additional regular jobs'" (quoted in Piven and Cloward, 1993: 388). That knowledge has consistently been ignored by the policy-makers. Workfare does work, however, at cheapening already distressingly cheap labour power, and it has been remarkably successful at diminishing the 'welfare' rolls (the Bureau of Family Services was wrong about that). Indeed, the latter was an explicit aim of the workfare aspect of PRWORA. States could fulfil their quotas of 'families engaged in work activities' by getting people off the 'welfare' rolls, full stop (see the italicised part of the quote above from the Office of Child Support Enforcement at the time). But workfare programs have been shown over and over again to fail in their stated objective of getting people into full-time, year-round jobs with adequate wages and benefits. They are, however, an excellent way of reducing the 'welfare' rolls because they mandate an impossibility—insisting that recipients get jobs even though they have applied for 'welfare' because they cannot get jobs.

Given that workfare's dismal record at getting people into jobs that will make them independent of 'welfare' has been well-known, even in official circles, for over half a century, it is not beyond the bounds of belief that workfare has nothing to do with work at all. Its primary purpose is not to get people into work (many of whom are already working anyway) (Morath, 2015); its primary purpose is to provide the opportunity for sanctions in order to 'end welfare as we know it' by reducing the 'welfare' caseloads. It is a central aspect of that bureaucratic disentitlement which allows the semblance of a welfare state while providing no such thing. 'Work first' (more Orwellian language) does not mean getting people jobs and then providing them with other services. It means focusing on bureaucratically devised activities which are named to suggest that they lead to employment—'job search', 'job clubs', 'assistance'—but which in fact do not. Then when people don't get jobs the harassment goes on and on and on until they can't stand it any more and stop turning up, or they lose their benefits by being sanctioned for breaking one of the many rules disguised as 'work activities'. The last twenty years of 'welfare reform' demonstrate that it cannot provide people with employment that would give them a way out of poverty (although the whole history of 'welfare' in the US had made that clear long before PRWORA—see below).

Privatisation

Another change is the level of privatisation allowed by PRWORA (although once again there is continuity with previous policies) (see below). The innovative aspect of PRWORA is the permission it gives States to contract out the whole of the TANF program to non-governmental agencies, including to large corporations:

> A State may—administer and provide services under the programs described [elsewhere] through contracts with charitable, religious, or private organizations; and provide beneficiaries of assistance under the programs … with certificates, vouchers, or other forms of disbursement which are redeemable with such organizations (SEC. 104 (a)(1)(A)(B), p.57).

For the first time private entities, for-profit corporations as well as non-profit organisations, could make decisions affecting the personal lives of the poor (Freedman et al, 2002; US GAO, 2002). Giving power to private corporations to operate 'welfare' systems has serious implications for the poor because the power to grant or deny benefits is coercive and private corporations care about nothing but the bottom line. As one commentator put it,

> The PRWORA opened the door to a number of large corporations adept at the art of pursuing federal largesse. Among the major contenders, and perhaps the most improbable one, is defense contractor Lockheed Martin, more accustomed to manufacturing weapons of mass destruction than calculating family needs budgets (Kennedy, 1998: 258).

But, of course, 'calculating family needs budgets' is not what PRWORA is about. Rather, its primary aim is to punish those who fail to thrive under a system stacked against them, and who better to administer the punishment than a multinational arms dealer.

Moreover, privatisation is also a way to disburse federal money for 'welfare' without offending 'States rights', which are not offended when public money ends up in private pockets. As the above-quoted commentator put it:

> It seems quite ironic that the states have urged devolution of welfare policy from the federal government and succeeded on the strength of the argument that local needs are best met by local services, only to vest operational authority in national, if not multinational, corporations. Devolution, after all, was supposed to result in decisions being made in state capitals, rather than corporate boardrooms (Kennedy, 1998: 266).

By 2003, it was not clear what the block grants had been used for, largely because the 'welfare' agencies kept only limited records and there was little research. What research there was found that the money was used for short-term programs that led to nothing of lasting value. It was clear where at least some of the money had gone—largely into private pockets: 'in their zest for services over [financial] support, states actually shifted government funds from the pockets of poor families to the pockets of private service providers' (Brodkin, 2003: 32).

There are few studies investigating 'welfare' privatisation. Most of the studies of privatisation in 'human services' have investigated prison management or job training, and most of those studies have found that private contractors are not more efficient or effective than public agencies. On the contrary, the studies consistently find that the public agencies perform at least as well as, if not better than, the privatised ones.

There is no recent information on the extent to which 'welfare' has been privatised (Butz, 2012). The only data available come from an audit by the General Accounting Office[348] in 2001. In that year, 13% of the TANF funds (more than $1.5 billion) had been allocated by States to contracts with non-governmental organisations, and 13% of that amount went to for-profit firms (US GAO, 2002: 3). In 2001, there was a great deal of variation between the States in the amount of TANF funds they had contracted out, ranging from no private contracting in South Dakota (the only State to retain sole governmental control), to 71% of TANF funds to private entities in Mississippi (the only State to have directed the majority of its TANF funds to private entities) and 74% in Washington D.C. (which is not a State). Several other States had privatised significant portions of their TANF budget in 2001—43% in Wisconsin and Idaho, 42% in New Jersey, 39% in Pennsylvania—but most States had privatised less than 15% of their TANF outlays (Butz, 2012: 46). At least at that time, it would seem that private contracting had not made any great inroads into the 'welfare' sector, given that 87% of the TANF funds were still in government hands; and it would seem, too, that for-profit companies had not made any great inroads either, given that 87% of the funds contracted out by State governments went to non-profit organisations—whether secular (national or community-based), or faith-based.

Whether that situation has subsequently changed is not known. The GAO collected the information through a special research project involving surveys and interviews as well as official documents such as audit reports and actual contracts. The research had not been replicated at the time of writing (2016).

What information there is on 'welfare' privatisation suggests that it has adverse consequences, both for the funding authorities, i.e. the federal and State governments (aka 'the taxpayer'), and for 'welfare' recipients. A study (Butz, 2012) examining administrative data in Florida for the period from

---

348. The name was changed to the General Accountability Office in 2004.

2000 to 2005 found that contracting 'welfare' out to private agencies did not improve client outcomes. For example, 'welfare' recipients with the for-profits were around one-fifth less likely to get jobs than those with public agencies or with non-profit organisations (p.128). The author of the study attributed the problems to secretive contracting procedures, weak contracts, loose oversight and self-reported results (p.147). He also said that, since 2008, 13 Regional Workforce Boards in Florida had terminated their contracts with private firms, and decided instead to keep the 'welfare' services in public hands. He believed that 'welfare' privatisation was now falling out of favour, and that it had been popular only for the period between 2000 and 2005 (p.147). However, this is not the case in Milwaukee County, Wisconsin, where private contractors were still administering the W-2 'welfare' programs (and earning big executive salaries and respectable profits) in 2016.

Non-profit and for-profit

The term 'private' applies to both for-profit and non-profit organisations, and definitions of 'privatisation' usually make no distinction. One definition, for example, interprets privatisation as 'the wholesale delegation of eligibility determinations for welfare programs ... to private parties', without identifying different kinds of 'private parties' (Stevenson, 2002: 546). Another interprets it as 'the array of strategies—such as contracting for services, the use of vouchers, and sale of public assets—to transfer responsibility for activities or functions from the government to the private sector'. The examples given of the private sector include both non-profits and for-profits: 'neighborhood nonprofit organizations ... churches [and] multinational corporations' (Freedman et al, 2002: 557). Yet another definition focuses on the change in values privatisation brings, and there is no suggestion that non-profits might differ from for-profit firms in the way they provided 'welfare': 'Privatization of Welfare: initiative to introduce market relationships into the bureaucratic production of public services where a standard of social justice is replaced by an ethos of economic costs and benefits' (Baldwin, 2010: 5n3).

It has been argued that the involvement of non-profit enterprises in the provision of 'welfare' is less problematic than that of for-profit firms. Not only do non-profits have more experience in and commitment to serving needy populations, the lack of the need to make a profit raises fewer concerns about their motives and efficacy (Kennedy, 1998: 257). Moreover, the study using 2002-2005 data in Florida (Butz, 2012) found that 'welfare' recipients were somewhat less likely to be sanctioned by losing their benefits altogether if they were with a non-profit organisation than if they were with a for-profit firm (and also less likely than if they were with a public provider), and more likely to gain employment.

However, any differences are likely to be minor. All service providers must comply with the terms laid down by PRWORA and they would cease to exist if they didn't follow the rules. The harshness of those rules can sometimes be ameliorated by common human kindness, but the rules themselves apply to all TANF providers without exception.

Moreover, the structuring of 'welfare reform' in line with 'predatory corporate forces' (Berkowitz, 2001) transformed non-profit organisations. As charitable, community and religious entities, non-profits originally operated on the assumption that they existed to serve the community, no matter how constrained they might have been by being deprived of resources and by the ideology of the undeserving poor. With 'welfare reform' they became subject to the values of 'the market', both in competition for funding with other service providers and in partnerships with firms whose primary interest is in making money for their shareholders and executives (Hasenfeld and Garrow, 2012). This is unlikely to have been an unintended consequence of 'welfare reform',[349] given the stranglehold the values of the market have over the hearts and minds of the policy-makers.

The problematic financial dealings that beset the W-2 program in Milwaukee County, Wisconsin (see below), were not confined to for-profit firms. Non-profit organisations also used the funding in ways that were found by the State audit bureau to be 'unallowable'; and they paid their chief executives salaries that made a mockery of any notion of community service. Moreover, the non-profits were also permitted to make unrestricted profits, and they often used those profits in the same way the for-profits did. The supposedly 'non-profit' Opportunities Industrialization Center of Greater Milwaukee, for example, used its profits to invest in a mobile phone company (Wisconsin LAB, 2001: 1-39). Another 'non-profit', United Migrant Opportunities Services, invested in real estate—'to retire two mortgages for buildings used for operations' and 'to purchase a vacant lot ... for future development, potentially for low-income housing'—and the money market—'to meet future agency operating needs' (Wisconsin LAB, 2001: 1-43). Employment Solutions (also 'non-profit') said that they had used around a half of the $9.5 million profit for services for 'disadvantaged and disabled residents ... senior citizens ... [and] families and children'. But they would not tell the State audit bureau how they spent the rest (Wisconsin LAB, 2001: 1-31),

---

349. 'An unintended consequence of welfare "reform" has been the transformation of the nonprofit sector' (Berkowitz, 2001).

and as a private entity they were not obliged to. YW Works, originally a for-profit subsidiary of the non-profit YWCA, flourished financially only after it changed its status back to non-profit.

So there is on the whole no need to make any distinction between for-profit firms and non-profit organisations when defining the category 'private', because the same rules and entitlements apply to all.

The decline in 'welfare' caseloads

Because there is little information on the extent to which 'welfare' provision has been privatised, it is not clear to what extent privatisation contributed to the decline in the 'welfare' rolls. Certainly, profits were tied to reductions—the more people who left the rolls, the greater the proportion of the up-front grant the organisation could keep.

For example, in Milwaukee County, Wisconsin, where the whole W-2 program was privatised, contracts with private agencies allowed them to keep as profit 10% of what remained of the budget at the end of the contract term (as well as the 7% of the whole budget which was designated as profit in the first place) (AFSCME, 2006: 13). Any funds not spent at the end of the contract period were defined as either restricted or unrestricted profit. Restricted profits were known as 'community reinvestment funds' and they had to be spent on services for people who were TANF-eligible; unrestricted profits 'could be spent for a variety of purposes' and the private contractors were not even obliged to disclose what they spent the money on. At the end of the initial contract period (September 1997 to December 1999), the unspent funds across all the W-2 agencies throughout Wisconsin amounted to $237.9 million out of a total State W-2 budget of $651.5 million, 'largely because of the unanticipated decline in caseloads'. Of that $237.9 million, $65.1 million was unrestricted profit (Wisconsin LAB, 2001: 5). The five Milwaukee agencies together were paid more than $26 million in unrestricted profits, money supposedly meant to aid low-income families (Rotker et al, 2002: 534). As one of the members of a panel monitoring the performance of the county's W-2 TANF program said, 'The profit motive was directly related to dumping people off the rolls ... You can't create an incentive like that and not expect people to take advantage of it' (Schultze, 2002a).[350]

350. The *Milwaukee Journal Sentinel* newspaper ran a campaign for a number of years, especially between 2001 and 2005, exposing the corruption in the privatised 'welfare' agencies. Most of their information came from the reports of the Wisconsin Legislative Audit Bureau, the state's auditing agency. The MJS is the source of much of this information about Wisconsin's W2 program. At the time of writing, the articles were freely available on the internet, but that is no longer the case. The existence of the articles can be confirmed by

Moreover, caseload reductions accelerated in Wisconsin after the introduction of its privatised W-2 program. Between 1997 and 2000, the numbers on the 'welfare' rolls dropped by just over 80%, the largest decline of any State (Piliavin et al, 2003: 3). Citing information from the Wisconsin Legislative Audit Bureau 2001 evaluation report, poverty advocates found that private agencies in Milwaukee imposed harsher sanctions on more people, and asked for fewer extensions to W-2's time limits, than did the publicly-administered agencies in the rest of the State (Rotker et al, 2002: 530). As one researcher found in relation to the pressures on workers in the privatised 'welfare' agencies in Wisconsin, '[i]f their professional goal is to clear cases (which in the privatized era no longer means to solve mothers' problems), then they are evaluated in their job performance based on how many mothers they get off the welfare rolls' (Baldwin, 2010: 256).

However, there is no national data on the consequences of privatisation for 'welfare' recipients and the poor more generally, nor on the effectiveness and efficiency of privatised agencies. The few studies that do exist are small qualitative case studies in particular States or localities, or State audit reports, none of which systematically examines privatisation and performance and its effect on recipients' outcomes across the country. Most of the privatisation research focuses on prisons (and on such services as garbage collection, building construction, and asphalt laying), and there is very little research on contracting arrangements within social service programs (Butz, 2012: 38, 177).

Nonetheless, what research there is suggests that, at best, privatisation makes no difference to the outcomes for 'welfare' recipients, at worst, that it is not only less efficient than public provision, but that it leads to inappropriate use of public money and outright corruption. A study using the 2001 figures reported by the General Accounting Office (Butz, 2012) found that the outcomes for TANF recipients were not usually improved by privatisation, whether the agency was non-profit or for-profit. People were neither working more nor earning higher incomes than those in the public sector. When a private agency was doing better than the public service, it was more likely to be a non-profit organisation than a for-profit firm. The study also found that those states with the highest amount of money invested in for-profit firms had the lowest full-time employment rates among TANF recipients in 2001. Mississippi, with the highest level of welfare privatisation of any State (and the lowest maximum cash benefit and the highest rate of

entering author's name into the journal's search engine, but the articles are now behind a paywall (http://nl.newsbank.com/sites/mwsb/).

poverty), had the lowest work participation rates among its TANF recipients. It also had the highest rate of sanctions (Butz, 2012: 124). While these findings are neither current nor representative of the whole country, they do suggest that privatisation does not improve matters for 'welfare' recipients (not that that is likely to concern the policy makers).

W-2

Privatisation of 'welfare' can be illustrated with an account of the management of Wisconsin's W-2 program (short for 'Wisconsin Works') in its early years in Milwaukee County. Wisconsin had been experimenting with its welfare program for 10 years before PRWORA was enacted. Through a series of waivers (i.e. exemptions from the federal regulations for 'welfare' provision—see below), the State had been imposing work and other requirements as conditions for receiving cash and services from AFDC, and these experiments were incorporated into W-2 under TANF (Courtney and Dworsky, 2006a-f).

It might be argued that a single case study, and one moreover which relies mainly on newspaper reports (i.e. the Milwaukee Journal Sentinel), is hardly typical of privatised 'welfare' overall. But these particular private agencies operate in other States as well as Wisconsin (as well as overseas, including Australia), and there are similar stories from the other sources quoted in this context. It is unlikely that privatised 'welfare' has been managed with any more effectiveness, efficiency or integrity elsewhere, given the profit motive and the system's foundational premise of contemptuous disentitlement for the 'welfare' recipients.

W-2 was first implemented throughout Wisconsin in September 1997. Its stated aim was 'to help participants achieve economic self-sufficiency through employment', and in pursuit of that aim it purported to provide 'job-search and other employment assistance, education and training, and help in overcoming barriers to employment' (Wisconsin LAB, 2001: 11). By June 2004, it had cost $1.5 billion (Wisconsin LAB, 2005a: 1, 3).

W-2 provided for four categories of 'help'.[351] One category, called 'transitional placements', involved 'work practice and training' for people deemed to be 'unable to perform independent, self-sustaining work or work [in] community service or trial jobs'. People in this category originally

---

351. Later a fifth category was added, involving 'unmarried women in the third trimester of pregnancy who have a medically verified at risk pregnancy'. The original benefit was $673. Information about the original benefit level is no longer available (https://dcf.wisconsin. gov/files/publications/pdf/11890.pdf).

received a monthly benefit of $628 (which was reduced to $608 by 2012). It should be noted that these stipends were less in dollar amounts in 2012 than they were for the same categories in 1997. So not only did benefits not increase in real terms and rise with inflation in the15 years between 1997 and 2012, the actual dollar amount was deliberately reduced.

Another form of 'help', called 'community service jobs', involved 'work experience and training' for people who were deemed to be not quite as incapable as those placed in the first category, because they were 'able to perform some job duties'. People in this category were 'expected to eventually move into trial jobs or unsubsidized employment'. The original monthly benefit was $673 ($653 in 2012). As well as the overall five-year limit on participation in TANF, there was a two-year limit on the length of time anyone could spend in either of these two categories.

A third category was called 'trial jobs' (later, Trial Employment Match Program). This was also a 'work experience and training' category, although they were actual jobs in the ordinary labour market. It was hoped that participants would keep their jobs at the end of the trial period—the jobs 'may become permanent, unsubsidized positions'. There was no benefit payment because the person was supposed to be earning a wage—'the participant earns not less than the State or federal minimum wage for every hour worked'—but the employer was paid up to $300 a month for each participant who was working full-time. The fourth category applied to mothers of new-borns up to the age of 12 weeks. They were 'not required to work outside of the home' and they received a monthly benefit of $673 (Wisconsin LAB, 2001: 3-4).

Milwaukee County in Wisconsin was the first place in the nation where core welfare services, including eligibility determination, were privatised after the passage of PRWORA (AFSCME, 2006). Milwaukee is the most populous county in the State, with around 80% of the State's TANF caseload (Piliavin et al, 2003). Its W-2 program was much praised by 'welfare reform' proponents (and 'objective' observers) for the enormous reduction in the 'welfare' rolls it achieved. When W-2 was launched in September 1997, there were 35,000 welfare cases on the books in Wisconsin; by the beginning of 2000, there were only 4,400 who were receiving cash payments, plus another 1,300 who were registered for W-2 services but receiving no cash payments (Schultze, 2000b).[352] The numbers subsequently rose again, although not to the original pre-PRWORA level. In July 2005, there were 9,224 families who

---

352. Some of those 35,000 had transferred to other programs—to Supplemental Security Income or the Kinship Care program (Wisconsin W-2 Monitoring Task Force, 2002: 9).

were getting monthly W-2 payments, and this was 3,317 families fewer than at the same time the previous year (Schultze, 2005e).

Not everyone approved of W-2, especially after the exposure in the press of the misuse of funds. One commentator referred to it as 'a welfare reform con game' and 'the bloated social policy known as W-2' (Kane, 2004b). But although some changes were made to the way in which W-2 operated, and at least two of the providers went out of business, neither the criticism nor the disreputable behaviour led to any changes that would have treated recipients more humanely.

Privatisation and corruption: the case of W-2

If what happened in Milwaukee County, Wisconsin, is any indication, the major beneficiaries from 'welfare reform' were the private providers, including those technically termed 'non-profit', and their executives, who used the TANF money to award themselves high salaries with bonuses on top of already inflated remunerations (Rotker et al, 2002). They also used the money for purposes that were later found to be inappropriate, if not illegal, and they were required to re-pay it. Some private providers found that 'welfare' was not so profitable after all and went out of business, while others continued to profit

There were five private 'welfare' agencies awarded contracts by the State to administer its W-2 program. The five agencies were: Employment Solutions; Opportunities Industrialization Center of Greater Milwaukee; United Migrant Opportunity Service (all non-profit organisations); Maximus; and YW Works (both originally for-profit firms although the latter subsequently became non-profit). Employment Solutions was the only one of the five to administer the program in two of Milwaukee County's six regions; the rest were allocated one region each.

Maximus

Maximus was the first agency to come under fire in the county press for the way it was using W-2 money. Maximus had originally put in a bid to provide W-2 'welfare' services in all six of the administrative areas of the county (Dresang, 1996). A for-profit provider of 'human services' based in McLean, Virginia, it was founded in 1975 by a former Defense Department analyst who had worked for the Department of Health, Education, and Welfare during the Nixon administration. By 1999, the company was a $319.5 million operation with more than 3,700 employees, located in more than 130 offices across the country and overseas. It had been the first private, for-profit firm in the country to be awarded a contract to operate in a 'welfare' system, in Los Angeles County from 1988 to 1993 (Berkowitz, 2001). It is the only W-2 agency traded on the New York Stock Exchange, and after it was awarded the W-2-contract in Milwaukee County, the share price increased more than two-thirds (Baldwin, 2010: 253). Altogether, Maximus had W-2 contracts worth $107.7 million between March 1997 (to help prepare for W-2 implementation) and December 2001 (Wisconsin LAB, 2000). During the first contract period (1997-1999), Maximus was paid more than $4 million in unrestricted profit (Wisconsin LAB, 2000: 34).

The first question about Maximus raised in the Wisconsin press, early in 2000, involved concerns that it was using W-2 money to fund its bids for TANF contracts in New York. Maximus' two TANF contracts with New York City worth $104 million, it was reported, were 'on hold after a judge called the selection process "corrupted"' (Schultze, 2000c). The reasons given for the freeze were: possible undue influence over the selection process, i.e. the contracts were awarded through 'an expedited "negotiated proposal" process rather than competitive sealed bids'; a proposal to use a former aide of the mayor as a subcontractor for 30% of the funds; and the failure of Maximus 'to disclose it had been part of a criminal investigation in West Virginia over the company's bid for a contract to develop a computerized child welfare system'. A court dealing with these issues had found them proven, although the City was appealing the decision. The article also noted that the Wisconsin Legislative Audit Bureau was reviewing allegations of employment discrimination raised by former Maximus employees, and that the company was being investigated for 'other, unspecified matters' (Schultze, 2000c).

The City's appeal was successful. The original court decision against Maximus in New York was overturned and Maximus went ahead with the contracts. The original lawsuit had been brought by the New York City Comptroller against the mayor of New York. In describing what was involved in that lawsuit, the General Accounting Office said that that original judicial decision had maintained that the New York City Human Resources Administration had violated city procurement policies in awarding TANF contracts to Maximus, namely, that HRA: had rejected proposals from highly-qualified organisations and recommended much less qualified organisations for awards; had contact with one particular organisation (presumably Maximus) before the request for proposals was made public; and had given this particular organisation information before it was available to any of the other interested organisations (US GAO, 2002: 25-6). There was no information in the GAO report about the reasons for the appeals court's overturning of the original decision.

These media reports inspired the Wisconsin Legislative Audit Bureau to expand the scope of its proposed review of Maximus to include questions relating to improper use of W-2 funds and other relevant issues (Wisconsin LAB, 2000). The audit found that 46 Maximus staff members had worked on projects in New York and elsewhere. The audit report noted that Maximus had reimbursed Wisconsin the sum of $18,068 earlier that year for 272 staff hours and other costs, although the audit found that the State should have been reimbursed only for 224 hours. However, the audit found another 500 hours associated with projects in other states, including 124 hours associated with the New York City project, for which Maximus agreed to reimburse Wisconsin the sum of $33,236. The audit also found that the sum of $138,840 in other costs charged to W-2 was unallowable, and that a further $276,407 was questionable.

Senator Gwen Moore was instrumental in getting the State to track Maximus' expenses (Schultze, 2000c). A staunch critic of 'welfare' privatisation, Senator Moore was a member of the Wisconsin Senate from 1993 to 2004 and a member for Wisconsin in the US House of Representatives since 2005. She is herself a single mother and former 'welfare' recipient. In early 2000, she was reported deploring the fact that so many of the families who had left 'welfare' had remained in poverty (Schultze, 2000a). At that time she was sponsoring two bills in the Wisconsin State legislature intended to ease some of the conditions of W-2. The first bill proposed to abolish the two-year time limit on participation in some of W-2's categories, leaving only the overall five-year time limit. The second bill proposed new uses for W-2 surplus funds, including public input into the ways in which the money should be spent, and review by a legislative committee before the money could be released. Most of the money ($97.4 million left over from the first two years of the program) was not being released. A spokeswoman for W-2 was quoted saying that the money was on hold because the agencies wanted it as a backup in case there wasn't enough money for the next two years (Schultze, 2000b). There was no further information in subsequent issues of the newspaper on the progress of Senator Moore's proposed legislation.

In June 2000, it was reported that a subsidiary of Maximus, MaxStaff Employment Services, was going to close down. The article also said that '[t] he state had previously dismissed concerns about the propriety of Maximus diverting W-2 clients to MaxStaff' (Dresang, 2000). However, on 31 August it was reported that the U.S. Equal Employment Opportunity Commission had found that MaxStaff had discriminated against female workers by paying them less than men. The Commission also found that, when MaxStaff was advised of the Commission complaint, they began hiring men at the lower rate (Pabst, 2000).

On 26 July, it was reported that Maximus was warned by State officials that it could lose its multimillion-dollar contract to run 'welfare' programs in Milwaukee because of the 'spending irregularities'. As a result of these irregularities, the State was withholding or re-claiming the sum of $7.6 million, comprising $3.2 million re-paid by Maximus the previous month for improperly billed expenses, $1 million for the company's June W-2 costs, $2.9 million worth of performance bonuses from September 1997 to 1999, and $500,000 the firm was claiming in W-2 surplus funds (Schultze, 2000d).

On 29 July, it was reported that the Legislative Audit Bureau had disallowed or questioned more than $415,000 in expenses claimed by Maximus, and identified another $1.6 million in spending with insufficient supporting documentation (Schultze, 2000e). Other irregularities involved $3,800 in restaurant bills for an executive director's lunches; $35,000 for a staff training conference at a holiday venue; and $23,000 paid to Broadway singer Melba Moore for performing at three events in June 1999, including a job-training graduation ceremony for former 'welfare' recipients. This latter expense was defended by a Maximus spokeswoman on the grounds that the singer was herself a former 'welfare' recipient and served as an inspiration for current recipients (Schultze, 2000e, f).

In October 2000, the head of the Department of Workforce Development announced that Maximus had to pay back $500,000 for improper spending of W-2 money, as well as spending another $500,000 'on extra services for the poor' as a way of making amends. This was a new head of the Department whose tenure had begun with the announcement of a 'crackdown' on private contractors. She was quoted saying that "[i]t is important to recognize that Maximus did not commit fraud or do anything illegal", and that "[t]he mistakes were the result of sloppy bookkeeping, and measures are being put into place to make sure it doesn't happen again". The journalist noted that this was the same language used by the company in explaining its 'mistakes'. Mistakes or not, Maximus was audited three times in 2000 (Schultze, 2000h), only to escape relatively unscathed.

Gwen Moore was not the only Wisconsin lawmaker to express concerns about how the privatisation of 'welfare' was being managed in that State. Towards the end of 2000, six members of the State legislature were calling for the termination of Maximus' $46 million W-2 contract, arguing that the $1 million deal the State arranged with Maximus was not sufficient punishment (Schultze, 2000i). Maximus' contract was not terminated, but two Wisconsin Congressmen requested the federal General Accounting Office in October 2000 to conduct an inquiry into practices by private companies hired to manage 'welfare' services. "'Hopefully'", one of them was reported to say, "'the GAO can shed some light on just how widespread these problems are and provide Congress with some insight as to how to prevent future misuse and abuse of public funds'" (Berkowitz, 2001).

The result was the GAO's report, *Welfare Reform* (US GAO, 2002), but the Congressman's hopes were doomed to disappointment. The GAO found that the federal Department of Health and Human Services did not analyse the State audit reports comprehensively enough to be able to identify problems with non-governmental TANF contractors, nor to monitor those problems effectively. The GAO recommended that HHS use the audit reports 'in a more systematic manner' in order to identify the nature and extent of the problems uncovered by the GAO's investigation. But HHS disagreed and refused to implement this recommendation. They did plan 'to identify ways to better assure compliance with audit requirements applicable to nongovernmental entities' (US GAO, 2002: 22), but how they expected to do this without adequate data analysis was not revealed.

The public exposure of Maximus' 'mistakes' did the company no harm. By 2005, it had been paid nearly $233 million during the eight years it had held W-2 contracts, the highest amount paid to any W-2 provider (Schultze, 2005c). In August 2003 it was granted part of United Migrant Opportunities Services' territory. The then secretary of the Department of Workforce Development was reported saying 'Maximus had experienced problems with W-2 in the past … for improper spending of W-2 administrative money', but that they 'had made progress since then' (Schultze, 2003a). In February 2005, it was one of two private providers to take over the $16 million contract and the caseload of Opportunities Industrialization Center of Greater Milwaukee after OIC's financial crisis (Schultze and Sykes, 2005). At that time, Maximus was the State's largest W-2 agency, with a 2004-2005 contract worth $86.2 million (Schultze, 2005a).

It is true that the company's contract was not automatically renewed for 2005-2006 because it failed to meet two of the seven performance standards. But they appealed the decision (Schultze, 2005d), and they must have won the appeal and had their contract renewed for 2006-2007, because they were still operating in March 2007 (Schultze, 2007). This is despite the fact that State auditors had raised questions in 2005 about $721,000 in bonuses paid to rank and file staff during Maximus' 2002-2004 contract, and had found that bonuses amounting to $41,000 paid to Maximus executives were illegal (Schultze, 2005f). They were required to re-pay most of the $41,000. The secretary of the Department of Workforce Development was quoted saying that bonuses to top executives were not allowed because of their already high base salaries. However, most of the employee bonuses were found to be allowable expenses (Schultze, 2005g).

By 2005 Maximus had improved its fiscal controls and financial management practices, according to the State Legislative Audit Bureau (Wisconsin LAB, 2005a). It was still in existence in 2016, 'celebrating 20 years of welfare reform'[353] and still operating the TANF program in Milwaukee, as well as workfare centres in more than 40 US states, and around the world in Australia, the UK and Canada.

Employment Solutions

The other four private W-2 contractors behaved no better than Maximus, although at least some of them appeared to lack Maximus' charmed life. Employment Solutions, non-profit and a subsidiary of Goodwill Industries, was particularly short-lived, even though to start with it was the State's largest W-2 contractor, with nearly $205 million in contracts in the first three years of W-2 (Schultze, 2001b). It was also the agency with the largest unrestricted profit for those three years—$9.5 million of the $65.1 million in profit across all W-2 agencies (Wisconsin LAB, 2001: 5). After a stream of revelations about misuse of W-2 funds in late 2000 and early 2001, Employment Solutions decided not to renew its contract beyond December 2001.

Like Maximus, Employment Solutions spent W-2 money that should have gone to cash assistance for the poor, on bidding for TANF contracts in other States. The sum of $140,000 was mentioned in the press on 14 September 2000—'the sum was repaid, agency officials say' (Schultze, 2000g). A special State audit report (prompted by the press reports on Maximus) found that $370,000 had been improperly billed to the State's W-2 program (Schultze, 2001a). Most of this money went towards soliciting business in other states, but around $97,000 was spent on staff parties and meals in restaurants ($31,186, including $1,250 for a musical performance for staff), legal bills ($4,130, most of it to find out if lobbying would jeopardise its non-profit status), and what the newspaper article referred to as 'other questionable or clearly forbidden purposes'. Around $15,000 was spent to develop a training manual that could not be found. Other unallowable expenses were flying its

---

353. http://www.maximus.com/blog/welfare-reform/part-1.

executives first class and paying out large sums in bonuses to employees. In 1999, $197,000 had been paid to 149 employees, and the single largest bonus recipient was the company's chief executive—he was paid $61,645 in three bonus payments that year. The agency paid back about $255,000.

Employment Solutions was one of three of W-2 agencies that had paid their staff nearly $2 million in bonuses between 1997 and 1999, with Employment Solutions paying out the largest bonuses (Schultze, 2001b). A spokeswoman for Employment Solutions was reported to have said that the managers' bonuses 'were linked to such things as converting old welfare cases to W-2 on time, interviewing new W-2 applicants within 24 hours and maintaining expenses within contract limits'. The executives' bonuses were not dependent on 'clients landing jobs and holding them for a month or more'—only the caseworkers' bonuses were based on this criterion, and there was no information in the article about bonuses received by the caseworkers (if any). The ruling against executive bonuses was not introduced until 2004 (Schultze, 2005g), so all the bonuses were legal. However, as a staff member of the non-profit Institute for Wisconsin's Future said, within the context of poverty they were 'obscene', given that '"[t]hat money is meant to help poor people"'. She also said that paying such bonuses was 'a dangerous practice' because it 'could lead to shoving people out of W-2 prematurely' (Schultze, 2001c).

At the beginning of June 2001 it was announced that Employment Solutions would not be renewing its W-2 contract. This was reported to be a voluntary withdrawal from the program. According to the secretary of the Department of Workforce Development, 'the decision by Employment Solutions to give up its right for contract renewal [was] a mutual one between the state and the agency' (Schultze, 2001c). And yet the reason why the contract was not being renewed involved 'additional disclosures of improper spending of public money intended to aid the poor'. The company had paid about $1.7 million in bonuses from 1997-1999, including $98,000 to its chief executive on top of his already large salary (see below). The agency was required to pay back an extra $135,439 for work improperly billed, on top of $344,901 it had previously paid back. A spokesman for the agency gave as a reason for not renewing their contract, 'the ongoing community criticism over the improper spending'. Presumably, neither the company nor the oversight agency would have had any problem renewing the contract if there hadn't been any public criticism. The improperly used funds were spent mainly on 'efforts … to solicit contracts in other states'. The company had to re-pay the money but there were no other sanctions. They were even entitled to 'a $2.6 million performance bonus … earned by meeting job placement goals for clients' (and remember that 'job placement goals' were measured by the proportion of the caseload 'engaged in work activities', and a high proportion could be achieved by getting rid of those couldn't participate in those activities). And once again, the culprit was supposedly sloppy book-keeping. According to the company spokesman,

> after extensive investigation, it still appeared the improper spending of W-2 money was the result of "a cascade of errors" rather than a deliberate attempt to defraud the state. "It reflects bumbling rather than trickiness".

State officials were reported to agree with him: 'they did not find evidence of deliberate misappropriation of the money' (Schultze, 2001c). Such beneficence was never applied to TANF's recipients, who were sanctioned en masse for the most trivial of 'infractions', or for none at all.

OIC

Opportunities Industrialization Center of Greater Milwaukee (OIC or OIC-GM) lasted a few years longer than Employment Solutions, until February 2005 (Wisconsin LAB, 2005a: 12), although it too eventually went out of business. It was the third W-2 agency in Milwaukee County to have significant levels of costs charged to the W-2 program questioned by the State Legislative Audit Bureau (Wisconsin LAB, 2005a).

OIC was founded in Philadelphia in the 1970s (or 1967—Schultze, 2003c) by a civil rights activist, the Rev. Leon Sullivan, and had a mainly African-American clientele. In 2004, just before it shut its doors forever, it had more than 350 employees, more than 80% of them black, making it one of the largest employers of black professionals in the state (Schultze and Sykes, 2005). At the end of that year, it had branches in dozens of US cities and ran programs in more than 18 countries around the world. (Kane, 2004b). By the time it went out of business in early 2005, OIC had been paid more than $230 million in W-2 contracts (Schultze and Sykes, 2005). It had also participated in every State 'welfare reform' experiment in Milwaukee County since 1988, and 45,000 families had passed through its W-2 program since 1997 (Schultze, 2003c). During the first contract period (1997-1999), OIC had been paid more than $4 million in unrestricted profit (Wisconsin LAB, 2000: 34)

Until the beginning of 2004 OIC largely escaped the kinds of criticisms directed towards the other private W-2 contractors, although not entirely. For example, the Legislative Audit Bureau's 2001 report questioned $67,000 OIC

449

spent on television ads (Schultze, 2001a), and noted that it had used its profit to invest in a mobile phone company (Rotker et al, 2002) (as it was legally entitled to do). It had also missed job placement goals but 'had made progress since then' (Schultze, 2003a). Earlier, in 1994 it had been investigated by the State in relation to another State program, in response to claims by former employees that records had been falsified to hide a low success rate. The investigation found no evidence of 'significant improprieties', but the firm's contract for job training was reduced from $4 million in 1993 to $2.8 million in 1994 (Schultze, 2003c).

OIC's troubles started in earnest when State Senator Gary George was indicted in November 2003 by a federal grand jury on charges that he took hundreds of thousands of dollars from two charitable organisations, one of them being OIC (Zielinski, 2003). Although OIC had become the State's largest W-2 provider by the first week of January, and it was not being accused of any wrongdoing in relation to George's indictment, it was required to accept close, on-site monitoring by a State administrator (whose salary it was obliged to pay), as well as special auditing of its use of W-2 money (Schultze, 2004a).

By September, OIC was being ordered to improve its performance or lose its contract (Schultze, 2004c). The reasons were: that its caseload was rising at a time when caseloads elsewhere were dropping; that it had improperly claimed reimbursement for some administrative costs; that it had failed six of 10 performance standards; and that its new managers were inexperienced. The company had a new set of managers because the former top officials had resigned after the former CEO, Carl Gee, was convicted in relation to the illegal payments to Senator George. The State was also querying aspects of several managers' salaries, and 'strongly recommending' that procedures be reorganised so that money could be shifted to services for clients. The State also required the company to repay $216,000, which had been billed to W-2 as 'legal fees' but which federal prosecutors were saying was used to pay George through one of OIC's lawyers.

In November, the *Milwaukee Journal Sentinel* reported that ex-CEO Carl Gee (who first became an executive director in 1972) had been paid $1.75 million between 1997 and 2003, while another executive, William Clay, had been paid $1.35 million (Schultze, 2004d). Both men had been involved in the kickback scheme funnelling W-2 money to ex-Senator George. Gee was convicted, while Clay was fired by OIC in August after he cooperated with federal prosecutors in connection with the scheme. In justification of his salary, Clay was reported to have said, "'Nothing in my salary takes a piece of bread out of one poor person's mouth'". OIC's new interim CEO was being paid $165,000 a year. The newspaper article also reported that state auditors had questioned $275,000 OIC had paid to the host of a local radio program.

In February 2005, OIC announced that it was going out of business (Schultze and Sykes, 2005). It was $2.3 million in debt, a shortfall that was not fully explained, and the state was going to take legal action to recover $2.2 million owed from money already paid OIC under the two-year 2004-2005 contract. The company's chief financial officer of seven years was facing federal charges for using OIC money to get $45,000 worth of mobile phones; and the previous year the State had ordered them to get rid of their auditing firm because it had been giving a false picture of OIC's finances for years. According to the interim CEO, there was an ongoing investigation by the federal attorney's office (and unspecified others) to determine whether other criminal charges were to be filed. The State was going to take over their W-2 operation, but the remaining $16 million contract and caseload of 1,650 families for this year was to be split between Maximus and United Migrant Opportunity Services.

UMOS

Like the other four initial W-2 providers in Milwaukee, United Migrant Opportunity Services[354] has had a chequered career although, like Maximus, it too was still in existence in 2016. During the first contract period (1997-1999), UMOS was paid more than $4 million in unrestricted profit (Wisconsin LAB, 2000: 34). It too was criticised in the 2001 Legislative Audit Bureau report which censured Employment Solutions. The auditors questioned $5,000 UMOS spent on a 'Fatherhood Summit', $23,250 spent on advertising connected with the Milwaukee Brewers (Schultze, 2001a), several real-estate purchases, and investments in money market accounts (Rotker et al, 2002).

Towards the end of the year, it was reported that UMOS was in financial difficulties because of growing W-2 caseloads (Schultze, 2001e). It was 'reshuffling its budget' and 'scrounging up money elsewhere', in order to avoid having a deficit of $1.2 million at the end of the year in the funds 'needed to pay benefits to the poor'. Among the projected solutions was an offer of help from OIC, whose vice-president, William Clay, was quoted saying he '"would certainly look favorably" on the idea of transferring some of OIC's anticipated surplus to UMOS'.

In 2003, UMOS lost part of its territory to Maximus, despite Maximus' own shortcomings. The reason was that UMOS had 'mishandled W-2 cases'

---

354. http://www.umos.org/.

and 'short-changed participants', for which it had been fined earlier in the year (Schultze, 2003a). Its fortunes did improve. Early in 2005 UMOS was the recipient of the remainder of OIC's contract and caseload (along with Maximus), at which time it became state's largest W-2 agency (Antlfinger, 2005). It failed to win an automatic renewal of its contract for 2006-2007 (along with Maximus and OIC), but it was successful when it put in a new bid (Schultze, 2005d). However, later in the year the audit bureau found that UMOS and YW Works had charged expenses to W-2 without providing receipts or other documentation. And it was in trouble again in 2009, when its contract for the next two-year period was reduced from $56.6 million to $19.1 million because it 'didn't score as well with its new contract proposal as did Maximus', which was to take over the central Milwaukee region from UMOS (Schultze, 2009).

YW Works

YW Works was originally a for-profit subsidiary of YWCA, which went into partnership with two other for-profit firms in order to manage its $40 million welfare-to-work contract (Berkowitz, 2001). Since January 2000 it has been a non-profit limited-liability corporation (Wisconsin LAB, 2005a), but when W-2 started, YW Works was the first of the social enterprises established by YWCA administrator, Julia Taylor, as a way of earning money for the non-profit YWCA. In 1999, Taylor was reported to be 'a star among non-profit leaders nationally', who had testified before the US House of Representatives' Committee on Government Reform. Her achievements in the field were praised by the then-governor of Wisconsin, Tommy G. Thompson, the chief architect of W-2. She had also won a one-year position as 'social entrepreneur in residence' at the University of Wisconsin-Milwaukee School of Business Administration. However, by 2002 every social enterprise she had created was on the verge of failing and YW Works was no longer a for-profit enterprise (Murphy, 2004).

Between September 1997 to December 2003 YW Works spent $140.4 million as a W-2 provider, received $4.8 million in unrestricted profits, and reported $2 million in community reinvestment fund expenditures (Wisconsin LAB, 2005a).

Along with the other four W-2 providers in Milwaukee, YW Works was evaluated by the Legislative Audit Bureau in 2001 (Wisconsin LAB, 2001).[355] The evaluation report noted that YW Works reported spending $1.1 million

---

355. This was the sixth and last of the series of reports evaluating the W-2 program produced by the Audit Bureau (Wisconsin LAB, 2001: 11).

on a plastics processing company that was intended to serve as a workplace-skills training centre, on a non-traditional employment and training program, and on a variety of other education and training activities and programs. At that time, YW Works was found to have sanctioned 48% of its clients, the highest proportion of any of the five agencies. Despite that finding, it was reportedly told 'in a Feb. 26 [2002] letter from a state W-2 official that it wasn't sanctioning enough new clients', although the figure mentioned as a target for the proportion of clients to be penalised was 15% to 20%. That instruction came after YW Works had taken on extra clients from Employment Solutions after the latter went out of business (Schultze, 2002b).

In August 2003, it was announced that YW Works was to be cut out of the W-2 program because of its financial problems (Schultze, 2003a), although later in the year YW Works was to get the largest proportion of the W-2 money shifted into Milwaukee County from other parts of the state (Schultze, 2003b). Nonetheless, it was not a W-2 contractor from January to June 2004 (Wisconsin LAB, 2005a), although it remained as a subcontractor to OIC (Schultze, 2004e). By the beginning of 2005, it was once again a prime W-2 contractor, with a $12.7 million contract along with Maximus ($86.2 million) and UMOS ($47.7 million) (Schultze, 2005a).

PIC

These problems with the spending habits of the private contractors arose because there was initially insufficient oversight of the expenditure aspects of the program. Although all W-2 contractors were audited annually, this was clearly inadequate. The private firm paid to monitor the program, the Private Industry Council of Milwaukee County, initially had contracts worth $7.5 million for program coordination and monitoring (Wisconsin LAB, 2001: 70). But it was not clear that the PIC was expected to oversee program expenditures. It had little guidance from the Department of Workforce Development; and until the media reports about the inappropriate billing of staff time to the New York bids, the Department had shown no concern with the ways in which W-2 money was being spent. Having encouraged the providers 'to spend the money in innovative ways', the Department gave them no further guidance about how that should (and should not) be done (Wisconsin LAB, 2000: 15).

The investigation by the Legislative Audit Bureau (Wisconsin LAB, 2001: 72-3) found that PIC's financial oversight was confined to checking each month that the contractors had not spent more than the budgets they had been allocated. PIC staff told the State auditors that they had tried to monitor the appropriateness of the contractors' expenditures, but that the contractors had refused to give them the information. PIC staff also said that the Department had told them not to investigate these particular financial activities. There was no documentation of any such agreement with the Department, but PIC's new contract starting July 1999 substantiated the PIC claim. It contained no financial monitoring responsibilities.

However, in September 2000 the Department of Workforce Development acquired a new head, who announced 'a crackdown' on the private contractors. She was reported to say that 'lavish spending and sloppy accounting [would] no longer be tolerated', and that the Department would be appointing its own auditors to monitor their spending (Schultze, 2000g). Perhaps it was this crackdown that led to the 2005 discovery of $41,000 in unallowable bonuses paid to Maximus executives during their 2002-2004 contract, and the financial peculations of Messrs George, Gee and Clay (when the latter two were executives of the Opportunities Industrialization Center of Greater Milwaukee).

Salaries

As well as publicising the financial peculations of the private W-2 contractors, the press also criticised the exorbitant salaries of their chief executives. Table 1 shows the salaries of the top five W-2 administrators in Milwauke in 2000.

Table 1 Salaries of the top five W-2 administrators in 2000

Name	Position	Organisation	Salary
William Clay	vice-president	OIC	$154,524
William Martin	vice-president	Employment Solutions	$146,204
Julia Taylor	executive director	YW Works	$138,482
Lupe Martinez	executive director	UMOS	$125,571
Jerry Stepaniak	vice-president	Maximus	$122,083

Source: Schultze, 2001d

By comparison, the median annual earnings of full-time male wage and salary workers in 2000 was $36,176 ($646/week), and $27,496 for women ($491/week). Nearly a quarter of women workers (24.5%) in the US were employed part-time, and 10% of men (p.2, Chart 2, p.3).[356]

In response, the 2001 State budget included a rule to limit the salaries of the top executives of the W-2 agencies to the amount the state governor

---

356. https://www.bls.gov/opub/reports/womens-earnings/archive/womensearnings_2000.pdf.

was paid, i.e. $122,406 a year (Schultze, 2001d). But it was doubtful whether that ruling would have any effect on executive salaries, because the limitation applied only to that portion of the salary paid out of W-2 funds. The 'welfare' executives were paid from other sources as well,[357] and in at least three cases the W-2 salary component was already less than the governor's pay.

And indeed, the ruling had no effect on keeping executive salaries within reasonable bounds. Taylor's salary had increased to $201,507 by 2001 (Murphy, 2004); and in 2003, the *Milwaukee Journal Sentinel* (Kissinger, 2003) was reporting that the salaries of all the top W-2 executives had kept increasing, 'some more than 100%'.

In 2004, The Legislative Audit Bureau (Wisconsin, 2005b) found that the private W-2 agencies in Milwaukee paid their executives much higher salaries than were paid to W-2 officials anywhere else in the State. Among officials earning more than $60,000 a year, those in the private agencies averaged $89,346, whereas they averaged $75,540 elsewhere. Eight officials in the private agencies were paid more than $100,000, whereas only one official outside Milwaukee was paid more than this. Maximus paid its top official, $145,455 (of which $74,082 was paid with W-2 funds), United Migrant Opportunity Services paid its CEO $170,000 (of which $82,263 was paid with W-2 funds), and OIC paid two of its vice presidents $151,278 ($79,103 and $87,893 of W-2 funds). (See also: Schultze, 2005e).

The efficacy and efficiency of W-2

The Wisconsin W-2 Monitoring Task Force (2002) found that private contractors were not at all effective in getting people into the kind of employment which would take people out of poverty. Although employment was given as the reason for the closure of roughly two-thirds of cases between 1997 and 1999, they were hardly the kinds of jobs that would make someone self-sufficient. Not all were full-time and they were very badly paid. A study cited by the Task Force had found that the average income earned by employed W-2 leavers in Milwaukee was $1,029 per month, just over $12,300 a year (if the job lasted a year). Another study using the 1999 tax returns of former W-2 recipients in Milwaukee came up with much the same information. Their average annual income ranged from $10,980 for OIC 'clients' to $12,979 for Maximus 'clients'. These income levels were $1,000

---

357. '[D]irectors of county human or social services agencies typically oversee other programs such as Medical Assistance, public health programs, food stamps, child care subsidies, child support, juvenile court services, and programs for the elderly and people with disabilities' (Wisconsin LAB, 2005b)

or more below the federal poverty level for a family of three (the size of the typical welfare family) (Wisconsin W-2 Monitoring Task Force, 2002: 11).

Although the supposed reason for the existence of W-2 is to get people into employment, during the first two years there were no formal performance standards which the W-2 providers had to meet in order to qualify for renewal of their contracts. And even when a standard was introduced during the second contract period (2000-2001), it was minimal—to place 35% of participants into jobs, either full- or part-time, which lasted a month. This was not very onerous for the contractors, who were given enormous sums of money and yet not expected to place even 50% of their caseload in employment, much less employment that paid a living wage. Neither was it a standard likely to lead to the 'welfare' recipients' self-sufficiency. From January to September 2002, the percentages of the caseloads placed in full-time employment were: YW Works, 15%; UMOS, 14%; OIC-GM, 14%; Maximus, 16%. In December 2002, only four of the 67 W-2 agencies across Wisconsin were on track to meet all the required standards, but the response of the Department of Workforce Development was to consider giving them more time, rather than sanctioning them or threatening not to renew their contracts (Wisconsin W-2 Monitoring Task Force, 2002: 21).

The Wisconsin W-2 Monitoring Task Force (2002: 17-18) compared the costs of AFDC in 1996 with the costs of W-2 in 2001, and found that W-2 cost around twice as much per recipient as AFDC had in its last year. The overall cost of W-2 was less than the last year of AFDC (around 62%), but that was because of the massive decrease in the caseloads. The average cost per case in 1996, counting both benefits and services, was $7,258 (in 2001 dollars), whereas in 2001 it was $14,653. The Task Force attributed this high cost per participant to the vastly increased cost of W-2 administration (in comparison with AFDC), in particular the greater numbers of W-2 management staff and the high salaries of the executives. In the last year of AFDC 80% of the funding had been spent on participants' benefits, whereas only 37% of the W-2 funding was being paid to recipients in the form of benefits in 2001, the other 63% being spent on administrative and program costs. The authors of the Task Force report commented that 'it appears that the money is often misallocated, being spent on administration and infrastructure costs of the agencies, not on benefits or services that directly help the families the program was created to serve' (p.18). (See also: Schultze, 2002a).

Still, whether or not privatisation had been successful depends on what criteria of success are being used. It has been argued that privatisation has been very successful, not for the 'welfare' recipients and ex-recipients who remain in poverty, and not necessarily for the State either, but for the private firms and their top management. As one commentator put it:

> After four years of welfare reform there is evidence that privatization has been successful, not for the people who were supposed to be moved out of poverty, but for corporate profiteers (Berkowitz, 2001). (See also: Rotker et al, 2002).

Conclusion

If W-2, Wisconsin's much lauded 'welfare program', is any guide, privatisation does not have a good record, even leaving aside the outright fraud. Private contractors were found to be using TANF money inappropriately in other ways too, at least until 2005, and especially in 2001, three to four years after the beginning of W-2. It is true that they were usually using the money in ways that were perfectly acceptable in private enterprise, e.g. staff parties, executive lunches and jaunts, advertising, flowers. But these activities were not helping the poor, either to find employment (the purported aim of the program) or to survive. They were eventually found to be 'unallowable', but it should have been clear from the beginning that these were morally reprehensible in a program supposedly serving the poorest of the poor.

Private contractors were also censured for using Wisconsin money to support bids to run TANF in other states, again, standard operating procedure in a commercial enterprise but not an acceptable use for W-2 money. It is also true that the amounts of the executives' salaries were not exorbitant in comparison with what executives are usually paid in private enterprise. But in comparison with what 'welfare' recipients are paid, and in terms of common humanity, it is grotesque—'obscene', as one commentator said.

Presumably the private 'welfare' contractors no longer spend TANF money on irrelevancies or to support bids in other states. Presumably, too, they no longer side-step the legitimate selection process by using undue influence over the decision-makers. But almost certainly the executive salaries have increased in line with inflation, while the benefits paid to recipients have in fact decreased in absolute figures, never mind keeping pace with inflation.

But the exposure of the suspect ways in which private contractors used public money intended to help the poor did not bring privatisation into disrepute. Even outright illegal behaviour could be explained away as an isolated incident, and not something inherent in a system designed to funnel billions of public dollars into private hands. For example, one of the authors of W-2 was reported to have said in relation to the OIC scandal, 'I don't think you can pull out one problem and then label everyone who is a private organization as not acting in good faith' (Schutze, 2004a).

Monitoring and auditing bodies kept finding serious problems when they were finally allowed to do their job, but rarely was any private contractor sanctioned. For example, agencies were supposed to be fined $5,000 if they failed to provide services to 'clients'. But the Department of Workforce Development was reluctant to hold contractors to the terms of their contracts. Up until 2002, the Department had investigated only one allegation of failure to serve, despite the large number of complaints received and at least 151 administrative findings that agencies had violated W-2 policies (Wisconsin W-2 Monitoring Task Force, 2002: 20). This reluctance was also demonstrated by the Department's willingness to allow the W-2 agencies more time to meet the standards contained in their contracts (p.121).

Another example of an attempt to sanction non-complying contractors involved a State law enacted in 2001 which required the 2002-2003 TANF contracts to contain a provision stating that contractors who submitted unallowable expenses had to pay the state a fine equal to 50% of the amount of those expenses (US GAO, 2002: 30-1). There were no subsequent media reports of any agency charged under this law. The Department of Workforce Development was reported to have stepped up monitoring in late 2004 (Schultze, 2005b), but it is unclear why they waited so long, given that the problems had started to appear at least as early as 2000. In August 2003, the Milwaukee County administration offered to take over the handling of all intake services for W-2. The State administration rejected the proposal, preferring to remain with the private providers (Schultze, 2003a).

The main point to note in conclusion to this discussion of privatisation is the difference between the way in which the private contractors are treated, and the treatment meted out to 'welfare' recipients. The leniency extended towards the defalcations of the private firms and their well-paid executives, stands in stark contrast to the harshness and frequency of the sanctions imposed on the poorest of the poor. As poverty activists have noted:

> While telling families that only work would pay, private contractors spent welfare funds for staff parties, Hollywood entertainers, expensive lunches for agency executives, flowers, and first-class air travel … Wisconsin's double standard is remarkable. While families face harsh sanctions if they fail to comply with even minor program rules, state officials chalked up the private contractors' blatant misuse of public welfare funds to "sloppy book-keeping". Then the state handed Maximus a new two-year contract' (Rotker et al, 2002: 531).

This contrast clearly exposes the values that motivate US legislators—the worship of wealth and power, combined with a hatred of those harmed in pursuit of it.

But in the last analysis, whether 'welfare' is privatised or not makes very little difference. As one researcher found:

> Although privatized welfare providers are not found to consistently induce superior employment outcomes among the general TANF population in Florida, the evidence … suggests that privatizing welfare administration also does not have particularly deleterious effects on disadvantaged clientele (Butz, 2012: 150).

The same values are enforced on all 'welfare' agencies, whether public or private, for-profit or not-for-profit. All 'welfare' providers are expected to reduce the rolls and to keep as many people off as possible; all are encouraged to apply forms of bureaucratic disentitlement; all are subject to the myth of employment as the way out of poverty; and all are committed to the ideology of individualism that holds the poor responsible for their own poverty. Given these common factors, the difference privatisation makes to the lives of 'welfare' recipients is minimal.

Chapter Seventeen: PRWORA's Precursors

Despite the changes PRWORA introduced, and despite widespread perceptions of PRWORA as innovative, 'welfare reform' retained the substance of what went before, based as it was on the age-old meanings and values attached to 'welfare' in the US system. True, there is no longer even a pretence that the national government has a responsibility to tackle poverty, given that the Act explicitly withdrew people's entitlement, but this means little more than that all the old right-wing resistances to 'welfare' had triumphed. The little that was changed made things worse for the poor in the US, but the compromises with capital made by the US legislators followed the same pattern as all the previous 'welfare' initiatives, whether federal or State. 'Welfare' has always been a term of opprobrium in the US among politicians doing the bidding of wealth and power, as well as in the mainstream media (owned by wealth and power), and among those citizens who allow themselves to be deceived into supporting interests which run directly counter to their own. As a consequence, every policy initiative for income support throughout US history has met with powerful resistance to helping 'the poor', and 'reforms' along lines similar to PRWORA.

While this resistance is not peculiar to the US—the right-wing mindset is multi-national after all—the antagonism towards 'welfare' in the US reaches heights unparalleled in any other nation, and not only among the economically powerful. What Piven and Cloward (1987: 7-8) term 'the Great Relief Hoax'— that welfare programs are ineffective and even worsen poverty because they discourage people from working—has been successfully perpetrated even among people who have the most to lose by believing it, i.e. workers in the low-wage economy churned between 'welfare' and poverty wages. Hatred of 'welfare' is one of the most successful confidence tricks in the western world, but it did not originate with PRWORA.

So despite the changes, the kinds of 'reforms' enshrined in PRWORA were not substantially different in kind from those that preceded it. As one commentator said of two of the immediate precursors to PRWORA:

> these proposals [Clinton's Work and Responsibility Act of 1994 and the Republicans' Personal Responsibility Act of 1995] essentially change nothing. Significant alteration of Western poor relief methodology is taboo (Backer, 1995: 341. See also: Backer, 1993).

For this author, 'welfare reform' must comply with what he called 'the static paradigm', which is based on the following assumptions: that the current socio-economic order already provides all that is necessary for a comfortable material existence for everyone; that poverty, therefore, is the fault of those who are poor; that the poor must be made to see the error of their ways, preferably through punishment; and that 'reforms' must always be cost-saving because 'welfare' is an unnecessary expense (Backer, 1995: 345-53). That a 'welfare' program must be subordinate to the labour market, that the 'solution' to poverty is a job, that unemployment is the fault of the unemployed, that all that is needed to get people into work is educationandttraining and punishment, are the perennial meanings and values motivating 'welfare'. Even the disentitlement that PRWORA demands is nothing new. PRWORA made explicit the assumption that has always informed 'welfare' systems—the right-wing conviction that people are responsible for their own poverty and the only 'help' they require is to be made to see that.

For example, in his 1962 State of the Union message, President Kennedy said that a proposed new 'welfare' program would be "'stressing services instead of support, rehabilitation instead of relief, and training for useful work instead of prolonged dependency'" (quoted in Steiner, 1966: 257). This use of declamatory pronouncements saying that, this time, they've got it right, is another aspect of continuity throughout all the supposed 'changes' in 'welfare'. Bill Clinton's oft-quoted remark about 'ending welfare as we know it' is one example, but Kennedy said much the same thing about his Public Welfare Amendments of 1962. They were "'the most far reaching revision of our public welfare program since it was enacted in 1935'", and they "'mark[ed] a turning point in this nation's efforts to cope realistically and helpfully with these pressing problems'" (quoted in Steiner, 1966: 42). But nothing changed then and nothing has changed now, because the meanings and values motivating 'welfare' have not changed. As the above-mentioned commentator put it,

> [a]ll American poor relief proposals orbit around certain paradigmatic assumptions from whose gravitational force they cannot break free.

> And, like a strong gravitational field, these assumptions—inherent in our conceptions of poverty and the poor—invisibly limit the meaning and possibility of transformation. Poor relief reform remains confined within the boundaries of the world [thus] created (Backer, 1995: 343).

But while those meanings and values are perennial (and consistently prevail whenever policy becomes reality), so too is the awareness that there is something wrong with seeing the problem in this way. For example, one critical commentator remarking on Kennedy's 1962 pronouncement on what a 'welfare' program would need to emphasise, pointed out that it wasn't a question of either services or support (etc.), that there would still be people who needed financial support no matter how many services they received. 'Outside the legislative hearing room', he said, it was not 'a realistic goal' to expect that 'people [would] become self-sufficient so that they no longer need assistance':

> for the victim of discrimination in education or in employment or in housing, for the helpless aged, for the chronically unemployed, unskilled worker ... the primary goal of public welfare is a reasonable subsistence. It is a goal that has yet to be achieved (Steiner, 1966: 259-60).

Fifty years later after decades of neo-liberal governmentality, not only is the goal not yet achieved, it is further away than ever.

Early history

PRWORA has precursors reaching back to the first ever federal government attempt to provide for women and children without male breadwinners, Aid to Dependent Children (ADC),[358] Title IV of the 1935 Social Security Act, and even earlier than that, in the various State and local provisions for widowed mothers and their children up to that time (not to mention 'a history of conflict over relief that goes back to the sixteenth century [in Europe]'—Piven and Cloward, 1987: 1). Individual States in the US began to establish 'Mothers' Aid' pensions for widowed mothers (along with pensions for the blind and the aged) early in the twentieth century. Prior to that time, provision for the poor ('relief') had not been a federal or Sate responsibility, but rather a local (county or city) one, just as it had been in Europe in medieval times. In fact, Mothers' Aid continued to be a local responsibility because few States contributed towards funding the local initiatives for 'poor relief', and the localities were not obliged to implement their States' programs.

---

358. The program was renamed Aid to Families with Dependent Children (AFDC) in 1962.

The terms and conditions of these Mothers' Aid pensions largely remained in place after the passing of the Social Security Act in 1935, the main difference being that the federal government now proposed to share the costs (together with the costs of providing for the blind and for the old who were not covered by the old-age insurance part of the 1935 Act). Linda Gordon tells us that

> [t]he enthusiasm for mothers' aid was so great that forty-six of the forty-eight states had passed such laws ... mainly within the decade 1910-20 ... The design of these programs was so influential that when, twenty years later, the depression provided an opportunity to establish a federal program—ADC—it simply added federal funds to the mothers'-aid model ... not only for ADC but for all the programs today called "welfare" (Gordon, 1994: 37).

Enacted under the administration of President Franklin D. Roosevelt as part of the New Deal economic programs implemented between 1933 and 1936, the 1935 Social Security Act[359] was a belated response to the depression of the late 1920s and early 1930s. It contained provisions for old-age benefits, unemployment compensation, maternal and child health services, public health, and aid to the blind, as well as Aid to Dependent Children. A dependent child was defined as 'a child under the age of sixteen who has been deprived of parental support or care by reason of the death, continued absence from the home, or physical or mental incapacity of a parent', and who was living with a relative. Despite the de-gendered language, the 'parent' who was dead, absent (etc.) was a father, and the law was regarded as a way of helping children who had lost their breadwinner. These children were referred to as 'orphans' even though their mothers were still alive (the terminology providing another example of the male supremacist belief that only men count). The 'help' was not generous—the maximum any family could be paid was $18 a month for the first child and $12 for each subsequent child (in contrast to the $30 a month the legislation provided for an aged or a blind person) (Piven and Cloward, 1993: 129).

The dominant view at the time was that mothers' responsibilities required that they stay at home to care for their children (Glassman, 1970) (as long as they were 'respectable' and not black). The ADC program was presented as a way of allowing mothers without breadwinners to do that. The legislation was acceptable to the extent that it was seen as a program for families headed by widows, whom even the right-wing could not hold responsible for their plight. But there was opposition to its support for mothers who

---

359. https://www.ssa.gov/history/35activ.html.

were divorced, separated or never married (and mothers who were black), and it was accused of encouraging women to leave their husbands. Particular opprobrium was reserved for women who bore children while they were already receiving 'welfare' payments.

Throughout the 1960s the program's caseload increased dramatically in size, the numbers almost doubling between 1960 and 1970. This increase had a number of causes: the migration from the rural South to the northern cities of millions of people (especially African-Americans) looking for work; increases in divorce and out-of-wedlock child-bearing; the court-ordered cessation of discriminatory State regulations like the 'suitable homes' and 'man in the house' rules; the success of the welfare rights movement in organising eligible claimants to make claims; and welfare officials and social workers who encouraged the poor to take advantage of public assistance (Blank and Blum, 1997).

But such a trend could not be allowed to continue and, as a way of stemming the flood, the late 1960s saw a number of attempts to introduce work requirements as a condition of federal funding, culminating in the Work Incentive Program (WIN for short), passed by Congress as part of the 1967 amendments to the Social Security Act. Similar work requirements were a central feature of 'welfare reform' proposals and federal legislation during the 1970s and 1980s, e.g. Nixon's Family Assistance Plan and President Carter's Program for Better Jobs and Income,[360] the 1981 Omnibus Budget Reconciliation Act (OBRA for short), and the 1988 Family Support Act. Although PRWORA may have toughened work requirements and demonstrated a greater obliviousness to history than anything that had gone before, it was not the first time work requirements had been introduced as a condition of receiving federal aid.

Waivers

Whether or not PRWORA expanded the States' capacities to design their own 'welfare' programs 'dramatically' (Handler, 2008: 4), the fact is that States had been developing their own programs for years under the federal 'waiver' system. The US Department of Health and Human Services regarded these waivers as 'the first phase of welfare reform', because 'many of the policies

---

360. Nixon's FAP was finally defeated in 1972, and Carter's program was proposed and defeated in 1977 (for details of the Carter program, see: Danziger et al, 1977). In relation to Nixon's 'welfare' policies, David Kennedy has pointed out that they were 'quite surprising in light of his conservative Republicanism. Nixon is the only President who ever proposed a guaranteed annual minimum income' (Kennedy, 1998: 252n90). It was this proposal which was primarily responsible for the defeat of the FAP.

and concepts included in state waiver requests were later incorporated into the Personal Responsibility and Work Opportunity Reconciliation Act (PRWORA) of 1996' (US DHHS, 2001).

Before the passage of PRWORA, under both the Bush and the Clinton administrations, states had been applying for, and being granted, 'waivers' that exempted them from the federal regulations for 'welfare' provision. Between January 1993 and August 1996 under the Clinton administration, 43 states had 'welfare' waivers approved by the Department of Health and Human Services (US DHHS, 2001). The waiver requests invariably asked for permission to introduce conditions for 'welfare' recipients that were harsher than the already harsh restrictions in the federal regulations, and reduced people's entitlement even further.

For years before the passage of PRWORA, the Department of Health and Human Services had been approving projects which substantially undermined federal eligibility criteria, such as requests for permission to impose time limits on benefit-receipt. To take another example: the federal regulations prior to PRWORA allowed for an exemption from participation in the Job Opportunities and Basic Skills (JOBS) so-called 'training' program (established under the 1988 Family Support Act), for AFDC recipients who were caring for a child under three, which could be reduced to a child under one if the State opted to introduce that restriction. Even so, some States applied to reduce the age of the child before which the mother was exempt even further (to 12 weeks—Delaware, Idaho, Iowa, Maryland, Nebraska). Utah and Michigan applied to have all the federal exemptions waived except those for recipients aged under 16 (US DHHS, 2001). This meant that 'welfare' applicants in those States were required to participate in JOBS even if (to list the federal exemptions) they were ill, incapacitated or aged, or already working at least 30 hours per week, or in the second or third trimester of pregnancy, or caring for an ill or incapacitated family member, or lived in an area where the program was not available, or were caring for a child under six and child care was not available. It also meant that 'welfare' claimants who were unable to participate in JOBS for the reasons listed were not eligible to receive any cash benefits.

On the face of it, this was not the intention of the original waiver legislation.[361] The stated purpose of section 1115 of the Social Security Act, introduced in 1962, was research. This section allowed the Secretary of the

---

361. The following is taken from Williams, 1994.

Department of Health, Education and Welfare[362] to waive a state's compliance with federal requirements in the interests of finding ways of improving the system: "'In the case of any experimental, pilot, or demonstration project which, in the judgment of the Secretary, is likely to assist in promoting the objectives of [the Act] ... in a State or States ... the Secretary may waive compliance with any of the requirements of section[s] [of the Act] ... to the extent and for the period he finds necessary to enable such State or States to carry out such project'" (Williams, 1994: 10). At the hearings prior to the bill's enactment, the Departmental Secretary said that the section was designed to "'make it easier for States to embark on imaginative pilot or demonstration projects which could lead to improved operations'". He also cited the President's "'welfare message to the Congress'" in which he rejected attempts "'to save money on welfare expenditures through ruthless and arbitrary cutbacks'" on the grounds that they were unsuccessful (pp.11-12).

But despite the alleged grounding of the waiver process in the need for research, there was little, if any, evidence for the effectiveness of these projects. Throughout the Bush and Clinton administrations waivers were granted indiscriminately, despite the lack of reliable data on what works and what does not (Peck, 2001: 100). And yet, it was these 'experimental, pilot, or demonstration projects' which were incorporated into PRWORA

The block grants to the States and the five-year limit on 'welfare' receipt do give the appearance of something different from what went before. But the waiver system had already allowed individual states to apply time limits; and the federal open-ended commitment was never stretched to cover the full extent of the need. It often happened that the states didn't manage to spend all the federal 'welfare' money they were entitled to, because they couldn't (or wouldn't) match the federal component.

Privatisation

PRWORA increased the level of permissible privatisation of 'welfare' services by paying non-governmental organisations, including for-profit corporations, for making financial eligibility determinations about 'welfare' claimants. But as Barbara Ehrenreich has pointed out, 'privatization was already under way, in a scattershot fashion, well before the advent of Clinton's welfare reform'. She gave a number of examples of contracts awarded to multinational corporations to operate aspects of the 'welfare' system:

---

362. Re-named the Department of Health and Human Services in 1980.

The defense contractor BDM International Inc. won a contract to automate New Mexico's welfare system as early as 1988; Lockheed was in the business of collecting child support and fingerprinting (or "finger-imaging", as the euphemism goes) recipients in various states; Curtis & Associates and the job-brokerage firm America Works were propelling recipients into the workforce in Buffalo, San Francisco, and other cities (Ehrenreich, 1997: 47).

As early as 1982, employers were being given tax credits if they hired people who were on the 'welfare' rolls, and throughout the 1980s, private contractors who ran job-training and job-placement services were eligible for subsidies and tax breaks. Moreover, prior to the passage of PRWORA several States included privatisation provisions in their waiver proposals (Brophy-Baermann and Bloesser, 2009).

And even earlier, in the early 1960s the Dallas-based Electronic Data Systems won the contract to process the Texas Medicare/Medicaid reimbursement claims. Founded by Ross Perot, a Texan who ran for President in 1992 and 1996, Electronic Data Services was the source of a large part of his fortune when he sold it in the 1980s. Perot's biographer referred to him as a "welfare billionaire" (Kennedy, 1998: 258-9).

PRWORA allowed corporations to directly interfere in the lives of the poorest of the poor, but the federal government was already allowing them to profit from the 'welfare' system prior to the passage of the 1996 Act. PRWORA extended that opportunity for profit but it didn't initiate it.

Children and their mothers

PRWORA's peculiar views on what is involved in supporting and caring for children are also not new. Originally the Mothers' Aid pensions that were established in individual States largely between 1910 and 1920 were intended to give money directly to women, just as their name implies. These State programs for assisting widowed mothers and their children were the first modern American public welfare programs. But they came under attack by the right wing on the grounds that they were 'a threat to the proper family, one headed by a man' (Gordon, 2008: 342). For that reason, Title IV of the 1935 Social Security Act, Aid for Dependent Children, meant exactly that— this federal aid was for the children, not their mothers. Any funding for the mothers had to come from the States under the same terms and conditions as Mothers' Aid. This changed in 1950 when a grant for the mother was added to the federal funding as a result of pressure on the federal government from the States wanting relief from the costs of aiding the ADC caretaker (Abramovitz, 1996: 316).

But there were other ways of ensuring that financial aid to women and children did not threaten one of the highest values of the right wing—male control of women. To the extent that such aid enabled women to leave distasteful marriages or violent husbands and live alone with their children, Mothers' Aid did hold out that promise. But that is not what happened in practice: it wasn't available to every woman who needed it, and it wasn't enough to live on. In the first place the pensions were largely available only to 'respectable' white women, i.e. to widows but not to mothers who were divorced, separated, deserted or never-married, nor on the whole to black women at all, especially in the southern states. That 'respectability' was monitored by social workers and officials who saw themselves entitled to intrude into a woman's home at any time of the day or night under 'suitable home', 'man-in-the-house' and 'substitute father' rules. Most States had such provisions, which refused assistance to any mother whose home failed to meet these standards. The 'failures' included bearing children out of wedlock, having alcoholic beverages or boarders or men in the house, and 'alien' methods of housekeeping and child care on the part of immigrants. In at least one State a mother could lose her pension if her children didn't get satisfactory reports at school (Gordon, 1994: 45-6).

Mothers' Aid wasn't available even to all the most 'respectable' of women. Because it was administered at the county or municipal level and the localities were not legally obliged to provide it, not all localities did so. Moreover, the local emphasis also continued the local prejudices, especially the racism. This was not confined to the southern States, but it was most virulent there. And the local emphasis could be used to justify refusing assistance to 'non-residents', to anyone who had recently moved into the area for whatever reason.

Moreover, despite claims that Mothers' Aid was intended to protect single mothers from the need to take paid work in the belief that children should have full-time mothering, the stipends were so tiny that they were never enough to live on. If the women and children were to survive they had to work, the children too, but clandestinely because they would lose their pensions if they were caught. Because of the need for secrecy and their extreme poverty, the women were ripe for exploitation and capital did not waste the opportunity. One of the few forms of work available was sweated piece-work (e.g. hand sewing, making artificial flowers) that paid less for harder work in worse conditions than factory labour. Often the children worked alongside their mothers, some of them as young as three years of age (Gordon, 2008: 343).

The focus on children instead of women not only did not help children, it was actively detrimental to their well-being. Withdrawing support from women who were found to be morally 'undeserving' meant their children starved too. As Linda Gordon put it, 'the ignominy laid on [mothers] reinforced a stingy attitude toward offering them aid. What would have benefited neglected children most was helping their [mothers]. In other words, overriding the rights of poor [mothers] did not usually lead to better fulfilment of children's needs' (Gordon, 2008: 342).[363]

As Gordon quite rightly said, the policy of child-only assistance is 'ludicrous'. She pointed out that 'the fiction of stipends for children only' was meaningless in its assumption that 'the caretaker could starve but the child would be well-nourished … the children get orange juice and cheese but the law requires the parent not to drink or eat these … the child with asthma gets treatment but the parent does not' (Gordon, 2008: 345). She argued that this focus on children at their mothers' expense had not been beneficial for children, as it cannot be, given that children's well-being is dependent on the well-being of their mothers.

The stinginess of the assistance, whether directed towards the children or their mothers, suggests that concern for children was not the real reason for the policy. As Gordon said:

> the United States arguably treats children worse than other countries of comparable wealth … The United States has become notorious for its wretched international record on basic child-welfare indices such as infant mortality rates, educational attainment, teenage pregnancy incidence, and poverty among children. A few comparative indicators: the United States has the second worst infant mortality rate in the advanced world (only Latvia does worse); the worst record for child poverty in the advanced world; and the lowest rate of overall social expenditure, at about three percent of GDP. It is difficult to reconcile these circumstances with the strength of the putting-children-first ideology (Gordon, 2008: 332-3).

And the situation has been getting worse. In 1960, the US had the 12th lowest infant mortality rate in the world, but by 1990, its ranking had dropped to 23rd, and to 34th by 2008 (Friedman, 2012). The infant mortality rate among African-Americans is over twice as high as the national average (13.63 per

---

363. Gordon says 'parents', but these parents were mostly women, and the ignominy and the stinginess of the assistance were largely driven by misogyny.

1,000 births in 2005, in comparison with 6.7 nationally). Friedman attributes the high rate in the US of 'congenital malformations and disorders associated with low birth-weight and short gestation', to factors which are the result of 'economic, ethnic, and racial disparities', in other words, poverty and racism. The concern for children is an ideological sham. Behind the sentimental veneer of supposedly 'putting children first' lie other agendas.

One of these is the cultural imperative which requires that women and children be under the control of men. To give women with children but without men an income sufficient to live on is to violate one of male supremacy's fondest beliefs—that women and children belong to men. This belief motivates the men who kill their wives and/or their children when the wives leave them; it motivates the 'men's rights' groups who threaten and harass the family courts, and demand 'shared custody' across the board even to the men who abuse their children; it motivates the gay male couples who use the bodies of women as 'surrogates' to acquire babies, thus dehumanising the most intimate and precious of human experiences—childbirth—and ignoring the emotional consequences for the women and children; and it motivates the 'transgender' men who claim they have been transmogrified into 'women', and then proceed to exercise their masculine sense of overweening entitlement to demand entry to women-only spaces and official recognition of their 'changed' 'gender'.

But there is another agenda, too, one which was to become more blatant in the second half of the twentieth century once women started entering the workforce in significant numbers. That agenda belonged to the powerful economic interests whose exploitation of women's labour was masked by the icon of the stay-at-home mother. Women had to be kept poor so that they could continue to supply a low-wage labour market. This was certainly the case for black women in the southern States where their labour in the fields and as domestic servants contributed far, far more to the economy than they were ever paid. But it was also the case for poor women in general who took in piece-work to supplement meagre pensions and keep themselves and their children from starvation and homelessness, and who had to remain silent about their exploitative work conditions because they were supposedly being paid to 'stay home with the children'. These two agendas—male control over women and children, and the economy's need for a highly exploitable workforce—dictated the form taken by the State Mothers' Aid laws in the second decade of the twentieth century, just as they were to dictate every 'welfare' initiative since.

Things could have been even worse. Mary-Jo Bane, former assistant secretary for children and families in the US Department of Health and Human Services (Bane, 1997: 52), said that the earliest version of the Republican 'welfare reform' bill made provision for the states to use the block grant money for orphanages. The wording in the Contract with America is: 'The state will use the funds for programs to reduce out-of-wedlock pregnancies, to promote adoption, to establish and operate orphanages, to establish and operate residential group homes for unwed mothers'. Clearly, these men knew (and didn't care) that 'welfare reform' would make it impossible for women to care for their children, and the orphanages were their ruthless (and dissociated) response to this. They had no qualms about taking children away from their mothers when the economy that had made those men rich had made the mothers too poor to care for their children. Bane refers to this as a 'stark recognition' on the part of the Republicans. The Democrats, she said, 'attacked this provision relentlessly' not, however, out of concern for the women and children, but because orphanages 'could never provide care for more than a small fraction of children affected by time limits or denials of benefits for other reasons'. So the Democrats, too, knew that 'welfare reform' would have horrendous consequences in the numbers of children who would be deprived of basic necessities, including food. Bane had resigned from the Department of Health and Human Services when PRWORA was passed because of her 'fears about what would happen to poor children' (Bane, 1997: 47).

The focus on children is nothing but a capitulation to the right-wing misogyny and callous ruling-class interests that have vitiated US 'welfare' policy all along. Families must not be headed by women and, more covertly, women must be available to work for the health of the economy whatever the repercussions for their own health and that of their children. Given how influential these two powerful interests were and continue to be, it is hardly surprising that 'welfare' fails to provide adequately for either women or children.

Bureaucratic disentitlement

Bureaucratic disentitlement did not originate with PRWORA.[364] Disentitlement has always been an intrinsic part of any 'welfare' system,

---

364. Other terms referring to the same phenomenon (listed from earlier to later discussions) are: 'churning' (Dehavenon, 1989-1990); 'discouragement' (Bennett, 1995); 'the dissuasion function of welfare bureaucracies' (Kennedy, 1998); 'administrative exclusion' (Brodkin et al, 2005); 'the revolving door' (Youdelman and Getsos, 2005); '"reformed" administrative

from medieval poor relief to the present day. The powers-that-be will always do the very least they can get away with to dampen down the social unrest caused by gross inequalities of wealth and power, that is, by domination. The aim of 'welfare' is never to abolish poverty because that would mean abolishing wealth; the aim of 'welfare' is to buy off the 'dangerous classes' who are threatening the ruling powers with riots and other forms of social disorder (Piven and Cloward, 1993). Those concessions appear to address the grievances of the poor while in fact changing nothing of any substance. That nothing has changed becomes obvious when new restrictions are introduced once the disorder has calmed down. As Piven and Cloward have noted:

> Poor relief was invented, and periodically expanded, to cope with widespread strife from below. And it was contracted or "reformed" in response to employer objections to an indiscriminate charity which intruded on labor market arrangements (Piven and Cloward, 1993: 421).

PRWORA introduced vicious new impositions which worsened the conditions of America's very poor still further, but it had been done before.

'Quality control'

One of the earlier forms of bureaucratic disentitlement was the federal Quality Control policy (Casey and Mannix, 1989). Originally established in the mid-1960s, it was a management tool aimed simply to measure the accuracy of claims processing, including claims that were erroneously rejected as well as errors of over-payment. In 1973 under the Nixon Administration, the federal Department of Health and Human Services revised the Quality Control system to one focused solely on over-payment. It did this by introducing sanctions for States with over-payment rates greater than a specified level (3%), and by abolishing the review of rejections altogether. The latter was restored in 1977, but only after claimant organisations had gone to court to force the Department to do so. However, the chief focus remained on claim approvals which could be shown to be unallowable. with little oversight of those that had been rejected without good reason.

At the same time as it placed the stringent requirements on the States, the Department abolished any protection from bureaucratic disentitlement, by repealing regulations that restrained State 'welfare' agencies from over-hasty rejection of people's claims. One of the regulations to be repealed stated that "'verification of circumstances pertaining to eligibility will be limited to what is reasonably necessary to ensure the legality of expenditures'".

---

practices' (Brodkin, 2006); 'administrative incapacity' (Handler, 2008); 'proceduralism' (Brodkin and Majmundar, 2010); 'informal diversion' (Hahn et al, 2012b).

Another requirement to be abolished had held States responsible for "'help[ing] applicants and recipients provide needed information'", and required States to "'obtain the information for them if … they themselves are unable to provide it'" (Casey and Mannix, 1989: 1385). The Department also repealed a regulation which was intended to curb the worst abuses in the practice of sending 'welfare' officials into people's homes. That regulation specified that officials were prevented from "'entering a home by force, or without permission, or under false pretenses; making home visits outside of working hours, and particularly making such visits during sleeping hours; and searching in the home, for example, in rooms, closets, drawers, or papers, to seek clues to possible deception'". As well as repealing this regulation, the Department told State 'welfare' agencies that home visits might be a way of reducing over-payments (Casey and Mannix, 1989: 1286).

Given the harshness of these changes, it is clear that their primary purpose was to reduce the 'welfare' rolls that had increased so much during the 1960s as result of activist campaigns, civil disorder among black populations, and Supreme Court decisions that many of the ploys used to keep people off the rolls were unconstitutional (Casey and Mannix, 1989: 1382). As one commentator has pointed out:

> The asymmetries in performance measurement had profound implications for street-level practice, providing incentives to pile on the paperwork and raise the burden of proof, but no penalties for piling paperwork too high, making the burden too heavy, or erroneously denying claims, regardless of one's actual eligibility for benefits. Under the guise of improving accuracy, the implementation of more rigorous bureaucratic procedures effectively limited access to assistance, closing the door to both proper and improper claims for help (Brodkin, 2006: 5).

In the 1980s, Congress asked the National Academy of Sciences to study the effects of the federal Quality Control policy. The request was made, not only (or not at all) because of the churning problem and the injustice of bureaucratic disentitlement, but because the problem was seen as an unfair imposition on the States. A State was liable for financial penalties if it had too high a proportion of claims that had been allowed when they should have been denied. It was argued that, at 3%, the proportion was set far too low. By the late 1980s, States owed the federal government around one billion dollars in unpaid penalties, with new penalties accruing at between $220 and $320 million a year (Casey and Mannix, 1989).

In 1986, two researchers submitted a study of churning in AFDC to the National Academy of Sciences' review (Casey and Mannix, 1986). These

473

researchers, described by one author (Dehavenon, 1989-1990: 245) as the leading experts on Quality Control, refer to bureaucratic disentitlement as 'verification extremism'. This is a reference to the chief way in which people are deprived of their entitlement to 'welfare', i.e. by being asked to provide large numbers of documents to 'verify' their claims.

The researchers had investigated national data on approvals, denials and reasons for the denials from 1972 to 1984, and found a three-fold increase over that time in denials for procedural reasons, i.e. the claimants had failed to fulfil bureaucratic requirements. They also found that most of those whose claims had been denied were in fact eligible on financial grounds. As well, they uncovered an increase in the routine use of home visits and the questioning of neighbours and landlords to verify claimants' eligibility (Casey and Mannix, 1986: 1385). Successful as these methods were in slashing 'welfare' rolls that had swelled during the 1960s (Piven and Cloward, 1993), the powers-that-be were still not satisfied. PRWORA added an extra dimension of bureaucratic disentitlement, and this succeeded beyond its framers' wildest dreams. But a 'welfare' system in name only with no substance to it has long been a dream of the arrogant, dissociated men spawned under capitalism.

Workfare and the perennial war against welfare

The workfare aspect of PRWORA also has a long history preceding this particular piece of legislation. It was a central aspect of state 'welfare' experimentation under the federal waiver system (Peck, 1998a: 536); and for all the lip service paid to children's need to have their mothers at home, work requirements have always been part of the US 'welfare' system, including Mothers' Aid pensions and ADC (Handler, 2002: 4).

The earliest recorded use of the term 'workfare' was in 1968 (Canzoneri, 1968). It is attributed to James Charles Evers (Safire, 1988; Peck, 1998b: 138), civil rights organiser and older brother of civil rights activist, Medgar Evers (who was shot and killed by a white supremacist in 1963). Evers did not use the term 'workfare' pejoratively, as a term of opprobrium in order to emphasise the point that 'welfare' was no such thing if it involved coercive work requirements. On the contrary, he thoroughly approved of what the word referred to. 'I believe in working', he is reported to have said during his 1968 Congressional campaign,[365] 'I always worked for everything I got'. The report covering the campaign said that 'workfare' was what Evers called one

---

365. He didn't get into Congress, but he did become mayor of Fayette, Mississippi the next year, the first African-American to become mayor in that state.

of his programs, and that 'he has said that everybody ought to work for what he gets'. This comment occurred in the context of 'the approach of a one-legged Negro man on a crutch'. Evers, the reporter continues,

> asks the man how much welfare he gets, and if he would be willing to work, handicapped though he is, if he had a job he could handle. The man says—perhaps reluctantly—that he is willing, and Evers replies quietly, "Then we're going to get work for you" (Canzoneri, 1968: 71).

Despite Evers' civil-rights activism, the word's coinage is clearly right-wing. There is the ritualistic invocation of the virtues of 'work', the blind belief in the power and ability of the individual to achieve anything no matter how great the obstacles, the ignoring of the structural, economic causes of poverty, the blithe disregard of the impediments that no one could possibly be powerful enough to overcome, and (not to put too fine a point on it) the deluding of self and other: 'Then we're going to get work for you'.

The right-wing lost no time in claiming 'workfare' as its own. William Safire, one of Richard Nixon's speech-writers, believed for some time that he himself was the originator of the word. Through his 'On Language' column in *The New York Times*, Safire was an acknowledged expert on political language usage, and in the 1978 edition of his *Political Dictionary*,[366] he defined 'workfare' as a 'conservative [i.e. right-wing] label for welfare reform'. He went on to say,

> in his nationwide television address on August 8, 1969, the President [Nixon] tried out a new word: "In the final analysis, we cannot talk our way out of poverty; we cannot legislate our way out of poverty, but this nation can work its way out of poverty. What America needs now is not more welfare, but more 'workfare'" (Safire, 1978: 799-800).

Actually, it was Safire himself who had tried out the new word in his role as presidential speech-writer. Later, when the word was included in the final volume of the Supplement to the Oxford English Dictionary, he learned that Evers had used it first (citing the *Harper*'s article—Canzoneri, 1968). 'That's all right', he said, 'I may not have been the first to use the word, but I had a hand in its nationwide launch and feel a stepfather's pride' (Safire, 1988).

The mainstream popularity of the term 'workfare' is fairly recent. A survey of articles in US newspapers from 1971 to 1996 (Peck, 1998b: 134-5) found that there were more references to workfare in 1995 (in the lead-up to PRWORA) than during the whole of the period from 1971 to 1980. The number of references started to rise in the 1980s, especially around the time

---

366. 'Workfare' doesn't appear in the first edition in 1968.

of earlier 'welfare reforms' such as Reagan's Omnibus Reconciliation Act of 1981 and Family Support Act of 1988, and the debate following on Clinton's 1991 promise to 'end welfare'. But the practice itself, whatever it is called, is an intrinsic part of the welfare state. Capitalist society cannot allow people to live comfortably unattached to the profit-making economy.

PRWORA's supporters often praise it for its mandatory work requirements as though such things had never existed before. For example, the Republican Committee on Education and Labor in the 111th Congress of the US House of Representatives, asserted that making 'individuals … work for their benefits' was the 'key reason why many former welfare recipients are leading independent lives today'. They went on to say: 'Under the old system, welfare families could expect a lifetime of cash assistance without engaging in constructive activities of any kind',[367] thus ignoring the fact that 'individuals' being required to work for their benefits had already been tried many times before over a period of at least 30 years. Leaving aside any questions about just how 'independent' people's lives are after leaving 'welfare' (not to mention not getting it in the first place), such wilful ignorance of history is typical of those for whom 'welfare reform' means abolishing it, but who won't say so outright.

Strictly speaking, 'workfare' refers only to the requirement that recipients 'work off' their benefits, i.e. to cases where the only recompense for the person's labour is the 'welfare' payment. (Under the principle of less eligibility, this must always be much less than the standard wage for the job, even when the 'welfare' recipient is doing a standard job). However, the term 'workfare' is also used for any requirement that recipients engage in employment or employment-related activities as a condition for receiving benefits. As one commentator put it: 'the term workfare is "now used in a much broader sense to include, as a condition of income support, the requirement that recipients participate in a wide range of activities designed to increase their employment prospects" (quoted in Peck, 1998b: 133). Sometimes this involves a policy of placing recipients in a job (at the going rate) as quickly as possible. This is commonly known as the 'work first' approach, that is to say, no consideration is given to any preparation for work such as education or training, nor to any other needs recipients might have. Sometimes it does involve education or training (as work-related activity), but not for long and never of a kind to lead to well-paid skilled jobs. Sometimes it simply involves recipients doing as they're told as 'volunteers' in not-for-profit community

---

367. http://archives.republicans.edlabor.house.gov/showissue.aspx?IID=15.

organisations or public employment, or even in some cases, for commercial enterprises. Because they are coerced, such activities are neither 'work' as it is commonly understood, nor 'volunteering' (which is called such because it is unpaid, not because it is voluntary). But such niceties have never been allowed to impede the lawmakers' enthusiasm for 'welfare reform'.

The first workfare programs were local (State, county or municipality), rather than federal; and State and local policies and practices often required that female heads of families work (Oliker, 1994: 196), even though Mothers' Aid pensions and ADC were supposedly designed to help widows remain at home with their children (as long as they were respectable and white). This was the jurisdictional level where employers had the most direct influence on welfare policy and the clearest perceptions of their interests in maintaining a readily accessible pool of low-wage labour.

One early example of a connection between welfare and employment concerns the so-called 'employable mother' rules. Louisiana was the first state to adopt an 'employable mother' rule, in 1943. This rule required that all ADC families with children over the age of six be refused cash assistance at harvest time so that their mothers had no financial alternative to working in the fields. Not only were county 'welfare' boards directed to deny all new applications, they were also required to close all existing cases (Piven and Cloward, 1993: 134-5, 138).

Calling these rules 'employable mother' partakes of the same Orwellian dissociation displayed by PRWORA's 'personal responsibility', 'work opportunities', 'reconciliation' and 'temporary assistance'. In actual fact these rules had nothing whatsoever to do with mothers' capabilities (real or imagined). They were a response to local labour conditions, in particular, the seasonal need in rural areas for people to work in the fields picking fruit or tobacco or cotton. It is no accident that the first 'employable mother' rule was introduced in a southern State (Louisiana). It was more characteristic of the southern States than the northern States, and was used primarily against black women. The rules were motivated by the need for field hands, a need more prevalent in the southern States than in the northern. But because the field hands had to be highly exploitable—the work never paid a living wage—and black, the rule was also motivated by a persisting slave-owner mentality. This mentality to this day remains stronger in the southern States than in the northern, although it is not absent there either. It is, in fact, the slave-owner mentality which motivates 'welfare reform'—the arrogant belief that the labour of some human beings can be exploited without adequate recompense, for the sole benefit of those who own the means of exploitation.

These State-level 'employable mother' rules were declared unconstitutional in 1968 (Piven and Cloward, 1993: 308). They were not workfare in the sense that they mandated employment-related activities in exchange for benefits. But they did serve the same function as workfare—to emphasise the message that recipients had no reliable entitlement to 'welfare' and that they had to be available for 'work' at any price, motherhood notwithstanding. Black women in the southern States had always been pressured to work, especially in the fields at harvest time, but the pressure came from the withdrawal of income support altogether, not from work requirements as a condition of that support.

WIN

Until the late 1960s there was no direct pressure at the federal level requiring recipients to take up employment as a condition of receiving benefits. During the 1950s, the major attacks on 'welfare' occurred mainly at the State level (Abramovitz, 1996: 322-3). But with the 1967 Work Incentive Program (WIN), federal 'welfare' policy itself became more punitive and more explicit about its purpose in 'regulating the labor force participation of poor and husbandless women' (Abramovitz, 1996: 336-41).

The timing of the first introduction of work requirements as a condition of federal funding (the late 1960s) is significant. The introduction of work and work-related requirements for claimants was the policy response to increasing caseloads, and there are historical reasons why the caseloads increased at that particular time. The activism of the civil rights and welfare rights movements were major contributors to the increases, together with the Johnson administration's War on Poverty, launched in 1964, especially its legal service arm. Not only did welfare rights activists encourage people to register, they also encouraged successful legal challenges to the more blatant forms of administrative exclusion. Cases heard in the Supreme Court of the United States led to the overturning of some of the more egregious of the State laws denying people's entitlements (Kennedy, 1998). Between 1966 and 1968, the Supreme Court handed down a number of decisions limiting what 'welfare' agencies could do, including restricting what could be used to assess claimants' eligibility and home suitability, and abolishing residence requirements, midnight raids and 'man-in-the-house' rules (Abramovitz, 1996: 334). But work requirements are seemingly perfectly legal, and they have always been a favoured way of reducing the 'welfare' rolls through bureaucratic disentitlement.

Initially participation in WIN was voluntary, but in 1971 it was made mandatory for recipients with school-age children. WIN brought official federal 'welfare' policy into line with common practice. It made work compulsory for AFDC mothers, and there was no longer any pretence that 'welfare' subsidised 'deserving' poor women to stay home to care for their children; or rather, the pretence and the ideological illusion of supporting motherhood existed side-by-side with the reality of coerced workforce participation. Those who failed to comply were to be sanctioned with a three-month reduction in their benefit or its withdrawal altogether.

As well as the work mandates under WIN, the 1967 amendments to the Social Security Act allowed federal aid to be still made available for widowed mothers and those whose husbands were unemployed, and the funds were not limited to any particular amount (they were not block grants) nor to any particular time period. But the amendments imposed a freeze on federal aid for mothers whose single status was the result of being deserted by their husbands or who gave birth to children outside marriage. This was the first time that a provision relating to out-of-wedlock births was introduced at the federal level. Although this provision was never put into effect and was finally repealed in 1969, it did appear in federal legislation and there was widespread support for it. During the 1950s, 19 States had excluded children from the ADC program if they were born to mothers who were already receiving benefits (Abramovitz, 1996). This was later to be referred to as a 'family cap', i.e. a cap on the number of children allowed in a family receiving 'welfare', or, as another commentator put it, 'barring aid to babies born to welfare mothers' (Brodkin, 1997: 27n4). PRWORA also includes a 'family cap' provision, although it's not mandatory: 'Under the new [1996] law, states have the option to implement a family cap … [i.e.] to deny cash benefits to children born to welfare recipients' (US CSE, 1996). By 2010, 21 states had introduced a family cap policy that restricted the benefits that could be paid to children born to a 'welfare'-recipient mother (Hasenfeld, 2010: 153).

WIN was not a success if judged by the criteria that supposedly motivated it—it neither got women into the workforce nor reduced the caseloads. There were a number of reasons for this. In the first place it was poorly funded and there were not enough places in the program for all recipients, not all of whom were women anyway. In 1971 38% of those enrolled were men. Because there were not enough places, States exempted some categories of mothers, especially those with pre-school children. These women can be regarded as the lucky ones because the exemption meant that they escaped the punitive sanctions, at least for a few years. There was also a reluctance on the part of the public assistance workers to impose work requirements on AFDC mothers, especially given the high cost and limited availability of child care (Abramovitz, 1996: 339-41). Moreover, policing women's participation was costly for the State agencies, poorly funded as they were. Simply handing over welfare cheques was much cheaper, and WIN in practice was often little more than a requirement that women register (Blank and Blum, 1997).

But the main problem which bedevilled WIN and every subsequent attempt to introduce workfare, was the nature of the workforce women were expected to enter. Not only were there too few jobs, those that did exist did not pay a living wage and hence were incapable of reducing 'dependency' on 'welfare'. And yet, despite WIN's lack of success, the 'reformers' kept trying, and they are still trying.

OBRA

The war against 'welfare' escalated at the federal level during the Reagan administration (1981-89). This is not surprising, given Reagan's well-known right-wing commitment and his concomitant detestation of 'welfare'. For example, part of his election campaign for the governorship of California involved his expressed intention 'to send the welfare bums back to work'; and during the 1976 presidential election campaign he constantly repeated his now-famous remarks about what the media referred to as a 'welfare queen'.

With the Omnibus Budget Reconciliation Act (OBRA) of 1981 and subsequent legislation, the Reagan administration did their best to 'end welfare as they had come to know it'. Budgets for the WIN programs were cut and hundreds of thousands of working-poor households were forced off AFDC. At the same time benefits for those remaining on the rolls were reduced. The administration wanted to repeal the WIN program altogether and replace it with a program which would have compelled recipients to work in exchange for welfare benefits ('workfare' in the narrow sense). This did not succeed, but Congress did allow States the option of introducing workfare. This was known as the Community Work Experience Program, and it allowed States to compel women with children as young as three to work at jobs they were assigned to in exchange for welfare benefits only. As well, States could design their own 'work-training' programs as Demonstration programs (Baum, 1991). Some of these programs, such as Greater Avenues for Independence (GAIN) in California and Employment and Training Choices in Massachusetts, were reported in the national media. The state OBRA programs became even better known when the Manpower Demonstration Research Corporation (which refers to itself only by the initials, MDRC) (see below) focused its research efforts on a number of them (Blank and Blum, 1997).

OBRA cut welfare payments as well as dramatically restricting eligibility for AFDC. This removed close to half a million families from the welfare rolls, despite being introduced in the midst of a recession. One of the main intentions of the OBRA legislation was to allow the States (and even smaller jurisdictions, e.g. a single agency) more leeway to design their own 'welfare-to-work' programs. Called 'OBRA Demonstrations', these local programs were allowed to waive federal rules about people's eligibility and entitlement. These were an earlier version of the waiver system in the early 1990s under the Bush and Clinton administrations and prior to the PRWORA legislation. Despite the fact that previous workfare programs had been markedly unsuccessful at getting people into work, under OBRA (with 90% federal funding) they proliferated at the local level during the 1980s (Peck, 2001: 91, 134)

The OBRA Demonstration programs were required to conduct evaluations, and it is this requirement which provided MDRC with the opportunity for its research. These Demonstrations differed from each other in a number of ways, but what they all had in common was that they were rigorously administered real, rather than purely formal, work mandates for mothers of school-age children (Oliker, 1994: 201). As Jamie Peck (2001: 91) said, 'Reagan effectively declared war on welfare with the Omnibus Budget Reconciliation Act'.

The cuts in 'welfare' expenditure under OBRA were couched in terms of reducing the budget deficit, as was the 2005 reauthorisation of PRWORA, the Deficit Reduction Act, which increased the work requirements yet again. Reducing the budget deficit is a favourite right-wing excuse for cutting spending on 'welfare' (or on anything else that might contribute to the common good). But the fiscal operations of sovereign currency-issuing governments such as the US federal government do not depend on 'budgets' (see chapter 10), and hence there is no economic need to reduce 'deficits'. There is, however, a *political* need motivated by right-wing hatred for those victimised by the capitalist economy. It is this that motivates 'deficit reductions', that is, spending cuts to those resources required for the common good. The US is not alone in this, it is standard operating procedure for governments everywhere. It is, however, a myth, or to use less euphemistic language, a lie. Lying in politics ('false news', 'alternative facts') has finally become a matter for public debate after so many years of neo-liberal service to inequality (i.e. domination). But it has always been useful for powerful vested interests, for as long as they have needed to disguise themselves as 'democracy'. The notion of government 'budgets' and the belief that they need to make 'savings' is one of those long-standing lies required to manage consent to conditions of domination.

FSA

The next piece of federal 'welfare' legislation was the Family Support Act (FSA) of 1988. The 'support' in the title did not mean that the government had a responsibility to support families, but rather, that parents had a responsibility to support their children—absent fathers to pay child support and mothers to get jobs. The workfare programs established under the legislation were to be WIN's successors and were known as Job Opportunities and Basic Skills (JOBS for short). They were to be operated by the States who were expected to provide education and training and at least two of four additional activities—job search, on-the-job training, work supplementation, and community work experience (Blank and Blum, 1997: 33). States had to keep at least 20 percent of eligible parents enrolled in these activities (Szanton, 1991: 590). All women whose children were over the age of two were deemed eligible, and those who were enrolled were compelled to participate under threat of having their payments stopped if they did not. The Act also allowed for federal funding for child care (Blank and Blum, 1997: 33); Medicaid and child care could be provided for a year after the former 'welfare' recipient had started work; and there were additional funds provided (to the States, not to the women) earmarked for employment-preparation services for women regarded as particularly hard to shift, i.e. those with few marketable skills and who had been on 'welfare' for extended periods of time (Szanton, 1991: 590-1).

One of the most important influences on the FSA was the National Governors Association. The States wanted the federal 'welfare' system 'reformed' for two reasons. The first reason was that they wanted more money from the federal government because the WIN appropriations had been reduced by more than two-thirds under the Reagan administration (from over $300 million in 1981 to under $100 million in 1986). The second reason was political—the governors believed there were votes in it. One governor was quoted saying: "'I have a pretty good idea of how my voters, whether they are bankers or construction workers, feel about … welfare reform … They support welfare reform'" (Szanton, 1991: 593). But the governors' real constituency was the bankers (not the construction workers), along with the rest of the 'business community', who believed that 'welfare reform' would mean 'better-prepared entry-level workers'.

One of the architects of the legislation was the Democratic Senator for New York, Daniel Patrick Moynihan (Baum, 1991). He made the same claims for the FSA's potential to end 'welfare' as Clinton was to make later. The FSA would mean that 'welfare' was no longer "'a permanent or even extended circumstance'", he said, "'it is to be a transition to employment'" (Szanton, 1991: 590). But the 1988 FSA was no more successful than any of the previous attempts at getting women into the workforce and reducing the 'welfare' rolls. It was never fully funded by the States. They were reluctant to match the federal funds and most of them didn't claim their full appropriations from the federal government. It was quickly eclipsed by the waiver system, whereby States could request permission from the federal government to vary the eligibility requirements (Blank and Blum, 1997).

Failure

Throughout the last half-century or more of federal government involvement in 'workfare' regulation (since WIN and the 1967 amendments to the 1935 Social Security Act), workfare has never been found to be successful, at least when judged by the criteria of workforce participation and poverty reduction.

The stated purpose of workfare is to get people off 'welfare' and into jobs, but these are not the same. People can be moved off 'welfare' without being moved into jobs. And while the system of workfare is very efficient at moving people off 'welfare', and even more so since PRWORA, its efficacy at getting people into jobs is disorganised to the point of chaos.

The way this works can be illustrated by an example from decades ago, described in a short 1971 article in the 'Notes and comments' section of the journal, *Social Service Review* (Anonymous, 1971).[368] The author deplored the then current attempts at 'welfare reform' by State legislatures. Because they were concerned only with cutting costs, the author said, the proposals seemed designed 'to make life just a little more miserable for those who must depend ... on public help', and to save money by discouraging anyone who might be thinking of asking for help.

The author described one such scheme in New York State. This involved requiring recipients who were judged to be 'employable' to come to offices of the State employment service to pick up their 'welfare' cheques rather than receiving them through the mail. The supposed rationale for this

---

368. This is the earliest citation of the term 'workfare' in the academic databases (Web of Science and Scopus) (viewed 9.6.'12).

move was to provide 'clients' with opportunities to contact job-placement counsellors as a way of getting jobs. This scheme was monitored at two agencies during its first eight weeks of operation by observers from an organisation called the Community Council of Greater New York, who also distributed questionnaires to the people who turned up. The author of the article described what happened:

> hundreds of clients appeared at the employment offices. Some were obviously feeble or ill. Some had received day passes from hospitals. Some brought medical certificates indicating that they could not work. Some had young children for whom child-care plans would be necessary before employment was arranged. Some had had to miss sessions of training courses in order to report. Some, after long waits in line, found no checks waiting for them. Others for whom there were checks—about 19 percent—failed to appear at all (Anonymous, 1971: 486).

There was no information available about how many people were provided with jobs. But the procedures used for defining who counted as 'employable' were clearly chaotic, as were the procedures for ensuring that eligible recipients got paid. The official explanation for the non-appearance of nearly one-fifth of those deemed 'employable' was that these were people who were already working and who had been committing some kind of fraud which the requirement to appear in person had exposed. The same official 'explanation' was still being given in relation to the people who didn't show up when they were referred to the GAIN program in the 1980s in Riverside, California: "'They're working already and it's not reported'" (Peck, 2001: 184; Riccio et al, 1994: 109).

But there are alternative explanations such as the compulsory nature of the activities required and 'the deliberate exploitation of uncertainty and fear' (Peck, 2001: 184). No attempt was made to find out why people hadn't appeared at the employment offices during those months in 1971. Nearly half (45%) of those who did appear and who answered the council's questionnaire said that they had found it hard to get to the office because of transport costs, illness, disability, or the difficulty of arranging child care. The report of the research recommended that the requirement to appear in person be repealed, or failing that, that it should be amended to go into effect only on three conditions: when the federal government develops a full-employment program; when unemployment declines; and when transportation costs are provided by law. The recommendations have never been implemented.

The 'disconnected': neither work nor welfare

The right-wing (whether in Congress, the mainstream media or academe) claim that the decreases in the 'welfare' caseloads are due to people getting employment. For example, a self-proclaimed 'strong supporter of tougher welfare policies' said: 'American welfare reform is best known for reducing the benefit rolls by 65 per cent and for sending millions of mothers out to work' (Besharov, 2008). But all the research shows that former 'welfare' recipients do not typically get jobs (see below), and many of those who do become employed are worse off because they are not paid a living wage and they lose the benefits they had on 'welfare' (e.g. Medicaid).

One of the consequences of a 'welfare reform' that abolishes entitlement is that a significant proportion of the American population of poor women and children have neither work nor 'welfare' nor any other forms of cash assistance such as SSI or unemployment benefits. They are referred to in the literature as 'disconnected', that is, whatever resources they are using to survive are not connected to the mainstream economy. This does not mean that they are part of a 'black' economy; it means that they 'are not receiving income from sources that are typically regarded as having the potential to meet a family's needs' (Moore et al, 2012: 99).

Michele Steinberg (1999) quotes US Senator, Paul Wellstone (D-Minn.), speaking in support of an amendment to the Defense Authorization Act for fiscal year 2000:

> Since August of 1996, 1.3 million families have left welfare. They are no longer receiving welfare assistance. That is 4.5 million recipients … the vast majority are children. On the basis of these numbers, too many people have deemed welfare reform a success … No one seems to know what has happened to these families. Yet we keep trumpeting the "victory" of welfare reform … I am worried that they are just disappearing and this amendment is all about a new class of citizens in our country. I call them "The Disappeared" (Steinberg, 1999: 10).[369]

That this is in fact what would happen as a consequence of 'welfare reform' should have been obvious, and was indeed obvious to many concerned observers. So obvious was it, that those responsible for the 'reform' can only have been heedless of the consequences, or worse, this is exactly the result they intended all along.

---

369. The publication within which this article appeared embraces one of the right wing's favourite missions—denial of global warming. This article, however, is not right wing, since it tells the truth about the disaster that is 'welfare reform' (http://www.larouchepub.com/eirtoc/site_packages/2007/al_gore.html).

Researchers from the Urban Institute couched the problem in the following terms:

> Some policymakers and advocates … are concerned that the reformed welfare system may have increased the number of families living without basic cash income. Under the reforms, families are more likely to lose benefit eligibility because of sanctions or time limits, and tougher work requirements may discourage or prevent some individuals from participating in assistance programs. State strategies to divert enrollment—such as requiring all eligible candidates to pursue job search activities before receiving benefits and instituting rules that make some immigrants ineligible—may also depress participation. Recent declines in program participation rates suggest that more eligible families are indeed staying away from welfare (Zedlewski and Nelson, 2003: 1).

This conciliatory statement tends to understate the problem, as is usual with the Urban Institute. It is true that they need to tread softly if they are to get any public hearing at all, just like any of the other organisations trying to ameliorate the worst of the 'reforms' while not alienating the powers-that-be. But 'welfare reform' is motivated by hatred and contempt for those who are victimised by the system. The most appropriate human reaction to that is outrage and a determination to tell the truth, not appeasement and a stance of disinterestedness and academic objectivity.

'Leaver' studies

It has been known since at least the beginning of TANF that there are women and children who have left 'welfare' without first acquiring other conventional means of support. For example, when the AFDC program was replaced by W-2 in Wisconsin in September 1997, 'a troubling 16%' (as the Wisconsin W-2 Monitoring Task Force put it) had not made the transition from AFDC to W-2 by June 1998, and had no other means of support (Wisconsin W-2 Monitoring Task Force, 2002: 9; IWF, 1998: 6).

This outcome is not surprising once it is recognised that caseloads did not decline because 'welfare' leavers got jobs that paid well, or even jobs of any sort. Between 1994 and 2001, for example, 'welfare' caseloads fell by three million, but the number of employed single mothers increased by only 1.1 million. Even if all the 1.1 million were former or potential 'welfare' recipients, this still amounts to only about one-third of the caseload decline (Besharov and Germanis, 2007: 43).

To put this another way: between 1995 and 2000, the number of 'welfare' recipients fell by 56%, while the proportion of single mothers who were employed rose by 18% over the same period (Moore et al, 2012).[370] Even though the two percentages are not strictly comparable—not all of that 18% of single mothers who eventually became employed would have been on 'welfare'—there is still a large discrepancy between the proportion who left 'welfare' and the proportion who gained employment. It is this discrepancy that contains the disconnected poor single mothers.

Most of the studies investigating the situations of poor women and children are what is known as 'leaver' studies, i.e. studies of former 'welfare' recipients. Their findings vary considerably. An MDRC study in a county in Ohio found that, between 1998 and 2001, there was an increase from 11% to 20% in the percentage of welfare leavers who had neither work nor welfare (Brock et al, 2002). Data from the 2002 National Survey of American Families also indicated that around 20% of those who had left 'welfare' were 'disconnected', i.e. had no employment, did not have an employed spouse, and were not receiving income support of any kind (Acs and Loprest, 2007). In 2003, an Urban Institute researcher estimated that around one in seven adults who had left 'welfare' were disconnected (Loprest, 2003). The Community Voices Heard research project investigating New York City's Employment Services and Placement program (Youdelman and Getsos, 2005) found that, according to the December 2004 VendorStats, an average of 36% of those placed in jobs through the TANF system had lost those jobs, did not return to public assistance and remained unaccounted for.

Other researchers (Besharov and Germanis, 2007: 33) estimated that as many as 40% of the mothers who had left 'welfare' were not working regularly, although they also quoted a figure of between 35% and 50% of ex-'welfare' recipients who had no jobs and hadn't returned to 'welfare'. Other figures quoted on the percentage of 'welfare' leavers who are unemployed are 36%, 37% and 43% (Loprest and Nichols, 2011).

National studies

Other studies use national data on poor single mothers in general, not simply data on those who are 'welfare' leavers. According to Urban Institute researchers, concern about the falls in the TANF caseloads and in the

---

370. The way in which the article frames this information is yet another example of the tendency in the literature to downplay the enormity of the disaster that is 'welfare reform'. The information about the 56% fall is stated factually without any adverbial or adjectival gloss. The 18% rise in employment is described as 'dramatic': 'a dramatic 18 percentage-point increase' (Moore et al, 2012: 93-4). But 18% is only a third of 56%. 'Dramatic' is much more appropriate applied to the fall in the 'welfare' rolls, than to the rise in employment among single mothers. This whole article is an excellent example of the dissociated nature of the 'welfare reform' research.

numbers of poor women who were actually receiving TANF was responsible for this broadening of the research focus to include the whole population (Loprest, 2003, 2011; Loprest and Nichols, 2011). By studying all low-income women, it was possible to reach those who were not locatable through the system. The most recent studies estimated the percentage of low-income mothers who were disconnected at between 17% and 20% (Loprest, 2011). That is, up to 20% of the US population of single mothers with incomes less than 200% of the federal poverty level had neither employment nor 'welfare'. The researchers said that there was evidence to suggest that there had been a substantial increase in the numbers of disconnected single mothers from 1990 through the mid-2000s. Another of these national studies was a 2008 study by the Congressional Research Service which found that 34% of poor single mothers—heading more than 1.3 million families—were neither working nor receiving cash assistance, and that this proportion had increased from 12% in 1991 (Edelman, 2010; Lower-Basch, 2011b).[371]

Bureaucratic disentitlement?

A number of studies have investigated the reasons why the women are disconnected from the mainstream economy. On the face of it, the evidence suggests that bureaucratic disentitlement is the reason for disconnection for only a minority of single mothers (although most studies have found that this minority is a sizeable one). An Urban Institute study involving interviews in 2002 with 95 extremely poor single mothers nationally (Zedlewski and Nelson, 2003: 8) found that only about 40% of the women said that they were not participating in TANF because of 'issues with the program'. The issues mentioned were: 'hassles with paperwork, poor treatment by caseworkers, not wanting to work 40 hours a week for a small welfare check, sanctions, or time limits'. Another study, this time in 2008 in Colorado (Farrell, 2009: 3), found that only around a third of the disconnected 'welfare' leavers reported leaving 'because of some issue they faced with the TANF program'. The issues mentioned in this study were much the same as those in the earlier study: 'Some respondents reported they left to avoid the TANF work requirements; others said they could not stand the hassles associated with getting a TANF check, including the paperwork that needed to be completed; some were

---

371. The study is: Gabe, Thomas (2009) *Trends in Welfare, Work, and the Economic Well-Being of Female-Headed Families with Children: 1987-2008*, Congressional Research Service, December. It was not possible to check this report. Until recently, most Congressional Research Service publications were not easily accessible by the public (Every CRS Report. com).

sanctioned or had a case closure due to non-compliance; and some reached the 60-month time limit'.

However, the way in which the findings are presented obscures the question of whether or not the women's disconnection was the result of bureaucratic disentitlement. Around one-third of the disconnected women had left TANF because they got jobs (and not because they had 'issues' with the program). But given that they were now unemployed, why had they not returned to TANF? The study did not ask the question. Instead, it asked why they weren't working, and some of the reasons given sound very much like bureaucratic disentitlement. These women were refused TANF despite the fact that there were very good reasons why they were not employed, including 'poor health' (26.5%), 'cannot find job' (23.2%), 'cannot find child care' (14.9%), 'pregnant or recently had baby' (8.3%) (Farrell, 2009: 6). But these are exactly the reasons why there is a need for a social safety net. The fact that nearly three-quarters of these women eligible for TANF were not receiving it suggests a system that is not providing a safety net, despite the clearly demonstrated need for it.

An Urban Institute study using data from the 2004 and 2008 SIPP[372] (Loprest and Nichols, 2011; Loprest, 2011) found an even lower proportion of low-income women who gave losing TANF as a reason why they became disconnected, only 11%. The main reason for disconnection was 'lost all earnings'—nearly 60% of the disconnected single mothers gave this as the reason for becoming disconnected. But 'lost all earnings' does not mean that they were not the victims of bureaucratic disentitlement. Again, the way the information as reported fails to ask why these women were not in receipt of TANF, given that they had lost all earnings. If they had no earnings, then they were eligible for TANF, at least on the financial criterion. Why, then, were they not receiving it? What was disqualifying these destitute women from TANF receipt? The report doesn't say because it doesn't ask the question. But clearly, something other than financial eligibility is at issue here.

The research findings do suggest that bureaucratic disentitlement is the reason why so many poor women and children are 'disconnected', however unclear the ways in which those findings are presented statistically. For example, the report of the Urban Institute research with extremely poor families (Zedlewski and Nelson, 2003) noted that:

---

372. The US Census Bureau's Survey of Income and Program Participation, which collects information on income (cash and non-cash) throughout the year, as well as on taxes, assets, liabilities and participation in government transfer programs.

[r]espondents who could not meet work requirements, including many with significant health problems, gave up on the program. Requiring parents to work a set number of hours when they have a health condition that makes such work impossible, or to repeat training courses or job search that have proven ineffective in leading to employment in the past, all to obtain a relatively small cash benefit, leaves struggling parents with little reason to participate in the TANF program (Zedlewski and Nelson, 2003: 37-8).

This account is still too individualistic. It gives these destitute women more agency than is allowed by a system deliberately designed to deprive them of it. The problem is that the requirements are impossible. People are driven away, they do not just 'give up' or decide not to participate because it's all too hard. They are faced with impossible demands with which no one could comply. Still, this account does acknowledge the bureaucratic disentitlement behind disconnection rather than disguising it as an employment issue.

Sources of income

The 'disconnected' women and children are not completely without resources, although the five-year New Jersey study (Moore et al, 2012: 103) found that their average income was less than $500 a month. They do have access to food stamps, charities and food banks, Medicaid, housing assistance (sometimes), child support from the children's fathers (sometimes), support from family members, and undocumented jobs in the informal economy. But these sources of support are not reliable, and neither do they provide a decent standard of living. It should be a national scandal that so many Americans have to rely on food stamps, charities and food banks for food, but it is not. Medicaid is only useful for health care—it doesn't buy the food or pay the rent. Child support is erratic (the children's fathers are poor too), and often the State takes the child support to recompense itself for the 'welfare' benefits paid to the women. Housing assistance when it comes is a boon, but it is not available for the majority of people who need it. And while having a job in the informal economy is usually frowned upon—'Some mothers who have left welfare, of course, may not be reporting their employment' (Besharov and Germanis, 2007: 43)—they are also notoriously exploitative. As commentators have noted, these resources do not add up to an adequate income:

> Although those who receive benefits from Supplemental Nutrition Assistance Program (SNAP; formerly the Food Stamp Program) or other small government benefits are connected in the sense that they receive social insurance income for which they qualify, this study

includes recipients of these programs as disconnected because the benefits of those programs alone are unlikely to meet a family's needs (Moore et al, 2012: 99).

Intermittent

It is true that these spells of disconnection can be intermittent. A study in New Jersey[373] found that one-quarter of the no work/no welfare group of leavers were back on TANF within a year, while another quarter had become employed. That still leaves half of the research sample without either work or 'welfare' at the end of a year. Subsequent stages of a five-year longitudinal study (Moore et al, 2012: 102) found that 44% of the sample had been disconnected at some time during the five years, although only 19% were disconnected at the time of two or more of the yearly surveys, and just 7% were disconnected across three or more surveys. Moreover, these percentages do not represent the same people from year to year. Nonetheless, the fact remains that many former 'welfare' recipients spend some time being disconnected after they leave TANF (Moore et al, 2012: 104), a not surprising finding given that, while 'welfare' might have changed (to the extent that it did), the US economy didn't. It is still an economy that demands a cheap labour market, often not even in the US at all, and maintains a reserve army of labour which ensures that wages at the bottom end remain below a basic living standard.

Conclusion

To conclude, the following example serves to illustrate the plight of the disconnected:

> Single mother with three children living in Georgia. Laid off from her job at a fast-food restaurant in January 2002, the mother says that her diabetes makes her feel ill and that she is often unable to work. She left welfare because she could not meet the work requirements and is uninsured. Her food stamps recently ended because she did not bring in the proper paperwork documenting the absent father's child support … Family has Section 8 housing assistance, which pays the entire rent. The absent father pays $300 per month (one-quarter of the poverty level), which, according to the respondent, is "as much as he can." When asked how the family will eat (considering it did not receive food stamps), the mother said she hoped that her ex-husband would buy the family food. She has a brother and sister who live nearby and provide moral support (Zedlewski and Nelson, 2003: 28).

---

373. Wood and Rangarajan, 2003, cited in Acs and Loprest, 2007.

These women and children are living proof of the unravelling of the social safety net in the US, and of 'the end of welfare'. While the safety net was never very safe, nor much of a net, PRWORA made things 'bitterly worse' (Albelda and Withorn 2001: 9). The women have neither work nor 'welfare' because they are entitled to neither. They are not entitled to 'welfare' because that is written into the legislation; and they are not entitled to employment because employment is not a right for anyone. Like the other PRWORA 'reforms', this disentitlement to any of the conventional forms of earning is not new, although the extent to which it has happened before is unknown. Many of the women refused 'welfare' under earlier bureaucratic disentitlements like the 'employable mother', 'man-in-the-house' and 'suitable home' rules, would have been unable to get jobs, given that that was why they applied for 'welfare' in the first place; and household surveys have always identified families who receive little or no cash income (Zedlewski and Nelson, 2003). But prior to 'welfare reform', single mothers were entitled (at least in theory) to return to welfare whenever their income fell low enough (Turner et al, 2006: 229). Under PRWORA with its sanctions and time limits, this is no longer the case and the disentitlement has become more blatant and entrenched. It would appear that the Supreme Court findings on the unconstitutionality of those earlier rules have had no influence on American legislators. Those who have the power to make a difference take no notice.

Chapter Eighteen: Poverty and 'Welfare Reform'

And yet the US economy, at least as it relates to the living standards of most of the population, is in dire straits. In the richest nation on earth, a *majority* of the population have experienced periods of economic insecurity at some point in their lives by the time they are 60 years of age. A news report in 2013 quoted Associated Press survey data to the effect that the proportion of the US population living a precarious existence had reached nearly 80%. 'Economic insecurity' was defined as a year or more of unemployment, reliance on government aid such as food stamps, and/or income below 150% of the poverty threshold (CBS News, 2013). Moreover, a 2015 study by The National Low Income Housing Coalition, using data from the US Department of Housing and Urban Development, found that there was no State in the country where a full-time worker on the minimum wage of $7.25/hour could afford a one-bedroom apartment at the going market rent (Bolton et al, 2015: 1). This is a not-insignificant number of people. At the time, there were an estimated 10.3 million extremely low income renter households in the US, one in four of all renter households. Three-quarters of these households (7.8 million) spent more than 50% of their income on housing costs, leaving them with little left over to meet other basic needs, including food (pp.5-6).

The 'welfare reform' that disentitled so many people from receiving cash benefits is hardly likely to rectify this situation. The US Office of Family Assistance reported that the proportion of families who were eligible to receive cash assistance on the grounds of their low income declined from 79% in 1996 (at the end of AFDC) to 32% in 2012. In other words, fewer than one-third of poverty-stricken American families are currently receiving cash assistance from TANF (US OFA, 2016b).

But then, ending poverty, or even reducing it slightly, was never a goal of PRWORA. The word 'poverty' does appear in the Act, but usually as a reference to 'the official poverty line'. For example, one reference occurs in a discussion in the first Section of the Act about 'the negative consequences of raising children in single-parent homes', i.e. more of those households are below the poverty line than the households of married couples (SEC. 101(9)(A), p.7). In true right-wing fashion this is purveyed as an intrinsic aspect of 'single-parent homes', instead of as a consequence of a society where men are paid more than women, child-rearing is not valued, and a low-wage economy is nourished to an extent unprecedented in the western world. Reducing poverty is not mentioned as a goal of the legislation, although the States are expected to submit to Congress reports which detail the extent to which they are meeting the objective of decreasing child poverty (among other things) (SEC. 411(b)(1)(B)(ii), p.46, SEC. 413(i), p.52). The fact that child poverty is a function of their mothers' poverty is not mentioned, and neither is the fact that their mothers' poverty is not ameliorated by employment in a low wage economy.

Under the ruthless mandate of the less eligibility principle, 'welfare' is prohibited from abolishing poverty, although the meanness of the US system has no equal in the Western world. No US State provides benefits that allow a minimal standard of basic financial security, or even come close to the miniscule official poverty level.

The poverty threshold, the official figure used to indicate the extent of poverty in the US population, is a fraction of what is needed for 'even just a basic, no-frills standard of living for American working families' (Bernstein et al, 2000: 3). And yet TANF benefits are a small fraction of that amount. As researchers from the Center on Budget and Policy Priorities put it:

> For those who do receive assistance from TANF, the benefits they receive remain quite low and are not enough to provide for basic needs. TANF benefits alone do not lift families out of deep poverty (i.e. 50 percent of the federal poverty line). In all states, TANF maximum benefit levels for a family of three are less—sometimes much less—than *half* of the Federal Poverty Level (Schott and Finch, 2010: 1—original emphasis).

In 2009, the poverty threshold for the annual income of a three-person household (the most numerous type of TANF household) was $17,285.

By way of contrast to the rest of the American population, the median[374] US household income in 2006-2010 was $51,914 (in 2015 dollars).[375] The median maximum benefit across all States in 2009 was $429 (in 2009 dollars). That's $5,148 a year, 28% of the official poverty line for that year and under 10% of the median US household income.[376] The lowest maximum benefit was Mississippi's, at $170 a month (i.e. $2,040 a year). In 2011, Mississippi also had the highest poverty rate in the nation, at 22.4% (the national average was 15.3%, according to the 2010 Census, U.S. Census Bureau),[377] and the highest child poverty rate (at 32%—the national average was 23%).[378] The State with the highest maximum benefit (not counting Alaska) was California ($776 or $9,312 a year). In a number of States even these paltry rates are lower in actual dollar figures (never mind inflation) than they used to be. For example, California's monthly benefit in 2004 had been $808 (US OFA, 2012: Table 12.7). At $673 in 2009, Wisconsin was one of the highest paying States, but that figure has since been reduced to $653. Between 1996 and 2011, the number of States paying maximum TANF benefits that were less than 30% of the federal poverty level increased from 17 to 30 (Zedlewski et al, 2012).

Just as the States vary widely in the amounts they pay in the form of cash assistance, so they also vary in the maximum amounts people can earn and still receive some cash assistance. The five States in the Urban Institute study (Hahn et al, 2012b: 11) set the maximum earnings a family of three could receive as follows: California $1,203; Washington $1,122; Michigan $815; Florida $393; Texas $401. The equivalent poverty level is $1,525 a month. Hence, even in the most generous States, people on what are officially recognised as poverty-level incomes are not eligible for TANF. Moreover,

---

374. The median—the level at which half the households are below and half above—is a more accurate indicator than the average, which is skewed by the inclusion of incomes at the top of the distribution ('the 1%') and hence makes it seem that the US population overall are wealthier than they are.

375. This information is no longer available on the US Census Bureau's 'Quick Facts' website, which is periodically updated. The median *personal* (not household) income in 2009 was $28,870 (in 2015 dollars), down from $30,436 in 2007, before the global financial crisis (https://fred.stlouisfed.org/series/MEPAINUSA672N). The difference between household (and family) and personal income is that households (and families) can contain more than one income-earning individual.

376. I don't know what proportion of the median household income the benefit amount is, since the dollar values are from different years.

377. https://www.census.gov/prod/2011pubs/acsbr10-01.pdf.

378. http://datacenter.kidscount.org/data/acrossstates/Rankings.aspx?ind=43.

since PRWORA became law, most of those who are eligible for 'welfare' are prevented from receiving any benefits, i.e. only 32% of poor people were receiving benefits in 2012.

To make matters worse from the standpoint of poverty alleviation, there has been a policy shift away from spending money on cash assistance and instead directing the money elsewhere. States are now spending more of their 'welfare' funds on 'overcoming barriers to work' than on providing cash assistance, even temporarily. By 2001, over half of the federal TANF money was being spent on non-cash 'services' purportedly designed to assist recipients to get jobs (Schram et al, 2010: 744-5). Since they do nothing of the sort, this spending can only be regarded as a massive waste of resources. But it serves to maintain the ideological fiction that employment is what it's all about.

In some States, TANF money is not even being spent on employment 'assistance', but instead is being diverted into other purposes (Hahn et al, 2012b: 23-9). Texas, for example, uses more than half its TANF funding for child welfare (i.e. services for abused and neglected children); while in Florida, child care is the largest spending category. These are important issues which are always underfunded, and directing TANF funding to them is allowed by PRWORA. But it means that the limited block grant funding is not available for providing the poor with even the most minimal income.

Measuring poverty

While poverty alleviation is not a goal of TANF, the fact remains that TANF receipt is intimately connected with income poverty of the direst sort. Hence it is legitimate to ask whether there have been any changes in poverty rates since the passing of PRWORA and the tightening up of eligibility requirements. This is not an easy question to answer. One reason for the difficulty is the fact that 'welfare', even before PRWORA, did very little to alleviate poverty (under the strictures of the less eligibility principle). The US is widely regarded as 'a welfare state laggard' with 'a threadbare social safety net' (Waddan, 2010: 243). So any changes in poverty rates, whether increases or decreases, are likely to be minimal.

Another reason is that measuring rates of poverty in the population, much less measuring changes in those poverty rates, is difficult and there is no consensus about how to go about it. All poverty lines—the point in the income continuum below which people are counted as 'poor'—are more or less arbitrary, and they exclude people whose income falls just above that line, even though they, too, might be regarded as 'poor' by other criteria (e.g.

lacking the resources to pay for basic necessities such as food, rent, utilities or transport). Income surveys are unreliable, and there is no general agreement about what should be included in 'income', or even that income is the best measure of whether or not someone is poor.[379]

The US poverty measure in particular is renowned for its limitations. The measure in use at the current time was adopted in 1969 and based on survey data from the 1950s. It is called the 'Orshansky index', named after Mollie Orshansky, a government statistician and economist in the Social Security Administration, who defined it in 1963 (Orshansky, 1965; Blank, 2008). The measure, which was adopted as the official federal measure of poverty by the Office of Equal Opportunity in 1969, involves costing a number of basic food items and multiplying by three to estimate a minimum cost-of-living. The original costing was based on the cheapest of four food plans developed by the US Department of Agriculture and claimed to be 'nutritionally adequate'; and Orshansky had decided on a multiplier of three because a 1955 food-consumption survey by the Department had found that households spent about one-third of their income on food.

There is general agreement that these are no longer adequate assumptions on which to base a poverty measure. The food multiplier is particularly out-of-date, both because food is now a much smaller proportion of household budgets than in the 1950s, and because food is only one necessity. By the early 1990s, the cost of food had dropped to less than one-sixth of the average household's budget (Citro and Michael, eds. 1995: 30), and hence it should be multiplied by six to estimate the poverty level, not three. As well, it was known from the beginning that the original food plan was suitable only for emergencies, that it was too sparse to support people for any length of time (Schram, 1995: 82). And while the cost of food has dropped relative to the cost of other necessities, the cost of housing has risen astronomically (Blank, 2008; Chan, 2007). The NAS report recommended that the cost of clothing and shelter also be included in calculations of poverty, plus 'a small amount of other needed spending—the multiplier' (Citro and Michael, eds. 1995: 23).

There have been attempts to change the way in which poverty is measured in the US. The NAS study (Citro and Michael, eds. 1995) was one such attempt, and it remains the reference point for subsequent attempts to update the measure. The Measuring American Poverty Act, introduced in 2009

---

379. ACOSS, 2003, 2004; Australian Senate, 2004; Citro and Michael, 1995; Harding and Szukalska, 2000; Harding et al, 2001; King, 1998; Manning and de Jonge, 1996; Saunders [SPRC], 1994, 1998, 2004.

(Harris, 2010), owed much to the NAS study. (The Bill was not enacted).[380] The Census Bureau has developed a Supplemental Poverty Measure which incorporates many of the NAS report recommendations. Calculations using the new measure gave a slightly higher poverty rate for 2010 than the official rate—16% and 49,094,000 people, rather than 15.2% and 46,602,000 people (Short, 2011: 6, Table 1).

But as long as people above the official poverty line are eligible for food stamps, that is, their incomes are not sufficient to enable them to feed themselves, then official poverty calculations in the US bear little relation to actual levels of deprivation. By the same token, the belief that the official level overstates the extent of poverty in the US because it does not include government provision of in-kind benefits such as food stamps, public housing or Medicaid, is also dissociated from the actual situation. As long as people are eligible for 'welfare' (which is always grudging and mean), they are still poor even if they are a little less poor than they would otherwise have been. One commentator noted that '[t]he cash provisions of AFDC and Food Stamps typically provide a standard of living far below (often only 50 percent) the official poverty threshold, which itself may[381] fall far short of contemporary social standards' (Epstein, 1997: 221-2). As Linda Gordon has said: 'believe me, if the federal government says you are poor, then you are very poor' (Gordon, 2008: 332).

Poverty lines do not capture everyone in the population whose income is insufficient to make ends meet. There are many more people than simply those whose incomes fall on or below the official poverty line, who do not have the resources for a safe and decent standard of living. This is even recognised in some official policies—for example, 200% of the poverty line is the income cut-off for eligibility for Medicaid and for 'services' under the W-2 program in Wisconsin (although not cash assistance) (Wisconsin LAB, 2001: 6), while households are still eligible for food stamps if their income is 175% of the federal poverty level (Ratcliffe et al, 2007: 6). These people would not be counted as among the poor in the Census Bureau surveys, and yet their income is not enough to buy food every day. As Schram (1995: 82) has pointed out, the official poverty line has come to be 'a reified entity disengaged from the realities of buying the necessities needed to achieve the generally accepted adequate standard of living'.

---

380. https://www.govtrack.us/congress/bills/111/s1625

381. The euphemising is relentless. The official poverty threshold *does* unequivocally 'fall far short of contemporary social standards'. There is no 'may' about it.

One attempt to establish an income line which would capture the disadvantage in a population to a more realistic extent, involves developing basic family budgets for an adequate standard of living for families of different sizes.[382] A review of such budgets in the US in the late 1990s (Bernstein et al, 2000) found that, for a three-person family, estimates varied between $20,000 and $40,000 in 1996 dollars (depending on where the family lived). The official poverty line at the time was $12,636, much less than this estimated budget.

Another study using budget methodology (Schwartz and Volgy, 1992, cited in Schram, 1995: 82-4) estimated that a four-person family in 1990 would need $20,658 to reach a 'threshold of self-sufficiency'. At the time the official poverty line was $13,360 for a household of four people. On the basis of their self-sufficiency standard, Schwartz and Volgy estimated that around 56 million Americans, or 22.8% of the population, were living below that standard in 1989. Moreover, using Orshansky's original methodology, but with the food budget multiplied by five (rather than the original three), gave a higher dollar figure than the authors' self-sufficiency standard—$22,300. On that criterion, there were 63 million people, or 26% of the population, whose incomes did not reach a basic standard of living in 1989. On the lower, self-sufficiency criterion, Schwartz and Volgy estimated the numbers of full-time, full-year workers below 'the lowest healthful level of the prevailing standard of living' at seven million people, rather than the official estimate of two million. But although the living standards estimated by developing family budgets are more realistic than official poverty lines, the less eligibility principle debars them from having any influence on 'welfare' policy.

While the official poverty rate understates the extent of deprivation in the US, it should be able to tell us whether or not what it does measure has changed because it is a consistent measure from year to year. According to the US Census Bureau, the official poverty rate rose for four consecutive years up to 2010, but there was no change between 2010 and 2011. And on this criterion it would seem that the financial situation of single mothers is no worse than it was when PRWORA was passed, but neither is it any better. In 1996, the poverty rate among single-mother families was 41.9%, and in 2011 it was 40.9%. The rate had dropped to 33% in 2000[383] (a fall which is attributed, at least in part, to the booming economy of the 1990s and the advent of more jobs) (e.g. Turner et al, 2006: 228). But incomes

---

382. For an Australian example, see: Saunders et al, 1998.

383. The US Census Bureau webpages from which these figures were taken no longer exist.

above the official poverty line in a low-wage economy do not mean the end of deprivation, and anyway the improvement didn't last. This should be evidence that poverty and unemployment are caused by the economy, not by the people who are poor and unemployed. But it is evidence that has no influence on the individualistic mindset that structures 'welfare' to coerce individuals into jobs without structuring the economy to provide those jobs.

Beyond the official poverty measure, there are indications that poverty has increased in recent years, although there is no way of knowing whether the 'welfare reform' legislation contributed to that increase. One of the Urban Institute researchers (Edelman, 2010: 3) believed that it had. He said in an address to House Ways and Means Committee that there had been 'a striking increase in extreme poverty' over the preceding decade. The numbers of those whose incomes were less than half the poverty line had increased from 12.6 million people in 2000 to 17.1 million in 2008, and he suggested that '[t]he shrinking of welfare must surely be a key factor in these disturbing trends about extreme poverty'. Another indication is the increase in the proportion of women and children who make up the homeless population, from 9% in 1987 to 34% in 1997 to 40% in 2001 (Roschelle, 2008: 194).

Moreover, it is known that most of the poor whose income makes them eligible do not receive any support from TANF (Hahn et al, 2012a: 4), and that America is supporting far fewer of its poor than before 'welfare reform'. Quoting the US Department of Health and Human Services' 2007 *Report to Congress* on 'indicators of welfare dependence', Moffitt (2008: 25) said that

> [p]articipation rates among financial eligibles dropped from around 80 percent in the early 1990s to 69 percent in 1997, and further dropped to 42 percent by 2004.

In other words, by 2004 the US nation was providing cash assistance to only 42% of the poorest of its poor citizens (down to 32% in 2012). Other researchers have put the proportion of the poor currently being assisted by 'welfare' even lower. Reporting to Health and Human Services, researchers from the Urban Institute said that,

> [i]n 2005, there were 7.6 million families living below the poverty line and millions more living just above it. The average number of families receiving TANF in any given month, however, is about 2 million (Acs and Loprest, 2007: xvi).

That's only slightly more than a quarter of those living below the poverty line who receive TANF in any month. That figure is an average across the nation. In 2008, percentages of the eligible poor who received 'welfare' differed widely from state to state, from 73% in California to 4% in Wyoming (Zedlewski and Golden, 2010: 3).

It is also known that poverty is widespread among those who have left 'welfare' for employment. To quote some of the research findings:

> Only 4-10 percent of jobs last eight quarters [i.e. 2 years] or more … [and] by any standard welfare recipients' jobs are poor ones. Over the life of the job—up to two years for our data—average cumulative earnings are only between $2,000 (for Atlanta) and $5,000 (for Chicago) … This figure is the sum of earnings for as long as the job lasts, up to eight quarters … in 1999 fourth-quarter dollars (King and Mueser, 2005: 2)

> Most welfare leavers earn between $5.67 to $8.42 per hour, with an annual average income between $8,000 and $16,000 (Handler, 2008: 20);

> almost 50% of TANF leavers [in the study] were not working and 70% of them were still living in poverty with a median annual family income of $10,000, 12 months after leaving welfare (Kim, 2010: 210)

A number of studies have found that incomes do not improve very much, if at all, when women leave TANF.[384] While 'welfare' leavers who are employed do have higher incomes than they did while in receipt of TANF, the increases are often cancelled out by the loss of benefits (Frogner et al, 2007). One study in Wisconsin (Cancian et al, 2002) found poverty levels of between 63% and 72% among 'welfare' leavers, based on their own incomes (i.e. not including the incomes of other members of the same household). On the whole, going off welfare does not result in enough work that is sufficiently highly paid to compensate for the loss of benefits—a telling indictment of the US low-wage economy.

A journalist summed up the current US economic situation—post-PRWORA and after the global financial crisis—using language more suited to its subject matter than the circumlocutions of academic research:

> although the economy has sputtered back to life in recent months, 8.3 percent of the workforce remains unemployed, and millions more have opted out of the job market altogether over the past few years. [In other words, although they have no paid employment, they are not counted in the unemployment figures.] Perhaps an even starker measure of America's poverty problem can be found in "food insecurity" data: after decades of success fighting hunger, the country is sliding back; ever more families cannot feed themselves. Forty-six million Americans subsist on food stamps, an increase of more than 14 million over the past four years, at an annual cost to the government of about $65

---

384. Burnham, 2001; Harkabus, 2010; Kilty, 2006; Shipler, 2005.

billion. The Food Research and Action Center estimates that another several million are eligible, making do without government assistance … only 40 percent of food stamp-eligible residents of San Diego are using the program. In Denver the figure is 46 percent; in Los Angeles, 56 percent … about 47 million Americans … are living at or below the poverty line. (That figure is up from 37 million before the recent housing crisis.) Of these, more than 20 million are living in what's called "deep poverty," with incomes that put them and their families at below 50 percent of the poverty line. More than 16 million children in the United States, 22 percent of the country's kids, live in poverty, the highest total since 1962 and the highest percentage since Bill Clinton took office in 1993. Even these sorry numbers, however, don't tell the full story. Additional millions of men, women and children in America are living below what economists like Dean Baker, co-director of the Washington-based Center for Economic and Policy Research, term a "living wage" threshold. Too affluent to qualify for most government assistance programs but too poor to make ends meet, they are working at jobs that provide few or no benefits and are thus perpetually at risk of falling into devastating debt (Abramsky, 2012).

Food stamps

The food stamp program (or SNAP as it is now called)[385] subsidises America's low-wage economy that pays starvation wages, and at least ensures that the problem of hunger in America is not worse. SNAP is now the core 'welfare' program in the US. It is still funded by the federal government, and more people are allowed to be eligible for food stamps than for cash assistance. As researchers from the Urban Institute said in their usual objective, just-reporting-the-facts fashion:

> Food stamps are an important component of low-income families' monthly resources, increasing the chance families are able to meet basic needs. Food stamps have been found to increase by 36 percent the purchasing power of a family of four supported by a full-time, year-round minimum wage worker … working families … are larger shares of [food stamp program] eligibles and of FSP participants now than in the early 1990s (Ratcliffe et al, 2007: 1).

Once again, the Urban Institute researchers fail to draw out the moral and political implications of the fact that 'a family of four supported by a full-time, year-round minimum wage worker' need food stamps to survive. Their

---

385. The 2008 Food, Conservation and Energy Act (the 'Farm Bill') changed the name of the food stamp program to the Supplemental Nutrition Assistance Program or SNAP as of 1 October 2008 (http://www.fns.usda.gov/sites/default/files/arra/070308.pdf).

research interest, like the research interest of all social policy researchers, is statistical. The following statement is typical:

> The food stamp participation model is based on a utility maximization framework where a household (1) participates in the FSP if the net benefit of participation—the benefit minus the cost—is greater than zero and (2) does not participate in the FSP if the net benefit of participation is less than or equal to zero. We estimate linear regression models for FSP participation (Y) for household i in state s at time t: $Y_{ist} = \alpha + \delta_1 \ 'FSP_{st} + \delta_2 \ 'WP_{st} + \beta_1 \ 'X_{ist} + \beta_2 \ 'S_{st} + \mu_s + \tau_t + \eta_t + v_{ist}$ (Ratcliffe et al, 2007: 13).

This is meaningless in the context of a focus on poverty as an injustice. Worse, it is a diversion from the real issue—the condemnation of an economy that waxes fat on starvation wages. That full-time workers need food stamps to feed their families is a national scandal. That is the real issue, not the cleverness of the statistical equations. But that cannot be said in any official context, so the statistics get cleverer and cleverer while the people get poorer and poorer.

The food stamp program was initially established in 1939 as a way of dealing with what the US Department of Agriculture presents as two social problems, but which is actually a single problem presented from two perspectives.[386] On the one hand there were food surpluses that were unmarketable, and on the other hand there was the reason why the food could not be sold, i.e. mass poverty caused by widespread unemployment. The original program operated through a system of orange and blue stamps. People on unemployment relief could buy the orange stamps with what they would normally use to spend on food, and for every dollar's worth of orange stamps someone bought, they received 50 cents' worth of blue stamps. The orange stamps could be used for any food purchases, but the blue stamps could only be used for food that the US Department of Agriculture had deemed to be surplus. This first phase of the program ended in 1943 because 'the conditions that brought the program into being … no longer existed'.

There was much debate in the 1950s about re-introducing food stamps, and in 1961 the Kennedy administration initiated food stamp pilot programs. These pilots eliminated the blue-stamp aspect of the program which required people to buy surplus food, but it kept the requirement that people buy their food stamps with the money they would normally spend on food, with the program providing extra stamps up to the value of 'a low-cost nutritionally

---

386. The information below comes from the USDA website (http://www.fns.usda.gov/snap/rules/Legislation/about.htm).

adequate diet'. These pilots were made permanent through the 1964 Food Stamp Act, the stated aims of which were: 'strengthening the agricultural economy and providing improved levels of nutrition among low-income households'. This Act prohibited the use of food stamps to buy alcohol or imported food. During the 1970s, variations to the program included limiting the amount of the stamps households could buy to 30% of their income, establishing temporary eligibility standards for disasters, and adding food-producing seeds and plants to the categories of eligible purchases.

The Food Stamp Act of 1977 eliminated the requirement that people buy their food stamps on the grounds that this was a barrier to participation in the program. As indeed it was. This change was implemented on 1 January 1979, and participation that month was 1.5 million more than the month before. During the early 1980s there were a number of cutbacks to the program, including allowing the States the option of requiring both applicants and recipients to engage in 'job search' as a condition of food-stamp receipt. Restrictions were slightly eased in the mid- to late-80s in recognition of the fact that the nation had a severe domestic hunger problem—the sales tax on food-stamp purchases was abolished, categorical eligibility was reinstituted (it had been abolished by the 1977 Act), the assets limit was increased, and the homeless were made automatically eligible.

PRWORA made a number of changes to the food stamp program. Not surprisingly, these erred on the side of callousness, including eliminating the entitlement of most legal immigrants, and putting a time limit for single people, of three months in every three years unless they were 'working at least 20 hours a week or participating in a work program'. The program was reauthorised by the Food Security and Rural Investment Act of 2002, which restored food-stamp eligibility for legal immigrants as long as they had been in the country for five years, qualified for disability payments, or were children.

In 2011, the numbers of recipients were the highest ever at a monthly participation rate of 46 million, with more than one in seven Americans receiving SNAP benefits (Simon, 2012: 4). By June 2012, initial estimates had put the numbers even higher, at 46,670,373, an increase of 0.4% since the previous month, and of 3.3% since June the previous year. In 2013, there were around 47.8 million people on food stamps (Goodman, 2013), although by July 2016, that figure had dropped to 45,507,071.

This drop in the numbers participating in the food stamp program was not the result of a drop in the amount of need. On the contrary, the need continues to rise while the right-wing US Congress does its best to deny entitlement.

The Agriculture Reform, Food and Jobs Act of 2012, for example, proposed to cut the food stamp program by around $20.5 billion, despite the fact that food stamp usage had increased by 70% between 2008 and 2013. Although the bill had not become law by May 2013, every Republican on the House Agriculture Committee had approved it. It was estimated that around two million people would lose entitlement to the program, including anyone who had ever been convicted of a crime.[387] A more recent example concerns the toughening-up of the three-month time limit on receipt of food stamps by childless people. The time-limit hadn't been in effect in most States since the global financial crisis (the 'Great Recession') because of high levels of unemployment. But because (official) unemployment rates were falling by 2016, fewer States and local areas were able to qualify for the waivers that allowed them to ignore the time limits. As a result, it was estimated that between 500,000 and 1 million people would lose entitlement to SNAP when the time limits in the original legislation were re-applied (Bolen et al, 2016).

Not surprisingly, the Republicans in Congress are constantly putting forward proposals to cut spending on food stamp programs (along with 'welfare' spending in general). For example, House Speaker, Paul Ryan, was reported in May 2016 to be still trying to cut more than $23 billion from SNAP, as a way of 'uniting the fractious Republican Party' (Akin, 2016). This was not his first attempt. When he was chairman of the House budget committee in 2014, he proposed a plan to cut $1 trillion from the program over 10 years. He was not a lone individual in proposing such spending cuts. In April 2016, the Republican Study Committee proposed a number of restrictions on food-stamp eligibility, some of them similar to those for TANF, i.e. block-grant funding and time limits (RSC, no date; Akin, 2016).

But attempts to cut food stamp eligibility have so far failed, not because Republicans have any concern for the poor, but because the program is a boon to the food industry. This is not surprising, given that food stamps originated as a method of selling off food surpluses, and given that they enable people to buy food they would not otherwise have been able to buy. Their benefit for the food industry was made clear in one of the arguments against Pennsylvania's proposal to apply an assets test to food stamp receipt (Lubrano, 2012), i.e. the amount of assets someone could have and still be eligible for food stamps. Applying stringent assets tests—$2,000 for a single person and $3,250 for a couple (these policies are never generous)—would mean that fewer people would be eligible for food stamps and hence that

387. http://www.care2.com/causes/the-new-farm-bill-shows-whats-wrong-with-u-s-food.html.

the sellers of food would have fewer customers. So the plan was 'widely condemned' by 'business leaders statewide', as well as by 'Philadelphia city officials … and advocates for the poor'. A businessman was quoted saying that the plan was '"mean-spirited" and "bad business strategy"':

> Jeff Brown, chief executive of Brown's Super Stores, which includes 10 ShopRites in and around Philadelphia … said 40 percent of his business depended on food stamps. Jobs in trucking, grocery stores, warehouses, and other areas will be hurt by the SNAP asset test, Brown added … Every dollar of food stamps generates $1.70 in economic activity locally, [a state official] said (Lubrano, 2012).[388]

Large corporations are well aware of the contribution the food stamp program makes to their profits. A food industry watchdog consulting group, Eat Drink Politics (Simon, 2012), found that three powerful industries had a major stake in the program: food manufacturers (using the word 'food' lightly) such as Coca-Cola, Kraft and Mars; supermarket chains such as Walmart; and large banks which contract with states to administer the Electronic Benefits Transfer system.[389] The so-called 'food' industries are resisting government attempts to prohibit the purchase of sugary drinks and snacks in order to limit SNAP to healthy food. So far the industries' lobbying efforts to prevent this happening have been successful, despite the supposed national concern with diet-related conditions such as obesity and type-2 diabetes, especially among the poor. The soda pop and candy lobbyists, not surprisingly, assert that their efforts are 'preserving food choice', although the choice they are attempting to preserve doesn't involve food, but rather edible substances that not only have no nutritional value but are actively harmful.

Its contribution to the economy is one reason why the food stamp program is so popular with the ruling elite as a method of 'welfare'. It is yet another way to channel public money into private hands. Republican resistance is not directed towards the program as such, but rather towards its 'expense'.

Another reason for its popularity is its role in humiliating people. As one feminist pointed out, food stamps immediately identify someone as 'poor':

---

388. The objections did not stop the assets test being introduced, although the amounts were raised to $5,500 for people under 60, and $9,000 for people 60 and over. The webpage containing this information no longer exists, probably because the State subsequently eliminated the assets test.

389. This allows a recipient to transfer their government benefits to a retailer electronically. Recipients apply for their benefits by filling out a form at their local food stamp office, and an account is established in the recipient's name into which food-stamp benefits are deposited electronically each month. Recipients receive a plastic card similar to a bank card, and a PIN.

Food stamps, used by many poor women for shopping, label her as poor and powerless in the marketplace. While the school free-lunch program forbids labeling of its recipients, the child's mother is labeled when buying her dinner at the supermarket (Glassman, 1970: 115-16).

The Australian equivalent of food stamps is the 'BasicsCard'.[390] The official rationale for this policy is that they are a way of quarantining 'welfare' payments so they cannot be used for such unacceptable commodities as alcohol, tobacco, pornography or gambling. They were originally introduced into the Australian 'welfare' system in the Northern Territory in 2007 as part of the federal government's intervention into the lives of Aboriginal people (and rolled out to other areas in Australia in 2012). Called the Northern Territory Emergency Response, the original intervention was officially justified by the need 'to protect Aboriginal children', supposedly in response to the findings of the *Little Children Are Sacred* report. However, the words 'child' or 'children' do not appear in the NT Emergency Response Act, but its many references to 'land' and 'area' indicate its true purpose, that is, as a land grab paving the way for mining companies to access Aboriginal land.

The Aboriginal people subjected to this form of surveillance were not consulted. The government continues to ignore the many protests pointing out that the cards restrict people's spending power far beyond the unhealthy commodities supposedly justifying their introduction. They can only be used at certain retailers—they can't be used at farmers' markets, for example—and they have none of the flexibility of cash. The government also ignores the findings of independent studies (e.g. Gray, 2015; Scott and Heiss, eds, 2015) showing that, at the very least, there is no clear evidence of the value of the program, and at worst that it has been a disaster for Aboriginal people. But the architects of programs like food stamps and the BasicsCard are not concerned about people's well-being. If they were, they would not impose such degrading conditions on people. Apart from the pandering to the food lobby, the overriding motivation is punishment, not for anything people have actually done, but for being living reminders of the dehumanising effects of the system that rewards the dominators so handsomely (at least in economic terms, and leaving aside any questions about the corrupting influence on the dominators' own humanity).

---

390. What follows is taken from Korff, 2016.

Chapter Nineteen: Research or 'Data Be Damned'[391]

Policy-makers take little notice of the findings of the huge volume of research evaluating the various 'welfare' policies installed over the years. Or rather, they take little notice when the findings do not confirm their own prejudices; and despite the fact that research is supposed to uncover non-prejudicial facts about the world, a significant amount of it does confirm what the powerful architects of 'welfare' want to know, at least on the surface. There is an unwillingness to know on the part of the powers-that-be, who simply ignore research results that contradict their own ideological presuppositions. But not only do 'welfare reformers' cherry-pick what they want to hear and ignore the rest, what they want to hear is too often built into the research process. The research itself is designed in such a way that only certain questions can be asked and only certain interpretations of the findings are allowed.

It is not a secret that 'welfare' programs are not based on empirical evidence uncovered by research, but on ideological assumptions impervious to the evidence. William M. Epstein (1997) attributed this to the inability of social science 'to create rational data' because of its methodical limitations, as a consequence of which it was prone to being 'influenced by political interests'. 'Indeed', he continued,

> the possible dominance of power over truth, to use ... [one] formulation for the tension between social preference and objective fact, has been the second major threat to the authority of the social scientist [the first being the inability to create rational data] (Epstein, 1997: 32).

It is the 'dominance of power over truth' that prevails in 'welfare reform'. This is not, however, simply a matter of 'social preference' prevailing over 'objective fact'. There can be general agreement about the facts, for example, that the billions of dollars spent on the 'welfare' system in the US has not

---

391. Stoesz, 1997: 69.

abolished poverty. But how that is interpreted and what policies follow from that fact, will vary according to which belief system is in operation. For the right wing, with their belief that 'there is no society',[392] it will be a fact about individuals and their 'dependency', self-inflicted because there is nowhere else it could have come from. From a genuinely human standpoint that acknowledges and resists domination, it will be a fact about an exploitative economy and a polity that operates in the interests of the rich and powerful. No amount of data creation, rational or otherwise, can adjudicate between those two positions. As Schram and Soss put it:

> Evaluations of public policy inevitably require political choices regarding which facts will be valued as indicators of success and which interpretations of facts will serve as a basis for judgment ... Welfare reform is now widely viewed as a success not because of the facts uncovered by researchers (which paint a murky picture) but because of a political climate that privileges some facts and interpretations over others (Schram and Soss, 2001: 50).

That political climate shows itself in the kind of research social policies are supposedly based on. A social policy advisor to the Republicans on the Ways and Means Committee in the US House of Representatives during the debate leading up to the passage of the 1988 Family Support Act, for example, believed that 'social science research ... played a significant role in bringing welfare reform to the top of the public agenda' (Haskins, 1991: 618). He specifically mentioned: Charles Murray's 1984 book, *Losing Ground*; a number of studies showing that more than 65% of families on 'welfare' would stay on it for eight years or more; and the work of the Manpower Demonstration Research Corporation (MDRC). The first two bodies of research—that which formed the basis for Murray's argument in his book, and the 65% finding—supposedly demonstrated the phenomenon of 'dependency' on the part of 'welfare' recipients, while the third supposedly showed what could be done about it.

The conclusion Murray drew from the research he cited—data on employment, crime, education and 'welfare'—was that government 'welfare' programs should be abandoned because their history showed that, far from lessening poverty, they had only increased it (Haskins, 1991: 618). But this conclusion arises, not out of the data itself, but out of Murray's right-wing focus on individuals and its deliberate ignoring of the ways in which people are systematically deprived of the necessary resources. Murray also

---

392. As Margaret Thatcher said in an interview with Woman's Own in 1987 (http://www.margaretthatcher.org/speeches/displaydocument.asp?docid=106689).

conveniently ignored the fact that 'welfare' is not meant to abolish poverty but to maintain it. It is meant to keep people desperate and penurious so that they have no alternative but to work in the low-wage economy that enables wealth to be accumulated in the hands of the few. By blaming the poor for their poverty and 'dependency', Murray showed himself to be one of the leading apologists for wealth accumulation. His thesis was avidly embraced by the wealthy 'welfare reformers' of the time (and by PRWORA's framers) because it emanated from the same ideological belief system, not because of the facts the research uncovered.

Much the same objection can be raised against the conclusion drawn from the 65% finding. Once again, the focus is on the individuals harmed by the system—the problem is their 'dependency'. There was no discussion of the economy in the research cited. But if there is such a significant proportion of people who remain on 'welfare' for years, it means that the economy cannot provide for the nation's citizens. No capitalist economy has ever provided for all its citizens, of course, but that fact is elided by arguments that locate the source of the problems with the victims, rather than with the exploitative system. It was not the research findings that generated the form taken by the 1988 Family Support Act, but rather the way they were interpreted by a US Congress beholden to the vested interests of the rich and powerful.

MDRC

The Manpower Demonstration Research Corporation (which refers to itself by the initials MDRC) is one of the most influential sources of the so-called research upon which 'welfare' policies are based. It describes itself as:

> a nonprofit, nonpartisan education and social policy research organization dedicated to learning what works to improve programs and policies that affect the poor … Once known primarily for evaluations of state welfare-to-work programs, today MDRC is also studying public school reforms, employment programs for ex-prisoners and people with disabilities, and programs to help low-income people succeed in college … Working in fields where emotion and ideology often dominate public debates, MDRC is seen as a source of objective, unbiased evidence.[393]

Its evidence supposedly demonstrating the effectiveness of welfare-to-work programs is regarded as 'scientifically respectable' (Peck, 1998a: 542), and it was not only cited as the research underpinning the JOBS program under

---

393. http://www.mdrc.org/about/about-mdrc-history.

the 1988 Family Support Act, it also played a part in what eventually became TANF.

Established in 1974 by the Ford Foundation in conjunction with a number of US government agencies, its purpose was to monitor the workfare-style programs that were being developed around the country during the 1970s and 1980s (Peck, 2001). In 1982, MDRC began an evaluation of eight OBRA Demonstration projects (Baum, 1991), and by the early 1990s, it seemed as though it had amassed considerable evidence about the performance of state welfare-to-work programs. According to Haskins, its research on State 'employment' programs was 'strikingly consistent' (Haskins, 1991: 620). It supposedly showed that a combination of 'job search' and 'work experience' led to increased income and employment and shorter spells on 'welfare', as well as to tax and 'welfare' savings. Its methodology was impeccable, viewed from the standpoint of mainstream social science: 'large sample sizes, multisite implementation, long follow-up period (three years), multiple measures of outcome, and randomization procedures' (Epstein, 1997: 168).

Its GAIN research (Greater Avenues for Independence), for example, involved three years of follow-up data for 33,000 people who were randomly assigned either to an experimental group (those in the GAIN program) or to a control group (those who were not in the program) (Riccio et al, 1994: xxi). The assumption was that any differences between the groups who participated in GAIN ('the experimentals'), and those who did not, were the result of the GAIN procedures. Its evaluation of the Californian GAIN program was one of the best known of MDRC's research studies (Riccio et al, 1994). Sites in six of California's 58 counties were extensively researched by the MDRC. It was widely hailed as a success (just as PRWORA was later), especially the program at the site in Riverside county, which became the '"most touted welfare-to-work program in the nation"' (quoted from U.S. *News and World Report*, 16 January 1995, in Peck, 1998a: 532).

The impression of success was at least partly conveyed by the way in which the results were reported. MDRC managed the influence it had on 'welfare' policy and programs through strategies of publication, publicity, and rhetoric. As one researcher put it: '[MDRC's] format of interpretation and publicity was simplified and oriented to vernacular persuasion. And the researchers adroitly publicized it before their analytical operations could be inspected and criticized by peers' (Oliker, 1994: 208). They went to great lengths to present their findings to the press and policy-makers in a variety of ways, 'in a flood of technical reports, pamphlets, press releases, summaries of findings, seminars, and briefings' (Szanton, 1991: 598), the chief message of which was that the Demonstration projects were on the right track.

There was a heavy emphasis on statistical significance as evidence for success. As Oliker (1994: 206) has noted, 'The summary presentation and the … emphasis on statistically significant rather than substantial results made a sanguine reading of the [research] very easy'. It did consistently find statistically significant differences in income and workforce participation between the experimental groups and the control groups. However despite the statistical significance, the differences were so small as to be insignificant in human terms; and the fact that workforce participation rates were not impressive, and there was very little (if any) impact on poverty, was downplayed in the way the research was written up.

The Preface to the eighth MDRC report on the GAIN program (Riccio et al, 1994), written by MDRC President Judith Gueron, was typical: 'GAIN can change the basic character of welfare to make it much more work-focused, and in doing so get people jobs, reduce welfare costs, and save taxpayers money', she said. The evidence for this was reported as follows: 'While, overall, GAIN increased single parents' three-year earnings by 22 percent and cut welfare payments by 6 percent, impacts were particularly large in one county [Riverside], where earnings went up 49 percent and welfare costs fell 15 percent' (Riccio et al, 1994: v-vi).

But this way of stating the facts is misleading. It reads as though GAIN participants' earnings increased by 22% over three years. But that '22 percent' is not the amount by which earnings increased, it's the difference between the average amount earned by the experimental groups and the average amount earned by the control groups, that is, those who participated in the GAIN program earned an average of 22% more over three years than those who did not participate. Moreover, Gueron did not mention the amount of money represented by that 22%—$1,414 over three years or $39 a month (Riccio et al, 1994: xxi, xxvii, 105, 125). That is what the GAIN groups earned on average over what the non-GAIN groups earned. The 49% difference in Riverside was $3,113 (or $86 a month over the three years) (Riccio et al, 1994: xxii, xxx, 118, 125). This is hardly the kind of evidence that proves that GAIN 'increased single parents' three-year earnings'. Technically it's correct, and 22% sounds like a big difference between the two groups. But the actual amounts of money tell a different story. They are so low it's hardly worth the bother of engaging with the program (not that the 'welfare' recipients had any choice—participation was compulsory).

Getting people jobs was also reported as statistical significance: 'GAIN increased the proportion of experimentals who were ever employed in year 3 by 6 percentage points above the control group rate. At the same time, a majority of experimentals as well as controls did not work at all during that year … For the six counties combined, automated official records show that 40 percent of experimentals had worked at some time during year 3 compared to 34 percent of controls, resulting in a statistically significant difference of 6 percentage points'. This was reported as evidence 'that GAIN can produce earnings gains, welfare savings, or both within a three-year period' (Riccio et al, 1994: xxx-xxxi).

However, it is evidence of no such thing if a majority of people in the experimental program did not work at all during the third year. This becomes even clearer if the same evidence is read in a different, less obfuscating, way: 60% of GAIN participants had no paid employment at all in year 3 (and 66% of non-GAIN 'welfare' recipients), while the other 40% had paid employment only 'at some time' during the year. In other words, by the third year of the experiment, no one, neither the GAIN participants nor the non-GAIN participants, had full-time work, much less work that paid a living wage. The employment record for the whole three-year period is reported in the same obscurantist way: 'A similar impact is found when the proportions of experimentals and controls ever employed over the entire three-year period are compared (57 percent versus 51 percent, respectively)'. The 'similar impact' refers to the fact that there is once again a 6% difference between the GAIN groups and the control groups. A little later it is acknowledged that 'almost half [of both groups] never worked during the entire three-year period'.

The reporting of GAIN's supposed effect on poverty levels was similarly upbeat: 'The analysis suggests that GAIN helped move some families out of poverty: 20 percent of the experimentals across the six counties, compared to 17 percent of the controls, had a combined income above the poverty line [in year 3]' (p.xxxiii). But the criterion for what counted as 'poverty' was the federal poverty line—'(In 1992, the poverty line for a single parent with one child was $9,190)'—a grossly inadequate measure of the income needed to buy even the basic necessities. People do not 'move out of poverty' when their incomes increase above the official poverty threshold. Even incomes double the poverty line are insufficient to provide for a decent standard of living in a rich developed nation like the US. Moreover, the researchers included food stamps as 'income' (as well as 'welfare' payments and earnings from paid work). If people need food stamps to feed themselves and their families, they can hardly be said to have moved out of poverty.

Not only was the research reported as a success story, with the touting of miniscule differences as major changes bolstered by tests of statistical significance, the research was constructed so that nothing of substance would be found. One example of this was defining 'poverty' in terms of the official poverty threshold, combined with assertions that incomes above the poverty line were 'moving families out of poverty'. Substantive issues such as the purchasing power of the income levels reported, the kinds of jobs people got, who was sanctioned (i.e. had their 'welfare' reduced or stopped altogether) and why, and the effect this had on people's lives, were downplayed or ignored altogether. Also excluded were such important considerations as the women's mental health, the time single mothers on workfare could spend with their children, the nature of their arrangements for child care and for the supervision of school-age children, whether or not the mothers could meet their obligations to care for their children and other relatives, and whether the women were sanctioned for giving priority to family responsibilities (Oliker, 1994: 202). The notion that enforced work requirements could undermine single mothers' family obligations and harm their children, which was central to 'welfare' policy in earlier years (at least rhetorically), was nowhere to be found.

The MDRC evaluation of GAIN (Riccio et al, 1994) did survey a sample of the participants in both the experimental and control groups. The primary focus of the survey was the difference between the GAIN and control groups on employment-related information (full-time or part-time, more or less than $200 a week, health benefits). The survey did ask questions about the effect of GAIN on respondents' quality of life, and found 'scant evidence of any effect on … aspects of these recipients' lives' (p.177). The only evidence that counted was, again, the narrow one of statistical differences between the GAIN groups and the control groups. Since both groups were 'welfare' recipients, it is not surprising that there were no systematic differences on such criteria as enough food, adequate housing and access to health care. However, the fact that GAIN made no difference to participants' quality of life is a scathing indictment of the program. That MDRC found it unremarkable—it was reported but not allowed to interfere with the overall message of success—is a prime example of the ways in which 'social science fails the poor' (Epstein, 1997).

And despite its reputation for methodological rigour, MDRC research excluded from its experiments those who were the hardest to place, i.e. long-term 'welfare' recipients and mothers with children under six years of age. Excluding long-term recipients meant ignoring those who were of most concern according to the political rhetoric of 'dependency', while excluding mothers with children under six discounted about two-thirds of the caseload. Both of these categories of recipients needed more intensive (and more expensive) services, and both were even less employable than the recipients who were included in the research. Their inclusion in the research would have further depressed the weak positive results, or even abolished them altogether.[394]

The report's final comment on the program was: 'GAIN, even operating at its best, was only moderately successful in moving people off welfare and out of poverty by the end of three years' (Riccio et al, 1994: lv). But if most of the participants were without employment by the third year, if few (or none) had liveable incomes, if it made no difference to people whose material circumstances were so dire, and if the research had excluded the most difficult-to-place segment of the 'welfare' caseload, then GAIN was not 'moderately successful' at all. It was, in fact, a rank failure.

And yet despite the weak results, these findings were trumpeted as proof positive of the success of workfare. It is true that MDRC were often careful in their interpretations and circumspect in their conclusions (Oliker, 1994). For example, Gueron said in her testimony before the Senate Committee on Labor and Human Resources that

> "Riverside's GAIN program has not eliminated welfare or transformed the earnings potential of welfare recipients. More people got jobs than would have gotten them without the program, and got them sooner, but they were usually not 'better' jobs and families were rarely boosted out of poverty" (quoted in Peck, 2001: 192).

Much of the responsibility for presenting the results of MDRC's research as a success story lies with the interpreters and popularisers of the reports— the media and the politicians—rather than with the researchers. However, MDRC must bear some of the responsibility for the ways in which the findings were interpreted, even though the researchers were careful to point out that there were limitations to the conclusions that could be drawn. Gueron (1996: 553), for example, acknowledged that workfare had a 'downside': it was difficult to find enough workplaces that would take 'welfare' recipients; some people were simply unable to work; it didn't develop people's skills or help them move into paid employment; it didn't discourage them from

---

394. Peck, 2001: 123n10, citing Block and Noakes, 1988.

applying for welfare (i.e. reduce the 'welfare' rolls); and it was more expensive for the government than simply handing over 'welfare' cheques. But she didn't present those negative consequences as a reason for dispensing with workfare. On the contrary, she listed some positive consequences as well—'it proved feasible to get people to work for their grants; participants viewed their work assignments as fair; and real work was done'—and concluded only that workfare had 'a mixed record' and that the effectiveness of any large-scale implementation of workfare 'remains unknown'. Such equivocation leaves the way open for workfare as a normal policy option, despite what the facts say.

It was an open secret that the projects were not succeeding in getting people into employment, nor in reducing their poverty. As a Senate Finance Committee staffer said: "'MDRC was important to the press exactly because no state program was all that clearly a success'" (Szanton, 1991: 598). MDRC have said quite clearly: 'There is little evidence that unpaid work experience led to consistent employment or earnings effects'.[395] The research they cite dates from 1993, but the situation is unlikely to have changed if New York City's ESP program in 2004 is any guide. As one commentator noted, the results fell far short of what the 'welfare reformers' were claiming (Stoesz, 1997), but that has not impeded the onward march of workfare as the solution to the 'welfare mess'. Three years after the 1993 research, workfare was to be PRWORA's chief strategy for 'ending welfare'.

---

395. http://www.mdrc.org/publication/unpaid-work-experience-welfare-recipients.

Chapter Twenty: Conclusion

Disentitlement

PRWORA is an example both of arrogant entitlement (and its correlative disentitlement) and of dissociation. The arrogant sense of entitlement belongs to the rich Congressmen who passed the legislation, together with their paymasters; the disentitled are America's poor, mainly women and children; and the dissociation is a divorce not only from the men's own humanity, but also from the reality of the real cause of poverty—the economic system which allows these men to become so rich and powerful.

The disentitlement of poor women and children was deliberate. It is explicitly stated in the Act. After PRWORA, the states are no longer obliged 'to provide assistance to needy families'. But then, they were not obliged to do so even before the Act was passed, if they didn't match the federal funding, or more formally through applying to the federal government to have their obligation waived.

The Congressmen's entitlement is covert, masked as it is by the disentitling ideology of the separative self as the human norm imposed on single mothers (who have no entitlement to assistance from the state because they could get a jobs if they tried), with its pronouncements of the virtues of employment (as 'the way out of poverty') and of the vices of 'dependency'. The lawmakers' real interests lie not only in their wealth and power and the profits which maintain it, but also in keeping that fact hidden. The focus on 'welfare' recipients displaces attention from the real cause of the 'welfare mess' and their own implication in it. But behind those rational (if reprehensible) interests lie even murkier motivations—hatred of the victims of the system that rewards these men so highly, and a continuing commitment to a slave-owner mentality which feels itself justified in exploiting people's labour if it brings the owners greater profit.

Dissociation

Single mothers (especially African-American women) are the prime target of the PRWORA legislation. All the single mothers and their children are desperately poor and they remain so, even after receiving 'welfare' and even though some of them have jobs. It is possible to work in the capitalist economy in the US, even to work full time, and not have enough money to buy food to feed everyone every day. And yet they supposedly need to be coerced into a 'personal responsibility' narrowly defined as paid employment in the labour market. The legislation is silent about the responsibilities the women are already shouldering—constantly having to find the necessities of life for themselves and their children without sufficient resources to pay for them, and more often than not in neighbourhoods made dangerous by desperate poverty. As Piven and Cloward pointed out:

> Many AFDC mothers … get their children up every morning and, because of the danger in the streets, walk them to school, walk them home, and keep them locked up in their apartments until morning. Forcing these overburdened women to [take up paid] work would mean adding the market job to the exhausting job of maintaining a home without funds or services, and all the while surrounded by dangerous and disorganized neighbourhoods (Piven and Cloward, 1993: 392-3).

Not only are the women's real responsibilities ignored in 'welfare reform', the reality of these women's lives is of no interest to the 'welfare reformers'. Or rather, the reality of these women's lives, the reality caused by the poverty created by the way the nation's economy is organised, is yet another occasion for punishment. Limited work experience and education, lack of child care, inadequate transportation, having to care for disabled family members, all increase the risk of being sanctioned (Hasenfeld, 2010: 160-1).

The women's real responsibilities towards their children were ignored by the Act's framers (and continue to be ignored) in favour of mythical 'jobs' which, even if they exist, are unlikely to pay a living wage. And because the women's real responsibilities are ignored, any conflict between the needs of the children and the demands of the job is resolved in favour of the job. The children's needs are often the reason why a woman is sanctioned, i.e. deprived of even the paltry resources 'welfare' gives. For example, if she fails to turn up for a 'work opportunity' because her child is sick or there is a crisis with her child care arrangements, her already meagre and grossly inadequate income is cut or abolished altogether. So PRWORA's 'personal responsibility' is demanded of those who already have responsibilities which far outweigh any responsibility the smug framers of 'welfare reform' will ever have to shoulder.

Another aspect of the dissociation of 'welfare reform' involves the myths that are promulgated about 'welfare' and its recipients. The notion of a 'welfare queen' spending her benefit on luxurious consumer items is ludicrous, as is the notion that anyone can become wealthy by getting multiple benefit payments. And yet this lie was spread far and wide by media outlets disinclined to do even the most basic research. Then there is the myth that 'welfare' recipients deliberately refuse to get jobs because they are lazy. These myths are outright lies and yet they are purveyed relentlessly by a media happy to scapegoat those who can't fight back.

Contrary to the belief of most commentators, PRWORA contained little that was new, certainly nothing so radical that it would end poverty as we have come to know it. It reproduced the same dehumanising pattern that has characterised the US 'welfare' system all along (and 'welfare' systems more generally, although the US case is the most extreme example). It also reproduced the individualistic ideology of poverty as a personality characteristic. PRWORA (like 'welfare' systems everywhere) maintained the focus on the people who are poor (usually designated 'families'), rather than on the economic system that requires poverty for its optimum functioning. To truly 'end welfare' it would be necessary to end the need for it, that is, to end poverty, and PRWORA certainly did not do that.

Twenty years on

By the time twenty years had passed, the dire predictions of its PRWORA's original critics had been realised. As already mentioned, because of Congress' refusal to provide for increases in the federal funding when the need increased, or even to link it to inflation, its value was a third less in 2016 than it had been 20 years earlier. By 2014 it was providing a safety net to far fewer families in need than the AFDC program it replaced, which itself never provided for all the poor. In 1996, AFDC had provided cash assistance to 68 of every 100 qualifying families, while in 2014 TANF was providing it to only 23 out of 100 such families, and in some States fewer than one-tenth of eligible families were receiving any money from TANF. The benefits women and children were receiving were anyway miniscule: less than half of the federal poverty threshold in every State, and in one-third of the States, under 20% of the poverty line. As a consequence, there was a rise in the numbers of people in deep poverty. This situation was exacerbated by the States' adoption of harsh eligibility policies such as time limits as short as 12 months and onerous work requirements as a condition for simply applying for assistance, and by TANF's failure to respond to the increased need caused by the global financial crisis. Moreover, the States overall were spending only half their TANF funds on the core welfare reform areas of basic assistance, work-related activities, and child care combined, while many States spent much less (Pavetti and Schott, 2016).

In an article called 'The failure of welfare reform: how Bill Clinton's signature legislative achievement tore America's safety net' (Weissmann, 2016), one commentator called this one of the most fundamental failures of 'welfare reform'. The program, he said, had become a 'slush fund' for repairing state budgets. Only 26% of the funding was directed to cash assistance, with the rest going to 'work-related activities and supports' (8%), child care (16%), administration (7%), refundable tax credits (8%), and 'other areas' (34%). Weissmann attributed this siphoning of money away from cash assistance to the program's inbuilt 'flexibility', which enabled States to treat the funding as 'an evaporating pot of money [with] carte blanche to spend it how they pleased'. Included among those 'other areas' the money was spent on, were measures supposedly intended to stem the 'flood' of 'out-of-wedlock births' that constituted the 'crisis in our nation': out-of-wedlock pregnancy prevention, including abstinence-only programs,[396] and encouraging two-parent families (Schott et al, 2015). While these are exercises in futility,[397] not to mention a gross interference in the lives of women and children, they are beloved of the right wing. They are intended to ensure that childbearing remains under men's control, although their effect is rhetorical rather than real. Nonetheless, as Weissmann said, 'TANF tore a hole in the safety net. That hole will just keep growing'.

Even right-wingers ('conservatives') have become critical of TANF in the light of how it has developed. By 2015, Peter Germanis, at one time a champion of 'welfare reform' and 'an ardent conservative' who served under the Reagan and Bush administrations, was being widely quoted saying that 'TANF is broken' (Germanis, 2015). In his 'personal statement' to members

---

396. 'Abstinence-only-until-marriage programs: ineffective, unethical, and poor public health' (Alford, 2007).

397. In 2011 the percentage of children born outside marriage in the US was the highest ever at 40.7%. A 2011 study of 9,000 young adults (26 to 31 years of age) found that 64% of mothers had had at least one of their children outside of marriage, while 47% had had all their children outside marriage (although some of the births had occurred when the women were living with a partner). Among the black mothers, 90% had had at least one child outside marriage, while the equivalent percentage for white women was 54% (Cherlin et al, 2014).

of Congress about the Draft Bill purporting to 'improve our social safety net', he said that the Bill failed to solve any of the program's real problems: 'When it comes to the TANF legislation', he said, 'Congress got virtually every technical detail wrong' (p.6):

> TANF was supposed to provide a safety net for the truly needy and a hand-up so families could achieve self-sufficiency. It has failed in to achieve these purposes and some states have enacted harsh policies without regard to the well-being of children, e.g., full family sanctions and very short time limits, just to use the savings to fill state budget holes (Germanis, 2015: 85).

He said that the bill solved none of the major problems: 'In fact, it is nothing more than rearranging the deck chairs on the Titanic' (p.74). However, the Bill's drafters insisted that it was 'the "biggest redesign of TANF in its history"', and nothing much is likely to change for the better, especially given a Trump presidency.

Not inadvertent

There is a tendency in the literature critical of PRWORA's 'welfare reform' to see the problems that have developed over the years as inadvertent. Pavetti and Schott (2016), for example, said, 'the program is not working as intended'. The flexibility built into TANF had led the States 'to spend the money in ways Congress never imagined', and the incentives for the States were 'poorly designed' (because they didn't require the States to be accountable for providing a safety net) (p.2). These commentators are arguing as though Congress simply made mistakes that could be rectified with sufficient information and encouragement. But this implication of inadvertence is not true. 'Welfare reform' has turned out exactly the way its architects intended. Nothing about PRWORA was inadvertent. What could be clearer, for example, than PRWORA's message to the States that they would be rewarded financially if they cut the 'welfare' rolls, and that they could use any and every means to achieve that goal without oversight or penalty? (Bach, 2011: 546) As one commentator said, 'One of the most important features of the block grant system is that if states reduce their welfare rolls, they keep the "surplus"' (Handler, 2008: 5).

The 'welfare reformers' knew what the consequences would be for poor women. They knew that putting time limits on benefit receipt would worsen poverty but they went ahead anyway (Stoesz, 1997), their sense of entitlement and their dissociation from any humanitarian impulses whatsoever overriding any sense of a common humanity. It is not necessary to read between the lines to find out that the framers of 'welfare reform' knew exactly what they were doing. Both parties in Congress 'heartily endorsed it' (Ehrenreich, 2010: 217), and the Republican Congressmen (some of whom may have been women)[398] had wanted even more stringent and punitive restrictions than those eventually contained in the PRWORA legislation, such as those contained in their 'Contract with America'.

Some of the policy makers have been brutally frank about what 'welfare reform' would do. For example, Jason Turner, New York City's Human Resources Commissioner and one of the architects of Wisconsin's W-2 (Schultze, 2000c), said openly that the 'reforms' he and Mayor Rudolph Giuliani had instigated were specifically designed to bring about 'a crisis in welfare recipients' lives, precipitating such dire prospects as hunger and homelessness' (address at the Nelson A. Rockefeller Institute of Government, 1998, cited in Bach, 2011: 546). The source cited did not say why Commissioner Turner was so keen to precipitate hunger and homelessness among 'welfare' recipients. No doubt this desire springs fully formed from the right-wing ideological belief that people who are poor are responsible for their own poverty and can be coerced into responsibility for ending it themselves, as well as from the cruelty that is inseparable from this type of masculine entitlement. And perhaps the Commissioner was sincere in his belief about where the responsibility for hunger and homelessness lay (as opposed to lying through his teeth). But whether lying or deluded, the framers of 'welfare reform' have no qualms about the misery they cause. In the logic of their right-wing ideology, claiming benefits was a 'choice'. Take that 'choice' away from people and they would have to get jobs, urged on by 'the spur of their own poverty' (George Gilder, quoted in Stoesz, 1997: 69).

Another example of brutal frankness was given by Robert Rector of the right-wing Heritage Foundation (quoted in Ehrenreich, 1997: 46-7). Speaking at a conference on 'welfare privatization' in Washington D.C. in March 1997, Rector praised the 'success' of 'welfare reform' in Wisconsin, where the caseload had declined faster than in any other State. (Wisconsin had started the process three years before the passage of PRWORA). This decline was due to what he approvingly referred to as '"application dissuasion"', that is, 'the imposition of work requirements so strict that "people never even walk in the door in the first place"'. In other words, bureaucratic disentitlement was deliberately built into the system. When Rector was asked what had happened to the nearly 40,000 families who were no longer on the rolls,

---

398. There were probably some women who voted for it, too, but the culture of masculinity can be embraced by women as well as men.

he said (ignoring the reams of research on just this issue) that "'poverty isn't bad for kids. Most of us had grandparents who were poor'". The real problem, he went on to say, is illegitimacy (the 'crisis in our nation' that so distressed PRWORA's framers). This had "'a decisive bad effect on kids'", he said, and in order for illegitimacy to end, 'welfare' must be abolished because it discourages the poor from marrying.

The US ruling class knew very well what they were doing in terms of their own interests. As one commentator pointed out, "'the desired outcome is reduced welfare rolls, regardless of what happens to those rejected for benefits or terminated from assistance'", and that outcome is desired because it brings in the votes. The 'welfare' constituency is not the poor women who are subjected to it, but the voters (Katz, 2008, quoted in Bach, 2009: 302n109).

The cheapening of an already grossly underpriced labour supply was another benefit for the US ruling class. A 2004 research report from the US Department of Agriculture (Hanson and Hamrick, 2004), estimated that, between 1996 and 2000, the flow of 'welfare' recipients into the labour force resulted in about 2.4 million new workers. While this had a positive effect on growth in employment and GDP, 'it put downward pressure on wages for low-skill occupations' (p.iii). So 'welfare reform', welcomed in low-wage populist circles out of resentment against 'welfare' recipients, was clearly against the interests of all low-wage workers. The Walmart family and the owners of the fast-food industry, however, were undoubtedly thrilled at this outcome. As for post-'welfare' poverty, these authors engage in the usual equivocation. 'Results are mixed', they say. Some households were better off, with incomes above 'the poverty level', while others were not (Hanson and Hamrick, 2004: 6). The criterion for being 'better off', however, is the federal poverty threshold and, as I have already argued, this is not an adequate measure of access to basic necessities. Moreover, the poverty measure is a household one: 'The earnings of other family members are an important factor in these results' (p.7). So while the women are no longer dependent on 'welfare', they remain dependent on someone. Hopefully, that 'someone' is not a violent male partner.

Such considerations have no influence on the policy-makers. 'Welfare reform' is serving its true purpose, which was neither to provide assistance to needy families, nor to promote job preparation and work, nor even to promote marriage, prevent out-of-wedlock pregnancies and encourage two-parent families (as stated in the legislation). The true purpose of 'welfare reform' is 'to ensure that labor stays on the market':

> Low-income people who apply for welfare today enter an arena that is organized to serve as a resource for employers: its purpose is to groom workers for hiring, make them as available as possible for employment, and actively push them into jobs. In this mode of "disciplining the poor", recipients are not just pushed into jobs by benefits that are too meager to compete with the worst wages – or even by forms of administrative *legerdemain* that deny access to benefits. Welfare programs are constructed to provide the poor with an experience of market incentives and logics and to teach self-discipline to workers who are expected to adapt to their plight on the lower rungs of the labor market (Schram et al, 2010: 744-5).

As the same researchers had argued earlier, 'welfare reform' is not just a moralistic attack on 'the poor' as punishment for their poverty. There are real material interests involved:

> by pushing the poor out of welfare and into low-wage work, employers hoped to lighten their tax burden and, more important, prevent tight labor markets from enhancing the bargaining position of labor or pushing wages upward (Schram and Soss, 2001: 54).

But beyond the interest in cheap labour power, 'welfare reform' creates scapegoats who can be used to deflect attention from the real cause of the people's woes, the capitalist economic system that uses and abuses people and discards them when it has no further use for them. These are the scapegoats needed if the domination that calls itself 'democracy' is to plausibly pass itself off as the interests of all. The hatred of 'welfare' characteristic of the US population (Gilens, 1999) is testimony to the success of this ploy. Aided by a mass media they own and control, the wealthy and their right-wing apologists have managed to dupe vast swathes of the US population into turning away from the real source of their woes. The advent of President Donald Trump is the lesson they won't learn this time either.

But beyond even these reasons (which are at least rational if we can accept the evil premises of masculine entitlement and dissociation), there are the emotions driving the policies. 'Welfare reform' is a form of bullying, and bullies get great pleasure from tormenting those who cannot fight back, whether in the playground, the corporate boardroom or the US Congress. Then there is the hatred the right-wing mind feels towards women whose child-bearing capacity is not under the control of men, combined with the continuing influence of a slave-owner mentality that condones disrespect towards black people and the violence against them, including routine murder. The dominant mentality which dictated the form 'welfare' should take throughout the history of the US, has not moved very far from the mentality of the slave-owner. PRWORA and subsequent attempts to 'redesign' it mandate what amounts to slavery—coerced labour which does not pay a living wage and which lacks any of the legislative protections of even the most menial job in the formal economy.

The solution to the problems of 'welfare reform' is to end poverty. But that would mean ending the limitless accumulation of wealth in the hands of the few. And that in turn means ending the arrogant entitlement and dissociation of the culture of male supremacy, and embracing instead the meanings and values of a genuine humanity and a universal respect that dehumanises no one. The possibility exists and the struggle goes on. But with a Trump presidency the future of America's poor, indeed of the whole US population and of the world, looks bleak indeed.

Epilogue

The main argument of this book is that the social world is organised in accordance with a culture of male supremacist masculinity characterised by unwarranted entitlement and a crazed dissociation from humanity (however else it might be organised). The five institutions I chose to illustrate how the values of masculinity permeate the social world—capitalism, fascism, surrogacy, transsexualism and US 'welfare reform'—do not appear at first sight to have anything in common. But if such disparate institutions can all be shown to subscribe to masculinity, then there is something seriously wrong with our modern, capitalist, 'democratic' societies.

Thankfully, male supremacy is not the whole of the social world. Alongside that masculinist reality there exists what I have called (for want of a better term) 'genuine humanity', a reality that runs counter to the dehumanisation of male supremacy and provides an alternative way of being in the world. This genuinely human alternative does not need theorising (because it does not cause the problems), but it is important to acknowledge its existence because otherwise it seems as though male supremacy is all there is. It is particularly important in a world that has seen decades of neo-liberal government policies pandering to the accumulation of wealth in the hands of the few, where global inequality has risen to a height unparalleled in history, where the biosphere is threatened with destruction, where unknown numbers of people are killed daily by a military-industrial complex unrestrained by any governance whatsoever, and where a Donald Trump can become president of the US and the US government comes wholly under the control of the right wing. It is vitally important to keep hold of the knowledge that these are dehumanising evils, and to refuse to pander to them simply because they seem to have triumphed. Male supremacy and its masculine arrogance and dissociation are not the whole of reality, no matter how prevalent they are.

Nonetheless male supremacy is ubiquitous, but when it operates within a democratic context with its ideological spin of 'freedom' and 'equality', it operates best when it remains hidden. The five institutions I chose are not publicly recognised as instances of domination, much less of male domination. Although fascism is usually repudiated,[399] the other four are largely accepted in the malestream. They have attracted criticism, although not as forms of male supremacy, except for surrogacy and transsexualism, which have been cogently criticised by feminism for the harms done to women by men's entitlement. But they have also been embedded in the social fabric as part of the world-taken-for-granted.

At the time of writing, the disastrous effects of the US economy on the US populace have thrown up yet another fascist demagogue and his henchmen, just as Germany did in the 1930s. There are farcical elements to this repetition of history,[400] with Trump himself a lazy, boorish buffoon. But his henchmen are no laughing matter. Take, as just one example, his choice of Mike Pence as vice-president. Pence was responsible for blocking disaster relief after Hurricane Katrina by demanding that it be paid for with budget cuts (American Bridge, 2016). He also chaired the Republican Study Committee that drafted a document recommending 'pro-free-market ideas for responding to Hurricane Katrina'. According to Naomi Klein, all of the recommended policies were 'straight out of the disaster capitalism playbook' (Klein, 2017). Paul Ryan, current Speaker of the US House of Representatives, was also one of the signatories to the document. Then there is Pence's typical right-wing stance against abortion, which is so obsessive he must take it personally. Perhaps, he's afraid it will be made retrospective with himself as the first candidate.[401] In that he is no different from the

---

399. Although not always. See, Sontag, 1974.

400. 'Hegel remarks somewhere that all great world-historic facts and personages appear, so to speak, twice. He forgot to add: the first time as tragedy, the second time as farce'. These are the opening sentences of Marx's *Eighteenth Brumaire of Louis Bonaparte* (1852). Marx was comparing the reign of Napoleon Bonaparte, Emperor of France from 1804-14, and again briefly in 1815 ('the first time') with that of his nephew, Charles-Louis-Napoleon Bonaparte, President of the Second Republic from 1848-52, and Emperor of the Second Empire as Napoleon III from 1852-70 ('the second time').

401. The right-wing claim that they are on the side of 'life' is clearly spurious. It is only foetal life they care about. They don't care about the lives of the women driven to backyard abortionists by the lack of safe affordable health care; they don't care about the lives of the myriads of people killed by US warmongering; and they fight alongside the National Rifle Association for the right to own the guns that have been used in so many massacres. I suspect that the right wing's obsessive concern for foetal life is caused by their fear and hatred of women outside the control of men. Foetal life is under women's control. It is

usual fundamentalist, right-wing 'Christians', to whose misrepresentations of reality he subscribes whole-heartedly. And it would seem as though he is going to have a disproportionate influence on presidential decision-making. Trump's campaign manager was reported saying in July 2016, before the actual election, that Pence 'will be handling the actual work of running the country. "He [Trump] needs an experienced person to do the part of the job he doesn't want to do."' (Pollitt, 2016).

The election of Trump is a replay of what happens when the economy creates 'surplus' populations, and it promises to be no less tragic than the first time round, both for the American people (most of whom did not vote for Trump) and for the rest of the world (none of whom had any say in the matter). The US already dominates the world, economically, militarily and politically. US corporate and military power seek to control the world economy, with military bases everywhere (Vine, 2015). At the end of 2016, the US was bombing seven countries—Afghanistan, Iraq, Libya, Pakistan, Somalia, Syria and Yemen—and had been for up to 15 years (Gordon, 2016b). Every US administration since World War Two has engaged in war crimes, specifically, unprovoked attacks on countries that posed no military threat to the US, while the Obama administration not only continued past policies, it exacerbated them. According to Noam Chomsky, 'If the Nuremberg laws were applied, then every post-war American president would have been hanged'.[402] (See also: Gordon, 2016a). In his view, 'the US is the world's biggest terrorist … [and] the greatest threat to world peace'.[403]

With that level of domination already in place, the arrival of Donald Trump and his minions in the most powerful position on earth promises to surpass even the Nazis in the devastation it can wreak. This is a possibility, not because the Trump administration is more evil than the Nazis, but because the weapons technology is so much more sophisticated and the earth's survival is so much more precarious. Trump feels entitled to transgress every norm of human decency, the public media reinforce this sense of entitlement by broadcasting his lies, slanders and detestable pronouncements far and wide; and he is aided and abetted by any number of equally entitled and dissociated men. His sense of entitlement is gargantuan, his dissociation from common

---

she who has the power of life and death over the foetus she is carrying, she whose body nourishes it, and she who decides whether or not to carry it to term. To the right-wing mind this is a power women ought not to have, so it must be curbed by law and society.

402. https://www.youtube.com/watch?v=NdD9uSrNFT4.

403. https://www.youtube.com/watch?v=vRbnPA3fd5U.

human decency is demented, and his contempt for women is monstrous; and everyone he has appointed to rule the nation, including the few women, shares the same values. With the ruling of the earth in the hands of men (and women) like that, humanity's future looks bleak.

References

*References marked with an asterisk * were originally found on the internet, although some of them are no longer available. I have not given the URLs because they would have to be typed in. Those references that are available can be viewed by entering the titles, keywords or key phrases into a search engine.

*AAP (2014) 'Couple who abandoned baby Gammy will be allowed to keep twin sister Pipah' *Australian Associated Press/The Guardian* 8 November

*ABC News (2015) 'Man charged over Sydney family law court bombings in the 1980s'

Aboulghar, M. A. and R. T. Mansour (2003) 'Ovarian hyperstimulation syndrome: classifications and critical analysis of preventive measures' *Human Reproduction Update* 9(3): 275-89

Abramovitz, Mimi (1996[1988]) *Regulating the Lives of Women: Social Welfare Policy from Colonial Times to the Present* Cambridge, MA: South End Press

*Abramsky, Sasha (2012) 'The other America, 2012: confronting the poverty epidemic' *The Nation* 25 April

*ABS (2009) 'Prisoners in Australia' Cat. No.4517.0. Canberra: Australian Bureau of Statistics

*ABS (2015) 'Prisoners in Australia' Cat. No.4517.0. Canberra: Australian Bureau of Statistics

*ACOSS (2003) *The Bare Necessities: Poverty and Deprivation in Australia Today* submission to the Senate Inquiry into Poverty and Financial Hardship Paper 127. Sydney: Australian Council of Social Service

*ACOSS (2004) *International Comparisons of Anti-Poverty Plans − Lessons for Australia* ACOSS Info 366. Sydney: Australian Council of Social Service http://www. acoss.org.au

*Acs, Gregory and Pamela Loprest (2007) *TANF Caseload Composition and Leavers Synthesis Report* submitted to the U.S. Department of Health and Human Services, Administration for Children and Families. Washington: The Urban Institute

*Acs, Gregory, Katherin Ross Phillips and Sandi Nelson (2003) *The Road not Taken? Changes in Welfare Entry during the 1990s* Washington, DC: The Urban Institute

*AFSCME (2006) *Safety Net for Sale: The Dangers of Privatizing Social Services* Washington: The American Federation of State, County and Municipal Employees

Ahlers, Rhodante (2010) 'Fixing and nixing: the politics of water privatization' *Review of Radical Political Economics* 20(10): 1-18

*Ahmed, Nafeez (2014) 'Nasa-funded study: industrial civilization headed for "irreversible collapse"?' *The Guardian* 15 March

*AHRC (2009) *The Sex and Gender Diversity Project—The Legal Recognition of Sex in Documents and Government Records: Concluding Paper* Sydney: Australian Human Rights Commission

Ajeet, Saoji and Kasturwar Nandkishore (2013) 'The boom in unnecessary caesarean surgeries is jeopardizing women's health' *Health Care for Women International* 34(6): 513-21

*Akin, Stephanie (2016) 'GOP wants to cut $23 billion from food stamps' *GW/Roll Call* 13 May

Albelda, Randy (2001) 'Fallacies of welfare-to-work policies' *Annals of the American Academy of Political and Social Science 577 – Reforming Welfare, Redefining Poverty*: 66-78

Albelda, Randy and Ann Withorn (2001) 'Preface' *Annals of the American Academy of Political and Social Science 577 – Reforming Welfare, Redefining Poverty*: 8-11

Albelda, Randy and Ann Withorn, eds (2002) *Welfare Reform, Poverty, and Beyond* Cambridge, MA: South End Press

*Alexander, Harriet (2014) 'Surrogacy laws damaging women's health' *The Sydney Morning Herald* 28 August

Alexander, Jeffrey C. (1990) 'Analytic debates: understanding the relative autonomy of culture', in Jeffrey C. Alexander and Steven Seidman, eds *Culture and Society: Contemporary Debates* Cambridge: Cambridge University Press. pp.1-27

*Alford, Bob (2003) 'What are the origins of Freddie Mac and Fannie May?' *History News Network* 19 September 2008

Alford, Peter and Paige Taylor (2014) 'Gammy's mum wants all sides on lie detector' *The Australian* 13 August

*Alford, Sue (2007) 'Abstinence-only-until-marriage programs: ineffective, unethical, and poor public health' *Policy Brief*, July. Washington: Advocates for Youth

*Allegretto, Sylvia, Marc Doussard, Dave Graham-Squire, Ken Jacobs, Dan Thompson and Jeremy Thompson (2013) *Fast Food, Poverty Wages: The Public Cost of Low-Wage Jobs in the Fast-Food Industry* University of Illinois at Urbana-Champaign and the Labor Center at UC Berkeley

*American Bridge (2016) 'Pence held hurricane Katrina relief funds hostage to push his political agenda' *American Bridge 21st Century* 29 August

*Amnesty International (2011) 'Brazil: indigenous leader killed in armed raid'

Anand, Sudhir, Paul Segal and Joseph E, Stiglitz (2010) 'Introduction', in Anand et al, eds

Anand, Sudhir, Paul Segal and Joseph E, Stiglitz, eds (2010) *Debates on the Measurement of Global Poverty* Oxford University Press

*Anderson, Mitchell (2011) 'Europe's own arms dealers and loan peddlers took down Greece' *The Tyee* 5 October

Anelauskas, Valdas (1999) *Discovering America As It Is* Atlanta: Clarity Press, Inc.

*Anna Maria (2014) 'Paedophiles and surrogacy' *annamaria.blogspot.com* 7 August

Anonymous (1971) 'Welfare "reform": 1971 style' *Social Service Review* 45(4): 482-5

*Anonymous (2012) 'Robert Peston ... life in the eye of a perfect storm' *Evening Standard* 4 October

Antlfinger, Carrie (2005) 'State seeks more W-2 providers: demise of the largest welfare-to-work agency in Milwaukee leaves its responsibility in hands of two remaining providers' *Milwaukee Journal Sentinel* 12 February

*Arditti, Rita (1990) 'Surrogacy in Argentina' *Issues in Reproductive and Genetic Engineering* 3(1): 35-43

Arditti, Rita, Renate Duelli Klein and Shelley Minden, eds (1984) *Test-Tube Women: What Future for Motherhood?* London, Boston, Melbourne and Henley: Pandora Press

*Arendt, Hannah (1951) *The Origins of Totalitarianism* second enlarged edition. Cleveland and New York: Meridian Books, The World Publishing Company, 1958

*Arendt, Hannah (1958) *The Human Condition* Second Edition. Chicago: University of Chicago Press, 1998

Arendt, Hannah (1971) 'Thinking and moral considerations' *Social Research* 38(3): 417-46

Argyrous, George and Frank Stilwell, eds (1996) *Economics as Social Science: Readings in Political Economy* Sydney: Pluto Press

*Associated Press (2014) 'Thailand's parliament approves bill banning commercial surrogacy' *The Guardian* 29 November

*Associated Press (2016) 'Some states cut back on unemployment benefits' *The Denver Post* 28 February

*Australian House of Representatives (2016) *Surrogacy Matters: Inquiry into the Regulatory and Legislative Aspects of International and Domestic Surrogacy Arrangements* Standing Committee on Social Policy and Legal Affairs

*Australian Senate (2004) *A Hand Up Not a Hand Out: Renewing the Fight against Poverty – Report on Poverty and Financial Hardship* Community Affairs References Committee Secretariat. Canberra: The Senate, Parliament House

Bach, Wendy A. (2009) 'Welfare reform, privatization, and power: reconfiguring administrative law structures from the ground up' *Brooklyn Law Review* 74(2): 275-324

*Bach, Wendy A. (2011) 'Responding to welfare privatization: new tools for a new age' *Clearinghouse Review: Journal of Poverty Law and Policy* 44(11-12): 545-54

*Backer, Larry Catá (1993) 'Of handouts and worthless promises: understanding the conceptual limitations of America systems of poor relief' *Boston College Law Review* 34(5): 997-1085

Backer, Larry Catá (1995) 'Welfare reform at the limit: the futility of "ending welfare as we know it"' *Harvard Civil Rights-Civil Liberties Law Review* 30(2): 339-406

*Bacon, Wendy and Elise Dalley (2015) 'Call for inquiry into women's refuge changes' *New Matilda* 27 March

*Baer, Paul, Tom Athanasiou, Sivan Kartha and Eric Kemp-Benedict (2008) *The Greenhouse Development Rights Framework: The Right to Development in a Climate Constrained World* Berlin: Heinrich Böll Foundation, Christian Aid, EcoEquity and the Stockholm Environment Institute

*Bailey, J. Michael (2003) *The Man Who Would be Queen: The Science of Gender-Bending and Transsexualism* Washington, DC: Joseph Henry Press

*Bailey, J. Michael (2005) 'Academic McCarthyism' *Northwestern Chronicle*

*Baker, Richard and Nick McKenzie (2014a) 'ANZ ethics under scrutiny over Cambodian sugar plantation loan' *The Age* 23 January

*Baker, Richard and Nick McKenzie (2014b) 'Uniting Church wants answers from ANZ over Cambodian sugar plantation' *The Age* 23 January

*Baldwin, Bridgette (2010) *Wisconsin Works? Race, Gender and Accountability in the Workfare Era Law, Policy, and Society* Dissertations. Paper 19

*Bane, Mary Jo (1997) 'Welfare as we might know it' *The American Prospect* 30, Jan/Feb: 47-55

Bannock, Graham, R.E. Baxter and Evan Davis (1992) *The Penguin Dictionary of Economics* Harmondsworth: Penguin Books

Baptist, Willie and Mary Bricker-Jenkins (2001) 'A view from the bottom: poor people and their allies respond to welfare reform' *Annals of the American Academy of Political and Social Science 577 – Reforming Welfare, Redefining Poverty*: 144-56

*Barbell, K. and M. Freundlich (2001) 'Foster care today' Casey Family Programs, Washington, DC

*Barlass, Tim (2014) 'When altruistic surrogacy goes wrong' *The Sydney Morning Herald* 10 August

Barrett, Michèle (1980) *Women's Oppression Today* London: Verso

Barry, Kathleen (2010) *Unmaking War, Remaking Men* Melbourne: Spinifex Press

*Barry, Kathleen (2013) 'Blowing up the Middle East: Obama's Syria and the masculinity of war' *Daily Censored* 6 September

Barry, Norman (1987) *The New Right* London, New York, Sydney: Croom Helm

Bauer, Fran (1996) 'Jobs issue takes center stage in debate over W-2: GOP says requirement to work is essential, while foes cry "slave labor"' *Milwaukee Journal Sentinel* 13 Feb

Baum, Erica B. (1991) 'When the witch doctors agree: the Family Support Act and social science research' *Journal of Policy Analysis and Management* 10(4): 603-15

Bauman, Zygmunt (2004) *Wasted Lives: Modernity and Its Outcasts* Cambridge: Polity

*BBC (2003) 'Derivatives—a simple guide'

Beauvoir, Simone de (1972[1953][1949]) *The Second Sex* translated and edited by H. M. Parshly. Harmondsworth: Penguin

*Bedard, Maurice (2016) 'Iceland sentences 26 corrupt bankers to 74 years in prison' *Loansafe.org* 8 January

Beechey, Veronica and Tessa Perkins (1987) *A Matter of Hours: Women, Part-Time Work and the Labour Market* Cambridge: Polity Press

Beeson, Diane and Abby Lippman (2006) 'Egg harvesting for stem cell research: medical risks and ethical problems' *Reproductive BioMedicine Online* 13(4): 573-79

Belliotti, Raymond A. (1988) 'Marxism, feminism, and surrogate motherhood' *Social Theory and Practice* 14(3): 389-417

*Benjamin, Harry (1999[1966]) *The Transsexual Phenomenon* New York: The Julian Press, Inc.

Benjamin, Jessica (1988) *The Bonds of Love: Psychoanalysis, Feminism, and the Problem of Domination* New York: Pantheon Books

Benjamin, Jessica and Anson Rabinbach (1989) 'Foreword', in Theweleit, 1989, pp.ix-xxv

Bennett, Susan D. (1995) '"No relief but on the terms of coming into the house": controlled spaces, disentitlements, and homelessness in an urban shelter system' *Yale Law Journal* 104(8): 2157-212

Bennett, Tony (2013) 'Introduction to the Routledge Classics Edition' in Bourdieu, 1984: xvii-xxii

Bennholdt-Thomsen, Veronika, Nicholas Faraclas and Claudia von Werlhof, eds (2001) *There is an Alternative: Subsistence and Worldwide Resistance to Corporate Globalization* Melbourne: Spinifex Press/London and New York: Zed Books

Bennholdt-Thomsen, Veronika, Maria Mies and Claudia von Werlhof (1988) *Women, The Last Colony* London/ New Delhi: Zed Books

Benston, Margaret (1970) 'The political economy of women's liberation', in Leslie B. Tanner, ed. *Voices from Women's Liberation* New York: A Signet Book, pp.279-92

Ber, Rosalie (2000) 'Ethical issues in gestational surrogacy' *Theoretical Medicine and Bioethics* 21(2): 153-69

Berger, Peter L. and Thomas Luckmann (1967) *The Social Construction of Reality: A Treatise in the Sociology of Knowledge* London: Allen Lane The Penguin Press

Bergmann, Barbara R. (1990) 'Feminism and economics' *Women's Studies Quarterly* 18(3/4): 68-74

*Berkowitz, Bill (2001) 'Welfare privatization: developing a poverty-industrial complex' *ZMagazine* July

*Bernstein, Adam (2009) 'Editor Irving Kristol, 89: architect of neoconservatism' *Washington Post* 19 September

*Bernstein, Jared, Chauna Brocht and Maggie Spade-Aguilar (2000) *How Much is Enough: Basic Family Budgets for Working Families Executive Summary*. Washington, D.C.: Economic Policy Institute

*Besharov, Douglas J. (2008) 'Two cheers for American welfare reform: lessons learned, questions raised, next steps' *www.policyexchange.org.uk*

Besharov, Douglas J. and Peter Germanis (2007) 'Welfare reform and the caseload decline' *Gender Issues* 24(1): 32-58

Bevir, Mark (1999) 'Foucault, power, and institutions' *Political Studies* XLVII: 345-59

*Bibby, Paul (2013) 'Please, just call me Norrie, this is a whole new agenda' *The Sydney Morning Herald* 1 June

*Bickers, Claire (2014) 'Baby Gammy drama: DCP aware of David Farnell's child sex convictions months before it became public' *Perth Now* 25 September

*Bindel, Julie (2007) 'My trans mission' *The Guardian* 1 August

*Bindel, Julie (2009) 'The operation that can ruin your life' *Standpoint* November

*Bindel, Julie (2015) 'Imagine a world without prostitution' *Byline* 14 April

Binder, Guyora (1996) 'The slavery of emancipation' *Cardozo Law Review* 17: 2063-102

*Bishop, Liz (2013) 'India's new surrogacy laws are only part of the equation' *OnLine Opinion* 14 March

*Blake, Emily (2015) 'As ID rules shift, transgender BCers break new ground' *The Tyee* 6 May

Blanchard, Ray (1985) 'Typology of male-to-female transsexualism' *Archives of Sexual Behavior* 14(3): 247-61

Blanchard, Ray (1989a) 'The classification and labeling of nonhomosexual gender dysphorias' *Archives of Sexual Behavior* 18(4): 315-34

Blanchard, Ray (1989b) 'The concept of autogynephilia and the typology of male gender dysphoria' *The Journal of Nervous and Mental Disease* 177(10): 616-23

*Blank, Rebecca M. (2008) 'Why the United States needs an improved measure of poverty', Testimony to the Subcommittee on Income Security and Family Support House Ways and Means Committee, Brookings Institution

*Blank, Rebecca M. and David K. Kovak (2008) 'Helping disconnected single mothers' National Poverty Center Brief 10

*Blank, Susan W. and Barbara B. Blum (1997) 'A brief history of work expectations for welfare mothers' *Welfare to Work* 7(1): 28-38

Block, Fred, Richard A. Cloward, Barbara Ehrenreich and Frances Fox Piven, eds (1987) *The Mean Season: The Attack on the Welfare State* New York: Random House

Block, Fred, Richard A. Cloward, Barbara Ehrenreich and Frances Fox Piven (1987) 'Introduction' in Block et al, pp.ix-xvi

Block, Fred and J. Noakes (1988) 'The politics of new-style workfare' *Socialist Review* 88(3): 31-58

Blum, William (2003a) *Rogue State: A Guide to the World's Only Superpower* London: Zed Books

Blum, William (2003b) *Killing Hope: US Military and CIA Interventions since World War II* London: Zed Books

Blum, William (2014) *America's Deadliest Export: Democracy: The Truth about US Foreign Policy and Everything Else* London: Zed Books

Bockting, Walter, Autumn Benner and Eli Coleman (2009) 'Gay and bisexual identity development among female-to-male transsexuals in North America: emergence of a transgender sexuality' *Archives of Sexual Behavior* 38(5): 688-701

*Bolen, Ed, Dottie Rosenbaum, Stacy Dean and Brynne-Keith Jennings (2016) 'More than 500,000 adults will lose SNAP benefits in 2016 as waivers expire', Center on Budget and Policy Priorities, 18 March

*Bolton, Megan, Elina Bravve, Emily Miller, Sheila Crowley and Ellen Errico (2015) *Out of Reach 2015: Low Wages & High Rents Lock Renters Out* Washington, DC: National Low Income Housing Coalition

Bolton, P. M. (1977) 'Bilateral breast cancer associated with clomiphene' *The Lancet* 310(8049): 1176

*Boot, Max (2016) 'Op-Ed: Conservatives ponder the future of the GOP under Trump' *Los Angeles Times* 13 November

Boron, Atilio A. (2006) 'The truth about capitalist democracy', in Panitch and Leys, eds, pp.28-58

*Borromeo, Leah (2013) 'India's e-waste burden' *The Guardian* 11 October

Bosanquet, Nick (1983) *After the New Right* London: Heinemann

Bourdieu, Pierre (1977) *Outline of a Theory of Practice* translated by Richard Nice. Cambridge: Cambridge University Press

Bourdieu, Pierre (1984) *Distinction: A Social Critique of the Judgement of Taste* London and New York: Routledge

Bourdieu, Pierre (1990) *The Logic of Practice* Stanford, Calif.: Stanford University Press

Bourdieu, Pierre (1991) *Language and Symbolic Power* edited and introduced by John B. Thompson, Cambridge: Polity Press

Bourdieu, Pierre (2001) *Masculine Domination* translated by Richard Nice. Cambridge: Polity Press

Boyle, Christine (2011) 'A human right to group self- identification? Reflections on Nixon v. Vancouver Rape Relief' *Canadian Journal of Women and the Law* 23(2): 488-518

*Brediceanu, Rebecca (2014) 'Gammy's future difficult to de-mystify' *UTS Law Research Centre News*, 7 October

Brenner, Arthur David (2001) *Emil J. Gumbel: Weimar German Pacifist and Professor* Boston: Humanities Press, Inc

*Brewster, Kerry (2013) 'Surrogacy laws may leave Australian babies stateless' *ABC News* 5 March

*Brock, Thomas, Claudia Coulton, Andrew London, Denise Polit, Lashawn Richburg-Hayes, Ellen Scott and Nandita Verma, et al (2002) 'Welfare reform in Cleveland: implementation, effects, and experiences of poor families and neighborhoods', in *The Project on Devolution and Urban Change* New York: MDRC

Brodkin, Evelyn Z. (1997) 'Inside the welfare contract: discretion and accountability in state welfare administration' *Social Service Review* 71(1): 1-33

Brodkin, Evelyn Z. (2003) 'Requiem for welfare' *Dissent* 50(1): 29-36

Brodkin, Evelyn Z. (2006) 'Bureaucracy redux: management reformism and the welfare state' *Journal of Public Administration Research and Theory* 17(1): 1-17

*Brodkin, Evelyn Z., Carolyn Fuqua and Elaine Waxman (2005) *Accessing the Safety Net: Administrative Barriers to Public Benefits in Metropolitan Chicago* Chicago: Sargent Shriver Center on Poverty Law

Brodkin, Evelyn Z. and Malay Majmundar (2010) 'Administrative exclusion: organizations and the hidden costs of welfare claiming' *Journal of Public Administration Research and Theory* 20(4): 827-48

*Brooks, Jamie D. (2007) 'Oprah on renting wombs in India: "It's beautiful"' *Biopolitical Times* 11 October

*Brophy-Baermann, Michelle D. and Andrew J. Bloeser (2009) 'Ending welfare as we didn't know it: the story of welfare privatization in California, New York, Texas and Wisconsin', a paper delivered at the Annual Meeting of the American Political Science Association, Toronto, Canada, 3-6 September

*Brown, Ellen (2008) 'Credit Default Swaps: evolving financial meltdown and derivative disaster du jour' Global Research, Center for Research on Globalization

Brown, Wendy (2015) *Undoing the Demos: Neoliberalism's Stealth Revolution* Cambridge, MA: MIT Press

*Buffett, Warren (2003) 'Chairman's letter', *Berkshire Hathaway Annual Report* 2002

Burchell, Graham (1993) 'Liberal government and techniques of the self' *Economy and Society* 22(3): 267-82

Burchell, Graham, Colin Gordon and Peter Miller, eds (1991) *The Foucault Effect: Studies in Governmentality* Chicago: University of Chicago Press

*Burchill, Julie (2013) 'Transsexuals should cut it out' *GenderTrender* 13 January

*Burkett, Elinor (2015) 'What makes a woman?' *New York Times* 6 June

Burnham, Linda (2001) 'Welfare reform, family hardship, and women of color' *Annals of the American Academy of Political and Social Science 577 – Reforming Welfare, Redefining Poverty*: 38-48

Burnham, Linda (2002) 'Racism in U.S. welfare policy: a human rights issue', in Gary Delgado, ed. *From Poverty to Punishment: How Welfare Reform Punishes the Poor* Oakland, CA: Applied Research Center, pp.121-38

Burton, Claire (1985) *Subordination: Feminism and Social Theory* Sydney: George Allen and Unwin

*Butz, Adam Michael (2012) *Privatization and Performance in the Implementation of Temporary Assistance to Needy Families* Theses and Dissertations—Political Science, Paper 1

Byrne, David (1997) 'Social exclusion and capitalism: the reserve army across time and space' *Critical Social Policy* 50, Vol.17(1): 27-51

Cahill, Damien (2004) 'Contesting hegemony: the radical neo-liberal movement and the ruling class in Australia', in Nathan Hollier, ed. *Ruling Australia: The Power, Privilege & Politics of the New Ruling Class* Melbourne: Australian Scholarly Publishing, pp.87-105

Cameron, Loren (1996) *Body Alchemy* Berkeley, CA: Cleis Press

Campbell, Beatrix (1987) *The Iron Ladies: Why Do Women Vote Tory?* London: Virago

*Campbell, Delilah (2013) 'Who owns gender?' *Trouble and Strife* 9 May

Campioni, Mia and Elizabeth Gross (1983) 'Love's labours lost: Marxism and feminism', in Judith Allen and Paul Patton, eds *Beyond Marxism: Interventions after Marx* Sydney: Intervention Publications, pp.113-41

*Cancian, Maria, Robert Haveman, Daniel R. Meyer and Barbara Wolfe (2002) 'Before and after TANF: the economic well-being of women leaving welfare' Discussion Paper no.1244-02. Institute for Research on Poverty, University of Wisconsin–Madison

*Cannold, Leslie (2006) 'Women can still say "no"' *OnLine Opinion* 24 November

Canzoneri, Robert (1968) 'Charles Evers: Mississippi's representative man?' *Harper's Magazine* 237, July, pp.67-74

*Carney, Scott (2010) 'Inside India's rent-a-womb business' *Mother Jones* Match/April

Casey, Timothy J. and Mary R. Mannix (1989) 'Quality control in public assistance: victimizing the poor through one-sided accountability' *Clearinghouse Review* 22(11, April): 1381-9

*CBS News (2013) '80 percent of U.S. adults face near-poverty, unemployment, survey finds' *CBS News* 28 July

*Chambelain, John (1965[1959]) *The Roots of Capitalism* Princeton NJ: D. Van Nostrand Company, Inc

*Chan, Andy and Jason Payne (2013) *Homicide in Australia: 2008-09 to 2009-10— National Homicide Monitoring Program Annual Report* AIC Reports, Monitoring Reports 21. Canberra: Australian Institute of Criminology

*Chan, Jenny and Ngai Pun (2010) 'Suicide as protest for the new generation of Chinese migrant workers: Foxconn, global capital, and the state' *The Asia-Pacific Journal*

*Chan, Sewell (2007) 'Mollie Orshansky, statistician, dies at 91' *The New York Times* 17 April

*Cheeseborough, Anthony J. (2002) 'The impact of welfare reform time limits on children and families: implications for reauthorization' *Journal of Public and International Affairs* 13

*Cherlin, Andrew J., Elizabeth Talbert and Suzumi Yasutake (2014) 'Changing fertility regimes and the transition to adulthood: evidence from a recent cohort' Department of Sociology, Krieger School of Arts and Social Sciences, Johns Hopkins University

*Chew, Kristina (2013) 'Fire engulfs poultry slaughterhouse, kills 119 in China' *Care2* 4 June

*China Labor Watch (2012) *Beyond Foxconn: Deplorable Working Conditions Characterize Apple's Entire Supply Chain* 27 June

Chodorow, Nancy (1978) *The Reproduction of Mothering: Psychoanalysis and the Sociology of Gender* Berkeley, Los Angeles and London: University of California Press

Chomsky, Noam (with Edward Herman) (1988) *Manufacturing Consent: The Political Economy of the Mass Media* New York: Pantheon Books

Chomsky, Noam (1999) *Profit over People: Neoliberalism and Global Order* New York, Toronto and London: Seven Stories Press

*Chomsky, Noam (2016) 'American power under challenge: masters of mankind' (Part 1) *TomDispatch* 8 May

*Christian Aid (2008) *Death and Taxes: The True Toll of Tax Dodging*

*Chui, Michael (2012) 'Derivatives markets, products and participants' *IFC Bulletin* No.35. Bank of International Settlements

Citro, Constance F. and Robert T. Michael, eds (1995) *Measuring Poverty: A New Approach* Panel on Poverty and Family Assistance: Concepts, Information Needs, and Measurement Methods, National Research Council. Washington DC: National Academy Press

*Clark, Andrew (2007) 'I should pay more tax, says US billionaire Warren Buffet' *The Guardian* 31 October

*Clark, Josh (2008) 'What are credit default swaps?' *HowStuffWorks.com* 1 October

Clinton, Bill (1994) 'Remarks by the President to officials of Missouri and participants of the Future Now program' Kansas City, Missouri, 14 June. *Social Justice* 21(1): 170-6

*Clinton, Bill (2006) 'How we ended welfare, together' *The New York Times* 22 August

Cockburn, Patrick (2014) *The Jihadis Return: ISIS and the New Sunni Uprising* OR Books

*Cohen, Margot (2009) 'A search for a surrogate leads to India' *The Wall Street Journal* 9 October

*Cohen, Steven (1999) 'Managing workfare: the case of the work experience program in the New York City parks department', a report prepared with the generous support of the PricewaterhouseCoopers Endowment on the Business of Government

Coleman, Eli, Walter O. Bockting and Louis Gooren (1993) 'Homosexual and bisexual identity in sex-assigned female-to-male transsexuals' *Archives of Sexual Behavior* 22(1): 37-50

Collins, Jane L. (2008) 'The spectre of slavery: workfare and the economic citizenship of poor women', in J. L. Collins, M. di Leonardo and B. Williams, eds, pp.131-151

Collins, Jane L., Micaela di Leonardo and Brett Williams, eds (2008) *New Landscapes of Inequality: Neoliberalism and the Erosion of Democracy in America* Santa Fe: School for Advanced Research Press

Collins, Jane L. and Victoria Mayer (2010) *Both Hands Tied: Welfare Reform and the Race to the Bottom of the Low-Wage Labor Market* Chicago and London: The University of Chicago Press

Connell, Raewyn (1995) *Masculinities* Sydney: Allen & Unwin

Connell, R. W. (2005) 'Change among the gatekeepers: men, masculinities, and gender equality in the global arena' *Signs: Journal of Women in Culture and Society* 30(3): 1801-25

Connell, Raewyn (2010) 'Two cans of paint: a transsexual life story, with reflections on gender change and history' *Sexualities* 13(1): 3-19

Connell, Raewyn (2012) 'Transsexual women and feminist thought: toward new understanding and new politics' *Signs* Sex: A Thematic Issue, 37(4): 857-81

Connell, Raewyn and Nour Dados (2014) 'Where in the world does neoliberalism come from? The market agenda in southern perspective' *Theory & Society* 43: 117-38

*Cooper, Caroline, Adam May and Anna Christiansen (2014) 'Desperate for a baby: scammed in global surrogacy's newest frontier' *Aljazeera America* 15 May

Coote, Anna and Beatrix Campbell (1982) *Sweet Freedom: The Struggle for Women's Liberation* London: Picador

*Corbyn, Jeremy (2015) 'Invest in our future' *Huffington Post* 8 July

Corea, Gena (1985) *The Mother Machine: Reproductive Technologies from Artificial Insemination to Artificial Wombs* New York: Harper and Row

Corea, Gena, and Susan Ince (1987) 'Report of a survey of IVF clinics in the USA', in Spallone and Steinberg, eds

*Courtney, Mark E. and Amy Dworsky (2006a) *Those Left Behind: Enduring Challenges Facing Welfare Applicants* Issue Brief 107, May. Chapin Hall Center for Children, University of Chicago

*Courtney, Mark E. and Amy Dworsky (2006b) *Barriers to Employment: Findings from the Milwaukee TANF Applicant Study* Chapin Hall Working Paper

*Courtney, Mark E. and Amy Dworsky (2006c) *Labor Market Outcomes: Findings from the Milwaukee TANF Applicant Study* Chapin Hall Working Paper

*Courtney, Mark E. and Amy Dworsky (2006d) *Income and Poverty: Findings from the Milwaukee TANF Applicant Study* Chapin Hall Working Paper

*Courtney, Mark E. and Amy Dworsky (2006e) *Economic Hardships and Food Insecurity: Findings from the Milwaukee TANF Applicant Study* Chapin Hall Working Paper

*Courtney, Mark E. and Amy Dworsky (2006f) *Child Welfare Services Involvement: Findings from the Milwaukee TANF Applicant Study* Chapin Hall Working Paper

Craigie, Emma (2010) *Chocolate Cake with Hitler* London: Short Books

Creed, Barbara (1993) *The Monstrous-Feminine: Film, Feminism, Psychoanalysis* London: Routledge

*Crouch, Brad (2014) 'South Australian gay couple travel to Thailand for birth of their surrogate twins' *news.com.au* 8 February, 2014

Crutzen, Paul J. (2002) 'Geology of mankind' *Nature* 415, 31 January: 23

*Cuthbert, Denise and Patricia Fronek (2014) 'Perfecting adoption? Reflections on the rise of commercial offshore surrogacy and family formation in Australia' Hayes and Higgs, eds, pp.55-66

Daalder, Hans (1984) 'In search of the center of European party systems' The *American Political Science Review* 78(1): 92-109

*Dabla-Norris, Era, Kalpana Kochhar, Nujin Suphaphiphat, Frantisek Ricka and Evridiki Tsounta (2015) *Causes and Consequences of Global Inequality: A Global Perspective* IMF Staff Discussion Note, SDN/15/13. Strategy, Policy, and Review Department, International Monetary Fund

Dalla Costa, Mariarosa and Selma James (1975) *The Power of Women and the Subversion of the Community* Bristol: Falling Wall Press

Daly, Mary (1978) *Gyn/Ecology: The Metaethics of Radical Feminism* London: The Women's Press

Danielson, Caroline and Jacob Alex Klerman (2008) 'Did welfare reform cause the caseload decline?' *Social Service Review* 82(4): 703-30

*Dannin, Ellen (2011) 'Crumbling infrastructure, crumbling democracy: infrastructure privatization contracts and their effects on state and local governance', Legal Studies Research Paper no. 14-2011 Penn State Law

*Danziger, Sheldon, Robert Haveman and Eugene Smolensky (1977) *The Program for Better Jobs and Income—A Guide and A Critique* a study prepared for the use of the Joint Economic Committee, Congress of the United States, Research on Poverty Reprint Series, Reprint 259, US Department of Health, Education and Welfare

*Darnovsky, Marcy (2014) 'Another scandal at a prominent surrogacy agency' *Biopolitical Times* 29 May

Dean, Mitchell (1994) '"A social structure of many souls": moral regulation, government, and self-formation' *Canadian Journal of Sociology/Cahiers canadiens de sociologie* Special Issue on Moral Regulation, 19(2): 145-68

Dean, Mitchell (1995) 'Governing the unemployed self in an active society' *Economy and Society* 24(4): 559-83

Dean, Mitchell (1999) *Governmentality: Power and Rule in Modern Society* London, Thousand Oaks and New Delhi: Sage Publications

*Dean, Sarah, Louise Cheer and Daniel Mills (2014) '"I will take care of Gammy on my own": Thai surrogate mother says she will take care of the critically-ill Down's syndrome baby as fundraising for his medical care tops $155,000' *The Daily Mail* 31 July, updated 3 August

*Dean, Sarah and Daniel Piotrowski (2014) 'Child protection services demand interview with paedophile father and his wife over baby Gammy case—as it emerges the couple met through a Chinese marriage agency when he left jail' *Daily Mail Australia* 5 August

*Deaton, Angus (2002) 'Is world poverty falling?' *Finance & Development: A Quarterly Magazine of the International Monetary Fund* 39(2), June

Deeming, Christopher (2014) 'Social democracy and social policy in neoliberal times' *Journal of Sociology* 50(4): 577-600

Deeming, Christopher and Bine Gubhaju (2015) 'The mis-measurement of extreme global poverty: a case study in the Pacific Islands' *Journal of Sociology* 51(3): 689-706

*Dehavenon, Mary Lou (1989-1990) 'Charles Dickens meets Franz Kafka: the maladministration of New York City's public assistance program' *Review of Law and Social Change* 27(2): 231-54

*Delong, J. Bradford (2007) 'Creative destruction's reconstruction: Joseph Schumpeter revisited' *The Chronicle Review* issue dated December 7

Delvigne, Annick et al (2002) 'Metabolic characteristics of women who developed ovarian hyperstimulation syndrome' *Human Reproduction* 17(8): 1994-6

*Demick, Barbara and David Sarno (2010) 'Latest news reports on the Foxconn suicides' *China Labour Bulletin* 26 May

*DeNavas-Walt, Carmen and Bernadette Proctor (2015) *Income and Poverty in the United States: 2014* Current Population Reports, P60-252, U.S. Census Bureau. Washington, DC: U.S. Government Printing Office

*Desmond-Harris, Jenée (2014) '8 sneaky racial code words and why politicians love them' *The Root* 15 March

Devor, Holly (1999) *FTM. Female to Male Transsexuals in Society* Bloomington and Indianapolis, IN: Indiana University Press

Dexter, Miriam Robbins (1990) *Whence the Goddess: A Sourcebook* New York: Athene Series, Pergamon Press

Dines, Gale (2010) *Pornland* Melbourne: Spinifex Press

Dinnerstein, Dorothy (1976) *The Mermaid and the Minotaur: Sexual Arrangements and Human Malaise* New York: Harper and Row

*Dirt (2010) 'Trans (male) violence—Camp Trans and Michfest 2010 (Part 2)'

*Dobbin, Murray (2015a) 'Downsize democracy for 40 years, here's what you get' *The Tyee* 26 January

*Dobbin, Murray (2015b) 'Corporate greed? Enough already' *The Tyee* 4 April

*Dobbin, Murray (2015c) 'Harper is right: this election is about security versus risk' *The Tyee* 25 July

Donnelly, Catherine (2010) 'Privatization and welfare: a comparative perspective' *Law and Ethics of Human Rights* 5(2): 1938-2545

Dresang, Joel (1996) 'Virginia firm bids to provide services to all of county: other proposals did not cover all six of W-2's administrative regions' *Milwaukee Journal Sentinel* 19 November

Dresang, Joel (2000) 'W-2 provider closing its staffing agency: MaxStaff, part of a state review, will drop its 70 employees next month' *Milwaukee Journal Sentinel* 9 June

*Duhigg, Charles and Keith Bradsher (2012) 'How the U.S. lost out on iPhone work' *New York Times* 21 January

*Dupor, William (2016) 'How does government spending affect inflation?' Federal Reserve Bank of St Louis 10 May

*Dworkin, Andrea (1977) 'Why So-Called Radical Men Love and Need Pornography', in Dworkin, 1988a, pp.214-21

*Dworkin, Andrea (1981) *Pornography: Men Possessing Women* London: The Women's Press

*Dworkin, Andrea (1983) *Right-Wing Women: The Politics of Domesticated Females* London: The Women's Press

*Dworkin, Andrea (1988a) *Letters from a War-Zone: Writings 1976-1987* London: Secker and Warburg

*Dworkin, Andrea (1988b) 'The ACLU: bait and switch', in Dworkin, 1988a, pp.210-13

*Edelman, Peter B. (2010) 'TANF and low-income family support: hearing before the H. Subcomm. on Income Security and Family Support of the H. Comm. on Ways and Means, 111th Cong., Mar. 11, 2010', statement of Professor Peter B. Edelman, Geo. U. L. Center

Edgar, David (1984) 'Bitter harvest', in J. Curran, ed. *The Future of the Left* Cambridge: Polity Press, pp.39-57

Edmond, Wendy and Suzie Fleming, eds (1975) *All Work and No Pay: Women, Housework, and the Wages Due* Bristol: The Falling Wall Press

Ehrenreich, Barbara (1997) 'Spinning the poor into gold: how corporations seek to profit from welfare reform' *Harper's Magazine* August, pp.44-52

Ehrenreich, Barbara (2003) 'Maid to order', in Ehrenreich and Hochschild, eds, pp.85-103

Ehrenreich, Barbara (2010[2001]) *Nickel & Dimed: Undercover in Low-Wage USA* London: Granta

Ehrenreich, Barbara and Arlie Russell Hochschild, eds (2003) *Global Woman: Nannies, Maids and Sex Workers in the New Economy* London: Granta Books

Eisenstein, Zillah, ed. (1979) *Capitalist Patriarchy and the Case for Socialist Feminism* New York and London: Monthly Review Press

Ekman, Kajsa Ekis (2013) *Being and Being Bought: Prostitution, Surrogacy and the Split Self* Melbourne: Spinifex Press

*Ellis, Ellen Deborah (1905) *An Introduction to the History of Sugar* a Dissertation Presented to the Faculty of Bryn Mawr College. Philadelphia: The John C. Winston Co.

*Ellis, Erle (2011) 'Forget Mother Nature: this is a world of our making' *New Scientist* 8 June

*Ellis, Erle (2013) 'Anthropocene' *The Encyclopedia of Earth* 3 September

*Emmerson, Glenda (1996) *Surrogacy: Born for Another* Research Bulletin no 8/96, Queensland Parliamentary Library, Brisbane

England, Paula (1993) 'The separative self: androcentric bias in neoclassical assumptions', in Ferber and Nelson, eds, pp.37-53

Epstein, William M. (1997) *Welfare in America: How Social Science Fails the Poor* Madison: University of Wisconsin Press

*Erinyes Autonomous Activist Lesbians (2010) 'Submission to the Australian Human Rights Commission's Consultation on protection from discrimination on the basis of sexual orientation and sex and/or gender identity: comment 143'

*Escobar, Pepe (2016) 'Dance to the Panama Papers "limited hangout" leak' *telesurtv* 5 April

*Ewing, Christine and Robyn Rowland (1990) 'Draft report on surrogacy issued by the Australian National Bioethics Consultative Committee—the debate on surrogacy in Australia continues' Reproductive and Genetic Engineering: *Journal of International Feminist Analysis* 3(2): (no page numbers)

*Eyres, James (2014) 'ANZ to cut ties to Cambodia bank' *The Age* 25 March

*Fader, Carol (2015) 'Fact check: is Florida drug-testing welfare recipients?' *The Florida Times Union* 29 May

*Falk, Gene (2016) *The Temporary Assistance for Needy Families (TANF) Block Grant: Responses to Frequently Asked Questions* Congressional Research Service, March

*Farrell, Mary (2009) 'Disconnected welfare leavers in Colorado', Research Brief 10 March. Falls Church, VA: The Lewin Group

*Farrelly, Elizabeth (2013) 'Not man nor woman, just a blur of genders' *The Sydney Morning Herald* 6 June

*Federici, Silvia (2010) 'The reproduction of labor power in the global economy and the unfinished feminist revolution' *caring labor: an archive* 25 October

*Feneley, Rick (2015) 'Chief Justice Diana Bryant confident commercial surrogacy will be legalised in Australia' *The Sydney Morning Herald* 30 April

Ferber, Marianne A. and Julie A. Nelson, eds (1993) *Beyond Economic Man: Feminist Theory and Economics* Chicago: University of Chicago Press

Ferber, Marianne A. and Julie A. Nelson, eds (2003) *Feminist Economics Today: Beyond Economic Man* Chicago: University of Chicago Press

Ferguson, Charles H. (2012) *Predator Nation: Corporate Criminals, Political Corruption, and the Hijacking of America* New York: Crown Business

*Ferguson, Sarah (2014a) 'Baby Gammy—surrogate mother disputes parents claims, focuses attention on Thai baby-making industry' *ABC 7.30 Report* 4 August

*Ferguson, Sarah (2014c) 'Baby Gammy's biological father's conviction details emerge' *ABC 7.30 Report* 6 August

*Fialka, John (1976) 'Reagan's stories don't always check out' *The Washington Star* 15 February

*FINRRAGE (1989) 'FINRRAGE responds to surrogacy report'

*First Post (2013) 'Why Indian surrogacy laws are ripe for exploitation by paedophiles' *firstpost.com* 11 June

Fitzgerald, Patrick (2016) 'PricewaterhouseCoopers settles a $5.5 billion crisis era lawsuit' *The Wall Street Journal* 26 August

Flanders, Laura, Janine Jackson and Dan Shadoan (1996) 'Media lies, public opinion, and welfare', in Diane Dujon and Ann Withorn, eds *For Crying Out Loud: Women's Poverty in the United States* Boston: South End Press, pp.29-40

Flax, Jane (1983) 'Political philosophy and the patriarchal unconscious: a psychoanalytic perspective on epistemology and metaphysics, in S. Harding and M. B. Hintikka, eds, *Discovering Reality: Feminist Perspectives on Epistemology, Metaphysics, Methodology, and Philosophy of Science* Dordrecht, Boston and London: D. Reidel Publishing Company

Flax, Jane (1990) *Thinking Fragments: Psychoanalysis, Feminism, & Postmodernism in the Contemporary West* Berkeley LA and Oxford: University of California Press

*Floyd, Chris (2015) 'The age of despair: reaping the whirlwind of western support for extremist violence' *Counterpunch* 13 November

Folbre, Nancy (1994) *Who Pays for the Kids: Gender and the Structures of Constraint* London: Routledge

*Ford, Clementine (2016) 'When male entitlement meets rejection' *Daily Life* 27 May

*Ford, Liz (2015) 'Sustainable development goals: all you need to know' *The Guardian* 20 January

*Forstater, Mathew (2004) 'Tax-driven money: additional evidence from the history of thought, economic history, and economic policy', Working Paper No.35

Foucault, Michel (1978) 'Governmentality', in Burchell et al, eds, pp.87-104

Foucault, Michel (1983) 'Afterword: the subject and power', in H. Dreyfus and P. Rabinow, eds *Michel Foucault: Beyond Structuralism and Hermeneutics* Chicago: University of Chicago Press, pp.208-26

Foucault, Michel (1984[1976]) *The History of Sexuality: Volume I: An Introduction* Harmondsworth: Penguin Books

Foucault, Michel (1991) 'Politics and the study of discourse', in Burchell et al, eds, pp.53-72

*Fowler, Alan R., SuSheila Dhillon and Brian Handal (2008) 'A brief history of the modern American mortgage market & today's financial crisis', Emerging Market Consulting Group

Fox-Genovese, Elizabeth and Eugene D. Genovese (1983) *Fruits of Merchant Capital: Slavery and Bourgeois Property in the Rise and Expansion of Capitalism* New York: Oxford University Press

Frankl, Victor (2004[1946]) *The Doctor and the Soul: From Psychotherapy to Logotherapy* London: Souvenir Press

Fraser, Steven and Joshua B. Freeman, eds (1997) *Audacious Democracy: Labor, Intellectuals, and the Social Reconstruction of America* Boston and New York: Houghton Mifflin Company

Freedman, Henry, Mary R. Mannix, Marc Cohan and Rebecca Scharf (2002) 'Uncharted terrain: the intersection of privatization and welfare' *Clearinghouse Review* 35, Jan-Feb: 557-72

Freud, Sigmund (1931) 'Female Sexuality', *Penguin Freud Library* 7, pp.367-392

Freund, Kurt, Betty W. Steiner and Samuel Chan (1982) 'Two types of cross-gender identity' *Archives of Sexual Behavior* 11(1): 49-63

*Friedman, Howard Steven (2012) 'US infant mortality rate higher than other wealthy countries' *Huffington Post* 25 June

Fritzsche, Peter (2009) 'Return to Soviet Russia: Edwin Erich Zwinger and the narratives of Barbarossa' *Kritika: Explorations in Russian and Eurasian History* 10(3): 557-70

*Frogner, Bianca, Robert Moffitt and David Ribar (2007) *How Families Are Doing Nine Years after Welfare Reform: 2005 Evidence from the Three-City Study*

Frost, Stephen and Margaret Burnett (2007) 'Case study: the Apple iPod in China' *Corporate Social Responsibility and Environmental Management* 14(2): 103-13

Frye, Marilyn (1983) *1*Trumansburg, NY: The Crossing Press

Galbraith, James Kenneth (2012) *Inequality and Instability: A Study of the World Economy Just Before the Great Crisis* Oxford University Press

Galbraith, James Kenneth (2014a) *The End of Normal: The Great Crisis and the Future of Growth* New York: Simon & Schuster

*Galbraith, James K. (2014b) 'Kapital for the twenty-first century?' *Dissent* Spring

Galbraith, John Kenneth (1975) *Money: Whence it Came, Where it Went* Harmondsworth: Pelican Books

*Gallagher, Anne (2014) 'Wombs for rent: a ruthless trade exploits the poor' *The Sydney Morning Herald* 5 August

*Gallus Mag (2013a) 'The function of "Transphobia"' *womenofthepatriarchy* 21 January

*Gallus Mag (2013b) 'Transgender rights: the elimination of the human rights of women' *GenderTrender* 11 July

*Geary, Kate (2012) *Our Land, Our Lives – Time Out on the Global Land Rush* Oxfam International

Gellner, Ernest (1994) *Conditions of Liberty: Civil Society and Its Rivals* London: Hamish Hamilton

George, Katrina (2008) 'Women as collateral damage: a critique of egg harvesting for cloning research' *Women's Studies International Forum* 31(4): 285-92

*George, Susan (1976) *How the Other Half Dies: The Real Reasons for World Hunger* London: Penguin Books

George, Susan (1984) *Ill Fares the Land: Essays on Food, Hunger and Power* London: Penguin Books, 1990

George, Susan (1990[1988]) *A Fate Worse Than Debt* London: Penguin Books

George, Susan (1999a) *The Lugarno Report: On Preserving Capitalism in the Twenty-first Century* London: Pluto Press

*George, Susan (1999b) 'A short history of neoliberalism', presented at the Conference on Economic Sovereignty in a Globalising World, Bangkok, 24-26 March

George, Susan (2008) 'Special report: We must think big to fight environmental disaster' *New Scientist* 18 October

*Germanis, Peter (2015) 'TANF is broken! It's time to reform "welfare reform" (and fix the problems, not treat their symptoms)'

Giddens, Anthony (1976) 'Introduction' to *The Protestant Ethic and the Spirit of Capitalism*, pp.1-12(b)

Giddens, Anthony (1994) *Beyond Radical Politics* Cambridge: Polity Press

Gilbert, Neil (1998) 'From service to social control: implications of welfare reform for professional practice in the United States' *European Journal of Social Work* 1(1): 101-8

Gilens, Martin (1999) *Why Americans Hate Welfare: Race, Media, and the Politics of Antipoverty Policy* Chicago and London: The University of Chicago Press

*Gilliam, Franklin D. Jr. (1999) 'The "welfare queen' experiment: how viewers react to images of African-American mothers on welfare' *Nieman Reports The Nieman Foundation for Journalism at Harvard University* 53(2)

Gilligan, Carol (1982) *In a Different Voice: Psychological Theory and Women's Development* Cambridge, Massachusetts and London: Harvard University Press

Gimbutas, Maria (1989) *The Language of the Goddess* New York: Harper and Row

Gimbutas, Maria (1991) *The Civilization of the Goddess: The World of Old Europe* San Francisco: HarperSanFrancisco

*Gittins, Ross (2014) 'Competition comes at a cost' *The Sydney Morning Herald* 15 October

*Gittins, Ross (2015a) 'Economists shouldn't be apologists for business' *The Sydney Morning Herald* 2 February

*Gittins, Ross (2015b) 'Long-term employment trends: retired workers happy to put their feet up' *The Sydney Morning Herald* 21 February

Glassman, Carol (1970) 'Women and the welfare system', in Morgan, ed., pp.112-27

*Global Witness (2012) *A Hidden Crisis? Increase in Killings as Tensions Rise Over Land and Forests* London: Global Witness Limited

*Gogarty, Brendan (2015) 'Criminalising dissent: anti-protest law is an ominous sign of the times' *The Conversation* 28 November

*Goldberg, Michelle (2014) 'What is a woman?' *The New Yorker* 4 August

*Golden, Olivia (2005) *Assessing the New Federalism: Eight Years Later An Urban Institute Program to Assess Changing Social Policies*

*Goldner, Loren (2007) 'Fictitious capital for beginners: imperialism, "anti-imperialism", and the continuing relevance of Rosa Luxemburg' *Mute* 21 August

*Goodman, John C. (2013) 'It's time for Congress to privatize the welfare state' *Forbes* 19 June

*Google Australia (2015) *Google Australia Submission to Senate Economics References Committee Inquiry into Corporate Tax, 2nd February* Senate Committee of Inquiry into Corporate Tax Avoidance, Submission 57

Gordon, Linda (1994) *Pitied But Not Entitled: Single Mothers and the History of Welfare 1890-1935* Cambridge, Massachusetts: Harvard University Press

Gordon, Linda (2008) 'The perils of innocence, or what's wrong with putting children first' *The Journal of the History of Childhood and Youth* 1(3): 331-50

Gordon, Rebecca (2016a) *American Nuremberg: U.S. Officials Who Should Stand trial for Post-9/11 War Crimes* New York: Hot Books

*Gordon, Rebecca (2016b) 'It's 2016: do you know where your bombs are falling? The forgotten war in Yemen and the unchecked war powers of the presidency in the age of Trump' *TomDispatch* 12 December

Gori, Gigliola (1999) 'Model of masculinity: Mussolini, the "new Italian" of the Fascist era' *The International Journal of the History of Sport* 16(4): 27-61

Gottschalk, Lorene Hannelore (2009) 'Transgendering women's space: a feminist analysis of perspectives from Australian women's services' *Women's Studies International Forum* 32: 167-78

*Gray, Stephen (2015) *The Northern Territory Intervention: An Evaluation* Melbourne: Castan Centre for Human Rights Law, Monash University

Green, David G. (1987) *The New Right: The Counter-Revolution in Political, Economic and Social Thought* Brighton: Wheatsheaf Books

*Green, Jessica (2011) 'London transgender conference cancelled after trans complaints' *Pink News* 19 April

*Greenberg, Mark (2009) 'It's time for a better poverty measure' *Center for American Progress* 25 August

*Greenspan, Alan (2002) 'Remarks before the Economic Club of New York' *The Federal Reserve Board* 19 December

Grenfell, Laura and Anne Hewitt (2012) 'Gender regulation: restrictive, facilitative or transformative laws?' *Sydney Law Review* 34(4): 761-83

Grogger, Jeffrey, Steven Haider and Jacob Klerman (2003) 'Why did the welfare rolls fall during the 1990's? The importance of entry' *American Economic Review* 93(2): 288-92

Gueron, Judith (1996) 'A research context for welfare reform' *Journal of Policy Analysis and Management* 15(4): 547-61

Guettel, Charnie (1974) *Marxism and Feminism* Toronto: Canadian Women's Educational Press

Guillaumin, Colette (1986) «Sexisme, pensée de 'la droite' ou pensée de 'droite'?» in *L'extrême droite contre les femmes: un recueil de textes et de documents* Paris: Maries-Jeannes (originally published in *Amazones d'hier, lesbiennes d'aujourd'hui* No 17: 38-41)

Guillaumin, Colette (1995) 'Sexism, a right-wing constant of any discourse: a theoretical note', in *Racism, Sexism, Power, and Ideology* London and New York: Routledge, pp.171-5

Gupta, Jyotsna Agnihotri (2006) 'Towards transnational feminisms: some reflections and concerns in relation to the globalization of reproductive technologies' *European Journal of Women's Studies* 13(1): 23-38

Gupta, Jyotsna Agnihotri (2012) 'Reproductive biocrossings: Indian egg donors and surrogates in the globalized fertility market' *International Journal of Feminist Approaches to Bioethics* 5(1): 25-51

*Gurría, Angel (2011) 'Remarks delivered during the press conference', OECD Secretary-General, launch of *Divided We Stand: Why Inequality Keeps Rising*, Paris, 5 December

Guttmann, Allen (1999) 'Sacred, inspired authority: D. H. Lawrence, literature and the fascist body' *The International Journal of the History of Sport* 16(2): 169-79

*Haberman, Clyde (2014) 'Baby M and the question of surrogate motherhood' *The New York Times* 23 March

*Hahn, Heather, Olivia Golden and Peter Edelman (2012a) 'Strengthening TANF for states and needy families', August. The Urban Institute

*Hahn, Heather, Olivia Golden and Alexandra Stanczyk (2012b) 'State approaches to the TANF block grant: welfare is not what you think it is', Working Families Paper 20, August. The Urban Institute

Hall, Stuart and Martin Jacques (1983) 'The great moving right show', in S. Hall and M. Jacques, eds *The Politics of Thatcherism* London: Lawrence and Wishart, pp.19-39

*Hamby, William (2012) 'Connecticut shooting, white males, and mass murder' *examiner.com* 14 December

*Hamilton, Clive (2008) 'Art or p-rn is not the question' *Crikey.com*, 26 May

Hancock, Ange-Marie (2003) 'Contemporary welfare reform and the public identity of the "Welfare Queen"' *Race, Gender & Class* 10(1): 31-59

*Handler, Joel F. (2002) 'Myth and ceremony in workfare: rights, contract, and client satisfaction', Research Paper No.02-21, UCLA School of Law

*Handler, Joel F. (2008) 'The rise and spread of workfare, activation, devolution, and privatization, and the changing status of citizenship' *Public Law & Legal Theory Research Paper Series*, Research Paper No. 08-05. Los Angeles: UCLA School of Law

Handler, J. F. and Y. Hasenfeld (1991) *The Moral Construction of Poverty: Welfare Reform in America* Newbury Park, CA: Sage

*Hanson, Kenneth and Karen Hamrick (2004) *Moving Public Assistance Recipients into the Labor Force 1996-2000* Food Assistance and Nutrition Research Report Number 40, Economic Research Service, United States Department of Agriculture

*Harcourt, Geoff (2014) 'Why treasurers should go back to economics school' *The Conversation* 19 August

*Harding, Ann, Rachel Lloyd and Harry Greenwell (2001) 'Financial disadvantage in Australia 1990 to 2000: the persistence of poverty in a decade of growth', Canberra and Sydney: NATSEM/The Smith Family

*Harding, Ann and Aggie Szukalska (2000) 'Making a difference: the impact of government policy on child poverty in Australia, 1982 to 1997-98', Canberra, National Centre for Social and Economic Modelling

Harding, Sandra (1981) 'What is the real material base of patriarchy and capital?' in Sargent, ed., pp.135-63

*Hardoon, Deborah (2015) *Wealth: Having it All and Wanting More* Oxford: Oxfam GB

*Harkabus, Jenna (2010) *Can Parental Work Eliminate Child Poverty?* Honors Thesis, Miami University

*Harris, Karen K. (2010) 'Acting on the data: the Measuring American Poverty Act' *The Shriver Brief* 28 April

*Harris, Katherine (2009) 'Exclusive: derivatives for dummies by the other Katherine Harris' *Dandelion Salad* 18 February

Hartmann, Heidi (1981) 'The unhappy marriage of Marxism and feminism: towards a more progressive union', in Sargent, ed., pp.1-42

Hartsock, Nancy C. M. (1985[1983]) *Money, Sex and Power: Toward a Feminist Historical Materialism* Boston: Northeastern University Press

Harvard Law Review (2005) 'Developments in the law: jobs and borders reviewed' *Harvard Law Review* 118(7): 2171-290

*Harvey, David (2003) *The New Imperialism* Oxford University Press

Harvey, David (2005) *A Brief History of Neoliberalism* Oxford and New York: Oxford University Press

Harvey, David (2006[1982]) *The Limits to Capital* Oxford: Basil Blackwell
Harvey, David (2007) 'Neoliberalism and the city' *Studies in Social Justice* 1(1): 2-13
Harvey, David (2011) *The Enigma of Capital and the Crises of Capitalism* London: Profile Books
Harvey, David (2014) *Seventeen Contradictions and the End of Capitalism* London: Profile Books
*Harvey, John T. (2012) 'It is impossible for the US to default' *Forbes* 10 September
Haseler, Stephen (2000) *The Super-Rich: The Unjust New World of Global Capitalism* Houndmills and London: Macmillan Press
Hasenfeld, Yeheskel (2010) 'Organizational responses to social policy: the case of welfare reform' *Administration in Social Work* 34(2): 148-67
*Hasenfeld, Yeheskel and Eve E. Garrow (2012) 'Nonprofit human-service organizations, social rights, and advocacy in a neoliberal welfare state' *Social Service Review* 86(2): 295-322
*Hasenfeld, Yeheskel, Toorjo Ghose, Kandyce Larson (2004) 'The logic of sanctioning welfare recipients: an empirical assessment' *Social Service Review* 78(2): 304-19
Haskins, Ron (1991) 'Congress writes a law: research and welfare reform' *Journal of Policy Analysis and Management* 10(4): 616-32
Hawthorne, Susan (2002) *Wild Politics: Feminism, Globalisation, Bio/Diversity* Melbourne: Spinifex Press
Hawthorne, Susan (2008) 'Somatic piracy and biophallacies: separation, violence and biotech fundamentalism' *Women's Studies International Forum* 31(4): 308-18
*Hawthorne, Susan (2016) 'Fragmented feminisms' labrys, éåtudes féministes January/July
Hawthorne, Susan and Renate Klein, eds (1991) *Angels of Power and Other Reproductive Creations* Melbourne: Spinifex Press
Hawthorne, Susan and Bronwyn Winter, eds (2002) *September 11, 2001: Feminist Perspectives* Melbourne: Spinifex
*Hayes, Alan and Daryl Higgs, eds (2014) *Families, Policy and the Law: Selected Essays on Contemporary Issues for Australia* Melbourne: Australian Institute of Family Studies
Hayes, M. G. (2013) 'Ingham and Keynes on the nature of money', in Pixley and Harcourt, eds, pp.31-45
*Hedges, Chris (2016a) 'Reform or revolution' *truthdig* 22 May
*Hedges, Chris (2016b) 'The mafia state' *truthdig* 4 December
Heilbroner, Robert (1996) 'Economics, political and otherwise', in Argyrous and Stilwell, eds, pp.viii-ix
*Henry, James (2012) *The Price of Offshore Revisited* Tax Justice Network
Henwood, Doug (2006) 'The "business community"', in Panitch and Leys, eds, pp.59-77
Hesse, Silke (1990) 'Fascism and the hypertrophy of male adolescence', in J. Milfull, ed., pp.157-75

Hewitson, Gillian J. (1999) *Feminist Economics: Interrogating the Masculinity of Rational Economic Man* Cheltenham, UK; Northampton, MA, USA: Edward Elgar

Higgs, Kerryn (2014) *Collision Course: Endless Growth on a Finite Planet* MIT Press

*Hill, Jess (2015) 'Suffer the children: trouble in the Family Court' *The Monthly* November

*Hill, Jess and Hagar Cohen (2015) 'How funding changes in NSW locked women out of domestic violence refuges' *The Guardian* 9 March

Hindess, Barry (1997) 'Politics and governmentality' *Economy and Society* 26(2): 257-72

Hoagland, Sarah Lucia (1988) *Lesbian Ethics: Toward New Value* Palo Alto, California: Institute of Lesbian Studies

Hollis, Martin and Edward J. Nell (1975) *Rational Economic Man: A Philosophical Critique of Neo-Classical Economics* London and New York: Cambridge University Press

Horkheimer, Max (1972) 'Traditional and critical theory', in Horkheimer *Critical Theory: Selected Essays* New York: Herder and Herder

*Hruska, Joel (2012) 'Apple's record profits built on grinding employees into dust – then blowing them up' *Extremetech* 26 January

Huddleston, Cindy and Valory Greenfield (2002) 'Privatization of TANF in Florida: a cautionary tale' *Clearinghouse Review* 35, Jan-Feb: 540-5

Hudson, Michael (2010) 'From Marx to Goldman Sachs: the fictions of fictitious capital, and the financialization of industry' *Critique* 38(3): 419-44

Hughes, Barry (1980) *Exit Full Employment: Economic Policy in the Stone Age* Sydney: Angus and Robertson Publishers

*Hunt, Jane (2016) 'Judge criticises lack of specific treatment for women who download child porn after Ardleigh woman, 20, is found with 1,200 indecent images' *East Anglian Daily Times* 13 October

Hüppauf, Bernd (1990) 'The birth of fascist man from the spirit of the Front: from Langemarck to Verdun', in Milfull, ed., pp.45-76

*Hurst, Daniel (2014) 'Australia's budget is deteriorating, says commission of audit head' *The Guardian* 15 January

*IMF (1998) 'Financial derivatives', Eleventh Meeting of the IMF Committee on Balance of Payments Statistics

Ince, Susan (1984) 'Inside the surrogate industry', in Arditti et al, eds, pp.99-116

Ingham, Geoffrey (1984) *Capitalism Divided? The City and Industry in British Social Development* Houndmills, Basingstoke: Macmillan Education Ltd

Ingham, Geoffrey (1996) 'Money is a social relation' *Review of Social Economy* 54(4): 507-29

*Ingham, Geoffrey (2000) '"Babylonian madness": on the historical and sociological origins of money', in J. Smithin, ed. *What is Money?* Routledge, Chapter 2, pp.16-41

Ingham, Geoffrey (2002) 'New monetary spaces?', in OECD, ed., pp.123-45

Ingham, Geoffrey (2004a) *The Nature of Money* Cambridge and Malden MA: Polity Press

Ingham, Geoffrey (2004b) 'The emergence of capitalist credit money', in Wray, ed., pp.173-222

Ingham, Geoffrey (2005) 'The social institution of money', in C. Calhoun, C. Rojek and B. Turner, eds *The Sage Handbook of Sociology* London, Thousand Oaks and New Delhi: Sage Publications, pp.154-73

Ingham, Geoffrey (2008) *Capitalism* Cambridge and Malden, MA: Polity

Ingham, Geoffrey (2013) 'Reflections', in Pixley and Harcourt, eds, pp.300-22

Innes, A. Mitchell (2004a[1913]) 'What is money?' in Wray, ed., pp.14-49

Innes, A. Mitchell (2004b[1914]) 'The credit theory of money', in Wray, ed., pp.50-78

*Ireland, Judith (2015) 'Fresh surrogacy concerns over boy abandoned in India' *The Sydney Morning Herald* 14 April

*Isquith, Elias (2015) 'Neoliberalism poisons everything: How free market mania threatens education — and democracy' *Salon* 16 June

*IWF (1998) 'Transitions to W-2: The first six months of welfare replacement' Working Paper, the Institute for Wisconsin's Future

Jaggar, Alison (1983) *Feminist Politics and Human Nature* Totowa NJ: Rowan and Allenheld

*Jamrisko, Michelle (2016) 'Modern Money Theory: radical economics is winning friends' *The Sydney Morning Herald* 14 March

Jeffreys, Sheila (1997) 'Transgender activism' *Journal of Lesbian Studies* 1(3): 55-74

Jeffreys, Sheila (2008a) *The Idea of Prostitution* Melbourne: Spinifex Press

Jeffreys, Sheila (2008b) 'They know it when they see it: the UK Gender Recognition Act 2004' *The British Journal of Politics & International Relations* 10(2): 286-302

*Jeffreys, Sheila (2011) 'The McCarthyism of transgender and the sterilization of transgender children' *GenderTrender* 20 April

*Jeffreys, Sheila (2012) 'Let us be free to debate transgenderism without being accused of "hate speech"' *The Guardian* 29 May

Jeffreys, Sheila (2014). *Gender Hurts: A Feminist Analysis of the Politics of Transgenderism* Abingdon, Oxfordshire: Routledge, Taylor & Francis Group

*Jet (1974) 'Alleged "welfare queen" is accused of $154,000 ripoff' *Jet* XLVII(13), 19 December, pp.16-17

*Jilani, Said (2016) 'John Kasich and the Clintons collaborated on law that helped double extreme poverty' *The Intercept* 14 February

Johnson, Richard (2007) 'Post-hegemony? I don't think so?' *Theory, Culture & Society* 24(3): 95-110

*Johnston, Jenny (2007) 'I bought my baby on the internet' *Daily Mail* 25 July

Johnston, Paul (1989) *Wittgenstein and Moral Philosophy* London and New York: Routledge

Jónasdóttir, Anna G. (1994) Judt, Tony (2010) *Ill Fares the Land: A Treatise on our Present Discontents* London: Penguin

Jung, Carl Gustav (1989) *Aspects of the Masculine* introduction and headnotes by John Beebe. London: Ark Paperbacks

*Kadmos, George and Phillip Anthony O'Hara (2000) 'The taxes-drive-money and employer of last resort approach to government policy' *Journal of Economic and Social Policy* 5(1)

*Kahney, Leander (2006) 'Judging Apple sweatshop charge' *Wired News* 13 June

Kalish, Rachel and Michael Kimmel (2010) 'Suicide by mass murder: masculinity, aggrieved entitlement, and rampage school shootings' *Health Sociology Review* 19(4): 451-64

*Kane, Elizabeth (1989) 'Surrogate parenting: a division of families, not a creation' *Reproductive and Genetic Engineering: Journal of International Feminist Analysis* 2(2): (no page numbers)

Kane, Eugene (2004b) 'Troubles at OIC smear founder's dream' *Milwaukee Journal Sentinel* 14 November

*Kanj, Jamal (2013) 'Modern day slave trade: America's offshore industrial sweat shops' *Global Research* 13 June

Kant, Immanuel (1990[1785]) *Foundations of the Metaphysics of Morals* translated, with an introduction by Lewis White Beck. New York: Macmillan Publishing Company

Kantor, MacKinlay (1955) *Andersonville* World Publishing Company

Kaplan, Alice Yaeger (1986) *Reproductions of Banality: Fascism, Literature and French Intellectual Life* Minneapolis: University of Minnesota Press

*Kapoor, Sony (2010) *The Financial Crisis—Causes and Cures* Brussels: Friedrich-Ebert-Stiftung/Bertelsmannstiftung/European Trade Union Institute

*Katz, Jackson (2012) 'Memo to media: manhood, not guns or mental illness, should be central in Newtown shooting' *Huffington Post* 18 December

Katz, Michael B. (2008) *The Price of Citizenship: Redefining the American Welfare State* Philadelphia: The University of Pennsylvania Press

Keller, Catherine (1986) *From a Broken Web: Separation, Sexism, and Self* Boston: Beacon Press

*Kelly, John (2016) 'The myth of inter-generational debt' *The Australian Independent Media Network* 5 July, 2016

Kennedy, David J. (1998) 'Due process in a privatized welfare system' *Brooklyn Law Review* 64(1): 231-306

Ketchum, Sara Ann (1989) 'Selling babies and selling bodies' *Hypatia* 4(3), 'Ethics & Reproduction', pp.116-27

*Khadem, Nassim (2014) 'Google Australia's tax bill jumps tenfold' *The Sydney Morning Herald* 1 May

*Khadem, Nassim (2015) 'We pay our fair share of tax and create jobs, say Google and Apple' *The Sydney Morning Herald* 5 February

*Kilian, Crawford (2014) 'On capitalism, we are all Pikettists now' *The Tyee* 30 April

Kilty, Keith (2006) 'Welfare reform: what's poverty got to do with it?' in Segal and Kilty, eds, pp.109-20

Kim, Jeounghee (2010) 'Welfare-to-work programs and the dynamics of TANF use' *Journal of Family and Economic Issues* 31(2): 198-211

King, Anthony (1998) 'Income poverty since the early 1970s', in Ruth Fincher and John Nieuwenhuysen, eds *Australian Poverty: Then and Now* Melbourne: Melbourne University Press, pp.71-102

*King, Christopher T. (2016) 'Testimony before the Subcommittee on Human Resources: Getting Incentives Right: Connecting Low-Income Individuals with Jobs', US House Ways and Means Committee, 1 March

King, Christopher T. and Peter R. Mueser (2005) 'Urban welfare and work experiences: implications for welfare reform' *Employment Research Newsletter* W. E. Upjohn Institute for Employment Research 12(3): 1-4

Kirkpatrick, Clifford (1939) *Woman in Nazi Germany* London: Jarrolds Publishers

Kissinger, Meg (2003) 'Top pay at W-2 agencies jumps: some salaries doubled since '96, reaching well into 6 figures' *Milwaukee Journal Sentinel* 16 March

Kitzinger, Celia (1987) *The Social Construction of Lesbianism* London and Newbury Park CA: Sage Publications

Klatch, Rebecca E. (1987) *Women of the New Right* Philadelphia: Temple University Press

Klatch, Rebecca E. (1994) 'Women of the new right in the United States: family, feminism and politics', in Valentine Moghadam, ed. *Identity Politics and Women: Cultural Reassertions and Feminisms in International Perspective* Boulder, CO: Westview Press, pp.367-88

Klein, Naomi (1999) *No Logo: Taking Aim at the Brand Bullies* Random House

Klein, Naomi (2008) *The Shock Doctrine: The Rise of Disaster Capitalism* Penguin Books

Klein, Naomi (2014) *This Changes Everything: Capitalism vs. the Climate* Penguin Books

*Klein, Naomi (2017) 'Get ready for the first shocks of Trump's disaster capitalism' *The Intercept* 25 January

Klein, Renate (1991) 'Women as body parts in the era of reproductive and genetic engineering' *Health Care for Women International* 12(4): 393-405

*Klein, Renate (2006) 'Rhetoric of choice clouds dangers of harvesting women's eggs for cloning' *On Line Opinion* 30 November

Klein, Renate (2008) 'From test-tube women to bodies without women' *Women's Studies International Forum* 31(3): 157-75

Klein, Renate (2009) *Radical Reckonings: Women's Lives, Men's Technologies* North Melbourne: Spinifex Press

*Klein, Renate (2015) 'Can surrogacy be ethical?' *ABC Religion and Ethics* 18 May

Klein, Renate D., ed (1989) *Infertility: Women Speak out about Their Experiences of Reproductive Medicine* London: Pandora Press; Sydney: Allen & Unwin; Boston: Unwin Hyman

Klein, Renate and Robyn Rowland (1988) 'Women as test-sites for fertility drugs, clomiphene citrate and hormonal cocktails' *Reproductive and Genetic Engineering* 1(3): 251-73

*Knight, Alex (2008) 'How capitalism is killing the earth' *End of Capitalism* 18 October. Originally published as 'Special report: How our economy is killing the earth' *New Scientist* issue 2678, 18 October 2008

*Knight, Alex (2009a) 'Is this the end of capitalism?' *End of Capitalism*
*Knight, Alex (2009b) '2. What is capitalism?' *End of Capitalism*
*Knight, Alex (2009c) '3. Why is it breaking down?' *End of Capitalism*
*Knight, Alex (2009d) '4. What comes after capitalism?' *End of Capitalism*
*Knight, Alex (2009e) 'Conclusion: the world we are building' *End of Capitalism*
*Knight, Alex (2013) 'The paradox of capitalism and magnetic revolutionary strategy' *End of Capitalism* 13 June
*Korff, Jens (2016) 'Aboriginal culture - Politics & media - Northern Territory Emergency Response (NTER) - "The Intervention"', *CreativeSpirits*
Kroeber, A.L. and Clyde Kluckhohn (1952) *Culture : A Critical Review of Concepts and Definitions* Vol.XLVII—No.1, papers of the Peabody Museum of American Archaeology and Ethnology, Harvard University. New York: Vintage Books
Kuhn, Annette and AnnMarie Wolpe, eds (1978) *Feminism and Materialism: Women and Modes of Production* London, Boston and Henley: Routledge & Kegan Paul
*Kumar, Manan and Ritika Chopra (2013) 'India's shame story: Israeli paedophile adopts girl through surrogate mother' *dnaindia.com* 8 June
*Kumar, P. C. Vinoj (2015) 'Giving a new life to many a childless couple and a livelihood for women renting their womb' *The Weekend Leader* 6(42), 19 October
*Lahl, Jennifer (2016) 'Europe moves to defend women and children' *The Center for Bioethics and Culture Network* 27 April
Laing, Lesley (2010) *No Way to Live: Women's Experiences of Negotiating the Family Law System in the Context of Domestic Violence* Faculty of Education and Social Work, University of Sydney
Lankford, Adam (2016) 'Race and mass murder in the United States: a social and behavioral analysis' *Current Sociology* 64(3): 470-90
*Lee, Stephanie (2013) 'Outsourcing a life' *San Francisco Chronicle* no date ('reported over 13 days in May and June')
Leed, Eric J. (1978) 'Class and disillusionment in World War I' *The Journal of Modern History* 50(4): 680-99
Leidholdt, Dorchen and Janice G. Raymond, eds (1990) *The Sexual Liberals and the Attack on Feminism* New York: Pergamon Press
Lemke, Thomas (2001) '"The birth of bio-politics": Michel Foucault's lecture at the Collège de France on neo-liberal governmentality' *Economy and Society* 30(2): 190-207
*Leopold, Les (2012) 'Vampire hedge funds are sucking Greece dry' *The Tyee* 20 January
*Levin, Josh (2013) 'The welfare queen' *Slate* 19 December
Levitas, Ruth (1986a) 'Introduction', in Levitas, ed., pp.1-23
Levitas, Ruth (1986b) 'Competition and compliance: the utopias of the New Right', in Levitas, ed., pp.80-106
Levitas, Ruth, ed. (1986) *The Ideology of the New Right* Cambridge: Polity Press
Leys, Colin (2006) 'The cynical state', in Panitch and Leys, eds, pp.1-27

Lightman, Ernie, Dean Herd and Andrew Mitchell (2008) 'Precarious lives: work, health and hunger among current and former welfare recipients in Toronto' *Journal of Policy Practice* 7(4): 242-59

Lightman, Ernie, Andrew Mitchell and Dean Herd (2010) 'Cycling on and off welfare in Canada' *Journal of Social Policy* 39(4): 523-42

*Ling, Lisa (2006) 'Lisa Ling investigates—wombs for rent' *oprah.com* 1 January

Lipset, Seymour Martin (1981[1963]) *Political Man: The Social Bases of Politics* Baltimore, Maryland: The Johns Hopkins University Press

Lipsky, Michael (1984) 'Bureaucratic disentitlement in social welfare programs' *Social Service Review* 58(1): 3-27

*Lohmann, Larry (2015) 'Neoliberalism's climate' *Corner House* 1 October

López, Ian Haney (2015) *Dog Whistle Politics: How Coded Racial Appeals Have Reinvented Racism & Wrecked the Middle Class* Oxford: Oxford University Press

*Loprest, Pamela (2003) 'Disconnected welfare leavers face serious risks' Snapshots of America's Families No. 3. Washington, DC: *The Urban Institute*

*Loprest, Pamela (2011) 'Disconnected families and TANF', November. *The Urban Institute*

*Loprest, Pamela and Austin Nichols (2011) 'Dynamics of being disconnected from work and TANF' May. *The Urban Institute*

*Lower-Basch, Elizabeth (2011a) 'Goals for TANF reauthorization' 24 January, *CLASP*, Policy Solutions that Work for Low Income People

*Lower-Basch, Elizabeth (2011b) 'Cash assistance since welfare reform' 21 January, *CLASP*, Policy Solutions that Work for Low Income People

Loxley, Andrew and Gary Thomas (2001) 'Neo-conservatives, neo-liberals, the new left and inclusion: stirring the pot' *Cambridge Journal of Education* 31(3): 291-301

Lubrano, Alfred (2012) 'Pennsylvania to impose asset test for food stamps' *The Inquirer* 10 January

*Lyngar, Edward (2015) 'Honduras is sold as a libertarian paradise – I went, and discovered a capitalist nightmare' *Alternet* 2 March

Macaldowie, A., Y. A. Wang, G. M. Chambers and E. A. Sullivan (2012) *Assisted Reproductive Technology in Australia and New Zealand 2010* Assisted Reproduction Technology Series No. 16. Cat. no. PER 55. Canberra: Australian Institute of Health and Welfare

*Macaldowie, A., Y. A. Wang, G. M. Chambers and E. A. Sullivan (2013) *Assisted Reproductive Technology in Australia and New Zealand 2011* Sydney: National Perinatal Epidemiology and Statistics Unit, the University of New South Wales

*MacDonald, Trevor (2015) 'Transphobia in the midwifery community' *The Huffington Post* 15 September

MacKinnon, Catharine (1987) *Feminism Unmodified: Discourses on Life and Law* Cambridge, Massachusetts and London: Harvard University Press

MacKinnon, Catharine (1990) 'Liberalism and the death of feminism', in Leidholdt and Raymond, eds, pp.3-13

MacKinnon, Catharine (1991[1989]) *Toward a Feminist Theory of the State* Cambridge, Mass.: Harvard University Press

Macklon, Nick S., Richard L. Stouffer, Linda C. Giudice and Bart C. J. M. Fauser (2006) 'The science behind 25 years of ovarian stimulation for in vitro fertilization' *Endocrine Reviews* 27(2): 170-207

*Maddison, Sarah and Emma Partridge (2007) 'How well does Australian democracy serve sexual and gender minorities?' Report no. 9, School of Social Sciences, Australian National University

Madeley, John (1999) *Big Business, Poor Peoples: The Impact of Transnational Corporations on the World's Poor* London and New York: Zed Books

Mahler, Margaret (1967) 'On human symbiosis and the vicissitudes of individuation' *Journal of the American Psychoanalytic Association* 15(4): 740-63

Mahler, Margaret (1974) 'Symbiosis and individuation: the psychological birth of the human infant' *Psychoanalytic Study of the Child* 29: 89-106

Mahler, Margaret, Fred Pine and Anni Bergman (2000[1975]) *The Psychological Birth of the Human Infant: Symbiosis and Individuation* New York: Basic Books

*Maiden, Malcolm (2014) 'Reserve Bank governor Glenn Stevens nails the "big question"' *The Sydney Morning Herald* 22 July

Males, Mike and Dan Macallair (1999) 'Striking out: the failure of California's "three-strikes you're out" law' *Stanford Law and Policy Review* 11(1): 65

Mangan, J. A. (1999a) 'Prologue: legacies' *The International Journal of the History of Sport* 16(2): 1-10

Mangan, J. A. (1999b) 'The potent image and the permanent prometheus' *The International Journal of the History of Sport* 16(2): 11-22

Mangan, J. A. (1999c) 'Blond, strong and pure: "proto-fascism", male bodies and political tradition' *The International Journal of the History of Sport* 16(2): 107-27

Mangan, J. A. (1999d) 'Icon of monumental brutality: art and the Aryan man' *The International Journal of the History of Sport* 16(2): 128-52

Mangan, J. A. (1999e) 'Epilogue: continuities' *The International Journal of the History of Sport* 16(2): 180-95

Mangan, J. A. (1999f) 'Global fascism and the male body: ambitions, similarities and dissimilarities' *The International Journal of the History of Sport* 16(4): 1-26

Mann, Geoff (2013) 'The monetary exception: labour, distribution and money in capitalism' *Capital & Class* 37(2): 197-216

Manning, Ian and Alice de Jonge (1996) 'The new poverty: causes and responses', in Peter Sheehan, Bhajan Grewal and Margarita Kumnick, eds *Dialogues on Australia's Future: In Honour of the Late Professor Ronald Henderson* Melbourne: Centre for Strategic Studies, Victoria University of Technology

Mantilla, Karla (2000) 'Men in ewes' clothing: the stealth politics of the transgender movement' *Off Our Backs* 30(4): 5, 8-9, 12

*Marchevsky, Alejandra and Jeanne Theoharis (2016) 'Why it matters that Hillary Clinton championed welfare reform' *The Nation* 1 March

Marcuse, Herbert (1971[1969]) 'Repressive tolerance', in R. P. Wolff, B. Moore Jr, and H. Marcuse (1971) *A Critique of Pure Tolerance* London: Jonathan Cape

*Marks, Alexandra (2003) 'Welfare reform, in times of both boom and bust' *The Christian Science Monitor* 22 August

*Marks, Robert E. (2013) 'Learning lessons? The global financial crisis five years on', Economics, University of New South Wales, Sydney, and University of Melbourne

*Marks, Robert E. (2015) 'Learning lessons? The Global Financial Crisis in retrospect' Australian Graduate School of Management, University of New South Wales

Martin, Randy, Michael Rafferty and Dick Bryan (2008) 'Financialization, risk and labour' *Competition & Change* 12(2): 120-32

*Martinez, Elizabeth and Arnoldo García (2000) 'What is "neo-liberalism"? A brief definition' *Global Exchange* 26 February

Marx, Karl (1976[1867]) *Capital: A Critique of Political Economy, Volume I* translated by Ben Fowkes with an introduction by Ernest Mandel. Harmondsworth: Penguin Books in conjunction with *New Left Review*

* Marx, Karl (2010[1894]) *Capital: A Critique of Political Economy, Volume III: The Process of Capitalist Production as a Whole* Institute of Marxism-Leninism, USSR/ International Publishers, NY/Marxists.org

*Mason, Priscilla (2015) 'First tampon for transgender women to hit shelves next month' *United Media Publishing* 6 July

*Matthews, Dylan (2014) 'Everything you need to know about the war on poverty' *The Washington Post* 8 January

*Matthews, Dylan (2015) '26 charts and maps that show the world is getting much, much better' *Vox.com* 20 March

*McLeay, Michael, Amar Radia and Ryland Thomas (2014) 'Money in the modern economy: an introduction' *Quarterly Bulletin*, Monetary Analysis Directorate, Bank of England

*McNeill, Heather (2016) 'Court rules baby Gammy's twin Pipah be raised by Bunbury parents' *WA Today* 14 April

Mead, Lawrence M. (1986) *Beyond Entitlement: The Social Obligations of Citizenship* New York: The Free Press

Mead, Lawrence M., ed. (1997) *The New Paternalism: Supervisory Approaches to Poverty* Washington, DC: Brookings Institution Press

Meagher, Gabrielle (1996) 'Gender in the economy', in Argyrous and Stilwell, eds, pp.38-40

Meagher, Gabrielle and Julie Nelson (2004) 'Survey article: feminism in the dismal science' *Journal of Political Philosophy* 12(1): 102-26

*Medew, Julia (2014) 'IVF pioneer Alan Trounson slams high cost of procedure in Australian clinics' *The Sydney Morning Herald* 23 August

*Medew, Julia and Mark Baker (2013) 'Making babies' *The Sydney Morning Herald* 19 October

Meek, James (2012) 'How we happened to sell off our electricity' *The London Review of Books* 13 September, pp.3-12

Mies, Maria (1982) *Lace Makers of Narsapur: Indian Housewives Produce for the World Market* London: Zed Books

*Mies, Maria (1988) 'From the individual to the dividual: in the supermarket of "reproductive alternatives"' *Reproductive and Genetic Engineering: Journal of International Feminist Analysis* 1(3): 225-37

Mies, Maria (1998) *Patriarchy & Accumulation on a World Scale: Women in the International Division of Labour.* London: Zed Books

Mies, Maria and Vandana Shiva (1993) *Ecofeminism* London: Zed Books; North Melbourne: Spinifex Press

Milfull, John (1990) '"My sex the revolver": fascism as a theatre for the compensation of male inadequacies', in J. Milfull, ed., pp.176-85

Milfull, John, ed. (1990) *The Attractions of Fascism: Social Psychology and Aesthetics of the 'Triumph of the Right'* New York, Oxford and Munich: Berg

*Millard, Elizabeth (2006) 'Is it ethical to own an iPod?' *Yahoo! News*

Miller, Peter and Nikolas Rose (1995)'Political thought and the limits of orthodoxy: a response to Curtis' *The British Journal of Sociology* 46(4): 590-7

*Miller, Shanelle (2014) '"I thought it would be easier to say Gammy died": Farnell daughter' *WAToday* 13 August

*Mishel, Lawrence and John Schmitt (1995) 'Cutting wages by cutting welfare: the impact of reform on the low-wage labor market', Briefing Paper, Economic Policy Institute, Washington

*Mitchell, William F. (Bill) (2001) 'The unemployed cannot find jobs that are not there!' Working Paper No.01-07, Centre of Full Employment and Equity (CofFEE), The University of Newcastle

*Mitchell, Bill (2009) 'The budget deficits will increase taxation!' *billy blog* 20 June

*Mitchell, Bill (2010a) 'Taxpayers do not fund anything' *billy blog* 19 April

*Mitchell, Bill (2010b) 'When governments are financially constrained' *billy blog* 17 September

*Mitchell, Bill (2012) 'Off-shore tax havens—be sure we define the issues correctly' *billy blog* 21 July

*Mitchell, Bill (2014) 'Solving tax avoidance will not cure the Eurozone of stagnation' *billy blog* 15 December

*Mitchell, Bill (2015) 'There is no need to issue public debt' *billy blog* 3 September

*Mitchell, Bill (2016) 'The case for re-nationalisation – Part 2' *billy blog* 21 July

*Mitchell, Bill (2017) 'When mainstream economists jump the shark and lose it completely' *billy blog* 23 January

Mitchell, William F. (Bill) and Warren B. Mosler (2002) 'Fiscal policy and the Job Guarantee' *Australian Journal of Labour Economics* 5(2): 143-59

Mitchell, Juliet (1966) 'Women: the longest revolution' *New Left Review* 1(40): 11-37

Mitchell, Juliet (1971) *Woman's Estate* Harmondsworth: Pelican Books

Mitchell, Juliet (1984) *Women: The Longest Revolution: Essays in Feminism, Literature and Psychoanalysis* London: Virago Press

Mitchell, Juliet and Ann Oakley, eds (1976) *The Rights and Wrongs of Women* Harmondsworth: Pelican Books

Mitchell, Juliet and Ann Oakley, eds (1986) *What is Feminism? A Re-Examination* New York: Pantheon Books

*Mitchell, Thom (2016) 'Explainer: Mike Baird's anti-protest laws—what are they and who hates them' *New Matilda* 7 March

*Mix, Jonah (2016) 'Mass killers don't have a warped view of masculinity—liberal men do' *@JonahMix* 13 June

*Moffitt, R. (2008) 'Welfare reform: the US experience', Working Paper13. Uppsala: Institute for Labour Market Policy Evaluation

*Mohammed, Amina (2015) '1. Deepening income inequality', Outlook on the Global Agenda

*Monbiot, George (2015) 'Follow your convictions – this could be the end of the politics of fear' *The Guardian* 28 January

Moore, Quinn, Robert G. Wood and Anu Rangarajan (2012) 'The dynamics of women disconnected from employment and welfare' *Social Service Review* 86(1): 93-118

*Moore, Suzanne (2013) 'It saddens me that supporting freedom makes me an opponent of equality' *The Guardian* 17 January

*Morath, Eric (2015) 'Get a job? Most welfare recipients already have one' *Wall Street Journal* 13 April

Morgan, Robin (1978) *Going too Far: The Personal Chronicle of a Feminist* New York: Vintage Books

Morgan, Robin, ed. (1970) *Sisterhood is Powerful: An Anthology of Writings from the Women's Liberation Movement* New York: Vintage Books

Morris, Bonnie J. (2005) 'Commentary: valuing woman-only spaces' *Feminist Studies* 31(3): 619-30

*Morris, Randa (2015) 'U.S. maternal death rate now highest in the western world, thanks to GOP war on women' *Addicting Info* 8 June

*Mosler, Warren (2010a) *Seven Deadly Innocent Frauds of Economic Policy* Valance Co., Inc

*Mosler, Warren (2010b) 'Taxes for revenue are obsolete' *Huffington Post* 25 May

Mosse, G. L. (1995) 'Fascist aesthetics and society', in A. del Boca, M. Legnani and M. G. Rossi *Il regime fascista. Storia e storiografia* Laterza, Roma-Bari

Mosse, George L. (1996) *The Image of Man: The Creation of Modern Masculinity* New York and Oxford: Oxford University Press

Motesharrei, Safa, Jorge Rivas and Eugenia Kalnay (2014) 'Human and nature dynamics (HANDY): modeling inequality and use of resources in the collapse or sustainability of societies' *Ecological Economics* 101: 90-102

*Motroc, Gabriela (2016) 'Iceland sentences 26 top bankers to prison' *Australian National Review* 21 January

Moynihan, Daniel Patrick (1996) *Miles to Go: A Personal History of Social Policy* Cambridge, Massachusetts and London: Harvard University Press

Mozes, M., H. Bogokowsky, E. Antebi, B. Lunenfeld, E. Rabau, D.M. Serr, A. David and M. Salomy (1965) 'Thromboembolic phenomena after ovarian stimulation with human gonadotrophins' *The Lancet* 286(7424) 11 December: 1213-15

*Mulligan, Casey B. (2009) 'Inflation and government spending' *The New York Times* 10 June

*Murdoch, Lindsay (2014a) 'Australian couple leaves Down syndrome baby with Thai surrogate' *The Sydney Morning Herald* 1 August

*Murdoch, Lindsay (2014b) 'Surrogate mother of abandoned Gammy vows to look after him' *The Sydney Morning Herald* 2 August

*Murdoch, Lindsay (2014c) 'Surrogacy clinic raided as agent admits 'confusion' over Gammy' *The Sydney Morning Herald* 7 August

*Murdoch, Lindsay and Rachel Browne (2014) 'Gammy's surrogate mother will not allow David and Wendy Farnell to take her baby boy' *The Sydney Morning Herald* 11 August

Murphy, Bruce (2004) 'Missions collide when non-profits try business: moneymaking pulls agencies into ethical, legal quandaries' *Milwaukee Journal Sentinel* 31 May

*Murphy, Damien (2010) 'Newsmaker: Gina Rinehart' *Sydney Morning Herald* 27 November

*Musil, Steven (2012) 'Putting a human cost on the iPad' *Cnet* 25 January

*Nair, Drishya (2013) 'Israel: authorities helpless as convicted paedophile adopts four-year-old girl' *International Business Times* 7 June

*Narayanasamy, Shen (2014) *Banking on Shaky Ground: Australia's Big Four Banks and Land Grabs* Melbourne: Oxfam Australia

NBCC (1990) *Surrogacy: Report 1* Commonwealth of Australia: The National Bioethics Consultative Committee

Nelson, Hilde Lindemann and James Lindemann Nelson (1989) 'Cutting motherhood in two: some suspicions concerning surrogacy' *Hypatia* 4(3), Ethics & Reproduction, pp. 85-94

Nelson, Julie A. (1993) 'The study of choice or the study of provisioning? Gender and the definition of economics', in Ferber and Nelson, eds, pp.23-36

Nelson, Julie A. (1996a) *Feminism, Objectivity and Economics* London and New York: Routledge

Nelson, Julie A. (1996b) 'Gender and the definition of economics', in Argyrous and Stilwell, eds, pp.194-200

Nicholson, Linda (1990) 'Introduction', in Linda Nicholson, ed. *Feminism/ Postmodernism* London and New York: Routledge, pp.1-16

*Nightingale, Demetra Smith and Kelly S. Mikelson (2000) 'An overview of research related to Wisconsin Works (W-2)', Washington: *The Urban Institute*

*Noeth, Bryan and Rajdeep Sengupta (2012) 'A look at credit default swaps and their impact on the European debt crisis' *The Regional Economist* April. Federal Reserve Bank of St Louis

*Nolte, Ellen and C. Martin McKee (2008) 'Measuring the health of nations: updating an earlier analysis' *Health Affairs* 27(1): 58-71

*NSW ADB (nd) 'Factsheet: transgender discrimination', Sydney: NSW Anti-Discrimination Board

*NSW Ministry of Health (2016) *NSW Domestic and Family Blueprint for Reform 2016-2021: Safer Lives for Women, Men and Children*

*Numapo, John (2013) *Commission of Inquiry into the Special Agriculture and Business Lease (SABL)* Port Moresby: Government of Papua New Guinea

Oakley, Ann (1974) *Housewife: High Value—Low Cost* Harmondsworth: Penguin Books

Oakley, Ann (1981) *Subject Women* London: Fontana Paperbacks

O'Brien, Mary (1986[1981]) *The Politics of Reproduction* London and New York: Routledge & Kegan Paul

*OECD, ed. (2002) *The Future of Money* Organisation for Economic Co-operation and Development: Paris

*O'Hehir, Andrew (2010) 'How the bankers fleeced the world' *Salon* 20 May

*Olding, Rachel, (2016) 'Family Court ruling: violent father given sole custody of child' *The Sydney Morning Herald* 17 April

Oliker, Stacey J. (1994) 'Does workfare work? Evaluation research and workfare policy' *Social Problems* 41(2): 195-213

Oliver, Kelly (1989) 'Marxism and surrogacy' *Hypatia* 4(3), Ethics & Reproduction, pp. 95-115

*Olusoga, David (2015) 'The history of British slave ownership has been buried: now its scale can be revealed' *The Guardian* 12 July

Orloff, Ann Shola (2002) 'Explaining U.S. welfare reform: power, gender, race and the U.S. policy legacy' *Critical Social Policy* 22(1): 96-118

Orshansky, Mollie (1965) 'Counting the poor: another look at the poverty profile' *Social Security Bulletin* 28(1): 3-29

Orwell, George (2000[1949]) *Nineteen Eighty-Four* London: Penguin Books

*Ostry, Jonathan D., Andrew Berg and Charalambos G. Tsangarides (2014) *Redistribution, Inequality, and Growth* IMF Staff Discussion Note, SDN/14/02

*Overell, Anne (2009) 'O'Keefe v Sappho's Party Inc' *QUT Wiki* 20 May

*Oxfam (2013) *Sugar Rush: Land Rights and the Supply Chains of the Biggest Food and Beverage Companies*

*Oxfam (2015) 'Extreme carbon inequality: why the Paris climate deal must put the poorest, lowest emitting and most vulnerable people first', 2 December

*Oxfam (2017) 'An economy for the 99%' *Oxfam Briefing Paper* January

Pabst, Georgia (2000) 'Job agency discriminated, commission rules' *Milwaukee Journal Sentinel* 31 August

*Paddenburg, Trevor, Emily Moulton et al (2014) 'Adult son of baby Gammy's father defends his dad over Thai surrogacy row' *news.com.au* 7 August

Pande, Amrita (2009) 'Not an "angel", not a "whore": surrogates as "dirty" workers in India' *Indian Journal of Gender Studies* 16(2): 141-73

Panitch, Leo and Colin Leys, eds (2006) *Telling the Truth: Socialist Register 2006* London: The Merlin Press

Park, Clara Claiborne (1967) *The Siege: The First Eight Years of an Autistic Child* New York: Harcourt, Brace & World

Parker, Philip J. (1982) 'Surrogate motherhood: the interaction of litigation, legislation and psychiatry' *International Journal of Law and Psychiatry* 5(3-4): 341-54

*Partridge, Emma (2014) 'Bunbury shaken by Gammy scandal' *The Sydney Morning Herald* 10 August

*Pascoe, John (2013) 'Issues of forced adoption and international commercial surrogacy', Chief Judge of the Federal Circuit Court of Australia

Patience, Allan (2015) 'Now is the time for all good men and women to come to the aid of the party' *The AIM Network* 10 November

*Pavetti, LaDonna and Liz Schott (2011) 'TANF's inadequate response to recession highlights weakness of block-grant structure: proponents wrong to see it as model for Medicaid, SNAP, or other low-income programs' *Center on Budget and Policy Initiatives* 14 July

*Pavetti, LaDonna and Liz Schott (2016) 'TANF at 20: time to create a program that supports work and helps families meet their basic needs' *Center on Budget and Policy Initiatives* 15 August

*Paxson, Christina and Jane Waldfogel (1999) 'Work, welfare, and child maltreatment', Working Paper 7343, National Bureau of Economic Research, Cambridge, MA

Pearson, Helen (2006) 'Health effects of egg donation may take decades to emerge' *Nature* 442, 10 August, pp.607-8

Peck, Jamie (1998a) 'Workfare in the sun: politics, representation, and method in U.S. welfare-to-work strategies' *Political Geography* 17(5): 535-66

Peck, Jamie (1998b) 'Workfare: a geopolitical etymology' *Environment and Planning D: Society and Space* 16(2): 133-61

Peck, Jamie (2001) *Workfare States* New York: The Guilford Press

Peck, Jamie (2010) 'Zombie neoliberalism and the ambidextrous state' *Theoretical Criminology* 14(1): 104-10

Peck, Jamie, Nik Theodore and Neil Brenner (2012) 'Neoliberalism resurgent? Market rule after the great recession' *South Atlantic Quarterly* 111(2): 265-88

*Percy, Tom (2014) 'Baby Gammy case shows the need for paid surrogacy here' *Perth Now* 2 September

Person, Ethel Spector (1999) *The Sexual Century* New Haven CT: Yale University Press

Peterson, Janice and Meg Lewis, eds (2000) *The Elgar Companion to Feminist Economics* Aldershot: Edward Elgar

*Pew Center on the States, The (2009) *One in 31: The Long Reach of American Corrections* Washington, DC: The Public Safety Performance Project, the Pew Charitable Trusts

Phelps, Linda (1971) 'Patriarchy and capitalism' *Quest* 2(2): 34-48

Phillips, Anne (1987) *Divided Loyalties: Dilemmas of Sex and Class* London: Virago

*Phillips, Gregory Erich (2015) 'Everything you need to know about the secondary mortgage market' *SmartAsset* 12 August

*Picchi, Aimée (2015) 'The shocking reach of U.S. child poverty' *CBS Money Watch* 11 September

*Pierce, Dale (2013) 'Modern Monetary Theory – An Introduction: Part 3 III. Taxing and Spending' *New Economic Perspectives* 24 April

*Piketty, Thomas (2013) *Capital in the Twenty-First Century* translated by Arthur Goldhammer. Cambridge, MA and London: The Belknap Press of Harvard University Press

*Piketty, Thomas (2016) 'Panama Papers: act now. don't wait for another crisis' *The Guardian* 10 April

*Piliavin, Irving, Amy Dworsky and Mark E. Courtney (2003) *What Happens to Families Under W-2 in Milwaukee County, Wisconsin? Report from Wave Two of the Milwaukee TANF Applicant Study* Chapin Hall Center for Children at the University of Chicago

Pine, Fred (2004)'Mahler's concepts of "symbiosis" and separation-individuation: revisited, reevaluated, refined' *Journal of the American Psychoanalytic Association* 52(2): 511-33

*Pinker, Steven (2011) 'Violence vanquished' *The Wall Street Journal* 24 September

Piven, Frances Fox (1997) 'The new reserve army of labor', in Fraser and Freeman, eds, pp.106-118

Piven, Frances Fox (2001) 'Globalization, American politics, and welfare policy' *Annals of the American Academy of Political and Social Science* 577 – Reforming Welfare, Redefining Poverty: 26-37

Piven, Frances Fox (2006) 'Foreword', in Segal and Kilty, eds, p.xix

*Piven, Frances Fox and Richard Cloward (1966) 'The weight of the poor: a strategy to end poverty' *The Nation* 2 May, reprinted in *Common Dreams* 24 March, 2010

Piven, Frances Fox and Richard Cloward (1987a) 'The historical sources of the contemporary relief debate', in Block et al, eds, pp.3-43

Piven, Frances Fox and Richard Cloward (1987b) 'The contemporary relief debate', in Block et al, eds, pp.45-108

Piven, Frances Fox and Richard Cloward (1993) *Regulating the Poor: The Functions of Public Welfare* Updated Edition. New York: Vintage Books

Pixley, Jocelyn (2004) *Emotions in Finance: Distrust and Uncertainty in Global Markets* Cambridge: Cambridge University Press

Pixley, Jocelyn (2013) 'Geoffrey Ingham's theory, money's conflicts and social change', in Pixley and Harcourt, eds, pp.273-299

Pixley, Jocelyn and Geoff Harcourt (2013) 'Introduction to positive trespassing', in Pixley and Harcourt, eds, pp.1-18

Pixley, Jocelyn and G. C. Harcourt, eds (2013) *Financial Crises and the Nature of Capitalist Money: Mutual Developments from the Work of Geoffrey Ingham* Houndmills and New York: Palgrave Macmillan

Plummer, Ken (1981) 'Homosexual categories: some research problems in the labelling perspective of homosexuality', in K. Plummer, ed. *The Making of the Modern Homosexual* London: Hutchinson

Polanyi, Karl (1957[1944]) *The Great Transformation* New York: Beacon Press

*Pollitt, Katha (2016) 'Mike Pence might be even worse for women than Donald Trump is: Trump's vice-presidential pick is a flaming reactionary' *The Nation* 31 July

*Pope Francis (2013) *Apostolic Exhortation Evangelii Gaudium* Rome: The Vatican

*Pritchett, Lant (2003) 'Who is not poor? Proposing a higher international standard for poverty', Working Paper 33, November. Center for Global Development

*Pritchett, Lant (2006) 'Who is not poor? Dreaming of a world truly free of poverty', The World Bank

*Pritchett, Lant (2015) 'The new global goals spell the end of kinky development', Center for Global Development 20 October

*Profitt, Hollis (2014) 'Cancel the Radfems Respond conference at Multnomah Meeting house' *change.org petition*

*Pun, Ngai (2012) 'Apple's dream, Foxconn's nightmare: suicide and the lives of Chinese workers'

*Pun, Ngai and Jenny Chan (2012) 'Global capital, the state, and Chinese workers: the Foxconn experience'

Quadagno, Jill (1994) *The Color of Welfare: How Racism Undermined the War on Poverty* New York: Oxford University Press

Quiggin, John (2010) *Zombie Economics: How Dead Ideas Still Walk among Us* Princeton and Oxford: Princeton University Press

*Quinlan, Daniel, Richard Baker and Nick McKenzie (2014) 'Deaths raise new questions on ANZ funding of Cambodian sugar projects' *The Age* 27 April

Rachels, James (1987) 'A report from America: Baby M' *Bioethics* 14): 357-65

Radin, Margaret Jane (1987) 'Market-inalienability' *Harvard Law Review* 100(8): 1849-1937

*Ralston, Nick (2013) 'Couple offered son to paedophiles' *The Age* 1 July

*Ramesh, Randeep (2010) 'Does getting tough on the unemployed work?' *The Guardian* 16 June

*Ratcliffe, Caroline (2015) 'Child poverty and adult success' Washington: *The Urban Institute*

*Ratcliffe, Caroline, Signe-Mary McKernan and Kenneth Finegold (2007) 'The effect of state food stamp and TANF policies on food stamp program participation' Washington: *The Urban Institute*

Ravallion, Martin (2010) 'How not to count the poor? A reply to Reddy and Pogge', in Anand et al, eds, pp.86-101

*Rawlinson, Kevin (2014) 'Interpol investigates "baby factory" as man fathers 16 surrogate children' *The Guardian* 23 August

Raymond, Janice (1980) *The Transsexual Empire* London: The Women's Press

*Raymond, Janice (1988a) 'The spermatic market: surrogate stock and liquid assets' *Reproductive and Genetic Engineering: Journal of International Feminist Analysis* 1(1))

*Raymond, Janice (1988b) 'In the matter of Baby M: rejudged' *Reproductive and Genetic Engineering: Journal of International Feminist Analysis* 1(2): 175-81

*Raymond, Janice (1989) 'The international traffic in women: women used in systems of surrogacy and reproduction' *Reproductive and Genetic Engineering: Journal of International Feminist Analysis* 2(1): 51-7

Raymond, Janice (1990) 'Reproductive gifts and gift giving: the altruistic woman' *Hastings Center Report* 20(6): 7-11

Raymond, Janice (1994) *Women as Wombs: Reproductive Technologies and the Battle over Women's Freedom* Melbourne: Spinifex Press

*Rea, Samantha (2016) 'I won't be referred to as "non-male" by the Green Party while women still suffer prejudice because of our female bodies' *The Independent* 4 April

Red Collective, The (1973) *The Politics of Sexuality in Capitalism* London: The Red Collective

Reddy, Sanjay G. (2005) 'Counting the poor: the truth about world poverty statistics', in Panitch and Leys, eds, pp.169-78

Reddy, Sanjay (2008) 'The World Bank's new poverty estimates: digging deeper into a hole' *Challenge* 51(6): 105-12

*Reddy, Sanjay G. and Camelia Minoiu (2007) 'Has world poverty really fallen?' *Review of Income and Wealth* 53(3): 484-502

*Reddy, Sanjay G. and Thomas W. Pogge (2002) 'How not to count the poor! – A reply to Ravallion' 15 August

*Reddy, Sanjay G. and Thomas W. Pogge (2003) *How Not to Count the Poor*

*Reddy, Sanjay G. and Thomas W. Pogge (2005) *How Not to Count the Poor* Eldis

Reddy, Sanjay G. and Thomas W. Pogge (2010) 'How not to count the poor', in Anand et al, eds, pp.42-85

Reese, Ellen (2007) 'The causes and consequences of U.S. welfare retrenchment' *Journal of Poverty* 11(3): 47-63

Reese, Ellen, Vincent R. Gledraitis and Eric Vega (2006) 'Welfare is not for sale: campaigns against welfare profiteers in Milwaukee' *Social Justice* 33(3): 38-53

Reiter, Rayna R., ed. (1975) *Toward an Anthropology of Women* New York and London: Monthly Review Press

*Reuters (2011) 'Ruth Madoff says couple tried suicide in 2008' *The New York Times* 26 October

Rhees, Rush (1970) *Discussions of Wittgenstein* London: Routledge & Kegan Paul

*Riccio, James, Daniel Friedlander and Stephen Freedman (1994) *GAIN: Benefits, Costs, and Three-Year Impacts of a Welfare-to-Work Program* New York City and San Francisco: Manpower Demonstration Research Corporation

Rizk, B. and J. Smitz (1992) 'REVIEW: Ovarian hyperstimulation syndrome after superovulation using GnRH agonists for IVF and related procedures' *Human Reproduction* 7(3): 320-27

Roberts, Dorothy E. (1996) 'Welfare and the problem of black citizenship: review' *The Yale Law Journal* 105(6): 1563-1602

*Robins, Brian (2015) 'Energy companies gouging households "because they can"' *The Sydney Morning Herald* 12 October

*Robinson, Eugene (2014) 'Paying for Bush's 2003 invasion of Iraq' *The Washington Post* 11 August

Rochon, Louis-Phillippe and Sergio Rossi (2003) 'Introduction', in Louis-Phillippe Rochon and Sergio Rossi, eds *Modern Theories of Money: The Nature and Role of Money in Capitalist Economies* Cheltenham, UK and Northampton, MA, USA: Edward Elgar, pp.xx-lvi

Roschelle, Anne R. (2008) 'Welfare indignities: homeless women, domestic violence, and welfare reform in San Francisco' *Gender Issues* 25(3): 193-209

*Rose, Andrew K. and Mark M. Spiegel (2015) 'Bond vigilantes and inflation', Working Paper 2015-09, Federal Reserve Bank of San Francisco

Rose, Nikolas (1993) 'Government, authority and expertise in advanced liberalism' *Economy and Society* 22(3): 283-99

Rose, Nikolas (1996) 'The death of the social? Re-figuring the territory of government' *Economy and Society* 25(3): 327-56

Rosenberg, Tracey (2011) *The Girl in the Bunker* Glasgow: Cargo

Rotabi, Karen Smith and Nicole Footen Bromfield (2012) 'The decline in intercountry adoptions and new practices of global surrogacy: global exploitation and human rights concerns' *Affilia* 27(2): 129-41

Rotker, Karyn, Jane Ahlstrom and Fran Bernstein (2002) 'Wisconsin works—for private contractors, that is' *Clearinghouse Review* 35, Jan-Feb: 530-9

Rottnek, Matthew, ed. (1999) *Sissies and Tomboys* New York: NYU Press

Rowbotham, Sheila (1972) *Women, Resistance and Revolution* Harmondsworth: Pelican Books

Rowbotham, Sheila (1973) *Woman's Consciousness, Man's World* Harmondsworth: Pelican Books

Rowbotham, Sheila (1974) *Hidden from History: 300 Years of Women's Oppression and the Fight Against It* Harmondsworth: Pelican Books

Rowbotham, Sheila (1977) *A New World for Women: Stella Browne—Socialist Feminist* London and Dallas, Texas: Pluto Press

Rowland, Robyn (1987) 'Making women visible in the embryo experimentation debate' *Bioethics* 1(2): 179-88

Rowland, Robyn (1990) 'Response to the draft report of the National Bioethics Consultative Committee (NBCC), Surrogacy', in Ewing and Rowland

Rowland, Robyn (1992) *Living Laboratories – Women and Reproductive Technologies* Sydney: Sun Books

Roy, Arundati (2002) *The Algebra of Infinite Justice* London: Flamingo

*Roy, Arundati (2003) 'The US invasion of Iraq: the most cowardly war ever fought in history' *Global Research* 19 June, 2014

*RSC (no date) 'Strengthening our safety net to empower people', The Republican Study Committee

Rubin, Gayle (1975) 'The traffic in women: notes on the "political economy" of sex', in Reiter, ed., pp.157-210

*Rubin, Shira (2013) 'Israeli horror as sex abuser adopts girl, 4' *The Jewish Chronicle* 6 June

*rubyfruit2 (2013) 'The silencing of radical feminists has to stop' *Sisterhoodispowerful* 19 January

Rudrappa, Sharmila (2010) 'Making India the "mother destination": outsourcing labor to Indian surrogates' *Gender and Sexuality in the Workplace, Research in the Sociology of Work* 20: 253-85

Ruml, Beardsley (1946) 'Taxes for revenue are obsolete', in Mosler, 2010b

*Rush, Emma and Andrea La Nauze (2006) *Corporate Paedophilia: Sexualisation of Children in Australia* Discussion Paper Number 90, The Australia Institute, October

Sachs, Karen (1975) 'Engels revisited: women, the organization of production, and private property', in Reiter, ed., pp.211-34

*SACOM (2010) 'Appeal by concerned international scholars: Create humane labor standards at Foxconn and end "stealth manufacturing" in Information Technology!' 8 June. Hong Kong: Students & Scholars against Corporate Misbehaviour

*SACOM (2011a) 'Foxconn and Apple fail to fulfill promises: predicaments of workers after the suicides' 6 May. Hong Kong: Students & Scholars against Corporate Misbehaviour

*SACOM (2011b) 'iSlave behind the iPhone: Foxconn workers in Central China' 24 September. Hong Kong: Students & Scholars against Corporate Misbehaviour

*SACOM (2013) 'Promise from Foxconn on democratic union is broken' Hong Kong: Students & Scholars against Corporate Misbehaviour

Safire, William (1978) Safire's Political Dictionary: An Enlarged, Up-to-Date Edition of The New Politics of Language New York: Random House

Safire, William (1988) 'Coiners' Corner' *New York Times* Magazine—'On Language', 17 July

Sahlins, Marshall (1976) *Culture and Practical Reason* Chicago and London: The University of Chicago Press

*Sales, Leigh (2014) 'Baby Gammy story takes startling turn as extreme options revealed' *ABC 7.30 Report* 17 September

Salleh, Ariel, ed. (2009) *Eco-Sufficiency & Global Justice: Women Write Political Ecology* London: Pluto Press; Melbourne: Spinifex Press

*Salomone, Jo (1992) 'Report on Australian national conference: "surrogacy-in whose interest?," Melbourne, February 1991' *Reproductive and Genetic Engineering: Journal of International Feminist Analysis* 5(1)

Sanford, Nevitt, Craig Comstock and Associates (1971) *Sanctions for Evil: Sources of Social Destructiveness* San Francisco: Jossey-Bass Inc., Publishers

Sanger, Mary Byrna (2003) *The Welfare Marketplace: Privatization and Welfare Reform* Brookings Institution Press

Sargent, Lydia, ed. (1981) *Women and Revolution: A Discussion of the Unhappy Marriage of Marxism and Feminism* Boston MA: South End Press

Saunders, Peter [SPRC] (1994) *Welfare and Inequality: National and International Perspectives on the Australian Welfare State* Cambridge, New York and Melbourne: Cambridge University Press

*Saunders, Peter [SPRC] (1998) 'Defining poverty and identifying the poor: reflections on the Australian experience', Discussion Paper No.84, Kensington: Social Policy Research Centre

*Saunders, Peter [SPRC] (2004) 'Towards a credible poverty framework: from income poverty to deprivation', Discussion Paper No.131, Kensington: Social Policy Research Centre

*Saunders, Peter [SPRC], Jenny Chalmers, Marilyn McHugh, Colette Murray, Michael Bittman and Bruce Bradbury (1998) *Development of Indicative Budget Standards for Australia* DSS Report 74. Budget Standards Unit, Social Policy Research Centre, University of New South Wales

Sawer, Marion, ed. (1982) *Australia and the New Right* Sydney, London, Boston: George Allen and Unwin

*SBS (2013) 'Aussie paedophile gets 30 years in US jail' *SBS News* 10 December

Schilt, Kristen (2006) 'Just one of the guys? How transmen make gender visible at work' *Gender & Society* 20(4): 465-90

Schilt, Kristen and Laurel Westbrook (2009) 'Doing gender, doing heteronormativity: "gender normals," transgender people, and the social maintenance of heterosexuality' *Gender & Society* 23(4): 440-64

*Schmidt, Lucie (2004) 'Effects of welfare reform on the Supplemental Security Income (SSI) program', Policy Brief No.4, October. Ann Arbor, MI: National Poverty Center

*Schmitt, John and Janelle Jones (2012) 'Where have all the good jobs gone?' Center for Economic and Policy Research July

*Schofield, Jack (2006) 'Inside the Apple iPod factories' *The Guardian* 13 June

*Schott, Liz (2007) 'Georgia's increased TANF work participation rate is driven by sharp caseload decline'. Washington: Center on Budget and Policy Priorities

*Schott, Liz and Ife Finch (2010) 'TANF benefits are low and have not kept pace with inflation: benefits are not enough to meet families' basic needs', Washington: Center on Budget and Policy Priorities

*Schott, Liz, Ladonna Pavetti and Ife Floyd (2015) 'How states use federal and state funds under the TANF block grant' Washington: Center on Budget and Policy Priorities

Schram, Sanford F. (1995) *Words of Welfare: The Poverty of Social Science and the Social Science of Poverty* Minneapolis and London: University of Minnesota Press

Schram, Sanford F. and Joe Soss (2001) 'Success stories: welfare reform, policy discourse, and the politics of research' *Annals of the American Academy of Political and Social Science* 577 – Reforming Welfare, Redefining Poverty: 49-65

Schram, Sanford F., Joe Soss, Linda Houser and Richard C. Fording (2010) 'The third level of US welfare reform: governmentality under neoliberal paternalism' *Citizenship Studies* 14(6): 739-54

Schrock, Douglas and Michael Schwalbe (2009) 'Men, masculinity, and manhood acts' *Annual Review of Sociology* 35: 277-95

Schultze, Steve (2000a) 'Wisconsin's top welfare-reform official transferring to state job in Wausau' *Milwaukee Journal Sentinel* 10 February

Schultze, Steve (2000b) 'Critics say W-2 hasn't done enough to stem ills of poverty' *Milwaukee Journal Sentinel* 11 February

Schultze, Steve (2000c) 'W-2 firm in spotlight for N.Y. work: state scrutinizes Maximus on use of reform money' *Milwaukee Journal Sentinel* 3 May

Schultze, Steve (2000d) 'State may take W-2 contract from Maximus: $7.6 million already has been withheld from human service firm' *Milwaukee Journal Sentinel* 26 July

Schultze, Steve (2000e) 'Audit says W-2 vendor billed state for Broadway singer, parties' *Milwaukee Journal Sentinel* 29 July

Schultze, Steve (2000f) 'Regulators accused of being easy on W-2 agencies' *Milwaukee Journal Sentinel* 1 September

Schultze, Steve (2000g) 'New W-2 director talking tough: she tells private agencies that spending will be monitored closely' *Milwaukee Journal Sentinel* 14 September

Schultze, Steve (2000h) 'Maximus to pay back $500,000: firm also plans extra spending for poor after audit' *Milwaukee Journal Sentinel* 14 October

Schultze, Steve (2000i) 'Lawmakers want Maximus fired' *Milwaukee Journal Sentinel* 27 October

Schultze, Steve (2001a) 'W-2 agency misspent $370,000' *Milwaukee Journal Sentinel* 17 February

Schultze, Steve (2001b) 'W-2 staffers given big bonuses' *Milwaukee Journal Sentinel* 28 February

Schultze, Steve (2001c) 'Agency getting out of W-2' *Milwaukee Journal Sentinel* 8 June

Schultze, Steve (2001d) 'State budget would limit W-2 executives' pay: measure is among provisions aimed at fixing the program' *Milwaukee Journal Sentinel* 22 June

Schultze, Steve (2001e) 'W-2 provider in financial pinch: UMOS deficit reflects state caseload rise' *Milwaukee Journal Sentinel* 31 October

Schultze, Steve (2002a) 'Study questions cost, effectiveness of W-2: agencies spent 63 cents on the dollar for program, administrative expenses' *Milwaukee Journal Sentinel* 21 December

Schultze, Steve (2002b) 'Benefits to W-2 clients docked unfairly: agency was pushed to raise sanction level, records show' *Milwaukee Journal Sentinel* 3 May

Schultze, Steve (2003a) 'YW Works cut out of W-2: state revamps county's welfare providers, dropping 1, reducing 1' *Milwaukee Journal Sentinel* 5 August

Schultze, Steve (2003b) 'County gains W-2 money: state shifts $11 million more here, prompts complaints others will be shorted' *Milwaukee Journal Sentinel* 9 October

Schultze, Steve (2003d) 'Opportunities Industrialization Center non-profit group has been awarded about $147 million' *Milwaukee Journal Sentinel* 20 November

Schultze, Steve (2004a) 'W-2 firm under close watch: fate of agency's contract lies in findings of state audit' *Milwaukee Journal Sentinel* 7 January

Schultze, Steve (2004b) 'W-2's poor stay poor, audit finds: most still earn poverty wages after leaving welfare program' *Milwaukee Journal Sentinel* 8 April

Schultze, Steve (2004c) 'State tells W-2 agency to improve: OIC given 10 days to devise corrective plan or lose contract' *Milwaukee Journal Sentinel* 23 September

Schultze, Steve (2004d) 'Former welfare execs' pay total in millions: in 1997-2003, Gee got $1.75 million, Clay $1.35 million' *Milwaukee Journal Sentinel* 13 November

Schultze, Steve (2004e) 'State postpones its decision on OIC's fate: troubled W-2 agency could see contract cut' *Milwaukee Journal Sentinel* 20 November

Schultze, Steve (2005a) 'W-2 plan criticized: providers take aim at Doyle's idea to reduce funding for program' *Milwaukee Journal Sentinel* 19 February

Schultze, Steve (2005b) 'W-2's poor stay poor, audit finds: most still earn poverty wages after leaving welfare program' *Milwaukee Journal Sentinel* 8 April

Schultze, Steve (2005c) 'Political winds rattle W-2: focus on jobs is shaky at times' *Milwaukee Journal Sentinel* 2 May

Schultze, Steve (2005d) '26 W-2 agencies fall short: 3 in Milwaukee among those failing to meet standards' *Milwaukee Journal Sentinel* 7 May

Schultze, Steve (2005e) 'Maximus bonuses hit $700,000: W-2 agency balks at releasing details, state says' *Milwaukee Journal Sentinel* 21 July

Schultze, Steve (2005f) 'W-2 bonuses appear illegal: Maximus leaders got $41,510 in tax funds' *Milwaukee Journal Sentinel* 4 August

Schultze, Steve (2005g) 'Maximus ordered to repay state for bonuses; Executives got $35,400 in tax funds' *Milwaukee Journal Sentinel* 5 August

Schultze, Steve (2007) 'Client's lawsuit puts W-2 in unfamiliar territory: agency goes to court to boot harassment case plaintiff from its rolls, but state says that may be overreach of authority' *Milwaukee Journal Sentinel* 3 March

Schultze, Steve (2009) 'W-2 clients get to pick agencies: aid covers more time in technical college classes' *Milwaukee Journal Sentinel* 16 October

Schultze, Steve and Leonard Sykes Jr (2005) 'Embattled OIC to close its doors: deep financial crisis is final blow to agency' *Milwaukee Journal Sentinel* 11 February

Schwalbe, Michael (2014) *Manhood Acts: Gender and the Practices of Domination* Boulder, CO: Paradigm

Schwartz, John E. and Thomas J. Volgy (1992) *The Forgotten Americans: Thirty Million Working Poor in the Land of Opportunity* New York: W. W. Norton

Schwartz-Nobel, Loretta (2002) *Growing Up Empty: How Federal Policies are Starving America's Children* New York and London: HarperCollins

*Scott, Amy (2007) '"Wombs for rent" grows in India' *Marketplace*

Scott, Rosie and Anita Heiss, eds (2015) *The Intervention: An Anthology* Vermont, Victoria: Concerned Australians

Scruton, Roger (1984) *The Meaning of Conservatism* London: The Macmillan Press

*Scrutton, Alistair and Ragnhildur Sigurdardottir (2015) 'Iceland convicts bad bankers and says other nations can act' *Reuters* 13 February

*Scully, Mary (2016) 'Mary Scully Reports', 29 May

Scutt, Jocelynne A. (1990) 'Book review: *Infertility: Women Speak out about Their Experiences of Reproductive Medicine*, by Renate D. Klein. Pandora Press, London, 1989; and *The Exploitation of a Desire: Women's Experiences with In VitroFertilisation—An Exploratory Survey*, by Renate Klein. Women's Studies Summer Institute - Deakin University, Australia, 1989' *Women's Studies International Forum* 13(6): 605-8

*Scutt, Jocelynne A. (1991) 'Whose surrogate? Surrogacy, ethics, and the law' *Reproductive and Genetic Engineering: Journal of International Feminist Analysis* 4(2): 93-107

Scutt, Jocelynne A., ed. (1988) *The Baby Machine. Commercialisation of Motherhood* Melbourne: McCulloch Publishing

*Seater, John (2008) 'Government debt and deficits' *Library of Economics and Liberty*

Segal, Elizabeth and Keith Kilty, eds (2006) *The Promise of Welfare Reform: Political Rhetoric and the Reality of Poverty in the Twenty-first Century* New York: Haworth Press

Segal, Lynne (1987) *Is the Future Female? Troubled Thoughts on Contemporary Feminism* London: Virago

Segal, Lynne, ed. (1983) *What is to be Done about the Family? Crisis in the Eighties* Harmondsworth: Penguin Books

Shalev, Carmel (1998) 'Halakha and patriarchal motherhood—an anatomy of the new Israeli surrogacy law' *Israel Law Review* 32(1): 51-80

*Shaxson, Nicholas, John Christensen and Nick Mathiason (2012) *Inequality: You Don't Know the Half of It* Tax Justice Network

Shipler, David K. (2005) *The Working Poor: Invisible in America* New York: Vintage Books

Shiva, Vandana (1992) *The Violence of the Green Revolution: Ecological Degradation and Political Conflict in Punjab* New Delhi: Zed Press

Shiva, Vandana (1997) *Biopiracy: the Plunder of Nature and Knowledge* Cambridge, Mass: South End Press

Shiva, Vandana (2000) *Stolen Harvest: The Hijacking of the Global Food Supply* Cambridge, Mass: South End Press

Shiva, Vandana (2001) *Patents, Myths and Reality* Penguin India

Shiva, Vandana (2002) *Water Wars: Privatization, Pollution, and Profit* Cambridge, Mass: South End Press

Shiva, Vandana (2005) *Globalization's New Wars: Seed, Water and Life Forms* New Delhi: Women Unlimited

Shiva, Vandana (2008) *Soil Not Oil* Cambridge, Mass: South End Press

Shiva, Vandana (2012) *Making Peace with the Earth* Melbourne: Spinifex Press

*Short, Kathleen (2011) *The Research: Supplemental Poverty Measure: 2010* U.S. Census Bureau, Economics and Statistics Division, U. S. Department of Commerce

Shragge, Eric, ed. (1997) *Workfare: Ideology for a New Underclass* Toronto: Garamond Press

Shutt, Harry (1998) *The Trouble with Capitalism: An Enquiry into the Causes of Global Economic Failure* London: Zed Books

Simmel, Georg (1908) 'On domination', in Simmel, 1971, pp.96-120

Simmel, Georg (1971) *On Individuality and Social Forms: Selected Writings* edited and with an introduction by Donald N. Levine. Chicago and London: The University of Chicago Press

*Simon, David (2013) 'There are now two Americas. My country is a horror show' *The Guardian* 8 December

*Simon, Michele (2012) *Food Stamps: Follow the Money. Are Corporations Profiting from Hungry Americans?* Eat Drink Politics, an industry watchdog consulting group

Singh, Ajit (1995) 'International requirements for full employment in advanced countries' *International Labour Review* 134(4-5): 471-96

*Sirico, Rev. Robert A. (2007) 'What is capitalism?' The Acton Institute

*Sloan, Kathleen (2016) 'India's new surrogacy law: much to applaud but major issues remain', Stop Surrogacy Now

*Smith, Adam (2007[1776]) *An Inquiry into the Nature and Causes of the Wealth of Nations* edited by S. M. Soares, MetaLibri Digital

*Snow, Deborah and Lindsay Murdoch (2014) 'Gammy surrogacy case fires up debate on bigger issues' *The Sydney Morning Herald* 9 August

*Snyder, Michael (2015) 'Goodbye middle class: 51 percent of all American workers make less than 30,000 dollars a year' *Washington Blog* 21 October

Solow, R. M. (1998) *Work and Welfare* Princeton, NJ: Princeton University Press

*Sontag, Susan (1974) 'Fascinating fascism', in *The Susan Sontag Reader* Harmondsworth: Penguin, 1982, pp.305-25

*South Commission, The (1990) *The Challenge to the South: The Report of the South Commission* Oxford, New York and Toronto: Oxford University Press

Spackman, Barbara (1996) *Fascist Virilities: Rhetoric, Ideology, and Social Fantasy in Italy* Minneapolis and London: University of Minnesota Press

Spallone, Patricia (1989) *Beyond Conception. The New Politics of Reproduction* London: Macmillan Education

Spallone, Patricia and Deborah Lynn Steinberg, eds (1987) *Made to Order. The Myth of Reproductive and Genetic Progress* The Athene Series. Oxford and New York: Pergamon Press

Spar, Debora L. (2006) *The Baby Business. How Money, Science and Politics Drive the Commerce of Conception* Boston: Harvard Business School Press

Stafford-Bell, Martyn A., Sam G. Everingham and Karin Hammarberg (2014) 'Outcomes of surrogacy undertaken by Australians overseas' *Medical Journal of Australia* 201: 330-3

*Stechyson, Natalie (2013a) 'And baby makes four' *Leader-Post* 26 September

*Stechyson, Natalie (2013b) 'Part 2: Patchwork of Canadian laws creates confusion in determining parental rights for gay and lesbian parents' *Leader-Post* 8 October

*Steinberg, Michele (1999) 'America's missing in action: Al Gore's genocide vs. the poor' *Executive Intelligence Review* 26(26): 25 June

Steiner, Gilbert Y. (1966) *Social Insecurity: The Politics of Welfare* Chicago: Rand McNally & Company

*Stelter, Brian (2011) 'Spotlight from Glenn Beck brings a CUNY professor threats' *New York Times* 21 January

Stenson, Kevin (1993) 'Community policing as a governmental technology' *Economy and Society* 22(3): 373-89

*Stevens, Glen (2014) 'Challenges for economic policy', address to The Anika Foundation Luncheon (Supported by Australian Business Economists and Macquarie Bank) Sydney, 22 July

Stevenson, Dru (2002) 'Privatized welfare and the nondelegation doctrine' *Clearinghouse Review* 35, Jan-Feb: 546-556

*Stockholm UN Association (2016) 'Response to the consultation relating different paths to parenthood', SOU 2016: 11

Stoesz, David (1997) 'Welfare behaviorism' *Society* March/April, 34(3): 68-77

Stoller, Robert J. (1984[1968, 1974]) *Sex and Gender: The Development of Masculinity and Femininity* London: H. Karnac (Books) Ltd.

Stoltenberg, John (1989) *Refusing to Be a Man: Essays on Sex and Justice* New York: A Meridian Book

Strassman, Diana (1993) 'Not a free market: the rhetoric of disciplinary authority in economics', in Ferber and Nelson, eds, pp.54-68

*Street, Paul (2015) 'Deleting crimes at the *New York Times*: airbrushing history at the paper of record' *Counterpunch* 24 July

Stuckler, David and Sanjay Basu (2013) *The Body Economic: Why Austerity Kills* New York: Basic Books

*Stuhmcke, Anita (1995) 'For love or money: the legal regulation of surrogate motherhood' *Murdoch University Electronic Journal of Law* 2(3)

Stulz, René M. (2010) 'Credit default swaps and the credit crisis' *Journal of Economic Perspectives* 24(1): 73-92

Summers, Anne (1975) *Damned Whores and God's Police: The Colonization of Women in Australia* Harmondsworth: Penguin Books

Sussex, Lucy (1991) 'Mother-of-all', in Hawthorne and Klein, eds, pp.95-127

*Sydney Morning Herald (2014) 'Gammy case demands background checks' *The Sydney Morning Herald* Editorial, 8 August

Szanton, Peter L. (1991) 'The remarkable "quango": knowledge, politics, and welfare reform' *Journal of Policy Analysis and Management* 10(4): 590-602

*Szego, Julie (2014) 'It sounds scary, but renting a womb makes sense' *The Age* 13 August

Tankard Reist, Melinda and Abigail Bray, eds (2011) *Big Porn Inc: Exposing the Harms of the Global Porn Industry* Melbourne: Spinifex Press

*Taylor, Ian and Lynn Sloman (2012) *Rebuilding Rail Transport for Quality of Life Ltd*

Theweleit, Klaus (1987) *Male Fantasies I: Women, Floods, Bodies, History* Cambridge: Polity Press

Theweleit, Klaus (1989) *Male Fantasies II: Male Bodies, Psychoanalyzing the White Terror* Cambridge: Polity Press

Thompson, Denise (1989) 'The "sex/gender" distinction: a reconsideration' *Australian Feminist Studies* no.10, Summer: 23-31

Thompson, Denise (1991a) *Reading Between the Lines: A Lesbian Feminist Critique of Feminist Accounts of Sexuality* Sydney: The Gorgon's Head Press

*Thompson, Denise (1991b) *The Radical Feminist Account of Domination* (pamphlet) UNSWorks, Library of the University of New South Wales [access under 'Links']

Thompson, Denise (1994a) 'Defining feminism' *Australian Feminist Studies* 20: 171-92

*Thompson, Denise (1994b) 'Asking questions about racism' (working paper) UNSWorks, Library of the University of New South Wales [access under 'Links']

*Thompson, Denise (1994c) 'What does it mean to call feminism white and middle-class?' (working paper) UNSWorks, Library of the University of New South Wales [access under 'Links']

*Thompson, Denise (1994d) 'Feminism and racism: what is at stake?' (working paper) UNSWorks, Library of the University of New South Wales [access under 'Links']

*Thompson, Denise (1996) *Against the Dismantling of Feminism: A Study in the Politics of Meaning* PhD Thesis, University of New South Wales [access under 'Links']

*Thompson, Denise (1997) 'Feminism and the problem of individualism' (working paper) UNSWorks, Library of the University of New South Wales [access under 'Links']

*Thompson, Denise (1998a) 'Individualising the social: or, whatever happened to male domination?' (working paper) UNSWorks, Library of the University of New South Wales [access under 'Links']

*Thompson, Denise (1998b) 'Feminism and the struggle over meaning' (working paper) UNSWorks, Library of the University of New South Wales [access under 'Links']

*Thompson, Denise (1999) 'The trouble with individualism ...: a discussion with some examples' (working paper) UNSWorks, Library of the University of New South Wales [access under 'Links']

*Thompson, Denise (2000a) 'What counts as feminist theory?' (working paper) UNSWorks, Library of the University of New South Wales [access under 'Links']

*Thompson, Denise (2000b) 'What can rights discourse cover up?' (working paper) UNSWorks, Library of the University of New South Wales [access under 'Links']

Thompson, Denise (2001) *Radical Feminism Today* London: SAGE Publications Ltd

*Thompson, Denise (2005a) 'Liberalism, human rights and a culture of domination: a feminist analysis—Introduction' Denise Thompson, Feminist Theorist

*Thompson, Denise (2005b) 'Liberalism, human rights and a culture of domination: a feminist analysis—Individualism: some distinctions' Denise Thompson, Feminist Theorist

*Thompson, Denise (2005c) 'Liberalism, human rights and a culture of domination: a feminist analysis—on domination' Denise Thompson, Feminist Theorist

*Thompson, Denise (2002a) 'Power and distaste: tolerance and its limitations' (working paper) UNSWorks, Library of the University of New South Wales [access under 'Links']

*Thompson, Denise (2002b) 'Marcuse and his critics' (working paper) UNSWorks, Library of the University of New South Wales [access under 'Links']

Times of Israel (2014) 'Cabinet approves "surrogacy equality" bill for gay couples' *The Times of Israel* 1 June

*TJN (2016) 'Tax havens & financial crisis' *The Tax Justice Network* April

Tovino, Stacey A. (2005/2006) 'Review: The Birth of Surrogacy in Israel by D. Kelly Weisberg' *Journal of Law and Religion* 21(1): 255-8

*Trans Women (2010) '"Let the trans women speak!" A response to Camp Trans' *Pink and Black Attack* no.6, pp.9-10

Turner, Lesley J., Sheldon Danziger and Kristin S. Seefeldt (2006) 'Failing the transition from welfare to work: women chronically disconnected from employment and cash welfare' *Social Science Quarterly* 87(2): 227-49

*Tymoigne, Éric and L. Randall Wray (2013) 'Modern Money Theory 101: A Reply to Critics', Annandale-on-Hudson, NY: Levy Economics Institute

*UK Government (2013) *Story of the Prison Population 1995-2009 England and Wales* Ministry of Justice Statistics Bulletin

*UK Government (2018) *Reform of the Gender Recognition Act – Government Consultation* LGBT Policy Team, Government Equalities Office

*UNDP (1997) *Human Development Report 1997* New York and Oxford: Oxford University Press

*UNDP (2002) *Human Development Report 2002: Deepening Democracy in a Fragmented World* New York and Oxford: United Nations Development Programme

*UNDP (2010) *The Real Wealth of Nations: Pathways to Human Development Human Development Report 2010, 20th Anniversary Edition.* New York: United Nations Development Programme

*UNDP (2013) *Human Development Report—The Rise of the South: Human Progress in a Diverse World* New York: United Nations Development Programme

*UN FAO (2013) *Trends and Impacts of Foreign Investment in Developing Country Agriculture: Evidence from Case Studies* Rome: Food and Agriculture Organization of the United Nations

*United Nations (2000) *Protocol to Prevent, Suppress and Punish Trafficking in Persons, Especially Women and Children, Supplementing the United Nations Convention against Transnational Organized Crime*

*United Nations (2013) *Inequality Matters: Report of the World Social Situation* ST/ESA/345. New York: Department of Economic and Social Affairs, United Nations

*United Nations (2015) *The Millennium Development Goals Report 2015* New York: United Nations

Unsworth, Barry (1992) *Sacred Hunger* London: Hamish Hamilton

*Upadhayaya, Venus (2013) 'Thousands of child-laborers dismantle e-waste in India's capital' *Epoch Times* 2 September

*US Attorney's Office (2013) 'Hogsett announces sentencing of Australian man in prosecution of international child exploitation conspiracy', 9 December. Department of Justice, U.S. Attorney's Office, Southern District of Indiana

*US CBO (2015) 'Estimated impact of the American Recovery and Reinvestment Act on employment and economic output 2014', Congressional Budget Office, February

*US CDC (2014) 2014 *Assisted Reproductive Technology National Summary Report* National Center for Chronic Disease Prevention and Health Promotion, Division of Reproductive Health, US Department of Health and Human Services, October

*US CSE (1996) 'The Personal Responsibility and Work Opportunity Reconciliation Act of 1996', The Office of Child Support Enforcement, Administration for Children and Families, U. S. Department of Health & Human Services

*US DHHS (2001) 'State welfare waivers: an overview' Department of Health and Human Services

*US GAO (2002) *Welfare Reform: Federal Oversight of State and Local Contracting Can Be Strengthened* Report to Congressional Requesters. Washington: United States General Accounting Office

*US Institute of Medicine (2013a) 'U.S. health in international perspective: shorter lives, poorer health' *Report Brief* January

*US Institute of Medicine (2013b) *U.S. Health in International Perspective: Shorter Lives, Poorer Health* Washington: National Research Council and US Institute of Medicine of the National Academies

*US OFA (2016a) *Characteristics and Financial Circumstances of TANF Recipients, Fiscal Year 2015* Office of Family Assistance, Office for the Administration of Children & Families, Department of Health and Human Services

*US OFA (2016b) *The President's Fiscal Year 2017 Budget: Strengthening the Temporary Assistance for Needy Families (TANF) Program* Office of Family Assistance, Office for the Administration of Children & Families, Department of Health and Human Services

*Van Gelder, Lawrence (1997) 'Noel Keane, 58, lawyer in surrogate mother cases, is dead' *New York Times* 28 January

*Vanstone, Amanda (2014) 'Rich versus poor is the wrong debate' *The Sydney Morning Herald* 13 October

*Victorian Government (2010) *Building Respect* Melbourne: State Government of Victoria

*Vigo, Julian (2013) 'Transcending the norms of gender: the left hand of darkness' *Counterpunch* 7-9 June

*Vine, David (2015) 'Garrisoning the globe: how U.S. military bases abroad undermine national security and harm us all' *TomDispatch* 13 September

Wacquant, Loïc (2002) 'From slavery to mass incarceration: rethinking the "race question" in the US' *New Left Review* 13, Jan/Feb, pp.41-60

Wacquant, Loïc (2009) *Punishing the Poor: The Neoliberal Government of Insecurity* Durham, NC: Duke University Press

Wacquant, Loïc (2010) 'Crafting the neoliberal state: workfare, prisonfare, and social insecurity' *Sociological Forum* 25(2): 197-220

Wacquant, Loïc (2012) 'Three steps to a historical anthropology of actually existing neoliberalism' *Social Anthropology* 20(1): 66-79

Wacquant, Loïc (2013) 'Constructing neoliberalism: opening salvo' *Nexus* 25(1): 1, 8-9

Waddan, Alex (2010) 'The US safety net, inequality and the Great Recession' *Journal of Poverty and Social Justice* 18(3): 243-54

*Wade, Matt (2016) 'Radical economic ideas grab attention amid low-inflation torpor' *The Sydney Morning Herald* 25 March

*Wahlquist, Calla (2014) 'Baby Gammy drama: Wendy Farnell, Gammy's twin sister Pipah return to Perth after funeral in China' *Perth Now* 30 September

*Wahlquist, Calla and Joe Spagnolo (2014) 'Gammy scandal: DCP confirms WA twin sister taken to China by mother Wendy Farnell' *Perth Now* 25 September

Waldron, Jeremy, ed. (1987) *"Nonsense Upon Stilts": Bentham, Burke and Marx on the Rights of Man* London and New York: Methuen

Wallerstein, Immanuel, Randall Collins, Michael Mann, Georgi Derlugian and Craig Calhoun (2013) *Does Capitalism Have a Future?* Oxford: Oxford University Press

Walters, William (1994) 'The discovery of "unemployment": new forms for the government of poverty' *Economy and Society* 23(3): 265-90

Waring, Marilyn (1985) *Women, Politics & Power* Wellington: Allen & Unwin New Zealand, Port Nicholson Press

Waring, Marilyn (1988) *Counting for Nothing: What Men Value and What Women Are Worth* Wellington: Allen & Unwin New Zealand, Port Nicholson Press

*Watkins, Thayer (2008) 'The nature and origin of the subprime mortgage crisis' Department of Economics, San José State University

Watson, William (2015) *The Inequality Trap: Fighting Capitalism Instead of Poverty* Toronto, Buffalo and London: University of Toronto Press

*Weber, Max (1927) *General Economic History* Chapter XXII, 'The Meaning and Presuppositions of Modern Capitalism', translated by Frank H. Knight, Greenberg, Publisher

Weber, Max (1964[1947]) *Max Weber: The Theory of Social and Economic Organisation* translated by A. M. Henderson and Talcott Parsons. New York: The Free Press

Weber, Max (1976[1905/1930]) The Protestant Ethic and the Spirit of Capitalism translated by Talcott Parsons. London: George Allen & Unwin Ltd

*Weber, Max (1978[1968]) *Economy and Society: An Outline of Interpretive Sociology* edited by Guenther Roth and Claus Wittich. Berkeley, Los Angeles and London: University of California Press

*Webster, Nick (2006) 'Welcome to iPod city' *The Daily Mirror* 14 June

*Webster, Stephen C. (2012) 'Perry "proudly" refuses health care to 1.2 million low-income Texans' *The Raw Story* 9 July

Weinbaum, Batya (1978) *The Curious Courtship of Women's Liberation and Socialism* York, PA, USA: South End Press

*Weissmann, Jordan (2016) 'The failure of welfare reform: how Bill Clinton's signature legislative achievement tore America's safety net' *Slate* 1 June

*We Own It (no date) 'Public services for people not profit'

*Werlhof, Claudia von (2015) 'Neoliberal globalization: is there an alternative to plundering the earth?' in Michel Chossudovsky and Andrew Gavin Marshall, eds (2010) *The Global Economic Crisis: The Great Depression of the XXI Century* Montréal: Global Research Publishers, pp.116-44

*West, Michael (2015a) 'Inquiry's roll-call of tax avoiders' *The Sydney Morning Herald* 6 February

*West, Michael (2015b) 'Google paying a fraction of the tax in Australia it should' *The Sydney Morning Herald* 9 February

Whitaker, Dan (2013) 'The uncatchable lizard' *History Today* 63(2): 29-35

*Williams, Eric (1944) *Capitalism and Slavery* Chapel Hill: University of North Carolina Press

Williams, Lucy A. (1994) 'The abuse of Section 115 waivers: welfare reform in search of a standard' *Yale Law and Policy Review* 12(1): 8-37

Williams, Raymond (1986[1973]) *Keywords: A Vocabulary of Culture and Society* London: Fontana Paperbacks

*Winkler, Anne E. (1993) 'AFDC-UP, two-parent families, and the Family Support Act of 1988: evidence from the 1990 CPS and the 1987 NSFH', Discussion Paper no. 1013-93, Institute for Research on Poverty, University of Wisconsin-Madison

*Winkler, Ute (1988) 'New U.S. know-how in Frankfurt—a "surrogate mother" agency' *Reproductive and Genetic Engineering: Journal of International Feminist Analysis* 1(2): 205-7

Winnicott, D.W. (1960) 'The theory of the parent-infant relationship' International *Journal of Psycho-Analysis* 41: 585-95

*Wisconsin LAB (2000) 'Letter of Transmittal', Madison: Legislative Audit Bureau, July

*Wisconsin LAB (2001) *An Evaluation: Wisconsin Works (W-2) Program* Madison: Legislative Audit Bureau, April

*Wisconsin LAB (2005a) *An Evaluation: Wisconsin Works (W-2) Program* Madison: Legislative Audit Bureau, April

*Wisconsin LAB (2005b) *Financial Management of Selected W-2 Agencies* Madison: Legislative Audit Bureau, July

*Wisconsin W-2 Monitoring Task Force (2002) 'A Report on W-2 implementation in Milwaukee County', W-2 Monitoring Task Force of the Milwaukee County Board of Supervisors, December

Wolff, Tobias Barrington (2002) 'The Thirteenth Amendment and slavery in the global economy' *Columbia Law Review* 102(4): 973-1050

*Wood, Robert and Anu Rangarajan (2003) 'What's happening to TANF leavers who are not employed? Trends in welfare-to-work', *Issue Brief* No. 6. Princeton, NJ: Mathematica Policy Research

Woolf, Virginia (1938) 'Three guineas', in *A Room of One's Own and Three Guineas* London: Vintage Books

*World Bank (1990) *World Development Report 1990: Poverty* Washington: International Bank for Reconstruction and Development

*World Bank (2015) 'World Bank's new end-poverty tool: surveys in poorest countries', *The World Bank* 15 October

Wray, L. Randall (2004) 'Conclusion: the credit money and state money approaches', in Wray, ed., pp.223-62

*Wray, L. Randall (2011) 'MMT: a doubly retrospective analysis', Keynote: CofEE Conference, University of Newcastle New Economic Perspectives 11 December

*Wray, L. Randall (2011-12) 'Modern money theory: a primer on macroeconomics for sovereign monetary systems' *New Economic Perspectives* 6 June

Wray, L. Randall (2013) 'A new meme for money', in Pixley and Harcourt, eds, pp.79-100

*Wray, L. Randall (2014) 'From the State theory of money to Modern Money Theory: an alternative to economic orthodoxy', Levy Economics Institute Working Paper No. 792

Wray, L. Randall, ed. (2004) *Credit and State Theories of Money: The Contribution of A. Mitchell Innes* Cheltenham, UK and Northampton, MA, USA: Edward Elgar

*Wroe, David (2016) 'Australian of the Year: Catherine McGregor sorry after saying David Morrison choice was "weak"' *The Sydney Morning Herald* 27 January

Wrong, Dennis H. (1961) 'The oversocialized conception of man in modern sociology' *American Sociological Review* 26(2): 183-93

*Youdelman, Sondra with Paul Getsos (2004) *Wages Work! An Examination of New York City's Parks Opportunity Program (POP) and Its Participants* Community Voices Heard

*Youdelman, Sondra with Paul Getsos (2005) *The Revolving Door: Research Findings on NYC's Employment Services and Placement System and Its Effectiveness in Moving People from Welfare to Work* a research project by Community Voices Heard

*Zagema, Bertram (2011) *Land and Power: The Growing Scandal Surrounding the New Wave of Investments in Land* Oxfam International

*Zedlewski, Sheila (2002) 'Left behind or staying away? Eligible parents who remain off TANF', Washington, D.C.: The Urban Institute, *Assessing the New Federalism Policy Brief* B-51

*Zedlewski, Sheila, Thomas Callan and Gregory Acs (2012) 'TANF at 16: what do we know?' *Low Income Working Families Fact Sheet* August. Urban Institute

*Zedlewski, Sheila and Olivia Golden (2010) 'Next steps for Temporary Assistance for Needy Families' *Brief* 11. Washington, DC: The Urban Institute

*Zedlewski, Sheila R. and Sandi Nelson (2003) 'Families coping without earnings or government cash assistance', *Occasional Paper* Number 64. Washington, DC: Assessing the New Federalism, The Urban Institute

Zielinski, Graeme (2003) 'George indicted on U.S. charges: Senator accused of taking $435,000 in kickbacks, illegal pay' *Milwaukee Journal Sentinel* 20 November

Ziervogel, Meike (2013) *Magda* Cambridge: Salt

Zucchino, David (1997) *The Myth of the Welfare Queen* New York: Scribner

Index

A

Aboriginal women 12
Aboulgar, M. A. 300
Abramovitz, Mimi 468, 478–479
Abramsky, Sasha 502
ABS 37
accumulation by
    dispossession 113–117, 245, as
    privatisation 117
ACOSS 497
Acs, Gregory 386–501
Acton, Baron Lord 185
advertising 52
AFDC 369, 413
AFDC-UP 386
Affordable Care Act 383, 401
AFSCME 438, 441
aggrieved entitlement 26
Ahlers, Rhodante 117
Ahmed, Nafeez 78
Aid to Dependent Children 462
Ajeet, Saoji 304
Akanksha clinic 255–260, 281,
    292–293, 305–307
Akin, Stephanie 505
Albelda, Randy 366, 367, 492
Albright, Madeleine 43
Alexander, Harriet 281
Alexander, Jeffrey C. 15
Alford, Bob 161
Alford, Peter 266
Alford, Sue 520
Allegretto, Sylvia 136
'alt-right' 32
American Civil Liberties Union 64
Amnesty International 116
Anand, Sudhir 137
Anderson, Mitchell 101
Andersonville 245

Anelauskas, Valdas 371, 401
Anna Maria 271
Anthropocene 80
anti-feminism 10, 50, 96, 264, 324,
    354, 358
anti-Semitism 193
Antlfinger, Carrie 452
ANZ Bank 114
Apple 97, 122–127
Arditti, Rita 269, 297
Arendt, Hannah 45, 53, 59, 64, 73, 92,
    108, 112, 152, 189–195, 239, 248
Augier, Marie 109
Australian Department of Foreign
    Affairs and Trade 339
Australian Government Department of
    Immigration and Border Control 278
Australian House of Representatives
    Standing Committee on Social Policy
    and Legal Affairs 284
Australian Human Rights
    Commission 337
Australian Institute for Family
    Studies 257
Australian Labor Party 31
Australian Senate 497
autism 222

B

Baby M 290–291
baby trafficking 249, 257
Bach, Wendy A. 421, 430, 521–523
Backer, Larry Catá 386, 393, 405, 412,
    461–462
Bacon, Francis 106, 166, 187
Bacon, Wendy 337
Baer, Paul 139
Bailey, J. Michael 317, 349
Baker, Mark 292, 297, Richard 115
balanced budget, myth of 175–180,
    181
Baldwin, Bridgette 373, 375, 436, 439,

582

Dirt 329, 330
disentitlement 5, 56, 58, 236, 246
dissociation 3–8, 14, 18, 21, 23,
    25–26, 31, 32, 41–48, 52, 56, 63–74,
    68, 75, 79, 80, 85, 86, 87, 88, 90, 91,
    92, 93, 96, 98, 101, 117, 123, 133,
    151, 154, 164, 182, 184, 185, 186,
    187, 191, 194, 195, 199, 203, 243,
    246, & fascism 227–232, 234–235
dissociation, masculine 374, 526,
    528, & academe 381, & Corporate
    America 371, & surrogacy 250, 260,
    264, 269, 270, 272, 287, 288, 295,
    296, 312, & transsexualism 315, 331,
    358, 360, & 'welfare reform' 384,
    393, 399, 412, 477, 518–520, 521,
    524
Dobbin, Murray 78
domestic violence 11–13, 24, 195, 247
Dresang, Joel 442, 444
DSM IV 66–68, 317, 319
Duhigg, Charles 122
Dunne, Sister Regis Mary 261
Dupor, William 176
Dwinger, Edwin Erich 206
Dworkin, Andrea 21, 40, 59, 63
Dworsky, Amy 440

E

economic insecurity, US 493
economics 151, 391, 424,
    capitalist 80–81, Keynesian 166,
    orthodox 102, 144–147, 156,
    164–165, 177, 181
Edelman, Peter B. 368, 423, 488, 500
Edgar, David 29, 35, 37, 39
Edmond, Wendy 85
Ehrenreich, Barbara 86, 150, 367, 420,
    466, 522
Ehrhardt, Hermann 205
Eisenstein, Zillah 85
Eisman, Steve 150

Ekman, Kajsa Ekis 292, 297, 304
Elias, Norbert 239
Ellis, Ellen Deborah 110
Ellis, Erle 80
Emmerson, Glenda 286
enclosures, of the Commons 105–108,
    113
Engelhardt, Tom 42
Engels, Friedrich 186
England, Paula 88–91
Ensler, Eve 326
entitlement 57–63. See
    also dissociation, & fascism 232–235
entitlement, masculine, aggrieved 283,
    318, 344, 349, 353, 360, 362,
    373, 374, & surrogacy 250, 270,
    287, 291, 296, 312, & the Family
    Court of Australia 283–284, &
    transsexualism 315, 318, 321–354,
    358, 360, 361, 470, & 'welfare
    reform' 371, 374, 412, 517, 521,
    522, 524
Epstein, William M. 386, 400, 498,
    508, 511, 514
'equality', spurious 254, 264, 293, 294,
    323, 527
Erinyes 343
Escobar, Pepe 130
euphemism 151, 380, 412, 467,
    481, 498, 'Anthropocene' as 80,
    Bourdieu 22, deletion of male agency
    as 13, denial of harm as 24, 'domestic
    violence' as 11, 195, 373, 'gender'
    as 9, 10, 315, Gittins 81, 'inequality'
    as 30, 119, 134, 'left' & 'right' as 31,
    'parents' as 383, plural form as 10,
    'set of ideas' as 22
euro 169
European Court of Human Rights 339
European Parliament 284
Everingham, Sam 257
Evers, James Charles 474
Evers, Medgar 474